Community, Culture and the Makings of Identity: Portuguese-Americans along the Eastern Seaboard

Community, Culture and the Makings of Identity: Portuguese-Americans along the Eastern Seaboard

Edited by Kimberly DaCosta Holton & Andrea Klimt

University of Massachusetts Dartmouth
Center for Portuguese Studies and Culture
North Dartmouth, Massachusetts
2009

PORTUGUESE IN THE AMERICAS SERIES 11
General Editor: Frank F. Sousa
Social Sciences Editor: Andrea Klimt
Editorial Manager: Gina M. Reis
Manuscript Editor: Richard Larschan
Copyeditors: Michael Colvin and Alexander Lee
Assistants to the Social Sciences Editor: Irene de Amaral & Sílvia Belo Oliveira
Graphic Designer: Spencer Ladd
Design Consultant: Mark Handler
Typesetter: Inês Sena

Community, Culture and the Makings of Identity: Portuguese-Americans along the Eastern Seaboard / University of Massachusetts Dartmouth

The publication of *Community, Culture and the Makings of Identity: Portuguese-Americans along the Eastern Seaboard* was made possible in part by a generous grant from the Government of the Autonomous Region of the Azores.

Printed by Signature Printing, East Providence, RI.

Library of Congress Cataloging-in-Publication Data
Community, culture and the makings of identity : Portuguese-Americans along the eastern seaboard / edited by Kimberly DaCosta Holton & Andrea Klimt.
p. cm. – (Portuguese in the Americas series; 12)
Includes bibliographical references.
ISBN 1-933227-27-3 (alk. paper)
1. Portuguese Americans–United States–History. 2. Portuguese Americans–United States–Social conditions. 3. Portuguese Americans–New England–History. 4. Portuguese Americans–New England–Social conditions. 5. Portuguese Americans–New Jersey–Newark–History. 6. Portuguese Americans–New Jersey–Newark–Social conditions. 7. United States–Emigration and immigration–History. 8. Portugal–Emigration and immigration–History. 9. New England–Emigration and immigration. I. DaCosta Holton, Kimberly. II. Klimt, Andrea. III. University of Massachusetts Dartmouth. Center for Portuguese Studies and Culture.
E184.P8C656 2008
305.86'91074--dc22 2008047367

Table of Contents

INTRODUCTION

9 *Lusophone Studies in the U.S.*
Andrea Klimt & Kimberly DaCosta Holton

CITIZENSHIP, BELONGING AND COMMUNITY

27 CHAPTER 1 *Citizenship, Naturalization and Electoral Success: Putting the Portuguese-American Experience in Comparative Context*
Irene Bloemraad

51 CHAPTER 2 *Multiple Layers of Time and Space: The Construction of Class, Ethnicity, and Nationalism among Portuguese Immigrants*
Bela Feldman Bianco

95 CHAPTER 3 *Divergent Trajectories: Identity and Community among Portuguese in Germany and New England*
Andrea Klimt

EXPRESSIVE CULTURE, MEDIA REPRESENTATIONS AND IDENTITY

127 CHAPTER 4 *Traveling Rituals: Azorean Holy Ghost Festivals in Southeastern New England*
João Leal

145 CHAPTER 5 *Dancing Along the In-Between: Folklore Performance and Transmigration in Portuguese Newark*
Kimberly DaCosta Holton

175 CHAPTER 6 *Images of the Virgin in Portuguese Art at the Newark Museum*
Lori Barcliff Baptista

203 CHAPTER 7 Viva *Rhode Island,* Viva *Portugal! Performance and Tourism in Portuguese-American Band*
Katherine Brucher

227 CHAPTER 8 *Salazar in New Bedford: History of the* Diário de Notícias, *New Bedford's Portuguese Newspaper*
Rui Correia

247 CHAPTER 9 *Media-Made Events: Revisiting the Case of Big Dan's*
Onésimo Teotónio Almeida

EDUCATION, SOCIAL MOBILITY AND POLITICAL CULTURE

265 CHAPTER 10 *Context or Culture: Portuguese-Americans and Social Mobility*
M. Glória de Sá and David Borges

291 CHAPTER 11 *The Political Culture of Portuguese-Americans in Southeastern Massachusetts*
Clyde W. Barrow

317 CHAPTER 12 *The Role of the School in the Maintenance and Change of Ethnic Group Affiliation*
Adeline Becker

WORK, GENDER AND FAMILY

337 CHAPTER 13 *Portuguese Labor Activism in Southeastern Massachusetts*
Penn Reeve

357 CHAPTER 14 *Kin Networks and Family Strategies: Working-Class Portuguese Families in New England*
Louise Lamphere, Filomena Silva and John Sousa

381 CHAPTER 15 *Unionization in an Electronics Factory: The Interplay of Gender, Ethnicity, and Class*
Ann Bookman

RACE, POST-COLONIALISM AND DIASPORIC CONTEXTS

409 CHAPTER 16 *The Shadow Minority: An Ethnohistory of Portuguese and Lusophone Racial and Ethnic Identity in New England*
Miguel Moniz

431 CHAPTER 17 *Stereotypes of the Tropics in 'Portuguese Newark': Brazilian Women, Urban Erotics, and the Phantom of Blackness*
Ana Yolanda Ramos-Zayas

461 CHAPTER 18 *Contested Identities: Narratives of Race and Ethnicity in the Cape Verdean Diaspora*
Gina Sánchez Gibau

497 CHAPTER 19 *Angola Dreaming: Memories of Africa among Portuguese* Retornados *in Newark, NJ*
Kimberly DaCosta Holton

525 CHAPTER 20 *Diasporic Generations: Distinctions of Race, Nationality, and Identity in the Cape Verdean Community, Past and Present*
Marilyn Halter

REFLECTIONS

557 *Current Trends and Future Directions in Portuguese-American Studies*
Caroline Brettell

569 **WORKS CITED**

643 **AUTHOR BIOGRAPHIES**

INTRODUCTION

Lusophone Studies in the U.S.

ANDREA KLIMT & KIMBERLY DACOSTA HOLTON

This volume has grown out of many years of conversations with colleagues and students.[1] Both of us teach courses concerning the Portuguese diaspora in our respective universities, and many of our students come from communities with long-established histories of immigration from Portugal and Cape Verde, and more recently from Brazil.[2] In many ways, this collection is the book we have been longing to teach—in the hope that it will encourage present and future generations of scholars to explore further the histories, cultures, and intertwined social dynamics of these immigrant communities. We have brought together previously-published but hard-to-find material along with new research by emerging scholars in an effort to consolidate our current understandings as well as spark future innovative research on Portuguese-American and other related communities. Our contention is that these research areas are particularly fertile, promising insight into understudied immigrant populations and the culturally complex and historically shifting interplay of race, ethnicity, nation and empire that characterizes the Portuguese-speaking diaspora.

The demographic narrative that underpins many studies of post-1965 immigration distinguishes this most recent U.S.-bound wave as originating out of Asia, Africa and the Caribbean in contrast to early 20th-century immigration originating primarily out of Europe.[3] Comparative studies across ethnic groups also argue that post-1965 immigrants to the U.S. have engaged in varied practices of incorporation into American society, whereas early 20th-century Europeans tended to follow more uniformly assimilationist trajectories (Rumbaut and Portes 2001). Portuguese immigrants have been largely absent from these analyses, perhaps in part because they muddy the waters of dichotomous constructs that have been used to distinguish between early and late 20th-century immigration to the U.S.

In contrast to the many cases used to substantiate the difference between these periods of immigration, Portuguese emigration to the U.S. spans both 20th-century waves. Described as a "national drama," a self-perpetuating cycle without end, and an integral component of the nation's social imaginary, massive emigration has significantly shaped the fabric of Portuguese society for over two centuries (Serrão 1977; Baganha and Góis 1999; Brettell 2003h). The emigrant constitutes a national symbol that frames the lives and outlooks of almost every Portuguese citizen, and leaving one's home to make a better life elsewhere has long been a viable option for members of all sectors of Portuguese society (Brettell 2003a; Feldman-Bianco this volume; Noivo 2000 and Rocha-Trindade). The resulting disapora in the U.S. and elsewhere around the globe thus encompasses recent immigrants as well as multiple generations of descendants and long histories of settlement. Exploring the Portuguese case thus offers the opportunity to understand the connections between both 20th-century waves of U.S. immigration and contributes important nuances to the entrenched scholarly portrait of these periods of immigration as largely separate and distinct.

The Portuguese nation has been increasingly defined as a deterritorialized entity that encompasses the far-flung diaspora as well as the former colonies in Africa, Asia and Latin America it once dominated (Baganha 1999; Feldman-Bianco 1992). This formulation, as politically charged and polemical as it is, also runs counter to the tendencies of U.S. immigration scholarship to evaluate waves of immigration according to First World vs. Third World dichotomies. The degree of acceptance—or adamant rejection—of the concept of the "Lusophone world" as a multi-continental, multi-racial harmonious whole depends upon the historical period, ideological purpose, and geographic and social space in which it is deployed. However, it is a straightforward fact that communities of people from both the Portuguese metropole and a myriad of one-time Portuguese colonies have settled alongside one another in the U.S. Exploration of this unique feature of the Lusophone case and the resulting inter-cutting of identities and relationships in the diaspora will, we hope, deepen and productively complicate the scholarly portrayal of 20th-century immigration to the U.S.

Decisions as to how to cast the scope of this collection evolved over the course of the project. Initially we had imagined a volume that would focus exclusively on the Portuguese-American experience and include articles on communities in all major regions of the country where the Portuguese have established themselves. Portuguese immigration is characterized by a striking persistence of extremely concentrated settlement patterns in coastal and central California, the northeastern seaboard and Hawaii—a result of the 19th-century whaling routes that included regular stops in the Azores and Cape Verde to pick up men and supplies, economic opportunities that encouraged Portuguese crew to jump ship in East and West Coast American ports, and patterns of tightly-linked chain migration that brought in subsequent generations of immigrants. Our aim was to further develop Williams's argument that very different local conditions led to significant variations in how immigrants and their descendants lived their lives and built their communities (Williams 2005). Such a framework would have allowed us, for example, to tease out the similarities and differences between the largely rural and agriculturally-based Portuguese-American communities characteristic of California, the primarily urban industrial communities of New England, the more recently established communities of New Jersey, and the relatively scattered communities built in the aftermath of Hawaii's plantation economy. Such comparisons are clearly essential to the development of an adequately nuanced analysis of the Portuguese-American case.

The final version of this project has, however, ended up being both narrower and wider in scope. When our search for contributions yielded an incredibly rich focus on East Coast communities, we decided to limit the geographic reach in order to extend the ethnographic depth of the collection. Our hope is that documenting the complex and varied histories of the communities along the Northeastern seaboard will provide the solid foundation for subsequent comparisons with the Portuguese immigrant experience in other regions of the U.S. and other corners of the globe. We also decided to widen the focus to include intersections with the communities of Brazilians, Cape Verdeans and African *retornados* that co-populate the region. As our thinking evolved over the course of this project, it became increasingly clear that Portugal's post-colonial history binds these immigrant groups together, as do contemporary projects of self-representation in the U.S. that can be oppositional, complementary or a combination of both. This volume thus brings together explorations of Portuguese and—although to a much lesser extent—other Lusophone or Luso-African populations that have settled in the immigrant hubs of the port cities and towns along the Northeastern seaboard in order to deepen our understanding of the interconnected nature of these communities.

Reframing the Field of Study

To learn more about the Portuguese-American experience, a seemingly obvious decision would be to focus the inquiry exclusively on Portuguese-Americans. The contributions to this volume make clear, however, that decisions about how to define a study population and set the parameters of investigation are often theoretically charged and potentially misleading, with each particular choice yielding insight into some areas while obscuring the answers or even our awareness of the questions in others. Theoretical breakthroughs are, in fact, usually accompanied by the reframing of decisions about whom to talk to and what questions to ask. Our hope is that the ways we as editors have framed this collection, as well as how the individual authors—especially those whose contributions are found in the sections, "Citizenship, Belonging and Community" and "Race, Post-Colonialism and Diasporic Contexts"—have established the parameters of inquiry, allow us to explore new and deeply relevant questions about the Portuguese-American experience.

Strategically structured comparisons offer ways to dislodge our often entrenched and sometimes misleading assumptions that certain immigrant trajectories and forms of belonging are natural, normal, and inevitable, while others constitute unusual anomalies unique to a particular group or situation. Bloemraad's comparison, for example, between naturalization rates among Portuguese immigrants in the U.S. and Canada allows her to explore why, despite similarly structured legal pathways to citizenship and analogous idealized narratives about being a nation of immigrants, these two neighboring liberal democracies differ markedly in the extent to which immigrants decide to pursue citizenship in their respective new homelands. The relatively low rates of naturalization among Portuguese in the U.S. have often been attributed to this particular immigrant group's lack of experience with participatory democracy—thus explaining their reticence to change citizenship according to shortcomings characteristic of the immigrants themselves.[4] That is, the assumptions that any immigrant can easily become an American citizen and that most would logically want to do so lead to the conclusion that something about the Portuguese must be making them less interested in and/or less capable of becoming U.S. citizens. Expanding the research scope to encompass the contrast with the much higher rates of naturalization among analogous populations in Canada allows us to see that it is particular U.S. governmental policies—not characteristics of this particular immigrant group—that significantly limit access to American citizenship. Klimt's comparison allows us to ask why the Portuguese in the U.S. have tended to create institutionally complete communities and make permanent commitments to their new homeland while compatriots in Germany have created actively transnational communities that entail a continued commitment to Portugal and adamant rejection of exclusive permanence in Germany or acquisition of German citizenship. Setting up research questions in such comparative terms enables us to move past assumptions that immigrant trajectories are uniform or unilineal and to interrogate social formations that, at least from the vantage point of southeastern New England, appear inevitable and universal.[5] Expanding the research scope to include the widely-scattered places in which Portuguese have settled around the world enables us to ask how the politics and power relations, economies and opportunity structures, and status hierarchies characteristic of any particular society shape the identities and communities of its immigrants. The answers, in turn, will deepen our understanding of the story of the Portuguese in North America.

Another way the essays in these sections extend our understanding of the Portuguese-American experience is by challenging the boundaries and categories commonly used to define the scope of social scientific inquiry. Feldman-Bianco makes clear that a portrait of Portuguese-American identity in New Bedford needs to extend beyond the confines of locally-rooted and ethnically-circumscribed interactions and take into account transnationally-enacted relationships, multi-sited and often multi-national communities, and the state-level actions of multiple nations (Glick Schiller et al. 1992). Her analysis has contributed to the theoretical debates about the on-going transnational nature of immigrant life and the concomitant research shift away from the often exclusive focus on geographically-bounded ethnic communities. Ramos-Zayas's investigation shows us that the social play of gendered stereotypes must be understood relationally.[6] That is, the association of traditional images of "decent" and "respectable" womanhood with Portuguese-American women in Newark's Ironbound neighborhood is part and parcel of the hypersexuality and exotic eroticism associated with Brazilian women living in the same neighborhood. To have focused the inquiry on only one or the other ethnic group and ignore the ongoing interactions between members of both groups would have been to miss the essential dynamic fueling both sets of stereotypes. Both Gibau and Halter focus primarily on the dynamics of racial and ethnic identities among Cape Verdean-Americans, but they also explore key questions about interactions between groups. Their analyses demonstrate that we can only make sense of what it might mean to be "black" or "Cape Verdean" in conjunction with questions about the shifting and often situationally specific meanings of being "white," "Portuguese," or "African-American." The editorial decision to include case studies of Cape Verdean as well as Brazilian immigrant communities in a volume primarily dedicated to investigating the Portuguese-American experience underlines the necessity of addressing questions about the complexly racialized and historical shifting boundaries around Portuguese nationhood. The ambiguities and arguments characteristic of these interconnected diasporic identities can only be understood in the context of Portugal's transformation from one-time empire to relatively peripheral player in a post-colonial world.[7]

Looking for and focusing on significant variations within a particular research population is yet another way to further refine our understanding of the Portuguese-American case. Holton, for example, noticed during her research on Newark's Portuguese-American community that a number of people in her study population originally came from the one-time Portuguese colonies of Angola and Mozambique (Holton, "Dancing", this volume). Her curiosity piqued, she decided to explore the outlooks of this particular subgroup whose life trajectories were so different from the majority of Portuguese immigrants in Newark who had come directly from their natal homes in continental Portugal. She found that despite being officially designated as "Portuguese-Americans," "European," and "white," these *retornados* thought of Africa as their beloved homeland, symbolically nurtured African components of their identities, and established social networks distinct from those of Portuguese-Americans from Portugal. The insights garnered from this framing of the research population points to the relevance of other dimensions of difference—place of origin, region of settlement, migration trajectory, social background, gender, to name just a few—that warrant further attention if we are to move past the analytically-limiting image of Portuguese-Americans as a generally homogenous group.[8]

An important point to keep in mind as we assess the various strategies for delimiting research populations is that the content and contours of any category are socially constructed and often vigorously contested. Deciding to focus an inquiry on Portuguese-Americans, for example, raises questions about who does and who does not "count" as "Portuguese-American" and what, if any, qualities constitute accepted characteristics of this category. Moniz directly addresses these questions by laying out the intense arguments Portuguese-Americans had with one another as to whether or not "Portuguese-American" should be an officially recognized minority status. The debate played out between differently positioned Portuguese-Americans who had opposing views on how to situate themselves collectively within a racialized maneuvering for resources and political voice. Moniz's analysis clearly demonstrates the insight gained from interrogating the very definition of a category—as well as the dangers of assuming that any particular set of parameters corresponds to an uncontested, unchanging social reality.

There are many ways to frame a field of study: geographically, temporally, demographically and analytically. The contributors to this volume each define their research scope in ways that provide better access to important questions, deciding for example: to follow a Portuguese-American band on its tour in Portugal—as opposed to just studying it in the immigrant context; to cast a comparative net that includes immigrant trajectories in different national settings and/or different historical eras—as opposed to focusing exclusively on a single locale or time frame; to include interactions between ethnic groups in a particular geographic setting—as opposed to focusing on only one particular group; or to interrogate the very nature of group boundaries—as opposed to accepting these categories as unambiguous characteristics of social life.

We anticipate that theoretically informed and innovative research strategies, such as those employed by the contributors to this volume, will continue to bring fresh insight into the history and culture of Portuguese-American and other related immigrant groups.

Formulating Alternative Arguments

One of the on-going fiercely argued theoretical conundrums in the social sciences concerns the relationship between culture and material conditions. With regards to the Portuguese, the argument has often been made that culture trumps context. That is, for example, lower rates of social mobility and educational success among Portuguese-Americans have been attributed to the cultural values and immutable "peasant mentality" thought to characterize this group of immigrants and their purported tendency to consider property ownership, physical labor, and family cohesion—rather than education, intellectual work, or individual ambition—as the most acceptable and expedient routes to prosperity and social success. In a similar vein, the generalized image of the Portuguese as passive workers, inward-looking and politically unengaged has been attributed to their life-long experience with political oppression under fascism in Portugal. Asymmetrical gender roles and patriarchal family structures found in the immigrant contexts have often been considered to constitute unchanged cultural patterns transplanted from communities of origin.

One of the ways the chapters in this collection—especially those in the sections "Education, Social Mobility, and Political Culture" and "Work, Gender, and Family"—offer alternative responses to the debate is to challenge the primacy given to cultural explanations. De Sá and Borges, for example, argue that lack of social mobility in southeastern New England is due largely to changing structural conditions and not, as is commonly asserted, to a culturally-specific aversion to pursuing higher education. They carefully document how "[a]s the last group to arrive, the Portuguese were kept at the bottom of the socio-economic hierarchy in order to sustain the economic viability of a declining industrial sector" characteristic of New England (de Sá and Borges, this volume, 265-266). In his analysis of political attitudes and behavior among Portuguese-Americans in southeastern Massachusetts,

Barrow also concludes that regionally-specific dynamics of economic decline—not the collective experience with political oppression and resulting fear of engagement—kept the Portuguese out of politics and "lock[ed] new immigrant groups into their disadvantaged position in the economy and society" (Barrow, this volume, 312). Reeve takes issue with the cultural explanation of political behavior by laying out how current low levels of union participation on the part of Portuguese immigrants are not due to any lingering reticence to becoming politically engaged, but to the very real nation-wide decline in the power of unions to improve the lives of their members—a historical shift of which Portuguese-American workers are only too aware. The emphasis is on understanding the opportunities and limitations created by the political, economic, and material conditions as key factors in shaping individual, familial, and community trajectories—and away from looking to culture as the primary explanatory framework.

Another way that the authors in this collection deepen our understanding of the Portuguese-American case is to assert the crucial need to move past cultural stereotypes. Together, these chapters make clear that developing a more accurate and nuanced analysis of the relationship between culture and context entails looking carefully at the actual patterns of belief and behavior and discarding the often firmly entrenched assumptions about this particular population. Barrow, for example, corroborates his argument countering widespread images of the Portuguese as politically apathetic and underrepresented by showing that Portuguese-American political attitudes are, in fact, quite similar to those of other comparable ethnic groups, and political representation in certain areas has, in recent years, actually increased significantly. In other words, Portuguese culture *per se* is not what was determining the political attitudes or behavior of immigrants and their descendants. Reeve challenges the widely-accepted portrait of the Portuguese as passive workers weighed down by past political oppression and traditional gender roles by documenting the active engagement of Portuguese-American men *and* women in the labor struggles of the not-so-distant but not-so-well-remembered past. The experience of fascism in Portugal was certainly real—but history shows us that it did not keep Portuguese workers from fighting for their rights in the U.S. Bookman's portrait of the crucial role women played in creating a unionized workplace not only pushes us past assumptions about the limitations of "traditional" gender roles, but shows how gender-specific ways of socializing and realizing commitments to family well-being actually made women highly effective organizers. Lamphere and co-authors' account of how Portuguese men and women juggled roles and responsibilities to meet the challenges of making a life in a new home demonstrates that cultural ideas about gender and family are subject to change and negotiation, and are not so immutable as to prevent people from figuring out new survival strategies in new contexts. De Sá and Borges turn on its head the assumption that Portuguese lack of interest in higher education contributed to lower rates of social mobility, showing that for many European groups, education, in fact, followed from social mobility, rather than preceding or facilitating the move into the middle class as is commonly assumed. They also clearly document the locally available alternative routes to middle-class status that have been successfully followed by a significant number of Portuguese-Americans in the region. Becker's essay shows how low expectations and negative stereotypes held by teachers undermined Portuguese immigrant children's ability to imagine and realize academic success—pointing, in other words, to how false assumptions about culture held by more powerful players rather than cultural values held by Portuguese immigrant families affected educational as well as more long-term social outcomes.

Theoretical arguments often proceed in pendulum swings, and countering the flaws of a particular perspective frequently entails pushing the whole approach entirely aside. In this case, some authors in these sections have sought to correct misleading, erroneous, and overly deterministic arguments about the role of culture in shaping individual and collective trajectories and their careful attention to political, economic, and social factors shaping people's lives significantly enhances our understanding of the Portuguese-American experience. We would like to suggest that productive possibilities for future research entail further interrogating the relationship between context and culture—coming back, that is, from one extreme swing of the pendulum. Thinking about the interplay between shifts in local and transnational employment opportunities; the nature of global interconnections and permeability of national borders; access to education, social support, and political voice *and* the continuities and transformations in ideas, values, and world views would help us move past a context *or* culture argument and towards a more nuanced understanding of how *both* are usually in play.

Connecting Performance, Representation and Power

Scholars of immigration often conceptualize expressive culture as a tool used for maintaining ties of migrants and their descendants to original homelands as well as straightforward evidence of cultural continuity across time and space. The essays in this volume—especially those in the section "Expressive Culture, Media Representations and Identity"—attempt to move beyond this traditional approach by exploring how performance, expressive culture, and media representations directly enter into dynamic and historically-particular plays for power, status, and visibility in receiving as well as sending communities. Volume contributors construe these performative acts as a conduit for the often politically-charged interchange between native and immigrant spaces, a means to negotiate varied social landscapes and aesthetic and communicative value systems, and an effective staging ground in negotiations for influence, power and political voice within local, national and transnational status hierarchies.

Just as Gilroy (1993), Vale de Almeida (2004), and Roach (1996) track how the exercise of power and the politics of difference figure into the movement of music, dance and ritual across transnational spaces linked by the Atlantic, contributors to this collection approach culture in motion as a dynamic force constantly imbricated in changing spatial and social alliances. Moving between native and adopted homelands, shifting expectations and hierarchies of ethnic and economic difference, expressive culture has the power to bridge gaps, forge coalitions or fuel conflict and misunderstanding. Building on Appadurai's argument as to the increased role of imagination during our modern era of unprecedented movement of people across space, these chapters indicate the possibility that expressive culture—a manifestation, after all, of the human imagination—plays a very high-stakes game in diasporic contexts, transnational exchanges and deterritorialized communities (Appadurai 1996).

One of the key arenas in which to explore the play between power and performance is at the level of the co-ethnic community. In Leal's account, for example, of how Azorean immigrants in East Providence celebrate the Holy Ghost Feast, he unpacks the inter-workings of the official feast hierarchies and the ways in which various ritualized roles serve to renew kinship ties and strengthen local community relationships. Through a detailed examination of the ritual components, he indexes the conflicting pressures of adaptation and authenticity and portrays this immigrant community as engaged in a dialogue with tradition while simultaneously working to translate the celebration to meet modern, site-specific demands and concerns.

Public displays of immigrant culture also engage with various wider levels of argument about political power and social position taking place in the towns, cities, and regions in which Portuguese immigrants have settled. Holton explores these arenas in her investigation of how folkloric performances figure prominently into the consolidation of a positive ethnic identity and audible political voice among the Portuguese in Newark, New Jersey. Not only does participation in folklore troupes help keep the second generation within the networks and traditional values of the Portuguese-American community, but she finds that folkloric performances give the Portuguese prominence within city and state-wide politics that celebrate and promote multiculturalism.[9] Taking a different route through city politics, Baptista analyzes the role of The Newark Art Museum in brokering new political and social alliances between municipal institutions and the local Portuguese-American community. She shows how the museum successfully drew in large numbers of Portuguese-Americans to see a major exhibit featuring Portuguese depictions of the Virgin and collaborated with local Portuguese-American leaders in the organization of the show. Not only was a meaningful connection forged between the historically insular ethnic population and a powerful city-wide institution, but "Portuguese culture" was represented via examples of both "high art" and "folk art" in one of the city's most visibly elite venues.

The jockeying for status and visibility and the politics of cultural performance often connect social dynamics across multiple national spaces. Bruchner demonstrates the complexity of these interconnections in her analysis of what happens when a Rhode Island Portuguese-American marching band goes on tour to a sister city in Portugal and culturally coded—and politically loaded—musical idioms are played in the music's and the musicians' place of origin. She describes how Portuguese hosts offered warm welcomes to one-time compatriots and the collegial exchange between fellow musicians and public officials in both sister cities gained political kudos and visibility. Her analysis reveals however, that a degree of competition and unacknowledged resentment underlay the interactions as Portuguese hosts maneuvered to show that they, in fact, played better and had a more authentically Portuguese repertoire than did their Portuguese-American guests. Attempts to define and lay proprietary claim to "Portugueseness" clearly shaped the dynamics around these transnational performances.

This volume considers representations and debates found in national and ethnic print media as yet another stage for public negotiations over representation, influence and power. Although quite different from the more commonly recognized venues of music, dance, art and ritual, images of ethnic groups presented in newspapers, television and radio stations can productively be viewed as a kind of public—and inherently political—performance. Almeida's contribution, for example, foregrounds the power of national and even international media to create and spread profoundly negative images of Portuguese-Americans and ignite deep and still unresolved conflict within the ethnic community. Sensationalist and, Almeida argues, at times deeply flawed journalistic coverage of a rape case involving a Portuguese woman and several Portuguese men in New Bedford, Massachusetts—all aimed at promoting media sales—led to serious cultural misunderstanding, increased ethnic prejudice and, in his terms, "the rape of a community." Correia's case study also features heated debate within the same Portuguese-American community of New Bedford, but he focuses on exchanges between compatriots in the *Diário de Notícias* (1919-1973), the only Portuguese language daily in the U.S. published for more than a few months. He follows the highly-charged arguments of the 1930s about the Spanish Civil War in which community leaders of opposing political ideologies battled with one another on the editorial pages of their local paper. Correia applauds the political evenhandedness of the *Diário*'s editors and the fact that this Portuguese-American paper actively fostered a freedom of expression that was stringently prohibited in Portugal by Salazar's fascist regime. He also notes how the realization of this freedom was, ironically enough, inhibited at times by tendencies towards political censorship in the U.S. Both Correia and Almeida make clear that the images and representations forged through printed words had real impact on the lives of immigrants and their families.

There are still many fascinating questions about the connection between the expressive culture, representation, and political power of immigrant and ethnic populations that await the attention of future researchers. What, for example, happens to ethnic identity and culture with increased incorporation into a "mainstream," and will ethnicity over third, fourth, fifth generations come to be expressed through primarily symbolic means? Will ethnic groups with different relations to political power develop different forms of expressive culture? And what aspects of ethnic culture will be retained, changed, or cast off as the political and social landscape shifts over time? Our hope is that this collection will provide some impetus to the continued exploration of the relationship between performance and power in Portuguese-American as well as other related ethnic communities.

* * *

The questions addressed in this volume point to a whole array of new and as yet unexplored questions regarding the history, culture and social dynamics of Portuguese-American and other interconnected communities. This still understudied case—which brings together the story of multiple waves of immigration spanning two centuries, close connections with a global diaspora, and the complex relationships of post-colonialism—has much to offer to our understandings of transnational migration and subsequent processes of identity and community formation among immigrants and their descendants. The contributors to this collection have clearly established the benefits of framing investigations of this particular case within larger debates that theorize the interconnections between culture, structure, and power as well as establishing research parameters that facilitate forays into new areas of study and analytically productive comparisons. And the ethnographic richness and productive interplay of their analyses indicate promising directions for future research.

Notes

[1] This introduction further develops the preface Andrea Klimt wrote to Jerry Williams's book, *In Pursuit of their Dreams: A History of Azorean Immigration to the United States,* entitled "New Directions and Future Possibilities: Understanding the Portuguese Immigrant Story" (2005). Many of the works cited in that piece as exemplary of future directions have been brought together in this volume.

[2] Andrea Klimt teaches courses on Portuguese immigration to the Americas at the University of Massachusetts Dartmouth and Kimberly DaCosta Holton teaches courses on the Portuguese diaspora and Portuguese literature and culture at Rutgers University Newark. Both universities are situated in close proximity to Portuguese-American communities and have student bodies that include significant percentages of Portuguese-Americans and Brazilian-Americans, and in the case of UMass Dartmouth, Cape Verdean-Americans.

[3] In 1965 The National Origins Act was repealed, spawning a new wave of immigration into the U.S. The restrictive National Origins Act, passed in 1924, limited new immigration to the U.S. to 150,000 people and established a quota system based on national origin.

[4] The immigrants who left Portugal before 1975, grew up under the Salazar regime and had no direct experience with participatory democracy.

[5] See Leal (2002) for an analysis of trajectories of Azorean identity in southern Brazil; Sarkissian (2000) for an account of the history of Portuguese identity in Malyasia; and Brettell (2003b) for a comparison between Portuguese communities in Toronto and Paris. Teixeira and da Rosa's collection, *The Portuguese in Canada* (2000), offers additional comparative possibilities.

[6] Noivo (1997) and Giles (2002) also offer useful arguments about gender dynamics within Portuguese immigrant communities in Canada.

[7] Other works that investigate the impact of the shifting status of empire and nation on Portuguese identity in the metropole as well as in the diaspora and post-colonial contexts are Sieber (2005), Sarkissian (2000), and Leal (2002).

[8] Williams (2005) focuses his attention on the differences between Portuguese-American communities in different regions of the U.S. He asks very useful questions about how significant differences in economic opportunity structures, settlement patterns, and place within local social arrangements have contributed to differences in patterns of social mobility, attitudes towards being "Portuguese," and degrees of cultural continuity. Even though all Azorean immigrants came from very similar backgrounds and with very similar aspirations, the economic and social conditions of the areas of the U.S. in which they settled were quite different from one another. The typical New England experience, for example, of living in urban, predominantly Portuguese neighborhoods and working in factories with few options for social mobility contrasted sharply with the tendency amongst Azorean immigrants in California to buy land, become independent and sometimes very successful farmers, and live in dispersed rural communities. The trajectory was different in yet another way in Hawaii, where Azoreans were imported as plantation laborers and found themselves on the bottom of a very stratified social hierarchy with few attractive options open to them outside of leaving for the mainland or becoming less "Portuguese."

[9] The film, *The Flight of the Dove,* directed by Nancy da Silveira, makes similar points as it shows how the Holy Ghost Feasts in Californian communities help keep people of Portuguese descent connected to one another and to a sense of "being Portuguese." A contrasting argument is made by Klimt, who argues that the visibility of expressive culture does not always correspond to increased access to political power (2005b). In the case she investigates in Germany, Portuguese folkloric performances gained a very high level of visibility on the local scene, but in a context where most Portuguese are not citizens and have no voting rights, that cultural prominence did not translate into political voice or pressure to change the status quo.

CITIZENSHIP, BELONGING AND COMMUNITY

CHAPTER I

Citizenship, Naturalization and Electoral Success: Putting the Portuguese-American Experience in Comparative Context[1]

IRENE BLOEMRAAD

Despite their large numbers in Massachusetts and Ontario, the Portuguese community is consistently described as politically "invisible" in the United States and Canada. Portuguese political apathy is variously attributed to low levels of education, socialization under a dictatorship that actively discouraged civic and political participation, factionalism within the community, the liability of newness or immigrant origins, or ingrained cultural traits that discourage political involvement. All these explanations presume that the problem of Portuguese immigrants' lack of political voice lies with the immigrants themselves.

In this chapter, I argue that while these obstacles are significant, accounts of Portuguese political invisibility have failed to consider how the political institutions and policies of the new home affect citizenship and electoral success. Portuguese immigrants in Canada, and especially the metropolitan Toronto area, are much less invisible than their compatriots in the United States. Portuguese immigrants in Canada are more likely to hold citizenship than those in the United States (Bloemraad 2002). Between 1980 and 2005, dozens of Portuguese-Canadians ran for office at all levels of government in greater Toronto, with at least seven winning seats on local school boards, two sitting in municipal government, two sitting as a member of Provincial parliament and, in 2004, Toronto residents elected the first Portuguese-born member of federal Parliament. In contrast, over this same period, only one Portuguese-American woman held elected office as a Somerville school board member and no Portuguese-American held city, state or national office in the immediate Boston metropolitan area (Bloemraad 2006). I will suggest that Portuguese-Americans' greater invisibility is due in part to the lack of government policies funding community organizations, the prevalence of a race-based discourse around multiculturalism and immigration, and the intersection of the Canadian political system with a unique group of left-wing Portuguese migrants living in Toronto.

I make these arguments based on a large-scale study of immigrant political incorporation in the United States and Canada. Here I bring together evidence based on census statistics, in-depth interviews with sixty-two Portuguese community members in the Toronto and Boston areas, an additional twenty interviews with government officials and community activists who work with Portuguese immigrants, and documentary data gathered from government and community-based organizations.[2]

This chapter is divided into three parts. In the first section, I outline the rationale—in many ways legitimate—that academics and community advocates provide to explain Portuguese political invisibility. Next, I show that despite the many commonalities between the Portuguese immigrant communities in greater Toronto and Boston, those living in Toronto enjoy higher levels of citizenship and greater success in electoral politics. The final section sketches out the reasons for the difference, focusing on government policies that provide resources to local community groups, multiculturalism discourse, legal practice, and the intersection between the political system and selective elite migration.

Portuguese Immigrants' Political Invisibility

Though understudied in North America, Portuguese immigration to the United States and Canada has been substantial and long-standing. In the United States, most Portuguese immigrants live in the Northeast or California (Allen and Turner 1988; Williams 2005), while in Canada, they largely settled in urban centers such as Toronto and Montreal (Teixeira and Da Rosa 2000; Teixeira and Lavigne 1992). I focus on Massachusetts and Ontario because both contain large Portuguese communities. According to the 2001 Canadian Census, Portuguese immigrants were the eighth-largest immigrant group in the province of Ontario (112,510 individuals, or 3.6 percent of all foreign-born residents) and in metropolitan Toronto (3.8 percent of all foreign-born residents). In Massachusetts, the 2000 U.S. Census counted 66,627 Portuguese-born individuals, the largest immigrant group in the state (8.6 percent of the total foreign-born population), and the eighth-largest group in metropolitan Boston (3.9 percent of all foreign-born residents).[3]

The movement of people from Portugal, especially from the Azores, to the United States began in the 19th century (Pap 1981; Williams 2005), while substantial Portuguese migration to Canada only began in the 1950s (Anderson and Higgs 1976; Marques and Marujo 1993). In the post-World War II period, however, the flows of people crossing the Atlantic Ocean to North America were very similar. Teixeira and Lavigne (1992, 5) estimate that in the late 1960s over 10,000 Portuguese migrated to the United States every year, while Canada—with a tenth of the U.S. population—welcomed approximately 6,000 per year, about two-thirds to three-quarters of whom hailed from the Azores. Another twenty to thirty percent of people come from mainland Portugal, often from the Lisbon area or northern Portugal, and smaller groups hail from Madeira or Portugal's former African colonies. Anderson (1983) confirms this pattern of predominantly Azorean migration for Toronto, while Ito-Alder (1980 [1972, 1978]) does the same for Cambridge and Somerville, the two most heavily Portuguese suburbs of the immediate Boston area. The bulk of Portuguese migrated to North America before Portugal's transition to democracy in the mid-1970s.

Overall, Portuguese immigrants look largely the same, whether they live in Ontario or Massachusetts (Bloemraad 2002, 2006). Age and gender profiles, marital status and business ownership patterns are nearly identical. Portuguese immigrants are largely ethnically homogeneous and almost all are Roman Catholic.[4] Before moving to North America, the majority engaged in subsistence farming, fishing or manual labor (Williams 2005). In North America, Portuguese workforce participation rates resemble those of the native-born, with many employed in manual and semi-skilled jobs such as cleaning, factory work and construction. The only demographic or socioeconomic difference that stands out is Portuguese-Canadians' somewhat higher median income as compared to those living in the United States, a difference that might be in part attributable to higher rates of unionization in Canada (Reitz 1998). In Toronto, many Portuguese men have found employment in construction, often in unionized positions, generating a decent income despite low levels of education. In the United States, fewer Portuguese work in non-residential construction, and they appear less likely to be members of a union. The difference in income probably drives, in part, slightly higher levels of homeownership in Canada.

Portuguese immigrants are noteworthy as one of the most residentially concentrated immigrant groups in both the United States and Canada (Allen and Turner 1988; Balakrishnan and Kralt 1987). Normally, geographic concentration facilitates political voice and electoral success (Pelletier 1991). Yet the Portuguese community is consistently described as politically "invisible" in the United States (Taft 1923; Smith 1974; Pap 1981; Valdés 1995; Almeida 1999) and in Canada (Anderson and Higgs 1976; Alpalhão and da Rosa 1980; Almeida 2000). Portuguese political apathy is variously attributed to low levels of education (Pap 1981), socialization under a dictatorship that actively discouraged civic and political participation (Anderson and Higgs 1976), factionalism in the community (Wolforth 1978), the liabilities of immigration and "newness" in a country, or ingrained cultural traits that discourage political involvement (Almeida 1999). Let's consider each in turn. [5]

Education and English Language Ability

A long history of political science scholarship shows that low levels of education depress electoral participation (Miller and Shanks 1996; Rosenstone and Hansen 1993; Verba, Schlozman and Brady 1995). Education generates political interest, information and skills, all of which correlate to political involvement. Education indirectly affects voting and campaign activity by increasing income, chances for recruitment and civic skills (Verba, Schlozman and Brady 1995, 433-36). Familiarity with the host society's predominant language—English in both countries, and French in certain parts of Canada—also facilitates citizenship acquisition and voting (Bloemraad 2002; Cho 1999).

An important reason for Portuguese immigrants' political invisibility consequently lies in relatively low levels of educational achievement and English language skills. In Toronto, the Portuguese have by far the lowest levels of educational attainment of any ethno-racial group. In 1996, over fifty-one percent of Portuguese between the ages of twenty-four to sixty-four had only primary schooling or none at all, and almost seventy percent had not completed high school, more than double the thirty-one percent among all Toronto residents (Ornstein 2000, 38). At the other end of the educational ladder, fewer than four percent held a university degree. Numbers in the United States are similar: in 2000, forty-five percent of Portuguese immigrants in Massachusetts had never attended high school; only thirty-seven percent held a high school diploma; and fewer than six percent held a university degree.[6] These numbers compare to six percent, eighty-five percent, and thirty-three percent, respectively, among the general population in the state. The census also tells us that more than half of Portuguese immigrants in the United States cannot speak English well, despite the fact that many have lived in the country for over thirty years. Similar linguistic barriers exist in Canada: Portuguese in Toronto are three-and-a-half times more likely than other Toronto residents to report an inability to carry out a conversation in English or French (Ornstein 2000).

Those with limited schooling express fear of the political system and blame a lack of knowledge for their reluctance to become involved. Maria, a Portuguese-American who migrated in the 1960s, is typical of many. In the Azores, she completed four years of schooling and helped on the family farm. In the United States, she works as a cleaner and found time to attend evening classes and achieve a high school equivalency diploma (GED). But despite decades in Boston, she has never voted: "I'm afraid to vote for the wrong person; I am not confident in myself.... I always feel that I am going to do a mistake or something." Political activists recognize the difficulty of mobilizing a community with limited education and English language skills, although lack of schooling can be a very sensitive, if not taboo, topic in the Portuguese community.[7]

Previous Political Socialization

Most activists feel that homeland experiences feed into political silence in the adopted country. One Portuguese-Canadian leader explained, "In the Portugal that they knew, you fended for yourself. You didn't expect anything from the state, except for the expectation that Salazar was going to take more and more away from you. You were not to trust the state, you were not to get involved. The further away you are, the farther removed, the better off." Another person elaborated, "Not only were they not allowed to vote, but they were not supposed to participate either. They are not used to using the vote to get into the decision-making circles." More than once, ordinary Portuguese immigrants would dismiss my questions about political participation with a wave of the hand. In interviews, adjectives such as "dirty" or phrases such as "can't be trusted" cropped up frequently: "A politician has to be a self-centered individual that will sacrifice friends, will sacrifice anything for the sake of achieving that end." Being in office makes elected officials "dilute the things they stand for." As one person put it, "Politics for a lot of Azoreans was considered what is called the 'realm of the witches'."

To a certain degree Portuguese attitudes mirror the feelings of native-born Canadians and Americans, but the Portuguese appear to hold more reservations about politics than other groups. Surveys of ethnic groups in Toronto find that Portuguese respondents express relatively little faith in the use of organized action or political parties to resolve problems; and while they are on average quite satisfied with life in Toronto, they are less likely than most other groups to feel that they have access to local politicians (Breton, et al. 1990; Goldfarb Consultants 1999).[8] Although North America is poles apart from pre-1974 Portugal, it takes significant convincing to change a lifetime of distrust and disinterest.

Internal Divisions and Community Solidarity

Community leaders consistently cite internal divisions as a major reason for lack of political success. This refrain focuses particularly on regional prejudices, especially between mainlanders and Azoreans, but also between Azorean islands or people from different villages on the same island. Such divisions, which revolve around perceptions of superiority and relative backwardness, divide Portuguese immigrants into distinct social networks and organizations. Remembering the cultural differences between mainlanders and those from the Azores apparent in her American classroom, one woman who migrated from mainland Portugal as a young child explained:

> When we were in grammar school, there were maybe twenty kids...of Portuguese background. Some came from the Azores, and some were from the continent, and they really didn't understand much about each other.... There was always this certain competition that the mainlanders always seemed to think that they were better than islanders. And then the people from the islands would think the girls from the main-

> land were really racy, because they could go out at night, and they could not go out at night. And islanders are very religious oriented....Where we came from [mainland]...we went to church, we listened to the sermon, but it wasn't that blind.

Class differences provide a second line of internal tension, although the strain is often latent rather than explicit. Ordinary immigrants allude to the gap between their own issues and the activities of prominent community members by using a shrug of the shoulder and a reference to "those guys." In most cases, differences in class, income and education do not produce outright clashes, but rather detachment between community subcultures organized around different occupation paths and social organizations.[9] For some, however, lingering resentment over class inequalities in the homeland colors perceptions of compatriots in the receiving society. As one Portuguese-American, a man of modest background who was able to work his way up into a white collar occupation in the United States, explained in talking about a local elite:

> [He] looks up to himself. He cares about everybody else, but appearances are also very important.... [I]f you have a problem communicating with people, and you only have your eyes focused to high-level type of society...[you can] forget. He or they cannot forget that the global community, the people themselves, are very important.... And when I say "the people" I mean the average people.

Prominent first-generation Portuguese often had access to education that was denied to the vast majority of their compatriots. The education gap between the community leaders I interviewed and the average Portuguese immigrant is striking. The North American environment equalizes such differences somewhat—working-class Portuguese buy houses and purchase the material possessions of the middle class—but divisions remain.

The Liability of "Newness" and the Immigrant Experience

Finally, the liability of being an immigrant and not having multi-generational roots—and political contacts—crops up repeatedly as an obstacle to political participation. Research on native-born citizens finds that those who move to a new town or neighborhood are less likely to participate politically than those with longstanding ties to their community since "[n]ew arrivals face the many demands of relocation.... They must reestablish themselves politically...[and] they must wait for new channels of political information and encouragement to develop" (Rosenstone and Hansen 1993, 157). The number of years of residence an immigrant has in his or her adopted country has a consistently positive correlation with electoral participation and naturalization (Lien 2002; Ramakrishnan and Espenshade 2001; Jones-Correa 2001).

Even though most Portuguese immigrants migrated more than thirty years ago, liabilities of newness affect the Portuguese because compared to other "white ethnic groups" with which they are contrasted, the Portuguese remain a largely immigrant group. One Portuguese-American who ran for office in Massachusetts explained that in his case, "Because I came at fourteen, I didn't have the school buddies, the friends from elementary school that would be your natural supporters." In contrast, other candidates did have these deep roots in the community. A Portuguese-born woman in Toronto who is active in politics made a similar observation, adding that such barriers made political involvement even harder for immigrant women:

> It's difficult because, no matter how you look at it, you don't always have the same connections. Even myself, who has been in different jobs, in different interactions with different people at different levels. I mean, I'm not in their circle. I don't play golf with them on weekends. I can't compete with their incomes, or with their power, or with who they know. I may have worked with them. I may call upon them to make a donation, but...I don't rub shoulders with these people.... I'm not part of that circle. I never have been, you know. I take a step in, I say hello, and I step out again.

Liabilities of newness affect ordinary immigrants as well as the small group of political activists who might contemplate standing for office.

Portuguese-Americans' Greater Political Invisibility

All of these reasons for political invisibility—lack of education and language skills, prior socialization, internal divisions and immigrant 'newness'—should affect Portuguese communities in the United States and Canada equally. Indeed, among the more than 100 migrant groups that have moved to North America, Portuguese immigrants appear among the most similar on either side of the 49th parallel. If political invisibility were only a function of immigrants' characteristics, we should find the same levels of citizenship and elected representation in Toronto and Boston.[10]

Citizenship and Naturalization

Citizenship acquisition, done through the legal process known as naturalization, is an important indicator of political incorporation. Citizenship denotes legal and symbolic membership in a country and it is a necessary prerequisite for voting almost everywhere in North America. To become a citizen, an immigrant must prove a certain number of years of residence (three in Canada, generally five in the United States), demonstrate basic knowledge of civics and English (or French in Canada), swear (or affirm) an oath of allegiance and show "good moral character," such as the absence of a criminal record. These requirements are largely the same in Canada and the United States. The benefits of citizenship are actually higher in the United States: U.S. citizenship makes it easier to sponsor relatives and provides guaranteed access to social welfare benefits, while Canadian law makes no such distinctions between Canadian citizens and foreign-born permanent residents.

Given the higher benefits of citizenship in the United States, it is surprising to see that whereas sixty-seven percent of Canadian residents born in Portugal held Canadian citizenship in 1996, only fifty-nine percent of Portuguese-born residents in the United States were American citizens in 2000. Moreover, these figures understate the extent of the naturalization difference because Portuguese migration to the U.S. Northeast is of slightly older origin than to Ontario. Since citizenship is strongly correlated with length of residence, we need to compare immigrants who entered North America at the same time. Figure 1 does this for Portuguese immigrants in Ontario and Massachusetts, using data from the 1990 U.S. and 1991 Canadian censuses.[11] For those with eleven to fifteen years of residence, citizenship levels in Ontario are double those in Massachusetts—fifty-two and twenty-six percent respectively. The gap diminishes for older cohorts, but even after thirty years of residence, Portuguese men and women living in Massachusetts are still less likely to be naturalized than compatriots in Canada.

FIGURE I

PERCENT OF PORTUGUESE-BORN ADULTS WHO HAVE NATURALIZED IN MASSACHUSETTS OR ONTARIO, BY PERIOD OF ENTRY (1990/91 CENSUS)

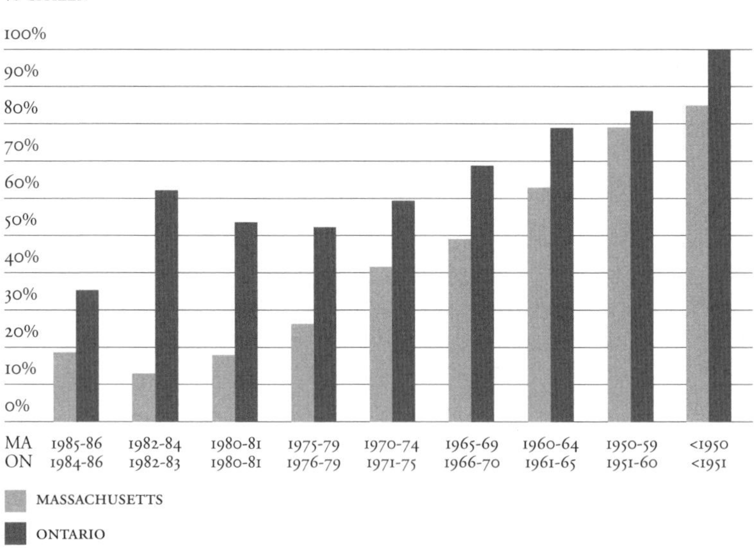

We can use statistical controls to further compare a Portuguese immigrant's probability of being a citizen in Ontario and Massachusetts. By using statistical modeling, we can artificially compare people with the same individual characteristics in terms of language ability, length of residence, income, gender and a host of other attributes to test whether individual differences among Portuguese immigrants in North America drive the naturalization gap between the two countries.

I report on the detailed statistical modeling elsewhere (Bloemraad 2002, 2006), but the upshot of the analysis is that even when we take into account all the things that might differentiate Portuguese immigrants in the two countries—such as Portuguese Ontarians' somewhat higher income—the probability that a Portuguese immigrant will hold citizenship is lower in Massachusetts. We can use a statistical model to imagine the "typical" Portuguese immigrant: a person who migrated to North

America in 1970 or 1971 at the age of twenty-four, who speaks English but only has completed elementary school, and who earns the median income of any Portuguese immigrant. Statistical simulation predicts that there is about a sixty-eight percent chance that this immigrant has acquired Canadian citizenship. The likelihood that this same person, living in Massachusetts, possesses American citizenship is forty-six percent. In sum, personal characteristics affect citizenship status, but where an immigrant lives matters significantly in predicting his or her odds of citizenship.

Electoral Success — Winning Office

An alternative measure of Portuguese immigrants' political presence is their ability to win elected office at all levels of government, from school boards to national legislature. Election to political office is, compared to naturalization, a much more elite level of political participation, but it can reflect the political strength of a community if that community throws its support behind an ethnic candidate. My interviews clearly suggest that many immigrants value political representation from their community for its symbolism, for the potential access it gives them to power brokers, and for the possible representation of substantive interests. As one Portuguese-Canadian activist argued:

> I feel that other politicians cannot take our cause equally well.... [I]t's the sense of belonging to a particular group. It has nothing to do with it being a Portuguese-Canadian group. It could be the group of the fifty-year-olds that make quilts.... It's the identification with a particular group, knowing the history, knowing some of the challenges and the issues and so on. Really having the interests of that group at heart. And that's what makes the difference.

Yet despite strong interest in ethnic representation, most Portuguese lament what they see as their community's lack of political presence on municipal, state/provincial and national decision-making bodies.

Importantly, these complaints seem more founded in the Boston area than in metropolitan Toronto. At least ten Portuguese-Canadians have held elected office in the Toronto area, from serving on local school boards to the 2004 election of Canada's first Portuguese-born member of federal Parliament, Mario Silva.[12] Also strikingly, all but one of these individuals is a first-generation immigrant, someone born in Portugal. Portuguese-Canadian advocates have some grounds for complaint—in the 1990s, Portuguese representation on Toronto municipal council, at just under two percent of all seats, was only half of the community's proportion in the city—but we see a clear trend to active and increasing electoral participation and success.

In comparison, in Boston or its immediate suburbs, Teresa Cardosa, a U.S.-born Portuguese-American, is the only person elected in the last twenty-five years. Given that Portuguese-Americans accounted for almost 4.5 percent of the population in Cambridge and over eight percent in Somerville in 1990, the lack of political representation is striking. The Portuguese community has had somewhat more success in politics in parts of New Jersey and California, but especially in the Californian case, these individuals tend to be the third- or fourth-generation descendants of Portuguese immigrants who came to the United States in the early 20th century. Their immigration experience has become so distant that comparisons to Canada's largely immigrant and second-generation Portuguese population become highly problematic.[13] It would nonetheless be useful, in the future, to make comparisons across Portuguese-American communities in the United States to see whether context effects make a difference today, since we have evidence that they did matter in the past (Baganha 1991; Williams 2005).[14]

How Does the Context of Reception Matter? Explaining Relative Invisibility

What explains Portuguese-Americans' relative political invisibility compared to Portuguese-Canadians? I highlight three factors, all of which point to the role played by receiving societies in immigrants' activities and interest in citizenship and politics.

Government Support and Organizations

First, we need to consider the role of government in facilitating the creation and maintenance of ethnic or immigrant community organizations. Civic associations, sports clubs, religious bodies, social service agencies and a host of others provide material and human resources, as well as a physical location, from which to mobilize people politically, even if the organization's primary mission is not at all political. For example, organizations can facilitate naturalization, especially for immigrants who face significant language or education barriers, by filling in forms, teaching civics and English as a Second Language, providing counseling and more generally offering encouragement to go through with the citizenship process (Alvarez 1987; Bloemraad 2006). Having numerous organizations in an ethnic community, or certain large, strong organizations, also facilitates participation in the formal electoral system. Politicians see such groups as an easy and efficient way to reach large numbers of potential voters (Marwell 2004; Parenti 1967).

In Canada, governments provide more support to immigrants and local community organizations than those in the United States, especially around immigrant integration such as job counseling, language instruction and translation/ interpretation assistance (Bloemraad 2006). For example, over the 2003-04 fiscal year, the Canadian federal ministry in charge of immigration, Citizenship and Immigration Canada, allocated $100 million to English language instruction to immigrant newcomers which, combined with other programs, meant that the federal government spent about $1,500 per new immigrant admitted (House of Commons 2003, 2, 6). No similar programs exist in the United States for immigrants such as the Portuguese, and while local or state governments offer some assistance, funding for these activities tends to be meager. In 2002, the Office of New Bostonians in Boston City Hall estimated that an immigrant faced a two-year wait for public ESL classes, with a somewhat reduced wait for priority clients such as those who have children in the city's public schools.[15] The Canadian government's official policy of multiculturalism, as well as comparable provincial and municipal policies, also provides financial and symbolic support to ethnic associations ranging from advocacy organizations to folklore groups. In the United States, governments favor more distant, neutral relations with immigrants, ethnic organizations, and community advocates. Only legally recognized refugees and asylees can access government-funded programs for resettlement. While the United States holds a strong ideology as a country of immigrants, its policy on community-building has been largely *laissez-faire.*

As a result, Portuguese Canadians in Toronto enjoy a relatively richer organizational infrastructure than in the Boston area (Bloemraad 2005,

2006). The groundwork for political mobilization is stronger. Although the number of ethnic Portuguese in Toronto and the Boston area are roughly similar—approximately 87,200 individuals in Toronto and 78,500 in metro Boston—there appear to be about six times more organizations in downtown Toronto than in the Cambridge/Somerville area of Boston. The organizational difference changes depending on the type of group considered, but we find many more political and professional associations, ethnic media, social service and advocacy groups in Toronto, even though Portuguese migration to Massachusetts has a longer history and more time to develop an organizational infrastructure.

It is worth noting that one of the biggest imbalances is around media organizations. Part of the difference reflects the two areas' relative importance as foci for the larger provincial or state Portuguese community. In Ontario, Toronto is a center for Portuguese activities, but in Massachusetts, larger and older Portuguese communities in New Bedford and Fall River produce newspapers and some radio programming that is consumed in the Boston area. However, greater regulatory support for multicultural radio and television programming in Canada also plays a role. In Toronto two locally-based TV stations are dedicated to the city's linguistic minorities, and various radio stations offer a multicultural selection of programming. While in some cases the Portuguese are only granted a few hours per day or per week on these multi-ethnic channels, the Toronto ethnic media have been a particularly fertile ground for community advocates and politicians: one former member of municipal government had a regular radio show before being elected; a former school trustee currently works as a newspaper journalist; and at least two elected school board members have worked on Portuguese-language television.

Without a clear policy in favor of multicultural broadcasting at the national or state level, ethnic communities such as the Portuguese in the Boston area are dependent on local authorities and the volunteer energies of community members. City governments in metropolitan Boston require cable companies to provide community television channels in return for distribution contracts and a few Portuguese-Americans have produced shows for these local stations. However, those active in ethnic media complain that distribution of the shows tends to be very localized given complicated cable agreements, and their efforts are largely amateur and require sustained community support—which often fails to materialize. As one person explained, "No one even helps.... I have a guy that used to come and videotape, control the camera, [but] he had other things to do.... It looks like everyone is busy, and they say 'I don't have the time.'" Lacking a local, professional ethnic media, many Portuguese immigrants in the Boston area watch RTPi, the international Portuguese broadcast station. While there is some local content on RTPi—mostly focused on southeastern Massachusetts—the lack of sustained local input makes it a poor vehicle for political mobilization.

In sum, government policies in Canada toward immigrant integration, the funding of community organizations and regulation of multicultural media facilitate participatory citizenship in Toronto, while the lack of similar efforts in the United States aggravates Portuguese political invisibility.

The Party System and Ideological Congruence

A second reason for the greater political visibility of Portuguese immigrants in Toronto lies in the relationship between local political structures and community elites. In Toronto, a stronger and more competitive party system, greater ideological diversity between parties, and more localized nomination procedures lower barriers to running for office and make elections appear more meaningful than in heavily Democratic Boston. Especially noteworthy is the activism of a small but vocal group of left-wing Portuguese-Canadians in Toronto, an advocacy presence absent in Boston.

While most Portuguese contemplating a move to North America did so for economic reasons, usually setting their sights on the United States, a small minority of elite Portuguese immigrants moved to Canada for political reasons. Most are from the mainland and were involved in the Communist party and its efforts to overthrow the Salazar dictatorship. In some cases, these individuals embraced the Communist party and its ideology. Others, a larger proportion, participated in networks or joined in events organized by Communists because there was no other organized, viable opposition to the dictatorship. In some cases these individuals' move to Canada was dictated by prior family ties, but in others, individuals avoided the United States because of Americans' perceived anti-Communism; Canada was seen as a relatively more welcoming country.[16] These people brought a Leftist mind-set to Canada that found a home in the New Democratic Party (NDP) and, for some, became reinforced by the Canadian union movement.[17]

For example, José Manuel left Portugal for political reasons. In his words, "The political police were after me. I thought I'd like to go there [to Canada]. I don't fit in with the American mentality. I had a friend who had escaped from the compulsory military service and he offered to take me to Canada." After entering Canada on a tourist visa, he confirmed his vague, positive notions about the country and decided to stay, regularizing his situation in 1972. He soon found a political home in the left-wing Portuguese-Canadian Democratic Association and, through friends at the Association and other political activities, he became heavily involved with the NDP, including a brief stint in elected office.

The individuals who chose Canada for political reasons influenced a larger group of future community advocates. Some current Portuguese-Canadian community leaders trace their political beliefs and activism to people like José Manuel. The left-wing group also created political opposition in the community by those with more conservative views. Such ideological cleavages split the Toronto Portuguese community, but from the viewpoint of political participation this competition has been positive: it spurred other Portuguese to run for office in opposition to the left-wing group. The left-leaning elite do not represent the political ideology of the majority of the community, which is probably Liberal, yet five of the ten Portuguese-Canadians elected to office are affiliated with the NDP, and their activism has spurred others to participate.

Similar dynamics are largely absent in Boston. Certainly some individuals involved in the anti-Salazar opposition migrated to Massachusetts, but these people did not find a similar home in the Democratic Party or the union movement of the Boston area, at least not to the point of standing for office. Often the most active Portuguese leaders in Cambridge and Somerville separate their community-based activism from mainstream politics. Armando, for example, is widely recognized for his leadership around community events, but when it comes to American politics, he participates by making campaign contributions and acting as a liaison between U.S. politicians and elites from Portugal, not ordinary Portuguese immigrants. For Armando, community participation is personal, while his political activities are "at a different level."

Strong local Democratic "machines"— party structures with loyalties to particular people—also make it difficult for the Portuguese to break into politics in places such as Somerville, which are often dominated by Irish- and Italian-Americans.

Multiculturalism, Immigration and Race

Finally, languages of race and ethnicity operate differently in Canada and the United States, and these discourses impede Portuguese immigrants' political visibility more in Boston than in Toronto. In Canada, the predominant language of multiculturalism is oriented to ethnicity, allowing Portuguese-Canadians equal standing to Chinese-Canadians, Italian-Canadians or Vietnamese-Canadians. In the United States, political multiculturalism tends to be understood in terms of broad racial groupings. In this context, the Portuguese are grouped with other white ethnic groups in Boston. This is problematic because these other "white ethnics"—notably the Irish and the Italians—have more distant immigrant pasts; almost all the Irish and Italian political elites in Boston are American-born. In their everyday lives, Portuguese immigrants face linguistic, cultural and socio-economic barriers like other immigrants, a majority of whom are racial minorities or Latinos. But when local advocates try to forge immigrant coalitions, the Portuguese are sometimes excluded because immigrant affairs are often equated with racial minority status.

Although the Portuguese are a European group, their status as "white" in American racial classifications was not a foregone conclusion. In Hawaii, the Portuguese historically have been considered part of the local non-white population rather than members of the European-origin "Haole" community, a distinction reflected in Hawaiian census reports from 1853 to 1930 (Geschwender, Carroll-Seguin and Brill 1988).[18] In Massachusetts, the presence of darker-skinned Cape Verdeans led some Americans to consider all Portuguese as "Black," an experience recalled by some of my older respondents. When Congress debated the inclusion of Latinos and Hispanics into federal minority programs in the 1960s and 1970s, many in the community felt that Portuguese immigrants should be included. One researcher who surveyed the Portuguese populations of Cambridge and Somerville in the 1970s summed up the general attitude when he argued:

> Whatever the national political logic of this position, it [the Hispanic category] is conceptual nonsense in terms of defining minorities as far as this local area is concerned. If speaking a different language, sharing a foreign cultural background, or being an immigrant population is sufficient reason to be considered a minority in the case of non-Black Hispanics, then the Portuguese are definitely a minority.... (Ito-Alder 1980 [1972, 1978], 25)

However, certain Portuguese elites opposed the designation, arguing for the distinctiveness of Portuguese culture vis-à-vis that of Hispanics. A letter stating such objections was sent to Congress and read into the Congressional Record. In subsequent legislation, the Portuguese were excluded from the Hispanic/Latino designation, while another European group, immigrants from Spain, was included (see Moniz, this volume).

Portuguese "whiteness" has had significant political consequences, notably in the lack of Portuguese linguistic assistance under the Voting Rights Act. The Act, passed by Congress in 1965, aimed to ensure African-Americans' access to the ballot box. Renewed in 1970 and again in 1975, the second renewal extended its guarantees to linguistic minorities. Asian, Hispanic and Native American groups successfully lobbied Congress to include provisions guaranteeing linguistic minorities access to ballots, instructions, and voter information pamphlets written in their own language, as well as to multilingual poll workers. Under the Act, a political jurisdiction contains a linguistic minority if 10,000 people or five percent of the population speaks a language other than English, and reports limited English competency as measured by the Census. In addition, the group must show a level of illiteracy above the national average. In Massachusetts, various Portuguese immigrant communities satisfy these provisions, but the Act limits its coverage to "persons who are American Indian, Asian-American, Alaskan Natives, or of Spanish heritage" (Sections 14 (c) (3) and 203 (e)).[19] In 2002, 296 municipalities and counties across the United States were required to make special linguistic accommodations (Kong 2002). In Massachusetts, Lawrence, Holyoke, Springfield, Boston, and Chelsea had to provide Spanish-language services to electors during the 1990s, but Portuguese-speakers received no special assistance.[20]

In contrast, Canadian multiculturalism is primarily ethnic. Groups are recognized based on national origin or, more rarely, by sub-national ethnicities if the group is relatively large and cohesive. A major advantage of such public rhetoric is that it accords well with most immigrants' self-perceptions. A Portuguese-Canadian woman who migrated from the Azores as a young girl still considers herself first and foremost Portuguese, rather than Canadian or Portuguese-Canadian. She nonetheless speaks approvingly about Canadian multiculturalism:

> What it means to me is different nations of people, different, all types of people gathered.... [I]t shows that everybody can get along together. It's not discrimination against anybody. We all feel that in some way we are important to each other. That this person is not better than [a] Portuguese person, not better than the next person. To me it's VERY important.

In both recognizing and legitimizing immigrants' difference, multiculturalism helps this woman and others feel that they have grounds to make claims on government and fellow citizens, and that they may do so despite their origins.[21]

The emphasis on ethnicity combined with the relatively universal nature of many Canadian settlement programs creates two contradictory impulses for community leaders: a sense of integration and welcome, but also fear of political isolation through ethnic "ghettoization." One Portuguese-Canadian told me, "I think official multiculturalism... is used to pander down, to buy votes and to kind of ghettoize a little bit. This whole ethnic thing also bothers me...because I think that's another way in which the immigrant communities are kind of marginalized and ghettoized." Noteworthy in this assessment is the respondent's belief that politicians seek to "buy votes" through such programs, a process of inclusion rather than exclusion. Fear of ghettoization leads community leaders in Toronto to encourage fellow immigrants to embrace Canadian citizenship.

In addition, when organizations receive money and legitimacy from government departments or programs called Multiculturalism or Citizenship, community advocates make an implicit link between government, inclusion and participation. From the point of view of leaders such as Célia, the state welcomes newcomers, and while it clearly could do more, a certain loyalty emerges:

> I know that a lot of people resent the multiculturalism policy; they feel that it ghettoizes us, and puts us into separate little communities, and it prevents us from fully integrating and so on. There is a bit of truth to that.... Having said that, however, on another level we have fought and we have gained, and other organizations have fought for services, social services, health care services.... A system that has had a lot of faults—that's why we're still lobbying and advocating for a lot of things—but a system that gives us, from what we hear from other jurisdictions and other countries, [a system] that I think has been incredibly good to newcomers in terms of trying to address a lot of the different needs.

Such sentiments encourage community leaders to mobilize in favor of citizenship and political participation in Toronto.

Conclusion

The comparison of Portuguese immigrants' political "invisibility" in the Boston area to that of their compatriots in Toronto teaches us two important things. First, Portuguese political invisibility is not inevitable. Along with a number of measures, Portuguese immigrants in Toronto have achieved significant political voice and political visibility. A large majority of the community holds Canadian citizenship and thus can access important political rights. While naturalization among Portuguese is lower than among many other immigrant groups in Canada, it is significantly higher than in the United States, and it has had a bigger effect on political outcomes, propelling at least nine Portuguese-born Canadians and one Canadian-born woman of Portuguese origin into elected office from the metropolitan area. There is no reason to believe that political invisibility is the necessary lot of Portuguese-Americans.

However, this chapter has also demonstrated a second important point: government policy, the local political system, and understandings of race-based multiculturalism in the United States and Massachusetts erect further obstacles to Portuguese political incorporation. These obstacles come on top of the already formidable obstacles of limited

English-language ability, low levels of schooling, distrust of politics, and a lack of long-standing political ties. Whereas past accounts of Portuguese political invisibility variously blame, or explain, Portuguese immigrants' lack of voice on their lack of interest, skills and resources, the comparison to the Toronto community shows that the social and political context in which immigrants find themselves exerts a powerful influence on voice and visibility. Hopefully future generations of Portuguese-Americans will be able to break into politics as they benefit from better language skills, more education, and economic mobility. For Portuguese immigrants, however, the obstacles are formidable.

Notes

[1] An earlier version of this paper was given at the Portuguese Studies Program, Institute of European Studies, University of California, Berkeley, April 23, 2004. In conducting this research, I gratefully acknowledge the financial support of the National Science Foundation (SES-0000310), the Canadian Social Science and Humanities Research Council, the Quebec Fonds FCAR, the Social Science Research Council, and Statistics Canada (Division of Housing, Family and Social Statistics).

[2] This chapter draws from and synthesizes results reported in Bloemraad (2002, 2005, 2006). The fieldwork was conducted between 1996 and 2001, largely in the downtown core of the city of Toronto and in Cambridge and Somerville, cities directly adjacent to Boston. These areas are historic sites of first settlement for post-World War II Portuguese immigrants and continue to have high proportions of Portuguese in their population. The sixty-two Portuguese-origin individuals interviewed fell into two groups: community leaders (eighteen in Toronto, thirteen in the Boston area) and ordinary immigrants (fifteen in Toronto, sixteen in the Boston area). Community leaders were identified by residents of Portuguese origin or they were selected because they held a position of leadership in a local community organization. Ordinary immigrants were selected through convenience sampling and referral; special effort was made to avoid recruiting through community-based organizations so as to not bias interviews toward those most active in the community. The interviews with regular members of the community were evenly divided between men and women. In line with what we know from census data, the majority of respondents had less than a high school education and hailed primarily from the Azores. Among community leaders, the proportion of men was higher, almost all had a university degree, and there was greater representation by 1.5- and 2nd-generation Portuguese. For further information about the research design and methods, see Bloemraad (2006).

[3] In Massachusetts, the historic centers of Portuguese-American settlement are the cities of Fall River and New Bedford in the southeastern part of the state. According to the 2000 U.S. Census, forty-seven percent and thirty-nine percent of town residents, respectively, report some Portuguese ancestry, compared to 7.5 percent for Somerville and 3.1 percent for Cambridge, Massachusetts. I discuss some of the implications of the large community in southeastern Massachusetts later in the chapter, notably around Portuguese media. It is worth emphazing that while Fall River and New Bedford have produced more Portuguese-American politicians—usually of native, not immigrant, birth—Portuguese-Americans are far from dominating local politics, a somewhat surprising situation given their numerical presence in the area.

[4] According to the 1991 Canadian Census (twenty percent sample), ninety-six percent of Portuguese-born adults in Ontario reported being Catholic. The U.S. Census does not include a question on religious affiliation, but a survey in southeastern Massachusetts in 1999/2000 found that ninety-five percent of Portuguese-American respondents reported being Roman Catholic (Barrow 2002).

[5] The first four explanations probably do help to explain differences between the Portuguese and other ethnic groups, and I consider them in-depth. The fifth explanation carries a cultural determinism that seems suspect. Almeida suggests that the political failings of the Portuguese probably stem from a general mind-set characterized by "a high degree of emotion [sic] life strongly connected to

and affecting their intellectual domain" (1999a, 237). He believes that Portuguese share such a cultural orientation with other Mediterranean cultures, but such an explanation flies in the face of Italians' over-representation in Toronto politics at all levels of government (Siemiatycki and Isin 1997). Almeida (2000b) also argues that those in Massachusetts and Ontario share the Portuguese psyche, yet we find important cross-national difference in electoral success.

[6] The Ornstein data are based on reported Portuguese ethnicity, and thus includes some Canadian-born Portuguese, while the U.S. data are only for immigrants. The Canadian data consequently understate the extent of the skill gap among Portuguese immigrants.

[7] In Toronto, former metro councilor Martin Silva, a Portuguese-Canadian, attributes his electoral loss in part to comments he made on Portuguese radio describing illiteracy as a significant problem for the community.

[8] To my knowledge no surveys exist that measure the political attitudes of Portuguese-Americans in the Boston area. A study of Portuguese-Americans in southeastern Massachusetts found relatively low levels of political interest in affairs outside the local community. Thus, whereas no significant differences existed between the political knowledge or activity of Portuguese-Americans and non-Portuguese in Taunton, Massachusetts, Portuguese-Americans were significantly less likely to know the name of the Massachusetts governor or to express interest in national affairs than non-Portuguese (Barrow 2002). The small number of people sampled (depending on the question, between fifty-three and 403 individuals) means that these results should be treated with caution.

[9] There is a clear educational gap between those individuals who are identified as community leaders and/or who hold formal positions of authority in community organizations, and the rest of the community. Among the leaders, most have a university education or some post-secondary training, while the majority of Portuguese immigrants have an eighth grade education or less. This probably feeds into a "brokerage" system, where community leaders speak for the community to the mainstream press and politicians. Some do this for political gain, while others do it for economic standing or to enhance prestige in the community (see also Brettell [1977] 2003g).

[10] Indeed, we can consider the similarities of Portuguese migration to be akin to a laboratory experiment. While ethical and practical considerations mean that immigrants cannot be randomly assigned to move to Canada or the United States, Portuguese migration offers a quasi-experiment of how the political and policy environment might matter.

[11] Because of the strong effect of length of residence and the lack of contemporary Portuguese migration, these differences attenuate somewhat in 2000.

[12] This count is based on interviews and published electoral returns, and it is meant to be exhaustive for the time period covered. It is possible, however, that it misses some elected Portuguese-Canadians, especially at the school board level. Because of Canada's historic compromise between English Protestants and French Catholics in the 19th century, there are four Toronto school boards: the "public" English and French ones (which were historically influenced by Protestantism) and the Catholic English and French school boards, which are supported through public taxes.

[13] Immigration researchers call those who are foreign-born and who physically migrate the "first" generation. The native-born children of these immigrants are the "second" generation, and the native-born grandchildren of the original immigrants are "third" generation. In some cases, researchers talk about the "1.5" generation, people born in another country but who migrated as children and who were largely educated and socialized in the country of residence. Because they are foreign-born, they are "first" generation in a legal and demographic sense, but their socialization as children and young adults makes their experience somewhat akin to "second" generation immigrants.

[14] Baganha argues that the social context of reception had a significant impact on how Portuguese did economically at the turn of the 19th century in Massachusetts, California, and Hawaii (1999). While the focus is on economic integration, she provides some impressionistic naturalization information, suggesting that contexts of reception possibly produced higher naturalization in California, lower levels of citizenship in Hawaii, and in-between results in Massachusetts.

[15] Telephone conversation with Office of New Bostonians, 17 December 2002.

[16] This perception has some basis in reality. In the United States, an individual must formally declare past Communist affiliation on the naturalization application. Past membership in the Communist party constitutes grounds upon which USCIS can refuse American citizenship. There is no similar question on Canadian citizenship forms.

[17] In the United States, there are two main political parties, the Republicans and the Democrats, while for much of the post-World War II period in Canada there were three parties: the right-of-center Conservatives, the centrist Liberals and the left-of-center New Democratic Party.

[18] Census reports distinguished between "Portuguese" and "other Caucasians."

[19] These provisions were renewed in 1982, 1992, and 2006.

[20] This includes, as well, the burgeoning Brazilian population in the state. The presence of a significant Brazilian community, a group from Latin America but which is not Hispanic, adds further complexity to the classification of minority communities.

[21] Canadian governments also address racial discrimination and institutional barriers by making a distinction between "visible minorities," a catch-all category that includes all non-whites, and non-visible minorities (whites).

CHAPTER 2

Multiple Layers of Time and Space: The Construction of Class, Ethnicity, and Nationalism among Portuguese Immigrants[1]

BELA FELDMAN-BIANCO

Introduction

Ever since the era of seafaring exploration in the 15th and 16th centuries, the world—rather than the nation-state—has been the spatial unit for the Portuguese. Starting with the voyages of discovery and the colonizing of new lands and later (since the 19th century) continuing with labor migration, the movement of people across the globe has been constitutive of the Portuguese experience. *Saudade,* a word that originated in the 16th century[2] has been associated with the unending Portuguese *wanderlust.* While loosely translated as "longing" and "nostalgia," *saudade* is in fact a cultural construct that defines Portuguese identity in the context of multiple layers of space and (past) time.

On the one hand, at the level of the self or the person, *saudade* has been viewed as "the soul divided throughout the world," (Pereira and Gomes 1976, 81) "the uprooted experience located between the desire for the future and the memories of the past," (Pereira and Gomes 1976, 112) or simply as "the memories which touch a soul."[3] This dimension of *saudade,* referring to the symbolic representations and social practices of a time and space prior to emigration, further shapes regional identity.

On the other hand, *saudade* as the collective memory of Portugal has been reconstituted as the essence of Portuguese national character and as the basis of the imagined political community (Anderson [1983] 1991). Within that perspective, collective temporal memory is invariably linked to the discovery era and to the subsequent history of immigration; while collective spatial memory encompasses the explorations and the long separations from relatives around the world.

By focusing on the multiple layers of time and space of *saudade,* my aim in this paper is to contribute to the ongoing discussions of transnationalism and transmigration (Glick Schiller, Basch, and Blanc-Szanton 1992; Basch, Glick Schiller, and Blanc-Szanton, n.d.; Kearney 1991). Towards that end, based on fieldwork research conducted in Portugal and New Bedford, a New England industrial city, I will, first, examine how the attempts made by Portugal's post-colonial state to create a global deterritorialized nation encompassing its dispersed populations have been rooted in the reinvention of the collective memory of *saudade* (Basch, Glick Schiller, and Blanc-Szanton 1991); and, second, discuss how immigrants have differentially conceptualized *saudade* as the basis of their personal and collective identities in the context of their specific experiences at the intersection of Portuguese and American cultures.

From that view point, I will analyze the differential constructions of class, ethnicity, and nationalism of Portuguese immigrants against the background of changes in the global economy and of evolving Portuguese and American policies of control from the 1920s to the present. Two distinct periods in this process of identity construction will be delineated.

In the first period beginning in the 1920s and 1930s, a period of world economic depression, Portuguese migrants were subjected to restrictive immigration laws and second-class citizenship status both in the United States and Portugal. In addition, they were faced with two conflicting and highly charged ideologies, and were confronted with the state policies of two different nation states. On one side were the pressures of the U.S. "melting pot"—policies and ideologies that stressed the supremacy of American society and American ways of life. Conflicting with these were the Portuguese colonial policies and ideologies, based on the superiority and pride of the Luzitan race, which cast aspersions on those who left Portugal, and emphasized the exclusive maintenance of Portuguese culture and language.

In the second period—the 1970s and 1980s—in the context of the increasing internationalization of the global economy, both the United States and Portugal changed their approach toward the Portuguese immigrant population. In the United States, cultural pluralism now prevailed, an ideology which recognized the persistence of Portuguese culture among immigrants but which continued to encourage their incorporation into the U.S. polity. Meanwhile, the Portuguese post-colonial state, broadening the constructs of "nation" and "nationality," gave immigrants dual citizenship rights and began to consider them "Portuguese spread around the world." In the end, the forms of control exercised by both the United States and Portugal over their migrant populations led to the politicization of ethnicity as well as to an intensification and redefinition of transnationalism.

By adopting the theoretical and methodological approaches outlined by Glick Schiller, Basch, and Blanc-Szanton (1992), I seek to bring a historical dimension to the recent inquiries which have emphasized that immigrants are increasingly becoming transnationals "creating a single field of social action that merge the home and the host societies into a single construction" (Glick Schiller, Bash, and Szanton 1992). Insofar as these findings are mostly an outcome of research conducted among the so-called "new immigrants" (like those from the Caribbean and South Asia), analysts have tended to limit the scope of their studies to a period characterized in the United States by the restructuring of "deindustrialization." While these "new immigrants" have replaced the Europeans as the major labor pool in the United States, segments of the Portuguese migrant population have settled for several generations in New Bedford and the surrounding region. Since the 1920s, they have constituted the major ethnic group of the city, comprising today [1980s] sixty percent of New Bedford's 110,000 inhabitants. The continuous renewal of Portuguese immigration to New Bedford allows, therefore, for a close examination of patterns of continuity and change between past and present migrations, particularly as they concern the interrelationship between transnationalism and the construction (and reconstruction) of class, ethnicity and nationalism in the context of the creation of a "global" Portuguese nation.

When I first began my historical analysis, I found that I was confronted with a paradox: domestic structures indicated that in the past as in the present, lived experiences of Portuguese migrants settling in New Bedford have tended to stretch between Portugal and the United States. In the context of this prevailing pattern, there has been since the late 1970s both an intensification of old and the emergence of new forms of transnationalism. Yet, my analysis of events at the grass-roots level, together with the delineation of the organization of the Portuguese settlement in New Bedford, led me to identify a simultaneous increase of their insularity as an ethnic enclave in the city. Although they may seem contradictory, the seemingly paradoxical trends can be shown to result from the same dynamic. The growing internationalization of the world economy is being accompanied by the re-imagining of political communities. These newly-conceptualized political communities may be spatially dispersed. In any one locale, the global trends may appear as a growing ethnic insularity. Thus, this paper is directed at unveiling this paradox in the context of a shifting world economy and of corollary Portuguese and American changing mechanisms of control of international migrants.

The Reinvention of Saudade *and the Creation of a Portuguese "Global" Nation*

At least since the advent of the Portuguese Republic in the 19th century, the concept of nation (including the construction of successive nationalisms) has been linked to Portugal's role during the seafaring era and to its (real or mythical, imperial or colonial) overseas dominions. Camões, the author of the *Lusiadas,* the epic poem of the Discoveries, was turned into the mythical embodiment of the nation and of Luzitan patriotism. After the 1974 Portuguese revolution and the loss of the last overseas dominions, governmental officials began to shift away from ideologies that recurrently portrayed an image of "Portugal, the colonizer" and that glorified the "Luzitan race."[4] Yet, we will see that these experiences have been built upon by the Portuguese state. While there are plans to celebrate the Quincentennial of the Portuguese discoveries during the year 2000, the image of Camões has become associated with an "Immigrant Portugal" (Carvalho 1931, 35). The Tenth of June, formerly known as "The Day of Portugal, Camões, and the Luzitan race" was reinvented as "The Day of Portugal, Camões, and the Portuguese communities" and, thereby, transformed into a celebration of the immigrant communities abroad.

According to a decree established in 1977: "This day, better than any other day assembles the necessary symbolism to represent the Day of Portugal. It harmoniously synthesizes the Portuguese nation, the Luzitan communities spread throughout the world and the emblematical figure of the genial epics."[5]

Thus, the emigrant communities spread around the world replaced the former colonial dominions in the new and expanded construction of a "global" Portuguese nation. In 1980, the then Minister Sá Carneiro defined Portugal as a populous nation scattered over the four corners of the earth, stating that, " We can only survive, we can only believe in Portugal and in Portugal's future if we think of ourselves as a nation that embraces both residents and nonresidents, all treated equally" (Aguiar 1986, 7).

Upon Portugal's entrance into the European Community, in conformity with the emerging construction of a "global" nation, emigrants were given dual citizenship status, including voting rights. In a meeting of the Council of Europe, Manuela Aguiar justified this broader construction of nationality in the following terms:

> Migration and changing countries of residence originate new connections, new bounds and new loyalties. But this does not mean that the deep roots that bind individuals to the land and culture of their fathers do not continue to be the structural element of their identity. For individuals, the main thing is to be doubly accepted and wanted because they accept and love two countries. It will therefore be of advantage for the states to regulate with one another the consequences of such twofold links.[6]

The creation of a Portuguese global nation reflects dramatic redefinitions of emigration policies. At least until the 1940s, emigrants—considered second-class citizens—were defined as "those passengers traveling second- and third-class by boat." Even after that definition was abolished, Portuguese officials still continued to consider emigration a "necessary evil" and to view illegal migration as a serious crime.[7] A major shift began to occur in the early 1960s, when Portugal's colonial state, taking into account the prevailing international division of labor, recognized the need for developing emigration policies within the framework of labor policies. In 1965, the Portuguese government established a national employment service, which made the government itself in charge of the recruitment, placement, and return of migrant workers. Later, with Portugal's entrance in the European Community, post-colonial governmental policies began to emphasize the human rights of laborers rather than the supply of labor. Furthermore, in preparation for the unification of Europe, the term "emigrant" was recently abolished and replaced by the expressions "Portuguese abroad" and "Portuguese spread around the world."

In the past, Portuguese emigrants were stigmatized and discriminated against. By designating emigrants as Portuguese abroad, the government recognized the transnational character of Portuguese emigration. However, in Portugal's everyday life, emigrants are still seen as individuals who have assimilated into the culture of the country to which they had emigrated. They are still pejoratively called "French," "Canadians," "Brazilians," "Americans." Yet, since the late 1970s (and particularly since the early 1980s), along with their newly-acquired full dual citizenship rights, Portuguese emigrants (or, the Portuguese abroad) have a dual responsibility: "to integrate in [to] the host society without assimilating and to establish the presence of Portugal in the world" (Aguiar 1986, 18).

With the inclusion of emigrants in the conceptualization of a "global" nation, emigration services were placed under the Ministry of Foreign Affairs. In addition, the central government created a Secretariat of Portuguese Communities with the aims of a) strengthening the persistence of Portuguese culture and language in the world; and b) economic, social and cultural cooperation among Portuguese communities abroad as well as among those communities and the different regions of Portugal. Similar divisions were formed by the autonomous regions of the archipelagos of Madeira and the Azores, and currently a department of Portuguese overseas communities (with the participation of representatives of different Portuguese communities abroad) is being organized.

Recognition by Portugal's post-colonial state of the transnational character of Portuguese immigration and incorporation of its dispersed population into the creation of a global deterritorialized nation is mirrored and reinforced by Portuguese poet Fernando Pessoa's image of Portugal as a "nation-ship aboard which we (the Portuguese) are already born departing," and thus "a Portuguese who is only a Portuguese is not a Portuguese" (Carvalho 1931, 32). The imagining of a Portuguese deterritorialized "global" nation has also been expressed in immigrants' poems. Consider this poem by João Teixeira Medeiros, who was born in

New England, lived in the Azores from age nine to twenty-two and then returned to New England:

> the word saudade who felt it
> who made it fit the Portuguese heart at large
> saudade has happiness and sadness
> feeling and voice
> saudade is very Portuguese
> it is an offspring of all of us
> saudade gives flavour to entire nations
> it is part of our daily life
> saudade will be present
> in any place where there are Portuguese flags
> saudade travelled with us in the sea
> as well as in the thousands of hinterlands
> it is with us in the airplanes
> saudade God help us
> has such a deep power
> it is like a hurricane spreading us
> in the little corners of the world[8]

In the context of the emerging world economic order, the Portuguese post-colonial state has reinvented and reelaborated the temporal memory of the exploration era into the present. At the same time, it included the dispersed emigrant populations in the new spatial conceptualization of an overseas Portugal. *Estamos todos espalhados pelo mundo* [we are all spread throughout the world] is a common statement among the Portuguese, which suggests that their lived experiences and imagery have stretched across the world. These experiences and imagery have provided a source of legitimacy for the creation of a "global" nation. Yet, Portuguese settled abroad (such as those in New Bedford) have differentially reshaped their self-identities in response to these policies.

"A Portuguese who is only a Portuguese is not a Portuguese" or "The Construction of a Portuguese Territory Abroad"

New Bedford is one of the many Portuguese "little corners of the world."

As such, it is part of a network of Portuguese enclaves in New England, a transnational space, which Onésimo T. Almeida calls "L(U.S.A.) land," "a portion of Portugal, surrounded by America from every side... a special nation composed of communities that are neither Portugal nor America ...[that are] rather a mixture of two cultures, a world between Portugal and America (Almeida 1987, 231).

For at least a century, labor migration, networks of kinship relations (including intercontinental marriage patterns), circulation of material and symbolic goods, and the constant reinvention of multiple layers of Portuguese (past) time and space in an American present, have merged this "world between Portugal and America" into a single social construction.[9] By focusing on the interrelationship between transnationalism and insularity, I will trace the historical processes and the cultural meanings through which this "world between Portugal and America" has in fact become a Portuguese "territory" abroad.

The Portuguese mark 1832 as the year they began to construct their "territory" in New Bedford. At that time, Azorean and Cape Verdean males increasingly provided the labor for whaling expeditions. However, mass migration of families (first from the Azores and subsequently also from Madeira and the mainland) began during the last decades of the 19th century, reaching its height in 1910. These immigrants were mostly composed of impoverished small landholders, landless laborers, and artisans fleeing poverty in a period of Portugal's major economic decline. There are indications that, initially, the Portuguese settling in New Bedford were predominantly involved with agriculture and craftsmanship. Some eventually managed to buy land in the outskirts of the city.

The local cotton mill industry, at that time at the vanguard of American industrialization, was initially based on a labor force mainly composed of English, Irish, and French-Canadian workers. It was only by the turn of the 20th century that the Portuguese, along with other Southern and Eastern European unskilled workers began arriving in large numbers to the area, as cheap labor in the cotton economy. By 1910, the Portuguese already represented forty percent of that labor force. Estimates further suggest that, by 1930, eighty percent of the Portuguese were cotton mill workers while fifteen percent were professionals and business people.[10] Even though there was a certain degree of stratification among the Portuguese, those who remained in the region were deeply affected—like other local residents—by the decline of the textile industry and the thirty-year-long depression of the New Bedford economy that was to follow.

While Portuguese immigration to New Bedford never ceased, in the late 1950s, the American government issued a special decree to facilitate the arrival of the Azoreans, in view of a drastic earthquake on one of the islands. Later, with the 1965 United States Immigration Act, successive contingents from the Azores, mainland Portugal, and Portuguese Africa have settled in New Bedford. Though to a lesser degree, Cape Verdeans, Hispanics, and (more recently) Koreans have also migrated to the area.

There are indications that the Portuguese arriving since the 1970s have tended to be more stratified economically, socially and educationally than the former contingents. In contrast to the bulk of the immigrants of the past who came to New Bedford in a bid to escape destitution, there are considerable numbers of middle-class Portuguese among the new migrants. While some emigrated to avoid the drafting of their sons during the colonial wars in Africa, others came to the United States "for the future of their children." Still others either left Portugal prompted by the Portuguese Revolution, or left Portuguese Africa in response to the independence of the African colonies. Some emigrated to New Bedford from other countries of the world.

Estimates indicate that sixty percent of today's 110,000 inhabitants of New Bedford are of Portuguese origin. These include the so-called Luso-Americans (descendants of the older contingents of immigrants from the Azores, mainland, and Madeira), many of whom have intermarried with members of the older immigrant groups (French-Canadian, English, Irish, Polish, Italians, etc.); American-born Portuguese, who moved, together with their parents, to Portugal prior to or by the 1930s, and have increasingly returned to New Bedford since the 1960s; as well as newer contingents of immigrants and their descendants, most of whom are linked by kinship to the older generations of migrants and their descendants. In addition, these figures include the Cape Verdeans, who, prior to the independence of Cape Verde, were part of the Portuguese community of New Bedford.

Today, the Portuguese of New Bedford are stratified economically, socially, and educationally. While fifty percent of the immigrant population is still composed of factory workers, Luso-Americans and segments of the immigrant population are represented in different sectors of activity in the region.[11] There has been, however, little political representation of these Portuguese within the American governmental echelons. Overall, in spite of their numbers, the bulk of the Portuguese immigrants still remains invisible in mainstream life in New Bedford. They live their daily routines within segregated (and self-segregated) neighborhoods.

Exploratory analysis of sixty oral histories and twenty-five genealogies suggests that the successive contingents of immigrants who have settled in New Bedford in different historical periods are linked among themselves through regionally-demarcated consanguineal and affinal kinship ties. In fact, there are indications that the more recent contingents of immigrants are ultimately members of the same families that emigrated to New England in the past.

The available data further suggest that, prior to the issuing of a series of increasingly restrictive immigration laws between 1917 and 1924, Portuguese immigrants (with their American-born children) moved back and forth between Portugal and the United States. While many settled permanently in New Bedford, others left Portugal to work for a few years either on the farms surrounding the city or in the local cotton mills with the aim of amassing capital to buy a plot of land in the homeland. Even though there were, at that time, successful entrepreneurship stories of immigrants returning to the homeland and investing their capital in local enterprises, these were solely the result of private initiative without any backing from the Portuguese state.

Later, during the decline of the cotton mill industry and the Great Depression that was to follow, return migration from New England to Portugal seems to have been relatively high: some immigrants returned to Portugal with their entire families, which in many cases included American-born children; others left their married offspring in the United States, returning to Portugal with their younger (American- and Portuguese-born) children. To a certain extent, even during the 1930s and 1950s, when restrictive American immigration quotas only allowed 500 Portuguese to enter the United States yearly, American-born Portuguese continued to move between Portugal and the United States, sometimes bringing along their Portuguese mates. In the same fashion, given the decline of New England's mill economy, some Portuguese offspring who had been left in the United States eventually returned to Portugal. Others, while remaining in the United States, went to Portugal to find mates. Still others moved from New England to other American regions, particularly California.

* * *

"Hello ... Goodbye ... my time to leave has come ..."[12] is the beginning sentence of a song that narrates how emigration has been constitutive of the everyday life in Portugal. In many regions of Portugal, and particularly in the Azores, the holding of American citizenship as well as access through kinship and marriage to "American papers" have been a valuable asset enabling individuals and families to move across, and live between, Portugal and the United States. Therefore, it is not by chance that American-born offspring of the Portuguese immigrants before and after 1930 as well as their relatives who have remained in the United States, have constituted the major connecting link between past and present contingents of Portuguese settling in the United States. Even in the 1960s, at a time when the Portuguese government was attempting to redirect the movement of labor migration from the United States to Europe, webs of kinship made way for the continuous arrival of new Portuguese contingents (mostly from the Azores and, to a lesser degree, Portuguese mainland) to the United States.

In this context, the continuous arrival of kin-related immigrants to the United States was facilitated, between the 1960s and the 1980s, by American governmental policies fostering chain migration. In fact, these policies enabled many families to reunite in New England and, at the same time, reinforced the common family strategy of choosing mates for their daughters and sons in the homeland.

In addition, the tendency of the local factories to engage in the paternalistic labor strategy of hiring family members of "docile" workers made way for the entrance of newly-arrived immigrants into the labor force. Therefore, independent of their class origins, many new arrivals found their first job opportunities in the labor-intensive factories which have progressively replaced the faded textile industry of the area.

Since recruitment tended to follow ethnic lines, the labor force in the local factories came to consist mainly of Portuguese male and female workers. Yet, particularly for some younger men and women, industrial work was merely the first channel of employment. The possibility of learning English to study a skill or to pursue further studies or of accumulating some capital (even if this meant working two shifts) provided them with an opportunity to enter other occupations, such as commerce, clerical work, or the liberal professions. In addition, some men were also able to leave the factory and make a livelihood in the local fishery (whose fleet is mainly composed of Portuguese mainlanders) and in construction work. However, for most immigrants, industrial work continued to be the main avenue of employment. In fact, until the turn of this decade, when many factories began to close down their local plants, it was not unusual to find immigrants working in the same factory, together with their relatives, for over fifteen or twenty years. But even within the factory, promotion was possible for those with a knowledge of English. While many immigrant workers speak only Portuguese, supervisors as well as union representatives are bilingual.

The advent of Social Security in the United States in the 1930s together with Medicare benefits for the elderly in the 1960s shifted the ideal from amassing capital to buy a plot of land in the homeland to the attainment of retirement in the United States and, thus, to the usufruct of the American structure of social benefits. This goal led to the postponement of return or, in many cases, to permanent settlement in the United States. Nonetheless, in view of the prevailing ideal of return, many "new" immigrants have kept their houses, land, and even cars in the homeland. At the same time, they have tended to buy, as soon as they could, a house in the United States, which symbolized in their own words, "their share of the American Dream." In view of this ever-postponed return to the homeland, their sons and daughters were able, at least since the 1970s, increasingly to pursue a U.S. education. Particularly those offspring who were able to earn a college degree have provided a brokerage role between immigrants and American institutions. In view of the prevailing ideology of cultural pluralism and of their bilingual and bicultural skills, many were able to enter occupations within the local governmental structure and the bilingual educational system as well as the Portuguese institutions which were created in the 1970s with the aid of American grants. At the same time, therefore, that this cultural brokerage has helped immigrants to cope with the American system and American institutions, it has further reinforced the insularity of the Portuguese within New Bedford.

However, particularly after the issuing of dual citizenship rights in Portugal, older immigrants have in fact returned to Portugal (and to a betterment of conditions), leaving younger relatives behind in the United States. These immigrants have lived simultaneously between Portugal and the United States, making full use of their dual citizenship rights (and of special privileges issued by the state to returning immigrants) and accumulated property in both countries. This trend seems to have intensified even more these days when, in view of the ongoing recession in the United States, larger numbers of retired immigrants are returning to the homeland.

Given Portuguese extended family patterns, this phenomenon made way for the intensification of a transnational family structure in which decisions of everyday life are dependent upon and encompass relatives living in Portugal and the United States. While younger members of these families often live more in the American milieu, taking into account that other bicultural and bilingual offspring often perform a brokering role for their Portuguese-speaking parents, this transnational family structure has tended to increase the isolation of these families within New Bedford.

In the past, Portuguese literature and oral histories have portrayed the arrival of trunks full of goods with the smell of America. Many immigrants still spend the year collecting goods and sending their trunk to Portugal, thereby laying claim to social prominence in Portugal by trying to assert their social mobility in the United States through these material goods. Formerly, this circulation of material goods was essential for the domestic economy of those relatives who were left behind in the homeland; now, however, immigrants are increasingly confronted with the higher social mobility of those relatives who were able to gain access to the free educational system of post-Revolutionary Portugal as well as to profit from the ongoing process of capitalist penetration. More and more, these relatives in Portugal request specific American brands, marking the transnationalization of consumption and of the domestic economy. In this context, the increasing incorporation of Portugal into the world economy and the betterment of standards of living in Portuguese regions also made for an intensification of visits of relatives living in Portugal to New England as well as for an increase in the circulation of material goods.

The Meaning of Portuguese (Past) Time and Space in Everyday Life at the Intersection of Cultures

These transnational networks which mark the Portuguese of New Bedford as members of a global nation encapsulate them and so insulate these immigrants within the social life of New Bedford. Symbols of the Portuguese past, in fact, of different layers of Portuguese time and space, are a constitutive part of immigrant neighborhoods in New Bedford. For instance, a layer of time, representing the Portuguese major role during the exploration era, (*i.e.*, the collective historical memory of the Portuguese) is found here and there: the 15th-century costumes of the Prince Henry Society (a type of Portuguese Rotary Club, formed in the 1980s); the many *caravelas* (the sailing ship of the discoverers) displayed in storefronts and homes; and the Prince Henry Monument in nearby Fall River. Another layer of time related to the past prior to immigration is reflected in the spatial organization of homes, with an American upstairs (represented by the symbols of consumption in the U.S.), a Portuguese downstairs (the major setting of everyday interaction and of social practices associated with the homeland), and in the yard, reproductions of Portuguese gardens. In the neighborhood outside the house are Portuguese stores.

Leisure-time activities include the continuation of the *serões* (storytelling and musical gatherings reminiscent of a strong oral tradition). The use of time and seasons may also place immigrants within a Portuguese world. While during the year, factory work shapes the lives of many, during the summer (as at the end of the harvest in rural Portugal), immigrants continue to ritualize their memories of the homeland in a succession of regional folk-religious festivals.[13] Discussions among family members, neighbors, and co-workers are filled with stories from the ethnic media (newspapers, radio, TV), which also bring Portugal into the everyday life of immigrants.

This sense of a certain immutability of time, given by the continuous incorporation of different layers of the past into the present, is perhaps characteristic of immigrant neighborhoods anywhere. In a way, these neighborhoods resemble still photographs of a past that was already lived and does not exist anymore in the homeland. Yet, these different layers of past time and space are dynamic representations of the ways in which immigrants cope with changing conditions of existence.

In the reconstruction of Portuguese identity on the level of the self or the person, the collective historical memory may, in some instances, permeate interactions with non-Portuguese, particularly in situations of discrimination. Self-esteem is reasserted by comparing the United States to the Portuguese mythical past in such ways as "How old is America? Who discovered America? And who are the Americans, anyway?"

Reconstructions of identity, which are mediated by symbolic representations of different layers of the Portuguese past, vary according to social class, regional background, generation, and gender.[14] Particularly, those women and men whose immigration history encompasses the transition from pre-industrial task-oriented activities in Portugal to industrial work in the United States tend to develop a romantic nostalgia, or *saudade da terra,* for their immediate past of non-industrial labor. The reinvention of their immediate past reflects their experiences with and perceptions of different rhythms and different meanings of time, work, and life in Portugal and the United States: from more natural rhythms to the time discipline of industrial capitalism.[15]

This romantic nostalgia for a past when work was intermingled with multiple dimensions of social intercourse gives meaning to hard lives marked by abrupt change—representing a strategy to resist total immersion in industrial time. Therefore, it is not by chance that they tend only to remember the beneficial aspects of their lives prior to migration.[16] In the context of dramatic changes caused by immigration and the pressures imposed by the regularities of industrial work, the homeland (which is remembered in terms of their village or region of origin) turns into Utopia. This romantic nostalgia is further translated into social practices associated with that past of non-industrial labor, such as gardening, wine making, sewing, embroidery. While during their work shift they are proletarians, in their free time they continue to be peasants and artisans. Above all, these symbolic representations and social practices of their past of non-industrial labor further provide the basis for self-reconstitution as Azoreans, Madeirans and mainlanders, thus demarcating their strong regional identities. In their everyday life, these regional identities tend to be stronger than (and sometimes conflict with) Portuguese national identity.

In contrast, American-born descendants of immigrants as well as younger immigrants who have advanced socially, educationally and economically, and who have become cultural brokers between immigrants and the larger American society have tended either to juxtapose their Portuguese and American identities or to shift progressively to an American identity. Endemic cleavages, expressing conflicting identities (in terms of regional origin, generation, and gender) mark the actions and interactions among these cultural brokers. Major divisions cut particularly across the relationships between immigrants and the so-called Luso-Americans (descendants of immigrants who settled in New Bedford before the mid-1950s). Yet, in their attempts to represent a rather heterogeneous (and probably nonviable) "Portuguese community," members of this stratum, particularly since the early 1980s, have tended to reinvent the Portuguese exploration era in their mobilization as an ethnic group striving to establish itself as a majority (not a minority) in the pluralistic society of New Bedford.

The past is, therefore, not a matter of fading memories and superfluous sentiment. Incorporated are the reimagings and reinventions of Portuguese identity, which both the Portuguese state and the transnational population play a part in producing. Perceiving themselves as a people spread throughout the world, the Portuguese immigrants make full use of their dual citizenship rights. In the context of the growing internationalization of the world economy, they make way for newly emerging forms of transnationalism. These immigrants have differentially re-elaborated their Portugueseness in the context of their concrete experiences of migration, changing work habits, and of the interconnection of lives lived between Portugal and the United States.

Reinventions of Portuguese Identity: Historical Processes and the Role of the Portuguese and American States

Contrasting American and Portuguese nationalisms—including different definitions of race—together with the immigrants' structural position in New Bedford is essential to gaining an understanding of the cultural and social processes underlying the construction of class, race, ethnicity, and nationalism as collective movements. In the 1920s and 1930s, the earlier years of settlement, as well as today, American officials have tended to view immigration essentially as a "race question" and be concerned with which racial strains of immigrants were desirable to U. S. society. After issuing highly restrictive immigration laws, a major Americanization campaign was launched to educate (white) immigrants to become part of American society and, thus, assimilate. Although the prevailing ideology did not include blacks, the major slogan was "America Belongs to Everyone."[17]

On the other hand, Portuguese ideologies linked to Portugal's mythical role during the seafaring exploration era recurrently emphasized the patriotic pride of the "Luzitan race." This pride was also based on the existence of their overseas colonies, whose populations were primarily defined culturally as Portuguese rather than in terms of genetic definitions of race. In this context, those who emigrated were considered a "necessary evil" and second-class citizens. Persons who left Portugal and settled in the United States (immigrants) were viewed pejoratively by both states, and faced discrimination from both governments: discrimination was implicit in the very concept of "immigrant."

At the time, the Portuguese were already the largest immigrant group in New Bedford. However, the so-called Portuguese colony was in fact composed of four distinctive groups: the Azoreans, mainlanders, Madeirans, and Cape Verdeans (who, as part of Portugal's overseas colonies were considered—and considered themselves—Portuguese). There was, in addition, a Luso-American contingent, which included descendants of the whalers and farmers who had settled in the region before the turn of the 20th century, some of whom had attained economic prosperity. While the Portuguese were highly stratified, the majority was part of the lower economic echelons of local society. Structurally, they were economically, socially and politically in a position inferior to other immigrant groups, particularly the English, Irish, French-Canadians, and Jews. Moreover, while immigration itself was considered to be a "race issue," the presence of Cape Verdeans within the Portuguese group further earned them the stigma of "Black Portugee."

This was a population that had already established transnational family networks and projects tying their aspirations for a better life to their connections in both worlds. Yet, in the context of the prevailing

Portuguese and American nationalisms, immigrants and descendants were continuously confronted with the necessity of choosing whether to continue to be Portuguese or to assimilate and become American. On the one hand, Americanization implied the rejection (and invisibility) of Portuguese identity, and avoided the issue of race. At the same time, it provided the possibility of gaining access to political, social and economic mobility within the United States. On the other hand, Portuguese nationalism stressed the maintenance of Portuguese culture and language and the superiority of Portuguese culture.

Americanization and naturalization classes were established in New Bedford with funds channeled by City Hall and with the support of the YWCA and local industries. Among the teachers recruited for the Americanization mission were descendants of immigrants of different national origins, including Portuguese. Apparently, Americanization leaders attempted to get support from inside the foreign groups. In conformity with those goals, the Portuguese-American Civic Society (a voluntary association composed mostly of leading Luso-American professionals and businessmen who were trying to gain access to American governmental institutions) began to play a major role in that campaign. However, there is evidence of some contention between their goals and those of the governmental forces promoting Americanization. The propaganda of the Civic Society advocated: "If you want to be a good Portuguese, become an American."

In contrast to the assimilative forces, the Portuguese daily paper, *Diário de Notícias,* a leading representative of Portuguese patriotic ideologies, systematically advocated the maintenance of Portuguese culture and language. Its editorials recurrently attacked the ongoing interethnic marriages, the tendency to anglicize Portuguese names, and the fact that Luso-Americans who spoke perfect English and whose names were anglicized were easily passing as Americans. The newspaper further called attention to those richer Portuguese families who tended to disconnect themselves from the so-called *colónia,* by, among other things, attending English—rather than Portuguese—masses.

The maintenance of Portuguese national identity and patriotism among Portuguese and descendants was a matter of concern for Portuguese governmental officials. A case in point is the report written in 1926 by a Portuguese consul regarding the inauguration of a monument in honor of a Luso-American, born in New Bedford, who died during World War I. Apparently, that monument was part of a campaign promoting a historical memory of Luso-Americans as "true Americans":

> Side by side with patriotism, and confused with it, there is what we can call COLONIALISM, (and) that is not the love for Portugal. I could verify that fact at the time of the inauguration of the monument to Walter Goulart, son of Portuguese and the first American soldier to die at war (Carvalho 1931, 273).
>
> The initiative of the monument was made by a committee composed almost entirely of the Portuguese of New Bedford. The American public officers classified Walter as a true American. With all my energy, I vindicated him for Portugal. I reclaimed him for us and I introduced him as Portuguese. I linked him to the motherland, our nation. For the members of the committee (composed primarily of Portuguese) and for many other men of our race present during that major ceremony, he was not an American, nor a Portuguese from Portugal. He was a Portuguese from New Bedford, a Portuguese from the Portuguese colony.
>
> Walter Goulart was for the Americans a true American. *The Boston Post,* publishing in 1924 the photo of Mr. Manuel Açores, emphasized in headlines that he was also a true American. Who are those among the Portuguese born in America and those naturalized Americans, who would in fact disagree with that classification? I cannot answer. (Carvalho 1931, 273-275)

During the celebration of the anniversary of the Portuguese Republic, held by a voluntary association in nearby Fall River, another governmental officer praised the ongoing resistance toward denationalization, and urged Portuguese and their descendants not to reject their ancestry:

> We should praise the Portuguese...who in the present circumstances have patriotically resisted denationalization...[as] Portuguese.... The motherland needs every sacrifice that we can make...even when she refuses us an easy economic life. We must imitate the great men, like Fernando de Magalhães, who, even when not well appreciated in their land, never forgot it....

> And even those who are forced by circumstances to change their juridical condition, as well as those who were born in America...those also can be a reason of pride for Portugal, if they don't negate their Portuguese ancestry. (Carvalho1931, 273-275)

The rejection of Portuguese ancestry became a major issue in New Bedford a few years later, in 1931, when the newspaper *Diário de Notícias* published a dramatic headline: "The Portuguese-American Civic Society Rejects the Portuguese Flag." From the newspaper's editorial and coverage, that event seemed to have divided the community:

> This civic association, composed of Luso-American professionals and businessmen, decided that the Portuguese flag should never appear in their club. This action represents an insult of a bunch of snobs who don't want to be Portuguese, and who in fact don't deserve to be Portuguese (and now) the majority of the Portuguese, who had become members of that organization in the hope of gaining political prestige for the Portuguese colony, are now ready to abandon it.[18]

After a sequence of editorials and pressure from the community, the Portuguese-American Civic Society called for an extraordinary meeting, in which the author of the proposal, a lawyer named Nunes, emotionally stated:

> I thought that the public exhibition of the Portuguese flag in the club whose members are citizens, could create antagonism among the natives, who are always ready to censor us and to call us foreigners... and this would be in a certain way an obstacle for us to gain the desired political prestige. We cannot antagonize the so-called American vote because we need their cooperation to win. I sincerely believe that by acting the way I did, I was fulfilling my duty with our club and towards our people. I thought that the subject was the club's affairs and not the public's affair. But if the well-being of the club and the well-being of the colony requires the presence of the flag in our public function, we will do it.[19]

Because of the pressure of many who attended the meeting, the decision was that the Portuguese flag was to continue to be exhibited in the club's public sessions. This dramatic event brings to the fore the pressures to reject (or at least to turn invisible) any symbols related to foreign ancestry, particularly by those who were trying to gain upward mobility and political power in the United States. It also makes clear that there were among the Portuguese in New Bedford countervailing forces to the assimilative pressures, although in this case they were not publicly acknowledged. Not only did the Portuguese state play a direct role in the life of the colony, but the familial transnational networks made identification with Portugal and Portuguese culture not a fading memory, but a continuing presence and orientation for the future. Nonetheless, oral histories suggest that the pressures to Americanize had a potent effect on the descendants of immigrants. In order to avoid discrimination, particularly the stigma of "Black Portugee," Luso-Americans tended to "pass" within the mainstream culture, even though in many cases they retained the Portuguese language and traditions. Some, but not all, intermarried into other immigrant groups, and—to some degree—"melted in the melting pot" (as defined by Luso-Americans).

* * *

In short, the "melting pot" policies emphasizing assimilation, the stigma of "Black Portugee," together with the Great Depression put major constraints upon the community. For many (particularly the descendants of immigrants), assimilation became a way to avoid discrimination, and issues pertaining to naturalization were major sources of conflict. Yet, in spite of the pressure of Americanization and of prevailing regional cleavages, the exploration era was present in the collective memory of the Portuguese. A case in point was the joint celebrations in 1932 of the fifth centenary of the Discovery of the Azores, the fiftieth anniversary of the Monte Pio Mutual Aid Society, and the centenary of the Portuguese colony of New Bedford. These events were extensively celebrated throughout New England with parades, lecture series, and exhibits.[20] In addition, under the auspices of the Monte Pio Mutual Aid Society, a committee composed of Madeirans, Azoreans, mainlanders, and Cape Verdeans published in Portuguese a book documenting the history of the Portuguese in New Bedford. On the basis of their own transnational experience, the authors resisted the prevailing polarization between the two competing national ideologies. Instead they saw the histories of New Bedford and different regions of Portugal as inter-related parts of a single construction.[21]

The Americanization process did not seem to have had a great impact on the immigrant working-class population. Those who remained in New Bedford after the restrictive immigration laws were coping with hard times. Many continued to keep in touch with their relatives in the homeland, and, when they could, sent remittances. For many, the symbolic representation and social practices associated with the past prior to immigration provided an outlet for self-expression. In the 1920s and 1930s, alongside the proliferation of regional voluntary associations and mutual aid societies, Portuguese schools were established. Radio programs and six Portuguese theater groups were formed. One of these groups (the more radical), the Popular Dramatic Group (linked to the anti-fascist Liberal Alliance in Portugal), was an offspring of both Portuguese involvement in the 1928 six-month-long strike against the ten percent reduction of wages in the local textile mills and of the fight against fascism in Portugal.[22]

In the 1970s, the Portuguese were still viewed as the "invisible minority" and the "case of the disappearing ethnics."[23] And, even today, many Luso-Americans (descendants of the older generations) are caught between feelings of shame and pride for their Portuguese ancestry. Furthermore, discrimination continues to permeate the fabric of social life in New Bedford. In the past as in the present, cultural misunderstandings have provided a main source of (sometimes) disguised and concealed discrimination in everyday life. In this context, the label of "greenhorn" has further stigmatized different contingents of immigrants upon their arrival in the United States. In particular, younger immigrants and children of immigrants recall how, by virtue different customs (including food and clothing styles) and language, they were invariably faced with prejudice at the intersection of cultures (and most flagrantly in the American schools). At the same time, regional and class differences have marked social boundaries among the immigrants themselves. Moreover, while in the past the "melting pot" policies were based on explicit discrimination, ongoing American multi-ethnic policies—reinforcing ethnic boundaries—have made way for increasing segregation and self-segregation. While segregation implies (and at the same time avoids) discrimination, in times of conflict and confrontation, social prejudices come dramatically into the open.

In the last decade, there has been an emerging reconstruction of class, race, ethnicity and nationalism among the Portuguese of New Bedford. This has been prompted by a complex mix of factors:

1. American pluralistic policies, emphasizing the allocation of resources through ethnic lines in the context of an ideology that, at least rhetorically, views "America as a nation of immigrants";
2. The arrival of new and more diversified contingents of immigrants;
3. The betterment of New Bedford's faded economy;
4. The relative improvement of the social, political, and economic position of the Portuguese in New Bedford; and
5. The recent redefinitions of the concepts of "nation," "nationality," "immigration," and "immigrant" by the Portuguese state in the context of Portugal's increasing incorporation into the world sys tem. Government officials have assigned new responsibilities to the so-called Portuguese abroad: to integrate in the host society without assimilating and, at the same time, establish the presence of Portugal in the world.

As a part of these strategies, the central government as well as those of Madeira and the Azores have strengthened their relations with leaders of the Portuguese communities abroad. Besides stimulating extensive celebrations of the Day of Portugal, Camões, and Portuguese communities, the Ministry of the Portuguese Communities has organized conferences with leading "citizens abroad" in different parts of the world, and has recently directed particular attention to the media, creating special TV and radio programs for the communities abroad. In similar fashion, the Emigration Divisions of Madeira and the Azores, whose local constituency is larger, have increasingly strengthened their ties with leading immigrants and Luso-Americans of their region. Visits of a variety of government officials (including President Mário Soares) to the region have been frequent. Mota Amaral, President of the Azores, visits New England (especially Fall River, a Massachusetts city a few miles from New Bedford) at least four times a year.

Even before the intensification of contacts between Portuguese officials and leading community leaders, Luso-American and immigrant business people have recurrently attempted to become part of the main political, economic and social streams of society in the United States. In spite of prevailing conflicts with an emerging stratum of bicultural Portuguese social workers (composed mainly of women), Portuguese leaders decided not to join the "Affirmative Action" program and, thus, established themselves as a part of the majority.[24] As such, they have distanced themselves again from the issue of race at a time when the Cape Verdeans, already independent from Portugal, had chosen the "minority" path. However, in the early 1970s, segments of this leadership took advantage of American federal and state funds to create an "Immigrant Assistance Center" and a Portuguese branch of the local public library (whose personnel of social workers and librarians are made up of bilingual immigrants who have pursued an education in the U.S.). In contrast to the 1930s, when a government report indicated a scarcity of Portuguese personnel and interpreters, New Bedford today has a bilingual structure. Portuguese-Americans and immigrants have begun progressively to occupy bureaucratic, social service and teaching positions in the city, and have acted as brokers between the community and the larger system. A few of them have also acted as brokers between Portugal, New Bedford, and the immigrants.

While in the past, the possibility of attaining upward mobility and political power demanded the rejection or invisibility of Portuguese identity and ancestry, today there is an inverse process. This may be illustrated by the formation of organizations like the Prince Henry Society mentioned earlier. This club, composed mostly of English-speaking Luso-Americans and immigrant professionals and business people, was named in honor of Prince Henry the Navigator. It is one of the few associations able to reunite Azoreans, Madeirans, mainlanders, and Luso-Americans.[25] Like the former Portuguese American Civic Society, the Prince Henry Society aims at playing a political, economic and social role in the region. In contraposition to the former civic association, the Prince Henry Society emphasizes the historical memory of the discoveries, and one of its goals is to promote Portuguese official culture. Besides honoring leading citizens of New Bedford, as well as the "Immigrant of the Year," this association also organizes concerts of classical music, art exhibits, and conferences. The emphasis on "high culture" is intended to enhance their own class position as representatives of Portugal in New Bedford, and at the same time, change the image of the Portuguese as peasants engaging in folk-religious festivals.

The following statements by the Director of the Portuguese Cultural Foundation of Rhode Island at the time of the inauguration of a monument honoring Portuguese explorers in Newport by President Mário Soares, summarizes the ongoing process:

> Like other cultures, the Portuguese are not only farmers and fishermen. They are part of a great heritage. A monument like this allows anyone who is interested to discover the world of the Portuguese, just as the Portuguese discovered the world of America 500 years ago. It is a culmination of a dream where the past becomes the present and the future.[26]

Rather than an obsession with Portugal's historical past, or a Utopian characterization of Portuguese fate, the reinvention of the discovery era into an American present represents a pragmatic cultural construction to change the image of Portugal and of Portuguese immigrants in the region. The Portuguese state as well as segments of the immigrant and Luso-American upper classes have vested interests in the ongoing reinvention of tradition (using Hobsbawm's definition of the term). On the one hand, the Portuguese state, by strengthening its relationships with the leading citizens of the Portuguese "communities" abroad, has tried to establish "the presence of Portugal in the world." On the other hand, those leaders, in their attempts to establish themselves as part of the mainstream of American society have made use of the reinvention of tradition to better their position within the realm of American multi-ethnic politics.

However, since the Portuguese leadership of New Bedford is highly differentiated and fragmented (in terms of region of origin, class, generation, gender, and particularly in terms of the differential experiences of immigrants as compared to the older and more established Luso-American stratum), the politics of the Portuguese state have ultimately intensified endemic cleavages insofar as different groups have competed among themselves to represent Portugal's historical past in the region.[27] At the same time, endemic cleavages further reflect and encompass regional countervailing interests in Portugal. In fact, since the Portuguese Revolution of 1974, the Azoreans (as well as the Madeirans) have tried to gain more autonomy in relation to the centralizing forces of the state. In that historical conjuncture, the Azorean government, together with Azorean intellectuals residing in the islands and abroad, has invented the tradition of *açorianidade* (or azorianity), the Azorean "distinct way" of being Portuguese. In New England, where the Azorean constituency is the largest, *açorianidade* has increased regional cleavages among leading citizens (including among Azorean immigrants). *Açorianidade* further enabled the Azorean government to seek the help of leading New England Azoreans in establishing international accords in the region as well as in gaining direct access to the higher echelons of American politics.[28] As part of their attempts to incorporate their dispersed populations, both the Portuguese state and the autonomous government of the Azores systematically award medals and honors to leading immigrants and Luso-Americans who have gained a certain celebrity in their spheres of activity in the United States.[29]

In the meantime, the bulk of Portuguese workers, who are themselves more vulnerable to the rhythms of capitalism, are presently facing once again the closing down of local plants, salary cuts, and unemployment. As we have seen, in their everyday life, these immigrants have tended to imagine Portugal in terms of their village of origin rather than in terms of that nation's remote historical past. Hence, the symbolic representations and the social practices associated with their immediate past prior to migration have shaped their identities as Azoreans, Madeirans, and mainlanders. These strong regional identities have been strengthened even more by regionally demarcated transnational networks of kinship. In spite of the endemic regional cleavages, which have been further intensified by ongoing American and Portuguese policies of control, these immigrants have mobilized themselves in the work-place as Portuguese workers facing discrimination within the American labor force. At the same time, as members of the American labor force, these workers have become increasingly aware that their present economic vulnerability is an outcome of the on-going process of "deindustrialization" since local plants have tended to relocate to other areas of the world in search of cheaper labor.[30] Taking into account the betterment of living standards in Portugal, these immigrants are beginning to realize that their "American Dream" (which they translate as their search for a "better future") lies presently in Portugal rather than in the United States.[31]

Conclusions

Immigrants the world over are known for their elaboration of images of home which become sentimentalized in song, story, and poetry. While these remembered and reinvented pasts have served as bolsters against the uprooting of migration, in the United States they have also become the stock in trade of ethnic politics. Using their reconstructed past to create a multi-class ethnic constituency, upwardly mobile immigrants have entered the U.S. political process. At first glance it would be possible to read the history of these Portuguese settlers as part of the fabric of U.S. ethnic history and to see the Portuguese of New Bedford as typifying an ethnic enclave insulated from the society in which they have settled and from connections with larger political and social currents. Earlier generations of Portuguese who migrated to the United States yielded to assimilative pressures when these pressures were dominant by learning English and by inter-marrying. However, they stood prepared to assume the role of an ethnic leadership when later generations needed representing in a redefined, culturally plural America. Certainly the memories of the past, preserved and invented, pervade the life of the Portuguese of New Bedford and contribute to the self-definition of the population.

However, underlying the apparent insularity of the Portuguese settlers is a series of paradoxes in which Portuguese ethnicity is found to be the product offered that extends far beyond that local community and encompass Portuguese and U.S. nation-building processes. It became clear that explaining the cultural identity of these Portuguese migrants requires a different reading of Portuguese immigrant history, one in which the racial constructions embedded in the nation-building processes of both the United States and Portugal take a prominent place. The constant recreation of historical memories, crystallized for Portuguese migrants in the concept of *saudade,* has its origins within Portuguese nation-building processes and represents a continuity of the relationship between the Portuguese migrants and the Portuguese state. And these nation-building processes themselves both reflect and reinterpret the changing relationship of Portugal to world capitalist forces. Yet Portuguese migrants, at the same time, have created themselves as inheritors of *saudade* in relationship to their experience of settlement and work within the United States.

In earlier generations, U.S. nation-building processes sought to incorporate immigrants through assimilation, but in the context in which foreignness and racial difference were stigmatized and in which Portuguese immigrants tended to be seen as dark-skinned foreigners. In response, while some upwardly mobile Portuguese migrants intermarried and assimilated, much of the working class of earlier generations of migrants developed and maintained transnational family networks that melded together their lives in the United States and Portugal into a single set of relationships. Through these transnational networks, migrants located themselves within Portugal, whose "imagined political community" was based on the supremacy of the Luzitan race and its overseas possessions. However, as emigrants from Portugal, the migrants were not fully welcome or secure in a Portugal which defined leaving the country as a betrayal of the state.

In the current conjuncture of capitalism, the Portuguese state has come to redefine itself as a global nation some of whose people live beyond the confines of the state. Central to this redefinition has been the legitimization of the transnational networks of its migrants as well as the very cultural construction of *saudade* at the very same time that U.S. efforts at immigrant incorporation have now given public acceptance to celebrations of ethnic communities as building blocks of the American social fabric. The incorporative strategies of both nation-states coincide with the interest of an educated stratum of "transmigrants" (Glick Schiller, Basch, and Blanc-Szanton 1992). Members of this stratum gain prestige and personal advantage by claiming to speak as representatives of an insulated Portuguese ethnic community of New Bedford without forswearing the benefits they obtain from remaining citizens in the Portuguese state. Whether it serves their working-class compatriots equally well to be incorporated into both settings, surrounded by the symbols of past glory but having a future of limited economic possibilities, is a different matter.

Acknowledgements

The field research in New Bedford discussed in this paper was undertaken during my tenure as University Professor of Portuguese Studies at the University of Massachusetts Dartmouth.

Different drafts of this paper were presented at: Columbia University (University Seminar on Cultural Pluralism); University of Coimbra (Center for Social Studies); Brown University (Center for Portuguese and Brazilian Studies); Lehman College of the City University of New York, and the New York Academy of Sciences. I profited from discussions with Drs. Emilia Viotti da Costa and David Montgomery. I am greatly indebted to Drs. Nina Glick Schiller, Linda Basch, and Cristina Blanc-Szanton for the framework they developed for the discussion of transnational migration. In particular, I am very grateful to Nina Glick Schiller for her input into the final version of this paper.

Postscript—July 2008

This article was originally published in 1992 and based on five years of fieldwork in the late 1980s.[32] My research was inspired by the multiple and contradictory images of Portuguese times and spaces that were imposing upon and, at the same time, contrasting with an American industrial setting. Metaphors of Portugueseness appeared to draw symbolic borders around the ethnic enclaves found within New England's small towns. And while I took into account the parallel and simultaneous processes of immigrants' incorporation into the American ways of life, my attention was focused on connections with the homeland and cultural constructions of *saudade* in the diaspora. This postscript offers me an opportunity to reflect on the various factors that shaped my research questions, outline subsequent developments in the lives of the New Bedford Portuguese, and lay out promising directions for future research.

The Original Research Context

With the distance of time, I have realized that my research questions were to some extent molded by my own life experiences. I am the daughter of Jewish immigrants from Russia and Poland who settled in São Paulo just before the Second World War. I grew up in a Jewish enclave in São Paulo which was similar in many ways to New England's ethnic neighborhoods. As is the case for many descendants of immigrants, I was exposed since childhood to conflicting cultural codes and values. I was also an immigrant in the U.S. throughout the 1970s at the time of the Brazilian dictatorship.[33] I moved to the U.S in 1969 with my husband at the time, who was awarded a two-year fellowship at New York University. We soon became aware that it would, for political reasons, be dangerous for us to go back to Brazil. As painful as it was to be in exile, we had to proceed with our lives in the U.S. This allowed me to pursue a much-desired doctorate in social anthropology, and given my husband's expertise in the medical field, it was not difficult for us to acquire immigrant status. Those years I spent in New York City were both very stimulating and very difficult. I greatly enjoyed the new milieu, studying anthropology at Columbia University, the new friends I made and my new life in the U.S. But I also deeply missed my family, my Brazilian friends and the Brazilian ways of life, which I tried to reconstruct by following events in Brazil, reading Brazilian novels, listening to Brazilian music and cooking Brazilian dishes. After I returned to Brazil in 1980, I missed the life that I had left behind in the U.S. When I began fieldwork on the Portuguese of New Bedford seven years later, I was still feeling very much divided between Brazil and the U.S. This ambivalence shaped my anthropological sensibility in my encounter with Portuguese immigrants and their descendants since their experiences of being integrally connected to multiple national spaces reflected my own personal experiences.

The historical conjuncture in which I conducted my initial research also significantly shaped my research focus. When I started fieldwork in New Bedford in 1987, a particular combination of factors was fostering the reconstitution of Portuguese culture and identity. During the 1960s, '70s and '80s, American policies promoting chain migration enabled new contingents of immigrants from the Azores and continental Portugal to settle in New England, and the period was marked by the replenishment of Portugueseness in the New England region. The ideological turn to multiculturalism in the U.S. further stimulated the politics of difference and the flourishing of ethnic identity. Furthermore, a 1985 change in Portuguese citizenship law favoring the bonds of descent and race and offering dual citizenship rights to emigrants and their descendants made way for the incorporation of the diaspora into the post-colonial nation. It was thus not by chance that the "ethnographic present" I encountered in New Bedford led me to examine the reconfigurations of Portugueseness in the diaspora.

My initial research was also shaped by and contributed to an emerging theoretical debate about how to frame analyses of transnational migration.[34] The development of a transnational approach to migration was a result of dissatisfaction with old prevailing paradigms centering either on the "ethnic enclave" or the "job market." While a focus on the so-called "up-rooted" limited the analyses solely to issues of acculturation and assimilation, studies centering on the job market tended to restrict investigation to the processes of immigrants′ incorporation into the (domestic) labor force of their country of settlement. In contrast, the transnational perspective on migration with its emphasis on social fields began to inspire research questions on the relationships between transnational migrants and their nation-state of origin. This paradigm enabled us to examine transmigrants as subjects and actors within the hegemonic processes of at least two nations, as well as to transpose the field of ethnicity well beyond the analysis of cultural diversity.

In contrast to other scholars who were examining the national projects of former colonies, my research centered on emigration from a former Empire. Portugal offered an interesting case given that it was an imperial (albeit subaltern) metropolis and, at the same time, a nation of emigrants. From my location in the United States, I could offer insight into one dimension of the reconfiguration of the Portuguese post-colonial nation—one that related to the incorporation of Portuguese emigrants into a global nation based on population rather than territory. My research shows how the incorporation of the Portuguese diaspora into the post-colonial global nation has replaced the former overseas colonies in the spatial (re)imagining of the former space of the empire. I was also able to document how in the past as well as in the present, Portuguese migrants simultaneously created ethnic enclaves in New England *and* created and maintained connections with their communities of origin. These seemingly contradictory patterns turned out to be constitutive of the dynamic interplay between globalization and localisms in this juncture of global capitalism.

After my return to Brazil in the early 1990s, I became involved with comparative research on the migrations of Portuguese to São Paulo, Brazil and Brazilians to Lisbon, Portugal. This comparison allowed me to examine the contradictions and ambiguities underlying the remodeling of Portugal from an imperial metropolis into a European post-colonial nation, and examine interrelated facets of this complex process of national redefinition including the incorporation of Portuguese transmigrants into the nation and Portugal's transformation into a destination for immigrants from its former colonies (see Feldman-Bianco 2001, 2007). My initial attempts at deciphering the meanings of the multiple layers of Portuguese times and spaces in New Bedford, together with the transnational perspective on migration, ultimately led me to conduct comparative research on the remodeling of nationalism in post-colonial Portugal in the context of ongoing debates on colonialism and post-colonialism.[35] This comparison includes the Portuguese of New Bedford, where I have continued to conduct intermittent research throughout the years. And, now, informed by my triangular perspective on Portugal's evolving sense of nation and the ongoing transnational practices in its diaspora, I turn to making sense of the changes taking place in this New England city over the last twenty years in light of the changes in the world political economy. Since these global changes have inspired a renewed interest in the study of the relationship between migrants and cities, I focus attention again on the interplay between global and local processes. As I will show, these dynamics are once again restructuring New Bedford as well as the incorporative practices linking migrants to this gateway locality and the new transnational initiatives and connections that are contributing to the economic and cultural reinvention of the city.

Economic Shifts

Once at the forefront of the global whaling (1815-1860) and textile industries (1880-1925), New Bedford has been striving ever since to attract manufacturing and service industries and, more recently, tourism. When I first arrived in the "whaling city" in the late 1980s, the effects of the short-lived "Massachusetts economic miracle" of the 1970s were still evident. The imposing structures of the abandoned textile mills, remnants of an era when the city was at the economic height of global capitalism, were occupied by labor-intensive factories employing contingents of newly-arrived immigrants, mostly from the Azores and continental Portugal. However, as I remarked again and again in my fieldnotes, the factories were, one after another, either closing down or leaving town. As part of related trends in the global economy, the local fishing processing houses were being incorporated into larger business. Successive attempts to save local industries—such as Morse Cutting Tools, the remaining tools and dies enterprise in town—were unsuccessful.

New Bedford has been confronting de-industrialization ever since the 1920s when local mills were moved to the American South in order to take advantage of the cheaper and un-unionized labor pool. In fact, the 1928 six-month strike, together with the Great Depression, is remembered by local inhabitants in connection with New Bedford's downfall as a leading city in the whaling and textile eras.[36] The decline of manufacturing and fishing of the last few decades points to another shifting positioning, or rescaling, of New Bedford within the current historical conjunctures marked by the flexibility of capital and labor, out-sourcing, and the on-going neo-liberal restructuring of cities.

These local processes have been state-wide. The 1993 NAFTA trade agreement led to an estimated loss in Massachusetts between 1993 and 2000 of 17,000 jobs (http://www.commondreams.org/news2001/0418-05.htm). Other regions within the state were able to cope with these global structural changes by diversifying their local economies and/or attracting high technologies. However, New Bedford, together with neighboring Fall River, has continued to depend heavily on industry. The impact of NAFTA on apparel industries throughout the 1990s caused local manufacturing employment to fall by a drastic 55.1 percent—a decline of 20,528 jobs in 1985 to 9,212 jobs in 1999 (Barrow and Borges 2001). The loss of manufacturing jobs is even greater if this period is extended to 2005, reaching sixty-one percent for a twenty-year period (de Sá 2008). Since the 1990s, commercial fishing was also greatly reduced because of increased legal restrictions that limited the number of fishing trips, while increasing the working hours at sea (Georgianna and Schrader 2005). The 3,069 fishermen working in 1993 decreased to a total of 2,088 by 2000, primarily because of a decline in the numbers of part-timer workers.

Consequently, in 1995, the state designated New Bedford as an "economically distressed" area after a Department of Housing and Urban Development report characterized the city as being "doubly burned" by population-loss and high unemployment and poverty rates. The report noted that the city "has lost more than 11,000 manufacturing jobs, and more than sixteen percent of the fishermen have lost their jobs during the few past decades" (*Brownfields Show Case Community Fact Sheet*). The percentage of the active population working in New Bedford decreased from sixty-five percent in 1985 to fifty percent in 2001, the year the city was ranked as the 348th lowest income community among the 351 municipalities in Massachusetts (Barrow and Borges 2001, 2).

As have other laborers around the world, New Bedford's working class has had to cope with the restructuring of global capitalism and the reorganization of work forces as "flexible labor" without long-term job security, benefits, unions or grievance procedures.[37] In this situation, many local citizens started to look for alternatives elsewhere. The population dropped from 99,222 inhabitants in 1990 to 93,768 in 2000. While some Portuguese decided to migrate to other regions of the United States, especially Florida, where the cost of living is supposedly lower,[38] others opted to return to their homeland, where economic conditions had improved after Portugal had joined the European Community.

For those who remained in New Bedford, the growing service sector, together with the declining manufacture industry, were the major employers in the city. While some Portuguese workers were able to keep their manufacturing jobs (de Sá and Borges, this volume), those who lost their factory employment because of NAFTA were entitled to learn new skills including the English language. Most began looking for employment in the service sectors in the city and surrounding region.[39] The majority of men went to blue collar trades, especially into construction work, while women tended to move into pink-collar occupations such as office work, child and elder care, and social work (de Sá 2008).

Thus, Portuguese laborers, as workers elsewhere, are now exposed to even greater economic vulnerability as they have entered flexible labor employment which does not offer job stability or social benefits. However, in a seeming paradox, they have advanced their position within the local working class. Upon the drastic decrease of immigration from the Azores and continental Portugal to New England, new contingents of immigrants from Latin America and the Caribbean have settled in the city and taken the unskilled jobs in the remaining factories and fish processing plants. Since most of these new arrivals from Guatemala,

Mexico, Nicaragua and, to a lesser degree, Brazil are undocumented migrants, they have became the local underclass, exploited by their employers and exposed to the stringent post 9/11 immigration policies, which make them victims of the increasingly frequent Homeland Security and workplace raids.

Leading Portuguese and Portuguese-American professional and business people have used their transnational social fields and practices to become involved in "the concerted efforts by local governance in partnership with state and federal governments, citizens and business organizations, non-profit agencies and institutions of higher education regarding the implementation of economic development policy" towards meeting, in the words of the incumbent mayor, "the 21st-century challenges" (Lang 2008).[40] By 1997, efforts to fund local initiatives for urban reinvention through attracting international investment bore fruit. Facilitated by leading Azoreans from New Bedford, Portugal's Ministry of Foreign Affairs (then headed by an Azorean) provided a $500,000 grant to the Whaling Museum for the construction of a special wing to portray the cultural heritage of the Azorean whalers of the city. This donation enabled the Azorean whalers to be finally incorporated into the historical heritage of the city's elite. There have also been attempts by the New Bedford Economic Council to attract Portuguese enterprises to the city's business park and free trade zone, resulting in, for example, the opening of Portuguese banks in the city. Directors of the Council have visited Portugal in search of investments and recently a delegation of government, education, and business leaders went to the Azores on a trade mission designed to strengthen its educational, cultural, and economic ties with the South Coast. It is important to note that access to the Azores also means access to European markets.[41]

Promoting New Bedford as a tourist destination—with multicultural and multiethnic attractions—has been another cornerstone of the city's economic revitalization efforts. And the Portuguese have become a visible and desirable component of the city's cultural heritage. As part of the city's Office of Marketing and Tourism strategies to attract tourists, Portuguese restaurants, bakeries, and summer festivals—including the Day of Portugal, which was, in the late 1980s, essentially a celebration by and for Portuguese-Americans—have been promoted as a constitutive part of the city's and the region's highly marketable "cultural diversity."

Policy Shifts

Harsh immigration policies equating immigrants to issues of national security began to be implemented in the U.S. five years before 9/11 in the form of the 1996 Illegal Immigration Reform and Immigrant Responsibility Act. Besides restricting immigrants' access to American social benefits, under this act, minor offenses have made individuals eligible for deportation, and deportations have become a major drama for documented and undocumented immigrants in this era of neo-liberal multiculturalism.[42] After 9/11 and particularly upon the issuing of the 2004 Patriot Act, legislation regarding undocumented migrants was tightened. In 2004 and again in 2007, New Bedford attracted national news coverage because of Homeland Security raids that were accompanied by deportations without due process or appeal. But, differently from in the past, the Azoreans under arrest were now largely ignored by the media as they had been replaced by the "Mayans" as the region's new scapegoats.[43]

With the aim of counteracting the restrictive immigration laws, bicultural community leaders started an extensive "naturalization" campaign in 1997 as a way of insuring that immigrants living in the U.S. had access to social benefits and political voice. The naturalization campaigns resonated with the politics of dual citizenship rights promoted by the post-colonial Portuguese state. These politics emphasized the incorporation of the Portuguese abroad in the localities of settlement while continuing to act as representatives of Portugal. Accordingly, the motto "to be a good Portuguese, it is necessary to be a good American," which had been employed during the Americanization campaign of the 1930s to persuade immigrants to assimilate into American society, was redefined by then President Mário Soares, in the 1980s, to stimulate biculturalism (Feldman-Bianco 1996).

The Luso-American Development Foundation (FLAD), a private, financially independent institution created by the Portuguese government in 1985 "to contribute towards Portugal's development by providing financial and strategic support for innovative projects by fostering cooperation between Portuguese and American civil society,"[44] also supported the ongoing naturalization campaign. In 1999, they launched a Portuguese-American Citizenship Project to promote citizenship and civic involvement in Portuguese-American communities across the U.S. Presently, seven of the eleven town councilors of New Bedford are of Portuguese descent, and an eighth is the widow of a deceased Portuguese member of the Board of Election Committee.

It is important to note that while most members of the successive contingents of immigrants from the Azores and continental Portugal settling in the city and surrounding areas since the late 1950s began their lives as factory workers or fishermen, they have experienced a gradual process of differential social mobility and unequal incorporation. Many have managed to attain retirement in the U.S. and thus access to the American structure of social benefits. Also, their sons and daughters were able, at least since the 1970s, to pursue an education. Some offspring who earned a college degree began to serve as cultural brokers between immigrants and American institutions. They benefited from the prevailing ideologies of multiculturalism and from their bilingual and bicultural skills by entering occupations within the local government structure, the bilingual educational system, and local and regional Portuguese institutions created, in the 1970s, with the aid of federal grants (Feldman-Bianco 1992). Others managed to open businesses or became professionals in various fields. And a few immigrants and descendants even became millionaires (de Sá 2008).

The Portuguese, who had been characterized in the early 1970s as an invisible minority and a case of disappearing ethnics (Smith 1974), seem to have enhanced their structural location in New Bedford, including within the realm of local politics. This improvement is a result of an interplay of complex factors, including the drastic reduction of immigration from continental Portugal and the archipelagos of the Azores and Madeira, the gradual process of incorporation of immigrants and their descendants in the region, the corollary process of upward mobility and suburbanization, and the fact that for the first time in over a century, the newest contingents of immigrants settling in the locality are not Portuguese.

Shifts in Culture and Identity

It is important to take into account the shifting position of the Portuguese state within the global economy and the increasing role of long-distance nationalism—especially by Portuguese-American bicultural and bilingual brokers—in changing the image of Portugal and the Portuguese within New England communities. This is a process that began with the entrance of the Portuguese post-colonial state into the European communitarian space in 1985. The ensuing efforts of the Portuguese state to incorporate its emigrants and their descendants into the nation provided members of a Portuguese diaspora with dual citizenship rights which in turn became an asset in places such as New Bedford.[45] Portuguese governmental officers have also progressively shifted their focus towards strengthening their relations with the affluent and influencial citizens of the diaspora who are capable of occupying positions of power in localities and countries of settlement as well as playing brokerage roles for Portugal's interrelated politics of culture and investments.[46]

In the past, Portuguese immigrants and their descendants were confronted with the choice of continuing to be part of Portuguese contingents or assimilating and becoming American (Feldman-Bianco 1992) Considering their association with Cape Verdeans migrants—who were, until the one-time colony's independence in 1975, part of the Portuguese community of New Bedford—the rejection (and thus invisibility) of Portuguese identity eluded the issue of race (and thus, the stigma of "Black Portugee"), providing them with the possibility of "passing" into the mainstream society, even though, in many cases, they retained the Portuguese language and traditions. Later, in the 1970s, as part of continued efforts to establish themselves as part of the majority, affluent and influential Portuguese-Americans decided not to make use of the Affirmative Action program (see Moniz, this volume) and distance themselves from a racially defined minority status—a path chosen by immigrants from the newly independent Cape Verde. In the last two decades, newer generations of upwardly mobile immigrants and descendants joined an already established stratum of Portuguese-Americans, some of whom had reasserted their Portuguese-American identities after the shift from assimilationist to multiculturalist ideologies in the U.S. Members of this stratum have revived the historical memory of the Discoveries and promoted the politics of high culture supported by the Portuguese state in order to enhance their own position as representatives of a "modern" Portugal—as opposed to the entrenched images of Portugal, consisting entirely of traditional and culturally conservative peasants.

As part of the politics of high culture of the post-colonial state, a Center for Portuguese Studies and Culture was formed in the mid-1990s at the University of Massachusetts Dartmouth. This center has played a major role in changing the image of Portugal and of the Portuguese in the region through a multiplicity of educational and cultural programs and activities including summer language programs; the establishment of a Department of Portuguese; the publication of English translations of Portuguese literary and scholarly works; the organization of seminars and conferences with renowned scholars and writers; the creation of an endowed chair; the formation of Portuguese-American archives to document the history of the Portuguese in the U.S.; and the launching of a new graduate program in Luso-Afro-Brazilian Studies. Indicative of the active transnational fields characterizing the region, the academic programs and the Center have received financial support from the state of Massachusetts, the Luso-American Development Foundation, the support of affluent Portuguese-Americans, as well as the Portuguese state. The University of Massachusetts Dartmouth has been one of the primary academic institutions facilitating the higher education of successive generations of Portuguese immigrants and descendants, and the Portuguese Department and Center have greatly contributed to the enhanced image of Portugueseness in the region.

Transnationalism

Any examination of the transformations that have occurred over the last twenty years in New Bedford—including the resurgence of Portuguese ethnicity—demands taking into account the active role played by its transnationally connected immigrant populations These connections have been fostered by the Portuguese state's granting of dual citizenship rights to its emigrants which not only connected the Portuguese migrants to Portugal in new ways, but allowed them access to the economic and political space of the European Community. A further consequence of these changes in the parameters of citizenship has been that the Portuguese state—including the Azorean regional government—has developed a notably stronger presence in New England. The private Luso-American Development Foundation, created by the central Portuguese government, for example, has come to play a major role during the 1990s in the channeling of grants to the region and the promotion of a Portuguese-American citizenship project. The intensified politics of culture and investments have provided venues to the affluent and influential Portuguese and Portuguese-Americans to gain power within mainstream U.S. politics, and allowed them to become brokers between the South Coast region and their homeland. The increased transnational reach of leading Portuguese immigrants and Portuguese-Americans to Portugal as well as to European communitarian space has strengthened their positions within the political and economic landscape of economically declining cities such as New Bedford and Fall River. These influential transmigrants have facilitated educational and economic partnerships with Portugal—especially with the Azores—and mediated the channeling of much-desired Portuguese and European Union funds to New Bedford and the region.

The image of the Portuguese in New Bedford and the surrounding region has clearly improved over the past twenty years. Key factors include the dramatic decrease of migration from the Azores; the arrival of new waves of immigrants from Latin America and the Caribbean who now occupy the lower ranks of the immigrant labor force; the disassociation of Portuguese from racially-marked Cape Verdeans; and the efforts at local universities to promote Portuguese "high" culture. However, it is the intensified connections of leading Portuguese-Americans and Portuguese immigrants with their original homeland and the increased presence of the Portuguese state within the political and cultural economy of this declining region that have significantly contributed to this new and more positive image of Portugal and the Portuguese.[47]

Questions for Future Research

Future research should, I would argue, continue to focus attention on this interplay between the global processes that are restructuring New Bedford and the incorporative processes linking immigrants to this gateway city. This perspective would allow insight into how transmigrants have confronted, mobilized against, negotiated with or conformed to projects of domination in specific historical circumstances and situations. In particular, this approach would help expose the paradoxes underlying current neo-liberal projects which are sustained by flexible labor and increasingly restrictive immigration policies of national security and immigrants' criminalization along with the promotion of multicultural ideologies and the politics of difference.

While the literature on transnational migration has tended to reify the "ethnic group," the "nation-state," and even "transnationalism," I suggest that future researchers avoid taking them for granted as units of analysis. Instead, looking at the interplay between processes of transnational migrants' incorporation and the restructuring of global capitalism would facilitate a critical analysis of how ethnicity, nationalism, transnationalism, multiculturalism, and difference are constructed at different historical conjunctures. Distinguishing, for example, between the ways in which immigrants and their descendants from the Azores, Madeira, and continental Portugal have reconstructed themselves as "Portuguese-Americans" and the different roles they and their local and transnational practices of incorporation have played in the restructuring of New Bedford would help us understand the making and re-making of New Bedford in the context of uneven capitalism. Another strategy in investigating the connections between the global processes restructuring New Bedford and immigrants' political mobilization and transnational practices, would be to foreground their historical particularity. Comparing key liminal events taking place in different global and local conjunctures—for instance, the 1928 strike vs. responses of labor in present neo-liberal times or the various era-specific approaches to the marketing of local heritage—would help unveil the continuities as well as the changing patterns of partial incorporation and/or exclusion of the "Portuguese" and other transmigrants in the city as well as the shifting position of New Bedford within the global political economy. Thinking comparatively across space and structuring research projects that encompass the social histories of other immigrant gateway cities would also certainly bring us a better understanding of the key role immigrants and their descendants have played in shaping the South Coast region. In any case, the shifting connections between Portuguese immigrants and their new and old homelands promises fertile ground for future research.

Notes

[1] This article originally appeared in Glick Schiller, Bash, and Szanton (1992, 145-174). A 2008 Postscript updates the findings of the original data. Endnotes have been reformatted to conform to volume style. My appointment as Endowed Chair in Portuguese Studies at the University of Massachusetts Dartmouth in the Spring of 2008 enabled me to prepare this postscript.

[2] For an etymological study of the origin of the word *saudade* the reader is referred to Vasconcelos (1922).

[3] As defined by a young Portuguese immigrant who attended my courses at the University of Massachusetts-Dartmouth.

[4] For a detailed analysis of the relationship between *saudade* and the construction of the Portuguese nation, the reader is referred to Lourenço (1978). Besides profiting from Lourenço's study, I further adopted Hobsbawm's formulation of "invented tradition" as "... a set of practices, normally governed by overtly or tacitly accepted rules and of a ritual or symbolic nature, which seek to inculcate certain values and norms of behavior by repetition, which automatically implies continuity with the past. In fact, where possible, they normally attempt to establish continuity with a suitable historic past." Hobsbawm (1983, 1).

[5] Quoted from the first Report of the Day of Portugal, Camões and the Portuguese Communities, 1977, 3 (author's translation).

[6] Aguiar, "Introdução à discussão sobre a dupla nacionalidade dos imigrantes do ponto de vista de um país de emigração," presented at a round table on immigrants' dual citizenship rights, Stockholm, September 6, 1985 (author's translation).

[7] A detailed analysis of Portuguese emigration rules and regulations are found in F. G. Cassola Ribeiro's works, as follows: *Emigração portuguesa: Regulamentação emigratória do liberalismo ao fim da Segunda Guerra Mundial.* Contribuição para o seu estudo. Secretária de Estado das Comunidades Portuguesas. Instituto de Apoio à Emigração e às Comunidades Portuguesas, Série Migrações, Política, Relações Internacionais, Porto, 1987. *Emigração portuguesa: Aspectos relevantes relativos às políticas adoptadas no domínio da emigração Portuguesa,* desde a última Guerra Mundial. *Emigração portuguesa: Algumas características dominantes dos movimentos no período de 1950 a 1984.* Secretária de Estado das Comunidades Portuguesas, Centro de Estudos, Série Migrações, Sociologia, Porto, 1986.

[8] Poem entitled *Saudade,* author's translation. While Portuguese experiences and the imagery of *saudade* have encompassed the world, the movement of Portuguese migration, historically linked by regionally demarcated networks of kinship, has followed the demands of labor in a changing global economy. From the last decades of the 19th century to 1960, Portuguese migrants settled primarily in the New World, mostly in Brazil and, to a smaller extent, in the United States, Venezuela, and Argentina. Subsequently, with the economic reconstruction of Europe and the creation of the European Community, there was a major shift in the direction of Portuguese labor. Since the 1960s and throughout the 1970s, Portuguese mainlanders have tended to move away from transoceanic towards intra-continental migration, settling increasingly in France, Germany, and Switzerland, among other European countries. Though in smaller proportions, through networks of kinship, they have continued to migrate to Brazil and the United States. During the same period, the Azoreans, while continuing to emigrate in large numbers to the United States, found new work alternatives in Canada, and to a lesser degree, Bermuda. In contrast, the majority of Madeirans began to settle in Venezuela and South Africa. In the 1980s, at the same time that the Portuguese emigration rate has steadily decreased, the United States became the major recipient of migrants from the Azores and the Portuguese mainland. J. C. Arroteia *(*1985) and J. Serrão *(*1982) provide detailed data on the movement of Portuguese emigration.

[9] This single construction further encompasses networks of kinship spread in other parts of the world. Among the Azoreans, the density of social relations also includes relatives settled in California, Canada, and Brazil; Portuguese mainlanders are mostly settled in Europe and Brazil; Madeirans are particularly in Venezuela, South Africa, and Brazil.

[10] Data come from *Os portugueses de New Bedford,* Montepio Luso-Americano, New Bedford, 1932 (a book published by the immigrants themselves as part of the celebration of the fifth centenary of the discovery of the Azores).

[11] The socio-economic position of Portuguese immigrants in Massachusetts was analyzed in detail by Maria da Gloria de Sá Pereira (1985).

[12] Song by Dionisio Costa, a Portuguese immigrant from Faial (Azores), who has settled in Taunton, MA.

[13] I have analyzed these festivals in "A reinvenção da memória em festas imigrantes" (The reinvention of memory in immigrant feasts), a paper presented at the International Seminar, Feasts: Tradition and Innovation, organized by Dr. M. B. Rocha-Trindade, at the Universidade Aberta, Lisbon, November 11-13, 1991. The reader is further referred to Cabral (1989).

[14] I have analyzed (with Donna Huse) gender as constitutive of the construction and reconstruction of immigrant identity in Feldman-Bianco and Huse (1996).

[15] This analysis is based on Thompson's distinction between "natural time" and the "time-discipline of industrial capitalism" (1967).

[16] I am drawing a distinction between "memory" and "tradition." Like Scott, I am suggesting that the reinvention of the memories of the past is directly related to the struggles in the present. See Scott (1985). On the subject, the reader is further referred to Williams (1973).

[17] Headline of a pamphlet distributed by the Portuguese-American Civic Association.

[18] In *Diário de Notícias*, a Portuguese newspaper of New Bedford (1917-1970s), January 15, 1931 (author's translation).

[19] *Diário de Notícias*, January 23, 1931.

[20] These events, extensively covered by the Portuguese newspaper, *Diário de Notícias*, brought to the fore the existence of deep cleavages among the Portuguese concerning the participation of the Cape-Verdeans in the celebrations. These cleavages were more profound in Providence, RI than in New Bedford.

[21] This book was published under the title *Os portugueses de New Bedford*.

[22] In the spring of 1928, 30,000 mill workers refused to accept a ten percent wage cut imposed on them by New Bedford's mill owners. The strike, the longest in New Bedford, lasted 6 months. As a result of a deep split between rival unions, the workers accepted a compromise of a five percent cut.

[23] From titles of papers by Smith (1976).

[24] Francis Rogers, a Harvard professor and himself of Portuguese descent, defends the "majority" path in Rogers (1974).

[25] Other associations reuniting Azoreans, Madeirans, mainlanders, and Luso-Americans include a Portuguese-American Business Association and a Portuguese Anti-Defamation League. Moreover, in spite of their regional cleavages, Portuguese workers mobilize together in the local unions.

[26] Quoted from the newspaper, *East Bay Window*, Newport, RI, March 1, 1989.

[27] These cleavages came flagrantly to the fore during the 1988 celebrations of the "Day of Portugal, Camões, and the Portuguese Communities" in New Bedford.

[28] In comparison to the policies of the Portuguese state, the Azorean government has played a more direct role in the region.

[29] Obviously, the Azorean government gives awards only to Azorean immigrants and Luso-Americans of Azorean descent.

[30] The 1988 Carol Cable strike in New Bedford is a case in point. In that strike, which was organized by the United Electric Union (U.E.), workers of Carol Cable's local plant (whose labor force was primarily composed of Portuguese immigrants) perceived the company's attempt to impose wage cuts and cancel workers' health insurance as "discrimination against the Portuguese." In that context, they further claimed that their salaries were already lower than those of the workers of other Carol Cable plants. In their meetings, they manifested their concern with the relocation of plants to other parts of the world. While the workers won that strike, Carol Cable closed its local plant in New Bedford one year later. Since then, numerous plants have closed their operations in the city.

[31] Younger immigrants in particular have said to me "A América está agora em Portugal" (America is now in Portugal) or "A América está agora nos Açores" (America is now in the Azores).

[32] This postscript was written in the Spring of 2008 and updates previous research.

[33] In March 31, 1964, a military coup ousted the democratically elected civil President João Goulart, at a time of intense political confrontations between the Brazilian right and left wings around issues regarding agrarian reform. The military ruled over Brazil for a period of twenty years, from 1964 to 1984.

[34] Debates on transnationalism were initiated by Nina Glick Schiller, Linda Basch, and Cristina Blanc-Szanton (1992).

[35] In the context of this comparative research, I started stimulating critical dialogues with anthropologists and historians from Brazil and Portugal, resulting in Feldman-Bianco (2001, 2002).

[36] The strike was at first prompted by an announcement of a ten percent wage cut which violated a pact between the mill owners and the local Textile Council to let the union leaders know in advance about wage cutting plans. The strike further exposed the cleavages between the skilled unionized English, Irish, and French-Canadian laborers and the lower-paid, mostly Portuguese, Cape Verdean, and Polish unskilled workers who sided instead with the leftist Textile Mill Committees (TMC) whose representatives came to New Bedford to challenge the Textile Council. The reader is referred to Daniel Georgianna's excellent detailed account of the 1928 strike (1993).

[37] This strategy is less possible within the neo-liberal restructuring of work because temporary employment leads to no employment-based pensions and reduced accumulation of Social Security retirement benefits.

[38] I thank Onésimo Teotónio de Almeida for this information.

[39] There are indications that with the downfall of manufacturing, service jobs have turned into the single largest employment in the municipality. Nevertheless, manufacture and retail still remain major employers in the city. Also high technology has emerged as a critical industry and it has been reported that even the area's traditional manufactures have introduced computer-assisted design and computer-assisted manufacturing processes (Barrow and Borges 2001).

[40] As part of the efforts economic revitalization, the New Bedford Economic Development Council—a public and private partnership—was formed to provide leadership and coordination for economic development initiatives; serve as a business liaison to city hall; and provide financing and educational opportunities in order to create and strengthen the economic development opportunities in Greater New Bedford. Efforts to attract tourists entailed the creation, in 1996, of a longtime desired National Heritage Park.

[41] As part of the educational dimension of the accord, an Azorean governmental grant will enable the digitalization of the *Diário de Notícias,* the region's Portuguese newspaper (1919-1970).

[42] Under the leadership of the New Bedford Immigrants' Assistance Center, programs were established with American and Portuguese funds to provide services to the deportees (mostly from São Miguel) and their families and to strengthen cooperation and informational exchanges between New England localities and Azorean officials.

[43] While thirteen undocumented immigrants working at a processing fishing industry were detained in 2004, home security agents arrested 300 women and men, mostly from Guatemala, Nicaragua, and Mexico in 2007. Smaller numbers of Brazilians and Azoreans were also among the detained. And since among those under arrest included a considerable number of mothers who were separated from their small children, their dramas called the attention of local and state authorities. It also mobilized the citizens of New Bedford, including leading labor unions and other community leaders.

[44] According to mission statement at the website (http://www.flad.pt/) of FLAD.

[45] Since the Schengen Regulation of Borders in 1991 and particularly upon the formation of a supranational Lusophonic Community of Nations (composed of Portugal and former colonies), governmental officers seem to have invested more and more in a neo-liberal agenda which includes the recreation of Portugal as a modern European nation. Consequently, through combined actions of the Ministry of Foreign Affairs, Culture and Economy, the government built a solid information industry tying the promotion of the Portuguese ancestral cultural patrimony to the ongoing politics of expansion in markets, tourists, and investments.

[46] In the same spirit, the Portuguese state has established the Camões Cultural Foundation in charge of disseminating Portugal's ancestral universal culture across the world, including traveling exhibits. (Feldman-Bianco 2001; 2007). Consequently, the FLAD Portuguese-American Citizenship Project should also be seen in relationship to both the Portuguese state's long-distance nationalism and the concerted efforts by affluent and influential Portuguese immigrants and Portuguese-Americans to increase the political power of the Portuguese as an ethnic group in U.S. mainstream politics.

[47] Portuguese immigrants and descendants have become part of the repositioning efforts of both the Portuguese state and the South Coast region. While Portuguese centers in the southeastern Massachusetts region have invested in the promotion of Portuguese high culture, local government has been marketing folkloric festivals and gastronomy, such as "A Taste of Portugal," as part of the cultural heritage of New Bedford in their efforts to attract tourists to the city.

CHAPTER 3

Divergent Trajectories: Identity and Community among Portuguese in Germany and the U.S.[1]

ANDREA KLIMT

That immigrants form geographically cohesive tight-knit ethnic communities and eventually become citizens with hyphenated identities in their new place of residence is widely held, at least in the U.S., to be a "natural" and inevitable process. It is difficult, for example, to imagine Portuguese immigration as having evolved into anything other than the large, vibrant, and institutionally complete Portuguese-American communities characteristic of southeastern New England. Those of us familiar with this area of the country think nothing of seeing travel agencies, food markets, flower and clothing shops, restaurants, banks, or any number of other small businesses that invoke Portugal, or more specifically the Azores, in their names, products, and décor. As residents of American cities, we automatically associate urban geographies with the temporally layered settlement of immigrants—the Chinatowns, Little Italies, and, at least along the coastal Northeast, the predominantly Portuguese parts of town are common and taken-for-granted frames of reference. The predominance of names such as Correia, Silva or Almeida in the phone book, voting lists, or in my case, on course rosters at the public university in southeastern Massachusetts where I teach, constitutes evidence of the progressive settlement and permanent shift of allegiances we assume automatically comes with the passage of time.

One of the ways in which we can gain a critical understanding of our closely-held assumptions about what happens when people leave one national sphere and go to live and work in another is to search for contexts in which the development of identities and communities have followed different routes.[2] To this end, I compare the life trajectories of migrants and histories of community formation in two very different corners of the

Portuguese diaspora—the U.S. and Germany. More specifically, I draw on my understanding of the Portuguese-American communities in southeastern Massachusetts, where I have lived for the past decade, and my research with Portuguese migrants in Hamburg, Germany, where I have intermittently been conducting fieldwork since the mid-1980s, in order to understand why these two relatively similar groups of migrants have organized their lives, relationships, and feelings of belonging in dramatically different ways.[3] Those Portuguese who arrived in the northeastern U.S. in the 1960s and '70s have largely oriented their lives to their new place of residence, often buying homes in the U.S., taking on American citizenship, and imagining their futures as anchored in their Portuguese-American communities. The Portuguese who arrived in Germany during the same period, despite having lived there now for almost four decades, continue to orient their lives, identities, and futures towards Portugal, generally not taking on German citizenship or investing in a home in Germany, and actively preparing for an eventual return "home."[4]

The central question of this analysis is how we can best account for the differences between these trajectories.[5] The strikingly different narratives of national belonging and legal frameworks around citizenship and transnational movement in Germany and the U.S. have clearly played a central role in shaping the divergent forms of identity and community characterizing these two populations. The different ways in which migrants to these two corners of the Portuguese diaspora initially conceptualized their futures has also affected what subsequent options and directions were and were not open to them—that is, the projects of leaving with the intent to eventually return vs. permanently settle abroad each created a momentum that, once begun, was difficult to redirect. Key differences in the physical and social geographies of the communities that migrants encountered in their respective receiving countries, the nature of the connections between receiving and sending contexts, and regionally-specific and historically particular opportunity structures in both communities of origin and settlement also all contributed to the divergence in forms of identity and community. The following comparison argues that differences in the dynamic interplay between these multiple factors has, over time, shaped how the Portuguese in Germany and the U.S. think about who they are and where they belong—and led to the very different configurations evident today.

The Portuguese in Germany—Forty Years of Non-Settlement

It is essential to situate the story of the Portuguese experience in Germany within the dramatic political and social transformations that have taken place over the past four decades. Economic trends of prosperity and recession, the reign and then end of the Cold War, and the increasing realization of a unified Europe have all shaped the life options and emergent identities of the first-wave migrants who arrived in Germany as well as those of their now adult children who have largely grown up in Germany.

The Initial Decades

The Portuguese in Germany, along with other southern European, Turkish, and Yugoslav migrants, were first recruited to work in Germany and other points in Western Europe in the mid-sixties and early seventies to meet the growing demand for cheap and accommodating labor. Germany, along with the rest of Western Europe, was in the throes of the post-war economic boom, and industry was flourishing. However, the German working-age population had been severely decimated by the war and the flow of people coming from Eastern Europe to work in the more prosperous West had been cut off by the sudden erection of the Berlin Wall in 1961 and the clamping down on emigration out of the East during the height of the Cold War. Germany thus turned elsewhere in the search for labor.

The migration to Germany of the so-called "guest workers" was tightly controlled by the state and strictly linked to employment. German law during this period carefully regulated migrants' movements: only spouses of migrants and their underage children were allowed to enter the country; residence permits were time-limited and linked to employment; and leaving Germany for more than three months meant forfeiting the possibility of reentry. Consequently, the migrants in Germany came from all over Portugal, and followed jobs, not friends and family, to their destinations abroad. The Portuguese population in Hamburg, where I did my fieldwork, consisted of people from every region in Portugal, and often individual migrant families were the only ones from their village or town to have left for Germany. Even siblings did not necessarily find themselves in the same city, or even the same country of Western Europe. The community in Hamburg was thus not tied to a particular place of origin in Portugal.

Most everyone expected this migration to be temporary and circular. The Portuguese who went to Germany and other points in Western Europe during this time planned to work abroad "a few years" in order to build a better future for themselves and their children in Portugal. They had no intention of settling permanently in Germany and all their efforts were directed towards improving their lives at "home." Even by the mid-1980s, when I started my research in Hamburg, all of the Portuguese migrants I knew, without exception, adamantly maintained a commitment to returning "home" to Portugal, even though most of them had already been abroad for at least fifteen years. Their sense of self was firmly linked to an anticipated return, and their resources and ambitions were all aimed at creating an improved life in Portugal. During this time, construction sites and grand, if half-finished, houses dotted the Portuguese countryside—the concrete markers of the absentee owners' firm intention to return as well as the anticipated social mobility earned through the years of hard work and deprivation abroad.

Saving enough money to build the home of their dreams and arrange a secure future in Portugal turned out, however, to be much more difficult than many had anticipated. Life in Germany was expensive, salaries did not stretch as far as they had expected, and new projects, such as the education of their children, continued to keep them in Germany for, as many said, *mais uns anitos*—"a few more little years." Remaining in Germany was, however, always cast as a postponement, never as a change of heart, and returning "home" remained a very definite goal. Annual trips home, nostalgic stories of village life, photos of the dream home in Portugal on the coffee table in Hamburg, and a studied lack of investment in life in Germany served as markers to themselves and everyone else of the steadfastness of their commitment to a future in their Portuguese homeland. The result was that in the mid-1980s, the first generation of Portuguese migrants had spent the better part of their adult lives away from "home," and the next generation had grown up abroad and was often more culturally connected in Germany than "at home" in Portugal. Yet all of them, regardless of generation or degree of comfort in Germany, planned to eventually return, and permanence in Germany did not enter into any migrant's serious considerations.

During this period, the Portuguese were literally invisible to most Germans in Hamburg. Given their relatively small number and the lack of concentration of the population in any one area of the city, there were no specifically Portuguese neighborhoods—the Portuguese constituted only three percent (a total of 77,000) of the foreigner population nationwide, and six percent city-wide (a total of 6,000).[6] While migrants generally lived in areas with low-cost housing, these neighborhoods were more generically associated with foreigners than with migrants of any particular national origin. Turkish kebab restaurants, Greek green grocers, and Yugoslav video stores dominated the street scene due to the large numbers of migrants from these countries, but stores catering to Portuguese tastes were few, scattered across the city, and relatively obscure. The church most Portuguese migrants attended was not specifically a Portuguese parish, but a German church that hosted a number of foreign-language masses. And the Portuguese priest traveled between several such churches in the wider Hamburg area to serve scattered congregations of Portuguese migrants. There were several Portuguese social clubs located in very different parts of the city, but migrants often had to travel quite a distance to attend Portuguese events.[7]

The continued commitment of Portuguese migrants during this period to an eventual future in Portugal made, in many ways, both economic and symbolic sense. For one thing, migrant earnings simply went much further in Portugal than they ever would in Germany, and acquiring a house and land was a much more attainable dream in rural Portugal than in urban Germany. Migrants felt—understandably enough—that moving up the social ladder and transforming financial gains into cultural capital were much more realistic possibilities in Portugal than in Germany. Many had left Portugal as impoverished peasants or landless rural laborers, and while they saw no possibilities for social mobility in Germany, they eagerly anticipated becoming respected members of the local elite upon their return "home." Portuguese migrants' continued commitment to return was also a practice through which they retained a sense of self-respect in Germany as their continued "Portugueseness" made their marginality within the German polity largely irrelevant.

The historically entrenched notions of Germanness made it very difficult in this period for Portuguese migrants to even imagine becoming part of the German nation. Biological descent was the ideological and legally encoded underpinning of German national belonging.[8] By this definition, "being" German was an innate and inherited quality, and while they might change their official designation, people who were not ethnically German could never, at least according to hegemonic understandings, really "become" German. Many migrants explained to me that even the acquisition of German citizenship would never change their status as perpetual foreigners, and blood lines, rather than any cultural transformation or shift in allegiance, determined the parameters of available categories.[9] Although there was increasing discussion during the 1970s and '80s about the need to "integrate" non-Germans and recognize the *de facto* multiculturalism of German society, even the most progressive arguments stopped short of pushing for the full incorporation of cultural difference into the German polity. Government policy deliberately aimed to maintain the temporary and liminal status of migrant workers, even in the face of their increasingly long-term presence within German society. German citizenship was difficult and expensive for Portuguese migrants to acquire—even if they had wanted it. Criteria for citizenship was onerous and clearly articulated expectations of cultural assimilation including:

> a long period of permanent residence and adequate accommodations; a good reputation; the capability to make a living for self and dependents without reliance on welfare; spoken and written German-language fluency; a "voluntary attachment" to Germany; a basic knowledge of Germany's political and social structures; no criminal record; and a positive commitment to the Federal Republic's "free democratic basic order" as well as a "positive attitude toward German culture." (Kvistad 1998, 150; See also Martin 1994)

Furthermore, the determination of whether a particular person met these criteria was subject to the discretion of local bureaucrats and, as there was considerable regional variation in how strictly they were applied, migrants could never be sure how their application for citizenship would be received. Legal measures during the 1970s and '80s were primarily intended to restrict entry and encourage permanent repatriation.[10] For those who stayed, the message was quite clear that national membership was reserved for those born German.

The Fall of the Wall

In 1992, when I next returned, Germany was a very different place than it had been seven years earlier. The Cold War was over, the two Germanies had just rushed headlong into reunification, and the western regions were reeling from the massive influx of refugees, asylum seekers, and ethnic Germans from the former German Democratic Republic, Eastern Europe, and the disintegrating Soviet Union.[11] Violent explosions of racist hatred were dramatically on the rise; declarations of "Germany for the Germans," "Turks to the gas chambers," and "Foreigners Out" were frequently found scrawled on public walls; and the media headlines carried almost daily accounts of aggression towards non-German residents.[12] The overall atmosphere was tense and arguments about the changing contours of Germanness and who had a right to participate in German society were ubiquitous. There were wide-spread demonstrations condemning xenophobia, and increasingly audible support for the acceptance of cultural diversity, but anti-foreigner sentiments were gaining a disturbing degree of respectability and political influence. Even though the Portuguese in Hamburg were not the direct target of violence, the people I knew all felt vulnerable and threatened by this turn of events.

In addition to this rise in xenophobia and virulent nationalism, Portuguese migrants also had to contend with the economic impact of the arrival of whole new categories of foreigners. The entry of over a million-and-a-half people into Germany between 1989 and 1992 significantly changed the dynamics of the job market. Migrant workers recruited in earlier decades, such as the Portuguese, were suddenly part of a much larger and more desperate pool of foreign labor. The sudden influx of newcomers from the East made affordable housing a scarce commodity and many people complained that certain consumer goods were hard to find and increasingly expensive. State resources earmarked for social welfare were also stretched quite thin given the extensive support allotted for asylum-seekers as well as newly-arrived ethnic Germans.

One of the main surprises that I encountered during this period was that almost all of the Portuguese who, at the end of 1985, had intended to remain only "a few more little years" in Hamburg were still there. Many were living in the same apartments and working the same jobs as when I had first met them eight years earlier. Except for the fact that many of the children I had known now had children of their own, most people's lives were remarkably unchanged. Despite the recent upheaval and xenophobic violence in Germany and the insistence with which they had, in 1985, declared their intent to return "home," they had not yet done so. Most migrants still strongly asserted their commitment to an eventual future in Portugal, continued to spend their annual holidays in Portugal, and nurtured relationships with friends and family who had remained in Portugal. They adamantly rejected the idea of "settling" in Germany or adopting German citizenship—even though by now many of them had lived longer in Germany than "back home," and some had seen their grandchildren born on German soil. And although the rhetoric of return was perhaps not as intense as it had been in earlier years, the eventual return home to Portugal was still the ultimate and most explicitly articulated goal of most migrants' lives.

The other surprise was that while many aspects of the lives of Portuguese migrants remained the same, the ways in which they thought about being in Germany had changed in significant ways. During this period, migrants were primarily worried how the intense arguments about national membership in Germany and the flood of newcomers would affect their positions within German society. A common response to this concern was to assert a kind of superiority over the new arrivals. Through their self-presentations as skilled, highly motivated, and reliable workers, as well as competent and able consumers—both highly valued qualities in the capitalist schema of the West—they substantiated claims to a continued presence in Germany that did not undermine their commitment to a continued Portugueseness and eventual return "home." Allying themselves with the West German ideals of diligence and hard work enabled Portuguese migrants to argue for their right to stay in Germany and to keep their jobs, but did not require any commitment to permanence, cultural assimilation, and acquisition of citizenship in Germany.

Through the idiom of being "good foreigners"—that is, being dependable, well-trained workers as well as capable consumers—the Portuguese attempted to deflect the brunt of German racism away from themselves, and assert their own version of their relationship to Germany and the Germans. Portuguese migrants repeatedly assured me that the recent surge of racism had not touched them personally. The Germans they came into contact with in the course of their daily lives had, after all, they said, lived and worked next to them for the last twenty-five years and had become accustomed to, if not necessarily enamored of their presence. In contrast to Turkish migrants—who, in addition to being by far the largest and most visible group of foreigners, were Muslim, came from what is still defined as officially outside of Europe, and had a racial identity that according to local categories was ambiguous—the Portuguese were by far the smallest and least visible group of foreigners and considered unambiguously "white," Christian, and "European." As such, the Portuguese migrants did not bear the brunt of German racism.

The assertions by Portuguese migrants about their right to reside in Germany did not rest on claims of "being" or "becoming" German or commitment to any version of permanent settlement in German society. As they had in their first two decades in Germany, Portuguese migrants continued to sidestep the widespread assumption that prolonged residence within a national space inevitably led to incorporation within that polity. They were also, however, engaging the intense arguments swirling around them during these turbulent years about who had a right to be in Germany. In their view, being good workers and competent consumers entitled them to stay on until *they* decided the time was right for their return "home" to Portugal.

Becoming "European"

By the time of my next extended visit in 1998, six years later, the drama of unification and its turbulent aftermath had largely subsided. Xenophobic sentiments were less threatening and overt. There had been no recent headline-grabbing violence and the arguments about who had a right to participate in German society had largely moved from the streets into more mainstream political arenas. The intense concern of the Portuguese about their positions within Germany characteristic of conversations in the immediate post-Wall years—had given way to more casual or amusing anecdotes about the aftermath of unification. One father told me with a chuckle how his daughter was one of the few children in her kindergarten class who could speak German—all the rest were children of recently arrived Polish families. People often exchanged stories about how impossible it had been after reunification to buy a used car, rent a reasonably-priced apartment, or even find a mattress in any of the department stores. But stories about racism or unpleasant encounters with East Germans—or any Germans for that matter—were absent or muted, and the earlier unease and feelings of vulnerability were no longer evident.

The major shift that figured prominently during the early 1990s in the self-conceptions and plans of Portuguese migrants was the changing nature of borders within and around "Europe." This has been an ongoing process: in 1986, Portugal was admitted into the European Union, but it was only in 1992 that full membership rights, including the freedom of movement across intra-European borders, came into effect. At that point, Portuguese migrants were able to move with relative freedom across national borders that previously had been tightly regulated, and they were presented with new options for how to configure their identities and arrange their families and communities across national spaces. The numbers of Portuguese in Germany had increased significantly as many people who had returned to Portugal in earlier years, as well as many first-time migrants, took advantage of the open borders. In Germany overall, the Portuguese population had increased from 77,000 in 1985 to over 125,000 in 1998, and in Hamburg, the 6,000 Portuguese in 1985 had increased to over 10,000.

Some analysts argue that this later cycle of migration was qualitatively different from that of earlier periods because of the politically different conditions in which it was taking place (Baganha 1999, 248). Within Germany, the regulations governing residence and work had loosened up significantly for citizens of EU countries, and state control over the movements of the Portuguese was decidedly less stringent—as Europeans they could move freely across borders within the EU. Access to social benefits had also become increasingly standardized across the EU. Of special interest to the Portuguese was that their pensions included contributions made from anywhere in Europe, and could be received regardless of place of residence. They were also able to vote for Portuguese seats in the European Parliament, although this seemed to hold little interest to the majority of Portuguese in Hamburg.

The increasing reality of "Europe" mitigated the rigid divide between staying in Germany and returning to Portugal and reduced the pressure to definitively decide between national spaces. Staying and returning were no longer such irreversible or mutually exclusive decisions and it was becoming possible for migrants to organize their lives more fluidly across national spaces and integrate the multiple localities of their identities and communities. "Being European" had given the Portuguese of all generations a new way to diffuse the tension between their continued stay in Germany and their commitment to staying "Portuguese." As it is becoming increasingly accepted for "Europeans" to live in one national space while "belonging" to another, the Portuguese could remain in Germany without calling their commitment to being Portuguese into question.

One of the ways the first generation of migrants responded to these transformations was in the timing of their planned return. The hopes of almost everyone of the first generation were still focused on returning "home" and on ensuring their economic survival in Portugal—and not, even after all these years, on settling permanently in Germany. The progressively easier access to German citizenship implemented over the course of the 1990s was, at least at the time of my last period of research in 1998, of little interest for most of this generation.[13] The timing of their planned departure from Germany had, however, shifted from earlier envisioned trajectories. Many migrants were carefully calculating their financial futures before making the return to Portugal as the cost of living in Portugal had risen substantially and accumulated savings were no longer adequate for retirement. First-generation migrants, most of whom were in their fifties, were planning to return only after they became eligible for their German pensions. As one woman told me, "I've stood it so long, I might as well wait a few more years."

Many second-generation Portuguese had grown up with strong parental expectations that they too would eventually return to Portugal. Now that they were adults and beginning to establish families of their own, they were experimenting with arenas of belonging and finding creative ways to avoid making a definitive choice between national spaces. Most second-generation Portuguese were fluent in German, had successfully established a career track, and developed a social niche in Hamburg, but asserted that they had no interest in making a permanent or exclusive commitment to German society. They rejected this possibility even though most had many more friends and connections in Hamburg where they had grown up, than in Portugal, which they primarily knew as vacation visitors. The possibility of acquiring German citizenship held little appeal as migrants felt it meant relinquishing, or in some way betraying their commitment to Portugal and staying Portuguese, and most expected

Portugal to continue being the state through which they received the benefits of national membership. Even the most politically active of this generation were primarily concerned with engaging Portuguese politics and encouraging the Portuguese state to tend to its deterritorialized population than with participating in German politics and arguing for migrant rights. The rhetorical commitment to return was central in their assertions of continued Portugueseness even though when and exactly under what circumstances they would actually leave Germany usually remained quite vague. "When I've finished my apprenticeship," "after I've got my degree," or, in words reminiscent of people in their parents' generation, "after we've finished building our house in Portugal" were all frequently heard refrains from second-generation Portuguese.

A common way for second-generation Portuguese to organize their lives across national arenas was to actively develop what some referred to as "geographic flexibility." They, like their parents, aspired to social mobility, but did so in different ways. Whereas their parents envisioned becoming members of the bourgeoisie in their natal villages, many of the second generation imagined using their German education to find good jobs in urban Portugal. One father who described his daughter as tied to the cultures of two countries, explained how her choice of career kept her "geographic options" open. She was planning to become a math teacher rather than a social worker, because math was the same thing in Portugal and in Germany, whereas social work was tied to nationally-specific programs and laws. Another way to realize this "geographic flexibility" was for second-generation Portuguese to acquire positions in either Portuguese firms doing business in Germany or in German firms doing business in various European countries, including Portugal. One young couple, for example, had accepted a three-year contract with a German company to work in their Lisbon office because they wanted to "try out" what it was like to actually live in Portugal. But, the wife added, they would never have accepted the offer without retaining the possibility of returning to Germany. As it turned out, neither she nor her husband was content in Portugal. He found the Portuguese work ethic too lax for his taste, people accused him of being too "German," and he was not able to "get anything done." The wife missed Germany, her friends, their home, the way of doing things. In Portugal, she spoke only German with their two young sons in the hope they would soon be able to return to Hamburg. Others' decisions of how to balance the Portuguese and German arenas of their lives were shaped primarily by family contingencies. One young woman who had already returned to Portugal to marry a man near her parents' village, had returned again to Germany after the birth of her second child. Her parents were still in Germany and she needed her mother's help with child care. Her husband also wanted to find a higher paying job than he was able to secure in Portugal, and, under the new regulations, was able to work in Germany without onerous restrictions.

Even the few people I knew who admitted to wanting to stay in Germany also kept open the possibility of someday returning to Portugal. Some said they would eventually go to work in Portugal "to see what it was like," while others were more pragmatic and said that if things did not turn out in Germany the way they hoped, they could always return to Portugal. The small number of Portuguese of this generation who had definitively relinquished the idea of a permanent return were, by and large, married to non-Portuguese. Their version of "geographic flexibility" was to continue the tradition of annual vacations in Portugal, but to locate their permanent "homes" in Germany.

If the permeability of borders within Europe and the notion of "Europeanness" eases the logistics of migrants' transnational existence and reduces the pressure to choose between national spaces, the direct question of "identity" remains a conundrum for many second- and third-generation Portuguese. As the following, rather meandering, comment by a young Portuguese born in Hamburg illustrates, the construction of belonging is an ongoing and rather doubt-ridden process:

> Well, I certainly don't feel German.... In first place, I feel as...as...yes, I am Hamburger. In second place, no ah parallel to being Hamburger, I'm Portuguese. I know—I'm Portuguese. But if someone asked me "Where do you come from?" I wouldn't say "I come from Lisbon or Guarda." I would say, "I come from Hamburg." And that would settle the matter. So, I feel myself to be a Hamburger, I feel myself to be Portuguese, and as a kind of overarching feeling I have something like Europe. I feel I belong to Portugal, but not so much that I would go to war for the Portuguese. So, I guess in the extreme situation, I'm not Portuguese.... Yes, that's so. So that is a statelessness.... Well statelessness is

> wrong. I have, well, legally I'm naturally according to my passport, I'm Portuguese. So, according to that I know, aha, "You are Portuguese."... Nowhere in the world would I say "I am German." I would just always say "I'm a Hamburger," or I would say, "I'm a European." Ah,...European is also kind of stupid.[14]

Nothing for this generation quite fits all the time. Being "Portuguese" is certainly affectively relevant, but does not cover extreme commitments such as going to war or the daily reality of living in Germany. Being "German" in any case is tainted and undesirable. The crimes of the Nazi era are very present in contemporary memory and inextricably tied to negative assessments of German identity and nationhood. As another young member of the second generation, who culturally and physically could have easily passed as German, told me, she would never get a German passport because "If somebody like Hitler ever comes again, I want to be sure I can leave quickly." Being "European" mitigates the pressure to reconcile geographic residence and national membership, but is at times too distant and abstract a concept. "Hamburger" reflects daily life and can be distinguished from the negativity of "Germanness," but in some instances is too circumscribed and local. The relationship between identity and place for the Portuguese in this corner of the diaspora thus continues to be reft with ambiguities, contradictions, and shifting contingencies.

The Contrast—Portuguese in the U.S.

When I tell my American students the German story, especially those whose parents came to the U.S. during the same time frame as the initial migrants went to Germany, they are surprised on a number of accounts. The identities of the Portuguese who live in Germany and the shapes of their communities have followed trajectories quite different from the paths followed by their families and compatriots in the U.S.

In contrast to the relatively scattered and low-profile presence of the Portuguese in Germany, Portuguese-American communities in the northeastern U.S. are highly visible, geographically concentrated, and institutionally complete. Many first-generation immigrants from Portugal as well as people of subsequent generations live in close proximity to concentrated Portuguese-American communities; shop at or own businesses that cater to a Portuguese-American clientele; belong to Portuguese-American parishes; participate in social clubs organized by people who trace their origins to the same island or region of Portugal; have access to Portuguese language newspapers and media that cover local events; can go to doctors, travel agents, lawyers, and social workers who speak Portuguese and primarily serve the ethnic community; and work with and live next door to people of Portuguese heritage.[15] Although the number of people of Portuguese descent is relatively small on the nationwide scene, the geographically very focused patterns of settlement have led to vibrant and highly visible Portuguese-American communities. The historical link of the Azores and Madeira to 19th-century whaling routes laid the foundation for present-day communities in southeastern New England; and the subsequent opening of significant regionally specific economic opportunities in textile manufacturing allowed for the burgeoning of these communities. The work place was the point around which immigrants settled, and whaling ports and then the textile mills became the focal points around which Portuguese-American communities were first established around the turn of the 20th century. The geographic contours, despite regional downturns in the economy, have remained remarkably stable over the century, and new Portuguese settlement in the U.S. continues to be concentrated in the areas that already encompass the large majority of the Portuguese-American population; New England, California, and more recently metropolitan New Jersey/New York.[16] There has been little secondary migration to other regions of the U.S., subsequent generations tend to remain close to established Portuguese-American communities, and new immigration tends to follow the same geographic routes. The result is that new immigrants as well as many members of subsequent generations tend to live within or at least in close proximity to well-established Portuguese-American communities. This is in marked contrast to the patterns of Portuguese migration to Germany that have been, and largely continue to be, characterized by geographic dispersal across the industrial centers of the country and a relatively low degree of family-mediated chain migration.

One of the points to emphasize in understanding the implications of these different histories is the relative role of family reconvergence. Almost all of the Portuguese I have come to know in New England are surrounded by extended family whose members reconvened in the U.S. through an extended process of chain migration. The American immigration system has long given precedence to family reunification—as opposed to employer recruitment—and allows naturalized immigrants to act as "sponsors" for family members and compatriots in order to facilitate their immigration to the U.S. Although long waits for the required permissions and papers are not unusual—sometimes involving several years—legal entry via family connections and eventual family reunification have been the predominant pattern characterizing Portuguese immigration. Weekly Sunday dinners at grandparents' homes with dozens of cousins, living on the same street as aunts and uncles, and having an extended local kin network are thus common patterns in Portuguese-American communities. Many people maintain connections with relatives who stayed "back home" or settled in other communities along the eastern seaboard, California or Canada, but the majority has numerous extended kin close by. This contrasts dramatically with Portuguese families in Hamburg who, until relatively recently, tended to consist only of parents who followed job contracts and their underage children. Aunts and uncles were often scattered throughout Western Europe, grandparents tended to remain in Portugal, adult children were not automatically allowed to join parents, and people from the same village or region were not connected to the same destination points.

Many of the students I have had over the past decade who are either first- or second-generation Portuguese-American nurture active connections with their or their parents' homeland, but they do so in ways that are quite different from the Portuguese in Germany of a similar age and background. The Portuguese in Germany have built a community that spans the geography of multiple nations in which most aspects of life—everything from deciding the location of a wedding celebration, finding employment, seeking someone to mind their children, choosing the site of a future home, to evaluating retirement options—play out transnationally. For the Portuguese communities of New England, however, the balance between national spaces is best understood as being firmly anchored in the U.S. with more circumscribed and intermittent connections to life in Portuguese spaces. Although some family celebrations and rites of passage are celebrated in the villages where people's families originated, most take place in the ethnic communities of New England.

While a few of my students may dream of getting a job and living the "good life" in the Azores—which, drawing on their vacation experiences and often nostalgic parental stories, they imagine as being less hectic and more sociable—by and large they pursue careers and imagine futures located in, or at least close to, the Portuguese-American communities in which they grew up. Some elderly couples have kept a house and land in the Azores as a vacation and retirement option, but most young people's parents envision living in closer proximity to their children and, at some point, grandchildren. I knew of no young adult who built a permanent home—for the present or the future—in Portugal. When in my *Portuguese in the Americas* classes I ask the question of whether anyone desires to emigrate from the U.S. or envisions living permanently elsewhere, a raised hand is a very rare exception.

Communication has certainly become cheaper and more fluid, and, as is the case in Germany as well as the U.S., phone conversations, the sharing of video images, and e-mail and iChat exchanges have become commonplace. But even though air transportation has become much more accessible in both places, the patterns of actual travel are markedly different. Visiting Portugal during the holidays or spending a school semester in Lisbon are not uncommon among my first- and second-generation students, but the pattern that predominates is the one-time special visit to see their or their parents' place of birth and re-connect with extended kin who had remained in Portugal. *The* trip to the homeland is often a very memorable and out-of-the-ordinary event, not part of the regular flow of life. In contrast to almost everyone I knew in Germany, no one I knew went on regular annual trips to Portugal or expected, as a matter of course, to spend summer holidays "at home" in Portugal.

The connections between ethnic and national identity, citizenship, and feelings of belonging are more complex, but still marked by key differences. Again, in contrast to the Portuguese in Germany—who almost to a person, have refused German citizenship despite its increasing accessibility—most of the students I have come to know over my years of teaching who were born in Portugal have become naturalized U.S. citizens. And obviously, all those born in the U.S. had American passports. A significant number also have Portuguese passports and think of dual citizenship as a normal and unremarkable status—one that has been allowed by Portugal since 1992. In the classroom discussions I provoked on how to articulate the connection between Portuguese and American identities, responses have ranged from assertions of a hyphenated identity that evenly connects Portuguese to American—an "I'm Portuguese-American" assertion—to a more strident emphasis on the Portuguese components of personal identity that place the American context more in the background—an "I'm Portuguese with an American passport" kind of response. But regardless of the variation, the "American" component is always somewhere in the mix—in contrast to the often outright rejection of any "German" component of personal identity, sense of belonging, or formal declaration of national allegiance.

Efforts emanating from Portugal to extend the parameters of national belonging to encompass the diaspora—or at least establish a continued connectedness with emigrants—have been felt within the communities of New England as well as Germany. In New England, for example, the presence of Azorean politicians is commonplace at local parades and celebrations, and Portuguese state money from the Ministry of Culture and other funding agencies, such as the Luso-American Development Foundation and Calouste Gulbenkian Foundation, have been instrumental in furthering regional programs of Portuguese language instruction as well as cultural events, publications, and university academic programs. The Azorean regional government has also actively reached out to the diaspora by organizing annual meetings of representatives of Azorean communities abroad, establishing cultural programs in the Azores for emigrants wanting to reconnect with their homeland, and creating an arm of government responsible for keeping up connections with the Azorean diaspora.[17] And as mentioned above, the transnational version of Portuguese national membership through the acquisition of dual citizenship has been actively pursued by many Portuguese-Americans. Although the particular enactments of transnational connections in New England differ from those in Germany, the pull into a geographically unbounded realization of Portuguese nationhood is felt in both of these centers of the Portuguese diaspora.

Comparative Insights ... And Further Questions

The majority of Portuguese who arrived in Germany in the 1960s and '70s left their homeland for the same reasons as did their counterparts who left for the U.S. during the same time period—they wanted to create better opportunities for their children than the endemically underdeveloped rural areas of Portugal could offer them. Some came to avoid the possibility of sons being drafted into the unpopular colonial wars in Africa, others were fleeing the oppression of the Salazarist regime—but in both cases, the large majority emigrated to escape poverty. Most of the members of both of these diasporic populations who emigrated as adults were peasants or rural laborers with few assets and minimal levels of schooling. The question that will be explored here is why, despite these basic similarities, they have configured their identities and communities in such different ways.

Ideological and Legal Frameworks of "Belonging"

Among the primary factors that have shaped the initial expectations and subsequent options of Portuguese migrants in Germany and the U.S. are the respectively very different conceptualizations of national belonging and histories of nation-building. Tracing the nuances and transformations of these national narratives over time is well beyond the scope of this article, but broadly speaking, the dominant self-understanding of Germany is—or at least has been until the past decade—of itself as a nation composed of a culturally homogenous population where "being German" rested on inherited immutable qualities. There was no accepted notion of "becoming German." Until the relatively recent, and much debated, constitutional changes in the 1990s opened up the naturalization process for second and third generations of foreigners, access to German citizenship had been a prohibitively expensive, bureaucratically daunting, and decidedly unappealing prospect. The migrants who were invited in during the "guest worker" program were invited as laborers, not as potential settlers, and certainly not as eventual "Germans." Over the course of their initial three decades in Germany, the legal restrictions around residence and work rights, strict regulation of family unification that kept extended families apart, tight control of borders that minimized reentry rights, limitations on property ownership that made it difficult for non-Germans to get home mortgages and start businesses, and governmental schemes that encouraged workers to "go home" during economic downturns made clear to foreign residents that full national belonging was not meant for them. Even though German citizenship has finally been made much easier to acquire, it continues to carry the negative baggage of history as well as hegemonic expectations of cultural assimilation. The Portuguese response is to say that they are not interested in staying anyway, and very few, regardless of generation, have, at least for now, availed themselves of their rights to German citizenship.

Dominant narratives cast the U.S., on the other hand, as a country made up of immigrants who transformed themselves into "Americans." The history of this narrative is certainly complex, reft by varying and, at times, quite intense xenophobic and nationally-specific anti-immigrant sentiments. During the 1960s and 70s, when this wave of Portuguese migrants was arriving, the era of ethnic hyphenation was just beginning to take hold—that is, the expectations of cultural assimilation had, at least for the time being and for immigrants from particular regions of the world, given way to celebrations of attenuated forms of cultural difference. Although their predecessors had encountered pressing expectations to "Americanize" and downplay differences of language and culture, members of this wave of Portuguese immigrants were received as potential settlers who would maintain an ethnic distinctiveness. Being "Portuguese-American" was a readily available identity that allowed for the conjoining of Portuguese and American cultural elements, and could be enacted by subsequent generations through ritual and symbolic means. In any case, the legal framework within which they moved allowed these immigrants to bring extended family to join them, have relative freedom of movement across national borders, access the financial support necessary for establishing home ownership or a business, and pursue a path towards full national membership that, for this wave of immigrants, was at least theoretically accessible.[18]

Besides the fundamental differences between national narratives, the lives of migrants in Europe are framed by formalized transnational connections that are wholly absent from the American context. The increasing reality of "Europe" as a legal and ideological entity has greatly mitigated the tension citizens of "European" nations experience when living in European Union member nations other than their own. "Being European" enables the Portuguese in Germany to lead a life that encompasses both German and Portuguese spaces, to actively navigate between opportunities and constraints of both national spaces, and to stay "Portuguese" while continuing to live in Germany. "Being European" grants the Portuguese living in Germany many of the rights and protections—freedom of movement across borders, rights to work, access to social services, etc.—otherwise acquired through citizenship. Since the reforms implemented in 2000, it is possible for Portuguese citizens and other EU countries to also hold German citizenship. However, it remains to be seen whether the option of dual citizenship develops into an attractive option for the Portuguese in Germany. Currently, the only clear advantage of acquiring German citizenship is the right to vote in national elections—and even the pull of that right is mitigated by the right to vote in European-wide elections as well as have official representation in the political process "at home" in Portugal.

The analogous solution developed by immigrants in the U.S. has been to institutionalize their continued connection to two different polities by acquiring dual citizenship after it was legalized in Portugal in 1992. The key difference with the possibilities of "being European" is that holding both an American and Portuguese passport does not convey a particular set of transnational rights, and only one country's set of obligations and rights are in effect at a time. (Which country's rules are in effect is generally determined by physical residence.) This legal framework allows for a form of transnational existence, but when compared to "being European," holding dual citizenship offers a much less robust set of practical advantages as well as a much less visible expression of identity and allegiance.

The other framework of belonging that is relevant to this comparison is that created by Portugal. Portugal has moved to increasingly incorporate its deterritorialized population into definitions of the nation, and it has become increasingly easier for the Portuguese residing abroad—even for long periods of time—to continue thinking of themselves as members of the Portuguese nation. Incorporation of dispersed populations into the national fabric has long been actively encouraged by both state and private institutions in Portugal: Portuguese banks facilitate the transfer of remittances and offer special interest rates to migrants; the Portuguese Catholic Church actively cultivates migrant congregations abroad; the state helps support Portuguese language schools for the children of migrants; and the interests of Portuguese living abroad are officially tended to by state agencies (Brettel [1982] 2003h; Baganha 1981; Feldman-Bianco, this volume). Both populations of migrants feel the pull into a geographically unbounded conceptualization of Portuguese nationhood, but they obviously have not responded in the same way to this pull.

The Momentum of Original Expectations

Different expectations were clearly created by ideological and legal frameworks. The Portuguese in Germany went as "guest workers"—that is, as explicitly temporary laborers with no claims to or expectations of settlement abroad. They left Portugal with the intent to return "home" and organized their lives around that goal. The experiences and subsequent actions of Portuguese who went to the U.S. during the same time period, on the other hand, were framed by expectations of permanent settlement. They followed several generations of migrants who had settled permanently in the U.S. and established extensive and permanent Portuguese-American communities that enveloped the newcomers into an all-encompassing and culturally familiar sphere.

It is important to understand that once begun, these visions of the future carried a momentum of their own. For example, financial resources gained through work abroad in Germany were, whenever possible, directed back towards Portugal, often resulting in the purchase of more land or the building of a home to return to. Very little investment was directed towards anchoring and improving life in Germany. In the U.S., the first investments usually were in a family home or the start of a business in the new place of residence, not at "home" in Portugal. Immigrants perhaps held onto land or homes in Portugal, but did not direct their available finances towards expanding or refurbishing their properties in Portugal. Such financial commitments, once made, continued to pull migrants in their respective—and divergent—directions and shifting course and the locus of investment along the way was not easy. Even if the Portuguese in Germany, especially those of the first generation, had decided after a decade or two abroad to center their futures more exclusively within German spaces and invest in building a home in Germany, much of their capital was already tied up in property in Portugal. Likewise, the Portuguese who had pursued a path of settlement in the U.S. but wanted to relocate the center of their lives to Portugal would face the challenge of liquidating property assets in one place and reestablishing them in another. Given that the cost of living and property ownership in

Portugal is no longer so very different from the parts of Germany or the U.S. where Portuguese migrants may be living, transferring the physical locus of "home" can, just financially speaking, be quite daunting.

Urban Geographies

Differences between the urban environments of Germany and the cities of southeastern New England contributed to the markedly different shapes of the respective communities. Given their low numbers, the Portuguese in Germany tended to meld into low-rent neighborhoods with high concentrations of foreigners from other countries; in Hamburg, the Portuguese I knew in the mid-1980s and early '90s more often lived next door to Turks, Italians, and Yugoslvs than fellow compatriots. Most lived near the factories through which they had secured their initial work permits, and given the nature of the state-organized recruitment process, the workforce at any particular place of employment tended to be composed of multiple nationalities. Neighborhoods with high concentrations of non-Germans were thus not exclusively composed of one nationality or another, and pockets of *auslaendervierte*l—or foreigner-neighborhoods—were scattered across the city. The scattered nature of urban settlement patterns was reinforced by the legal restraints on ethnic business ownership as up until Portugal gained full membership in the European Community in 1992, there had been limitations on non-German ownership of businesses. So, even in the areas where Portuguese migrants did tend to live, there were very few, and often not very visible, businesses owned by and catering to Portuguese residents. And there was no commercial center that Portuguese living in outlying neighborhoods could come to congregate in and make, even sporadically, their own.

As is the case in Germany, the numbers of Portuguese immigrants in the U.S. is, compared to that of other national groups, very small. However, the geographic concentration of settlement patterns within a small number of regions in the country, the tight networks established through chain migration, and the tendency to live in the vicinity of a few particular industries has led to the formation of visible and vibrant Portuguese-American communities. The migrants arriving in the '60s and '70s thus encountered well-established and multi-generational communities that mitigated the need to interact with an

English-speaking and culturally very different environment. Furthermore, the establishment of family-owned small businesses has long been a favored route of economic survival and social mobility pursued by immigrants to the U.S. Around areas of Portuguese settlement there are thus extensive, geographically concentrated, ethnically specific and highly visible commercial areas that bring together Portuguese-Americans on a regular basis—even those subsequent generations who moved out to more affluent and less ethnically concentrated neighborhoods can symbolically renew their connections by returning for special celebrations or shopping for Portuguese goods and foods. These centers of residence and commerce help create a continually reinforced sense of connection with fellow ethnics and a community buffered from the expectations of the wider society.

Spatial and Temporal Proximity—And the Significance of Regional Origin

One of the arguments often offered in explanation of the multifaceted and tightly-woven transnational character of the Portuguese in Germany is simply geography—Germany and Western Europe are closer to Portugal than the U.S., making frequent visits and multiple forms of connection much easier to realize. There is obviously some truth to that, but dramatic changes in the modes and cost of travel and communication over the past few decades have decreased the relevance of geography. Traveling to the Azores or to Lisbon from the East Coast of the U.S., while still more expensive than a flight from Western Europe, has become much more affordable, and charter flights are readily available in the summer months. And the ease of phone and electronic communication has shrunk the distance from natal villages and friends and family in Portugal, regardless of where in the world a Portuguese emigrant might be living. Even as space has become physically and virtually compressed, the fundamental differences between the sporadic and shorter visits and ongoing but not closely intertwined connection with Portugal characteristic of the American context versus that of annual extended visits and the maintenance of integrated lives across national spaces characteristic of the German context have remained. Geography thus does not seem to be the crucial factor behind the continuing difference in the shape of these two diasporic communities.

The other component to understanding relative proximity is time. Even if the travel time has been compressed to a point where the difference between going to Portugal from the U.S. or Germany is not that significant, a key factor to take into consideration is that in contrast to the predominant American pattern of a two-week vacation, the norm in Germany is five or six weeks of vacation, usually taken in a single block. Spending significant time away from work is not as difficult or unusual in Germany as it is in the U.S. Organizing significant amounts of time in Portugal on an annual basis poses daunting logistical difficulties for most people contending with the usual expectations of an American workplace.

While at first glance the greater logistical ease with which Portuguese in Germany can occupy both the Portuguese and German spaces of their transnational lives seems to contribute significantly to the differences between these two communities, an interesting wrinkle enters the argument when differences in regional origin are considered. After giving a talk about the German situation to Portuguese-American students at Rutgers University in New Jersey, I did not encounter the surprise I usually received from my Portuguese-American students at the University of Massachusetts Dartmouth. In trying to make sense of this response with my colleague, Kimberly DaCosta Holton, who now teachers at Rutgers in the Portuguese and Lusophone World Studies Program, I learned that the Portuguese immigrants in New Jersey tend to maintain patterns of connection that in some respects are quite similar to those of their compatriots in Germany.[19] That is, annual visits "home" are expected and commonplace, building a home in Portugal is not unusual, and it is not uncommon for people to consider a permanent return. Among the key differences between these two communities is that in New Jersey, Portuguese-Americans are primarily first- and second-generation migrants from the continent—as are all the migrants in Germany—whereas in southeastern New England the majority trace their origins to the Azores and range from being first- to fifth-generation immigrants.

This of course leads to the question of whether regional origin is at the crux of the factors fostering the different trajectories of identity and community. Like all seemingly simple explanations, this one leads to much more complex questions. Are, for example, the available economic options that would favor a return or tighter integration between sending and receiving national spaces more favorable on the continent than in the Azores? More specifically, as I will lay out in greater detail below, it is possible that there are significant differences between the regions in prospects for white-collar jobs that would appeal to the better-educated second generation as well as attractive business opportunities for returning first-generation migrants, such as job options in companies that operate in both national spheres. Another possibility—although one that I feel has less explanatory force and will not pursue in depth here—is that the history of experiences with return migration and cultural notions of "home" prevalent on the continent are simply different from those commonly shared in the Azores. In any case, rather than considering the transnational balancing act in generic terms—that is between Portugal and Germany, and between Portugal and the U.S.—it appears that a more differentiated exploration of how that balance plays out with regards to regionally specific histories, cultures, and opportunity structures would be a rewarding line of inquiry.

In the European context, it was Germany's post-war boom and Portugal's long-term stagnation that prompted the first wave of "guest workers" to go north. At that time the strength of the *mark* over the *escudo* made building a better future in Portugal with a "few years" of labor in Germany a viable possibility. Claims to status, respect, and success were—and continue to be—much easier for migrants to enact in Portugal as prodigal sons returning home than as perpetual foreigners in Germany. Over the years, however, the periodic recessions and retrenchments of the German economy have undermined the ability of the Portuguese to get and keep well-paying jobs. Recent trends in Germany to automate production and downsize the labor force have hit older Portuguese workers especially hard, and created a much more competitive job market for younger workers. Keeping their options open in Portugal is thus a necessary balance to the uncertainties of the German labor market, whether through negotiating an early retirement, opening a family business at "home," or finding a job in Portugal's service and professional sector. Life in Portugal has, on the other hand, become increasingly expensive, and savings earned in Germany no longer guarantee economic security in Portugal. Furthermore, the availability of well-paying, white-collar jobs the second generation has been trained for in Germany educational opportunities for their children, and amenities to which they have become accustomed are very limited in their villages or towns of origin. Maintaining a transnational way of life has thus become a way for the Portuguese in Germany to hedge their bets and increase their chances of being able to create and maintain a comfortable standard of living.

Many of these contingencies apply to how members of the third wave of Portuguese immigrants in southeastern New England have arranged their lives across a transnational nexus. The local New England economy has certainly seen its share of recessions and economic downturns since their arrival several decades ago. The question that awaits more systematic exploration is what kinds of balancing opportunities the Azores offers in contrast to that of continental Portugal. The Azores has seen remarkable economic development over the years, and the long endemic emigration has been transformed into a pattern of immigration from less prosperous regions. Many of the islands' construction workers are from Eastern Europe, most towns feature a Chinese dry goods store, and Cape Verdeans have become a ubiquitous presence in lower-paid service sectors. Crushing poverty no longer characterizes the countryside and the more urban areas are relatively prosperous and offer many modern amenities. Clearly, life in the Azores offers its attractions.

One of the differences between the Azorean and continental context that may contribute to the divergent ways in which migrants from these areas balance the geographies of their lives is the range of easily available options. On the continent, there is a wider space within which migrants and their children can realize connections with Portugal and being Portuguese. Many second-generation migrants, for example, pursue opportunities in the modern metropolises of Lisbon or Oporto or the next larger town over from their parents' village—the realization of their transnational community is not limited to one particular rural arena. The Portuguese population on the continent in general has also shifted from the small agricultural communities of the interior to the more service, industry-based economies of the coastal regions that offer jobs second-generation migrants would find appealing.[20] In the Azores, spatial relations are much more circumscribed. On two of the islands—São Miguel and Terceira—there are medium-size cities, otherwise the other islands have, at most, a mid-sized town. Life is still primarily rural and traveling between islands to order to participate in a more varied urban economy, while certainly much easier than in the past, still entails not insignificant amounts of time, effort, and money. The arena, in other words, in which an immigrant from the U.S., especially a second- or third-generation descendant, might actualize a transnational life is much more limited in the Azores than on the continent.

* * *

As with any complex social and cultural process, there are multiple factors that shape the ways in which Portuguese migrants and their descendants in Germany and the U.S. fashion their communities, assert their identities, and pursue their futures. This comparison has aimed to underline an understanding of identity and community among transnational migrants as contingent, historically particular processes that do not necessarily follow a unilinear, uniform, or inevitable path. It is clear that the frameworks of legal and ideological belonging, the inherent momentum of initial trajectories, the nature of physical and social geographies in both receiving and sending contexts, relative proximity between national spaces, and shifting balances between regionally-specific economic opportunities and constraints have conjoined to create very different trajectories among these two broadly comparable migrant populations.

Notes

[1] This chapter also appeared in *Portuguese Studies Review* 15(2), 2007, released 2009.

[2] See Brettell ([1982] 2003b) for a comparative analysis of Portuguese community formation in Paris and Toronto; Bloemraad (2006) for a comparison between attitudes amongst Portuguese immigrants towards citizenship in Canada and the U.S.; Leal (this volume) for a comparison between Azorean identity formation in New England and southern Brazil; and Klimt (2004) for a comparison between the trajectories of Portuguese in France and Germany.

[3] I conducted my initial fieldwork in Hamburg, Germany from 1983-85, and returned in 1992 and 1998 for subsequent periods of fieldwork. My understanding of the Portuguese-American experience in southeastern Massachusetts comes in large part from having taught at the University of Massachusetts Dartmouth since 1997. I regularly teach a course called *Portuguese in the Americas* in which students conduct primary research in the local Portuguese-American communities. A central course project is to collect an oral history of a person of Portuguese origin – this may include first as well as subsequent generations of Portuguese-Americans. Over the years, my students have collected a total of about 250 oral histories. Students also conduct research on some aspect of the Portuguese-American community, and projects have addressed a wide array of cultural, historical, and sociological questions. Many of my students are of Portuguese descent and class discussions explore many of the issues addressed in this chapter. As a resident of the area for over a decade, I am very familiar with Portuguese neighborhoods in both Rhode Island and Massachusetts, and regularly frequent Portuguese stores, celebrations, and events. My university's Center for Portuguese Studies and Culture, where I serve as a Board member, is closely connected with the Portuguese communities of Massachusetts, and many of my colleagues are involved in the Portuguese-American community surrounding the University of Massachusetts Dartmouth. I also draw extensively on published research and conversations with other scholars who work on Portuguese-American topics. See especially Bloem-

raad (2006), Feldman-Bianco (1994), Holton (2004), Leal (this volume), Moniz (this volume), de Sá and Borges (this volume), Thomas and McCabe (1998), and Williams (2005). For work on Portuguese migrants in Canada, see Teixeira and daRosa (2000) and Oliveira and Teixeira (2004).

[4] This article draws extensively on earlier articles of mine on the German situation. See Klimt (2000, 2005) for more extensive analysis.

[5] See Klimt & Lubkemann (2002) for a general argument regarding the value of comparative analysis in the Portuguese case.

[6] The major groups of foreigners in Germany in 1985 were Turks (1,401,000), Yugoslavs (591,000), Italians (531,000), Greeks (280,000), and Spaniards (153,000). Figures are drawn from the 1985 *Statistisches Jahrbuch für Die Bundesrepublik Deutschland* and *Statistische Berichte für die Hansestadt Hamburg.*

[7] This is a marked contrast with other larger groups of non-Germans, especially the Turks. The Turkish communities in Germany are extremely large, internally quite varied, institutionally quite complete and extremely visible. See Chapin (1996), Faist (1999), and White (1997).

[8] For more extensive reflections on German national identity see Brubacker (1992) and Fijalkowski (1998).

[9] See Klimt (2004) for a comparison between the national ideologies of France and Germany and the impact on identity formation of Portuguese migrants in each country.

[10] During the mid-1980s, the federal government, for example, aggressively encouraged migrant repatriation by offering cash pay-outs of pension contributions to Portuguese (and Turkish) migrants who agreed to permanently leave Germany. About a quarter of the population did in fact take advantage of this program, and returned to Portugal during this time. The Portuguese population in Germany dropped from 99,500 in 1983 to 77,000 in 1985.

[11] Between 1990 and 1992 almost 900,000 people applied for asylum in Germany; about 400,000 ethnic Germans resettled in Germany each year; and in the year after the fall of the Berlin Wall, over half-a-million East Germans moved West. See Martin (1994, 215).

[12] Between mid-1991 and the end of 1993, over 4,000 anti-foreigner incidents were reported. The arson attacks in the West German cities in 1992/93 led to the death of eight Turkish residents. See Martin (1994).

[13] German citizenship law has undergone numerous revisions in the last several decades and as of January 1, 2000 it allows for much more flexible access to German citizenship than had previously been the case. Currently a child born in Germany to non-German parents automatically acquires German citizenship at birth if at least one parent had lived legally in Germany for at least eight years prior to birth or had a permanent residence permit. A child must choose between German nationality and the nationality of his/her parents before age twenty-three. Dual citizenship is allowed for most citizens of other EU countries, including Portugal, and in special cases where relinquishing the other citizenship is not possible or entails excessive hardship. The extent to which Portuguese and members of other EU countries avail themselves of German or dual citizenship, and the meanings people attach to citizenship in these circumstances are key questions for future research.

[14] Heuer (1995, 140), author's translation.

[15] Brettell ([1982] 2003b) develops the concept of institutionally complete communities in her comparative analysis of Portuguese settlements in Canada and France.

[16] See Williams (2005) for a description of settlement patterns in different regions in the U.S.

[17] See Leal (2008b) for an in-depth analysis of how ties are created between the Azores and diasporic communities. See also Brucher (this volume) for an interesting case study of connections forged through musical performances between New England Portuguese-American communities and continental Portugal.

[18] Laying out the differences in legal frameworks encountered by Portuguese migrants in Germany and the U.S. is not to minimize the realities of anti-immigrant sentiment in the U.S. Immigrating to the U.S. also often involved long waiting periods—especially for immigrants coming in later decades. See Bloemraad for an analysis of the lack of support given to immigration incorporation in the U.S.

[19] Personal communication with Professor Kimberly DaCosta Holton, Director of Portuguese and Lusophone World Studies Program, Rutgers University, Newark. See also Holton (2004).

[20] See Costa Pinto (1998) for an overview of recent economic and demographic transformations in Portugal.

EXPRESSIVE CULTURE, MEDIA REPRESENTATIONS AND IDENTITY

CHAPTER 4

Traveling Rituals: Azorean Holy Ghost Festivals in Southeastern New England[1]

JOÃO LEAL

The scene is a large room. There are two laptop computers and a printer on a table between piles of printouts of lists and photocopies of maps downloaded from Yahoo. Two cell phones can also be seen. The two computer screens have an Access file open with names, addresses, more names and credits and debits in English. Three men sit at the table, two of them are unshaven and bleary-eyed as if they had been up all night. The third has just come out of the shower—his hair is still wet and he looks freshly shaven. Laid out on nearby tables are rows of raw meat hygienically sealed in transparent plastic bags, different types of breads and biscuits on small plastic plates, and bottles of wine. This food is being loaded onto pick-up trucks and will be delivered door-to-door by teams of two men who, equipped with lists and maps, will sort out problems they might have about finding the way with their cell phones. In this hectic scenario with dozens of people rushing about, orders and counter-orders, cars coming and going, the most surprising element is the way in which these visible signs of technology and modernity blend with practices and representations linked to time-honored tradition.

What I have just described is the general atmosphere surrounding the distribution of *pensões*, the Portuguese name given to a gift of raw meat, sweetbread, and red wine that are part of the *Império Mariense*, a Holy Ghost festival organized by Azorean immigrants from the island of Santa Maria,[2] currently living in East Providence, Rhode Island where thirty-five percent of the population is of Azorean origin. The sophisticated and ultra-modern equipment—computers, databases, cellular phones—is thus used within the traditional ritual framework of the Holy Ghost festival.

This article seeks to explore the dialectics between continuity and change, between tradition and innovation, that are indissolubly intertwined in the Mariense Holy Ghost festival of East Providence. After addressing the dialectics reflected in the formal structure of the festival, the paper examines the transnational and bifocal identities of *Mariense* immigrants in relation to the sociocultural meanings of the ritual. The concluding discussion draws on Stuart Hall's characterization of diasporic identities as anchored both in tradition and translation as a way of understanding the hybridity of Mariense Holy Ghost festivals in the U.S.

"Back Home": Holy Ghost Festivals and Tradition

Holy Ghost festivals are a central aspect of Azorean culture. They originated in continental Portugal during the 14th century. According to their "myth of foundation," Holy Ghost festivals were formally initiated by Queen Saint Isabel, the wife of King Dinis, in Alenquer (a town in central Portugal). They spread throughout central and southern Portugal, and then to Madeira and the Azores (and later to Brazil). While in continental Portugal and in Madeira, Holy Ghost festivals entered a process of gradual decline throughout the 19th and 20th centuries, in the Azores they have become a central and distinctive ritual of the islands. They are currently celebrated in every parish of the archipelago, and constitute an important aspect of the religious and social lives of Azoreans and a central component of the identity of individuals and communities in the Azores.

In the Azores, the festival lasts for seven to eight weeks, taking place between Easter Sunday and Pentecost and Trinity Sunday.[3] It consists of a number of ceremonies in honor of the Holy Ghost and is centered around the Holy Ghost Crown, a silver crown topped by a dove representing the Holy Ghost. Formally independent of the Catholic Church, the festival has as its main protagonist the *imperador* [emperor]. The ritual, which is characterized by a wide diversity of forms in the different islands of the archipelago, is particularly elaborate and includes a series of religious celebrations, such as processions and prayer sessions in honor of the Holy Ghost. The most important of these ceremonies is the *coroação* [coronation], which takes place at the end of Mass and culminates in the literal crowning of the *imperador* by a priest or of a child chosen by him. In addition to these religious ceremonies, Holy Ghost festivals include a variety of meals, food gifts, and the distribution of beef, bread and *massa sovada* (made with wheat flour, sugar, eggs, and butter) to a considerable number of people and households.[4]

Given their importance in the Azores, Holy Ghost festivals occupy a central place in the Azorean diaspora in the United States, which constitutes ninety percent of the Portuguese-American population.[5] Recreations of the Holy Ghost festival in the U.S. have played an important role in the maintenance of symbolic ties between immigrants and their homeland, and the construction of a sense of community and Azorean-American ethnicity among the immigrants.

Available figures show the importance of Holy Ghost festivals in the Azorean diaspora in New England. According to information provided by the directors of the Grandes Festas do Divino Espírito Santo of Fall River—an annual festival that brings together dozens of Holy Ghost brotherhoods from all over New England, and is also attended by some brotherhoods from California and Canada—there are sixty Holy Ghost brotherhoods active in the states of Massachusetts and Rhode Island. Holy Ghost festivals are celebrated every weekend between Holy Ghost Sunday and the beginning of September in both states, and on several weekends, there are Holy Ghost festivals taking place simultaneously in three or four different neighborhoods.[6]

This re-creation of Holy Ghost festivals in the U.S.—which began during the first wave of Azorean migration between the 1870s and the 1930s, and reached its peak during the second wave of migration in the 1960s and 1970s—has followed certain patterns. The most important of these is connected to the segmentary nature of Azorean local and transnational identities. Although people identify themselves as Azorean, this more general level of identification is relatively recent and coexists with a stronger sense of loyalty towards the island and the parish. Immigration has reinforced the importance of these loyalties. Indeed, both access to the American green card and settlement in the U.S. were greatly dependent on pre-existing social networks operative at the level of the parish or, in the case of smaller islands, at the level of the island. It is precisely this segmentary logic that governs the re-creation of Azorean Holy Ghost festivals in the U.S. Apart from the recently created pan-Azorean Grandes Festas do Divino Espírito Santo of Fall River, Holy Ghost festivals in the U.S. have been organized by groups of immigrants coming from specific Azorean islands and/or parishes.

Mariense *Impérios* [empires] or Holy Ghost festivals organized by immigrants coming from the island of Santa Maria are a good example of this trend. The first Mariense *Império* in New Enlgand was founded in 1927 in Saugus, Massachusetts by immigrants from Santa Maria who had arrived during the first immigration wave. Other *Impérios* were launched during the second immigration wave in other towns of New England: in Hartford, Connecticut in 1976; in Hudson, Massachusetts in 1978, where the Mariense represent eighty percent of the local Azorean population; and, more recently, in Bridgewater, Massachusetts.[7]

The East Providence Holy Ghost festival is part of this pattern of re-creating Mariense *Impérios* in New England towns with significant groups of immigrants from Santa Maria. Among the city's Azorean population of 15,000, which stems mainly from the island of São Miguel, there is also a small group of 1,000 immigrants from Santa Maria. Initiated in 1986, the *Império* was founded by some of the more active members of the Mariense community in East Providence. One of its founders, Manuel Braga, wrote a detailed account of the foundation of the *Império*:

> On the day of the *Império Mariense* in Connecticut [in 1986], José P. Cunha and José M. Resendes [two immigrants from Santa Maria living in East Providence] went out to have some Holy Ghost soup, and were nostalgically recalling the Mariense Holy Ghost festivals of the past. As they were talking to one another, they suddenly came to the conclusion that they too could also organize an *Império* in East Providence. Although the Mariense population there was rather small, all that was needed was good will.
>
> José P. Cunha spoke to John Medina, who thought that the idea was a good one, and then they both spoke to Manuel F. Braga, João F. Braga, João L. Marques, José M. Braga and Manuel S. Braga. They had a first meeting but were too few to be able to appoint a committee. They decided then to appeal to all the Marienses in East Providence and surrounding areas to see if they could set up a committee to start off the project they had in mind.
>
> As a result eighteen people…turned up and a committee was appointed.... The committee…held a general meeting in which thirty-eight people took part and approved a plan for the launching of the association they intended to form. The association was registered so

> that they could take the first steps towards organizing a Holy Ghost festival. While some people thought that the first festival should be held in 1987, others insisted that the *Império* should take place that very same year, which was 1986. This issue divided both the committee and the general meeting. Voting took place and the majority decided that the first *Império* should take place that year. (Braga n/d, 1)

The association, which in 2001 had 200 members, was named Mariense Holy Ghost Brotherhood. Initially, the *Império* took place on the premises of other Holy Ghost Brotherhoods in East Providence, but in 1998, the Mariense Brotherhood moved into its own premises at the Mariense Cultural Center. As well as organizing other activities, such as dinners based on traditional Mariense menus, the Brotherhood also rents out the premises to Azorean immigrants for events, like weddings, showers, or anniversary celebrations. However, the main activity of the Brotherhood is, of course, the *Império Mariense*, which takes place since 1998 on the first weekend of July.

The structure of the East Providence festival is directly inspired by *Impérios* back in Santa Maria.[8] Thus, as is the case in Santa Maria (and generally throughout the Azores), the Holy Ghost is symbolized by a silver crown. The main protagonist of the festival is the *imperador*, who is helped by some twenty to thirteen *ajudantes* [helpers]. Among those *ajudantes* are the *ajudantes grados* [major assistants]: the *trinchante* [carver], the *mestre sala* [master of ceremonies] and two *briadores* [councilors]. One of the more important *ajudantes* of the *Império* is the *pagem de mesa* [table page], who is a child, usually the *imperador*'s son, nephew or grandson. During the festival, music is provided by the *folia*, a traditional musical group composed of three musicians. In the East Providence festival, the *folia* is backed up by one or two Portuguese-American brass bands.

As in Santa Maria, the most important occasion of the *Império* is the so-called *dia de Império* [the day of the *Império*], which takes place usually on the first Sunday in July. Among the ceremonies that take place on *dia de Império*, the most important is the *coroação*, which is preceded and followed by two processions. After the *coroação* and throughout the day, a number of distributions of food open to all who wish to join the celebration take place. Inside the premises of the Mariense Cultural Center, *Sopas do Espírito Santo* [Holy Ghost Soup], a soup made of beef and wheat bread, is served. Outside, the *ajudantes grados* are in charge of distributing throughout the day slices of *massa sovada* [sweet bread] and glasses of red wine to anyone who asks for them. In the morning, usually before Mass, Holy Ghost Soup is delivered to the homes of some twenty to thirty elderly or sick people who cannot attend the *Império.* Finally, just as in Santa Maria, the celebrations of *dia de Império* also include musical attractions and stalls with food and drinks.

Besides *dia de Império* celebrations, East Providence Holy Ghost festivals also include, as in Santa Maria, a number of preliminary ceremonies and celebrations. In the week prior to *dia de Império,* the rosary is prayed each night at the *imperador*'s house where the crown is kept in a decorated altar. Meals are also offered to the assistants, especially in connection with the preparation of the food at the Mariense Cultural Center. On the eve of *dia de Império,* members of a procession attended by the *imperador,* the festival queen, her maids of honor, and several other members of the Mariense brotherhood carry the crown from the *imperador*'s house to the Mariense Cultural Center.

Every Mariense involved in the celebrations insists on how scrupulously the ritual sequence of the *Impérios* back home is replicated by the East Providence festival. The directors of the Mariense Holy Ghost Brotherhood emphasized this point to me during our conversations in May 2000. In a room decorated with nostalgic photographs of wheat-threshing, maize harvest, and *Impérios* of the 1950s, they told me that the aim of the *Império Mariense* was to reproduce the *Impérios* of Santa Maria. One of the directors even suggested that in East Providence the Mariense *Império* was even more faithful to Mariense tradition than most *Impérios* in present-day Santa Maria, and noted that "perhaps we are better organized than they are there." This idea was constantly repeated to me during my fieldwork and people noted that: "it is here, on this side of the ocean, that tradition is alive;" "tradition in Santa Maria is coming to an end;" "*Impérios* here are more complete [than in Santa Maria]."

The claims of many Marienses in East Providence emphasize the alleged fidelity of this festival to the original format of *Impérios* back in Santa Maria. The local *Império* is regarded, in some respects, as more authentic than the original Mariense Holy Ghost festivals in Santa

Maria, as some of the more traditional aspects of the ritual can also be found in the U.S. This is the case of a ceremony called *provimento da mesa* [opening of the meal] where, on the *dia de Império*, the distribution of slices of sweet bread and red wine is initiated. Many of the people in East Providence who gather to watch this ceremony stress the ways in which it is carefully performed according to the traditional requisites. That is also true of the *caldo da meia-noite* [midnight broth], a distribution of Holy Ghost soup that takes place on the eve of *dia de Império*. Considered one of the most picturesque aspects of the *Impérios* in the Azores, its performance in East Providence becomes a means for claiming the authenticity and fidelity to tradition of the local *Império Mariense*. The debates about the genuineness of the flavor of Holy Ghost soups and the musical performance of the *folia*, whose members sometimes come from Santa Maria, further attest to the constant monitoring of the ritual's authenticity by both the organizers and the audience. What seems to be at stake is the extent to which the ritual performance in the diasporic setting is a faithful facsimile of the original *Impérios* of Santa Maria.

This traditionalist discourse is, ironically enough, also the driving force behind changes that have been introduced into the East Providence festival in order to make it look more authentic. This is the case with the decorated arches put on top of pick-up trucks used to distribute the *pensões*; these arches are inspired by similar ones that in Santa Maria decorate the ox carts prominent in some *Impérios* processions. This is also true of the small Holy Ghost flags the assistants carry with them when they distribute the *pensões*. Although these small flags are used in Santa Maria, they are employed in a different ritual sequence of the *Império*. Thus, in both cases, actual transformations in the ritual are legitimated by reference to tradition.

The continuation of tradition by future generations is one of the main concerns of the activists involved in organizing the East Providence Holy Ghost festivals. As in other contexts, there are constant complaints that younger generations no longer want to have anything to do with homeland traditions. The musical program of the *Império* is thus specifically aimed at engaging young people in an attempt to counter the prevailing tendency among the children of first-generation immigrants to assimilate into American society and distance themselves from the homeland culture.[9] To this end, younger musical artists whose repertoires do not primarily consist of Portuguese music are usually invited to perform. A special celebration directed and performed by children was also launched in 1998 as part of the festival in order to encourage the younger generation to continue Azorean traditions. Inspired by the *Impérios de Crianças* [Children's *Impérios*] that take place in Santa Maria on Saint John's day,[10] this celebration is a kind of small-scale *Império* in which children themselves carry out all the preparations and ritual sequences of an *Império.*

"Away from Home": Innovation in the Holy Ghost Festivals

Despite all the emphasis on tradition and fidelity to the original ritual, East Providence Holy Ghost festivals are also strongly affected by changes, innovation, and cultural creativity. While some of these changes are acknowledged by the directors of the Mariense Brotherhood, the prevailing discourse tends to downplay innovation and to emphasize traditional continuity. However, behind the cultural purity that the participants demand of the ritual, one can also find significant transformations.

First of all, the organizational structure of the celebrations has been transformed in the diasporic context. One of the major changes relates to the weakening of the role of the *imperador* as the main organizer and sponsor of the festival. In Santa Maria, *Impérios* are the direct result of individual promises made to the Holy Ghost which exchange the favor solicited and granted to the individual for the hosting of an *Império.* Although the community also participates actively in funding the festival, it is the *imperador* who assumes the basic responsibility for its organization and funding. The share of the *imperador* in underwriting an *Império* represents between forty and seventy percent of the total expenses, which in the 1980s amounted to about $18,000. Through the appointment of a special assistant known as the *copeiro* [butler], the *imperador* also has a decisive role in the organization of the festival.

In East Providence, however, this dual role of the *imperador* as the sponsor and the main organizer of the festival has substantially weakened. His role becomes primarily a ceremonial one and his organizational and funding responsibilities are transferred to the board of the Brotherhood. In financial terms, while the *imperador* usually pays for the meat needed for preparing the Holy Ghost soup, the bulk of expenses of the *Império*, which can amount to some $30,000, is borne by the Brotherhood. It is also the board of directors of the Brotherhood that chooses and supervises the assistants of the *Império*, except for the *ajudantes grados* and the *pagem de mesa*, who are generally chosen by the *imperador* from among his immediate family. Finally, in the event that there are no promises, it is the Brotherhood directors who choose the *imperador* from amongst their members.

A second set of transformations is found in the ritual sequence of the Mariense *Impérios*. The major change has been the introduction of the *domingas* ("domingas" is the feminine plural of "domingo," the Portuguese word for Sunday), which are borrowed from São Miguel's Holy Ghost festivals. The *domingas* consist of preliminary ceremonies during each of the seven weeks prior to *dia de Império*. Each *dominga* has its *mordomo*, who keeps the Holy Ghost crown at his house for one week. During the week, a number of rosaries are said at the *mordomo*'s house, and on Sunday after Mass, a lunch is usually held at the Mariense Cultural Center. This lunch, which is attended by 50 to 150 guests, must include Holy Ghost soup. At the end of the meal, items offered by the guests are auctioned. The profits, which may amount up to $3,000, are used to pay the expenses of the *Império*. *Mordomos* are usually chosen among those who volunteer for the job, and the expenses associated with the *domingas* are usually supported by the respective *mordomo*.

Another major change in the ritual of the *Impérios* is the introduction of the distribution of *pensões* described at the beginning of this paper. This distribution consists of door-to-door distribution of a *pensão* composed of five pounds of raw beef, wheat bread, sweet bread, biscuits, and a bottle of red wine. These *pensões* are given in return to all those who have made gifts of twenty-five dollars to the *Império*. The motivations behind these gifts are diverse: some are given as a result of individual promises to the Holy Ghost; others are generated by a more generic devotion to the Holy Ghost; and still others are given to help fund the *Império*. These gifts, which can total as many as 700, constitute an important part of the revenues of the *Império*. Besides these standard *pensões*, there are also the *pensões grandes* [large *pensões*], which include a bigger piece of raw beef and one *pão leve* (a kind of sponge-cake). They usually number between thirty to forty for each ritual, and are given in return to those who made gifts of over $250 to the *Império*. The distribution of *pensões* takes place one week before *dia de Império* and, as we have seen, is carried out by groups of two assistants carrying a small Holy Ghost flag.[11]

Finally, a third group of changes relates to some of the *Império*'s ritual forms, especially in the organization of processions. New figures, absent from the Holy Ghost festivals in Santa Maria, have been added, such as the *rainha da festa* [festival queen] and her maids of honor, who are usually chosen from among second-generation children and teenagers. Local authorities are also represented in the processions. Additional Holy Ghost silver crowns, as well as several Holy Ghost banners and flags, have also been introduced into the ritual. Underlying this series of changes is the desire to add a more dramatic sense of spectacle to the *Império* processions. These innovations tend to transform the processions into complex operations, and, as a consequence, they now require their own organizing committee directly appointed by the Board of Directors of the Mariense Brotherhood.

Transnationalism and Bifocal Identities

To sum up, Mariense *Impérios* in East Providence are as much about tradition as they are about innovation. This apparently contradictory anchoring in both tradition and innovation reflects the ambiguous and contradictory status that characterizes the lives of Mariense migrants in the U.S. As is the case of other Azorean communities in New England, the Mariense community can be seen as a transnational ethnic community, unstably located between the country of origin and the host country. Migrants are as involved with the host country as they are with their country of origin, maintain multiple relations and identities that cross national borders, and construct their identities in a context of structural ambiguity (Basch, Glick Schiller, and Szanton Blanc 1994). Much like the Mexican immigrants studied by Rouse, Mariense immigrants have become:

> skilled exponents of a cultural bifocality that defies reduction to a singular order. Indeed, in many respects...they [too] have come to inhabit a kind of border zone, especially if we follow Américo Paredes in recognizing that a border is "not simply a line on a map but, more fundamentally, ...a sensitized area where two cultures or two political systems come face to face." (Rouse 2002, 163)

In celebrating the traditional dimensions of the *Impérios*, Mariense migrants try to recreate the homeland in their host country, injecting a dose of "Azoreanness" into their lives in the U.S., and maintaining a bifocal identity that keeps their East Providence and Santa Maria communities connected. The innovative side of *Impérios* is about creating ties with the host country and adjusting a traditional discourse to fit the codes and representations of a new socio-cultural context. In that sense, East Providence *Impérios* "reveal more about making a home abroad, than about reconstructing the original loss" of home (Boym 2001, 328).

Thus, some of the changes introduced in the ritual sequence of *Impérios* constitute adaptations to the constraints, expectations, and codes of the larger Azorean-American community that the Mariense immigrants have joined. In fact, the Azorean-American community in New England is dominated by immigrants coming from the island of São Miguel, the largest island of the Azorean archipelago. Micaelenses control most immigrant organizations and constitute the majority of local Portuguese-American political leaders. The ritual and festive calendar of the Azorean-American community is also strongly influenced by distinctive aspects of Micaelense folk culture, such as *Romarias Quaresmais* (Lent processions which exist only in São Miguel) or the cult of *Senhor Santo Cristo* [Holy Christ, the Lord]. In the case of the Holy Ghost festivals, the Micaelense variant predominates in all the Azorean communities in New England.[12] This means that the majority of New England Holy Ghost festivals are organized by Micaelense brotherhoods, and follow the traditions of São Miguel. Of particular relevance for this discussion, Holy Ghost festivals organized by immigrants from other Azorean islands are strongly influenced by the Micaelense version.

Some of the changes that have been introduced to the Mariense *Impérios* are thus due to the influence of the Micaelense way of celebrating the Holy Ghost. The increased importance of the Brotherhood in the organization of the festival to the detriment of the *imperador*, the introduction of *domingas* and *pensões*, are all changes that reflect the importance these three aspects have in São Miguel Holy Ghost festivals. So, even though the focus is explicitly on preserving Mariense characteristics, the *Impérios* have undergone significant transformations in response to the new ethnic context in which they are now performed.

The emergence of a pan-Azorean identity under Micaelense aegis has tended to weaken the segmentary logic inscribed in the Mariense *Impérios*.

Besides being dominated by Micaelense immigrants, members of the ethnic community are also actively engaged in a dialogue with American culture. Changes in the form of the Holy Ghost procession have developed through contact with the American conventions and norms around "parades."[13] Of particular note is the presence in the East Providence festivities of the Portuguese, American, and Azorean flags at the head of the parade, closely followed by local political authorities such as state representatives, the mayor and members of the City Council and School Committee. These features are absent in the traditional Holy Ghost processions of Santa Maria. The introduction of new characters, such as "the festival queen" (or *rainha da festa*) and her maids of honor, usually dressed in long, white or pastel formal dresses, with the skirt covered by one or two layers of tulle, red or blue mantles and tiaras topping sophisticated hairstyles, although sometimes rationalized with reference to Queen Saint Isabel, reflect, as Carty (2002) has convincingly argued, the American conventions for beauty queens and civic parades.

Other aspects of the festival also illustrate the importance of this dialogue with American culture. Along with folkloric groups who perform and enact Portuguese or Azorean traditions, American pop music and rock-and-roll artists are also invited to the Holy Ghost festivities. The combination of "homeland flavors" and "fast food" in the stalls is another example of this coexistence between the commitment to tradition and the process of innovative cultural blending. Alongside the *malassadas* [fried dough], *caçoila* [marinated pork], smoked sausage, and other Azorean traditional dishes, one can also find hot dogs, hamburgers, and other quintessential American snacks.

Impérios, as the immigrants themselves, are unstably located in the intersection of distinct cultural universes between which their protagonists and their audience move. The bifocality that characterizes the migrant condition also characterizes Mariense *Impérios*, and behind the tradition that connects the immigrants to their country of origin lies innovation which ties them to the new ethnic context.

Kinship, Neighborhood, Work and Community: Old and New Forms of Sociability

Impérios in Santa Maria are an important ritual tool for the cyclical assertion and reinforcement of networks of social relationships, and are strongly connected to the language of gift and reciprocity (Leal 1994). It is through gifts and counter-gifts of food, through meals and other forms of food-sharing, that *Impérios* in Santa Maria contribute to the reassertion of social ties within family, kin, neighborhood, and larger social units such as the parish or the island.

Mariense Holy Ghost festivals in the U.S. also play a fundamental role in reinforcing family and kinship connections, but in ways that are shaped by the dialectic between tradition and innovation. Kinship is central to understanding the social dynamics of the Mariense Brotherhood in East Providence. The Brotherhood is directed by two main bodies: the Executive Committee in charge of the administration of the Brotherhood and, most importantly, the organization of the *Império*; and the Board of Directors who constitute a kind of fiscal council with authority in financial areas.[14] One of the most relevant aspects in the composition of these two bodies is that the majority of their members belong to one of three extended Mariense families: the Amarals, the Sousas and the Bragas. Although the actual functions of the *imperador* in East Providence are less relevant than in Santa Maria, they are also strongly dependent on the language of kinship. Some of the *imperador's* assistants are chosen from among his close relatives, especially in the case of the major assistants and of the festival queen and her maids of honor. Female members of the *imperador*'s family play an important role in preparing food for the festival. And *Impérios* are important occasions for reuniting the *imperador's* extended family living in different areas of the U.S. and Canada. The language of kinship is also important in the *domingas*. Many of those who help to prepare the food for the Sunday lunch are relatives of the *mordomo* in charge of the *dominga,* and most of the guests at these Sunday lunches are also relatives of the *mordomo* or his wife. Thus, as is the case in Santa Maria, the East Providence *Impérios* continue to provide a relevant context for the cyclical strengthening of kinship ties and demonstrate the enduring importance of kinship among Mariense immigrants in the diasporic context.

Mariense *Impérios* in East Providence also ritually assert the island as a major social unit in Azorean-American social life. Besides the fact that the majority of the members and directors of the Mariense brotherhood share a common Mariense background, several other aspects of the *Império* also demonstrate the importance of island-specific identification in the organization of the festival. Participation of Mariense immigrants, both through *pensões* and through *pensões grandes*, is of great importance,[15] and distribution of Holy Ghost Soup that takes place in the morning of *dia de Império* goes to immigrants from Santa Maria.

The shared connection to Santa Maria is also reinforced through participation of the East Providence Holy Ghost Brotherhood in Mariense Holy Ghost festivals throughout New England. Holy Ghost brotherhoods in New England usually send delegations consisting of board members, the *imperador*, and the festival queen to Holy Ghost festivals with which they have a close relationship. The Mariense Holy Ghost Brotherhood in East Providence, for example, participates in the *Impérios* of Hartford, Connecticut and Bridgewater, Massachusetts. The Mariense *Império* in Saugus, Massachusetts served as the gathering point in the past for the Mariense diaspora in North America. But, even today, with a total of five Mariense *Impérios* taking place in New England, Mariense *Impérios* in general, and the East Providence *Império* in particular, continue to be attended by hundreds of Mariense immigrants living in different towns and neighborhoods in New England. Bus excursions to visit the different *Impérios* are often organized, and, in some cases, the realization of an *Império* provides the occasion for more formal gatherings of Mariense immigrants in the U.S. This was the case in 2002 with the third Bairros meeting[16] in the U.S., which brought together over 200 people in Hudson, Massachusetts on the same day as the local Mariense *Império*.

Thus, as in Santa Maria, *Impérios* keep a strong local dimension, reasserting the centrality of island origins for individual and group identity under the new immigrant conditions. They are key in the construction, maintenance, and celebration of the deterritorialized Mariense community in the U.S. Even as they maintain strong connections to social ties and groups related to the country of origin, Mariense *Impérios* have also been affected by the new sociological environment of the host country. The most relevant modification in this respect is the decline of the importance of the parish in organizing Mariense *Impérios* in the diaspora. In Santa Maria, the parish is one of the fundamental social units for promoting Holy Ghost festivals (Leal 1994, 107-127). However, in the U.S., due mainly to the low numbers of Mariense immigrants, the home parish has lost its importance as the primary locus for the social identification of individuals and groups. The declining importance of residential neighborhood in the diaspora must also be noted. In Santa Maria, both close neighbors and hamlet neighbors are fundamental to the working of *Impérios* (Leal 1994, 77-104). In the U.S., during the 1960s and 1970s, when Azorean immigrants tended to live in densely-populated ethnic enclaves, neighborhood retained some importance in the social networks of the Mariense diaspora. But with the recent suburbanization of a large number of immigrants, neighborhood has lost its centrality as an organizing principle. As a result, the importance of neighborhood connections in Mariense *Impérios* in the U.S. has substantially declined.

At the same time, new social networks closely linked to the new American social and cultural environment have acquired an important role in East Providence Mariense *Impérios*. Social networks based on the workplace, which are absent from *Impérios* in Santa Maria, have become very important in American *Impérios*. This centrality of workplace connections is particularly evident in the distribution of the *pensões*. The great majority of *pensões* not distributed to fellow-Mariense, almost 500 out of a total of 700, are circulated among the Azorean workmates of the directors and other activists of the Mariense *Império*. This shift reflects the sociological importance of industrial and post-industrial forms of work in the U.S. as opposed to the Azores; besides being a means for earning a living, work is a major focus for personal identity and social relations in American society (Sennet 1999). In the case of Mariense immigrants, this increased importance of workplace connections is reinforced by the close relationship between ethnicity and employment (Portes & Manning 1999, 88-96). Many small businesses, for example, that are owned by Portuguese-Americans in sectors such as construction, gardening, auto repair, and restaurants, primarily employ Portuguese-American workers. There are also some local non-immigrant owned companies that recruit primarily Azoreans as employees. The American Insulated Wire Corporation, based in Pawtucket, Rhode Island, for example, employs so many Portuguese that it sends representatives to Portuguese-American events such as the local celebration of Portugal Day.

The Mariense *Impérios* in the U.S. also reflect the importance of a larger pan-Azorean identity within the social lives of individuals and groups throughout the diaspora. As we have already seen, the importance of the overarching Azorean framework under Micaelense aegis is evident in some formal changes that the *Impérios* have undergone, such as the introduction of *pensões* and *domingas* into the Mariense versions of the ritual. Participation of non-Mariense Azoreans in the *pensões* and the celebrations of *dia de Império* also points to the significance of pan-Azorean networks. This inclusion of non-Mariense in the Mariense *Impérios* is the result of the mixing Azorean immigrants from different islands at the workplace as well as the increasing inter-marriage between Mariense and non-Mariense Azoreans. In the East Providence Mariense *Império*, for example, Mariense are clearly dominant among the organizers, but a significant number of directors and assistants from other islands, but who are married to immigrants from Santa Maria, actively participate in the *Império.*[17]

Conclusions

Addressing the contemporary "fragmentation of identities," Stuart Hall (1992, 274) has stressed the way in which globalization has "a pluralizing [and contradictory] impact on identities" (Hall 1992, 309):

> While some identities gravitate towards…tradition, attempting to restore their former purity and recover the unities and certainties which are felt as being lost....[O]thers accept that identity is subject to the play of history, politics, representation and difference, so that they are unlikely ever again to be unitary or pure; and these consequently gravitate to what Robbins (following Homi Bhabha) calls "Translation." (Hall 1992, 309)

Impérios reveal the importance that these social and cultural identities, rooted both in tradition and translation, have in the Mariense ethnic community.

Tradition is mostly evident in the way in which the *Impérios* are consciously recreated as a replica of Holy Ghost festivals in Santa Maria. This traditionalist rhetoric emphasizes connections to the homeland and reflects the importance that Santa Maria continues to assume as a primary source of identity for individuals and groups in the diaspora. The relationship between *Impérios* and the cyclical assertion of networks of social relationships, such as kinship and local identity, linked to the traditional Mariense social landscape must also be emphasized.

At the same time that they dialogue with tradition, *Impérios* are also actively engaged in a work of translation. Their formal structure has been transformed and a number of innovations, reflecting the new cultural context in which they now take place, have been introduced. At the same time, they have also adjusted to new forms of sociability, linked to the work place and to a larger Azorean-American ethnicity, which characterize the new social environment in which Mariense migrants now live.

Notes

[1] This paper is based on research carried out as part of the project "USA and Brazil: Processes of Transnationalization of Azoreaness" within the framework of the Centro de Estudos de Antropologia Social (ISCTE), Lisbon. The project was generously funded by the Fundação para a Ciência e a Tecnologia (FCT), Fundação Luso-Americana para o Desenvolvimento (FLAD) and Fundação Calouste Gulbenkian (FCG). During the period of my field research in the U.S., I was a guest of the Department of Portuguese and Brazilian Studies at Brown University, and I am especially thankful to the Department Chair, Onésimo Teotónio de Almeida, for his valuable help. I would also like to thank the members of the Board of Directors of the East Providence Mariense Holy Ghost Brotherhood as well as all the *Império* assistants. Special thanks are due to Tony Amaral. I also thank Bianca Feldman-Bianco for her suggestions and proposals. Previous versions of this paper were published in 2004 ("A Pomba e a Águia: as Festas do Espírito Santo nas Comunidades Açorianas dos EUA," *Actas do III Colóquio "O Faial e a Periferia Atlântica nos Séculos XV a XX,"* Horta, Núcleo Cultural da Horta/ Câmara Municipal da Horta/ Casa da Cultura da Horta, 153-174) and in 2005 ("Travelling Rituals: Azorean Holy Ghost Festivals in the United States," Capo, J. & J. Leal (eds.), "Challenges of Migration to the Nation-State," *Narodna Umjetnost (Croatian Journal of Ethnology and Folklore Research)* 42 (1), 101-124).

[2] Santa Maria, one of the nine islands of the archipelago of the Azores, has an area of ninety-seven square kilometers and a population of approximately 5,000. Throughout the paper I will use the Portuguese adjective "Mariense" to refer to people (or things) from the island of Santa Maria.

[3] Pentecost Sunday and Trinity Sunday take place respectively seven and eight weeks after Easter Sunday.

[4] For further information on this topic, see Leal (1994).

[5] According to the U.S. 1990 Census, there were 900,000 individuals of Portuguese ancestry living in the USA, of which ninety percent are usually assumed to be of Azorean origin. Of these 900,000 individuals, 232,000 were born in Portugal. Thirty percent (approximately 275,000) lived in California, and thirty-five percent (approximately 317,000) in the states of Massachusetts and Rhode Island. In New England, the Azorean immigrants settled in three main areas: in Cambridge and Somerville in the outskirts of Boston; in southeastern Massachusetts; and in the state of Rhode Island. Cities with particularly large numbers of Portuguese immigrants are Fall River, with 46,000 Portuguese-Americans who make up fifty percent of its population, and New Bedford, with 45,000 Portuguese-Americans who make up forty-five percent of its population. In the state of Rhode Island,

especially in East Providence, Pawtucket, etc., there are some 76,000 Portuguese-Americans, approximately ten percent of the total population of the state.

[6] Holy Ghost festivals are also of great importance among the Azorean immigrants in California. See Goulart (2002).

[7] The Bridgewater Holy Ghost festival was initiated in the 1930s by immigrants from São Miguel island. It was only recently that the festival began to be organized by people from Santa Maria. No precise date was given to me about this recent change in the ritual, but it must have occurred in the mid 1990s. There are also records of a Mariense *Império* taking place in Taunton, MA in the 1970s, but this festival has apparently come to an end. In California, there are two Mariense *Impérios*, in Redlands and in Oakdale. The first festival was initiated in 1919 and the second in 1997. More recently, a group of Marienese have initiated an *Império* in St. Petersburg, Florida. In Canada there are at least two Mariense *Impérios* in Brampton and in Galt, both in the state of Ontario.

[8] Since the specific contents of *Impérios* in the five parishes of the island of Santa Maria present some diversity, the East Providence festival uses as its main source of inspiration the *Impérios* of the parish of Santo Espírito.

[9] One of the canonical formulations of the law of the second generation was proposed by Hansen. According to him, the second-generation immigrant "wanted to forget everything: the foreign language that left an unmistakable accent in English speech, the religion that continually recalled childhood struggles, the family customs that should have been the happiest of all memories" (Hansen 204). See Kivisto and Blanck for a revaluation of Hansen's thesis (1990). See also Portes & Rumbaut (1996, 232-268 and 2001) for current debates on second generation.

[10] See Leal (1984, 58) on Mariense *Impérios de Crianças.*

[11] Although there is a similar distribution of food in Santa Maria, both its name, *irmandade* [brotherhood], and its main characteristics are very different from *pensões.* In East Providence, as a result of the introduction of *pensões*, *irmandade* has lost its former importance; the same occurs in the Mariense *Impérios* of Bridgewater, Hudson, and Saugus.

[12] For a presentation of the Micaelense variant of Holy Ghost festivals see Leal (1994, 182-185).

[13] On the "parade" as an American genre of marching, see, for instance, Ryan (1989).

[14] The first has five members elected for one year, and the second has nine members who serve two-year mandates; four of the mandates in the board of directors are renewed on even-numbered years while the other five are renewed on odd-numbered years.

[15] Ten percent of the number of pensões—84 out of a total 700 in 2001—come from Mariense immigrants. The contribution of Marienses is of even greater importance in the case of *pensões grandes*; in 2001, out of a total of twenty-seven of these *pensões*, twenty-one came from individuals born in Santa Maria.

[16] Bairros is a very common last name in Santa Maria and there are many people who argue that it is a last name that can only be found in Santa Maria, or among people of Mariense ancestry.

[17] This Azorean dimension of the Mariense *Impérios* and also of the Mariense community is again under Micaelense aegis. The most common relations both at the workplace and through intermarriage are those that the Mariense tend to establish with the numerically and culturally dominant group within the New England Portuguese-American community, the Micaelense.

CHAPTER 5

Dancing Along the In-Between: Folklore Performance and Transmigration in Portuguese Newark[1]

KIMBERLY DACOSTA HOLTON

Introduction

Twentieth-century Portugal has witnessed many governmental strategies for promoting nationalist ties among lusophone communities in far-flung continents. During the Estado Novo (1926-74), dictator António Salazar drew a unifying rhetorical frame around distant colonies, defining them as interior to the body of the nation despite their severed geographic circumstance—Angola and Mozambique were not, for example, colonies but rather domestic appendages, "overseas provinces." This rhetorical formulation pointed not only to Salazar's imperialist ambitions, but also to the desire for an inclusive nation-state, one which viewed overseas *and* domestic citizens as working parts in the same rambling collective. Following World War II, the Portuguese state actively cultivated ties to Portuguese emigrants living in North America and northern Europe. Emigrant remittances contributed greatly to the health of the Portuguese economy, particularly in times of great expenditure such as the colonial wars of the 1960s and '70s (Brettell 2003a, 2003h). Since the collapse of the Estado Novo dictatorship in 1974 and the end of the colonial empire, Portuguese emigrant communities around the world have been the object of increased governmental attention and funding. Maria Baganha (2001) has suggested that the state simply transferred the object of its traditionally exterior focus from the overseas colonies to emigrants in diaspora.[2] Feldman-Bianco (1992) argues that this post-1974 shift points to a reconceptualizing of the nation as defined by people as opposed to places.

Revivalist folklore performance figures prominently in the intensification of the relationship between emigrants and the Portuguese state in the late 20th century. Both private and public institutions in Portugal strategize emigrant preservation of national customs throughout the world as an essential tool for increasing Portugal's geopolitical visibility and maintaining ties between Portuguese migrants and their native homeland. As I will argue in this essay, the existence of emigrant folklore groups called *ranchos folclóricos* ensures a constant traffic of goods and services, performers and publics, between Portugal and Portuguese communities in diaspora. Revivalist folklore is both a vehicle for the economic and emotional linking of emigrants to Portugal, and a tool for achieving what Rumbaut and Portes (2001a; 2001b) term "selective acculturation" within the United States.

Selective acculturation among immigrant groups, as Rumbaut and Portes define it, is marked by a "paced learning of the host culture along with retention of significant elements of the culture of origin" (2001b, 309). In their extensive anthology analyzing fourth-wave experience of "segmented assimilation" across an array of U.S. immigrant groups, scant mention is made of the role of expressive culture in processes of adaptation to new national contexts. I would argue, however, that in the Portuguese-American community of northern New Jersey, selective acculturation cannot be understood without considering the way in which it is communicated and reinforced through performance.

Folklore performance supports both Portuguese and U.S. e/immigration policies by invigorating Portuguese language use, moral values, and endogamy while simultaneously celebrating Luso-American commercial success and rising political visibility in New Jersey. Portuguese folklore performers enact a "back and forth" dynamic between Portugal and the U.S., where home and host society become "a single area of social action" (Margolis 1994, 29). New Jersey folklore groups depend upon transnational media and transmigrants, "those who claim and are claimed by two or more nation states," (Glick Schiller 1999, 96) for their survival. Many New Jersey *rancho* members return from Iberian holidays armed with costumes, video tapes of folklore performances, and "gifts" of new songs and dances donated by childhood friends from hometown *ranchos*—the material with which groups in diaspora update and strengthen performance repertoires (Interview by author, Tony Cardoso, Februrary 13, 2003).

New Jersey *ranchos folclóricos* dance along the transmigratory in-between, reinforcing core Portuguese values while performing ethnic traditions on American soil—an expression of difference accepted and often celebrated within the multicultural context of Newark, NJ and its surrounding areas. Newark, a city which has struggled for decades to recover from the devastating effects of the 1967 uprisings, has turned a history of racial strife into a platform for image-overhaul, where tropes of peacability between diverse ethnic groups form the foundation of a new post-1967 identity. Newark's growing arts scene reflects this diversity, and the city's renaissance has been tied to the development of large-scale arts infrastructure (Strom 2002; 2003) as well as the proliferation of smaller-scale ethnic festivals and parades (Holton 2003b). The annual Portugal Day Parade and its display of *ranchos folclóricos* figure prominently in Newark's arts-driven revival. The fact that Portuguese folklore has been able to thrive in Newark and accompany Luso-American commercial success and political empowerment serves as a testament to Newark's post-1967 transformation. *Ranchos* forward an image of Newark as a city that welcomes diversity and allows varied immigrant groups to maintain autochthonous traditions within northern New Jersey's hearty regional embrace.

New Jersey folklore performance radiates out toward both sides of the Atlantic, imbricated simultaneously in processes of U.S. adaptation and the maintenance of ties to Portugal. In constant dialogue between sending and receiving contexts, emigrant performers both live and enact transnationalism. This paper examines the struggles within the Portuguese community of northern New Jersey over issues of assimilation, the state policies and pressures which catalyze selective acculturation's dynamic of national duality, and the ways in which folklore performance affirms and makes visible this transmigratory dialectic.

This article is based on three years of ethnographic fieldwork (2000-03) in the Portuguese-American communities of northern New Jersey. In addition to participant observation of numerous New Jersey *rancho* rehearsals and performances, I have conducted ethnographic interviews with folklore dancers, musicians, directors and festival organizers primarily from the Sonhos de Portugal Rancho of Kearny, NJ and the Danças e Cantares de Portugal Rancho of Elizabeth, NJ.[3] This article is also informed by research at the Rutgers-Newark archive of the Ironbound Oral History Project, a store of primary audio, visual and textual documents containing over 250 interview transcripts with Portuguese-speaking immigrants of northern New Jersey[4] and the Newark archives of the

Luso-Americano biweekly newspaper. Finally, this research into New Jersey folklore performance is consistently ghosted by my long term ethnographic investigation (1993-present) of *ranchos folclóricos* and political change in 20th-century Portugal.[5]

Assimilation Debates

Folklore performance figures prominently in recent debates within the Portuguese community concerning the extent to which Luso-Americans should become integrated into mainstream U.S. society and culture. The NJN documentary entitled *Ironbound: Ties to Portugal* (1999) illustrates several vectors of this discourse, situating folklore performance on one side of what the film portrays as the assimilation/anti-assimilation binary. Midway through the film, the camera focuses in on a large dinner table filled with *bacalhau* [codfish] and *vinho verde* ["green" sparkling wine]. Seated at the table in the midst of an intense debate are several of Newark, New Jersey's Luso-American community leaders: Linda Rodrigues, a university professor; Armando Fontoura, Essex County Sheriff; and Licínio Cruz, a local judge and co-owner of Cruz Construction Company. At issue is the move by some Portuguese families out of the Ironbound—Newark's "Little Portugal" neighborhood.

"Why do our people leave the Ironbound?" asks Professor Rodrigues, who still lives in the neighborhood.

"For the American Dream," Sheriff Fontoura says with a smile.

"And I don't have it?" Rodrigues asks in disbelief.

"You have it. You left the Ironbound too, may I remind you, my dear. You went to graduate school...."

"But I came back," Rodrigues asserts, "My parents stayed here."

"As soon as they could, my parents left," Judge Cruz says, "My father saw a better future for his family in the suburbs."

"When Lee's father left, the Ironbound was still good," says Fontoura.

"It's still good. It's still good, here, okay, Armando?" Rodrigues asserts over the rising din.

"Look," Fontoura says, "let me ask you something. What's wrong with our people here in America—this is the melting pot—marrying within the American society, ours sons and daughters marrying Jewish-

Americans, Italian-Americans, Irish-Americans? That's the American way, that's what we do, that's the way it's supposed to be."

The controversy continues as Luís Nogueira, then director of Newark's Sport Clube Português, wonders aloud if intermarriage will result in the loss of the Portuguese language and culture, causing Newark's Luso-Americans to be "phased out."

As if in answer to anxiety over the dilution of Portuguese ethnicity, the film quickly cuts from the dinner table to a clip of an enormous feast sponsored by the Sport Clube Português in Newark. *Sardinhas* [sardines] and *leitão* [suckling pig] rotate from large spits as hundreds of people gather at picnic tables, speaking in Portuguese. The camera pans from the barbecue to a heated soccer game where two players are arguing over a foul the referee never called. Then the camera switches to a folklore performance going on beside the barbecue where a large, well-rehearsed *rancho folclórico* begins a whirling dance for a cheering public. This segment of the film ends with the Sport Clube director speaking into the camera:

> We put everything together in one event, we play soccer, dance folklore, we do the barbecue.... For a change, we have a different kind of unity. A lot of people remember the feasts and the parties from back home in Portugal.... It's in our blood, it's part of our culture. (*Ironbound Ties* 1999)

The crisis point I describe not only involves tension over demographic changes within the Portuguese enclave in the Ironbound, but also over the more generalized process of assimilation and its effects on ethnic identity, solidarity, and sociability. In the film, the expressive markers of Portuguese ethnicity—soccer, religious devotion to Fátima, *fado* and folklore—are all spliced together in an amalgamated portrayal of ethnic purity, anathema to Sheriff Fontoura and others' call for assimilation. From the perspective of the film's producers, performing folklore is a means to fight *against* integration and ethnic dissolution. As I will argue in the last section of this paper, the reality of folklore's role with regard to assimilation is more nuanced and dialectical, contributing to both sides of the film's binary formulation.

Assimilation has been a hot topic of debate among anthropologists and sociologists who study America's post-1965 fourth wave of emigration—widely acknowledged as the United States' most profound demographic transformation in a century[6] (Rumbaut and Portes 2001a, 7). Traditional Chicago School models of linear assimilation which theorize the seamless loss or absorption of ethnicity into white mainstream society over the course of three generations of socioeconomic ascent have recently been challenged by scholars who present a more complex and varied portrait of ethnic adaptation (Rumbaut and Portes 2001a; 2001b). Rumbaut and Portes argue that the second generation of fourth-wave migrants undergo what they term "segmented assimilation" where "outcomes vary across immigrant minorities" and where "rapid integration and acceptance into the American mainstream represent just one possible alternative" (2001a, 6). Based on studies of thousands of second-generation immigrants from diverse ethnicities, Rumbaut and Portes describe the varying coordinates along the trajectory ranging from complete assimilation to oppositional ethnic plurality.

The Portuguese immigrant community of northern New Jersey, I would argue, falls in the middle of this trajectory, practicing what is termed "selective acculturation" which is "commonly associated with fluent bilingualism in the second generation … [and] absorption by second-generation youths of key values and normative expectations from their original culture and concomitant respect for them" (Rumbaut and Portes 2001b, 309). The measures of ethnic assimilation employed by Rumbaut and Portes center on issues of bilingualism, patterns of sociability and the dynamics of co-ethnic communities.

In the case of Portuguese Newark, what specific factors have shaped the dynamic of selective acculturation? I would argue that in addition to factors such as a condensed urban settlement pattern,[7] and a tightly-knit, relatively homogenous co-ethnic community, State policies on e/immigration have also contributed greatly to the way in which the Luso-American community of northern New Jersey integrated into mainstream American society while retaining key values of the country of origin.

State Policies, Language Use and Selective Acculturation

As Bela Feldman-Bianco (1992) argues, Luso-American immigrants have experienced shifting pressures from both the U.S. and Portuguese governments with regard to assimilation. In the 1920s and '30s, Portuguese migrants "were subjected to restrictive immigration laws and second-class citizen status in both the United States and Portugal" (Feldman-Bianco 1992, 146). Conflicting national ideologies also left immigrants torn: the U.S. "melting pot" formulation which guided immigrants into an ideal of swift and total assimilation versus the superiority and pride of the Lusitanian race proffered by the Portuguese government which encouraged the "exclusive maintenance of Portuguese culture and language" (Feldman Bianco 1992, 146).[8]

By the 1970s, however, both countries had changed their official stance vis-à-vis Portuguese migration. The U.S. repealed the 1924 National Origins Quota Act in 1965, dissolving strict, limitations on emigration according to country of origin. Cultural pluralism, an ideology which encouraged the maintenance of diverse ethnic traditions and values within the North American polity, came to dominate the U.S. approach. This ideology also dominates Newark's city government rhetoric today. In describing Newark's ongoing revitalization, Mayor Sharpe James stated in 2004, for example, "Our greatest strength lies not in bricks and mortar, but in our rainbow of peoples and cultures whose diversity and energy have fueled our rebirth and growth. Sample our restaurants, visit our cultural attractions, meet our diverse people" (2004). The Portuguese Ironbound section of the city is often singled out for its active participation in Newark's post-1967 recovery (James 2002). Boasting low crime rates, generally well-maintained residential buildings, and a booming commercial district replete with ethnic restaurants and shops, the Ironbound's "Little Portugal" figures prominently in Newark's narrative of urban renewal and multicultural acceptance[9] (Rae-Turner and Koles 2001, 153-54; Grogan and Proscio 2001, 137-38).

The post-colonial Portuguese state also enlarged its concept of nation in recent decades to include Portuguese emigrants around the globe. Portugal passed a law in 1981 permitting dual nationality and allowing Portuguese emigrants who had lost their native citizenship to regain it. As Irene Bloemraad points out, nowadays it is almost impossible for a Portuguese emigrant to claim singular non-Portuguese citizenship; "if a Portuguese swears the [U.S.] oath of allegiance today, the state of Portugal will continue to consider that person a Portuguese national. Many immigrants therefore find themselves in a situation of *de facto* dual citizenship" (Bloemraad 2002, 205, Holton's brackets). The change in both U.S. and

Portuguese ideology toward Portuguese emigrants residing in the U.S. set up the conditions for selective acculturation. It is in the interest of both states, according to current policies, for Portuguese-Americans to recognize an allegiance to both sending and receiving contexts.

The Portuguese government has not confined its overseas focus solely to issues of emigrant citizenship. In 1996, it also created a special consultative council, the Conselho das Comunidades Portuguesas (CCP; Council for Portuguese Communities) comprised of 100 elected representatives from varying international hubs of Portuguese emigration who gather regularly to communicate their concerns directly to Lisbon.[10] The Portuguese government also began giving increased cultural support to Portuguese in diaspora following the revolution of 1974. In several well-publicized visits to Newark in the 1990s, for example, Portugal's Prime Minister António Guterres and Secretary of the Portuguese Communities, José Lello, gave speeches suggesting that the immigrant community both maintain Portuguese customs and traditional values abroad, while simultaneously committing to their current geographical locale, through increased assimilation, U.S. citizenship procurement, and political participation. Former Prime Minister Guterres spoke at the inauguration of the new Portuguese Consulate of Newark in 1998 promising,"We [the Portuguese government] will do our best to be present here, but you [Luso-Americans] must strongly participate in the civic and political life of the United States" (*Ironbound Ties* 1999). Five years later, the Ministro dos Negócios Estrangeiros e das Comunidades Portuguesas [Minister of Foreign Commerce and Portuguese Communities], António Martins da Cruz, reiterated this very same message in a 2003 address to Luso-Americans in Danbury, Connecticut. Reporting on the event, Henrique Mano writes, "Martins da Cruz asked the Portuguese to integrate themselves into their adopted homeland, but also encouraged them to keep the umbilical cord tied to their country of origin" (2003, 8).[11] Cruz elaborates by suggesting that:

> the best way not to forget Portugal is to teach your children and grandchildren, the new generation, Portuguese culture and language. The best way to keep the nation of Portugal always present here is to speak Portuguese, to have *ranchos folclóricos*, and to have groups which prolong our culture here.(Mano 2003, 8)

In this statement, Martins da Cruz names folklore performance as an important vehicle for conjuring the nation of Portugal on American soil, and keeping Portuguese culture alive while integrating into U.S. society.

This official stance urging immigrants to both stay connected to Portuguese culture while becoming assimilated agents in their adopted homeland is accompanied by an aggressive campaign by the Instituto Camões to solidify Portuguese language acquisition in emigrant communities abroad—particularly among second- and third-generation immigrants. The Instituto Camões plan, which involves supporting some community language schools, university Portuguese Studies programs and the founding of Portuguese Language Centers around the globe, aims to increase the number of Portuguese speakers throughout the world, so that Portuguese, currently the sixth most spoken international language can become a vital communicative vehicle in the world of business, international trade, and foreign relations. According to this plan, immigrant communities act as both linguistic incubators of future Portuguese language vitality, and intermediaries between Portugal and the immigrants' newly adopted homelands.[12]

The change in U.S. and Portuguese policy toward i/emigrants occurs concomitant with a surge in Portuguese migration to the U.S. Emigration from Portugal to the U.S. rose dramatically between 1965-80, (see Figure 1). This surge is due to a variety of exogenous and endogenous factors, including economic hardship, political instability and colonial

FIGURE I

PORTUGUESE EMIGRATION TO THE UNITED STATES BY DECADE (1891-1990)

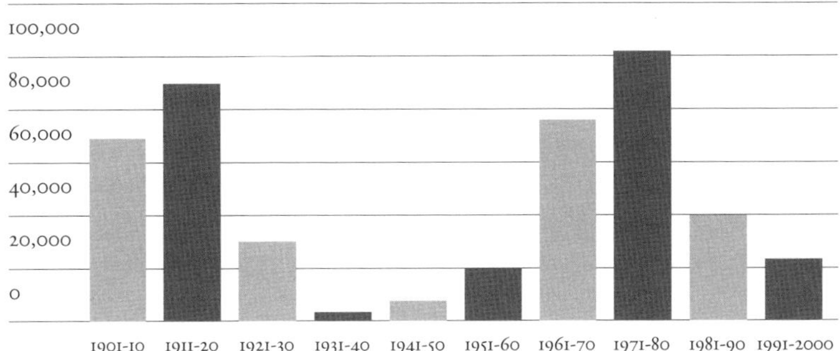

Source: Immigration and Naturalization Service, 2002

war in Portugal, the U.S. repeal of the 1924 National Origins Quota Act in 1965, and a softening of the 1974 northern European labor market which resulted in the redirection of Portuguese emigrants previously destined for France, Germany, and Belgium.[13]

During the period between 1960 and 1980, many Portuguese destined for the U.S. settled in New Jersey. According to the 1990 Census, New Jersey boasts the fourth largest population of Portuguese, behind California, Massachusetts, and Rhode Island, in that order (see Figure 2). New Jersey is distinguished by having the highest proportion of continental Portuguese and an extremely high concentration of recently-arrived Portuguese emigrants (see Figure 3). Upon analyzing the 1980 census numbers for New Jersey, we can see that eighty-three percent of the population of foreign-born Portuguese arrived between 1965-80.[14] Another indicator of New Jersey's relatively newly arrived Portuguese population is the large percentage of Portuguese families who speak Portuguese in the home. According to the 1990 U.S. census data illustrated in Figure 2, out of a population of 56,928 Portuguese in New Jersey (first ascendancy only), 55,285 people aged five or older speak Portuguese in the home (Vicente 1999, 61-66). A much greater proportion of New Jersey Luso-Americans have thus retained native language use relative to the Portuguese communities in Massachusetts, Rhode Island and California—native language use, of course, being an essential component of selective acculturation.

FIGURE 2

NUMBER OF LUSO-AMERICANS AND PORTUGUESE LANGUAGE USE BY STATE, 1990

	General Population	*Luso-American Pop.*	*Port. Lang. Use**
CALIFORNIA	29,760,021	275,492	78,232
MASSACHUSETTS	6,016,425	241,173	133,373
RHODE ISLAND	1,003,464	76,773	39,947
NEW JERSEY	7,730,188	56,928	55,285
HAWAII	1,108,229	39,748	1,110

Source: 1990 U.S. Census of Population, Detailed Population Characteristics, adapted from Vicente 1999

** This category indicates the number of Luso-Americans who still speak Portuguese at home*

FIGURE 3

CITIZENSHIP AND YEAR OF IMMIGRATION FOR NEW JERSEY'S FOREIGN-BORN PERSONS BY COUNTRY OF BIRTH: 1980

Place of Origin	*Foreign-Born Population of NJ*	*1975-80*	*1970-74*	*1965-69*	*1960-64*	*1950-59*	*Before 1950*
AZORES	219	15	84	50	16	25	29
CONTINENTAL PORTUGAL	28,234	7,520	9,788	6,021	1,886	1,126	1,893

Source: 1980 US Census of Population, Detailed Population Characteristics

The cultural and lingual vibrancy of northern New Jersey's Portuguese population is also evident in the built environment. Throughout Newark's East Ward Ironbound section, and interspersed throughout the downtown areas of neighboring towns of Elizabeth, Kearny, Hillside, Perth Amboy, and Bellville, Portuguese-owned businesses announce themselves through bilingual signs, often incorporating the colors of the Portuguese flag and other emblems of national identity such as the 16th-century caravel and the one-eyed portrait of Luís de Camões. Many apartment buildings in these areas feature ceramic tiles of Fátima and the three shepherd children, red clay roofs, elaborate urban gardens of fig trees and grape arbors, and mosaic stone sidewalks reminiscent of urban Portugal. In the business districts of Newark, Kearny, and Elizabeth, many retail shops, banks, and professional offices post signs announcing "*Fala-se Português*" ("Portuguese Spoken Here"). The local ATM machines have a Portuguese language option, and the Portuguese community has its own Lusophone yellow pages.

The concentration of Portuguese residents in Newark—the city's largest foreign-born ethnic group according to the 1990 census (Vicente 1999)—has allowed for a staggering number of Portuguese businesses to flourish.[15] This robust commercial presence has a double effect of serving the monolingual foreign-born population while obligating the second- and third-generation Portuguese and ethnic outsiders to become conversant in the language/culture in order to navigate the area as consumers and fellow merchants. This in turn feeds the educational programs funded by the Instituto Camões by populating them with students who feel they must know Portuguese to break into the northern

New Jersey job market. The multi-contextual and quotidian use of Portuguese in northern New Jersey, as a language of commerce, religion, and domestic life, has created a structure of mutually reinforcing linguistic joists which facilitate the maintenance of the language into the second and third generation. This feature of New Jersey's Portuguese community is directly attributable to both state policies and ideologies with regard to late 20th-century emigration.

In conclusion, the post-1974 Portuguese government has asserted a two-pronged policy of cultural preservation and U.S. assimilation, while the U.S. has welcomed Portuguese immigrants by repealing the 1924 National Origins Quota Act in 1965, and forwarding a post-civil rights era agenda of multiculturalism.[16] These state ideologies create a hospitable environment for the "retention of significant elements of the culture of origin," "fluent bilingualism in the second generation," and the perseverance of "key values and normative expectations from the original culture"—the primary components of selective acculturatio, according to Rumbaut and Portes's definition. The ethos of transnational hybridity is reflected in the built environment of northern New Jersey and the large quantity of Portuguese-owned businesses that thrive throughout the region. The transmigratory dynamic of living between two national contexts, where home and host society commingle in a "single arena of social action" is also facilitated by the predominance of newly-arrived immigrants in the community, the high density of Portuguese in northern New Jersey, and their settlement in self-contained urban enclaves.[17]

Dancing Along the In-Between

Portuguese immigrants in northern New Jersey gain social and cultural capital by "keeping their feet" in two national contexts. The adroit navigation between Portugal and the U.S. has resulted in commercial success and political empowerment within New Jersey's Portuguese community, which, in turn, requires making visible one's commitment to both originary and adopted homelands. This is where revivalist folklore performance becomes a vital part of transmigration, imbricated as it is in the commercial and political life of northern New Jersey's Portuguese community and in national emigration ideologies.

Within northern New Jersey's Luso-American community, selective acculturation must be examined alongside performative manifestations of ethnic identity. Folklore performance is a consistent presence in debates over Portuguese assimilation. Remember the Connecticut speech, where Foreign Commerce Minister Martins da Cruz singles out *ranchos folclóricos* in his appeal to Luso-Americans to "keep the umbilical cord tied to Portugal" while integrating into the U.S. Revivalist folklore performance invigorates Portuguese language use, moral values, and endogamy while, at the same time, celebrating Luso-American commercial success and political ascendancy. Folklore groups depend upon transmigrants and transnational media for the creation and periodic renewal of their performance repertoire and costumes, the restoration of musical instruments and historical props, the recruitment of performers and publics, and the exchange of ideas and advice among folklore groups throughout the Portuguese diaspora. Northern New Jersey's thriving folklore scene is both an expressive symbol of and practical means towards the achievement of selective acculturation.

Rancho performance in diaspora differs greatly from *rancho* performance within the bounded space of Portugal. Portuguese *ranchos* have fought social stigma due to folklore's association with the fascist regime that controlled Portugal from 1926 to 1974. Following the 1974 revolution that ended fascism, Portuguese *ranchos* overhauled costumes, musical repertoire and choreography to rid folklore of its ties to fascist cultural policy. Shedding fascist spectacle that had turned folklore dancers into whirling national flags, reformed *ranchos* now meticulously research turn-of-the-century tradition using ethnographic methodologies. Reformed *ranchos* perform historically reconstructed dances drawn from the locality in which performers live. Revivalist folklore in Portugal today combines scholarship with performative expression (Holton 1999; 2005).

The hundreds of *ranchos folclóricos* that exist in Portuguese immigrant communities of northern Europe, Brazil, South Africa, Southeast Asia, Canada and the U.S., however, have not, for the most part, experienced fascist stigma nor undergone post-revolutionary cultural reform. *Ranchos* in the diaspora generally do not conduct ethnographic research; rather they recreate dances from books, videos, television programs or in consultation with other folklore groups in Portugal. Some perform the nation *not* the locality, using amalgamated costumes and repertoire sampled from all of Portugal's twelve regions, as is the case in Hamburg, Germany (Klimt 1992; 2000). Other *ranchos* combine Portuguese folklore with performance traditions from their current cultural environment, as is the case in Malaysia's Portuguese Settlement (Sarkissian 2000). Still other *ranchos* select one region to represent, as is the case with many *ranchos* in New Jersey, and this region, Minho, acts as a synecdoche for the nation as a whole.[18] Although at first glance they appear similar to Portugal's fascist troupes of the 1950s in their patriotic celebration of the nation, *ranchos* in diaspora construct "Portuguese" identities to differing political and social ends.

There are currently sixteen active *ranchos* in northern New Jersey.[19] New Jersey *ranchos*, like their Portuguese counterparts, are comprised of amateur musicians and dancers who perform reconstructions of traditional songs and dances from the late 19th century. Typically composed of thirty to thirty-five members, New Jersey *ranchos folclóricos* feature eight to ten pairs of dancers, a section of instrumentalists called the *tocata* and several vocalists. The dancers are typically the youngest members of the group—ranging in age from five to thirty years old. The musicians, usually older men in their forties and fifties, play instruments such as the accordion, concertina, clarinet, various forms of guitars and percussion, depending on the regional repertoire. The vocalists perform alone or in pairs. *Ranchos*, both in Portugal and the United States, often operate under the auspices of larger cultural associations or social organizations.

Ranchos typically rehearse weekly throughout the fall and winter and perform regularly during the spring and summer months at festivals and religious and civic celebrations. *Ranchos folclóricos* are often hired to mark the observance of *both* American and Portuguese holidays, such as São Martinho, 25 de Abril, Fátima celebrations, Father's Day, Mother's Day, and the Fourth of July. Many New Jersey *ranchos* also perform in secondary schools throughout the state, at Newark colleges and universities, and in International Folklore Festivals throughout the U.S. New Jersey *ranchos* occasionally travel to Portugal to perform or to other Portuguese emigrant communities in Europe, South Africa and the Americas. The primary focus of the New Jersey *rancho* performance calendar, however, is Newark's enormous Portugal Day Festival which takes place annually during the week of June 10. Most *ranchos* appear in the cacophonous weekend parade alongside their own floats, while also performing in other festival programming throughout the week.

One of the ways northern New Jersey's community of 72,196 Portuguese immigrants (F. Santos 2002b) maintains transnational links between Portugal and the U.S. is through what Appadurai (1996) calls "global mediascapes." Folklore dancing is just one expression of globalized associationism that ties in to other media-driven activities such as reading the Portuguese immigrant newspaper, watching the International Portuguese cable channel, and listening to Portuguese radio programs. This lusophone mediascape not only furthers the goals of Instituto Camões linguistic ambitions, it also creates "communities of sentiment" where through the collective cultural consumption of videos, TV, audio cassettes and newspapers, "groups of people begin to think and feel things together" (Appadurai 1996, 8). Through Lusophone mediascapes, *ranchos folclóricos* maintain contact with their homeland and with other Portuguese immigrant communities around the globe. This mediascape becomes an essential tool for both *rancho* repertoire building and *rancho* promotion; immigrant *ranchos* learn new songs and dances from watching TV, and gain visibility from appearing on Portuguese cable. Folklore performance, as it exists within a well-developed system of cultural consumption and reproduction, is an ideal vehicle for maintaining ties to Portugal and the Portuguese diaspora, while asserting a political and cultural voice in the U.S.—the twin goals of the Portuguese state policy after 1974.

Virtual travel between Portugal and the U.S. is also complemented by real trips home. Although the Luso-American population is considered more permanently situated in the U.S. compared to Portuguese communities in northern Europe who describe their emigrant lives as "temporary" (Klimt 1992), many of New Jersey's Portuguese return regularly to their birthplace and dream of Iberian retirements. Over one third of the Luso-Americans interviewed for the Ironbound Oral History Project reported visiting Portugal annually. Many in this group still maintained family homes or newly purchased apartments in Portugal. *Retornados*—those who had emigrated to Lusophone Africa and were forced to return to Portugal after 25 de Abril, later moving to the U.S.—comprised the population that returned to Portugal least frequently.

Among the second-generation Luso-Americans, all had been to Portugal at least once, and some returned annually with their parents or alone to visit grandparents.[20]

According to the *rancho* performers I interviewed, returning to Portugal contributes significantly to the health and maintenance of the folklore group. As Joe Cerqueira (Interview by author, Dec. 18, 2003) describes:

> The costumes of all of New Jersey's *ranchos* come from Portugal, all of the *ranchos* that exist today got their costumes in Portugal. The only *rancho* that didn't buy their clothes there was Barcuense in 1977—but the *ranchos* today all clothes, all pieces of the costumes, as well as the musical instruments came from Portugal.

In addition to the regular purchase and restoration of costumes, props and musical instruments, *rancho* members also report returning to Portugal for repertoire acquisition. Tony Cardoso (Interview by author, Feb 13, 2003), Director of Sonhos de Portugal describes how they acquired the song, "Vida de Emigrante" [Emigrant's Life]:

> Tony: One of the musicians we had in our group is now back in Portugal for good. But before he moved back he brought us that music … it's been one of our favorite dances.
> Kim: So he wrote the music?
> Tony: He didn't write the music. He used to perform with a group in Portugal, and it was one of the people in that group that taught him the music. The dance was also given to us too by…Toto was his name. It was very difficult in the beginning to learn it, but we picked it up.

The fact that Cardoso's Luso-American *rancho* was given a song about emigration by a folklore troupe in Portugal illustrates how transnational interchange truly dominates the experience of most *ranchos* in northern New Jersey, and the way in which sending and receiving contexts become "a single arena of social action" (Margolis 1994, 29). Portuguese *ranchos* sing about emigration, and American *ranchos* sing about Portugal. The double utopia described by Feldman-Bianco and Huse (1998) resonates in this example.

Folklore dance in New Jersey is also a way for Portuguese-born parents to instill distinctly Portuguese moral values in their second- and third-generation "American" children and grandchildren. Folklore dance encourages the maintenance of conservative moral values such as monogamy, respect for authority, and celebration of an agrarian lifestyle abandoned by immigrants who moved from Portuguese rurality to U.S. industrial urbanism throughout the 1960s, 1970s, and 1980s.[21]

Paired dancers in New Jersey *ranchos* tend to be second-generation descendants chosen by the *rancho* directors in consideration of uniform height, skill, and age. However, another factor, not often verbalized, influences the constitution of pairs—that is, many dancer pairs court each other (Carvalho 1990, 30). Public courtship in Portuguese immigrant families is a charged issue. Many second-generation Luso-Americans interviewed for the Rutgers-Newark Ironbound Oral History Project describe being subject to strict parenting and disciplined guidelines for dating: children should ideally choose a Portuguese-American partner.[22] Once a partner is chosen and courtship becomes public, children should stay with this partner, preferably until marriage. [23]

Luso-American college-age students also describe strict parental monitoring of courtship, especially for daughters. Dating in the presence of adult family members, acquaintances, or at the very least other peers, is preferable to going out on a date alone. Given these guidelines, dancerly participation in *ranchos folclóricos* increases the chances of finding a Portuguese mate (Carvalho 1990). Jessica Moreira (Interivew by author, Dec. 15, 2003), a nineteen-year-old dancer in the Danças e Cantares de Portugal Rancho, describes the courtship of couples in her group and the familial pressures she feels to find a Portuguese mate:

> Jessica: Well, actually one of them, the girl, was dancing and then I guess they started going out and she brought her boyfriend to the group so they could stay as partners. And then another couple, they've been [*rancho*] partners since they were five. They started in the Rancho Infantil and they've been partners for ten years now. She's twenty and he's eighteen, and they started going out about a year ago.
>
> Kim: Would you say it's important to your parents that you date a Portuguese guy?
>
> Jessica: Yes.

> Kim: Why?
> Jessica: I don't know, my father thinks the Portuguese are better than everything else, he just regards us as way up there, I guess cuz he's in … construction, the Portuguese just kind of strive a little more and he see *os outros* [the others] as *preguiçosos* [lazy].
> Kim: Do you think the *rancho* is a way to ensure that you….
> Jessica: Even if he doesn't say it directly, I know he wants me to go out with a Portuguese guy…. The *rancho* is to keep myself involved, to keep myself going, keep the culture going. (Interview by author, Jessica Moreira, Dec. 15, 2003, author's inserts)

While Jessica's father's rationale for preferring a Portuguese husband for his daughter is due to a belief in Portuguese industriousness, some other second-generation teenagers cite language as the primary reason for wanting a Portuguese mate. Sonia DaCosta (Interview by Maria DaSilva, April 16, 2001), interviewed for the Ironbound Oral History Project, states that marrying outside the Portuguese community would cause problems in her extended family. "I want my husband to be able to talk to my parents and grandparents," she says. Folklore performance not only "keeps the culture going" among younger generations through the rehearsal of Portuguese songs and dances, it also "keeps the culture going" by fostering Luso-American friendships and endogamous pairing. Dancing folklore also facilitates adult supervision of public courtship and exerts social pressure on couples to maintain their relationships and work toward marriage.

In addition to promoting endogamous courtship practices, *ranchos folclóricos* also instill in second-generation dancers a respect for their rural heritage and the traditional gender roles that come with it. *Ranchos,* both in the U.S. and in Portugal, reconstitute popular songs and dances created by a nameless, faceless collective of peasants at the turn of the 19th and 20th centuries. Rurality, seen from the vantage point of Portuguese immigrants living in Northeastern U.S. cities, becomes a utopian space (Feldman-Bianco and Huse 1998). *Rancho* songs and dances hearken back to a static, fictionalized past, where social hierarchies are unquestioned and rural life is stripped of the backbreaking labor and economic impoverishment that often characterized the quotidian life of agrarian workers. *Rancho* dancers carry onto the stage agricultural tools long obsolete, in a material celebration of peasant lifestyle. These "objects of ethnography," in Barbara Kirshenblatt-Gimblett's (1991) sense of the term, are stripped of their utility, framed as aesthetic mementos or theatrical props. Through song lyrics that remember bucolic courtship and camaraderie, and choreography that has dancers, arms akimbo, whirling around and around in dizzying reveries, *ranchos folclóricos* invoke rural life in its most idealized form.

Many New Jersey *rancho* members come from families of Portugal's rural North (Carvalho 1990, 12), and *rancho* dancing promotes an embodied albeit "invented" (Hobsbawm and Ranger 1983) celebration of this ancestral past. Jessica Moreira, for example, describes a float that members of her Portuguese Youth Group—many of them second-generation *rancho* dancers—constructed for the Portugal Day Parade:

> We had Minho represented with the brick stove. We had the smoke machine inside, so it was smoking the *chouriços* [smoked sausage], it looked so pretty.... And of course for Minho we had the girl and the guy dressed in *rancho* outfits. And then we had Trás-os-Montes represented with a *carro de mão* made out of wood with hay on it ... and we had Nazaré with a fish net with dried fish ... and we had a girl with the *sete saias* [seven skirts] and a *peixeiro* [fishmonger]. Do you know the story of the *sete saias*? I'm such a dork, I know all this stuff. Well, the *peixeiras* [fishmongers] in Nazaré have *sete saias* because the *peixeiros*—their husbands used to go out to sea for seven months and every month they used to take off a *saia* and then when they were at their last *saia*, they know their husbands are coming home. (Interview by author, Dec. 15, 2003, author's inserts)

In the float, Portugal's regions were each represented by a pair of Luso-American teenagers dressed as Portuguese peasant archetypes. These couples were further described by the props characteristic of rural life according to region—a cart of hay, a brick stove, a fishing net. This Portuguese Youth Group float celebrates rural peasant life in all of its regional diversity while also embodying idealized patterns of conservative sociability. The story of the *sete saias* is a powerful illustration of this—the wife waiting patiently (and chastely) for her husband, shedding one skirt at a time, invoking her body as a calendar to mark the husband's return. According to the *sete saias* sequencing, it is only the husband who will enjoy the *peixeira*'s full state of undress.

"Não é para ti" [It is not for you], a dance frequently performed by Sonhos de Portugal, playfully exhibits female chastity. Throughout the choreography, young male dancers try to kiss their female partners and are snubbed with the dramatic wag of an index finger and a kerchiefed shooing. Dressed in long skirts and kerchiefs, female *rancho* dancers role-play traditional constructs of rural femininity.[24] Male dancers, typically dressed in long pants and vests adroitly guide their female partners through *viras*, strong hands placed firmly on the small of their partners' backs in a symbolic display of masculine power and leadership. In many *viras,* the men and women dance in pairs in single broad circle. Individuals occasionally break off and dance with other partners or form smaller foursomes of men and women circling rapidly in quadrants of autonomous unpaired movements. These dancerly breeches, however, are always followed by the resumption of male/female pairing and a return to the permanent partnerships where boyfriends and girlfriends end up in the proper pre-marital embrace. *Rancho* costumes and choreography present an anachronistic portrait of traditional gender roles, flying in the face of the high incidence of female industrial labor and increasing rates of university study among Portuguese immigrant women living in the U.S.[25] *Rancho* dancing contributes to the maintenance of conservative moral values, traditional gender roles, and the celebration of rural ancestry despite the urban relocation and concomitant liberalizing forces faced by many Portuguese immigrants living in the northeastern United States.

In addition to catalyzing ties to Portugal and solidifying Portuguese ethnic identity, *rancho* dancing also becomes a vehicle to demonstrate assimilation and social prestige within the United States. Many immigrants experience a double-edged lack of prestige. In the northeastern U.S., many Portuguese immigrants are blue-collar workers who have shown, until very recently little socioeconomic mobility. In Portugal, emigrants who return home for summer vacation or retirement are often ostracized as uncultured *nouveaux riches* who return from years of U.S. labor speaking neither Portuguese nor English well, with a bent toward conspicuous consumption (see Cole 1991 and Brettell 2003a). According to many immigrant *rancho* members, performing folklore helps mitigate this stereotype of Portuguese emigrants, boosting their status, both within the Luso-American community and in Portugal. As one dancer explained:

> We are not rude people who went away only to make money, as most people might think; we are able to cultivate forms of traditional music and dance even better than *ranchos* in Portugal. *Ranchos folclóricos* are evidence that migrants have culture." (quoted in Carvalho 1990)

Dancing in a Portuguese *rancho*, according to Rutgers Newark college student Brian Santos, raised his social standing within a New Jersey public high school. Brian, who dances in the *rancho* Sonhos de Portugal recalls a performance that took place in Kearny, New Jersey:

> My friends in high school were always really interested in it. There's an international festival every year at the high school and when I was a student there, we performed. Basically, it is one day dedicated to all the different cultures represented in the school, and there are different performances from different cultures and the Portuguese is always one of the most popular. We always got standing ovations, everyone always loved it, the teachers, the students, they would always call us on stage and ask us lots of questions. (Interview by author, May 19, 2002)

Brian's testimony shows the effects of the 1974 Ethnic Heritage Act which encourages multicultural celebration, even at the high-school level and where, particularly in a diverse region like northern New Jersey, children of immigrants raise their social capital by performing ethnic difference in a public context. Brian explains that, contrary to some of the kids in Portugal who get teased by their peers for performing in *ranchos*, dancing folklore is seen as "cool" by many of his New Jersey friends, Portuguese and non-Portuguese alike. His family is also very supportive of his participation in folklore because "It shows that I am involved in our culture" (Interview by author, May 19, 2002). Brian, then, receives concentric circles of social kudos by dancing folklore starting with the most intimate social context, that of the nuclear family, radiating out into larger rings of friends, neighbors, classmates, teachers, and administrators. Brian even articulates the stature of his *rancho* within a national framework:

> We actually are considered professionals, we're in the Hudson County Book of Professional Entertainers, so anyone who is looking for a certain musical group can find us there. You know we're also in the Library of Congress, in Washington DC. We're documented in there! (Interview by author, May 19, 2002)

Rancho director Tony Cardoso echoes this story of broad recognition and visibility:

> We've danced at the Statue of Liberty.... [W]e were even invited to perform at Giants Stadium.... We've also been on Portuguese TV and even the American FOX channel, you know FOX 5.... [I]t was really something for the kids to be on a major channel, to be on national TV. (Interview by author, Feb. 13, 2003)

In addition to celebrating ethnic difference and catalyzing social prestige and visibility, *rancho* performance is intimately linked to Luso-American commercial success and emergent political power in northern New Jersey. Many *ranchos* are officially tied to cultural organizations. The *ranchos,* Sonhos do Portugal and Os Sonhos Continuam, for example, are affiliated with the Portuguese Cultural Association in Kearny, NJ. Danças e Cantares de Portugal is affiliated with the Portuguese Instructive Social Club in Elizabeth, New Jersey. The Rancho Folclórico da Casa do Minho is affiliated with the Casa do Minho in Newark. Some groups, however, are also officially or unofficially linked to prominent Luso-American merchants and entrepreneurs. The Rancho Folclórico "A Eira" for example, is linked to Bernardino Coutinho, owner of the Coutinho Bakery chain and founder of the Portugal Day Parade. Sonhos de Portugal and Os Sonhos Continuam are linked to Licínio Cruz, a district judge and co-owner of the successful Cruz Construction Corporation.

Links to prominent community leaders can mean a variety of advantages for *ranchos* in northern New Jersey. Tony Cardoso emphasizes the financial and logistical support his *rancho* has received from Cruz Construction:

> Cruz over the years has supported the group with money and outfits at times.... Every year they make a contribution when it comes to Portugal

> Day in Newark. They not only give the truck trailer to the group, they also supply the wood every single year…to build it, to supply the wood, which is a couple thousand dollars, and another couple thousand for other materials. [The float] takes about three days to assemble. (Interview by author, Feb. 13, 2003)

The bond between Cruz Construction and Sonhos de Portugal is fortified and made visible not only during the enormous Portugal Day Parade,[26] but also through annual performances at the company picnic and other business functions sponsored by Cruz Construction. Similar to the commercial *padrinhos* Portuguese *ranchos* cultivate, New Jersey *ranchos* often share personnel with their corporate sponsor. Tony Cardoso, for example, has worked for Cruz Construction for decades. He sees his role in the *rancho* and in the company as symbiotic and mutually constitutive. Cruz construction not only lends Sonhos de Portugal financial assistance, but also the social cachet that comes with being linked to a successful Portuguese-American business. Sonhos de Portugal, in turn, symbolically enacts the company's commitment to Portugal and to its Luso-American employees through the performance of 19th-century popular traditions—traditions that help an emigrant workforce cohere overseas while advertising the company's services and ethnic provenance.

Ranchos folclóricos play with mnemonic function—calling up memories of summer *festas* in the North of Portugal for Portuguese emigrants far from home (Interview by author, Joseph Cerqueira, Oct. 23, 2002). At the same time, *ranchos* help a community in diaspora, caught up in the liminal moment of performance, forget their current geographic circumstance, transported back in time and space, as if reversing emigration. *Ranchos* in an immigrant context encourage both mnemonic recall and erasure. However, bonds between Luso-American entrepreneurship and folklore performance add a charged symbolic layer to collective memory not present in the Portuguese context. *Rancho* performers, barefoot on stage holding hoes and pitchforks exist in marked contrast to their corporate *padrinhos*, successful navigators of America's industrial Northeast and exemplary portraits of the American Dream attained. *Ranchos* in this context become a measuring stick for the success of the emigration project—an initiative often fueled by the desire to leave an impoverished agrarian plight for a place that promises industrial opportunity and social mobility. The staged celebration of rural life, a misty unreality, exists in metonymic tension with the figure of New Jersey's Luso-American entrepreneur, men dressed in three piece suits driving expensive cars, their economic rise often the product of successful urban businesses. The symbolic tension created by the relationship between *ranchos folclóricos* and their commercial sponsors is nowhere better illustrated than the Portugal Day Parade where barefoot dancers in peasant garb march alongside sleek white limousines, marking both experiential distance and emotional proximity between rural past and urban present, in a complex homage to two national contexts.

In addition to intimate ties to emigrant entrepreneurship, *rancho* performance has been a consistent presence at celebrations of Luso-Americans' rise to political power in New Jersey. There has been much ink spilled in attempt to document and theorize the historic lack of political participation among the Portuguese in the United States (Almeida 1999; Barrow 2002; Marinho and Cornwall 1992; Moniz 1979). Casual debates on the topic often arrive at the same conclusion; voting is not part of the Portuguese culture due to the fascist government which stifled political agency from 1926-74. However, as Onésimo Almeida (1999) rightly points out, lack of political participation throughout Portuguese emigrant communities predates the installation of the Estado Novo. As recently as 1996, the authors of a proposed documentary entitled, "Newark's Silent Majority: Citizens Without a Voice," describe the situation in the Ironbound:

> More than fifty years ago they started coming, drawn by the hope of a promising future in a bountiful country. Today they find themselves possessing the material things the country offered, but missing the joy and power of a people who govern themselves. Newark's Portuguese-Americans don't vote.... They have turned the Ironbound into an inner-city paradise, but have never elected one of their own to the City Council. And they are bitter about it. The Ironbound is a dumping ground and its people whipping boys for cynical politicians who revel in Luso-American political impotence, never failing to ignore it. (Lancellotti and Gardner, quoted in Almeida 1999)

Lancellotti and Gardner's depiction of Newark's Portuguese in 1996, however, no longer reflects the reality of the community today. Since the late 1990s much has changed. The Portuguese government installed a new and improved Portuguese Consulate in a prestigious building on the outskirts of the Ironbound in 1998. Official ribbon-cuttings attended by the Portuguese Prime Minister and Luso-American leaders became the forum for a revitalized campaign aimed at increasing political participation among Luso-Americans. In November 1998, Augusto Amador became the first Portuguese-American councilman elected to office in the history of Newark. And in May 2002, with the election of Governor James McGreevey, Dina Matos McGreevy, a Portuguese-American activist, became New Jersey's First Lady. The Portuguese government even recognized this change during a 2003 "Seminar on Participation and Citizenship" in Lisbon, citing the increase in Luso-Americans elected to political office as a model upswing in civic engagement ("Martins da Cruz Quer Luso-Descendentes" 2003).

Since the late 1990s, as Newark's Luso-Americans have raised their political visibility, and received increased attention from the Portuguese government, *ranchos folclóricos* have served as the expressive mascot of Portuguese ethnicity in action. Many of New Jersey's *ranchos* have performed at voter drives, election parties and alongside campaign speeches. In fact, in May 2002, newly-elected New Jersey Governor James McGreevey, hosted a party on the lawn of the Governor's mansion in celebration of Portugal Day and marked by the performances of three Newark *ranchos*. Reviews and color photographs of these *rancho* performances made their way into the mainstream local press as well as the Lusophone mediascape, announcing, in the words of several journalists, the political arrival of the Portuguese.[27] In 2003, Portugal Day was again celebrated at the Governor's mansion—this time the *ranchos,* Os Sonhos de Portugal and Os Sonhos Continuam comprised the featured entertainment. In addition to the rapid-fire footwork of the *rancho* dancers which commanded rapt attention from the large crowd of Portuguese-Americans, there was a costumed dancer who captured the public's fancy. Teetering on the edge of the performance space, dressed from head to toe in a tiny embroidered *rancho* costume the color of the Portuguese flag, was two-year-old Jacqueline McGreevey, the daughter of New Jersey's Irish-American governor and his Portuguese-American wife. As the diminutive figure clapped her hands in time to the accordion's animated melody, raising her arms in emulation of the other second-generation dancers, expressive culture embodied political ideology. As the Portuguese government reminds any Luso-descendent who will listen, " [politics] and the preservation of cultural roots are not incompatible" ("Martins da Cruz Quer Luso-Descendentes" 2003).

Conclusion

In summary, *rancho* dancing enculturates a new generation of Portuguese-Americans according to the moral values of their parents' homeland. Second-generation Luso-Americans perform romanticized choreographies of rural life, where their parents' experience of back-breaking agricultural labor and poverty in northern Portugal is obscured by the festive presentation of ethnic heritage in an adopted homeland. Through the execution of paired dance steps, the vocalization of popular song lyrics, and the adherence to contemporary rehearsal practices, folklore dancing models conservative behavior such as the maintenance of traditional gender roles, respect for authority, and monogamy. Folklore dancing also provides children of immigrants with a pool of endogamous courtship possibilities, while affording them informal adult supervision of weekend social activities. Second-generation Luso-American dancers make a visible commitment to their ethnic heritage through folklore performance, which, in turn, grants them positive social reinforcement in family, school, and neighborhood contexts.

Revivalist folklore performance ties into U.S. immigration ideologies. As a result of legislation such as the 1965 repeal of the National Origins Quota Act, the passage of the 1974 Ethnic Heritage Act, and the general valorization of post-civil rights era multiculturalism, the United States has witnessed the proliferation of "ethnic celebrations, a zeal for genealogy, increased travel to ancestral homelands, and greater interest in ethnic artifacts, cuisine, music, literature and, of course, language" (Halter 2000, 5). *Rancho* dancing participates in this trend, revealing New Jersey's Portuguese population as, "exotics at home, hidden in plain sight" (di Leonardo 1998), a part of the state's ethnic diversity which local officials work to promote. Through the celebration of its ethnic neighborhoods and multicultural arts programming in municipal parks and the New Jersey Performing Arts Center, Newark has pinned much of its hopes for urban revitalization on the "marketing of ethnic heritage," a late 20th-century North American phenomenon that anthropologists are increasingly theorizing as part and parcel of American modernity (di Leonardo 1998; Halter 2000). Portuguese *rancho* performance, a consistent presence at "Diversity Day" festivals on New Jersey college and secondary school campuses, Newark's Portugal Day Parade and other U.S. folklore festivals play into both municipal and federal ideologies celebrating ethnic difference and inclusivity.

Changes in Portuguese state emigration ideology also undergird the development of *ranchos folclóricos* in diaspora. Once seen as traitors to their homeland, Portuguese emigrants are now the object of increasing state support and attention. In numerous high profile visits to Newark in the past ten years, Portugal's political leaders have urged Luso-Americans to fortify ties to their homeland while becoming actively engaged in America's political and civic life. Both private and public institutions in Portugal have sponsored initiatives that aim to affect this hybrid policy; U.S. naturalization campaigns are funded alongside Portuguese language schools throughout immigrant communities in the U.S. Northern New Jersey's second-generation Luso-Americans have been marked by this two-pronged policy, practicing what Rumbaut and Portes term "selective acculturation." Along the lines of Rumbaut and Portes's definition, Luso-Americans in Newark exhibit a high rate of bilingualism in the second generation, balancing assimilation into mainstream American society with the retention of core values and cultural practices from their parents' native context. Given New Jersey *ranchos*' relationship to Luso-American entrepreneurs and campaigns for U.S. political participation, revivalist folklore in diaspora reflects Portugal's emigration ideology. *Rancho* performers enact a commitment to their ancestral home through the restoration and dissemination of Portuguese tradition in diaspora while celebrating the success of the emigration project through association with Luso-American business leaders and their growing political clout within New Jersey.

Rancho dancing participates in a chain link of lusophone media production and consumption which strengthens and perpetuates the vitality of the Portuguese language and of Portuguese expressive culture, catalyzing communities of sentiment around the globe that can imagine themselves as an ethnic collective, despite geographical separation. New Jersey *rancho* scouts and enthusiasts travel to Portugal regularly, ensuring a constant transatlantic traffic in goods, services, and people related to the thriving revivalist folklore industry. Folklore performance links Portugal and the United States on myriad levels, offering transmigrants a way to process national, lingual, and cultural plurality through the lens of expressive tradition.

Notes

[1] This article was previously published in *Portuguese Studies Review*, 11(2), 2004: 153-182. Research for this article was made possible by generous grants from Rutgers University's Cornwall Center for Metropolitan Studies and the Institute on Ethnicity, Culture and the Modern Experience. Earlier versions of this paper were presented at the Society of Dance History Scholars annual conference in 2002 and the American Portuguese Studies Association Conference in 2002. I am grateful to Caroline Brettell, Salwa Castelo Branco, Andrea Klimt, and Tim Raphael for reading earlier drafts of this paper; Fernando Santos and Maria do Carmo Pereira for their kind assistance in accessing *Luso-Americano* back issues; Jessica Moreira and Susete Cesário for helping with transcription; and all the performers who shared their experiences with me, particularly Tony Cardoso and Joseph Cerqueira. Any errors are my own.

[2] This shift is also reflected in the official language used to describe new governmental departments post-1974. What used to be called the Secretary of the State of Emigration (Secretária do Estado da Emigração) was changed to the Secretary of the State of Portuguese Communities (Overseas) (Secretária do Estado das Comunidades) (Baganha 2001; Feldman-Bianco 1992).

[3] As is the case in Portugal, many New Jersey folklore performers move from *rancho* to *rancho* throughout the course of their performance careers. Reasons for leaving a *rancho* can include personality conflicts with fellow performers or *rancho* directors, a desire to join friends, spouses or other family members in a neighboring *rancho*, or geographical relocation. Several of the performers I interviewed had been members of other groups, including the Rancho Folclórico Roca-o-Norte of Newark, NJ and the Rancho Folclórico de Barcuense of Newark, NJ before joining their current *rancho*.

[4] The Rutgers-Newark Ironbound Oral History Project was founded by the author in 2001 as means to document the Portuguese-speaking population of northern New Jersey, a community which has received little scholarly attention. To date, student researchers have conducted and transcribed over 250 oral history interviews with Portuguese-speaking immigrants residing in northern New Jersey. These semi-structured interviews, typically one to two hours in duration, contain information as to the date and reasons for migration, strategies for adaptation, plans for return migration, expressive manifestations of ethnic and cultural identity in the U.S., conflict and collaboration within the Portuguese-speaking community of northern New Jersey, among other topics.

[5] See Kimberly DaCosta Holton (1999; 2003a; 2005).

[6] Rumbaut and Portes argue that today's era of mass immigration—"now overwhelmingly non-European in composition…[raises] serious questions about the applicability of explanatory models developed in connection with the experience of European ethnics [earlier in this century]" (2001a, 5). It is evident here that Rumbaut and Portes view European migration as a phenomenon of the past. This is not, however, the case with Portuguese migration to the U.S.—particularly to the state of New Jersey—which saw a surge in the 1960s and '70s, due to a variety of factors from the colonial wars and political instability in Portugal to the U.S. repeal of the quota system in 1964. The Portuguese have been called an "invisible minority" in the U.S., due to low levels of civic engagement and political participation. The Portuguese remain an invisible minority, I would argue, also due to scholarly inattention to these communities. In a modest attempt towards visibility, this chapter examines Portuguese immigrant communities as part and parcel of the fourth-wave migration to the U.S.

[7] For an excellent study on the settlement patterns and social dynamics of the Portuguese-Canadian community, see Teixeira (1999).

[8] Feldman-Bianco argues that during the 1920s and 1930s the Portuguese state viewed emi-

grants as "second-class citizens" and traitors to their country for having left (1992, 146-47). Other scholars document widespread social stigmatization of Portuguese emigrants upon returning home throughout the 20th century (Brettell 2003a; Cole 1991). Although the economic success of the emigrants in mid- to late 20th century made the State dependent on the remittances of the Portuguese abroad, this symbiosis did little to lessen the migrants' difficult reentry into Portugal for holidays or retirement: "they are still pejoritively called 'French,' 'Canadian,' 'Brazilians,' 'Americans'" (Feldman-Bianco 1992, 150).

[9] For more on the history of Newark and the evolution of the Ironbound section, see Rae-Turner and Koles (2001) and Cunningham (1988).

[10] There is a feeling among many CCP representatives that the Portuguese government has not used the emigrant think-tank to its fullest potential. Hoping to augment the visibility and political influence of Portuguese communities in diaspora, select CCP members have even proposed the creation of the Partido do Emigrant [Emigrant Party] in order to secure elected seats for emigrants in the Portuguese Parliament. See for example, Fernando Santos (2002a) and "*Conselho das Comunidades Portuguesas*" 2003. For more on CCP's history, see "*Com Onze Tarefas para Cumprir*" 1997.

[11] Unless otherwise noted, all translations are my own.

[12] The U.S. immigrant communities are particularly important elements in this plan because, unlike Portuguese communities in France and Germany, whose migratory leave-taking is consistently framed as "temporary" (Klimt 1992), Portuguese immigrants in the U.S. tend to reside permanently in their host country. For a comparative analysis of European state involvement among their emigrant populations, see Vicente (1999).

[13] Maria Baganha and Pedro Góis argue that northern Europe basically reversed its "open door"policy with regard to immigrant laborers in the mid-1970s "promoting the integration of previously-arrived immigrants while discouraging the arrival of new emigrant labor. In other words, permiting family reunification and prohibiting economic emigration" (1998, 235).

[14] Of course, the numbers in Figures 1, 2, and 3 do not include the large proportion of emigrants who left the country clandestinely and settled in the U.S. as undocumented aliens. Although there have been no systematic studies of undocumented Portuguese emigrants, Maria Baganha has estimated, for example, that illegal emigration to France and Germany between 1950 and 1988 comprised at least thirty-six percent of total emigration to those countries (Baganha 1998, 192). If we extrapolate to a U.S. context, adding data from the Ironbound Oral History Project where close to half of the interviewees arrived in New Jersey illegally, it is clear that these official numbers do not accurately quantify the number of Portuguese living in the region.

[15] Maria do Carmo Pereira (1996) has conducted an exhaustive study on the history of Portuguese business and commerce in northern New Jersey. Acording to her research, during the 1970s, 360 new Portuguese businesses were created, among them fifty-six restaurants, thirty-seven construction companies, forty automobile service stations, and twelve import/export retail establishments. From 1981-90 there was close to double the amount of new Portuguese businesses established. Out of 691, 148 were construction companies, forty-four automobile service stations, thirty restaurants, and eighteen travel agencies (52-9).

[16] Obviously, the extent to which the U.S. is a hospitable receiving context depends not only on the historical moment, but also varies according to country of origin. These variances are fully explored in Rumbaut and Portes 2001. The attacks of September 11th and the legislation these events provoked, of course, also mitigate the ideology of multicultural pluralism, sparking a new and yet unfolding phase in the United States' approach to immigration.

[17] Another factor which contributes to the dynamic of selective acculturation is the tightly-knit, co-ethnic community of the Ironbound which has a history of intense intergroup support and assistance. This relatively homogenous community is not generally characterized by conflict generated by racial, class, and regional tensions. New Jersey's population is overwhelmingly continental (see Figure 4, for example) with a strong regional orientation toward the North of Portugal.

[18] The vast majority of New Jersey *ranchos* identify themselves with the northern province of Minho. In António Medeiros's 1995 article, "Minho: Retrato Oitocentista de Uma Paisagem de Eleição," he argues that beginning in the last half of the 19th century, the region of Minho is imbued with mythic characteristics of primordialism, acting as a synechdoche for the nation and regional repository of national memory.

[19] These *ranchos* include Rancho Folclórico "A Eira" (adulto and infantil), Rancho Folclórico Roca-o-Norte, Rancho Folclórico Aldeia Velha do Sport Clube Português,Rancho Folclórico dos Camponeses do Minho do Sport Clube Português, Rancho Folclórico da Casa do Minho, Rancho

Infantil "O Futuro" da Casa do Minho, Danças e Cantares de Portugal, Os Sonhos Continuam, Sonhos de Portugal, Rancho Folclórico Barcuense, Grupo Folclórico Belas Ilhas, Rancho Folclórico Raízes de Portugal, Recordações de Portugal, Rancho Infantil de Union, Rancho Folclórico da Casa do Ribatejo.

[20] Two of the second-generation interviewees had even moved back to Portugal for junior high-school due to their parents' fears of violence in Newark area schools, only to return to the U.S. after the parents had changed their minds.

[21] João Carvalho suggests that *rancho* song texts "express the patterns of behavior the community wishes to perpetuate. These are childraising, obedience to parents, courtship strategies …" (1990, 39). I wish to argue that, in addition, the embodied process of performing in a *rancho* ensures cultural reproduction of "Portuguese" moral values.

[22] Many interviewees described a curious duality in the discipline their parents employed. In the U.S., household rules for socializing were much more restrictive than they were when the families traveled to Portugal for the summer.

[23] Public courtship can mean bringing the boyfriend/girlfriend to family functions and being seen with this partner in "public" (within the Portuguese community).

[24] This practice cites a fictional "pseudo past," an idealized construct; for, as many anthropologists note, 19th- and 20th-century women, particularly in the north of Portugal, often performed heavy agrarian labor, while men went off to war or in search of work (Brettell 1986).

[25] Many immigration historians, even dating back to the first wave of Portuguese emigration to the U.S. document high rates of female industrial labor (Taft 1969). A recent study of immigration, between 1960-80, documents a surprising trend where university attendance is higher for Luso-American women than it is for Luso-American men (Mulcahy 2001).

[26] The Portugal Day Parade in Newark, organized each year by Bernardino Coutinho and his family, has exploded in popularity. What started on June 10, 1980 as a one-day event to "unify the Portuguese community" on the anniversary of Luís de Camões's death has ballooned into a week-long event with an operating budget of $600,000 and a total spectatorship of well over half-a-million people (Bernardino and Alberto Coutinho, Interview by Vanessa Monteiro, October 16, 2002).

[27] See, for example, "A Drumthwacket foi Sábado 'Uma Casa Portuguesa, Com Certeza.'" *Luso-Americano,* June 2002 5:8.

CHAPTER 6

Images of the Virgin in Portuguese Art at The Newark Museum

LORI BARCLIFF BAPTISTA

On November 16, 1997, The Newark Museum unveiled the exhibition *Crowning Glory: Images of the Virgin in the Arts of Portugal/Coroa de Glória: A Virgem na Arte Portuguesa* to critical acclaim. The exhibition was a significant highlight of *World Festival I: Portuguese Words and Ways,* the first annual international performance festival organized by the New Jersey Performing Arts Center during their inaugural season. The festival brought together performance and visual artists from Portugal "...and the many nations and regions with which that country has shared cultural cross-currents: Angola, Brazil, Cape Verde, Goa, Guiné-Bissau, Macau, Mozambique, São Tomé and Príncipe and more" (*World Festival I* 1997, 19). *Crowning Glory* featured eighty "authentic objects" relating to the Virgin Mary, one of Portugal's most powerful cultural symbols (The Newark Museum 1998). The exhibition offered a glimpse into artistic and devotional practices relating to the Virgin Mary across six centuries, five continents, shifting colonial circumstances, and multiple forms of display and interaction. It was the first principal exhibition in the United States to examine Portuguese artistic traditions across such an expansive and inclusive temporal, geographic, and political scope.

Museum staff involved in presenting *Crowning Glory* expressed how the display objects, educational programs, and festival activities transformed community relations as well as the space of the museum. Art critics and journalists lauded the showcase, deeming it revolutionary for its mix of fine and folk art, diasporic outlook, and its social and historical interpretation of objects of devotion.[1] The exhibition caused a stir within Newark's notoriously insular Portuguese immigrant community, which came out in droves to view the exhibition and participate in related programs and activities.

In this essay, I examine museum mission statements, newsletters, internal reports, curatorial outreach strategies, video documentation of the exhibit as well as exhibit catalogues and grant reports to understand how The Newark Museum attempted to forge a new relationship with the city's Portuguese immigrant community. I also interviewed the museum director, museum staff, curators, collaborators, and an advisory member to further this query. I review coverage of the exhibition in mainstream English-language press and the *Luso-Americano*, the nationally distributed Newark-based Portuguese language newspaper, to understand how critics interpreted the exhibition and presented it to their respective audiences. As part of a related, long-term research project, I carried out fieldwork in Murtosa and Fátima, Portugal, where I witnessed and documented religious devotional practices; this research informs my analysis of the Newark exhibit. Additionally, I conducted surveys and interviews with participant-spectators from Portuguese communities in Newark and Elizabeth to gauge the local impact of the exhibition.

I contend that a powerful alchemy of exhibit form, content, context, and targeted outreach created an unprecedented dynamic of museum interest and participation among the Portuguese-speaking community of Newark. *World Festival I: Portuguese Words and Ways* was a multidimensional event that attracted multiple sponsors, participants and audiences. The eight-month-long international festival was touted as a celebration of "the creative legacy and heritage of Portuguese-speaking peoples" (*World Festival* 1997, 19). Prior to the festival, some of the city's arts and educational leadership felt that they had not yet been able to serve the Portuguese community. Although Newark's Portuguese population constituted the largest foreign-born ethnic group in the city, according to the 1990 census, this community had received surprisingly little scholarly attention. Aside from the Portuguese language newspaper *Luso-Americano,* the history of Portuguese immigration to Newark was not well-documented. Some fledgling partnerships and programs that sought to address these deficiencies were strengthened by the interest generated by the festival and exhibition. Of note is the growth of the Portuguese and Lusophone World Studies program at Rutgers University—Newark Campus, and the subsequent founding of the Ironbound Oral History Project.[2]

Portuguese immigration to Newark can be traced back to the early 20th century. Newark historians note the arrival of Portuguese and Spanish "refugees" who trickled into the Ironbound district during the 1920s, and another wave of Portuguese immigrants during the 1940s. More recent data show that Portuguese immigration to Newark peaked from 1960-1980. Unlike the predominance of islanders in the New England and California communities, most of Newark's Portuguese immigrants are from mainland Portugal. While the community is home to some Azoreans, *lisboetas,* and *ribotejanos,* the vast majority came from rural agrarian northern regions such as Minho, Trás-os-Montes and Alto Douro, Coimbra and Centro—most notably from Viseu. A significant concentration hails from the Aveiro region of the northern state of Beira Litoral. In the course of my fieldwork, Portuguese Ironbounders have often called attention to Newark's large population of immigrants from the Concelho de Murtosa, one of Aveiro's traditional fishing and farming districts.

Most of Newark's Portuguese immigrants are not educated elites. Some of those who arrived in the Ironbound during the 1920s and 1940s did so by boat and by way of Brazil. Many came to Newark as political and economic refugees fleeing the oppressive regime of António Salazar. Those who flew into JFK airport after the April 25, 1974 military coup that deposed the fascist dictator, Marcelo Caetano did so for primarily economic reasons, with the benefit of relaxed government emigration regulations and the burden of supporting a family. When they arrived in the Ironbound, they sought out familiar social networks for living accommodations and work. Portuguese men were often employed in the construction trades and at Newark and New York shipping docks, and many women took up jobs in domestic service. At various times both men and women worked in Ironbound factories. A few who were committed to religious orders in Portugal transferred to Portuguese Parishes in Newark and Elizabeth to continue their service to the Roman Catholic Church.

Some became entrepreneurs. A number of Portuguese immigrants who arrived during the 1940s successfully launched businesses selling necessary goods, such as fuel and ice, to their neighbors. Later waves opened bakeries, restaurants, markets, and cafés to cater to the needs of a relatively young Portuguese community with a strong taste for home. Many immigrants became Ironbound homeowners. While Newark fought to recover from post-industrial decline and the 1967 riots, the Ironbound neighborhood thrived on its self-sufficiency. The Portuguese community in Newark is well known for its endeavors to renovate and develop its surroundings almost to the point of self-gentrification. It is entirely possible to work, shop, eat, worship, bank, marry, live, and die without ever speaking English or leaving the neighborhood except to travel back and forth between Portugal and Newark.

During my fieldwork, many of Newark's Portuguese-Americans with whom I spoke conceded that language, spatial practices, and cultural differences tended to separate the Portuguese community from the rest of the city. This dynamic has been a source of disappointment to municipal and arts leaders because the Ironbound is within walking distance of the city's downtown arts district and has long served as a dining and cultural destination for many Newarkers. *World Festival I: Portuguese Words and Ways* presented an opportunity to invite this community out, and showcase and celebrate it on a grand scale. The Newark Museum made significant contributions to this perfect storm of convergences, and mounted an ambitious exhibition that dared to envision an inclusive Lusoworld comprised of intersecting communal cultures.

Combining ethnographic and archival methods and analysis, I offer my assessment of how various constituencies conceived, participated in and responded to the exhibition, *Crowning Glory.* Moving from an understanding of how culture and identity work through efficacious symbols, I consider how the exhibition engaged spectators through various modes of display and interaction shaped by the Museum's guiding principles and curatorial practices. I suggest that the exhibit made a significant impact upon many Portuguese immigrants because they were able to connect visual representations of the Virgin to their personal experiences of religious rituals, artisanal practices, and the dynamic social processes of diaspora. The exhibit's targeted outreach strategies and innovative curatorial selection and presentation of objects succeeded in bringing together a major arts institution and an important swathe of Newark's multiethnic population into new relationships of dialogue and exchange.

Exhibition Scope

Crowning Glory opened in the Newark Museum's Eweson and Brady Galleries on November 26, 1997 and closed on February 8, 1998.[3] According to The Newark Museum's report to the Geraldine R. Dodge Foundation, "the exhibition featured eighty authentic objects, many of which had never been shown in the United States, borrowed from Portugal's leading museums, churches and private collections" (*Report to the Geraldine R. Dodge Foundation* 1998). These objects were displayed alongside colorful liturgical banners from local parish churches and a video installation of a candlelight procession in honor of Our Lady of Fatima. Viewed as a whole, this collection represents a wide-ranging tribute to the importance of the Virgin Mary throughout Portuguese history, visual arts, and devotional practices. The scope of this display demonstrates how Marian iconography crossed social class, traversed continents, blended with symbolism from other cultures, and was adapted to various past colonial contexts and present immigrant contexts.

Arranged thematically, and not chronologically, the exhibition included representations of the Virgin Mary in media as diverse as ivory carvings, cut paper, polychromed ceramic tile, and video display. Historical and contemporary objects were grouped together based upon common subject matter, regardless of artistic styles, conventions, place of origin or age. *Crowning Glory* opened with a 19th-century folk painting depicting a religious procession in Minho, Portugal, and closed with a video projection of a Marian procession that took place at Our Lady of Fatima Church in Newark's Ironbound neighborhood earlier that year. The annunciation, the mythology of the Virgin and Child, and the Virgin's function as intermediary were prominently featured in the exhibition.

Many of the exhibit images flesh out scriptural gaps in the depiction of Mary. "The power of the idea of the Virgin, and the deep need that her cult fulfills, stimulated the quest for narratives beyond those provided by the scripture" (Dodds and Sullivan 1997, 27). Accounts of the Immaculate Conception, her perpetual virginity, and her Assumption into heaven became a part of popular consciousness through apocryphal accounts which "provide a cosmic, but also a domestic narrative within which the Virgin might be imagined" (Dodds and Sullivan 1997,

27). The book of James fleshed out the fragmented details of Mary's life, making her at once accessibly human and divine.

Mary's human qualities, particularly those dealing with her maternal role, enjoy special resonance in the Portuguese-speaking world, and were highlighed in the Newark exhibit. One of the most commonly evoked domestic mythologies of Mary throughout the Portuguese colonial empire was that of the Virgin and Child. The exhibition featured five objects explicitly titled "Virgin and Child," and countless others that expanded upon her maternal role. A medieval depiction of the Virgin in polychromed limestone as an elegant yet full-figured Portuguese woman made its way into the exhibition alongside 16th-century sculptures in polychromed wood that portray her as a hearty Portuguese peasant; in a number of these works she is shown breastfeeding the Christ child (Dodds and Sullivan 1997, 31).

Sixteenth and 17th-century Namban and triptych images of the Virgin painted by Japanese new Christians meld Italian and Portuguese representational styles with Momoyama sensibilities (Dodds and Sullivan 1997, 32-33, 130). A 20th-century Angolan sculpture depicts the Virgin and Child in a traditional format, with the mother balancing the child on her hip. However, the sculptural form is draped in a highly stylized mantle common to traditional Angolan *Nkangi* carving (Dodds and Sullivan 1997, 78-79, 128).[4] In a 17th-century version of the Virgin in India, she is carved out of ivory cradling the Christ child in one arm while holding a rosary in her other hand (Dodds and Sullivan 1997, 79-80). An interpretation of the Virgin and Child, popular in 19th-century China, showcases her with Asian features and wearing an indigenous crown and adornments (Dodds and Sullivan 1997, 27). A Franciscan Congregation in Lisbon loaned a 19th-century ebony-colored statuette of Our Lady of Aparecida to the Museum for the exhibition. Officially recognized by the Catholic Church as the patroness of Brazil in 1930, Our Lady of Aparecida appears as an Afro-Brazilian Mary carved from wood with a gold crown studded with pearls and semiprecious stones. A long velvet robe decorated with gold fringe shrouds her dark, oval face and drapes her shoulders (Dodds and Sullivan 1997, 77, 154).

Icons carved out of precious materials such as limestone, marble, ivory and silver reflect the material wealth of those who commissioned them, as do elaborate oil paintings inlaid with precious metals. The great conquests of the 15th and 16th centuries yielded a tremendous amount of wealth for Portugal that benefited the "high bourgeoisie of Lisbon" and Portuguese nobility, mostly centered in southern Portugal (Dodds and Sullivan 1997). The majority of the citizens of the pastoral central and north of the country did not, however, benefit from the largesse of empire-building. Folk objects crafted by rural artisans in the northern regions were often made with simpler materials.

The exhibition's embrace of diverse images of Mary with a wide array of phenotypical characteristics and featured in varied material circumstances also challenged the notion that the Luso world was uniformly and unproblematically Catholic. Simple wood sculptures, polychromed ceramic tile, and oil-on-wood folk art compositions reflect class disparities and the uneven distribution of resources throughout the Portuguese empire and at home. Objects crafted in other parts of the Portuguese empire drew attention to the evangelization process that attempted to erase indigenous cultural practices. Early Jesuit missionaries sent to Goa:

> insisted that Indian converts must give up their distinctive costume and insignia and must dress and act like the Portuguese. They even had to give up their names and adopt not only a European Christian name but also a Portuguese surname. In short, they had to give up their Indian culture and become, in effect, Portuguese. (Bernard 1991, 88)

Such endeavors were successful in converting few members of the lower castes and were ineffective in persuading most of the native population to convert to Christianity. Later Jesuit evangelical missions immersed themselves in the stratified caste system that lent structure to Indian society, and worked within it to promote a form of conversion through "adaptation and acculturation" (Dodds and Sullivan 1997, 80). Their successes in converting Brahmans and high-caste Hindus during the 17th and 18th centuries are evidenced by the "rich materials and elegant effects of Christian images" produced during that time (Ibid, 81). These exhibition objects conjure the colonial period and its implied history of Christian conversion by force.

The Portuguese conquest of Brazil was also furthered by state initiatives to Europeanize Brazilian natives through Christian conversion. When Portuguese efforts to maintain order and control over their burgeoning sugar plantations and brazilwood harvests fell short, Dom João III centralized the dysfunctional *capitanias* system under the governance of Tomé de Sousa. The Portuguese king sent Jesuit missionaries with de Sousa to convert the native slave laborers to Christianity. In her description of Our Lady of Aparecida, Jerrilyn Dodds suggests that "Mary's comforting maternal presence was perhaps as appealing to an oppressed native population, who could have understood little of theology, as it was for illiterate Europeans of the Middle Ages" (Ibid, 77). If we expand our definition of domestic to include not only that which pertains to the household, but also to the nation, it is not a stretch to imagine why the mythology of mother and child resonated across the expansive colonial empire so strongly and for so long. The nation depended upon women's physical and symbolic labor to reproduce and sustain it. As Radhika Mohanram argues in her essay *Woman-body-nation-space,* "the nation is always embodied, and the idealized body within nationalistic discourse is always gendered"(1999, 59).

The exhibition was revolutionary in its restaging of religious objects to reflect the syncretism of native and Portuguese spiritual, artistic, and cultural practices, and its implied history of force, coercion, and interchange. In his review of the exhibition, *New York Times* art critic, Holland Cotter, asserted that this manner of grouping was a relatively new convention, derived from "[r]ecent museological thinking on the presentation of non-Western cultures—with objects and ethnological fieldwork displayed side by side—[that treat] displays of Western religious art… as part of a continuing tradition rather than a relic of the past" (Cotter 1997). Rather than imposing a chronology that begins and ends with the golden age of Portugal, the exhibition used the Virgin as a point of convergence for artistic, religious and cultural practices that preceeded the arrival of the Portuguese, were transformed by Portuguese encounters, and continue to survive.

The regional, racial, and ethnically diverse iconography of *Crowning Glory* attracted the interest of Luso-Americans who construct their present selves in relation to a diverse set of others, both within their communities of origin and within Newark's diverse population. In many ways, the inclusive and intersectional nature of *Crowning Glory* resonated within Newark's diverse social environment.

Curatorial Strategies for Community Involvement

With more than 270,000 residents, Newark is the largest and most populous city in New Jersey. Over eighty percent of the city's population is African-American and Latino, and over a third of the city's population lives in poverty.[5] Political designations separate the city into five wards named for their geographic locations—North, South, East, West and Central—but most residents identify with familiar neighborhood monikers associated with local histories, streets, communities, and activities.

Early colonists called the approximately four-square-mile swath of land that comprises the city's East Ward, "Dutch Neck" for the Dutch who settled the city in 1666, then "Down Neck," for the way that the Passaic River curved to look like a goose neck. It was deemed worthless except as grazing ground for livestock. Irish immigrants came to the area in the early 19th century to build the railroads and canals. The neighborhood was eventually nicknamed the Ironbound in the early 20th century because the elevated railroad tracks to the west and the factories to the east spatially separate the neighborhood from the rest of the city.

Historically, the city's poorest residents lived in the Ironbound and labored in its factories. Throughout the 19th and 20th centuries, the space functioned as a port of entry and transition into American mainstream culture for German, Italian, Polish, Spanish, Chinese, Cuban, and Portuguese immigrants. Most recently, immigrants from Brazil, Ecuador, and Mexico have taken up residence in the neighborhood. The East Ward is home to the largest Portuguese-speaking community in the state of New Jersey, and one of the largest communities in the United States. Countless visitors to the Ironbound have encountered its "Portugueseness" while visiting one of the neighborhood's many Portuguese restaurants or participating in the revelry of *Dia de Portugal*, the Portugal Day festival. However, the neighborhood remains known as the Ironbound or Down Neck, not Little Portugal. Railways, waterways, modern highways, and Newark Liberty International Airport have made an indelible imprint upon the neighborhood's urban landscape. They also symbolize the transitory patterns of the many ethnic groups that have crossed its borders.

Taking into account the city's rich demographic history, the foundational mission of The Newark Museum was to embrace cultural difference and connection throughout the globe by presenting devotional art "in a broad context of use and practice" (Price 2004, 71). Founded in 1909 by John Cotton Dana, The Newark Museum acquired a major collection of Tibetan Buddhist objects in 1911. Dana spearheaded the "new museum" in the United States that connected objects and ideas with the needs of its community. The value of objects was tied to their use, which was meant to be educational. As Dana himself states, "the goodness of a museum is not in direct relation to the cost of its building and the upkeep thereof, or to the rarity, auction value, or money cost of its collections. A museum is good only insofar as it is of use" (Peniston 1999, 65). For Dana, display objects were best utilized as teaching tools to promote cultural fluency. Objects of daily life, customs of "neighbor people" and exhibitions were viewed as a means of stimulating a two-way dialogue, *not* as representation. This dialogue privileges the quotidian contemporary alongside "high art," a commitment recognized by Kirshenblatt-Gimblett in *Destination Culture,* in which she notes The Newark Museum's commitment to showing folk and popular art without consideration or apology, and where the "in context" forms are perceived as unpretentious because they are not the product of art movements (Kirshenblatt-Gimblett 1998, 228).

Dana envisioned the new museum as a "living, active, effective institution," attentive to the changing needs of its community (Peniston 1999, 57). For such an institution "to make itself alive," he advised that the living museum must continuously teach and advertise. Dana counseled that once the museum began to teach, it would necessarily begin to form alliances with "present teaching agencies, the public schools, the colleges and universities, and the art institutions of all kinds." He suggested that a good museum might learn how to better serve its patrons through the example of a great city department store. It should be centrally located, easily reached, and open to all at the times when they wish to visit it. In addition to freely and courteously interacting with its publics, a good museum should display its most attractive and interesting objects, and borrow others of interest upon request. Dana believed that guides should be provided to visitors free of charge. He also believed that museum collections should be classified according to patrons' needs and knowledge, and that a good museum should be flexible enough to change its exhibits in accordance with changes in subjects of interest, tastes in art, and "the progress of invention and discovery" (Peniston 1999, 57).

The *Crowning Glory* exhibit took John Cotton Dana's progressive ideas about the sociocultural role of the urban museum to heart. A select group of art historians, community leaders and diplomatic officials worked together to connect Marian iconography, The Newark Museum, and a notoriously insular ethnic enclave into relationships of exchange, dialogue and cross-cultural learning. The exhibit's guest curators, Jerrilyn D. Dodds,[6] Chair of the Department of History and Theory and Professor of Architecture at The City College of New York, and Edward J. Sullivan, a noted Iberianist and authority on 20th-century Latin American art, worked closely with Maria de Lourdes Simões de Carvalho, International Relations Deputy Director of the Portuguese Ministry of Culture's Office; Museum Project Supervisor, Ward L.E. Mintz; Exhibition Coordinator, Julia Robinson; Exhibition Designer, David Palmer and Natátia Correia Guedes, official art historian of the Vatican to Portugal.[7]

More importantly for the purposes of this paper, however, Newark Museum leadership assembled another team of collaborators drawn from the Portuguese-American community, reflecting a longstanding museum commitment to opening lines of communication with the diverse communities it aims to serve. In the case of *Crowning Glory,* the museum convened a twenty-five member advisory committee, comprised of Portuguese-Americans with ties to the Ironbound to help determine what exhibition subject matter would best engage Newark's Lusophone community.

Although one might assume that the committee was comprised of an elite cohort of Portuguese arts patrons, in fact, members were generally local Portuguese-American civic, business, religious, and academic leaders. The group also represents a diverse collection of interests, affiliations, and points of view with very personal connections to both Portugal and Newark. Not unlike the Newark community that the museum hoped to serve, many of the advisory members were immigrants or first-generation Newarkers with familial ties to small rural villages in northern Portugal. Their individual successes and class mobility were well documented in local English and Portuguese language media.

The first Portuguese-American ever elected to any public office in the city of Newark, Augusto "Auggie" Amador, served on the *Crowning Glory* advisory committee. A former PSE&G employee, the East Ward councilman is commonly referred to as the "favorite son" of Murtosa, Portugal, Newark's sister city.[8] Auggie, who arrived in the United States in 1966, was elected to the Newark Board of Education in 1993, and to his first term as City Council Member in 1998.[9] Committee member, Albert Coutinho was appointed to the Newark Public Library Board of Trustees in 1994, and elected President in 1998. Coutinho also bears the distinction of being the first Portuguese-American to serve in the New Jersey State Assembly; he was elected in 1997.[10] Licínio "Lee" Cruz, was another committee member. A successful Judge and owner of Cruz Construction—a business founded by his late father—Cruz was born in Portugal's Coimbra region, and emigrated to the United States as a child.

In numerous conversations and interviews, Museum Director Mary Sue Sweeney Price emphasized the tremendous insight that she gained about the Portuguese community from Linda Rodrigues, a trustee of both The Newark Museum and the Newark Public Library. The Museum's report to the Dodge Foundation credits Linda M.A. Rodrigues for her role as scholarly consultant and liaison to New Jersey's Portuguese residents. "As a young girl growing up in Newark's Portuguese Ironbound district, Dr. Rodrigues divulged her family's reluctance to cross the area beyond her immediate neighborhood which included The Newark Museum. She hoped her work on this project would erase the line of demarcation for residents in the Portuguese-American community" (The Newark Museum 1998).

Advisory committee members served a practical function; they spoke the language, knew the people, social networks, institutions and vehicles of communication through which to reach them. They were border-crossers themselves, having grown up in the neighborhood, attended the local schools and churches, then ventured out into the worlds of politics, law and education. They were also recognizable, credible embodiments of the American dream.

While the politics and poetics of museum display are often the focus of scholarly attention, the seemingly mundane or administrative aspects of event coordination are often overlooked. In a 2006 interview, Linda Nettleton, then the Assistant Director of Family, Youth, and Adult programs, remembered the process by which the Education Department staff connected with community members to work through the logistical details of scheduling, transportation, and communication. Nettleton and Ward Mintz met with advisory committee member, Albert Coutinho to brainstorm about how to make the exhibition as accessible as possible to the Portuguese community. Coutinho's experience coordinating the logistics of the Portugal Day Festival was of great relevance. From their practical discussions with Coutinho and other advisory committee members came the coordination of shuttle busses from the local churches to the museum, connections to church organizers, and the hiring of bilingual (Portuguese-English) and trilingual (Portuguese-English-Spanish) docents. Collaborative efforts supplemented by the institution's longstanding educational and marketing networks enabled program initiatives to far exceed their projected goals. According to the January 1998 Education Department highlights report:

> January was an interesting month for the division. It marked an untraditional level of interest in a special exhibition.... The special exhibition which has generated such interest focused on a subject traditionally problematic in public education—religion—and turned it into something surprisingly current and topical. Since its opening in December, *Crowning Glory: Images of the Virgin in the Arts of Portugal* has attracted 13 school groups, reflecting 260 students. This unprecedented participation is attributed to a marketing effort that targeted area Catholic, public and Portuguese schools (public schools are the primary audience) and the Portuguese community at large. Lectures, concerts, family activities and workshops were conceptualized and devised as complements to the exhibition display. Building upon community relations, education staff worked to create special Friday programs for senior citizens, as well as the popularly attended Portuguese Cultural Family Festival. (*The Newark Museum Education Department Highlights Report* 1998)

Both children and adults participated in workshops as diverse as figure drawing and fishing-boat sculpture, an interactive game matching exhibition objects with a world map depicting sites of Portuguese cultural and linguistic heritage, and decorative tile making. In my interview with Ms. Nettleton, she fondly reflected upon the magnitude of the Portuguese community response to the Portuguese Cultural Family Festival. The day-long event was attended by 3,873 children and adults. It featured bilingual and trilingual tours, *fado* and Portuguese folk music, traditional dance performances, tile painting workshops, storytelling, traditional crafts, and discussion groups, followed by light refreshments featuring the foods of Portugal in the main courtyard. A shuttle bus provided ongoing transportation between The Museum, St. Benedict's Church, and Our Lady of Fátima Church. As the Family, Youth, and Adult Programs section of the monthly report indicates:

> For the first time, extended families came to our family festival bringing aunts, uncles, grandparents and family friends. There were many more adults than children at this festival primarily because the Portuguese community chose this as the main programming event of the exhibition *Crowning Glory.* A personal invitation to the pastors of the Portuguese Apostolate inviting parishioners to attend this event coupled with the shuttle bus that rolled out the welcome mat and made access to the Museum easy, resulted in an unprecedented response from the Portuguese community. Thousands of people walked through the exhibition and enjoyed the Court as if in the middle of a Portuguese village. (*The Newark Museum Education Department Highlights Report* 1998)

To be sure, the success of the exhibition is vested in the intersections of those who negotiated across cultures. The diligence of museum leadership, curators and staff in procuring evocative objects and organizing accessible and engaging events and activities also contributed to its success. But, in the end, it was not only the administrative and logistical outreach that succeeded in accessing a previously distant population; it was also the exhibition's relationship to Portuguese immigrants' embodied practices that allowed spectators to forge emotional connections to exhibit objects and, by extension, to The Newark Museum.

Exhibit Images Connect to Immigrant Practices

Visitors' first and last encounters with *Crowning Glory* were with documentations of embodied Portuguese devotional practices. As spectators entered the gallery of The Newark Museum, the first object that they encountered was the approximately twenty by twenty-four-inch 19th-century oil-on-canvas painting, "Procession" [*Procissão*], by the Swiss-born portrait and genre painter, Augusto Roquemont (1804-1852). Roquemont, who arrived in Portugal in 1829, died in Porto in 1852.

Many of the images that he created portray local Portuguese folk traditions. According to art historians, António José de Almeida and Edward J. Sullivan, "Procession" depicts the ceremonial aspects of a procession of an image of the Virgin Mary common to the Minho region. They describe the rustic village landscape, compositional elements, and devotional practice represented in the painting. Noting the presence of bier carriers processing down a steep incline, carrying images of a holy bishop and a statue of the Virgin and Child, de Almeida and Sullivan suggest:

> This genre painting, which evokes a sense of small-town life, is filled with picturesque and colorful scenes rendered in a serpentine composition. It documents a practice that has long been at the heart of Portuguese devotion to the Virgin, and that continues today. (Dodds and Sullivan 1997, 94)

Encountering the painting on the pages of the catalog, I attended to the details of context, color, and composition before attempting to follow the narrative provided by de Almeida and Sullivan. At first glance, I was struck by the solemnity of the procession. The color palette of the painting is comprised of warm, earthy tones. However, muted greens and blues breathe life into the orangy-browns of the harsh terrain; clusters of trees and shrubs soften the edges of Minho's rocky landscape. The subdued colors are contrasted with glints of silver that temper the austere setting. As sunlight parts the clouds, it strikes the staffs of the crucifix, enlivening the white of the holy bishop and virgin and child atop a billowy puff. These flashes of white likewise accent the occasional shirtsleeve, headscarf, apron or vest.

In the foreground of the painting, three very animated male drummers, fervently playing a bass and two snares, head up the procession. The dark-haired set form a triangle, sidestepping in harmony with each other at a landing, as the processors wind down a crude, dusty path. Knees bent, the lead drummer faces the exhibition spectator at an angle as he sets the pace for the march. His face is contorted with the effort of coordinating tempo, rhythm, and melody. His right arm is raised and poised to strike the belly of his *zé pereira* [bass drum] with his mallet. The tail of his red *lençol* [head scarf] disappears behind him. Gazing out into the distance, a bare-headed-bearded snare-drummer, sporting a dark vest and khaki-colored jacket, taps out the rhythmic patterns of the march on his *caixa.* A second snare-drummer rounds out the trio. Crouching slightly to face the other two, he rests a large cylindrical drum on his haunches.

A cohort of four elderly men wearing red capes over their simple clothes follows the trio. Each bears a staff of the crucifix. One disconcertedly motions forward, a look of agitation etched upon his face. Perhaps he is anxious about the pace of the procession; perhaps there is an obstacle up ahead. As he thrusts forward, I realize the contrast between fluid and arrested movement in the work. The remaining three staff-bearers have come to a halt. The man is irritated that the drummer has slowed the entire processional by stopping for a drink. Just to their left, a drummer and three staff-bearers have momentarily derailed the procession, breaking with formation to drink from the water sellers. A woman dressed in a simple white blouse, dark skirt, red *lençol,* and shawl is squarely stationed in a shaded area. Arms crossed in front of her, she dutifully holds an earthenware pitcher in her relaxed left hand. The drummer, head thrown back, appears to drink thirstily from a glass. The staff-bearer, next in line, taps the drummer on the arm to hurry him. This realization jolts me to look at the painting differently; I jog my memory for a recollection of the processionals that I have witnessed in Murtosa and remember the hot sun, dusty paths, sweaty musicians, tired children, and vendors selling snacks and trinkets.

Lingering with the image a bit longer, I am able to piece together bits of the narrative thread alluded to by the art historians with my own experience of Portuguese religious processions in Murtosa. The 2002 feast of Santo António in Montes, one of Murtosa's four *freguesias,* included elements of sacred and secular practices. Liturgical banners and icons of saints were mounted on biers and carried by devotees. A women's group carried a statue of Our Lady of Fátima, flanked by flowers. Several other clusters of women processed carrying liturgical banners featuring the Virgin, preceded by young girls dressed as the Virgin. Men wearing dark suits draped in scarlet robes proudly bore U.S., French, and Portuguese flags, symbols of their ties to Murtosa, the Church, and each other. These contemporary flag-bearers marched alongside members of the marching band who sported crisply starched blue and white uniforms, not traditional costumes. The military-style marchers kept time as the devotees made their way to the church at the center of town. I recognized several Newarkers in the procession, including a gentleman whom I had last seen from a café window on Ferry Street, the Ironbound's main thoroughfare. A careful review of my archival video also confirmed the presence of two women who marched alongside the musicians, carrying plastic jugs of water.

The mountainous terrain, red vests, *lençóis*, and other, perhaps more subtle, visual cues work together to signify 19th-century *Minhotos* in this particular work of art. They also serve as precursors to the Minho's bright red, royal blue, and gold *traje à vianesa* [Viana peasant woman costume], fashionable among Portugal's northern populations during the turn of the century. Fernando, one of my community advisors, assured me that his own grandmother regularly wore a *lençol* to pull her hair back as she went about her daily farming tasks. On a long wall in her beach house in *Torreira*, a *murtoseira* woman proudly displays her mother's *lençóis* alongside her own artistic renderings of local landscapes. As Holton suggests in her study of transnational *ranchos folclóricos,* traditional peasant clothing such as the *lençol* and the *traje* have been resignified as folkloric costumes that circulate as regional signs of Portugueseness: "The *traje à vianesa*...has been reproduced and sold in tourist shops throughout Portugal and abroad. The appealing design has come to emblematize Portuguese folklore and was widely 'cited' in *rancho folclórico* costumes throughout the country during the Estado Novo" (Holton 2005, 240). The *traje à vianesa* is commonly viewed in context when donned by *ranchos folclóricos,* who regularly perform during *Dia de Portugal* (Portugal Day) and other festive celebrations. Versions of the *traje* are donned by most of the sixteen active *ranchos* in the Ironbound, and act as a synecdoche for Portuguese identity in Newark. It is especially recognized in the Ironbound because a significant number of immigrants hail from the northern provinces of Portugal.

Roquemont's painting aptly conveys the sacred and secular aspects of devotional practice and folk life. The practice of connecting to the Catholic Church through local relations—the parish priest and the local bishop—is also signaled in the painting. The materiality of the setting and the embodied practice of walking along a steep path in the hot sun, albeit for divine purposes, is a performative act that many of Newark's Portuguese and Portuguese-Americans can relate to, and that I have witnessed. While religious procession is a recognizable event in the life of many Portuguese villages, Minho's *traje à vianesa* is also emblematic of Portuguese "national representation, particularly abroad" (Branco and Branco 2003, 5). To further layer and connect history, tradition, and contemporary practices, the exhibition closed with bright liturgical banners from Newark and Elizabeth parish churches, and a video of a candlelight procession from Our Lady of Fátima in Newark. Just as the folk-life bier carriers in Roquemont's painting fought to balance the weight of a sacred statue as they processed down a mountain path in 19th-century Minho, 20th-century Portuguese-Americans such as António Pereira, a native of Salvaterra do Mar, bore the burden of *Nossa Senhora de Fátima* on his shoulders as he processed down the front steps of the Newark parish.

When interviewed, Sr. Pereira proudly stated that he was a member of the Sagrado Coração de Deus, the Sacred Heart of God, a church association within Newark's Our Lady of Fátima Parish responsible for processions in March and October of each year, as well as other devotional activities. He asserted that he identified most strongly with the very old liturgical banners featured in the exhibition:

> *Eu gostei particularmente...bandeiras a representar diversos, diversos... santos e o próprio Cristo, bandeiras que estão guardadas em museus em Portugal e foram trazidas aqui para a comunidade ter a oportunidade de ver; coisas que já com muitos anos, mas muito bem preservadas que toda a gente gostou muito de—eu principalmente gostei muito de ver esses objectos de arte, principalmente...as bandeiras que são transportadas pelos membros das associações nas procissões que se faziam antigamente e que até hoje se fazem e que estavam bem demonstradas e muito bonitas.*[11]
>
> I particularly liked...banners that represented many, many...saints and even Christ himself, banners that were kept in museums in Portugal and were brought here for the community to have an opportunity to see; things that were very old, but very well-preserved that everybody liked a lot—I primarily liked to see those art objects a lot, primarily the...banners that are carried by members of the associations in the processions that were done in the old times, and that even today are done and that were well-presented and very beautiful.

Not all reactions of the patrons were as festive. According to an internal museum report, members of a Portuguese-American family from Atalaia were moved to tears by their encounter with an *ex-voto* painting featured in the exhibition.[12] *Ex-votos* are votives or holy offerings made in order to fulfill a vow. *Ex-voto* works are usually small panel paintings or statuettes donated as a token of remembrance, entreaty or thanks by individual believers or communities, and hung at sites of pilgrimage or holy places.[13] The 18th-century *ex-voto* of the Virgin and Child with Ship [*Nossa Senhora da Atalaia*] documents the miracle performed by Our Lady of Atalaia in Atalaia, Portugal on November 11, 1894 (Dodds and Sullivan 1997, 172). According to accounts passed down through oral traditions, sailors prayed to the Virgin to spare them from a tumultuous storm that left them shipwrecked. One of the forbearers of the family from Atalaia was purported to have been onboard the ill-fated ship, and survived the storm. Their encounter with the object triggered an intense emotional response.

The exhibition left a space for individuals like Sr. Pereira and the family from Atalaia to forge deeply personal connections with particular objects. Sr. Pereira expressed his pleasure in seeing objects related to the procession not only because they are artifacts of an ancient tradition that he proudly carries on, but also because he would not normally have access to them at home in Portugal. The family from Atalaia connected to an *ex-voto* painting, a remembrance of traumatic events linked to their family history. A symbol of the faith that saved their relatives' lives in 19th-century Portugal was in a museum in 20th-century Newark. These experiences of diaspora are not a part of the grand historical narrative of Portuguese empire, but are unwritten encounters "inscribed in the creative arts, material culture, and oral traditions" (Butler 2001, 212).

The image of Our Lady of Fátima, an artifact with contemporary resonance and affect that was prominently circulated throughout the exhibition, grew out of devotion to Our Lady of the Rosary. The cult of Our Lady of the Rosary,[14] which is said to have its origins in the 11th-century Dominican Order (De Montfort 1954), was represented in the exhibition in a progressive series of ceramic tile, oil-on-wood and gold-leaf compositions which have greatly impacted contemporary representations of the Virgin in Portugal (Dodds and Sullivan 1997, 175-80). In the spring of 1916, when Europe was deeply embroiled in World

War I and religion was under fire in Portugal's First Republic, an apparition appeared to three shepherd children near Fátima, in north-central Portugal. Warning them to pray in preparation for the coming of the Virgin Mary, the apparition visited with them several times before the Virgin herself appeared to them for a total of six times in 1917, each time carrying a message: first, for them to recite the rosary every day to bring about world peace, and subsequently, to reveal to them what has come to be known by the Roman Catholic Church as the three secrets of Fátima.[15]

The first image of Nossa Senhora do Rosário de Fátima, a polychromed wood statue, was commissioned from the workshop of Fânzeres de Bragas by a devout merchant. The commission was assigned to the best maker of sacred images in the workshop, J. Thedim, who also consulted with the three children who themselves experienced the visions. The first statue of Our Lady of Fátima, which has become the most duplicated iconic representation of Portugal, was delivered to its donor in May of 1920. He subsequently donated it to the Capelinha das Aparições [Chapel of the Apparitions], in Fátima where it remains to this very day.

This is a familiar statue to Newark's Portuguese immigrants, many of whom fulfill promises to the Virgin, leave flowers at her altar in Newark, and make annual pilgrimages to her shrine during their summer vacations in return for her blessing. Each of the many times that César Augustus and Maria Cecília have picked me up from the airport in Lisbon and driven to Murtosa, they have asked if I would like to stop at the national shrine to Fátima on our way home. I have overheard many summertime conversations between Newark women in the Pardelhas market about past and upcoming pilgrimages made to Fátima on their knees. When asked in English if she has a home town, or a place outside of the U.S. that she relates to, Rosário Pereira paused before mentioning Salvaterra do Mar, Portugal, the place where she was born and currently has a vacation home. When this question was restated in Portuguese to ask if there is a place outside of the U.S. where she *"tens obrigações?"* [has obligations] she quickly added Fátima: *"Quando estou de férias, preoccupo-me...em fazer visitação a Fátima. O Sanctuário de Fátima, por exemplo."* [When I am on vacation, I am concerned...with making visits to Fátima, the shrine of Fátima, for example].[16] Her husband António commented that he, like many Portuguese, is very proud that Our Lady appeared in Portugal.

As part of the exhibition, Archbishop Theodore E. McCarrick of the Roman Catholic Archdiocese of Newark arranged for the Pilgrim Statue of *Nossa Senhora de Fátima* to be enshrined in public view in the Cathedral Basilica of the Sacred Heart in Newark on November 29-30, 2007. The Pilgrim Statue had not been in the United States for about fifty years. It traveled to various parish sites around the Archdiocese before returning to Portugal in February 1998. In many ways, the tour of the Pilgrim statue was a seminal event in the life of the exhibition. There was something palpably exhilarating about seeing such extraordinary objects from home in a place where one would never imagine them to appear. Sra. Pereira spoke with pride about seeing objects from "*nosso país*" [our country], in Newark.

As *Crowning Glory* curator Jerrilynn Dodds foregrounds in the documentary film that was produced in relation to the exhibition, art historians often complain about Fátima's image as being too plain, bland and sweet, in contrast to the powerful, emotional Mary of the Portuguese past. Despite the drastic reconfiguration of the post-war, post-colonial Lusophone world, the tranquil image of Our Lady of Fátima remained relatively consistent. In response to critiques of the docile likeness of Fátima, Dodds proposes a second reading. She imagines the serenity of the icon as reassuring to people during turmoil and chaos. For many of Newark's Portuguese-American immigrants, perhaps Fátima portrays the turmoil of a displaced sense of Portugueseness.

Over the last century, a set of cultural practices have become emblematic of "Portugueseness" (see Almeida 2004; Arenas 2003; Klimt 1989, 2002; Gemzoe 2000; Hatton 1999, 2002; 2005; Sarkissian, 2000; Teixeira and DaRosa, 2000). Twentieth-century dictator António Salazar famously argued that one could sum up Portuguese identity using three F's: "Fátima for religion, *Fado* songs for nostalgia, and Football (soccer) for the glory of Portugal" (Birmingham 1993, 160). Cultural practices such as the three F's are often deployed to bind a people dispersed throughout the world, and distinguish them from others through the schema of imagined community. Mediated by multiple social structures, cultural contexts and taste preferences, each of these "Portuguese" practices is produced for and consumed by audiences with multiple allegiances.

While Portuguese religious art bears the mark of various European artistic movements, Portugal arguably has one of the richest traditions of devotional culture of any European country. Its central image and national icon is the Virgin Mary. Deemed the "Patroness of fledgling nations," and inextricably linked to the formation of European national identities, the name of the Virgin was invoked by the Portuguese government and burgeoning empire throughout history to justify or sanctify a cause, thereby metaphorically linking the "identity and fate of an earthly realm" with the Kingdom of Heaven (Dodds and Sullivan 1997, 25). In her introduction to the catalog, Dodds frames the goals of the exhibition by affirming the significance of the Virgin in Portuguese tradition:

> Many European nations harbor deep connections with the figure of the Virgin Mary....Portuguese devotion to the Virgin, and many of the images that bear witness to it, have, however, their own character. In reading images of the Virgin Mary—both those shared by the European tradition and those unique to Portugal—we hope to unravel a few fragments of the Portuguese collective consciousness. It is a consciousness softened by the image of the Virgin as a child, pierced through with the sword of her sorrows, a consciousness thrilled by the advocacy, the intervention, of the vision of an invincible queen in the conquests of a small, powerful nation. (Dodds and Sullivan 1997, 25)

In her description, Dodds intimates that the exhibition aims to explore a number of intersecting power relations. The power of the state, in appropriating the icon for its colonial projects is certainly one focus. But the resonance of the Virgin in this exhibition also attests to the creative power of marginalized and dispersed peoples to sustain themselves through times of hardship, change, and transformation. In *Yoruba Ritual*, performance scholar Margaret Thompson Drewal suggests that repetition within ritual functions to provide continuity between the past and present, relating individual agents' interpretations, inscriptions, and revisions. The personal connections to Marian devotion expressed by countless people who remembered *Crowning Glory* far exceeded any outreach goals that the organizers could have set. As Michael Schudsen suggests:

> One of the reasons a symbol becomes powerful is that—sometimes more or less by chance—it has been settled on, it has won out over other symbols as a representation of some valued entity and it comes to have an aura. The aura generates its own power and what might originally have been a very modest advantage (or even lucky coincidence) of a symbol becomes, with the accumulation of the aura of tradition over time, a major feature. (Schudsen 2002, 145)

Conclusion: Negotiating the Codfish Curtain

The Newark Museum is located on Washington Street, separated from Broad Street only by the pie-shaped green of Washington Park. New Jersey Performing Arts Center is located on Center Street, which intersects Broad Street just past the irregular swath of Military Park. Further south, the city's gold-domed Beaux Arts City Hall and the once illustrious commercial district are beginning to experience revitalization after decades of urban decline. If Broad Street is the main thoroughfare around which civic life clusters, the Ironbound literally and symbolically relates to it as a proximate yet marginal space.

Newark's Ironbound functions as a site of memory and transit for many of its immigrant residents. While the Ironbound is presently experiencing an influx of immigrants from Brazil, Ecuador, and Mexico, it nostalgically resonates in what performance scholar, Joseph Roach, theorizes as "collective social memory" as a Portuguese ethnic enclave. This may be due in great part to how local publics have experienced the Ironbound over the course of the last twenty years through its restaurants and the Portugal Day Festival. However, it is well documented that the neighborhood was the site of transition for successive waves of Irish, German, Polish, Italian, and African-Americans ethnic enclaves for the past 200 years (see Cunningham 2002). Despite the traces of the previous groups that remain embedded in the artifacts they have left behind, these groups are, in Roach's terms, selectively forgotten. These communities have not been critically engaged over time because of the relative inaccessibility of historical records and their less vivid traces. Likewise, the newer immigrant groups are perhaps less visible to residents who visit the neighborhood because they do not fit within the nostalgic frame of the Ironbound as a Portuguese ethnic community.

Class status, generational differences and regional affiliations are often collapsed or elided in celebratory narratives that idyllically characterize Newark's Lusophone community as "bombarding the senses with a vibrant foreignness"[17] or as "an ethnic neighborhood of forty to fifty years ago,"[18] forever frozen in the ethnographic present. Homeownership, business success, and a newfound freedom of speech and political engagement are often cited as markers of Newark's Portuguese immigrants' attainment of the American dream. There is however, a palpable tension between the attainment of the American dream and the loss of "Portugueseness." Given the complex circulation of people, ideas, and cultural practices, one can begin to intimate that "Portuguese" Newark has a complicated relationship with its religious, political, and cultural institutions with the city in which it is located, and with itself.

As a public display meant to stimulate a dialogue with its Portuguese immigrant community, *Crowning Glory* was not only a form of cultural representation "revealing deeply held ethos and belief" (Harnish 2005, 16). It also operated within the realm of the *World Festival* in which the nature of the inclusive, celebratory events could be seen as a staging ground for any number of other agendas, most notably the negotiation of ethnic, social, and political identities. Spectators perceived the exhibition through different interpretive schemes based upon experience, some conception of themselves, and their connection to the dynamic social processes of diaspora. *Crowning Glory* was formally situated alongside live performances of Portuguese, Cape Verdean, Angolan, Brazilian, and Mozambican music, dance, and theatre; photographic and cartography exhibitions at New Jersey Performing Arts Center, corporate office buildings, New Jersey Institute of Technology, and Rutgers University, the first international Portuguese literary conference at Rutgers-Newark; the future home of the Portuguese and Lusophone World Literatures program; a Portuguese cooking class hosted by the Adult School of Montclair, a neighboring suburban community; the Portugal Day Festival, a week-long public celebration of Portuguese culture; as well as concerts, expositions, and other special events.

In his introduction to the *Crowning Glory* catalog, Portuguese Prime Minister António Guterres acknowledges the Portuguese-speaking community in Newark as having set down its own roots in Newark, yet remaining connected to the spiritual traditions that have emanated from Portugal. Culture is invoked as a mediating force or intervention; perhaps the arts can do what politics have not been able to do,; that is, reimagine Luso-world relations. Guterres sees Newark's arts and cultural institutions as acculturation tools and the World Festival as "a bridge across different visions of the world to a state of mind very dear to us, one that is always in our hearts" (*World Festival I* 1997, 9). He views the exhibition in terms that pervade the imagination of the spectator:

> [the] exhibition…expresses…what neither word nor book can, that is, the deeper side of human nature, in which resides a nostalgia for things difficult to define, and which echo the murmurs of dimensions lost to conscious memory but not totally accessible to human beings. (Dodds and Sullivan 1997, 13)

In *Exhibiting Cultures: The Poetics and Politics of Museum Display*, Ivan Karp notes: "The 'living' dimension of the festival is the feature most frequently cited when the festival and the exhibition are contrasted" (Karp 1991, 281). As a primarily visual artistic medium that inspired identification with devotional practices, *Crowning Glory* was juxtaposed against the live performing bodies on the *World Festival* stages. However, as mounted by a living institution, *Crowning Glory* critically engaged diasporic representations of Portugal's national icon "to evoke in the viewer the complex and dynamic forces from which it has emerged, and for which it may be taken by the viewer to stand" (Greenblatt 1991, 42). Past Portuguese devotional practices were further linked to contemporary Luso-Newark through the exhibition's inclusion of a range of educational events and festivities. Such an approach reaffirmed the "native" spectator's dialogical encounter while upholding The Newark Museum's predilection for "in-context" display.

As a steward committed to the use of objects in context, TNM attempted to bridge the cultural politics of Newark's largely working- class Luso-American community and the city's then revitalizing downtown district. As a result of the Museum's guiding principles and interactive display practices, *Crowning Glory* had a consciousness-transforming resonance, a power that reached out beyond the formal boundaries of display.[19] This resonance effectively pulled back the "codfish curtain"[20] that spatially and discursively cordoned off significant numbers of Luso-Americans from Newark's civic and cultural life.

Notes

[1] See Holland Cotter, "ARTVIEW: A Gently Captivating Superstar Who Helped Rule an Empire," *The New York Times,* Dec. 21, 1997; Santos 1997, 1, 4-6; Ronald Smothers, "In Newark's Museum, an Exhibit Honors the City's Portuguese," *New York Times* (late edition East Coast), 4 December 1997:15.

[2] The program was founded by Professors Asela and Elpidio Laguna-Diaz in the early 1990s as a response to the increased numbers of Portuguese-heritage students enrolling at Rutgers-Newark. Professors Laguna-Diaz successfully procured funding and support from Newark's Portuguese Consulate, the Instituto Camões, the Foundation for Luso-American Development (FLAD), and the JP Fernandes Memorial Fund to start a program offering instruction in Portuguese language and literature. As a part of *World Festival I,* they hosted New Jersey's first International Conference on the Literature of Portugal and the Lusophone World. In 2000, they hired Portuguese literary and cultural studies scholar Kimberly DaCosta Holton who founded the Ironbound Oral History Project in order to document the immigration experiences of Portuguese and Brazilian residents of northern New Jersey. The project has produced over 250 oral history interviews, conducted and transcribed mostly by Rutgers Newark students.

[3] Major funding for the exhibition was provided by the *Gabinete das Relações Internacionais* (GRI) of the Portuguese Ministry of Culture. Additional major grants were awarded to the museum by the Rockefeller Foundation, the Geraldine R. Dodge Foundation, the Luso-American Development Foundation/*Fundação Luso-Americana para o Desenvolvimento,* Mr. and Mrs. Sherman R. Lewis Jr., The Newark Museum Volunteer Organization, the Dunphy Family Foundation, Banco Espírito Santo, Inc./North America, Rev. Monsignor William N. Field, the Most Reverend Theodore E. McCarrick, Vera G. List, Scot Spencer, and an anonymous donor in Honor of the Honorable Armando B. Fontoura. Major funding for education programs was contributed by The Prudential Foundation. The Newark Museum also acknowledged in-kind support from the Catholic Archdiocese of Newark and Continental Airlines. The Newark Museum also used the occasion of the exhibition to highlight its own ongoing *Cultural Crossings* series and distinguished permanent collection in a companion exhibition, *Images of the Sacred Feminine in the Newark Museum Collection.* This companion exhibition more broadly explored the sacred feminine across religious, cultural and temporal constructions.

[4] Nkangi are early Christian religious images molded into wood or brass by Angolan craftsmen.

[5] Excerpted from A. Baptista's 2006 presentation, "Toxic Tour: The Ironbound, Newark, New Jersey. Environmental Justice in American Cities," presentation for the Ironbound Community Corporation.

[6] Dodds is also a specialist in the study of medieval Iberian architecture created by Christians under Muslim rule and Muslims under Christian rule. According to the November/December 1997 Newark Museum newsletter: "Because of [Dodds]…unusual focus, she became interested in the ways groups create artistic identities and how those identities change when they confront people different from them." See "Newark Museum Exhibitions and Events" in the N*ewsletter of the Newark Museum.* November/December 1997:1.

[7] While curatorial authority was vested in the vision of the distinguished scholars, many aspects of the exhibition were meticulously and diplomatically negotiated through the Portuguese government and Cultural Ministry. Museum Director Mary Sue Sweeney Price emphasized the significant assistance and cooperation of the Portuguese Ministry of Culture's Office of International Relations, most notably the interventions of Director, Dr. Patrícia Salvação Barreto, and Deputy Director, Ms. Maria de Lourdes Simões de Carvalho who helped to procure display objects for the exhibition from museums, churches, and private collections throughout Portugal and Macau.

[8] Baptista, Unpublished field notes documenting ethnographic fieldwork on Portuguese identity constructions. Newark and Portugal, 2001-2006.

[9] As Portuguese businessman Fernando Santos explained in a 1974 *Star Ledger* Article, most of Newark's Portuguese immigrants "came from small towns and fishing villages and they were often left out of elections." Political leaders have gradually emerged from the community to represent the interests of immigrants and new citizens who have revitalized the industrially zoned neighborhood. See Clifford Feng, "Portuguese Overthrow is Felt in Newark." *The Star Ledger* 19 May 1974.

[10] Coutinho's legendary commitment to his community is in many ways linked to the success of Newark's Portugal Day Festival, New Jersey's largest ethnic festival. Founded in 1979 by his father, Bernardinho Coutinho, owner of Coutinho's Bakery, the festival is commonly referred to as the largest celebration of Portuguese culture in the world (See the Official Newsletter of The Newark Public Library "Trustee President: A Community Leader" *The Second Century* (1999) 10:1; and Maria Isabel João's discussion of the origins and evolution of the Portugal Day Celebration (See "Public Memory and Power in Portugal [1880-1960]: Reflections on Centenary Commemorations in Portuguese Studies" (2002) 18: 96-121.

[11] Audiotaped Interview with António Pereira, 2007, 26 July.

[12] Especially noted in the January 1998 *Education Department Highlights,* a monthly report produced by the Newark Museum Education Department. Photocopies.

[13] ex-voto. Answers.com. The Concise Grove Dictionary of Art, Oxford University Press, Inc., 2002. http://www.answers.com/topic/ex-voto, accessed August 6, 2007.

[14] The Rosary, which is both an object of worship and comprised of silent and vocal prayer, is commonly described as a meditation on the life, death, and glory of Jesus Christ and of his Blessed Mother. It is comprised of fifteen groups of ten Hail Mary prayers, headed by one Our Father. As one prays, one touches each of the 165 corresponding individual beads.

[15] The three secrets of Fátima are the prediction of the start of World War II, the rise of new communist regimes, and the assassination attempt on the life of Pope John Paul II. The first two predictions were revealed in 1942, with the latter kept under lock and key by the Vatican until 2000.

[16] Audiotaped interview with Rosário Pereira, 2007, 26 July.

[17] Jacket cover text and voice over narration in the NJN documentary *Ironbound Ties to Portugal.*

[18] Buros, "Little Portugal: Page of History in Newark." *The New York Times,* October 7, 1987.

[19] Bachelard's idea of resonance, which includes the possibility of understanding and making connections with other feelings, is combined with reverberation, that is, a change being effected by a transformation of consciousness. This "resonance-reverberation" couplet yields what Lionnet considers to be the ultimate identification with the image, where subject-object duality occurs.

[20] Linda Rodrigues, a Newark Museum Trustee, Newark-Ironbound resident, specialist in Portuguese Literature, and Professor at the New School for Social Research, as quoted by Ronald Smothers. "In Newark's Museum, an Exhibit Honors the City's Portuguese." *The New York Times* (late edition East Coast), 1997, 4 December:15.

CHAPTER 7

Viva Rhode Island, *Viva* Portugal! Performance and Tourism in Portuguese-American Bands

KATHERINE BRUCHER

On July 1, 2005, the Lusitana Band of Cumberland, Rhode Island triumphantly marched through the narrow streets of Penalva do Castelo, Portugal, kicking off a seventeen-day concert tour.[1] The forty musicians from this community band had not slept since leaving Rhode Island the previous evening and now played in near total darkness. The Lusitana Band's director, Gary Sebastião, called for the band to perform the street march "Joaquim Merim" by Portuguese composer, Miguel de Oliveira, followed by "Vinho do Porto" [Port Wine March] by Ilídio Costa. The musicians knew these marches well from performing them at parades back in New England, but these two pieces are also common to the repertoire of many bands in Portugal. Thus, the Lusitana Band announced not only its presence in Penalva but also its connection to the Portuguese tradition of *bandas filarmónicas*, or amateur community wind bands.[2]

These mixed wind and percussion ensembles perform music for various religious and secular functions such as saints' day feasts, processions, parades, and concerts. Ensembles range in size from twenty to eighty musicians, and typical instrumentation includes piccolo, flutes, clarinets; alto, tenor, and baritone saxophones; trumpets and trombones; baritones or euphoniums; marching horns (also called mellophones or *trompas*), tuba, bass drum, snare drums, and cymbals. Since their inception in the mid-19th century, *filarmónicas* have defined themselves as amateur music organizations closely tied to the communities where they were founded. While *filarmónicas* have always traveled regionally to perform, in the late 20th century, *filarmónicas* began to tour internationally (Brucher 2005). Portuguese ensembles toured diasporic communities, while ensembles located abroad traveled to the Azores or continental Portugal. In this essay, I analyze the Lusitana Band's 2005 trip to Portugal to illustrate how music, travel, and tourism are entwined with cultural, economic, and musical ties between Portugal and its diaspora. The band's trip suggests ways that tourism contributes to a transnational Portuguese identity.

Despite the difficulty of playing in the dark with little sleep, the parade in Penalva de Castelo represented the culmination of almost two years of planning and musical preparation for this trip. Initial planning began as conversations between Angelo Correia, the president of the Lusitana Band's board of directors, and Leonídio Monteiro, mayor of Penalva de Castelo (Correia 2005). The stated goal of the trip was to commemorate and strengthen pre-existing ties between Cumberland's diasporic community and the town of Penalva de Castelo. Many of the musicians in the band and members of its board of directors come from Penalva or nearby towns and villages in Beira Alta. Since the late 19th century, immigrants from Penalva and surrounding Beira Alta migrated to work in the textile mills in Rhode Island. Cumberland's Portuguese community is predominantly continental, unlike the majority Azorean neighborhoods and social clubs elsewhere in Rhode Island and southeastern Massachusetts.[3] Individuals settled in Cumberland as they followed family members and employment opportunities.

Band members emphasized that the trip was a chance to reconnect with their Portuguese heritage. Although there are all kinds of different band members with varying degrees of attachment to Portugal in the Lusitana Band, in this essay I will focus primarily on the experiences of returning emigrants and those who identified as Portuguese-Americans. Some members had emigrated from Beira Alta while others were second- and third-generation Portuguese-Americans. Of this group, younger musicians had different levels of facility with the Portuguese language. A minority within the band could be characterized as "outsiders" in this community—either musicians of Azorean background with little experience with continental Portuguese culture or non-Portuguese. For some individuals—second- and third-generation Portuguese musicians included—this was their first trip to Portugal. For many musicians, the trip was, in the words of Sabrina Boulay, a second-generation Portuguese-American and a long-time member of the Lusitana Band, "a way to see Portugal, learn more about our heritage, and appreciate where our culture comes from." Boulay's comments demonstrate the ways that travel and tourism framed the trip, although the band's schedule was planned around a series of concerts and parades.

Once the band arrived in Portugal, the municipality of Penalva provided lodging in a half-finished hotel that would become Penalva's first tourist lodging upon completion, a coach bus and driver, meals, and excursions. In addition to performing concerts and playing for local parades and processions, the band toured locally in Beira Alta and traveled to places considered emblematic of Portuguese culture and history, such as the Shrine of Our Lady of Fátima, the monastery of Batalha, the city of Coimbra and beaches along the Atlantic coast. In many ways, the trip mirrored the return of individual Portuguese emigrants to their natal villages in the trip's emphasis on staying in the *terra*, visiting places like Fátima, going to the beach, and participating in local festivals. Brettell has documented how emigrants living in France return to Portugal for holidays (Brettell 2003c), and likewise Klimt, has shown that Portuguese emigrants in Germany also planned regular trips back to Portugal during the summer months (Klimt 1989; 2000). Certain destinations such as the Shrine of Fátima have become a ritual part of emigrants' trips home. Many of the emigrants in Cumberland returned to Portugal with less frequency than emigrants living in Europe for various reasons, including the expense of traveling from North America and less vacation time provided by American employers.

The trip also highlighted the transnational ties between Cumberland, Rhode Island and Penalva de Castelo. The two cities are sister cities in recognition of the long-standing connections between the communities. This relationship acknowledges the cultural, economic, and social ties created and sustained through transnational circulation of people, ideas, and goods (Glick Schiller, Basch, and Stanton 1992, 1). Upon our immediate arrival in Penalva de Castelo—before our evening parade—members of the local government greeted the ensemble at a short ceremony held in Penalva's town hall. There, the mayor of Penalva, Leonídio Figueiredo Gomes de Monteiro, welcomed the band. In his speech, he expressed his wish that the band enjoy its stay in the Beira Alta region by appreciating the beauty of Portugal and exploring what Penalva had to offer. His speech emphasized that the musicians were there to visit Penalva and experience Portuguese culture as much as they were there to perform. David Iwuk, the mayor of Cumberland, also spoke. Iwuk is not Portuguese, but his wife emigrated from Portugal to the United States as a young girl. They accompanied the band on the trip, in part, because three of their children play in the ensemble. Iwuk's speech emphasized the cultural ties between the two sister cities that have grown from over a century of migration. Iwuk concluded with remarks that placed the band firmly in a transnational context: "I have just two words: *Viva a* relationship between Cumberland and Penalva. *Viva* Rhode Island! *Viva* Portugal!"

This paper examines the Lusitana Band's trip within the context of *turismo de saudade* and the negotiation of transnational identities. *Turismo de saudade*, sometimes defined as "ethnic tourism" (Holton 2005b, 82), is a term coined by Portugal's tourist industry to describe emigrants who make annual or semi-annual trips back to Portugal. In recent years, "saudade tourists" have become an important target market within the Portuguese tourist industry (Antunes, Concelho dos Ministros 2005, 188). Emigrants often blur the distinction between tourism and transmigration when they visit their natal communities (Coles and Timothy 2004; Duval 2002); and in a country, where roughly one-third of the population resides outside national borders, emigrants represent a large potential market.[4] By linking tourism to the notion of *saudade*, often translated as "longing" or "nostalgia," tourism becomes a new way for emigrants to experience Portuguese culture. *Turismo de saudade* evokes two key symbols within Portuguese culture: the concept of "*saudade*" (Feldman-Bianco 1992; Leal 2000) and the figure of the "*emigrante*" (Brettell 2003h). João Leal and Bela Feldman-Bianco discuss the ways that *saudade* has come to signify the "essence of Portuguese national character" (Feldman-Bianco 1992, 146) and functions as "a metaphor for Portugueseness among Portuguese emigrants" (Leal 2000, 278). I argue that, conceptually, *turismo de saudade* places narratives of Portuguese travel and identity in the framework of contemporary tourism.

Turismo de saudade reimagines the figure of the emigrant as a tourist. In this case, the tourism industry—local governments and tourism boards, restaurants, hotels, and travel agencies—invites returning emigrants to step outside the realm of the everyday and view Portugal with a "tourist gaze" (Urry 2002, 1, 3). The viewpoint of the tourist focuses on points of difference and departure from the everyday experiences. However, *turismo de saudade* also suggests that the emigrant's sending community views him or her in a different light. The figure of the *emigrante* often evokes stereotypes of the emigrant, assimilated to a foreign culture, returning to flaunt material wealth (Brettell 2003h; Feldman-Bianco 1992). Instead of viewing returning Portuguese as *emigrantes*, it suggests that local officials pursuing economic development embrace them as tourists. The Lusitana Band's trip offers an opportunity to explore the slippage between the figure of the *emigrante* and the tourist against a transnational landscape spanning Rhode Island and Portugal. Individual experiences on the trip revealed tension between musicians' expectations and perceptions of Portugal and those of their host community. Rather than revealing a simple binary between tourist and *emigrante*, the travel experiences of musicians could be categorized as at least three different registers of travel: the touring concert musician, the emigrant returning home, and the tourist.

The Lusitana Band's role as a performing group both complemented and complicated the musicians' roles as tourists. The schedule of concerts provided an itinerary for the trip and gave the musicians an opportunity to interact with several different local communities. The band's performance of marches well-known to both audiences in New England and in Portugal points to the way that musical performances span both time and space to connect diaspora to the homeland (Sarkissian 2000). Klimt and Lubkemann emphasize that the construction of diasporic identities relies heavily on cultural performances (Klimt and Lubkemann 2002). The band's formal performances support these arguments; however, the Lusitana Band's performances in Portugal inverted the expected relationship between tourists and musical performers. In most accounts of tourism and performance, tourists attend performances showcasing music and dance representative of ethnic or regional identities (Bruner 2005, 86-87; O'Neill 2003; Sardo 2003; Sarkissian 2003). These authors document the ways in which cultural shows—performances developed for tourist audiences—have shaped musical repertoire, performance practices, and perceptions of the culture. Within Portugal, tourism has influenced musical traditions (Castelo-Branco and Branco 2003). For example, *ranchos folclóricos* and other "folk" traditions have adapted repertoire to fit the formats and expectations of shows for tourists in regions such as the Algarve (Sousa 2003).

The Lusitana Band, on the other hand, was cast in the role of performer, not audience member. The experiences of touring musicians have been explored to a lesser degree in literature on music and tourism. In his 1994 essay on Turkish Black Sea musicians' tour of the west coast of Ireland, Stokes critiques the construction of the passive musical tourist, and lays the ground for exploring the dynamics of cultural exchange in musicians' experience of a new music culture (Stokes 1994). However, touring Portuguese-American *filarmónicas* present a somewhat different case. Musicians and audiences assume that they share at least some aspects of Portuguese culture. It is, rather, not an exchange between cultures, but an exchange within a transnational community.

The Lusitana Band performed musical repertoire that signifies a Portuguese identity in the United States to an audience that was generally more familiar with Portuguese *filarmónicas* and performance practices than audiences back home. In New England, the Lusitana Band could be described as what Slobin calls a "micromusic" viewed against the backdrop of a broader Anglo-American culture (Slobin 1993, 11). However, in Portugal, the band was no longer a "subcultural sound," but one that audiences measured against their expectations and knowledge of *filarmónica* performances at summer festivals. The juxtaposition of performing and touring often provided the grounds for discussions of Portuguese and Portuguese-American identities among both musicians and audience members. The tension between the roles of *emigrante*, tourist, and visiting musician often pointed to the various ways that people perceived the relationship between homeland and diasporic cultures. The Lusitana Band's tour provides a case study for exploring the construction of sameness and difference within the transnational networks that connect Cumberland to Penalva.

This paper draws on ethnographic research I conducted with the Lusitana Band from 2005–06. However, it explores issues of identity, migration, and diaspora that I began to research when I conducted fieldwork (2001–05) with *filarmónicas* in Portugal for my dissertation (Brucher 2005). I played alto saxophone with the Lusitana Band on the trip to Portugal. I had first played with the Lusitana Band when I was an undergraduate at Brown University in Providence, Rhode Island. The band had been my introduction to Portuguese culture, so I felt that, in some sense, my research on *filarmónicas* had finally come full circle. When I went to graduate school for ethnomusicology and began to consider a research topic in Portugal, Alcides Luís, a member of the Lusitana

Band, suggested that I contact the bandleader in his hometown, Covões. My experiences during several summers (2001, 2002, 2004, 2006) and one year working with the Banda de Covões (2002–03) led me to consider the role of emigrants in the support of *filarmónicas.* This 2005 trip offered the opportunity to experience Portugal from the perspective of emigrants visiting from America. On the trip, we spent nearly all of our time together—eating, riding the bus, performing, touring sites, and hanging out in the local café—and I had many opportunities to observe, participate, and discuss the trip with musicians and their family members. Conversations from these occasions yielded insight into how individual musicians felt about their experiences in Portugal. After our return, I interviewed additional band members as well as retired bandleaders in an effort to better understand the history of the Lusitana Band. This article is part of a larger project that explores the role of *filarmónicas* in Portugal and in diaspora communities in the construction of identities within local, regional, and transnational spheres.

The Lusitana Band: Sounds of Portugal in New England

The Lusitana Band has dedicated itself to performing music for Portuguese communities in southern New England since immigrants from Penalva de Castelo founded the band in 1926.[5] During oral history interviews, retired conductors Al Cardoso and João Lopes Soares offered detailed information about the band's activities and membership since its founding. Both casual discussions and formal interviews with current members provided insight into how musicians value the band's relationship to Penalva de Castelo and view the band as a way of creating and expressing Portuguese identities.

In 1921, immigrants from Penalva founded Clube Juventude Lusitana, a social club and mutual aid association. Five years later, in January 1926, the club started the band. The first group of musicians was probably all immigrants from continental Portugal. Club members recruited António Lança, a Portuguese musician working in Fall River, Massachusetts, to be the band's first director. Lança's duties included directing performances, rehearsing the band, and teaching solfege and instrumental lessons. The band's repertoire included marches and processionals for use at feasts and concert pieces, such as arrangements of Portuguese songs and dances and transcriptions of light classical works, many of which were composed or transcribed by Lança. By October of the same year, this amateur group had begun performing for Portuguese-American community events in Cumberland.

According to Al Cardoso, the band went through many "versions" in its first few decades. Cardoso joined the band in the early 1930s, when many members were young boys like him—the children of immigrants who had moved to Cumberland. The group disbanded during World War II,[6] but musicians revived it again in 1952. After the United States eased immigration restrictions in 1965, the band benefited from an influx of musicians who came during the second wave of Portuguese immigration in the 1960s and 1970s (Williams 2005, 110–11). Many of these musicians had learned to play their instruments with bands back in their hometowns in Portugal, and they brought their musical experiences and musical repertoire to the United States. In the late 1960s, Manny Sebastião, father of the band's current conductor, Gary, emigrated as a young man from Esmolfe, a small village near Penalva, to Cumberland. As a boy, he learned to play the trumpet with the Banda de Penalva do Castelo. After arriving in the United States, he initially played with the Açoriana Band, a *filarmónica* in Fall River, Massachusetts. In the early 1980s, Sebastião followed the Açoriana Band's director, João Soares, when he left to direct the Lusitana Band. In 1952, at age thirty-two, Soares emigrated from a village in Beira Alta after he had married his wife, a Portuguese-American whom he had met one summer when she visited Portugal with her family. He already had a musical career as a trumpeter in a military band and conductor of the *filarmónica* in his village. Musicians like Sebastião and Soares have helped the Lusitana Band maintain many musical practices and some of the same repertoire employed by *filarmónicas* in continental Portugal. These traditions continue to be taught to second- and now third- generation musicians in the Lusitana Band.

Today, the band's membership includes both immigrants and second- and third-generation Portuguese-Americans. About fifty men and women, ranging in age from pre-teens to retirees, perform with the band on a regular basis. Many of the younger musicians also play in their junior-high, high-school, or college bands; whereas most of the older musicians are immigrants who learned in their hometowns in Portugal. Today, the majority of the musicians live in Cumberland or nearby towns.

Musicians described many reasons for joining the band. The older immigrants like Sebastião, Soares, and Alcides Luís said that they joined the band, in part, because they had always played with *filarmónicas* back in their *terra*. Music has always played an important role in their social lives, and once they were in the United States, *filarmónicas* provided a community of other people that shared experiences as musicians and immigrants. The band and larger social club also provided an organization that aided adaptation to a new national context. Younger musicians, such as Pedro, a high school student who came to Cumberland with his family in 1990, said that his parents wanted him to play with the band because they wanted him to maintain a strong sense of Portuguese culture. Second- and third-generation Portuguese-Americans such as Sabrina Boulay identified the band as a way to maintain a sense of Portuguese heritage.

Family, school, work, and neighborhood friendships influenced musicians' decisions to join the band. Although I have not formally surveyed the band membership, family relationships clearly drew many people to the band. Al Cardoso and João Soares looked through old photographs of the band during their interviews, and both men identified fathers and sons, brothers and cousins from year-to-year in the band. In pictures taken since the 1970s, they also identified mothers, daughters, and sisters in each photograph of the band. The Sebastião family is a good example of how kinship plays an important role in the band. Manny joined the band as an adult, and both his son and daughter played in the band as children. His son Gary now conducts the band. In addition, Manny's wife, Maria, serves as vice president of the band's board of directors, and now Gary's teenage daughter plays with the band, too. However, other kinds of social relationships also figure prominently in musicians' decisions to join the Lusitana Band. Al Cardoso said that he joined the band because the musicians rehearsed across the street from his father's grocery store. Other men worked together in one of Cumberland's many mills. Today, the band offers students a chance to socialize together after school, but also outside of their parents' direct supervision.

The Rhode Island band asserts a strong connection to Penalva de Castelo. Paintings of the church and main square of Penalva decorate the band's rehearsal room in the basement of the Clube Juventude de Lusitana's social hall. However, the Lusitana Band also includes both Azorean and non-Portuguese musicians. Portuguese diaspora communities often appear insular (Feldman-Bianco 1992), but the Lusitana Band appears to be an exception among *filarmónicas* in southern New England.[7] The non-Portuguese musicians tend to know club members from work or school. I joined the band as an undergraduate because Matthew McGarrell, the director of bands at Brown University, performs regularly and recruits undergraduates to play with the band during the summer months. McGarrell initially learned about the Lusitana Band when Brown University asked him to hire a Portuguese band to perform for Mário Soares's honorary degree ceremony. On the 2005 trip, a few non-Portuguese musicians from outside the band—some from Brown University, some from other Portuguese bands—joined the ensemble to complete instrumentation and reinforce weak sections. A few regular musicians suggested that including non-Portuguese musicians was a relatively recent phenomenon; but Al Cardoso noted that the band began to admit non-Portuguese musicians as early as the 1950s, when several Polish immigrants from Cumberland joined the band. Gary Sebastião sees the non-Portuguese musicians as positive contributors to the band. Rather than diluting the band's function as a Portuguese social group, Sebastião views the inclusion of outsiders as part of the band's mission to promote Portuguese culture. In the band, non-Portuguese musicians have the opportunity to play music by Portuguese musicians, attend Portuguese cultural events, and ideally, learn to speak at least a few words of Portuguese.[8] According to Sebastião, this increases awareness and understanding of Portuguese culture and attests to the strength of Portuguese culture in its appeal to musicians who do not have Portuguese ancestry.

The Clube Juventude Lusitana, the band's parent organization, maintains an important presence in Penalva, through yearly donations to different charitable causes in the community. For example, in March 2006, at the annual Penalva dinner, admission tickets raised money to support a retirement home in Penalva and a separate raffle held during the dinner raised $1,500 to buy books for Penalva's new municipal library. The circulation of money and material goods has played an important part in the transnational experience of both emigrants and those who stayed in Portugal. Music and musical groups have played a central role in this transnational economy. All of the *filarmónicas* that I worked with in Portugal had benefited from emigrants' donations to buy instruments and uniforms, build rehearsal halls, and support travel.

Emigrants assert a presence in their hometowns through their donations to local charities—whether the *filarmónica,* local library, or community center. Many musicians interpreted Penalva's efforts to be a good host and provide for the band as a gesture of thanks for the Lusitana Club's ongoing support for the Penalva community.[9]

The 2005 trip was not the Lusitana Band's first trip to Portugal; the band had traveled to Portugal in 1993. Although my article does not explore this first trip in depth, the trip set an important precedent for the 2005 tour. In 1993, the band also toured Beira Alta, but it stayed at a school in the nearby town of Mangualde because, at that time, Penalva did not have any place to host the musicians. The trip was a major achievement for the band, as it showed that the group had both the financial means and community support in Cumberland and Penalva necessary for such an undertaking, and it set the stage for the 2005 trip. The itinerary for both trips was organized around communities with direct ties to the band through emigration. In 1993 and 2005, the band played a series of concerts in villages in the *concelho* of Penalva as well as in nearby *concelhos* that also had sent emigrants to Cumberland. The band also gave concerts in Covões, a village in the Beira Litoral *concelho* of Cantanhede, because Alcides Luís came from Covões and had played with the Sociedade Filarmónica de Covões with his father before emigrating to Rhode Island in the late 1960s.

The band is proud of both of its trips, and, already, board members have begun discussing a possible tour in a few years. The tours presented an inexpensive way for individuals to make such a trip. Musicians paid only one-third of their plane fare (about $300), and the band raised the balance from the fees it received for performances and from community fundraisers, such as dinners and raffles. Band director Gary Sebastião suggested that the trip was important to many individuals in the band because "people got to see family. They don't always have a chance to go back [to Portugal] as often as they would like. They have a chance to see family and things they miss." For most of the musicians in the band, a subsidized trip to Portugal was a unique opportunity. Most musicians come from working- or middle-class families, and trips to Portugal, even when visiting family, are major expenses.[10] Several band members extended their stay in Portugal by a week or two if they could afford additional vacation time. Some musicians' families joined them on the trip. In this manner, musicians already participated in *turismo de saudade* by spending more time visiting Portugal. Sebastião stressed that the band's non-Portuguese members also benefited from the trip: "[The] people that aren't Portuguese…got to see rural Portugal as well as industrial and bigger cities. They could see what Portuguese communities are all about." The opportunity to travel is an important attraction for members. The experiences of band musicians echo those of dancers in *ranchos folclóricos* documented by Holton (2005a). Travel for performances provided a chance to see different parts of Portugal and also facilitated sociality within the group (Holton 2005a, 135–7). Likewise, Maria João Vasconcelos, an ethnomusicologist and band musician in Portugal, also found that musicians joined *filarmónicas*, in part, because bands offered opportunities to travel both within Portugal and abroad to perform for Portuguese communities elsewhere in Europe and South America. For groups such as the Lusitana Band, sustaining Portuguese culture is a major goal. Through travel, the band collapses the space between homeland and diaspora, giving its members a way to connect with Portugal physically. However, travel also offers musicians a chance to experience new locales and to spend more time with each other outside their everyday lives back in Cumberland.

Performing Portugal and America in Penalva

The Lusitana Band performed a series of fifteen concerts during the seventeen-day tour. The band's performances in Portugal differed significantly from its usual summer schedule of religious processions and secular parades. In the United States, the band usually performs for processions at *festas* in Rhode Island and Massachusetts. The band occasionally plays concerts, but most of its performances and its repertoire are given over to functional marches and processionals. In Portugal, the band often played a few marches during the *entrada*—a short parade to announce the band's presence—but the majority of the performance took place on a stage. The concerts often took place as part of community events such as a celebration of the Feast of Saint Peter, the opening of a new community center, and a local art fair. These programs often included other musical groups from the area such as *ranchos folclóricos*, *tunas*, and choruses. In Portugal, both secular and sacred community celebrations often include outdoor concerts that feature musical groups ranging from wind bands to folklore ensembles to rock bands.

Since the Lusitana Band plays only a few concerts during the year back in the United States, the band had the unusual opportunity to develop its concert repertoire. The Lusitana Band approached concerts with Portuguese ensembles with great seriousness. When the Lusitana Band performed in Covões with the local *filarmónica,* the Sociedade Filarmónica de Covões, the director made it clear that audience expectations differed in Portugal by urging the band "not to screw up. These people actually know what a band is supposed to sound like." Sebastião programmed music exclusively by Portuguese composers, with the exception of Karl King's band classic, "The Princess of India Overture. Filarmónicas" have performed this piece since, at least, the 1950s.[11] He drew on pieces common to Portuguese band repertoire, such as concert marches and *rapsódias*—medleys of Portuguese folksongs.[12] Sebastião described the philosophy underlying his musical choices:

> My program followed this basic idea: we wanted to show that we could play, that we were a good band, and give [audience members] something they could relate to.... I programmed the shorter marches and the rhapsodies because I wanted to give them something that the common man could relate to. For example, there was a man at one concert that sang along to one of the songs.... I wanted to give [people] something they could enjoy and that would show our technical ability.

Rapsódias portuguesas play a key role in the repertoire of *filarmónicas.* A *rapsódia portuguesa* differs from a rhapsody in Western art music. *Rapsódias portuguesas* vary in length from ten to twenty minutes and include several Portuguese songs and dances with contrasting meters, tempi, and orchestration. Audiences and performers usually regard *rapsódias* as relatively difficult due to the technical ability and stamina needed to play them. The titles of some *rapsódias* refer to Portugal, such as "Sonhos de Portugal" [Dreams of Portugal] and "Um Abraço de Portugal" [An Embrace from Portugal]. Others refer to specific regions of the country—"Romarias do Norte" [Pilgrimages of the North] (1993) or "Rapsódia Durense" [Rhapsody of the Douro]—or a mythic past—"Recordações do Passado" [Memories of the Past].[13] The pieces provide a panoramic view of Portuguese folk songs and regions of the country. Sebastião identified *rapsódias* as a significant aural reminder of Portugal for audiences and musicians alike: "[*Rapsódias*] have both songs from years ago and [...] new folk songs from modern times. Most people recognize these pieces when we play them, and it keeps the culture going. [In the United States] especially, the older folks hear them and remember how things were. The newer generation hears them and learns this is what our culture is about." *Rapsódias* are one way that the band communicates its identity as a Portuguese cultural institution through its musical repertoire.

On the tour, the *rapsódias* were clear crowd-pleasers. The band often played "Sonhos do Portugal," followed immediately by "Rapsódia Durense." "Sonhos do Portugal" gives its audience a sampling of well-known Portuguese folksongs and dances often performed by folklore groups. The piece begins with a march and then segues to a *chula*. From the *chula*, it changes to a mournful *fado* that features a baritone horn solo. Once again, the tempo quickens as the band shifts to a *bolero*. After the *bolero*, the meter changes from duple to triple when the piece moves into a *vira*. The finale is a *marcha popular*, a brisk two-step associated with the celebrations of the *santos populares*. "Rapsódia Durense" follows a similar pattern of tempo and meter changes that correspond to popular genres of folksongs and dances. At the band's concerts in and around Penalva, audience members often paired off and danced to these arrangements of folksongs rendered for the concert stage. This was striking since bands usually do not expect their listeners to dance.[14] Despite abrupt shifts in tempo and meter as the band moved through each piece, the audience members danced along, often pausing to readjust their steps to match the meter. Other audience members sang along to songs they recognized, especially during "Sonhos de Portugal."

The Lusitana Band demonstrated the degree to which it was familiar with works by Portuguese composers, and that it shared a common repertoire with Portuguese *filarmónicas*. However, its concert repertoire differed significantly from the Portuguese *filarmónicas* in what it lacked. The night the Lusitana Band shared a concert with the hometown Banda de Penalva illustrated some of these differences. The Lusitana Band played the first half of the concert and presented what had become, by this point in the trip, our standard program of marches and *rapsódias*:

"Joaquim Merim" (march), "Sonhos do Portugal" (*rapsódia*), "Rapsódia Durense" (*rapsódia*), "Amigos de Penalva" (march), and "Presidente António Conde" (march). The Penalva Band performed the second half of the concert, and the Lusitana Band listened from the crowd. The Penalva Band also started with a concert march but soon branched into other musical realms. It finished its set with an arrangement of "When the Saints Go Marching In." Some musicians from the Lusitana Band reacted with amusement at hearing what they considered an American standard, but others expressed a mixture of disappointment and surprise. One even remarked, "Why would I want to come all the way to Portugal to hear this music?" In this exchange, the Penalva Band fell short of what this listener—someone who had played with the band for several years—perceived as "authentic" Portuguese band music. I was unable to confirm that the Penalva Band selected "When the Saints Go Marching In" as a nod to its American visitors, but Portuguese bands often program arrangements of popular music from all over the world. Arrangements of Beatles songs, ABBA's greatest hits, and standards such as "When the Saints Go Marching In" signal a band's ability to adapt to a wide range of genres, and Portuguese band audiences generally react positively to international pop music.[15] Additionally, *filarmónica* directors sometimes strategically program pieces that sound "Portuguese," such as *rapsódias,* alongside popular music that they believe will resonate with emigrants conversant with popular culture in France, Brazil, Venezuela or North America. Band directors know that emigrants often donate money to the bands in their *terra* and seek their support, and playing to audience members' transnational experiences is a proven method (Neves 2004).

The Lusitana Band inverted the typical relationship between visitor and performer at *filarmónica* concerts. The emigrants played a program of Portuguese music for an audience of local *filarmónica* musicians and their community. In effect, the Lusitana Band presented the opposite of what one might have expected—the band performed nothing that pointed to an American identity, and instead, highlighted its connections to Portuguese traditions. When performing for *festas* in Rhode Island, the band provides music for occasions that celebrate an ethnic cultural identity. However, in Portugal, a program of music by Portuguese composers did not resonate with their audiences in the way that it might for Portuguese-American audiences. When I spoke to musicians in the Covões band whom I have known for several years, they diplomatically said that the Lusitana Band must not have as much time to practice with busy American schedules. Perceptions of American lifestyles framed musicians' evaluation of the Lusitana Band's musical skills. While the comments were intended to be polite, they suggested the stereotypes of *americanos*—always busy, preoccupied with material wealth, and unfamiliar with Portuguese culture. Likewise, when the musicians in the Lusitana Band listened as audience members, they did not embrace "When the Saints Go Marching In" as a symbol of what the Penalva band perceived as their American identity. As members of a *filarmónica,* many musicians felt it was their duty to perform primarily Portuguese repertory. In this case, attempts to evoke a diasporic Portuguese identity through repertoire resulted in musical miscommunications. The two bands' performances and the audiences' reactions point to the difference in the host's and the visitor's interpretations of what constitute appropriate music for *filarmónicas* and how it relates to Portuguese identity.

Exchanging music traditions also took a literal form for Lusitana Band and the Banda de Penalva. Before the last number at each concert, representatives of the village hosting the event addressed the band and its audience. Usually a local leader presented the president of the Lusitana Band with a plaque with the community's crest, and in exchange, he gave them a commemorative plate with the band's emblem. However, at the end of the first official concert of the tour, the president of the Banda de Penalva—also an employee of Penalva's municipal government—came forward and gave the Lusitana band a score to a march, "Os Amigos de Penalva" [The Friends of Penalva], by Vítor Santos. After the concert, the Lusitana Band's director looked over the score, commenting that it was more interesting to receive a score than a commemorative plaque. He decided that we should perform it six days later at the concert with the Penalva band as an expression of gratitude to the town. The march is idiomatic of duple meter, up-tempo street marches, and it is simple enough for the band to learn within a few rehearsals. This piece of music has since become a signature piece in the Lusitana Band's repertoire. To the musicians, it provides a sonic reminder of the tour. We rehearsed the march in the afternoons and performed it nightly at concerts throughout the second week of the trip. The circumstances under which we learned the piece made the march standout from the other pieces in the repertoire. To audiences, the title announces the band's ties to Penalva. Sebastião has programmed the march on occasions such as the band's annual dinner at the Lusitana Club. He believes that the piece will help audience members identify with both the band and their own roots in Penalva: "The title tells people who aren't in the band about Penalva. They might hear it and say, 'I like that song, what was it?' and we'll say, 'Oh, it's Penalva' and they'll start to think about Penalva and where they're from. The title stirs up talk and memories." The march evokes both the band's historic ties to Penalva as well as its more recent experiences there.

Most musicians highlighted their positive experiences as touring musicians. The musicians in the Lusitana Band responded to the trip with enthusiasm. In interviews, musicians commented that Portuguese audiences appreciated the band in ways that their North American audiences do not. Band member, Sabrina Boulay, emphasized audiences' positive responses to the band on both trips to Portugal: "I think the audiences there really appreciated us… Back at the club, they like us, but they take us for granted." The director also noted that the band appeared to receive a warmer-than-usual reception in Portugal, and likewise, attributed this to Cumberland audiences' familiarity with the ensemble, adding, "Like they say, you have to leave your hometown to get recognition.... Appreciation is strong in both places, but I think you'll find in most places that you get more accolades when you leave your hometown." Musicians who attended the trip in 1993 reported similar reactions from audiences in Portugal. Al Cardoso summarized, "They treated us like royalty."

The role of touring musician sometimes conflicted with local audiences' perceptions of visiting *emigrantes.* While musicians felt welcomed in Penalva, I noted that face-to-face interactions with musicians from other bands were limited. For instance, few musicians from the Penalva Band spoke with the Lusitana Band musicians and, when the bands shared a concert, the two did not socialize together as a group. On occasion, some musicians felt some hostility, at least from the audience. One musician reported that someone on the street shouted at him in English, "What? You think you're too good for the other band?" when he left the Penalva band's concert to store his instrument. In this case, the use of English points to the notion that the descendants of *emigrantes* speak Portuguese poorly. In other cases, audience members wanted the visitors to prove their cultural and musical competence. Another musician recalled that someone in the audience struck up a conversation with a challenge, "Tell me how many possible scales are there in the key of Do?" He quizzed the visiting musician's transposition skills before the conversation shifted to amicable territory. Once again, stereotypes of *americanos*—emigrants to the United States—as wealthy or poorly acquainted with Portuguese customs and language fueled some of these exchanges (Brettell 2003h; Holton 2005a). Although the local government had officially welcomed the band as performers and tourists, some townspeople received the visitors from America more as *emigrantes*, not visiting tourists. Although the band's musical tour was a major event for Penalva, community members viewed the band as part of the ongoing flow of people between Penalva and Cumberland.

Transnational Tourists

Musicians' activities offstage provided other opportunities for individuals to demonstrate their connection to Portugal and in doing this, negotiate social status both within the band and in their hometowns in Portugal. Performing blended with touring as travel to performances also included sightseeing. The itinerary was planned around concerts in villages and towns with which the band had a direct connection—often through musicians or board members who had emigrated from these communities. These concerts often included lunch or dinner in a local restaurant as well as stops at local landmarks. For example, when the band traveled to Covões, a village in the *concelho* of Cantanhede to play two evening concerts, the *concelho* treated us to a bus tour of an industrial park, lunch in a seaside village of Tocha, an hour on the beach, and a brief stop at Covões's own "Statue of Liberty," a twenty-foot replica of the Statue of Liberty erected after September 11, 2001, by a family that had emigrated to New Jersey. Another day, a sightseeing trip to Torre, the highest peak in the Serra de Estrela, also included stops in villages where two of the band's board members had come from. These towns provided buffets for musicians that included the local wine, *queijo de serra* [Serra de Estrela cheese], and *presunto* [smoked ham], and the band played impromptu parades in both villages despite afternoon temperatures surpassing one hundred degrees Fahrenheit.

These parades and concerts were often a source of pride for the musicians and the townspeople hosting the event. They provided opportunities for these immigrants to demonstrate to the band their social stature within their hometown as reflected by the welcome the band received. To hometown audiences, a visit from the band showed their social position within the Lusitana Band and, by extension, Cumberland's diasporic community. Concerts outside Penalva demonstrated considerable social power within the band, since concerts scheduled within the host *concelho* of Penalva took priority. When the band attracted a sizeable audience in Satão, a *concelho* north of Penalva, the president of the band smiled broadly, and announced how happy he felt to bring the band to his hometown. Performances in hometowns also touched off competition among musicians as they strived to show that their community could show better hospitality than others.[16] "It's not Penalva, but I think it's pretty nice," said one band member of her hometown, only to later criticize another small village where the band played at the request of another band member.

The pretense of showing the band a new place in Portugal provided a venue for emigrants to negotiate for social capital both within their hometowns and within their social circles in Cumberland. Caroline Brettell and Andrea Klimt have both documented the care that emigrants take to demonstrate the material wealth that they have accumulated through working abroad (Brettell 2003a; Klimt 2000). The musicians' and board members' efforts to show off the band to their hometowns resonates with Glick-Schiller, Basch, and Szanton-Blanc's observation that "one way migrants keep options open is to continuously translate the economic and social position gained in one political setting into political, social, and economic capital in another" (Glick-Schiller, Basch, and Szanton-Blanc 1992, 12). In the context of the trip, emigrants demonstrated not only material wealth, as shown by the community's ability to finance a transatlantic trip for more than forty people, but also social capital and status within the diasporic community.

Some excursions focused exclusively on sightseeing. These trips, organized by Penalva's municipal government, illustrated *turismo de saudade* as the band visited both major national sights and local landmarks in Penalva. For instance, the town arranged for a coach bus to take the band on a day trip to Fátima, the caves at Mira de Aire, and the Monastery of Batalha. Other excursions showed local highlights in Penalva. The town arranged for a guided tour of the Casa de Insua, a local manor house in the village of Insua, followed by a tour and lunch at Penalva's cooperative winery. The tour of the Casa de Insua emphasized the mansion's neoclassical architecture and ornamental garden. This contrasted sharply with a board member's account of what it had been like to work for the Duke of Insua during the 1950s. Many of the musicians and their families had emigrated to Cumberland for economic opportunities and to escape the hardships of agricultural life in Penalva, but the tour encouraged a more romantic view of Portugal's history. In this case, the tour emphasized nostalgia for grandeur of a lost era divorced from the realities of servitude to the Duke and subsistence farming. *Turismo de saudade*, while encouraging Portuguese-Americans to embrace their heritage, places unpleasant aspects of Portuguese history—often the very factors that contributed to the decision to emigrate—at a distance. Sites like the Casa de Insua are recast as the heritage of Beira Alta and a destination for tourists interested in Portuguese history.[17] The band's sightseeing trips encouraged a tourist gaze, emphasized what Portugal had to offer visitors, and suggested an easygoing lifestyle. The musicians embraced this, and within a few days, the trip became an extended musical party. To be sure, people rehearsed and took concerts seriously; however, the schedule took the shape of touring by day, performing concerts in the evening, and socializing in the bar near our hotel or dancing at clubs in the nearby provincial capital at night. Soon, people were playing in every sense of the word: playing their instruments, playing games while going out, and in some sense, playing at what it might be like to live in Portugal.

Conclusion

The tour of Portugal achieved several ends. First of all, it yielded musical improvements and social prestige for the Lusitana Band. Musicians said that the trip transformed the band: it brought them closer to Penalva, and it bettered the band musically and brought them together socially. Dan Vasconcelos, a saxophonist on the trip, described what he called the band's "drastic improvement," which he attributed to the frequent performances, extra rehearsals, and socializing: "We went to Portugal a ragtag bunch of musicians, and we became a band by the end." One musician identified the trip itself as a reason to devote more time to music, telling the band director during an extra rehearsal in Penalva, "I'd go to rehearsal every night in the States if we got to do this all the time. If you promise to take us to Portugal every year, I'd rehearse two times a night, in fact." The band could claim the trip to Portugal as a badge of honor because it showed that it had sufficient resources and support from both its home community in the U.S. and its host community in Portugal to make such as a trip possible. Newly acquired repertory like "Amigos de Penalva" resonates for musicians and audience members alike. Back in New England, the band uses the possibility of travel to Portugal as a tool to recruit new members.

The trip drew attention to individuals and institutions in both Penalva and Cumberland. It achieved political ends for both municipal governments as it reinforced the "sister city" relationship. Furthermore, at the time of the trip, both Mayor Figueiredo and Mayor Iwuk were running for re-election in their communities. Neither man cast his public appearances with the band as campaign stops, but both candidates gained exposure within the emigrant community and additional public forums to discuss their goals for continuing the relationship between the two towns. The generosity of Penalva's municipal government made a strong impression on the musicians from Cumberland. Perhaps, recreational organizations in Penalva such as the band or local *rancho folclórico* could expect reciprocal treatment in Cumberland if they visit the United States.

The visitors from Cumberland also benefited the local economy in Penalva. Forty musicians, board members, and musicians' family members provided a temporary influx of business. While the community invested substantial financial resources in hosting the band, the visitors bought things at local markets, ate in local cafés, and drank in the local bars. The municipal government wants its investment in the band's trip to pay long-term dividends as well. The hotel owner hopes that once construction is completed, band members and their friends and family will return to Penalva and stay in his hotel. While a few band members' families own houses in this area, many do not. On the last night of the trip, the hotel owner hosted a party for the band in the basement of the hotel—

which he had rushed to finish for this occasion—and he gave every guest a framed photograph of the band in full uniform, standing in front of his hotel. In the photograph, the building is clearly unfinished—windows are missing from the first floor and construction materials are visible in the background. Laundry hangs over the second- and third-story balconies, since Penalva has no laundromats in town. Nonetheless, the photograph links the visiting Rhode Island band to Penalva's nascent tourist industry.

Penalva plans to develop tourism as a local industry, and promotes this region as a family-friendly destination. The town government emphasized the potential of tourism to both help Penalva retain its residents and draw people to it. Unlike other areas of Portugal, Beira Alta did not have the infrastructure to expand economically after Portugal joined the European Union, and young people, although they emigrate overseas in smaller numbers, still move elsewhere within Portugal to find employment once they finish high school or college. The local government has identified returning emigrants as one obvious place to market the region. The president of Penalva shared his hope that one day people will come from Cumberland not only to vacation, but eventually, to work in Penalva, reversing a century's trend of emigration abroad.[18]

Moreover, Penalva's focus on *turismo de saudade* echoes the goals of the Portuguese government to include emigrants and their descendants in the nation-state through culture. The government sponsored Comunidades Portuguesas, or Portuguese Communities, aims to unite the Portuguese diaspora worldwide by encouraging Portuguese citizens and their descendants to keep dual citizenship, speak Portuguese, and maintain Portuguese culture. *Turismo de saudade* extends the practice of encouraging travel to Portugal and understanding Portuguese culture as a form of economic development. Emigrants have long contributed to the Portuguese economy, and *turismo de saudade* presents one more way of reinforcing economic and cultural ties. In returning to Portugal, the Lusitana Band traced the lines that the government imagines to connect the diaspora to its homeland.

The Lusitana Band's journey from Cumberland, Rhode Island to Penalva do Castelo, Portugal and back again indicates a complex relationship between tourism, ethnic identity, diaspora, and transnationalism. The figure of the tourist, rather than that of the emigrant, encompasses a range of relationships to Portugal, including those of

Portuguese-Americans for whom *festas* in Rhode Island had previously provided their only experiences of Portuguese culture. A trip like this one encourages even those who are a few generations removed from Portugal to continue to return. The band used the trip to perpetuate its connections to communities in Portugal while simultaneously promoting its identity as ethnically Portuguese within the diaspora community in Rhode Island. However, the musicians' experiences challenged presumptions of a common culture and heritage implicit in a diasporic Portuguese identity. Because the Lusitana Band's trip inverted the usual relationship between audiences, musical ensembles, and tourists, it provides a rich case study for further examining how performance and travel reconstitute the relationship between Portugal and its diaspora. *Turismo de saudade* offers a lens for interpreting fluidity of the relationship between homeland and diaspora.

Notes

[1] I would like to thank the members of the Lusitana Band and its board of directors for the opportunity to play with the ensemble on this trip. Matthew McGarrell also provided invaluable support by facilitating introductions, offering comments, and providing hospitality.

[2] For further background on *filarmónicas*, see Brucher (2005), Freitas (1946), Lameiro (1997, 1999).

[3] Immigrants from continental Portugal went to Cumberland for many of the same reasons that Azorean immigrants decided to emigrate to Rhode Island. The availability of jobs as unskilled laborers in the textile mills attracted many new immigrants to urban Rhode Island (Williams 2005, 52). The group of immigrants that founded the *Clube Juventude de Lusitana* in 1921 resulted from chain migration from this region of Beira Alta.

[4] An article available online through ICEP's PortugalNews service, declares that the market of emigrants and luso-descendants "arriving with money in their pockets like *saudades da pátria*, is already awaking diverse interest." In the article, representatives of Sojopor and the Associação Nacional das Regiões de Turismo describe returning emigrants as an untapped market for Portugal's leisure economy (Antunes 2000, my translation).

[5] The ensemble's history is documented in a two-page summary of the band's activities.

[6] According to Cardoso, the ensemble disbanded during this period for lack of musicians. During this period, the musicians in the band were all men, and many musicians went to fight for the U.S. military in World War II.

[7] Dan Vasconcelos, a musician who has played with several *filarmónicas* in Massachusetts and Rhode Island, observed that the Lusitana Band is the only one that has regular members that are not Portuguese. Other *filarmónicas* do not have policies barring non-Portuguese musicians, but they do not invite outsiders to perform with them.

[8] The Lusitana Club sponsors a language school that receives funding from the Camões Institute. Although band members are not required to attend the language school, Sebastião drew a parallel between the band's and the language school's efforts to promote Portuguese culture and language. Sebastião runs bilingual rehearsals in Portuguese and English, and he encourages musicians to use Portuguese music vocabulary.

[9] Kimberly Holton discusses a similar emphasis on reciprocity and feeling "well-received" during *rancho folclórico* events (2005a, 122).

[10] I have no specific data on the socioeconomic profile of band members, so this is based on general observations. Both Correia and Sebastião stated that the trip was important because it allowed musi-

cians to travel who might not otherwise have the opportunity. Many musicians commented on the generosity of the band and the community in Penalva for making the trip financially possible.

11 *Filarmónicas* in Portugal have played "Princess of India Overture" in Portugal for several decades. In *I Concurso Nacional de Bandas Civis*, Pedro de Freitas lists at least three different bands that included "A Abertura Princesa de Índia" by K. L. King in their competition programs (1965: 255, 259, 274). Although Karl King is a well-known American composer, it is possible that musicians brought this piece to *filarmónicas* in the United States from bands in Portugal. João Soares, director of the Lusitana Band from 1982 to 1998, recalled conducting this piece with the Lusitana Band (2006).

12 Although some composers, Ilídio Costa for example, compose their own melodies, most base *rapsódias* on well-known songs and dances. Even Costa follows common forms and rhythms that render his songs recognizable to audience members familiar with Portuguese folk music.

13 These titles were taken from concert programs or public announcements at concerts in Portugal and did not include the date of composition or publisher's information. Many scores to popular band music circulate as photocopies of manuscripts rather than as items purchased from music publishing houses.

14 During several summers of fieldwork at concerts in the Beira Litoral region of Portugal, I rarely saw adult audience members dance to *rapsódias*. Occasionally people sang along if the band played an arrangement of a particularly well-known song.

15 At concerts that I attended in Portugal, pieces by non-Portuguese composers, pop arrangements, and transcriptions of classical works often complemented repertoire that bands regard as distinctly Portuguese such as *rapsódias*.

16 Holton proposes hospitality as one way for analyzing how Portuguese communities receive and interact with outsiders (Holton 2005a). In the case of the Lusitana Band, discussions of hospitality framed competition and demonstrations of social power. For example, musicians and board members immediately noted if a community hosting the band provided food or drink and evaluated the community based on this. Musicians frequently described Penalva's reception of the band in terms of the town's generosity towards the band.

17 Dean MacCannell discusses the phenomenon of reconfiguring what were once elements of everyday life as history and tradition in tourist attractions (MacCannell 1999). Barbara Kirschenblatt-Gimblett further explores the impetus for recasting places or ethnographic objects as tourist destinations. She argues that detachment, fragmentation, and contextualization are necessary for the production of a museum site (1998). In Portugal, perhaps, the best example of the recasting of everyday life as museum site is the village of Monsanto. In 1938, the village won the *Concurso de A Aldeia Mais Portuguesa de Portugal* [Contest for the Most Portuguese Village in Portugal], a nationwide competition sponsored by the Estado Novo. Local leaders transformed the village into living museum of Portuguese traditions and attracted national and international attention of folklorists, journalists, and tourists (Felix 2003). Although Monsanto is an extreme example, it points to the way that the creation of a museum site tends to separate it from the very history and tradition that it represents.

18 Leonídio Monteiro spoke about the potential for tourism during a speech at a *sessão solemne* [formal ceremony] at the Câmara Municipal de Penalva July 9, 2005. He also made similar comments during his welcoming remarks to the band July 1, 2005.

CHAPTER 8

Salazar in New Bedford: Political readings of *Diário de Notícias*, the only Portuguese daily newspaper in the United States*

RUI CORREIA

On July 22 1946, *Time* magazine devoted its cover and a long article to the Portuguese head-of-state, António de Oliveira Salazar. In this article, Percy Knaught wrote that the Salazarist regime was inspired by Mussolini's fascism, painting it as dictatorial and corrupt and deploring Portugal's neutrality during World War II.[1] Following this hail of criticism, *Time* magazine was banned in Portugal, and its Lisbon correspondent, an Italian journalist by the name of Saporiti, was forced to leave the country.

This incident serves as one of many revealing examples of the way in which all Portuguese print media was subject to the robust and watchful eye of government censors after the overthrow of Portugal's First Republic in 1926.[2] Regarded as a catalyst for the social fragmentation in the country's recent past, the press was reconceived under Salazar as a tool for national reunification, needing to be patriotically led by those who shared the government's plan to unite all Portuguese in the pursuit of the much-acclaimed national resurgence. Dark memories of the political crisis of the First Republic were more than enough to show, with a little demagogical maneuvering, how freedom of expression and democracy could undermine the nation's economic and social progress. Any overt public opposition was regarded as subversive at a time when social and parliamentary dissent was thought to produce political failure. The political discourse of those in power emphasized social unification as the primary political objective of the dictatorship—a political concept that was not in disrepute then, as it is today.

In this plan to crush all political opposition, any transgression constituted a challenge to Salazar's rule. Portuguese newspapers were subject to close state control, and showing alternative versions of events was extremely difficult and risky for anyone in Salazar's day. Merely perusing one of these newspapers could have dire consequences. The free press only operated secretly or from abroad. Many Portuguese emigrants or exiles of varied political persuasions sought to create a means of communication that would give voice to those who disagreed with the political agenda of the Portuguese dictatorship. It was beyond Portuguese borders that these voices condemning the regime, or simply expressing impartiality and political pluralism, made themselves openly heard in print.

We find one such example in the U.S., where the Portuguese-American community in New Bedford, Massachusetts had been publishing the country's only daily Portuguese-language newspaper since 1919. The New Bedford *Diário de Notícias* had the largest readership among Portuguese-American communities and was the most important cultural reference for Portuguese immigrants and their descendants in the U.S., especially in New England. The newspaper only recently ceased publication in 1973, after an uninterrupted fifty-four year history, with some 330,000 pages written exclusively in Portuguese. It produced articles in Portuguese by local writers, republished news from Portuguese newspapers, and translated items of interest to the Portuguese community, or "colony" as it was called. Every edition featured an epigram boasting that it was "*o único jornal diário portuguez nos Estados Unidos*" [the only Portuguese daily newspaper in the United States]. The paper was extremely popular and regularly featured expressions of appreciation from its readers.

The *Diário* opened its columns to the most illustrious writings from contemporary Portugal, reflected the political and cultural diversity of New Bedford's Portuguese-American community, was committed to promoting the Portuguese immigrant community, and stood as a bastion of tolerance and resolve in times of great political and commercial pressure. This historical source therefore provides us with a Portuguese-American view of Portugal as well as of the Portuguese-American community itself.

Analyses of the Portuguese presence in the U.S. have been limited, sometimes more than necessary, to studies of a sociological or anthropological nature. One of the reasons for the prevalence of this type of approach is the lack of written sources that would allow us a historical examination of the thoughts and actions of New England's Portuguese throughout the 20th century. The *Diário de Notícias* is one of the few written sources that enables us to expand our vision of the Portuguese community of the U.S.[3] An examination of the articles generated by this community shows that, contrary to popular stereotypes, the Portuguese-Americans in New Bedford asserted a fiercely-articulated national dignity.

This article is part of a more comprehensive study that focuses on this remarkable historical source both because of its singular significance as a written document and the unforgivable scholarly neglect—a disinterest which merits redress. An unparalleled archive featuring a virtually complete, albeit uncatalogued, collection of the *Diário de Notícias* exists at the University of Massachusetts Dartmouth, while a microfilmed copy of this collection is available at the Boston Public Library.[4] Not a single collection exists in Portugal. The *Diário de Notícias* deserves more widespread examination as its articles include not only daily reports on the quotidian lives of Portuguese immigrants but also in-depth ideological, literary, and political discussions.

In each edition, we come into contact with a dynamic, politically-informed community that included a Portuguese-American elite comprised of doctors, clergy, teachers, attorneys, and politicians, including former government officials who had fled Salazar's political police. The *Diário de Notícias* welcomed the opinions of the whole political spectrum of New Bedford's Portuguese-American community. Far away but never cut off from Portugal, its pages conveyed the ideas of monarchists, republicans, socialists, liberals, and fascists who wrote about Portugal and the Portuguese. As articulated in its first editorial, however, the *Diário* went far beyond mere politics or ideology to give us an insight into "the social movement of our immigrant communities throughout the United States in general and in New England in particular."[5] Indeed, it provides us with a record of all the Portuguese-American community's activities and debates between 1919 and 1973.

For example, the *Diário de Notícias* published a long, scathing, almost instantaneous response to the piece in *Time* magazine condemning *Time*'s writer for being too circumspect and restrained in his attacks on Salazar's regime.[6] The newspaper's ideologically eclectic outlook was fundamentally different from the press in Portugal before the 1974 revolution ended the country's authoritarian regime. The paper's significance lies in its independence and democratizing stance, striking a sharp contrast with both the censored press in Portugal and communist underground publications. A systematic study of the *Diário de Notícias* thus gives us an overview of the community's political diversity, especially regarding the controversies that brought Portuguese-Americans in New Bedford into fierce debate with one other. Paradoxically, they achieved solidarity with one another by debating shared problems in the pages of their newspaper, and the community's intellectual elite was practiced in critical reflection. As exchanges in the *Diário* make quite clear, the community supported democratic ideals—a particularly notable undertaking as it contrasted so starkly with Portuguese reality. The polemics and reflections on a far-away homeland examined here reveal the cultural identity and complex dynamics of the Portuguese-American community in New Bedford in the mid-20th century.

The Thirties: The Political Matrix

One of the most intense and revealing moments in the history of New Bedford's Portuguese-American community occurred in the 1930s, a time of impassioned political, controversy involving substantially different ideologies and actively militant, sometimes even extremist, political views. Indeed, the examination of hundreds of articles for the present study reveals far more political controversy in the thirties than in any other decade in the *Diário de Notícias*'s publication run.

This is not altogether unexpected as the 1930s constituted a period of social, political and economic turbulence in the United States. These were years of crisis resulting from the Stock Market Crash of 1929, Roosevelt's New Deal, the Depression, and years of merciless limitations on immigration through the Emergency Quota Act (1921), Immigration Basic Law Act (1924), and Immigration National Origins Formula Act (1929). The last of these, based on a prospective immigrant's nationality, managed to reduce the admission of immigrants to the U.S. to 150,000 a year and totally excluded Asians. The 1930s was the only decade of the 20th century in which more people left than entered the United States.[7]

The 1930s was also a period of substantial change in Portugal. It was marked by the emergence of the Estado Novo under Oliveira Salazar as *Presidente do Conselho* [Chairman of the Council] in 1932, and by Portugal's reassertion of its empire with the 1933 publication of the *Acto*

Colonial. These were the years when the ideology, political programs, and institutions of the Estado Novo were built.

These were also the years of growing political tensions world-wide. With Adolf Hitler's appointment as chancellor of the German Reich in 1933 and his subsequent conquest of Austria, Czechoslovakia and Poland; Mussolini's annexation of Ethiopia in 1935; Josef Stalin's rise to power and his brutal political purges; Japan's conquest of China; and the outbreak of the bloody Spanish Civil War in 1936 and eventual triumph of Franco, the opposition in Portugal found clear reasons for energetically speaking out against all types of dictatorial regimes. The decade ended with the invasion of Poland and the beginning of the Second World War. The war was the result of fervent ideological activism that divided people all over the world and obliged them to make moral, civic, and patriotic choices.

It was during these times that the *Diário de Notícias,* like other regional ethnic newspapers, took part in a series of debates that threw openly oppositional liberals into conflict with the defenders of the Estado Novo. The heated disputes in the pages of the *Independente, Novidades* and *Diário de Notícias* are still rememberd by those who recall these newspapers. Indeed, the controversies resulted in important personal alliances and enmities that were later reflected in other debates. Most of these disputes, however, are irrecoverable, as no one thought to collect and restore original editions of these newspapers or put them on microfilm. Only New Bedford's *Diário de Notícias* and Fall River's *Novidades* were, to any extent, saved.[8] The clashes, for example, between Laertes de Figueiredo, a fervent anti-Semite, and Ferreira Martins, a journalist, republican and teacher, exemplify the political disputes of the period that ended up in print. The front-page dispute between João Camoesas, a physician and former Minister of Education living in exile in Taunton, and Manuel Caetano Pereira, a physician and Vice-Consul of Fall River, lasted over a year. This row was sparked by a simple article paying tribute to Afonso Costa, the former prominent Portuguese Prime Minister, after he had died, and moved on to a debate about Portugal's position on the Spanish Civil War, leading to lengthy and heated discussions concerning the Portuguese-American community itself.

The debates were followed attentively by *Diário de Notícias* readers who, as they often voiced their support for the different arguments, revealed the political dynamics of the Portuguese-American community. These discussions were not limited to the printed page; they reached the streets and resulted in altercations sometimes requiring police intervention, illustrating the limitations on freedom of expression in the U.S. of the 1930s. These debates reveal the existence of a concerned, activist, engaged community—an image that contrasts sharply with the stereotype of acquiescent indifference normally associated with Portuguese-American immigrants. The record found in the newspaper shows a community that was attentive to what was going on in their country of origin, rallying people and resources to the defense of the Portuguese or Portugal, condemning the advance of all totalitarianism, and politically so involved that they formed the region's most important electoral base.

The Spanish Civil War

Understanding the key debates in the Portuguese-language press means revisiting the origin of these controversies within American society. We see increased attention to the role of patriotism in people's daily lives when faced with a severe economic and ideological crisis; the moral acceptance of a certain radical, right-wing conservatism; and the drawing of a crucial distinction between liberalism and communism. These perspectives, along with the position of Portugal as well as the U.S. vis-à-vis the emergence of imperialism in Italy, Germany, and Japan was the subject of intense debates in the *Diário de Notícias*. These were the issues that, years later, also moved to the center of American public opinion. While, for Americans, a response to the tragedy of Pearl Harbor in 1941 was the first time many confronted the issues leading up to WWII, the debate in the *Diário de Notícias* had already begun much earlier, as the readership assessed Portugal's assertion of neutrality in October 1939.[9] This neutrality was highly criticized as it jeopardized the centuries-old diplomatic alliance with Britain. The specificity of the Portuguese-American debate further enriched ideological discussion in the thirties, especially with regards to the Spanish Civil War. For most Americans, with the exception of some informed and very engaged sectors, the Spanish Civil War was not considered to be of vital importance. For the Portuguese, however, this debate was immeasurably relevant and serious as it involved the acceptance or rejection of the new totalitarian and fascist doctrines, questions that would later become the central theme of American society and politics.

The controversy about the Spanish Civil War offers us insight into political dynamics of New Bedford's Portuguese-American community. In order to understand the nature of the controversy, it is important to become familiar with the life of one of the most active writers in the Portuguese-American daily, João Camoesas.[10] As former minister of the republican government, Camoesas attracted the attention of the Portuguese-American community as soon as he arrived in New Bedford. In 1930, the paper noted that "[h]aving given a sterling performance in the medical admissions exam required by law, Dr. João Camoesas is now the new physician of our community."[11] His reputation as a republican party minister stirred the Portuguese population so much that in February 1930 they decided to organize a public unveiling of a portrait of Camoesas at the Clube Republicano Português. The companion article covering the event noted reigning enthusiasm and the presence of many republicans.[12]

The sudden prominence of the recently-arrived João Camoesas did not go unopposed and there was some hostility to his ascent within the local community. As we will see, Camoesas suffered countless public attacks, some of which resulted in rather bizarre episodes, such as the enigmatic and still unsolved mystery of his portrait's theft three years after its unveiling, following the dogged refusal by the Clube Republicano Português's board to hang a portrait of General Óscar Carmona, President of Portugal. At a time when "communists" were ostracized, the *Diário de Notícias* published many articles, most of them at the instigation of Manuel Caetano Pereira, Vice-Consul in Fall River, a Catholic conservative who attempted to brand Camoesas a communist. Continued public accusations that Camoesas was a communist went far beyond the pages of the newspaper. In its January 28th, 1938 edition, the *Diário de Notícias* announced the cancellation of a series of lectures organized by the Popular Culture Committee scheduled for January 30th at the Fall River Ateneu where Camoesas had been invited to speak. At a general meeting, Ateneu directors had decided not to rent out its hall for lectures. António Abrantes, secretary of the meeting, tried to change their minds, but his motion was rejected. Abrantes immediately tendered his resignation, and Francisco A. Santos was elected to take his place.[13]

Camoesas appealed at once for Portuguese-American liberals to unite against what he considered to be a serious affront to freedom of expression. He complained of the social persecution he had suffered as an outspoken critic of the political dictatorships in Portugal and Spain, and said that the time had come to join forces. He felt that the attempts to malign him and sabotage his political career by accusing him of being a communist could also lead to persecution by the American authorities, whom he accused of having orders to obstruct all liberal movements in Fall River. In January 1938, Camoesas sent out an appeal for liberals everywhere to unite, a clear indication of the social and political pressure he was under:

> Everyone who has read my articles knows that I do not advocate Portugal's joining an Iberian soviet republic, that I have not insulted the Catholic Church, that I am not a communist, in short that these and other accusations are stupid, bald-faced lies. Nonetheless, with a terrifying lack of scruples and maniacal tenacity, people continue to accuse me of convictions to which I have never subscribed and have repeatedly denied. People have even gone so far as to publish no doubt distorted translations of some of my articles about communism to exploit the fear of the Fall River Chief of Police and place this employee of democracy in the service of Salazar's dictatorship.... Recourse to such measures shows, first, that our enemies realize that reason is not on their side. It also shows how low they are prepared to stoop. Finally, it is obvious that they are afraid that the people may listen to us. I would like to draw the attention of all liberals to this. Have no doubt that you are feared and that there are those who would nullify your actions by accusing you of subversion.[14]

The Fall River Police wasted no time and banned the lectures and the Ateneu refused to rent out its hall. The *Diário de Notícias* received a letter from the Ateneu's former secretary, António Abrantes, asking that the paper inform its readers of the cancellation of the lectures. Accompanying his somewhat sarcastic request, Abrantes enclosed a leaflet with the themes and dates of the public lectures: "On January 30th, Dr. João Camoesas will speak on 'SCHOOLS' and their role in human progress. The second lecture will take place at the same venue on Sunday February 13 at the same time and its subject will be 'The Pernicious Effects of

Alcoholism' on domestic and social life by the same speaker."[15] In pointing out that the subjects of the lectures were clearly of a civic nature and that Camoesas had been invited because of his experience as a physician, the article stressed the arbitrary, unwise, and anti-democratic nature of the ban.

On February 18th, 1938, the Fall River *Herald News* published an article entitled "Police Here Will Stop All Gatherings of Communists—Police Chief Declares He Will Not Move From His Stand." It contained an interview with Chief Abel J. Violette, who explained in detail why he had banned Camoesas's meeting. The interview confirmed Camoesas' theory that dubious translations of his writings had been sent to the police chief, leading him to the conclusion that Camoesas was a communist and had insulted Americanism and Abraham Lincoln. The *Herald News* articles read:

> "No ministerial association or any other group is going to make me deviate in the least from my opposition to Communism," declared Chief of Police Abel J. Violette today in announcing that he would assume the responsibility for preventing the showing of the motion picture *Heart of Spain* last Friday night in UTW Hall. Chief Violette declared he was not influenced by any fraternal or civic organization in banning the picture and that he stopped its presentation when his attention was called to its proposed showing by the Board of Police because he assumed that Dr. João Camoesas, Taunton, "who I know is a Communist as I have read his writings," was going to speak there.
>
> WILL STOP REDS HERE: "It is nothing new for the Police Department to oppose Communists," said the chief. "The department has driven them from pillar to post for the past twenty years, since the days of the IWW. Every time I can legally stop a Communist meeting here I am going to do so. I urge all persons in charge of the renting of halls to refuse to rent them for Communist meetings. If I know of any Communist meeting being held in this city, I will have men there to arrest any speaker whose remarks are subversive to the government."
>
> INSULT TO AMERICANISM: Chief Violette said the greatest insult to Americanism that Dr. Camoesas made in making arrangements for the showing of the alleged Communistic picture of the Spanish situation was in announcing the meeting was to be held under the auspices of the

> "Friends of Abraham Lincoln." "Lincoln died a martyr to democracy and he was a most religious man." said Chief Violette. "And it 'got' me to find Communists trying to worm their way into this city as friends of that great man. It happens that I was born on Feb. 12, as was Lincoln, and I have read much about him. I know what he stood for and I'm not standing for Communists."[16]

The article referred to the showing of a movie that had never been mentioned by any of the organizers of the session or announced in the leaflets that the *Diário de Notícias* had published at the request of António Abrantes.

The *Diário de Notícias* immediately published a translation of the *Herald News* article, including the interview with Chief Violette in which he labeled João Camoesas a communist and "former parliamentarian and minister of the Portuguese Republic deposed by the present military dictatorship."[17] The article in the *Diário de Notícias,* clearly designed to dignify Camoesas, gives us important information concerning the intervention of the Protestant community in Fall River:

> Chief Violette's statement is a response to the protest published a few days ago by the Association of Protestant Ministers against the arbitrary way in which the authorities of this city, in violation of the law guaranteeing freedom of expression and assembly, have recently prohibited two sessions in which Dr. Camoesas was to have spoken in support of the democratic form of government.[18]

We know of Camoesas's relationship with the Protestant community, as in June 1936 he had given a lecture on "The Cause of the Civil War in Spain" celebrating the eleventh pastorate of Reverend João P. Santos, pastor of Fall River's Portuguese Baptist Church.[19]

Camoesas's sabotaged lecture eventually took place at the headquarters of the Liberal Portuguese Alliance in New Bedford. António Abrantes made sure that this well-attended talk was noted, and the *Diário de Notícias* took up the cause and devoted its front page and all of page three to coverage of this controversial event. The moment was charged with emotion and Camoesas, who received a passionate standing ovation, took care to congratulate the *Diário de Notícias* on its publication of his writings and thoughts as well as those of the defenders of other political convictions:

> In spite of yesterday's stormy weather, by 3 p.m. the hall of the Aliança Liberal Portuguesa was completely full of liberals of all factions, who were there to hear one of the most brilliant lectures that, in the opinion of many, had ever been given in our midst. The former Minister of Education and parliamentary deputy of the Portuguese nation was anxiously awaited. When he entered the headquarters of Aliança Liberal Portuguesa he received a long round of applause. Then, after Dr. João Camoesas had greeted his large audience and praised the impartiality of the *Diário de Notícias* for publishing articles by liberals and their opponents, he began his lecture. "Compatriots and friends, let me begin our conversation by thanking you from the bottom of my heart for your warm welcome. Humble by nature and not in the habit, for a long time now, of allowing myself to be carried away by applause, I cannot ignore the welcome I have had the honor to receive here today. I take it as a sign of the awakening of old Portuguese virtues that the brutality of unwarranted persecutions has spurred more than all my written and spoken words."[20]

Camoesas also spoke of the social and political framework in the Portuguese-American community, pointing to the deep rift that divided Portuguese immigrants in New England:

> We must face current realities courageously and deal with them with the greatest of candor. Trying to ignore or avoid them complicates rather than simplifies them. Let us confess here and now, without euphemisms, that the Portuguese of New England are divided and often fight and attack each other. This deplorable situation is not new and already existed when I began my long exile in this country almost nine years ago.[21]

He ended his talk with a fervent appeal against the fanaticism promoted under Salazar:

> Wake up and work for yourselves and your children. People, like individuals, are the product of their own actions. Don't expect anyone to save you. In our country's history, saviors have always been villains who

not only enslaved the people but also drove them mad, making them wear the blindfolds of ignorance and animalizing them with the stimulants of fanaticism. Our ancestors were great because they earned their greatness and did not trust messiahs.… Dr João Camoesas received prolonged ovations at the end of his lecture. Before he arrived, António Abrantes and António Sameiro also spoke and were applauded.[22]

Manuel Caetano Pereira accused Camoesas of trying to play the martyr and, in an article about the affair, asserted his opposition to Camoesas's writing and justified the police chief's action:

He learned absolutely nothing from the lesson of Fall River. Anyone else would have learned a useful lesson for the past, present and future. Instead of learning, President Camoesas unlearned. He saw in the lesson of Fall River a "satanic conspiracy," "dreadful persecution!"... The documents published prove that all this is completely false. They prove that there was no "conspiracy." Discussing with the authorities a public matter that everyone is discussing and that is of interest to the community, never has been and never will be a "conspiracy," and never has been and never will be an "accusation," and never has been and never will be something that people should be ashamed of. The Fall River authorities acted within the law and regulations of the city, abiding by the Constitution, and acting justifiably for the good of the community.[23]

In a second opinion piece in the *Diário de Notícias*, Caetano Pereira condemned Camoesas for the Fall River incident, attributing his gesture to an ineptitude that was uncharacteristic of such a politically experienced person. His article also introduces another of Camoesas's opponents, the lawyer Francisco J. Carreiro:

On February 11,…the Fall River News section of the *Providence Journal* reported that the movie *Coração na Espanha*, which has been banned in several cities and the showing of which triggered protests in others, will be screened this evening at the U.T.W. hall.... The audience will be addressed by...Dr. João Camosesas from Taunton, the former minister of education in Portugal.... How does President Camoesas, a foreigner, dare to associate his person and his ideas with a communist propaganda

> film that has already been banned in several American cities and that has aroused protests in those where it was shown? Is this not very unwise on the part of President Camoesas?… Counselor Francisco J. Carreiro commented, "…As for Camoesas, the issue is not communism or fascism. For some time now, this gentleman, who is not a citizen of our country, has been preaching rebellion to the people in his articles and speeches. The issue here is peace and order in our community."[24]

Meanwhile, in an article insulting Camoesas and in clear support of Caetano Pereira, A. Leal Furtado, a local Camoesas antagonist, sent out a serious warning to the Taunton physician that his opponents were trying to have him forcibly deported. He stated, "[w]e have even discovered that the American authorities are very surprised that, as the Portuguese government is 'cruel, tyrannical and bloodthirsty,' it has not withdrawn Dr. Camoesas's diplomatic passport. The authorities are right to be surprised."[25] Camoesas's response was firm: he denied ever having subscribed to communist ideals; reiterated his stance as a Christian Democrat; gave explicit examples of occasions on which his opponents had misconstrued his statements in order to convince people he was a communist; and refuted allegations by Caetano Pereira and Leal Furtado. He had never left Taunton to go to the Fall River lecture and had never, therefore, come up against any police officers. He accused his opponents of distorting his positions and resorting to vile slurs.[26]

In order to defend himself against the machinations of Leal Furtado and Counselor Carreira, Camoesas spoke about his time in Africa, giving details that proved the legality of his presence in America. He had an official document published to refute the accusation that he was in the U.S. out of the good will of the Salazar government:[27]

> In the almost nine years that I have lived here, I have never had occasion to regret my choice of place of exile. The Americans of all categories with whom I have had contact have always treated me with deference and attention that are hard to forget. Many have even said how pleased they would be to see me join the ranks of their fellow citizens, while still respecting my reasons for remaining loyal to a country whose government and representatives persecute me instead of protecting me as they should. I can also truthfully say that my loyalty to Portugal involves sub-

> stantial material losses that make it something of a very expensive luxury. Finally, sad rather than offended, I would like to point out that only some people who call themselves Portuguese, at no inconvenience to me but with clear moral discredit to themselves, have dared to question my legal right to reside in the United States.... As a result, like so many others, I have been the victim of the most cowardly, merciless wrongs. The brutality went so far as to prevent me from stopping in Lisbon to say goodbye to members of my family, some unfortunately for the last time, when I came back from Africa on my way to the United States.[28]

Meanwhile, on March 1st, the *Diário de Notícias* wrote that the banning of Camoesas's meeting might result in internal disciplinary action against Fall River's Chief of Police. The editorial included the chief's response:

> "I will welcome the action with which I have been threatened to clear up this matter once and for all," Chief Abel J. Violette told us today, saying that a man claiming to be a lawyer by the name of John Landfield, of 18 Milk St., Boston, had visited him the day before and threatened to sue him for banning the movie *Coração de Espanha* on the grounds that it was communist and was going to be screened at the UTW Hall of this city on February 11.[29]

This development was later confirmed in an article entitled "Two Fall River Officials, the Mayor and Chief of Police, Sued for Banning the Showing of a Film about the Spanish War."[30] Translated from an unnamed Boston newspaper, the article reported that the Civil Liberties Committee of Massachusetts had brought civil suit against Mayor Alexander C. Murray and Chief of Police Violette over the incident with Camoesas.

The political debate in the Portuguese-language newspapers in the thirties made the vanguard wonder what to think and do regarding the new social doctrines that were appearing around the ideological legacy generically known as "liberal" or "republican" in Portugal. It also raised questions about the totalitarian legacy born out of anti-communism that would have dissimilar influences in Portugal and America in decades to come. Fascism, Nazism, republicanism, anarchism, socialism and communism were concepts that went beyond mere intellectual theories or political labels and had come to constitute concrete realities affecting people's daily lives. They were real professions of faith that stirred up fierce rivalries and intense debates around what were fundamentally different social ideals.

The Portuguese-American Debate

The *Diário de Notícias* opened its columns to the Portuguese-American community's greatest ideological debate of the 1930s. We find evidence of positions that, on one hand, placed the Portuguese homeland on a nostalgic pedestal and, on the other, adamantly rejected a dictatorship diametrically opposed to American rights to freedom of expression and assembly. The country, whose hospitality, freedom, and prosperity all Portuguese immigrants accepted and admired, and that was considered a bastion of democracy, served as a significant yardstick for assessing and critiquing what was happening in Salazar's Portugal.

This debate can be traced back to the first two decades of the 20th century when Portugal was unable to maintain its parliamentary democracy. The successive crises and armed uprisings during this period led to Gomes da Costa's disorderly coup in 1926, which aimed to restore the state's authority. In this context, how do we draw a line between necessary, transitory authoritarianism and a permanent denial of democratic freedoms? What position should we take with regard to the Portuguese government's political program that was so far removed from American or British-style liberalism? What can we say about the collaboration between Spain's fascist forces and the Portuguese government during the Spanish Civil War, a period in which well-known Americans were fighting for the restoration of democracy in Spain? This fascism was regarded with apprehension in the United States. As Harold L. Ickes, Secretary of the Interior under Roosevelt, noted in 1938, "Fascism is the most treacherous and dangerous enemy that we must prepare to fight as soon as possible."[31] Further, he doubted "the motives or intelligence of those who want us to join forces against the almost imaginary danger of Communism, while Fascism is knocking on the door of our citadel of freedom."[32]

From the Portuguese-American point of view, Portugal in the thirties was on the ideological threshold between liberalism and conservativism. The question was how far could a nation compromise its citizens' individual liberties in order to guarantee its economic recovery. To what extent could this strategy be legitimately deployed without turning into the totalitarian greed characteristic of other countries in Europe? These were questions that other countries were already grappling with and that the U.S. would soon have to confront.

The U.S. during this time was by no means a secure haven for its immigrants. The harsh economic crisis was considered by many to be an eloquent demonstration of the failure of its political system. In February 1938, in an article entitled "*O Século*—The Greatest Destroyer of Morale in Portugal," João Mattos, one of the writers of *Diário de Notícias*, berated the paper for being a "[c]hampion of all lies made up by unscrupulous people. It has been amusing itself for a while now, for lack of anything better to do, by insulting the great American Nation and its illustrious president, His Excellency Mr. Franklin Delano Roosevelt."[33] Mattos wrote that the journalist João Pereira da Rosa, "ignorant and short-sighted, hurls veiled insults to show the superiority of Dictatorships, regimes of crime and oppression, over Democracies, regimes of goodness, freedom, love and fraternity."[34] He accused the writer of knowing nothing about the country he was insulting, unlike other journalists who could give a truer vision of the U.S.

As we can see, the political position of the Portuguese in America was essentially ambivalent. The more conservative Portuguese-American intellectuals in the thirties found in the Estado Novo and Oliveira Salazar a second chance to recover the lost progress of the Portuguese nation. Their stance was, however, shaken by the fact that Salazar's regime was an anti-liberal dictatorship, and, as such, repugnant to American sensibilities. On the other hand, the more liberal faction was constantly called on to explain that one was no less patriotic for advocating a different system of government for one's country. Affinity to the Portuguese homeland did not, they argued, preclude condemning Portugal's political system and its affinities with Europe's totalitarian regimes.

Defense of American democratic ideals also did not keep Portuguese immigrants from leveling critiques at their host society. The U.S. was admired for being free and welcoming, but the American system was criticized for reserving only menial jobs for an overwhelming majority of the Portuguese-American population. Very few members of the Portuguese community held prominent positions. A number of episodes involving the Portuguese community in the thirties plainly showed that the local authorities did not always demonstrate the tolerance enshrined in the Constitution and that freedom was clearly limited. The U.S. did not readily tolerate being the target of attacks from non-natives, even when the critiques were justified.

We cannot say, however, that there was any kind of rift between American authorities and the Portuguese-American community during this period. On the contrary, they were very close. In the different elections in the thirties, the Portuguese vote was recognizably more than enough to decide who would govern the city, and so this electorate received abundant gestures of deference from the authorities, who always showed due consideration to Portuguese-American people, organizations and initiatives, regardless of their political orientation.

Some bonds united—at least to a certain extent—the different political sensibilities of Portuguese-Americans. The daily editions of the *Diário de Notícias* show that, according to the Portuguese community, Americans either regarded Portugal in an unfavorable light or were completely indifferent to things Portuguese. This was a constant offense to the immigrants' sensibilities, and the community welcomed any initiatives that increased the visibility of Portugal and the Portuguese-American community. From fostering tourism to parades on Portugal Day to visits by Portuguese warships to the World's Fair in New York, everything was designed to draw attention to a distant homeland that was to be respected and defended. Even so, these events were not enough for people to abandon long-held political principles or even to build temporary bridges between the different political factions in New Bedford.

* * *

We find richly dissimilar and charismatic voices in the *Diário de Notícias,* and the paper welcomed them all throughout its almost six decades of existence. Discretion and equanimity marked its posture at all times, and while there were virulent arguments, almost all of them came from its writers who jousted one another, each determined to stand up for his convictions. The *Diário de Notícias* witnessed but did not instigate these controversies. It never avoided a dispute and always expressed opinions. Pagination and layout details suggest that the editors of the *Diário de Notícias* were not afraid to foster debates, as they regularly placed controversial articles side-by-side in provocative ways. These seemingly technical decisions strengthened the paper's image of impartiality and independence from the political ideas it covered. The front page on May 27, 1938, a critical date, clearly illustrated this concern for impartiality. One column featured an article on friendly telegrams exchanged by General Francisco Franco and General Óscar Carmona, in which Portugal officially recognized the new Spanish government.[35] The middle columns featured a report on the accidental bombing of Cerberre and Port Bou on the French border by "Fascist war planes."[36] The right-hand column described a ceremony by exiled democrats in Paris in honor of Afonso Costa, whom the article called "one of the most vigorous builders of Portuguese democracy"[37] and a distinguished statesman forced into exile by Salazar. These and many other articles show the care taken by the *Diário de Notícias* to ensure a complete, multi-faceted vision of political and social realities.

At a time in history when there were calls to espouse or reject some ideology or other every day, the *Diário de Notícias* staunchly resisted the temptation to adhere to the institutional interests of either its country of origin or its host country. It was able to remain equidistant between militant opposition and the status quo and kept its doors open to all genuine currents of opinion, but closed them, as far as possible, to anonymous malevolence. Over the years, the paper responded with determination to any attempts to break its neutrality. Thanks to its fifty-four years of steadfast defense of freedom of expression, the *Diário de Notícias*, the only Portuguese-language daily ever published outside Portugal, is an eloquent, lasting illustration of the historical role that Portuguese-American periodicals played in the defense of democratic ideals. These journalists and writers demonstrated careful attention, acuity, opportunity and patriotic spirit in their reporting of what was happening in Portugal and the world and what was being said and written about Portugal. The *Diário de Notícias* would achieve considerable public recognition from President Harry Truman when in June 1949 he sent a letter paying tribute to the newspaper's coverage of Portuguese-American troops in World War II and noted that the paper "has been an effective force in championing our democratic system."[38] We can certainly say that the *Diário de Notícias* constituted a forum of free dialogue concerning Salazar's regime, where all sectors of opinion could defend their ideas, resulting in a real pluralism of convictions that was unparalleled in Portugal.

Notes

*This article was translated from the Portuguese by Wendy Graça.

[1] Knaught, Percy. 1946. *Time* magazine, July 22, U.S. Edition, Vol. XLVIII No. 4.

[2] May 28th, 1926, is the date of the decisive right-wing military coup conducted by General Gomes da Costa, that put an abrupt end to an embryonic liberal Portuguese First Republic, thus allowing the National Dictatorship to begin, which would later lead to the Estado Novo under Salazar's rule.

[3] It is not possible to read most of the Portuguese-language newspapers published before 1940. With the exception of the University of Massachusetts, Dartmouth Library holdings of the New Bedford *Diário de Notícias* and the Boston Public Library holding of *Novidades*, there is not a single complete collection of periodicals in Portuguese in any of the many libraries in New England. The disappearance of newspapers like *O Independente, A Voz da Colónia, O Popular, A Tribuna,* and *O Colonial* is particularly troubling. At best, we find only a few editions of these papers or, at worst, we find no trace at all. We know from other sources that they contained heated debates and local discussions.

[4] We would like to stress the important role of the Boston Public Library where the Massachusetts Newspaper Program is based. In 1986, it began to collect and preserve ethnic newspapers, microfilming them and making them available to the public. The Massachusetts Newspaper Program is part of the United States Newspaper Program sponsored by the National Endowment for the Humanities, which aims to create a guide to help the academic community locate and catalog all extinct newspapers ever published in the United States.

[5] "Alvorada Jornal Diário," *Alvorada*, January 1, 1919, 1:2.

[6] *Diário de Notícias*, 23, 24, 25 July 1946.

[7] M.E. Glade and J.R. Giese, *Immigration: Pluralism and National Identity*, Public Issues Series, Social Science Education Consortium, 1989. Concerning this sudden limitation of Portuguese immigration, Euclides Goulart da Costa, Consul-General of Portugal in Boston in 1936, in the presence of Cardinal Cerejeira, who was visiting New Bedford, bemoaned "the fact that the colony had ceased to grow due to a shortage of new blood from the homeland to enliven it." In "A Homenagem dos Portugueses de New Bedford ao Senhor Cardial Patriarca de Lisboa," *Diário de Notícias*, September 16, 1936, 5274:1.

[8] The Boston Public Library has a microfilmed collection of some editions of the Fall River *Novidades* from 1917 to 1948, when it closed down. It only has *O Independente* for 1942 on microfilm.

[9] An unofficial note from the government confirming its neutrality in the World War: "Fortunately, the duties arising from our alliance with Great Britain, which we wish to confirm at such a grave moment, do not oblige us to abandon our neutrality in this emergency." In "Portugal perante o conflito europeu," *Diário de Notícias*, May 10, 1939, 6198:1.

[10] João José da Conceição Camoesas was born on March 13, 1887 in the town of Elvas, where he graduated from high school and was owner and editor of the regional newspaper, *A Fronteira.* He was a prominent member of the Portuguese Republican Party, head of the Lisbon Municipal Department of Hygiene and was elected parliamentary deputy for Elvas and for Portalegre. He was appointed Minister of Public Education in 1923 in the government of António Maria da Silva. He held the same position in the government of Domingos Pereira in 1925. After the 1926 revolution he was deported to Angola in 1928; and in 1930 he went into exile in the U.S. He settled in Taunton, Massachusetts where he set up a medical practice. He died there on November 12, 1951.

[11] "Os portugueses na América," *Diário de Notícias*, May 13, 1930, 1023:1.

[12] An excellent and prolific speaker, João Camoesas name is linked to a number of social projects for Portuguese-Americans, such as the founding of the Aliança Liberal Portuguesa [Portuguese Liberal Alliance], a regional political association, and a cooperative defending the economic and social interests of Portuguese immigrants that he called Acção Social Portuguêsa [Portuguese Social Action], a project to which Camoesas devoted much energy. See "Acção Social Portuguesa—Aspecto Económico," *Diário de Notícias*, November 19, 1937, 5633:1, 2.

[13] "O Sr. Dr. João Camoesas não vai falar no Ateneu Português em Fall River" [Dr. João Camoesas will not be speaking at the Ateneu Português in Fall River] *Diário de Notícias*, January 19, 1938, 5690:1.

[14] João Camoesas, "Anotação á Margem—Reflexões para os liberais,"*Diário de Notícias*, January 29, 1938, 5691: 1.

[15] An article covering the controversy states, "Some people, for whom the words 'Popular Culture, School and Education' inspire terror, played the despicable role of informers upon hearing of the issue and went running to the police, denouncing everything that is communist and accusing Dr

João Camoesas of being a creature who does nothing else but spread Stalinist doctrines." *Diário de Notícias*, January 19, 1938, 5691:1.

[16] "Police Here Will Stop All Gatherings of Communists—Police Chief Declares He Will Not Move From His Stand," *Fall River Herald News*, February 18, 1938:1.

[17] "O chefe de Polícia de Fall River classifica de comunista o Dr. João Camoesas, antigo ministro do regime democrático português," *Diário de Notícias*, February 19, 1938, 5709:1.

[18] Ibid.

[19] "O Sr. Dr. Camoesas vai realizar uma Conferência em Fall River," *Diário de Notícias,* June 24, 1937, 5510:1.

[20] "A Conferência do Dr. Camoesas na séde da Aliança L. Portuguesa," *Diário de Notícias*, February 21, 1938, 5710: 1.

[21] Ibid.

[22] Ibid.

[23] Manuel Caetano Pereira, "Ao de leve—Em defesa da Verdade a bem da Colónia—I. Mais um mártir?", *Diário de Notícias*, February 23, 1938, 5711: 1.

[24] Manuel Caetano Pereira, "Ao de leve—Em defesa da Verdade a bem da Colónia—II. A Lição de Fall River," *Diário de Notícias*, February 26, 1938, 5714: 1,7.

[25] A. Leal Furtado, "Em louvor do Dr. Reineta," *Diário de Notícias*, March 1, 1937, 5716: 1.

[26] João Camoesas, "Anotação à margem—Chagas à vela," *Diário de Notícias,* March 4, 1938, 5719: 1,8.

[27] João Camoesas, "Anotação à margem—Documento Elucidativo," *Diário de Notícias*, March 14, 1938, 5727: 1,5.

[28] João Camoesas, "Anotação à margem—Documento Elucidativo," *Diário de Notícias*, March 14, 1938, 5727: 1,5.

[29] "A supressão do filme "Coração de Espanha" em Fall River—A atitude do Chefe de Polícia daquela cidade contra a sua exibição traz-lhe ameaça de processo," *Diário de Notícias*, March 1, 1938, 5716: 1.

[30] "Foram processados dois oficiais do município de Fall River—O Mayor e o Chefe de Policia são acusados de prohibirem a exibição dum filme da guerra espanhola," *Diário de Notícias,* March 3, 1938, 5718: 8.

[31] "Ickes diz que o Fascismo é o pior inimigo—pede acção agora; afirma que o perigo comunista é imaginário,'" *Diário de Notícias,* April 4, 1938, 5745: 1.

[32] Ibid.

[33] "O Século": o maior destruidor da moral em Portugal," *Diário de Notícias*, February 15, 1938, 5705: 1.

[34] Ibid.

[35] "O Reconhecimento do Govêrno de Espanha pelo Govêrno Português—telegramas trocados entre o Generalíssimo Franco e o Sr. Presidente da República," *Diário de Notícias*, May 27, 1938, 5790:1.

[36] "Os Fascistas bombardearam uma vila francesa—Os oficiais da fronteira crêem que a invasão foi acidental," *Diário de Notícias*, May 27, 1938, 5790: 1.

[37] "No primeiro aniversário do falecimento do Dr. Afonso Costa—como foi comemorada a lutuosa data pelos exilados políticos em Paris—O discurso do Dr. Bernardino Machado," *Diário de Notícias*, May 27, 1938, 5790: 1.

[38] "Uma Mensagem de Sua Exa. o Presidente Harry S. Truman ao *Diário de Notícias,*" *Diário de Notícias*, July 18, 1949, 9152: 1.

CHAPTER 9

Media-Made Events: Revisiting the Case of Big Dan's[1]

ONÉSIMO TEOTÓNIO ALMEIDA

In 1983, in the city of New Bedford, Massachusetts—home of a Portuguese community of over 100,000 people largely from the Azores—a gang rape took place at a local bar called Big Dan's in a rundown section of the city. A description of the incident in Wikipedia offers a brief synopsis, a kind of collective memory of the events:

> Cheryl Ann Araujo (1961-1986) was an American rape victim whose case became national news, and was the basis of the 1988 film *The Accused.* Araujo was gang-raped at age 21 by four men on a pool table in a tavern while other patrons watched but did not interfere. During the prosecution, the defendants' attorneys used cross-examination of Araujo to such an extent that the case became widely seen as a template for "blaming the victim" in rape cases. The case also raised tensions between the Portuguese-American community and other ethnic groups in New Bedford. Her case was widely known as the Big Dan's rape. Cheryl Ann Araujo's oldest daughter turned 3 on March 6, 1983, and the 21-year-old mother, both daughters and their father had thrown a party to celebrate. After the festivities had died down and the girls were put to bed, Araujo left her home to buy cigarettes. Her usual spots were closed, so she stopped at Big Dan's tavern in New Bedford, Massachusetts. Two men approached and demanded that she follow them out of the bar. She refused and proceeded to leave on her own when she was subsequently grabbed from behind and manhandled onto a pool table where the two men were joined by two other men who took turns raping her. The patrons in the bar heard cries for help, and some applauded the men. None came to Araujo's aid. Eventually Araujo freed

> herself, whereupon she ran half-naked into the street screaming that she had been raped. Three college students passing by in a van came upon Araujo in the street and drove her to the nearest hospital. Six men were originally charged with the rape, and four were ultimately convicted of the crime in a trial that attracted international attention. The rapists received sentences of 9 to 12 years. A fictionalized cinema treatment, *The Accused* (1988), starring Jodie Foster and Kelly McGillis, was based on the case. Foster won an Academy Award for her portrayal of the character based on Araujo.[2]

This transformation into a national and international story began when the local newspaper, *The Standard Times*, reported the events with grand histrionics that even a year later could not be confirmed. The *Times* reported a rape perpetrated by six men over two hours against a woman who simply stopped at the bar to buy cigarettes. The paper also spoke of at least a dozen bystanders who not only witnessed the crime, but also applauded the drama. Later on a group of women, led by a Luso-American woman, organized a vigil calling the attention of the media to the incident. The event took on even more of a life of its own when, for the first time in the U.S., the trial was broadcast on television. Until then, only sketch artists were allowed to draw the portraits we have been accustomed to seeing in the press and on television, and not even photographers could enter the courtroom.[3] During the trial, 10,000 Portuguese from Fall River and surrounding communities organized a march in front of City Hall, protesting the bias of many of the media reports, where generalizations and prejudicial judgments were directly or indirectly being made about the community. Many of those who marched were upset at the distorted coverage of the events being offered by the media that differed wildly from versions circulating within the community. Also many thought that the event was not much different from similar stories happening throughout the U.S., many of them on college campuses.

In June of 1995, the Azorean Forum, a civic group that organizes debates on a variety of social and political issues, assembled a roundtable of commentators to revisit the case, taking advantage of the greater media awareness of the event garnered by the release of a documentary film on the same subject by Diana Andringa, a journalist from the Lisbon-based *Diário de Notícias*. Adelaide Baptista,[4] João Luís de Medeiros,[5] and I were asked for comments on the film. João Luís Medeiros could not attend but sent a text expressing very much the same point of view as the one presented here.[6]

Instead of giving the history of the long process, I opted instead to focus on a few important documents that collectively convey the essential facts of the case. This dossier opens with a letter of mine directed to *The New York Times* in March of 1984:

On the Ethics of Media-Made Events

> The alleged rape case in "Big Dan's" bar, New Bedford, Mass, provides us with a poignant case for analysis of the media's power to create events.
>
> Events are indeed built upon some facts. But to create a good media-made event one has to be selective. One must choose only some of the facts, and not necessarily distort them, for they can be presented with relative accuracy. They must, however, be transposed to another context and, to be powerful, they must be used to serve a cause that carries momentum.
>
> Take the "Big Dan's" story. Supposedly (and so the story event has been spread everywhere for a year), six men for two hours raped on a pool table an innocent woman who just happened to stop at bar to buy a pack of cigarettes. If this were not bad enough, fifteen men watched and cheered from the bar counter.
>
> The story was super. A black and white case of an innocent victim of six Latin villain male chauvinists. The New Bedford *Standard Times* did not blink. It had a story right from the victim's mouth. Soon, the whole nation had an ugly but beautiful example, usable for many purposes, because it provided both prototype and symbol for those concerned with the escalation of violence in the U.S.; for the feminists and the defenders of women's rights; and, still, for the observers and analysts of our collective moral behavior who are alarmed over the apathy and growing withdrawal and neutrality of witnesses to crimes.
>
> In New Bedford, however, and in the surrounding community, those who know the city's neighborhoods and its immigrant subculture had

doubts about the media's "facts" from the very beginning and soon came to know another version of those "facts." Concern over this discrepancy was voiced by a considerable number of people in the community, but it was done in a non-English language and consequently not widely heard. Even when heard, moreover, the voices presenting the other side of the story were dismissed as obvious indications of either a sign of the acceptance of male freedom or machismo in Portuguese culture ("the Portuguese are Latins, therefore..."), or, a sheer case of turning the blame on the victim.

Journalist after journalist passed through New Bedford and reproduced the accuser's story, not bothering to listen to the version of the accused. They did not allow any of the people they heard in the community to spoil with different "facts" the "nice" story that would carry their journalistic masterpieces to print.

Now the trial is on. From six, the number of alleged rapists has been brought down to four, and no longer is there any mention of successive rapes. From an episode lasting two hours, we are now left with one lasting fifteen minutes. From an inadvertent stop to buy cigarettes, we now hear that the woman had several drinks and had even offered to buy drinks for the guys. She did not, apparently, go there to buy cigarettes. The erstwhile cheering crowd is not even mentioned. And there seems to be more to come.

But this letter is not an attempt at proving the innocence of the alleged rapists, but simply an effort to de-mythicize the case built up by the media. If the "Big Dan's" case is an instance of rape, it is now evident that the truth of what happened there differs greatly from the wildly inflated account hitherto purveyed by the media. As it appears now, it is an ugly case of rape (as Prosecutor Raymond Veary put it, "a story without heroes") but one that is by no means deserving of the national attention it has received, especially in light of all the other crimes the nation has been witnessing. Most of the Portuguese in this country come from the islands of the Azores—where rape is rare. A tired cliché around southeastern New England pictures them as Catholic, traditional, hardworking, and law-abiding. This immigrant community, with an exemplary public record for decency, now sees its name in the national news on a daily basis associated with a mode of behavior which, even if it were accurately described (and it is not), would in no way mirror the community, not to mention the fact that it takes place in a well-known bar of ill repute, where a subculture has established itself, against the will of the community.

But whose fault is this? Who is to blame for this publicizing only one side of the story, promoting an inaccurate stereotype of a community to a nation that readily believes that Latins are male chauvinists (and thus potential rapists), and that for the most part even ignores the very presence of that community in the country, not to mention its "moral" record, precisely because it never makes news (for it has a history of a quiet, though active, low-profile presence—a virtue which in turn is responsible for its having let the story grow wild in the devouring power of the media)? Causes need motivating prototypical examples, but the media and the defenders of those causes do not have the right to create them just because their potential existence will help such a cause.

Such interested groups have an undeniable obligation to double-check their facts so that victims are not immolated for their causes. This is particularly the case when stories happen to arise in environments, cultures or small worlds with which they are not familiar. When the story seems too good to be true, extra caution is in order.

Journalists and editors claim to know all this. "Mistakes happen," they will answer. But few of them have the bravery to come out and apologize. That is the nature of news. And thus victims are doubly victimized, as a result of the moral cause of the times, and the cause of journalism.

* * *

The letter, addressed to the *Op-Ed* page of *The New York Times* was never published. I called the newspaper twice. At first they informed me that the text was scheduled to be printed shortly. After a week I called once more only to be told that despite the importance of the article, its window of opportunity had closed. An international story had captivated public opinion and taken the available space at the newspaper—a confirmation, ironically, of exactly the subject matter of the article itself.[7]

The following month, *The New York Times* published an article by Jonathan Friendly entitled "The New Bedford Rape Case: Confusion Over Accounts Of Cheering At Bar." Here we reproduce some excerpts:

> Alan Levin, a reporter for *The Standard Times* of New Bedford, Mass., tried to find out who did the cheering. So did Fred Bayles, a reporter for The Associated Press. So did a score of other reporters, from the television networks and the news magazines and the big national newspapers, sent to New Bedford, to write about the reported gang rape in Big Dan's Tavern.
>
> The image of a barful of patrons cheering while a woman was raped was what made the event particularly horrible and especially newsworthy. The picture that emerged at the trial of the six men[8] ultimately charged was quite different, and it affirmed the version offered by the bar owners three weeks after the attack [in contrast to what the press stated in accord with the victim's account]....
>
> In interviews, the reporters said they were bothered by the disparity between the first accounts, based on what the woman told the police, and the version that began to emerge two or three weeks later. But they said they were busy covering the flow of events such as the arrests, the protest marches and the ethnic tensions in the community that they had little time to go back and try to alter the public vision of what had happened.
>
> "Initial impressions stay on," Mr. Bayles said.
>
> In the calmer atmosphere of the trial, the woman acknowledged differences in her testimony and her report to the police, but said she had been distraught at that time of the report.

The article by the writer for *The New York Times* continues under the heading "Reports in Error":

> Journalists and academics interviewed said they could not recall another case in which such a crucially newsworthy element of a story, one that strongly influenced public opinion, was subsequently found to be so misleading....
>
> John M. Impemba, a *Standard Times* reporter who now works for *The Boston Herald*, said the woman's description was consistently evoked by the prosecutor, Ronald A. Pina, in the first two weeks after the assault. "We asked, 'Why can't you give us a number?'" Mr. Impemba said, "I can't."

Friendly, after acknowledging the fact that three weeks removed from the crime, the lawyer for the proprietor of the bar had already denied the existence of the fifteen onlookers applauding, remarks:

> But the story had momentum, and reporters were so busy chasing new developments that they had little time to worry about a matter that was an accepted "fact."
>
> "It is difficult to deflate the scale of a story" once it has attracted national attention, noted Dudley Clendinen, a reporter for *The New York Times* who wrote the paper's first full-scale article about the incident and the city. That story, which attributed the account to the woman's report to the police, said she had been "tormented and raped beyond count by a group of men" at Big Dan's while "the rest of the men in the bar stood watching, sometimes taunting her and cheering."
>
> His article appeared 10 days after the rape, and *The Times* had no other major articles on the case until Feb. 5, just before the trial started nearly a year later. That later article said, in the 17th of 22 paragraphs, that the initial police account might have been exaggerated.
>
> *The Times'* articles about the trial testimony noted the discrepancy, but its March 18 and March 23 reports of the convictions reiterated the victim's description of cheering patrons and omitted the testimony that the only cheering was by the two men who were acquitted.

"In retrospect, we should have been more specific," said David R. Jones, the national news editor. The last *Times* account of the sentencing March 26, pointed out the difference between the early reports and the defense's description.

Even when it became clear before the trial that the initial account was at least open to question, that fact was subordinated in articles. *The Los Angeles Times*, in an article last month as the trial neared an end, was apparently the first major news organization to call direct attention to the discrepancy.

Jon Katz, executive producer of the CBS Morning News program, said the program tried to address the discrepancy after the verdicts through a joint interview with one of the prosecutors, Robert Kane, and one of the defense lawyers, Judith Lindahl. In that interview, Mrs. Lindahl said the initial story "was in fact a year-long opening statement,[9] and it planted in the public mind and, indeed, the minds of the jurors a view of the case which simply was not true."

Despite the evidence, the impression of a tavern crowded with hooting onlookers persists, even among journalists who have been following the case.

The Cable News Network telecast several hours of testimony every day of the month-long trial. Asked later why the network found the case so interesting, the executive producer, Larry LaMotte, cited the brutality of the crime and the upheaval in the community.

"And of course," he said, "there was the cheering."

After having read the article in the *The New York Times*, I again wrote a letter to the editor of the newspaper, which again was not published:

Providence, April 16, 1984
Dear Sir,
I was satisfied, yet surprised, to see your article (April 11) accusing the media of failing in their responsibility in the Big Dan's rape case, specifi-

cally the fact that the journalists never addressed the issue of what really happened being different from the initial reports.

I found the reporters' explanations quite laughable. According to your article they were "bothered by the disparity" but "were busy covering the flow of events such as the arrests, the protest marches and the ethnic tensions in the community that they had little time to go back and try to alter the public vision of what had happened."

This is an insulting mystification. If they were in truth so occupied by the events, they would have realized that the agitation in the community was precisely the discrepancy between what the community knew of the case and what the media was doing with the information.

The reporters (and I spoke with many) did not want to hear anything that was not sufficiently appetizing to constitute "news." The protest marches were simply a culmination of this: a community absolutely revolted with the media's manipulation. The media never wanted to rectify the situation. (Of that I am a witness.)

One final impression: your article declares that *The Los Angeles Times* was the first newspaper of great circulation to call the discrepancy to the attention of the readers. *The New York Times* could have done so much earlier. On March 13 (when the trial was still underway), I sent an article entitled "On the Ethics of Media-Made Events" to your Op-Ed page which took up the very topic of the behavior of the media in this case. It was delicately communicated to me that other events were slightly more urgent and deserving of the *Times'* attention.

Now, after the media's milking of the case until the very last drop, some elements of the media come forward saying they were mistaken. It's never too late, right? Nevertheless, the damage suffered by the Portuguese community is irremediable.

* * *

With the passing of time, the public began to slowly forget the Big Dan's rape case and, as anticipated, with calming of the collective nerves someone would revisit the issue with a critical eye missing from the reporting. The measured analysis actually came from a feminist researching the way the media treated victims of sex crimes in the last decade. In her book, *Virgin or Tramp*, Helen Benedict identifies the tendency to paint victims as either virgins or trash and reviews the problematic dynamics of media coverage of the Big Dan's case:

> [T]he press was indirectly responsible for the Portuguese turning against the victim. Without Portuguese reporters or speakers, the local American papers were unable to portray the community in a non-stereotypical way, unable to find people who had not blindly turned against the victim, and unable to win the trust of the victim's family and friends in order to represent her side. The result was that the case polarized into the liberal American media versus the New Bedford Portuguese, which filled the local people with such a sense of injustice that they turned on the victim as a scapegoat. This was not entirely the press's fault, but it was certainly exacerbated by its failures....
>
> As a result, the media came in for a lot of blame in post-case analyses, some of it undeserved, much of it well-earned. With all this criticism in mind, I asked the reporters on the case what they thought, in retrospect, of their coverage of Big Dan's.
>
> Ellsworth of *O Jornal*, who is now a lawyer, said she thought that her paper had done a good job and that she was particularly impressed with the *The Standard Times* reporters: "They were these unassuming, quiet, relatively unsophisticated people compared to the out-of-town press. They would just sit in the press room and not say a whole lot and write stories that were better than anything else anyone was putting out." She was less impressed with the out-of-town press: "I remember being appalled at the patronizing, nasty attitude that some of the out-of-town reporters had about the defendants. About the victim, too, but primarily about the defendants.... I couldn't actually hear the trial sometimes because these guys and women were making jokes and yuk-yuking. I said to myself, "How hypocritical. Here are these nice liberals moaning and groaning about what happened to this poor victim, and what they really feel is that the defendants are trash, the victim is trash and this is a big circus." Ellsworth added that

she did not think that condescending attitude showed in the reporters' stories, but it is possible that the Portuguese thought otherwise, which might have contributed to their resentment toward the American press and, by proxy, the victim.

Estes, who still works for *The Boston Herald,* said this about her paper's coverage: "That was a period of time when editors here didn't have a lot of qualms about anything. Rupert Murdoch had just bought the paper. Now it's transformed, but we had Murdoch-style editors then. They were trying to make an impression and no holds were barred."

Kukielski of *The Providence Journal,* said he did not know what else his paper could have done on the victim's side, but wished his paper had stepped back more from the case: "I would have liked to do more analysis along the way. When I look back over my clips, I remember how the story was shooting off like a skyrocket in all different directions. I wish there had been more opportunity to put these things in context."

A solution to this confusion could have been to assign someone to do a weekly news analysis of the story. The analysis could have been done by an editor, a columnist, an ombudsman, a reporter not on the case, or a guest writer with some expertise on the subject of sex crimes. The analyst could have explained the technicalities of the charges, the myths of rape, the methods of attorneys, the history of discrimination against the Portuguese, and could have kept an eye on the balance of the reporting. It is possible that an aloof, outside eye could have prevented the reporters from dwelling so unfairly on the anti-victim side and from allowing their class prejudices to inflame the Portuguese.

Charig, one of those "unassuming" reporters Ellsworth praised, had this to say about the Big Dan's case and its coverage: "I've never seen a case where everybody came away so hurt and so disillusioned.... I've covered a lot of court cases and I don't think I have seen one where there was less sense of justice. So many lives were torn to shreds." (Benedict 1992, 145)

Benedict concludes the chapter with the observation that:

> As a result, the Big Dan's case will not be forgotten. It revealed the raw underside of American society—the conflict between men and women, the suspicion of everyone toward victims, and the mutual hatred between settled Americans and those seen as foreign, lower-class, non-white, or "other"—and it revealed the way those elements can seduce and bias the press. The themes of class, race, and gender prejudice come up again and again in sex-related crimes, as will be seen in the next two cases, and they point to a reason why these crimes are so significant as mirrors of our society: They are not just stories of isolated, bizarre cases, they are stories that lay bare the forces underlying all our social interaction. As such they are essential for the press to cover wisely and well. (1992, 145)

I suggest that in addition to the subheading in Andringa's film of "A Case of Rape in a Community," we add "and the case of a rape of a community."[11]

* * *

To prove once again that myths rarely die, journalistic coverage of the incident by a newspaper in Ponta Delgada decided to completely ignore the facts I cited in my commentary.[10] Instead of referring directly to them, the journalist repeated what other papers such as *The New York Times*, *The Los Angeles Times*, and others had said before their corrections and subsequent self-criticism.[12]

Facing yet another wave of repetitive clichés, this time in the native land of the demonstrators, I sent the following letter to the *Açoriano Oriental*:[13]

> Ponta Delgada, July 3, 1995
> To the Editor-in-Chief:
>
> The report in your newspaper of the session of the Azorean Forum dedicated to the revisiting of the gang rape case in New Bedford, Massachusetts, twelve years ago, known as "Big Dan's," included various inaccuracies, many of which are important; but the nucleus of my criticism and primary motivation for this interposition is, without having directly cited my work, the very title of your report is an affirmation I made at the time of the case....

My work was not simply an accusation of the American media. Yes, I read excerpts of self-critical texts of the treatment of the case by the American media. It is not an everyday occurrence that *The New York Times* and *The Los Angeles Times* publish corrections because of their acceptance at face value of essential facts that weren't confirmed. It was never doubted that there was a crime, but there were many as to the reasons for attributing the ensuing circus to the case.

I gather that the excerpts I read were eloquently written. I even cited the work of a feminist, Helen Benedict, *Virgin or Tramp*, published in 1992 by the Oxford University Press, a series of criticisms and harsh self-assessments of the journalists and social scientists saying more or less what was stated in the corrections of those cited newspapers. I purposely referenced mostly women to accentuate the idea that the opinion wasn't one biased by gender. The journalists were from newspapers such as *The Providence Journal* and *The Boston Herald*. Benedict's book sought to analyze the treatment of the victims by the press and it concedes as understandable the subsequent reaction by the population against the media.

That was precisely my message and the message of the texts I cited, but nowhere in the reporting of the *Açoriano Oriental* can these contentions be found. In view of this fact, I find myself obligated to do so personally.

One last note concerning the piece by the *Açoriano Oriental*—("Nothing guarantees that in present day Azores a case of rape similar to Big Dan's will not occur; though perhaps an act the population of the Azores would not defend.") First: This statement reveals that the author continues to be ignorant of the motivations that led the populace of New Bedford to the streets, another fact apparently beyond the scope of the report's subject matter. Second: It seems clear then that those Portuguese demonstrators, in their majority of Azorean origin, specifically São Miguel, emigrated to America evidently from the moon.

Appreciative of the opportunity presently afforded to me, I send my regards,

O.T.A

The journalist responded by repeating his positions, but included the following surprising information: "The journalist Diana Andringa was quite clear in declaring that she obtained a statement 'off the record' by a man present at the bar during the rape saying in effect there were more people present as well."[14]

This is surprising because neither the court nor the journalists Alan Levin of the New Bedford *Standard Times* or Fred Bayles of the Associated Press (nor countless others as revealed by the *The New York Times*) could confirm or obtain such information, but a Portuguese journalist did so relying on an anonymous telephone call which she assumed came from a witness to the crime. It seems then that the credibility of such information on the part of the journalist of the *Açoriano Oriental* is ostensibly apodictical.[15]

Contrary to the assumptions of the organizers of the Azorean Forum, it still seems premature to look at the bare facts of the case independently of ideological passions. Be that as it may, those who look at this case through the lens of the Portuguese media, who themselves parroted the debate in the American media for over a year, at the very least will find included in these documents a motive for new reflection on the subject.[16]

During a round of colloquia at Brown University with regard to the media attended by players from the national stage, Howard Kurtz of *The Washington Post* criticized the media for being "too slow in the admission of its errors" (Kurtz 1995, 10). He noted that, "We are excellent at covering crises, arriving at the scene of a bank robbery, and disappearing in the ensuing calamity" (Kurtz 1995, 10). The significance of such a revelation is self-evident.

Notes

[1] A Portuguese-language version of this article appeared as "O Caso do Big Dan's—revisitação seguida de algumas considerações sobre acontecimentos 'media made,'" Arquipélago/Ciências Sociais, 9-10 (1996), pp.161-176.

[2] http://en.wikipedia.org/wiki/Cheryl_Araujo, January 29, 2008.

[3] To this day, no cameras or video equipment are allowed in U.S. Federal Court.

[4] A professor at the University of the Azores who lived in the U.S. for many years.

[5] A member of the Portuguese community of Fall River and former deputy to the Portuguese Parliament, Lisbon.

[6] "O tristemente famoso caso 'Big Dan's': Uma disputa em família?" *Açoriano Oriental*, June 1, 1995. João Luís de Medeiros is a former representative in the Portuguese *Assembleia da Républica* or parliament, who lived in Fall River and now resides in California.

[7] I then sent the article to the *Columbia Journalism Review*, which I knew was preparing an edition dedicated to "Ethics and Social Communication." The reason given for not printing the article

was entirely more plausible: "Given the fact that *The N*[ew] *Y*[ork] *Times* had (though tardily) examined the myth of the multitude who applauded, it seems to me that I must pass up the chance to publish your text—more so since our special edition of May/June is already submitted for printing and your text would only publish in the July edition." The letter was signed Spencer Klaw, Director (April 19, 1984).

[8] *Sic*, there were only four.

[9] In the legal sense of the term.

[10] Diana Andringa's film seemed quite balanced in its approach to the diverse points of view. However, in its repeated use of images from the rape scene of *The Accused* starring Jodie Foster as a *leitmotif*, during the opening and closing of each scene, it left the viewer with the impression that the same had occurred at Big Dan's. Those who followed the trial on television know that is not the case. The film *The Accused* sought to fictionalize the Big Dan's event but never made any reference to the Portuguese due to the lobbying by the Portuguese-American Congress directed at Warner Brothers, using all of its influences to distance the Portuguese communities from the crime. Nevertheless what Warner Brothers wisely decided not to do, the Portuguese journalist found acceptable in her opinion. At the conclusion of the debate with Diana Andringa, where she revealed she agreed with my position except for my stance against the women who protested against the crime, I told her that was our only disagreement. I believed the feminists should rightly fight against machismo but not take a case like Big Dan's, where no one came out unblemished, and "cleansed" it of inconvenient facets in relation to their position, to accomplish their ends. "It's a case where each side came out sullied"—I explained, to which Diana Andringa concurred.

Another fictionalization was put forth by Greg O'Brien in *Boston Magazine*, which became a fictional relation of the events from the victim's perspective, where the author let his imagination run wild, but not without retaining the localization of the case ("Rape in New Bedford" 75(8): 1983). In the "Letters to the Editor" section of the same publication, my criticism was published: "'Rape in New Bedford,' by Greg O'Brien/ August/ was astonishing, not in content but in what it revealed about *Boston Magazine's* journalistic standards—not bad compared to the *National Enquirer*, with one exception: the *Enquirer* does not pretend to do anything but trashy yellow journalism that makes quick bucks" (75(11): 1983, 13).

[11] "A violação de uma comunidade," *Açoriano Oriental*, July 1, 1995.

[12] There were other, in fact, on various levels. My thick *dossier* includes an article by a woman, Anita Kostecki, "Pointing the Finger: Portuguese Identity and the Big Dan's Rape Case," in the feminist publication *Cleavage—The Brown Undergraduate Journal of Women's Studies*. After stating that the rapists deserved to be punished for their crime, it concluded with the following affirmations: "I believe that, overall, the Portuguese community was right to protest against the treatment it received as an ethnic group from other individuals. The crime was sensationalized by the press in response to the desires of the American middle class.... The crime maintained a 'comfortable distance' from mainstream American culture by its association with a minority group. White American men and women could voyeuristically survey undesirable roles. But this voyeurism and comfort occurred at the expense of the identity of the Portuguese community and its ethnic brio. As a demonstrator put it: 'It doesn't matter to me if those individuals were innocent or guilty; what hurts is what this case did to my people'" (1987, 22).

[13] Published July 5, 1995. In the cited article, João Luís de Medeiros recalled that during the first trimester of 1983, the Massachusetts authorities were informed of sixty-two cases of rape, twelve of which were considered gang rape. The writer commenced his revisiting of the case thusly: "Hence we witness the great tactical failure. In 1983, apparently, no one was able to translate, in a socio-culturally clear manner, the intentions of the demonstrators: 'No to Rape—Yes to Justice'. To media-conscious Americans, a tremendous doubt was still in the air concerning the demonstrators. Were Portuguese immigrants definitively in favor of or against rape? It was precisely that question which the female intellectual observers of our ethnic group, perhaps indoctrinated in the emotional fervor of their militancy against domestic 'machismo,' which they claimed to know all too well—it was these very women who, in the end, refused to recognize the reality of the situation with the knowledge, courage, and tolerance required of one who in her anxiety to chop down the tree, burned the forest..." *Açoriano Oriental*, July 1, 1995.

[14] "A violação de uma comunidade," *Açoreano Oriental*, July 1, 1995.

[15] The response also contained other misinformed and misunderstood assertions which I refrain from clarifying at this time.

[16] During the height of the attention given to the case, I published an article in *O Jornal* with

the intention of calming the waters by offering facts that were left out by the Portuguese media in their reports (*O Jornal*, March 29, 1984 and May 11, 1983). Joana Godinho replied to my article with "*O Direito de Dizer Não*" (The Right to Say *No*). My text "*Contra Argumentos Não Haja Factos"* (Against Arguments There Can Be No Facts) and my reply to the journalist "*Aindo o caso do Big Dan's e as sucessivas confusões*" (More On Big Dan's and the Ensuing Confusion) can be found in Almeida (1987, 171-178). Joana Godinho at the time lived in North Carolina, a two-hour trip by airplane from New Bedford, and followed the event in the media, as did the journalist at the *Açoriano Oriental*.

EDUCATION, SOCIAL MOBILITY AND POLITICAL CULTURE

CHAPTER 10

Context or Culture? Portuguese-Americans and Social Mobility

M. GLÓRIA DE SÁ AND DAVID BORGES

Most immigrants begin their lives in America as members of the working class. Moving into the middle class is synonymous with reaching the fabled American Dream, which some reach faster than others. Since American society is assumed to be open and democratic, differences in social mobility among different ethnic groups are usually attributed to differences in skills or human capital (Borjas 1985, 1994; Chiswick 1979; Portes 1992), for which education is the most common indicator (Becker 1993; Blau and Duncan 1967; Sewell and Hauser 1980). Although this assumption has been challenged and criticized (see Rumbaut 1999), it continues to be central to the understanding of ethnic social mobility in the U.S., especially as it pertains to European groups arriving at the turn of the 20th century (Alba and Nee 1999). Among these groups, even Italians, who arrived with considerable cultural and educational handicaps, became part of the middle class by the last quarter of the century by attaining educational parity (Alba 1985 and 1990; Lieberson 1980; Lieberson and Waters 1988). But the Portuguese, who were also part of this wave, have remained primarily working class. According to most observers, and in conformity with the canonical assimilation perspective, the reason for this was a lack of education.

Referring to early 20th-century Portuguese immigrants, Bannick (1971) pointed out that they had the lowest educational levels of any group arriving between 1899 and 1910, while McGowan (1976, 18), writing during the second wave of Portuguese immigration, affirmed that "an examination of the literature on the Portuguese in New England readily shows that there has been little change in the last fifty years." A quarter of a century later, at the dawning of the 21st century, not much seemed to have changed (Barrow et al 2002; Borges 2005; Huff 1989), leading Marinho to conclude that in southeastern Massachusetts "there has been no change in educational attainment from 1977 to the present" (2002,161).

The majority of researchers have attributed the low social mobility of the Portuguese to a cultural heritage that places little value on education (McGowan 1976; Sharkansky 1960; Taft 1969), arguing or implying that there is something inherent in Portuguese culture that makes education seem irrelevant to most. Indeed, by looking at the history of education in Portugal, which until the 1960s provided only four years of compulsory, free education to its citizens, one can see how such a conclusion seems plausible. But, while these facts lend credence to the cultural hypothesis, lack of comparative research has led to a tendency to ignore other possible explanations, including the role of contextual factors.

Most of what is known about the educational patterns of the Portuguese comes from studies done in urban areas plagued by high drop-out rates and low general levels of educational achievement, such as Fall River and New Bedford in Massachusetts. Although most studies point out that low levels of education are endemic to these communities, suggesting a possible negative impact of community characteristics on the education of the Portuguese population, it is frequently assumed that causality runs the other way. That is, that the low levels of education of the Portuguese are responsible for the particular community's economic woes.[1] In most studies and commentaries, the Portuguese are portrayed as irrational, present-oriented actors who fail to understand the connection between education and future economic achievement, sacrificing their children's education to meet consumption needs and acquire status symbols, like furniture, cars, and, above all, home ownership (McGowan 1976; Noivo 1993).

As critics of straight-line assimilation have pointed out, conclusions like these rest on assumptions which have not been adequately substantiated by empirical findings: namely, that movement into the middle class is possible for all groups, that education is the vehicle, and that those who fail to follow this path do so for irrational or selfish reasons. Contrary to the canon, however, the historiography of immigrant groups shows that the classical path of social mobility has been, to a large degree, a myth (Gans 1992). For most European groups, middle-class status did not come until the second or third generation and educational success did not precede, but rather followed economic success (Greer 1972). Portes and Zhou (1993), for example, argue that assimilation into the middle class is only one of the possible paths of incorporation into American society. They state that the process varies not only with group characteristics, but also with the conditions encountered in places of settlement. Depending on contextual factors, three major paths are possible. While assimilation into the white middle class may be the most desirable, when this path is blocked, groups adopt alternative paths. Some adjust by seeking refuge in established ethnic enclaves in which success is measured by co-ethnic standards, while others assimilate into the urban underclass.

According to most researchers (e.g. Alba 1985; Alba and Nee 1997; Lieberson and Waters 1988; Perlmann and Waldinger 1997), the assimilation into the white middle class experienced by the immigrants arriving in the early 20th century was, in large degree, the result of the favorable structural conditions encountered by these groups, in particular the expanding industrial economies of the large industrial cities of the Northeast, and the immigration hiatus of the mid-20th century. In this context, as new groups arrived, they took their place at the bottom of the occupational ladder, pushing earlier arrivals upward. Social mobility was a generational process. New immigrants took unskilled jobs, children of immigrants occupied skilled manual positions, and grandchildren of immigrants moved into professional occupations. The erosion of the industrial economy in the second half of the 20th century, however, has made movement into the middle class increasingly difficult for those who arrived at the tail end of the industrial expansion (Lieberson 1980). With the disappearance of the traditional ladders of social mobility offered by the factory system, latecomers who did not possess the human and social capital necessary to enter the new post-industrial economy directly were trapped in economically depressed areas without much opportunity for upward social mobility (Waldinger 1996).

We contend that the later scenario applies to the case of the Portuguese of southeastern Massachusetts. Their opportunity for moving into the white middle class was negatively affected by the timing of their immigration relative to the arrival of other European groups, and to the area's economic restructuring. As the last group to arrive, the Portuguese were kept at the bottom of the socioeconomic hierarchy in order to sustain the economic viability of a declining industrial sector and the mobility needs of other groups. Blocked from acquiring the status symbols associated with WASP middle-classness, such as college degrees and professional occupations, due to the area's lack of economic growth, the majority sought social recognition within the Portuguese ethnic enclave, where success was measured by relative economic prosperity, especially ownership of property. Far from being irrational, selfish or caused by an inability to shed a peasant mentality, this strategy helped Portuguese immigrants achieve many of the economic characteristics of the middle class[2] and prevented them from falling into the ranks of the underclass to which their lack of formal schooling might relegate them.

Much of the research linking the education and social mobility of the Portuguese to cultural values has been restricted to communities (e.g., New Bedford, Fall River, and Taunton, Massachusetts) where the residential concentration of Portuguese ethnics is so high as to lead some to call it "The Portuguese Archipelago." Although valuable, these studies are limited by their historical and geographical scope, leading to generalizations that may misrepresent the level and the process of socioeconomic mobility among the Portuguese in general. This focus has led to a stereotype of the Portuguese as hardworking, uneducated, and passive in terms of social and political aspirations (Barrow 2002; Moniz 1979; Smith 1974), ignoring the fact that in other areas of the country, the same Portuguese have been described as ambitious, entrepreneurial, and politically successful (Baganha 1991; Warrin and Gomes 2001; Williams 2005).

Using a comparative approach in terms of time and geography, this research proposes that, contrary to the common perception generated by studies of the Portuguese Archipelago, the Portuguese of the U.S. experienced significant social mobility in the last quarter of the 20th century, and that their modest showing in southeastern Massachusetts is the result of a process of adjustment to the contextual constraints of the area.[3]

The Portuguese Archipelago

According to the U.S. Census, 232,472 of the residents of Massachusetts in 2000, or 4.3 percent of the state's total population, claimed Portuguese as their primary ancestry.[4] More than half of these live in the "Portuguese Archipelago,"[5] an area that cuts a swath across the eastern and southern sections of southeastern Massachusetts and consists of twenty-one cities and towns in Bristol and Plymouth Counties (Figure 1). Thirty percent of the residents of this area are of primary Portuguese ancestry, which is nearly three times the size of any other ancestry group in the region. In fact, the Portuguese Archipelago accounts for 14.4 percent of all persons of primary Portuguese ancestry in the United States.

The initial flow of the Portuguese into this area began with the whaling industry of New Bedford in the 19th century, but massive immigration is associated with the development of the region's textile and apparel industries, and occurred in two distinct waves, one which peaked around 1920 and another around 1970.

FIGURE I THE PORTUGUESE ARCHIPELAGO

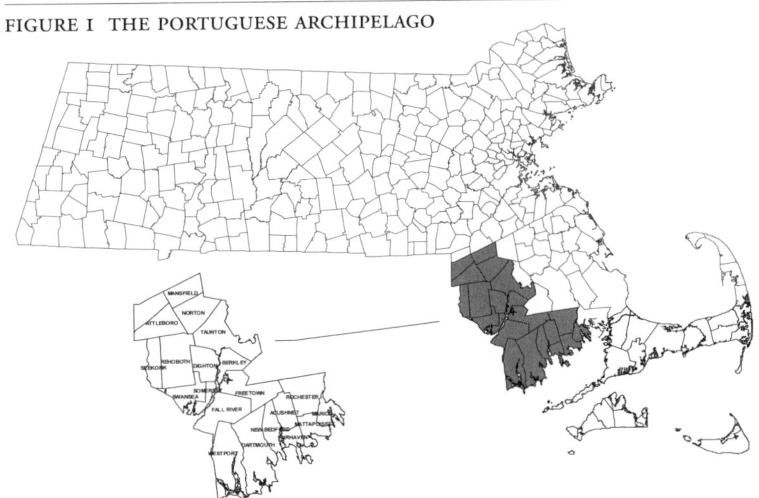

The industrial history of the region goes back to 1811 with the opening of Globe Manufactory in Fall River. By the end of the 19th century, Fall River and New Bedford were among the top manufacturing cities in the nation. The availability of mill jobs drew vast numbers of immigrants. By 1900, for example, Fall River had the highest percentage of foreign-born residents of any city in the entire country. Around this time most of the mill workers were French Canadians who had replaced earlier groups like the English and the Irish. These had moved into other occupations or out of the area (Baganha 1995; Pap 1981; Silvia 1976; Williams 2005). In the next two decades, as Canadian immigration began to dwindle, newly-arrived Portuguese immigrants replaced Canadians in the mills, entering at the bottom of the occupational ladder and settling in ethnically segregated neighborhoods.

For more than a century, the economic base of the Portuguese Archipelago has been heavily dependent on manufacturing, and the job market has always been volatile with wide fluctuations in employment. Although at the turn of the century the area enjoyed a period of extraordinary economic and population growth, the rate of expansion came to a halt in the 1920s. Following a series of labor strikes and the passage of restrictive immigration laws, most of the textile mills closed or left for the South, immigration became practically non-existent, and the economy of the Portuguese Archipelago entered a period of decline that has lasted until the present. While other areas of the state diversified their economies by attracting aerospace, electronics, defense, and medical research firms, in the Portuguese Archipelago new industries did not emerge to compensate for the loss of traditional jobs. The closing of the mills, the anti-immigrant sentiment of the times, labor unrest and the general economic conditions of the Depression made life so dismal that America became more a place to leave than a destination to come to. Many Portuguese returned to Portugal with their children. According to Pap (1980, 83), between 1922 and 1932, the number of Portuguese entering the U.S. was 11,589, while the number of those who left was 25,466. Without new immigrants coming in to push them up the occupational ladder, the children of early Portuguese immigrants replaced their parents in the surviving factories and the group remained where it had started—at the bottom (Silvia 1976).

The industrial decline continued through the Great Depression and World War II despite some defense-related expansion in response to the Cold War (Center for Policy Analysis 2001), but the area was not able to create middle-class job opportunities nor educational resources necessary to achieve them. In 1950, for example, New Bedford had the lowest median education of any city of 10,000 or more inhabitants in the U.S. (Gilbert 1989, 57), and until the middle of the 1960s, when most of the textile mills had already left the area, the only institutions of higher learning in the Portuguese Archipelago were the New Bedford Textile School and the Bradford Durfee Textile School in Fall River. Those born into middle-class families could use their class resources to further their education by going elsewhere, but working-class children, like the majority of the Portuguese, were stuck.

In the sixties and seventies a large influx of new Portuguese immigrants arrived, adding their numbers to the existing Portuguese working class. Their cheap labor allowed the area to hold on to a large proportion of its industrial base, while other areas of the state were losing theirs. In 1985, for example, manufacturing still accounted for about forty-three percent of total employment in Fall River and New Bedford, whereas for the state as a whole it was only twenty-one percent. But this dependence on manufacturing meant that the irreversible process of deindustrialization had a stronger negative impact in the region than anywhere else in Massachusetts. "From 1983 to 1990, New Bedford and Fall River suffered the most significant manufacturing job losses in the state, accounting for 12.5 percent of the state's total manufacturing job loss" (Center for Policy Analysis 2001, 2). Between 1985 and 2005, New Bedford lost sixty-one percent of its remaining manufacturing jobs and Fall River lost fifty percent. The loss had a devastating effect on the local economy. Between 1985 and 1999, total employment in New Bedford declined by more than twenty-nine percent, while rates of unemployment were almost double the state average. In 1991, for example, unemployment reached over sixteen percent and by 1999 the city's poverty rate became one of the highest in New England, with 14.6 percent of the city's residents living below the official poverty level.

Despite the creation of Southeastern Massachusetts University and Bristol Community College in the 1960s and the availability of bilingual education in the 1970s, college remained beyond the reach of most. In 1997, tuition at the University of Massachusetts Dartmouth was $4,151—almost twelve percent of the median family income of New Bedford ($35,708). By 2007, it had risen to $8,592 or almost sixteen percent of the median family income ($55,200 in 2006). Portuguese families, whose income is frequently too high to qualify for financial aid but not high enough to afford easy access, face particular constraints.

Thus, while Massachusetts has the most highly-educated population in the country, and one of the most developed post-industrial economies in the world, in 2000, the Portuguese Archipelago had one of the lowest rates of educational attainment in Massachusetts, and was still largely dependent on manufacturing employment. Within this area of relative disadvantage, the Portuguese stand out as much for their relative educational and occupational deficits as for their relative income advantage.

Educational Achievement

From 1980 to 2000, the proportion of Portuguese with a high-school diploma increased by twenty-three percentage points, going from thirty-two to fifty-five percent (Figure 2).

FIGURE 2

HIGH-SCHOOL GRADUATES BY PRIMARY ANCESTRY: PORTUGUESE ARCHIPELAGO, 1980-2000 (PERSONS AGE 25 AND OVER)

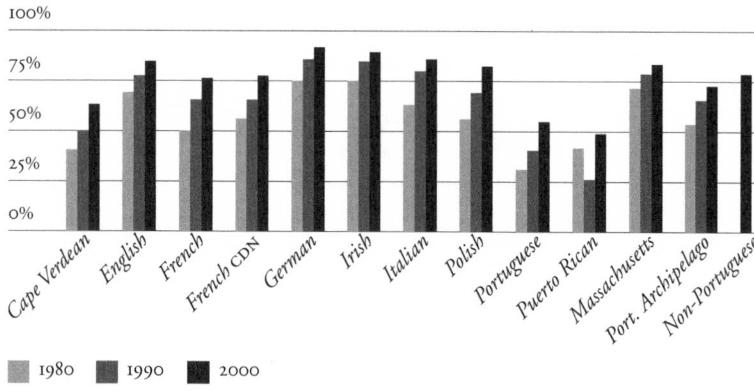

Source: U.S. Census Bureau PUMS 5% File, 2000

This was the third largest increase among the region's major ancestry groups and higher than the average improvement of eighteen percentage points. Despite these gains, however, the percentage of Portuguese who had a high-school diploma remained significantly lower than that of nearly all other major ethnic groups. For example, in 2000, only fifty-five percent of the Portuguese residents possessed a high-school diploma, compared to eighty percent of non-Portuguese, seventy-three percent of the region as a whole, and eighty-five percent statewide.[6]

FIGURE 3

HIGH-SCHOOL GRADUATES BY NATIVITY: PORTUGUESE ARCHIPELAGO, 2000 (PERSONS AGE 25 AND OVER)

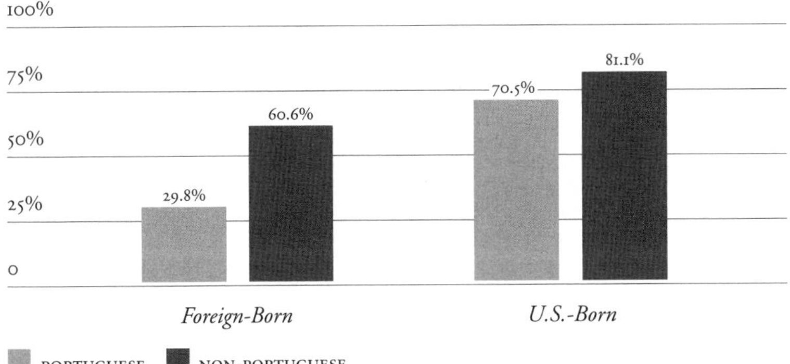

Source: U.S. Census Bureau PUMS 5% File, 2000

Some of the gap results from the difference in educational levels between foreign-born and U.S.-born Portuguese and from the higher proportion of immigrants among the Portuguese than the non-Portuguese (thirty-seven vs. twelve percent), but the disadvantage remains even after accounting for these factors. For example, in 2000, only thirty percent of Portuguese immigrants had a high-school diploma, compared to slightly more than seventy percent of their American-born counterparts, a difference of almost forty-one percentage points (Figure 3). In comparison, among non-Portuguese, about sixty-one percent of foreign-born have a high-school diploma compared to eighty-one percent of the U.S.-born, a difference of about twenty-one percentage points. Nativity differences among the Portuguese are twice as wide as among non-Portuguese, but both U.S.- and foreign-born Portuguese have much lower levels of high-school completion than their respective counterparts.

While the Portuguese have made one of the highest group gains in terms of high school education, they have realized only a small improvement in college graduation. From 1980 to 2000, the percentage of Portuguese with a Bachelor's degree or higher increased by barely five percentage points, compared to thirteen percentage points region-wide, and sixteen percentage points statewide. This is a very small gain, considering the low levels of college graduation among Portuguese in the 1980 baseline year.

FIGURE 4

BACHELOR'S DEGREE OR HIGHER BY PRIMARY ANCESTRY: PORTUGUESE ARCHIPELAGO, 1980-2000 (PERSONS AGE 25 YEARS AND OVER)

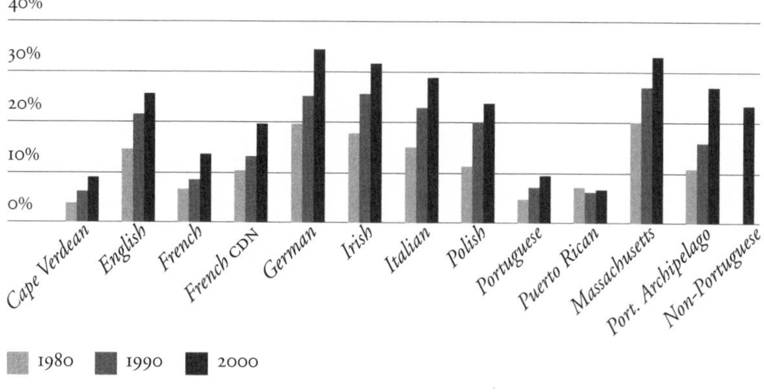

Source: U.S. Census Bureau PUMS 5% File, 2000

In 2000, fewer than ten percent of Portuguese held a Bachelor's degree or higher (Figure 4). This compared to almost twenty-four percent of the region's non-Portuguese, about twenty-seven percent region-wide, and thirty-three percent state-wide.

FIGURE 5

BACHELOR'S DEGREE OR HIGHER BY NATIVITY: PORTUGUESE ARCHIPELAGO, 2000 (PERSONS AGE 25 AND OVER)

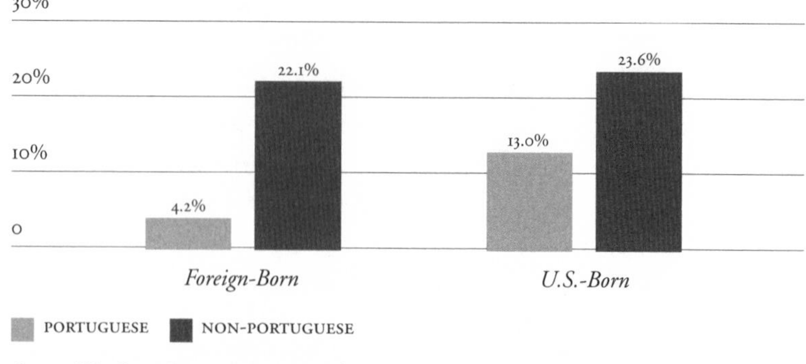

Source: U.S. Census Bureau PUMS 5% File, 2000

As was the case for high school education, differences in college attainment between the Portuguese and other groups cannot be explained by nativity differences alone (Figure 5). Even though the percentage of U.S.-born Portuguese attaining a Bachelor's degree or higher (thirteen percent) is more than three times that of foreign-born Portuguese (four percent), within nativity groups, four-year college graduation rates are significantly lower for Portuguese than for non-Portuguese groups.

FIGURE 6

HIGH-SCHOOL GRADUATES BY AGE GROUP, 2000

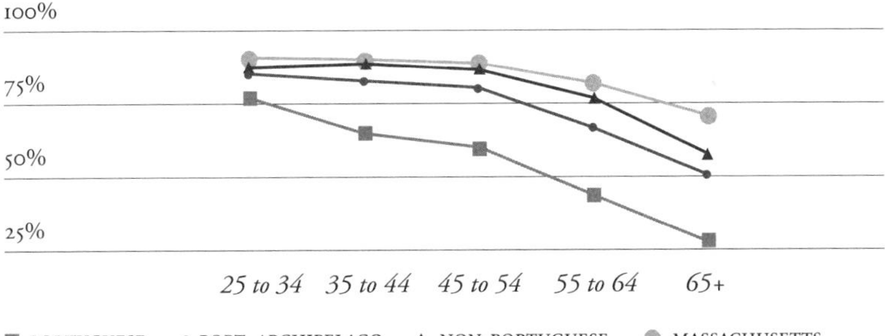

Source: U.S. Census Bureau PUMS 5% File, 2000

As mentioned earlier, educational opportunities have expanded in both Portugal and Massachusetts since the 1960s. These transformations, allied to the slowing down of Portuguese immigration, should theoretically have made education not only more desirable among the Portuguese, but also more attainable. In light of these developments, one would expect younger Portuguese to have higher levels of education than older cohorts and be more similar to the comparison groups than their older counterparts.

Figure 6 shows this to be the case for high-school education. Younger Portuguese are more likely to have graduated from high school than older ones. In addition, the younger the cohort, the closer they are to non-Portuguese region and state averages. However, even in the youngest Portuguese cohort, the rate of high-school graduation is lower than the region, state, and non-Portuguese rate.

While the figures on high school attainment show a narrowing of disadvantage for the Portuguese younger groups, no such trend is apparent in college attainment data. If anything, the gap between the Portuguese and the area's non-Portuguese is slightly wider for those under age forty-five (Figure 7), suggesting a worrisome trend of downward mobility for the younger generations.

FIGURE 7

BACHELOR'S DEGREE OR HIGHER BY AGE GROUP, 2000

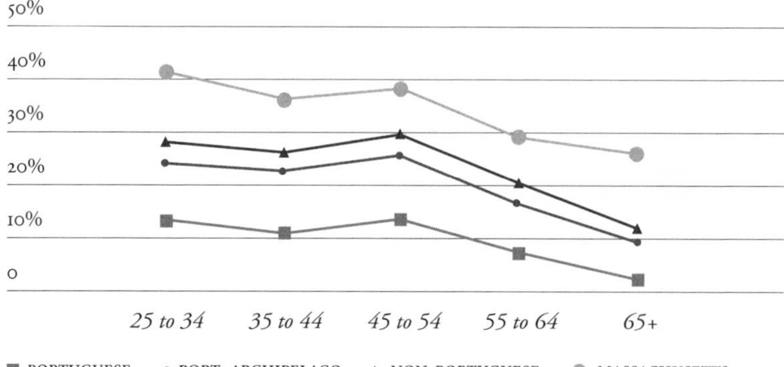

Source: U.S. Census Bureau PUMS 5% File, 2000

Overall, census data for the last quarter of the 20th century show that despite significant increases in the proportion of high school and college graduates, the Portuguese of the area have not caught up with other white groups, especially in terms of college graduation. In fact, the data indicate that the college education gap is widening. Some of the disadvantage is the result of the low levels of education of the Portuguese immigrants, and the larger proportion of immigrants among the Portuguese than among the general population; but Portuguese-Americans also have lower levels of education than their native counterparts.

Occupation and Income

Despite the significant loss of manufacturing jobs in the area over the last thirty years, many Portuguese continue to work in this sector. In 2000, a quarter of the area's Portuguese were employed in manufacturing, compared to less than fifteen percent of the total population. Other significant areas of employment were retail (thirteen percent), health care (eleven percent), and construction (ten percent). Professional services accounted for only three percent of total employment among the Portuguese, compared to five percent of the total population.

FIGURE 8

WAGE/SALARY INCOME: PORTUGUESE ARCHIPELAGO, 1999

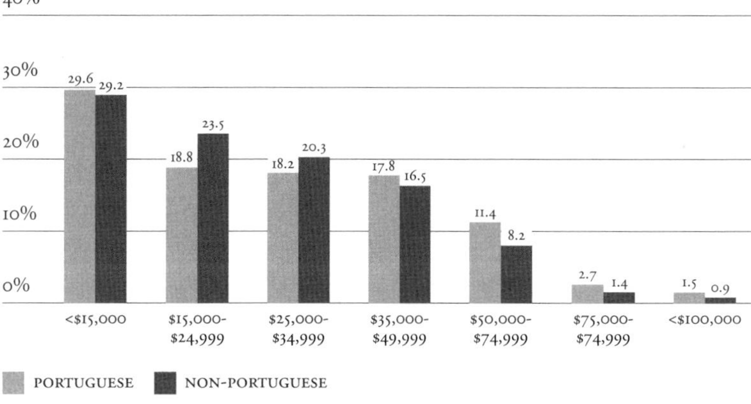

Source: U.S. Census Bureau PUMS 5% File, 2000

Since the Portuguese have comparably low levels of education and are found primarily in low-prestige jobs, an obvious hypothesis is that their wages and incomes are also lower than those of other residents in the area. However, an analysis of income and wages for 1999 shows that the Portuguese compare well with non-Portuguese. This is especially true of New Bedford and Fall River, where in 1999 median family income was about $40,000 for the Portuguese, but only around $37,000 for the general population. A similar pattern is found for individual income. In fact, for wage and salary incomes above $35,000, the percentage of Portuguese in each wage category is actually higher than those for non-Portuguese residents of the Portuguese Archipelago (Figure 8). Over thirty-three percent of all Portuguese had wage and salary income of $35,000 or more compared to only twenty-seven percent of non-Portuguese. Even those without a high-school diploma are well represented in middle- to high-income categories. A possible reason for this finding is that the Portuguese tend to concentrate in relatively high-paying occupations like factory work, construction, fishing, and blue-collar trades like carpentry and mechanics. Another possible explanation is that Portuguese families, although not different in size from the country's average,[7] are likely to have a greater number of workers, since the Portuguese have a higher-than-average rate of participation in the labor force (Mulcahy 2003).

Although it is commonly assumed that there is a clear, positive relationship between education and income, and that education explains most of the socioeconomic differences among groups, research about the area's Portuguese shows that their case does not fit the theoretical model. For example, Pereira (1985), who analyzed the income attainment of Portuguese men in Massachusetts and Rhode Island in 1979, found that education was a very poor predictor of income for the group, and that returns from education were lower for the Portuguese than for the general population. Twenty years later, this appeared to be still the case in the Portuguese Archipelago.

FIGURE 9

WAGE/SALARY INCOME OF $50,000 OR MORE: PORTUGUESE ARCHIPELAGO, 1999

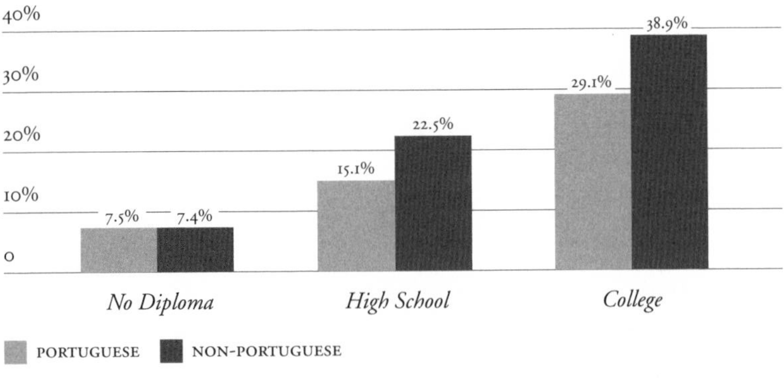

Source: U.S. Census Bureau PUMS 5% File, 2000

Our analysis shows that while maintaining low levels of education, the Portuguese have a slight advantage over non-Portuguese, at higher levels of education they earn less than their non-Portuguese counterparts (Figure 9). In 1999, Portuguese men without a high-school diploma were as likely as non-Portuguese to earn incomes of $50,000 or more, but the percentage of high school and college graduates in this income bracket was much lower for Portuguese than for non-Portuguese. Only twenty-nine percent of Portuguese college graduates earned this much, compared to thirty-nine percent of non- Portuguese.

In summary, analysis of income and wage data for the Portuguese Archipelago shows that, on average, the Portuguese earn more than would be expected from their average education, perhaps due to their concentration in the better-paying blue-collar jobs. However, the data also indicate that education pays less for the Portuguese than for others. This pattern seems to be associated with the fact that the Portuguese are disproportionately concentrated in the least lucrative and dynamic sectors of the economy (Pereira 1985; Borges 2005), suggesting lack of access to structures of power (Barrow 2005), which may be related to their late arrival in the area, lack of social capital, and discrimination.

Patterns and Trends Outside the Portuguese Archipelago

In our introduction we argued that the patterns that characterize the Portuguese Archipelago may underestimate the overall level and the rate of improvement in the social mobility of the Portuguese. To investigate that assertion we now examine the characteristics of the Portuguese in other places of residence.

FIGURE 10

PERSONS AGE 25 AND OVER WHO COMPLETED AT LEAST 12TH GRADE 1970-2000

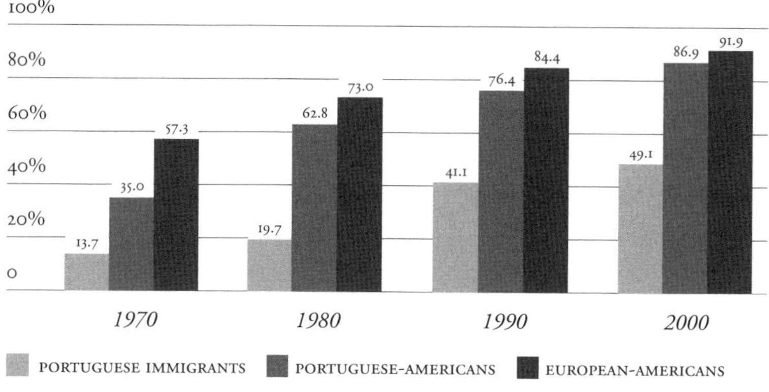

Source: IPUMS (U.S. Census Bureau): 1970, 1980, 1990, and 2000

Educational Achievement

Comparing the data presented in Figures 10 and 11 to those in Figures 2 to 5 confirms that the educational profile of those living in the

Portuguese Archipelago is not typical of the Portuguese as a whole. In the Portuguese Archipelago, educational levels are lower, educational gains over time slower, and educational disadvantages relative to other groups greater than at the national level. For example, in 2000 the proportion of high-school graduates in the Portuguese Archipelago was barely thirty percent for immigrants and seventy-one percent for Portuguese-Americans (Figure 3). In contrast, at the national level, it was about forty-nine percent for immigrants and eighty-seven percent for Portuguese-Americans (Figure 10). Nationwide, from 1980 to 2000, the proportion of high-school graduates increased by twenty-four percentage points for natives and twenty-nine for immigrants (Figure 10), compared to twenty-three percentage points for both immigrants and natives in the Portuguese Archipelago (Figure 2). At the national level, in 2000, only five percentage points separated Portuguese-Americans from other white natives of European ancestry (eighty-seven vs. ninety-two percent, Figure 10), whereas in the Portuguese Archipelago, the difference was twice as wide (seventy-one vs. eighty-one percent). In fact, in 2000, high-school attainment for Portuguese-Americans in the U.S. as a whole (eighty-seven percent) was higher than among non-Portuguese natives in the Portuguese Archipelago (eighty-one percent).

FIGURE 11

PERSONS AGE 25 AND OVER WITH AT LEAST 4 YEARS OF COLLEGE 1970-2000

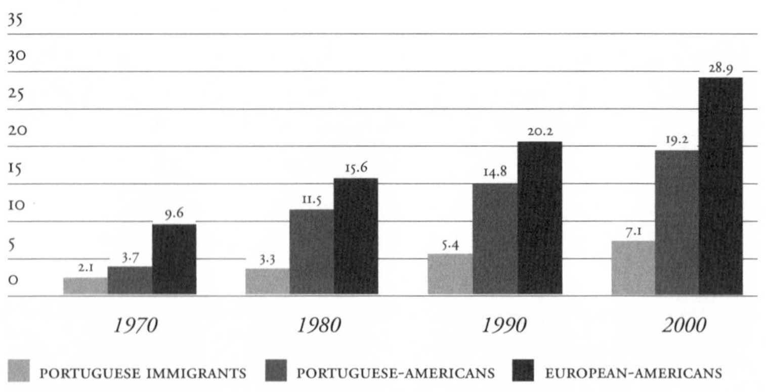

Source: IPUMS (U.S. Census Bureau): 1970, 1980, 1990, and 2000

Similar differences between local and national patterns are evident for college attainment. In 2000, about seven percent of all Portuguese immigrants in the U.S. had a college degree (Figure 11) compared to only four percent of those residing in the Portuguese Archipelago (Figure 5). For Portuguese–Americans, the rate of college attainment was about nineteen percent at the national level, but only thirteen percent in the Portuguese Archipelago. Rates of increase in college attainment over time are also higher at the national level. From 1980 to 2000, the proportion of college graduates nationwide increased by 3.8 percentage points for immigrants and by 7.7 percentage points for Portuguese-Americans (Figure 11). In contrast, in the Portuguese Archipelago gains averaged only 4.7 percentage points for both natives and immigrants combined (Figure 4). Finally, while at the national level the proportion of Portuguese-Americans with a college degree is about two-thirds of the rate for other white European-Americans (nineteen vs. twenty-nine percent), in the Portuguese Archipelago it is barely more than half of the rate of other natives, including racial minorities (thirteen vs. twenty-four percent) (Figure 5).

FIGURE 12

HIGH-SCHOOL GRADUATES BY PLACE OF RESIDENCE, 2000

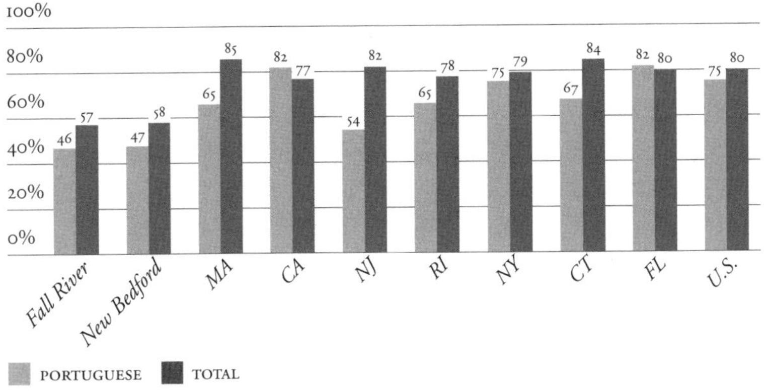

Source: U.S. Census Bureau, American Fact Finder

Despite being heavily influenced by the characteristics of the residents of the Portuguese Archipelago, given that they constitute over fourteen percent of the total Portuguese of the U.S., national-level fig-

TABLE I

OCCUPATIONAL DISTRIBUTION OF PERSONS AGE 16-70 BY GENDER, GROUP AND YEAR, 1970 AND 2000

		Professional & Technical	*Farmers*	*Managers*	*Clerical*	*Sales*	*Craftsmen*	*Operatives*	*Services*	*Non-Prof. Laborers*
					MALES					
PORT. IMMIGRANTS	1970	3.2	1.9	4.5	2.6	1.7	20.7	33.1	11.8	20.4
	2000	6.5	1.2	10.2	6.4	3.1	26.2	21.7	8.2	16.5
PORT. AMERICANS	1970	7.7	3.7	6.0	5.2	6.0	24.0	26.1	9.5	11.7
	2000	15.1	1.6	11.5	10.4	7.3	20.2	14.3	11.6	8.0
EUROP. AMERICANS	1970	13.5	3.3	9.9	7.1	7.0	24.0	18.9	7.4	9.1
	2000	21.7	2.1	14.6	7.7	7.2	18.9	12.7	8.9	6.1
					FEMALES					
PORT. IMMIGRANTS	1970	1.2	0.3	0.3	7.8	3.3	2.4	72.4	11.4	0.9
	2000	11.9	0.3	5.0	21.4	5.0	5.2	25.6	23.4	2.2
PORT. AMERICANS	1970	7.8	0.2	2.5	28.1	8.0	2.4	29.9	19.8	1.4
	2000	26.2	0.4	8.5	33.9	7.1	1.0	4.6	17.2	1.2
EUROP. AMERICANS	1970	15.6	0.3	3.0	36.4	9.1	1.8	13.9	18.2	1.8
	2000	29.7	0.4	9.6	30.2	7.1	1.6	5.0	15.3	1.2

Source: IPUMS (U.S. Census Bureau), 1970 and 2000

ures cast significant doubts about the accuracy of the cultural hypothesis. If indeed culture were the most important factor, the educational profiles of the Portuguese should be similar regardless of place of residence. Clearly, this is not the case; residing in the Portuguese Archipelago depresses educational mobility. Figures 12 and 13, which compare high-school and college rates for Fall River and New Bedford to those of the top seven states of Portuguese settlement in 2000 provide additional support for this hypothesis.

FIGURE 13

BACHELOR'S DEGREE BY PLACE OF RESIDENCE, 2000

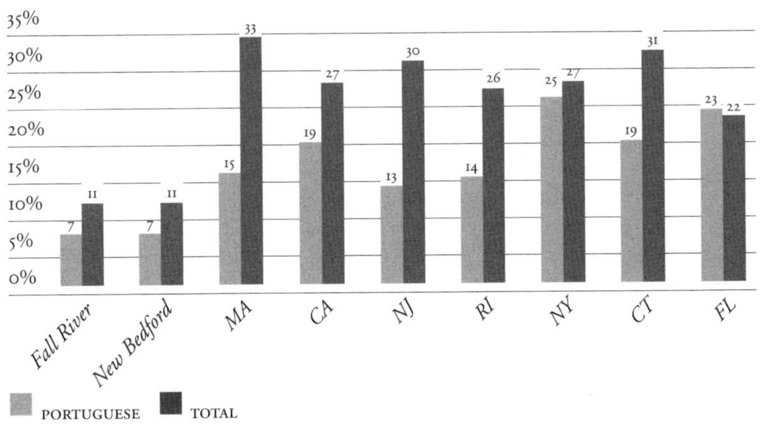

Source: U.S. Census Bureau, American Fact Finder

As Figure 12 indicates, rates of high-school graduation among the Portuguese varied widely, ranging from forty-six percent in Fall River to eighty-two percent in California and Florida. In these two states, the percentage of high-school graduates among the Portuguese was actually higher than among the general population. While the levels of high school attainment were lowest in Fall River and New Bedford, as expected, the relative disadvantage (i.e., the difference between the Portuguese and the general population) was greatest in New Jersey. In part, this is due to the fact that more than half of the Portuguese population of New Jersey is foreign-born (the highest of any state); but even there the proportion of high school graduates was considerably higher than in Fall River and New Bedford (fifty-four vs. forty-seven percent).

Geographical differences are even more pronounced relative to college education. In 2000, the percentage of college graduates ranged from seven percent in Fall River and New Bedford to twenty-five percent in New York (Figure 13), and the discrepancy cannot be adequately accounted for by differences in the percentage of the foreign-born. Although the state with the lowest percentage of college graduates (New Jersey with a thirteen percent proportion of college graduates) was also the one where immigrants constitute the largest proportion of the Portuguese population (fifty-four percent), the relationship did not hold for other places. For example, the proportion of college graduates in Florida was more than three times that of Fall River (twenty-three vs. seven percent) and yet the proportion of immigrants was about the same in both locations (thirty-one percent in Fall River and thirty percent in Florida).

As Figures 12 and 13 dramatically show, when it comes to education, the Portuguese of Fall River and New Bedford are more disadvantaged relative to their co-ethnics living elsewhere than they are relative to the general population of Portuguese Archipelago, confirming that they are not typical of the majority of the Portuguese in the U.S. and indicating a negative impact of the region. This negative impact is not confined to education: it extends to other areas of social mobility, including occupational prestige and income.

Occupation and Income

Whereas other immigrant groups arriving around the turn-of-the-century were able to move into white-collar occupations after World War II, by the end of the 20th century, the majority of the Portuguese of the U.S. were still doing blue-collar work. In the last quarter of the century, however, they were able to move from semi-skilled to skilled manual occupations and make some inroads into more prestigious jobs, such as professionals and managers (Table 1).

While for most of the century, the number one occupational category for Portuguese men and women was that of "operative,"[8] (Mulcahy 2003), by century's end this was the number-one occupation only for immigrant females (twenty-six percent). By 2000, "craftsmen"[9] was the number-one occupational category for Portuguese men, both immigrant (twenty-six percent) and native (twenty percent). For Portuguese-

American women the number-one occupation was "clerical" (thirty-four percent).

Despite this concentration in skilled manual jobs, the proportion of Portuguese doing professional and technical work has increased substantially. From 1970 to 2000, it doubled for men; increased by more than a factor of three for Portuguese-American women; and by a factor of ten for Portuguese immigrant women. In 2000, "professional and technical" work was the number-two occupational category for Portuguese-Americans, comprising fifteen percent of males and twenty-six percent of females. Among immigrants, it accounted for almost seven percent of males and twelve percent of females. In contrast, in the Portuguese Archipelago, less than three percent of all Portuguese were found in professional services (Borges 2005: Figure 8). Although the proportion of Portuguese doing professional and technical work is substantially lower than the equivalent figure for other European-Americans, national figures indicate that the Portuguese-Americans are not too far behind.

Overall, Portuguese women, especially those born in the U.S., have experienced more occupational mobility than Portuguese men. In fact, in 2000, American-born Portuguese women had virtually the same occupational structure as their other European-American counterparts. Portuguese immigrant women have also made considerable progress. From 1970 to 2000, for example, the proportion of factory workers among them declined by about sixty-four percent. Much of the outflow has been channeled into non-professional service occupations, such as home health aide and cleaner, but a large proportion involves movement into occupations requiring higher levels of human capital like clerical and professional work. From 1970 to 2000, nationwide, the proportion of Portuguese immigrant women in clerical occupations went from eight to twenty-one percent, and the proportion of professionals rose from one to twelve percent.

The higher occupational mobility experienced by women appears to be related to economic restructuring. Left without well-paid blue-collar alternatives to their traditional occupations in the needle trades, Portuguese women moved into the increasingly available white-collar "female" jobs, like secretary and teacher, by dramatically increasing their levels of education since 1970. Men have been slower in moving into white-collar occupations and acquiring education in part because they have been able to find well-paid work in blue-collar occupations like the construction trades.

FIGURE 14

MEDIAN FAMILY INCOME, 1999

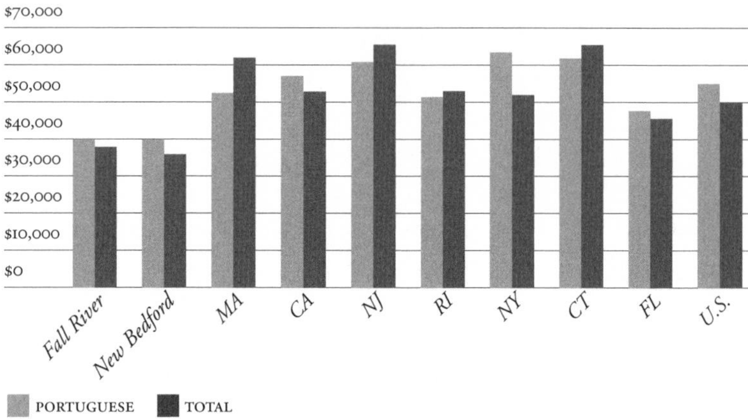

Source: U.S. Census Bureau, American Fact Finder

These strategies have allowed the Portuguese to do relatively well in terms of income (Figure 14). In 1999, the median family income of the Portuguese exceeded the national average by more than $5,000 ($55,100 vs. $50,046). They also did better than average in California, Florida, and New York. Even in high-income states like Connecticut and New Jersey, the Portuguese did relatively well. There was, however, significant geographical variability, with median family income ranging from $38,872 in New Bedford to $63,370 in New York State. But even though the residents of New Bedford and Fall River had lower incomes than their counterparts living elsewhere, they had a clear advantage over other residents of the Portuguese Archipelago.

As was the case with education, data on occupation and income by place of settlement indicate that the residents of the Portuguese Archipelago have significant disadvantages relative to their co-ethnics living in other areas of the country. They have made smaller educational and occupational gains and their incomes are significantly lower, despite being higher than the average for the area.

Discussion and Conclusions

Historical data on education, occupation and income by place of residence confirm that the experience of the residents of the Portuguese Archipelago is not typical of the Portuguese living in other parts of the country. Compared to their counterparts, the Portuguese of southeastern Massachusetts have experienced significantly lower levels of social mobility. Rather than being the result of irrational decisions caused by a culture that places little value on education, the evidence indicates that the low educational levels of the Portuguese of the area are the result of rational strategies aimed at coping with the constraints of local job markets and educational opportunities. Blocked from moving into the middle class by the needs of a shrinking industrial economy, their relatively late arrival in the area, and discrimination in education and other areas of public life (Barrow 2005; Barrow, Sweeney, and Borges 2002; Gilbert 1989), the Portuguese of southeastern Massachusetts adjusted to life in the area by seeking refuge and validation in the ethnic community. By maximizing their income through high rates of labor-force participation (Mulcahy 2003), concentration in the better-paid blue-collar occupations, and investing in home ownership, they were able to avoid falling into the underclass, despite low levels of formal education and declining economic opportunity.

Contrary to common belief, the Portuguese of the area do not seem to value education less than other groups. If anything, they seem to value it more than non-Portuguese residents (Barrow, Sweeney, and Borges 2002, 126), but decision-makers in the Portuguese Archipelago may not always have found it in their best interest to educate the Portuguese. This fact did not go unnoticed by a man who is known for his unkind opinions of the Portuguese. Writing about the educational conditions of Fall River around 1920, Taft stated:

> So far as recent school reports show the educational policy of recent years, there seems to be a curious conflict between a desire to keep the children in school longer, and a fear lest what they learn shall make them dissatisfied with the life of a mill operative.... Is the educational problem of Fall River to make "educated" people love to tend looms? Or is it to make them dissatisfied with the cotton mill, and if so, who is to tend the looms? (Taft 1969, 231-232)

Fifty years later, the conflict had not been resolved. While McGowan (1976, 94) asserted that the "major cause of early school leaving among Portuguese immigrants is parental pressure" because, according to one of his informants, "[i]t does not take long for an immigrant parent to realize that if he takes his child out of school at age sixteen, buying him off with a car, he obtains another productive member of his family unit" (McGowan 1976, 71). Fall River school superintendent, John Correiro (cited in Ribeiro 1982, 89-91), attributed the low educational achievement of the Portuguese in Fall River in the 1970s to lack of role models in the first wave of immigration; the fact that school counselors provided Portuguese students with minimal information regarding college programs, financial aid and scholarships; and the lack of affordable schools in the area. These explanations are echoed by countless private accounts of area residents. Similar arguments have been made in accounting for educational differences among other ethnic groups, including Jews in small cities. While the exceptional educational achievement of the Jews is usually attributed to cultural factors, Morawska (1994) credits their educational success to the role played by free, public schools like New York's City College. While those who settled in large urban centers like New York and Chicago moved into the middle class through education, those who settled in blue-collar towns like Johnstown, Pennsylvania were discouraged from pursuing education, opting instead for income maximization.

In her study of economic and educational achievement among the Portuguese of Fall River in the early 1970s, Gilbert (1989) also challenges the cultural explanation and emphasizes the bounded rationality of the Portuguese. She points out that, historically, the economy of southeastern Massachusetts has been characterized by a lack of occupational opportunities for persons with high levels of formal education, and an abundance of jobs requiring barely any formal education. Within this context, social recognition is not acquired through educational achievement and assimilation into mainstream society; rather, through the ownership of property and the admiration and respect of family and co-ethnics. Given these contextual factors, states Gilbert (1989, 24), "lack of participation in schooling makes a lot of sense."

> [T]here are jobs available for those without a high school diploma, and there is no guarantee that a diploma will ensure a better job in Fall River.

> Individuals who go to college run the risk of educating themselves out of the city's capacity to employ them; leaving Fall River means leaving family and friends. (Gilbert 1989, 133)

The Portuguese Archipelago has been both a gateway and a trap for the Portuguese. On the one hand, the area's industrial economy provided the group with opportunity for reaching a high degree of economic success despite very low levels of education. On the other, lack of affordable schools, information, guidance, and white-collar jobs, coupled with low returns from education, denied them both the opportunity and the incentive to acquire the educational requirements for reaching middle-class status. Those who settled elsewhere fared comparatively better.

Nationwide, from 1970 to 2000, the educational attainment of the Portuguese increased substantially for both immigrants and natives. Rates of high school graduation among immigrants increased by a factor of almost three for men, and by a factor more than four for women. For Portuguese-Americans, the rate of high-school graduation more than doubled, placing them very close to other European-Americans. Rates of college completion also increased during this period. While in 1970, only two percent of the women and five percent of the men had graduated college, by 2000, about seven percent of immigrants and nineteen percent for those born in the U.S. had college degrees. Occupationally, there has been a nationwide movement into more prestigious, skilled jobs, with native women having become virtually indistinguishable from other European-Americans. Economically, they are also doing relatively well. Median household, family, and per capita income are higher for the Portuguese than for the general U.S. population, and so are the average value of their homes and rate of home ownership. Therefore, although for most of the 20th century, the Portuguese of the U.S. remained trapped in the ranks of the working class, they entered the 21st as members of the middle class.

This study pointed out what appear to be significant contextual effects on the social mobility of the Portuguese, and challenged the view that their socioeconomic disadvantage is due primarily to cultural factors. Yet, could it not be reasonably argued that the Portuguese are not culturally homogenous, that they differ culturally according to community of origin, for example, and that it is these different origins and their association with particular places of settlement that are responsible for the patterns encountered? With the data available to us, we could not answer this question. However, it is relevant to emphasize that the value of research is not just to provide answers, but to stimulate further inquiry. Future research on the social mobility of the Portuguese should concentrate on exploring the patterns outlined here and the questions that they raise, through a combination of methodologies that combine the rigor of quantitative, comparative analysis with the richness of community-level, qualitative approaches.

Notes

[1] See for example, "New Bedford's Reality—The Struggle for an Educated Workforce," *The Boston Globe,* April 24, 2005; and "Educational Lag Carries Cost for Portuguese," *The Standard Times,* September 25, 2005.

[2] Following Joseph Kahl and Dennis Gilbert (Gilbert and Kahl 1998; Gilbert 2003) we conceive of social class as a composite of education, occupational prestige and wealth.

[3] The study utilizes U.S. Census data, including the U.S. Census Bureau SF3 files, PUMS 5% File; the U.S. Census Bureau, Summary File 4; and the Integrated Public Use Microdata Series (IPUMS) files from the Minnesota Population Center, University of Minnesota. Although the heterogeneity of the data does not permit perfect comparability across time and space, it nevertheless allows for the exploration of hypotheses, which can be pursued more thoroughly in future studies.The general term "Portuguese" refers to both individuals born in Portugal and to those born in the U.S. of Portuguese parentage or ancestry. "Portuguese-American" designates individuals born in the U.S. of Portuguese parentage (prior to 1980) or ancestry (from 1980 onward), and "Portuguese Immigrants" designates individuals born in Portugal. The same logic applies to the definition of other ethnic groups.

[4] Ancestry refers to a person's ethnic origin or descent, cultural heritage, or the place of birth of the person or the person's parents or ancestors before arrival in the United States. In the U.S. Census, the term "primary ancestry" includes persons who report only Portuguese as their ethnic group or persons who report Portuguese first and then some other group. The term "secondary ancestry" includes persons who report Portuguese second and some other group first (2000 U.S. Census of Population and Housing).

[5] The definition of the Portuguese Archipelago is based on the Public Use Microdata Area (PUMA) definitions from the U.S. Census Bureau for 2000.

[6] "Non-Portuguese" refers to all residents who are not of Portuguese ancestry.

[7] In 2000, average family and household size was three for both the Portuguese and the total U.S. population.

[8] This occupational category includes semi-skilled, blue-collar jobs, such as apprentices in various trades, various types of machine operators and general factory work.

[9] Skilled production workers like carpenters, plumbers, electricians, and machinists.

CHAPTER 11

The Political Culture of Portuguese-Americans in Southeastern Massachusetts

CLYDE W. BARROW

There are major bodies of scholarly work in political science, sociology, and ethnic studies that analyze the political culture of African-Americans, Latinos, Asian-Americans, and many other ethnic or nationality groups in the United States,[1] but the potentially significant political role of Portuguese-Americans in selected areas of the country has received very little attention from scholars in these fields (Marinho 1992; Pap 1981; Adler 1972). Even within the confines of Massachusetts, which has a significant Portuguese-American population, there are notable works on the political culture of the Irish (Handlin 1977; O'Connor 1995), Germans (Goethe Society 1981), African-Americans (Jennings and King 1986), and Latinos (Hardy-Fanta 1993), but until recently Portuguese-Americans have commanded little interest outside the field of immigration studies (Williams 2005), labor studies (Bedford 1966, 1995; Silvia 1973; Borges 1990), and comparative literature.[2]

Despite the relative dearth of empirical information on Portuguese-American political culture, there are many commonly held assumptions, including the belief that Portuguese-Americans: 1) are less politically active than other ethnic groups; 2) have low levels of political knowledge; 3) have a high level of distrust in government; and 4) do not have a distinctive political identity comparable to that of many other ethnic, racial, or nationality groups in the United States.

Furthermore, journalists, public officials, educators, and others have long offered a well-honed list of "historical" and "cultural" explanations for these alleged characteristics. For example, it is commonly asserted that because Portugal and the Azores were governed by an authoritarian dictatorship from 1926 to 1974, Portuguese immigrants do not have a history of political participation and have therefore failed to develop a participatory civic culture in the U.S. Life under an authoritarian dictatorship is said to have fostered high levels of distrust in government, and this aversion to "politics" leads to low levels of political knowledge and creates a cultural disincentive to becoming citizens of the United States. It is often assumed that many Portuguese immigrants intend to return to the home country and thus do not place any importance on becoming citizens or on participating in the American political process. For the same reasons, it is often argued that Portuguese-Americans are more involved in "non-political" civic associations such as church, nationality groups, fraternal organizations, and athletic clubs that reinforce their segregation within ethnic enclaves.

In contrast to explanations that invoke an anecdotally-based historico-cultural determinism, other explanations of Portuguese-American political culture invoke well-established sociological explanations based on current socioeconomic status. It is well-established that low levels of political participation in the United States are strongly correlated with low educational attainment and low incomes (Wolfinger and Rosenstone 1980). Since there is an unusually high percentage of Portuguese-Americans in southeastern Massachusetts who are employed in low-skill, low-paying jobs (Huff 1989), it follows that Portuguese-Americans would not be expected to participate in politics at the same level as many other ethnic, racial, or nationality groups with higher levels of educational attainment.

The empirical findings reported in this chapter suggest that much of the conventional wisdom about Portuguese-Americans and politics is simply ethnic mythology or ethnic stereotype. We find that Portuguese-Americans are not less politically active than other ethnic groups, but that they are a hybrid variant of what Sidney Verba and Norman H. Nie (1972) have called "the voter specialist" in American politics. We also find that Portuguese-Americans articulate a hybrid political ideology that is best described as economically liberal (i.e., supportive of government activism in the economy), socially liberal (i.e., supportive of individual and group rights), but culturally conservative (i.e., traditional moral values).

Definitions and Methodology

Political culture is a "set of attitudes, beliefs, and feelings about politics" attributable to a particular nationality or other group (Almond and Powell, Jr. 1978, 25). The concept of political culture originated among comparative political scientists in the early 1960s, who were seeking to describe the commonalities and peculiarities of political behavior among the citizens of different nations (Almond and Verba 1963; Pye and Verba 1965; Almond and Verba 1980). The concept has been increasingly used to describe the specific political behaviors of different social groups within nations, whether defined by class, race, ethnicity, gender, region, generation, or language. Political cultures are constructed and develop over time, but for that reason they are partially shaped by the experiences that delimit a nation's or a group's history, and partly by the ongoing contemporary processes of social, economic, and political activity (Almond and Powell, Jr., 1978, 25). Political culture is now frequently defined through the use of public opinion surveys, although other methods of measuring political culture include elite interviews and the analysis of the public statements, speeches, and writings of political and cultural leaders.

This chapter summarizes the results of three public opinion surveys conducted by the University of Massachusetts Dartmouth Center for Policy Analysis in 1999 and 2000 in collaboration with the Center for Portuguese Studies and Culture. The purpose of these three surveys was 1) to determine levels of political and civic participation among Portuguese-Americans and to measure their sense of political efficacy, 2) to measure levels of satisfaction with their position in the local economy, and 3) to measure their attitudes on major cultural and social issues in the United States.[3] The civic participation and political efficacy survey, the economic satisfaction survey, and the social and cultural issues survey were each administered to adult (age 18 and over) residents living in the Portuguese Archipelago of southeastern Massachusetts.

Southeastern Massachusetts consists of forty-eight cities and towns in Bristol, Plymouth, and Norfolk Counties. The region is 1,224 square miles in area and has a population of 1,045,843 (U.S. Census 2000). The major cities in the region, which account for about 42.3 percent of the region's population, are Attleboro, Brockton, Fall River, New Bedford, Plymouth, and Taunton.[4] A Portuguese Archipelago, consisting of twenty-one cities and towns in Bristol and Plymouth Counties, cuts a swath across the eastern and southern sections of southeastern Massachusetts.[5] This Portuguese Archipelago has a total population of 516,612 (U.S. Census 2000). The major cities in the area, which account for about fifty-five percent of the area's population, are Attleboro, Fall River, New Bedford, and Taunton.

More than thirty percent (30.5) of the residents in this ethnic archipelago (N=132,376) are primarily of Portuguese ancestry, which is nearly three times that of any other ancestry group in the area.[6] Approximately half of Fall River's residents (49.6%), 43.0 percent of Dartmouth's residents, 41.2 percent of New Bedford's residents, and 39.4 percent of Somerset's residents claim Portuguese as their primary ancestry (U.S. Census, 2000). Other communities in this archipelago, including Acushnet, Swansea, Westport, Dighton, Fairhaven, Taunton, and Seekonk have more than twenty percent of their residents who are primarily of Portuguese ancestry.[6]

A total of 401 telephone interviews were conducted for the civic participation and political efficacy survey from June 1, 2000 to July 14, 2000.[7] A total of 400 telephone interviews were conducted for the economic satisfaction survey from April 15, 2000 to May 13, 2000. A total of 400 telephone interviews were conducted for the social and cultural issues survey from August 7, 2000 to October 11, 2000.

In the political efficacy survey, more than a quarter (28.6%) of the respondents identified themselves as Portuguese, Portuguese-American, or Cape Verdean. The majority of respondents (65.2%) were female. The average age of respondents is 45.0 years with median family incomes between $25,000 and $45,000. Portuguese respondents had significantly lower levels of education in comparison to non-Portuguese respondents with more than eighty-eight percent (88.4%) of non-Portuguese respondents having a high-school diploma or GED, while only 57.4 percent of Portuguese-American respondents had a high-school diploma or GED.[8] More than a quarter (28.2%) of non-Portuguese respondents had a bachelor's degree or higher, while 13.0 percent of Portuguese-Americans had a bachelor's degree or higher. A fifth of respondents (20.9%) primarily spoke a language other than English (mainly Portuguese) and 13.3 percent were not born in the United States. Only 12.5 percent of the foreign-born respondents report that they have lived in the country for fewer than ten years, while almost two-thirds of these respondents (65.6%) report living in the United States for twenty years or more.[9] The demographic characteristics for respondents to all three surveys were very similar, and, with the exception of females being over-represented in all three samples, the numbers and characteristics of respondents were roughly comparable to those reported in the 2000 Census. Every effort was made to insure the methodological validity of the findings, but as with all forays into new areas of inquiry, it is risky to overgeneralize our findings about Portuguese-Americans in southeastern Massachusetts. The purpose of the studies was not to provide a definitive answer to the question, "who are the Portuguese?" but to stimulate discussion among Portuguese-Americans about their political future and to catalyze further interest among social scientists in the study of Portuguese-American political behavior and ethnic identity.

Political Engagement and Economic Success

There are always exceptions to every generalization, but on the whole, Portuguese-Americans in southeastern Massachusetts have lower-than-average levels of formal educational attainment when compared to the U.S. and Massachusetts population. They occupy predominantly blue-collar occupations, but like other Americans they have low levels of union membership. The Portuguese remain overwhelmingly Catholic, although our survey findings suggest that the Catholic Church exerts little direct influence on their political behavior, and it does not constitute a significant source of political information for Portuguese-Americans. As with most residents in Massachusetts, the Portuguese are heavily Democratic in their political party identification, and yet, as I discuss below, there is an identifiable tension between the "Portuguese ideology" and the current policy orientation of the Democratic party.[10]

In many ways, Portuguese-Americans exemplify the model minority in the United States. The Portuguese arrived in the United States with little education and few skills, but became a mainstay of the fishing and manufacturing industries in southeastern Massachusetts (Rodrigues 1990). They have a strong work ethic and believe that a good education and working hard are the keys to personal economic success. However, a higher-than-average percentage of Portuguese-Americans still work in blue-collar jobs that require lower levels of educational attainment and these jobs provide lower-than-average incomes. Nevertheless, Portuguese-Americans report that they were generally satisfied with their economic progress over the previous five years (1995-2000), have a better standard of living than their parents, and they are optimistic about the prospects of their children to be better off than they are. A large majority of the region's Portuguese-Americans are satisfied with their jobs and, in a strong economy, there was little concern about the prospect of unemployment. Despite a massive wave of deindustrialization that swept the southeastern Massachusetts region less than a decade earlier, Portuguese-Americans seem to have adapted with a great deal of resilience and have shown the ability to adapt quickly to changing economic conditions, particularly in their increased recognition of the importance of education in the new economy (see Gilbert 1989). These findings suggest that despite being disproportionately concentrated in the lower rungs of the region's economic hierarchy, most Portuguese-Americans view themselves as living "the American Dream."

Nevertheless, the Portuguese-Americans who responded to our surveys also recognized that pockets of poverty and unemployment still exist in the region, and that the region's public schools will have to be improved to realize the optimistic expectations they have about their children's futures. Hence, our surveys found that Portuguese-Americans were concerned about the nation's lack of progress in reducing poverty, expressed doubts about the quality of public education, and, importantly, considered it the government's responsibility to insure economic equity. Moreover, these anxieties are not abstract concerns for many of the Portuguese in southeastern Massachusetts.

The sample size in a fourth survey conducted in 1999-2000 is not adequate to draw a definitive conclusion, but a survey of Portuguese-Americans in the city of Taunton, Massachusetts found that about thirteen percent of them were unemployed at a time when the state and local unemployment rates were below four percent (Barrow 2002, Chapter 2). Significantly, this survey by the Center for Policy Analysis did not measure "unemployment" using the official U.S. Bureau of Labor Statistics definition, but simply asked whether a person was employed (including as a homemaker). The large number of unemployed, using our broader definition, suggests that many Portuguese-Americans may be chronically unemployed (and perhaps unemployable with current skills) and, for that reason, they simply do not register in official statistics.[11]

Moreover, while Portuguese-Americans in southeastern Massachusetts report that they are generally satisfied with their job security and the physical safety of their workplaces, nearly half (46.7%) are not satisfied with their chance for promotion. This concern could be an effect of their low educational attainment, their concentration in declining and downsizing manufacturing industries, or subtle forms of ethnic discrimination. While a large majority of Portuguese-Americans, like other Americans, are satisfied with their health care benefits, approximately one-third (32.8%) were not satisfied with those benefits and more than a third (36.7%) were not satisfied with their current medical and family leave benefits. Similarly, nearly one-third (30.0%) were dissatisfied with their current pension benefits. Although a majority of the region's Portuguese-Americans are satisfied with their current earnings, more than a third (36.4%) are dissatisfied with their earnings.

Thus, there is a significant pocket of economic discontent among Portuguese-Americans that is largely concentrated among persons holding low-wage jobs and having low levels of educational attainment (usually less than a high-school diploma). This pocket of discontent also consists disproportionately (usually more than half) of Portuguese who are foreign-born, and since many of these persons are not U.S. citizens, they are not eligible to vote. Therefore, the potential political alienation of this disaffected group of Portuguese-Americans is not likely to register in normal electoral politics. Our survey findings document that these are the very people who are least likely to vote, the least likely to belong to political or civic organizations, the least likely to contact government officials, and the least likely to be politically informed at even the most basic level.

This is an important finding because our surveys also indicate that when the Portuguese become U.S. citizens *and register to vote*, they tend to vote in comparatively high proportions (contrary to conventional wisdom), although like most Americans they vote with low levels of basic political information. For example, one-third of the respondents in our Taunton survey could not name the mayor of Taunton or the governor of Massachusetts; and these findings were replicated in a second, larger survey of the region's entire Portuguese Archipelago. These low levels of political information are strongly correlated with low levels of educational attainment and low incomes, which leads to the intriguing hypothesis that these respondents may be the same group of Portuguese-Americans that have low levels of political efficacy and who express dissatisfaction with their current economic conditions.[13]

Moreover, despite recognizing the importance of education to economic success, their overall satisfaction with the quality of public schools suggests continuing difficulty in adjusting to a constantly rising performance bar in the United States. Southeastern Massachusetts has some of the lowest performing schools in the Commonwealth of Massachusetts as measured by chronic absenteeism, high-school drop-out rates, standardized test scores, and rates of college attendance (Borges and Barrow 2000). It is quite notable that persons with lower levels of educational attainment are more likely to be dissatisfied with the quality of public schools.

Voter specialists are political participants who confine their political activism to regularized voting and occasional efforts to persuade others how to vote. Portuguese-Americans are hybrid voter specialists insofar as their voting behavior (and other forms of political participation) are more intently focused on *local* elections, where they have neighborhood enclaves, access to Portuguese-language media, and a greater probability of finding Portuguese-American candidates running for office. The Portuguese clearly express a stronger attachment to local politics than to national politics, despite the fact that issues such as immigration reform, deportation, deindustrialization, trade policy, unemployment, and the regional economy's overall performance, which directly affect large numbers of Portuguese-Americans in southeastern Massachusetts, are largely beyond the control of local governments and local politics.

Nevertheless, our findings indicate that Portuguese-Americans who are registered to vote turn out to vote in comparatively high proportions for all types of elections, but they are also hybrid voter specialists in the sense that they are more likely to make particularized contacts with government officials than most Americans, especially with local government officials. Particularized contacts consist of direct contacts with government officials, such as phone calls, individual or small group meetings, personal conversations at political or cultural events, or even informal encounters with government officials. In comparison to other groups in southeastern Massachusetts, Portuguese-Americans prefer direct contact with elected officials and such contact is facilitated by the large the number of bilingual Portuguese-Americans holding public office in the region as state legislators, mayors, city councilors, town selectmen, and school committee members.

Thus, Portuguese-Americans also express their greatest sense of political efficacy at the local level. However, it is interesting that while Portuguese-Americans are much more likely to make particularized contacts with government officials than the average American, the vast majority also feel they need an intermediary or political connection to help them make that contact. This finding suggests that Portuguese-Americans who are elected to office, as well as other civic leaders, provide an important conduit between Portuguese-Americans and their governments. It also reinforces the need for strong civic and political associations in the Portuguese community to facilitate these contacts on a wider basis (see Bloemraad 2006).

The idea that strong civic associations make a difference to political participation and political efficacy is supported by other evidence. Aside from the small number of persons who are simply "not interested in politics," the vast majority (85.7%) of Portuguese-Americans who are U.S. citizens, but not registered to vote, state that they are interested in registering if the opportunity is made easily available, if someone would show them how to register, and if literacy assistance is available to help them fill out the registration form where language is a problem. This finding indicates that among Portuguese-Americans who are already U.S. citizens, a fertile ground exists for voter registration campaigns, particularly if these campaigns are tied to local electoral races involving Portuguese-American candidates. Given their stronger attachments to local government, these campaigns are likely to be most successful when organized around races for the state legislature, city council, mayor, selectman, and school committee.

Our findings also indicate that the more salient differences in occupation, income, and education are between foreign-born and U.S.-born Portuguese than between U.S.-born Portuguese and other Americans. This finding suggests that the Portuguese are assimilating into the U.S. economy and become involved in local politics by the second or third generation, even while maintaining a distinct ethnic culture and a living language in their neighborhoods, sports clubs, and fraternal orders. However, when the Center's surveys are compared to earlier studies of

Portuguese-Americans in southeastern Massachusetts, it is clear that membership in Portuguese political organizations has been decreasing over the last twenty-five years, while membership in various civic associations, particularly sports clubs and social clubs, has been increasing during the same period (Marinho 2002). One inference from this finding is that in contrast to many other U.S. ethnic or racial groups (e.g., African-Americans or Mexican-Americans), Portuguese ethnic identity is evolving into a predominantly social or cultural identity and not a political one (see Cabral 1989).

This conclusion is further supported by our finding that a majority of Portuguese-Americans in southeastern Massachusetts do not think it is necessary for a person to be a member of a particular ethnic group to represent that group's interests.[14] Only twenty percent of the Portuguese-Americans surveyed felt strongly that being of the same ethnicity made a difference in an elected official's ability to represent a particular ethnic group. This may be an increase from the six percent reported in Marinho's 1977 study, but it is difficult to tell whether this is a real increase or merely the effect of slightly different questions. Regardless of how this methodological question gets resolved in the future, our findings also reveal that seventy-three percent of the Portuguese-Americans surveyed believe that they are well represented in important government and business institutions in southeastern Massachusetts.

Nevertheless, the empirical findings of a later study suggest that in proportion to their numbers in the population, Portuguese-Americans are actually "underrepresented" by approximately fifty percent in state and local political, educational, and cultural institutions (Barrow and Galipeau 2005). These findings of a 2005 study by Barrow and Galipeau indicate that Portuguese-Americans occupy only two percent of state level decision-making positions, while they are 4.3 percent of the state's population. At the local level, Portuguese-Americans occupy seventeen percent of important decision-making positions in the Portuguese Archipelago, and selected towns of Cape Cod, although they constitute 30.5 percent of the area's population.

However, this finding should be qualified with the observation that most Portuguese-Americans in Massachusetts are still first-generation immigrants or second-generation ethnics. Thus, despite being "underrepresented" in a strict sense, it is encouraging to note that Portuguese-

Americans are best represented in local government positions (19%), although they remain less well-represented in local school committees (15%). Similarly, at the state level, Portuguese-Americans have achieved near parity by occupying three percent of the state's legislative positions, but they occupy only two percent of the state's educational decision-making positions (trustees, boards, presidents, chancellors), and statistically have less than 0.5% of the executive and judicial positions at the state level. However, this is a typical pattern of political succession—another component of the American Dream—where ethnic groups win office at the local level, parlay that experience into state legislative campaigns, and then eventually secure appointments to executive and judicial offices. While Portuguese-Americans are not strictly represented in proportion to their numbers in the population, they are nevertheless far from a disenfranchised or disprivileged group in the political arena.

Ethnic Identity

Our findings on Portuguese ethnic identity are intriguing, but equivocal. There were many statistically significant differences between the responses of Portuguese and non-Portuguese respondents on questions related to ethnic identity. Portuguese respondents are more likely to think of themselves as members of a particular ethnic, racial, or nationality group than are the variety of non-Portuguese respondents, who as a group have generally resided in the United States for a much longer period of time. Portuguese-Americans are also more likely to report experiencing ethnic discrimination, with nearly a third (32.0%) of Portuguese-Americans reporting they have felt discrimination because of their ethnicity or race. Yet Portuguese-Americans are about evenly divided over whether applying to the federal government for official "minority" status would create better educational and job opportunities than those available to non-minority groups.

At the same time, a higher percentage of Portuguese respondents felt that racial and ethnic groups should maintain their distinct cultures as compared to the region's non-Portuguese respondents. A majority of Portuguese respondents felt that racial and ethnic groups should maintain their distinct cultures (52.7%) in comparison to non-Portuguese respondents (31.2%). This feeling is particularly strong among foreign-born Portuguese (70.3%)

as compared to Portuguese who were born in the United States (44.6%), although even the latter still report a stronger attachment to their ethnic identity than most non-Portuguese. Yet, at the same time, a large majority of Portuguese-Americans also said they think of themselves as "just an American," even though a higher percentage of Portuguese respondents consider themselves members of a particular ethnic, racial or nationality group (24.6%) than non-Portuguese respondents (3.2%). Notably, Portuguese respondents who were not born in the United States are far more likely to identify with a particular ethnic, racial or nationality group (50.0%) than Portuguese respondents who were born in the United States (12.7%), which suggests that a certain degree of social and cultural assimilation is occurring among the second and subsequent generations of Portuguese-Americans.

In this respect, the Portuguese seem to have embraced a "mosaic" concept of American identity, which does not put their sense of being "Portuguese" in conflict with being "American" (see Fuchs 1991). The characteristics identified by the region's Portuguese as most important to being an American, in order of importance, are U.S. citizenship, the ability to speak English, and being born in the United States. This concept of being "American" explains why a large number of Portuguese-Americans—particularly, the foreign-born, those without U.S. citizenship, and those who speak English poorly—may continue to feel marginalized in their adopted country and have a stronger sense of Portuguese identity. They are "non-American" by their own definition of what it means to be American. While a foreign-born individual may learn English and obtain U.S. citizenship, it is only their children—born in the United States—who are perceived as "truly" and "completely" American, even within the Portuguese-American community.

Consistent with this finding is the fact that a surprisingly large majority of both Portuguese and non-Portuguese respondents favor a law making English the official language of the United States. It is certainly true that Portuguese respondents are more likely than non-Portuguese respondents to oppose a law making English the official language of the United States, but foreign-born Portuguese are the only group in our sample to strongly oppose the adoption of an "English-only" law. Similarly, while all groups agree that rates of immigration to the United States should remain the same or decrease, the only significant pocket of support for increased immigration was among foreign-born Portuguese-Americans.

In this respect, the region's Portuguese-American community is deeply fractured between a politicized minority who feel that Portuguese ethnicity should be constituted as a political identity, versus the substantial majority who now view Portuguese ethnicity as primarily a social and cultural identity. Our survey results indicate that the politicized minority currently finds its strongest base of support among foreign-born Portuguese, and this is the same group that is most likely to feel that they do not get enough attention from government. Of course, due to statutory barriers such as non-citizenship, language barriers, and education levels, this paradoxically is the very segment of the Portuguese community that is least likely to be politically active in any form. In fact, Portuguese-American respondents to our surveys report that they are less "interested in politics" than other ethnic groups, and this finding is particularly true of the foreign-born and especially if they are not U.S. citizens. Furthermore, while the politicized minority overlaps with the sub-group that expresses discontent about its economic situation, the two groups are distinct enough to raise questions about whether they can combine in sufficient strength to realign Portuguese ethnic identity in a political direction, particularly since many among the economically dissatisfied are currently non-political (see Breton and Minard 1960).

Political Power

Even if Portuguese-Americans were to agree on a distinct political identity, to become citizens in larger numbers, register to vote in larger numbers and therefore vote in larger numbers, what is their potential impact on the regional politics of southeastern Massachusetts? Independent of whether mobilizing Portuguese-Americans would lead to the election of more Portuguese-American candidates, there are some potentially significant impacts. For instance, at a time when party identification, particularly among Democrats, has been weakening at both the state and national levels, Portuguese-Americans remain staunchly loyal to the Democratic party and the economic tenets of New Deal liberalism.[15] Nearly all (96.6%) Portuguese-Americans in southeastern Massachusetts who voted in the 1996 U.S. Presidential election voted for Bill Clinton.

This is a landslide Democratic majority that is unmatched by any other ethnic group except African-Americans. It is a particularly striking majority when compared to other white caucasian voters in the United States, including blue-collar workers, whose support for Democratic candidates is much weaker than that reported by Portuguese-Americans with the same demographic characteristics.

However, Portuguese-American support for the Democratic party cannot be taken for granted because it is clear that a psychological and ideological disjuncture is emerging between them. Despite their stated preference for the Democratic party, Portuguese-Americans' psychological attachment to the Democratic party appears to be weakening, which is not only consistent with a long-term statewide and national trend of declining party identification and "split ticket" voting, but with key elements of assimilation theory. As adopted by political scientists, assimilation theory suggests that first-generation immigrants who become citizens gravitate to the liberal wing of the Democratic party, which is perceived as ethnically pluralistic and as the party of the working class. Second-generation ethnics, particularly those who achieve some degree of middle-class economic or professional success, loosen their ties to the Democratic party and begin to adopt less liberal views. By the third generation, the ethnic group becomes a microcosm of the U.S. political party and ideological spectrum, where political and ideological divisions within the ethnic group, based on socioeconomic differences, are wider than the ethnic differences between comparable socioeconomic sub-groups in a similar position (Dahl 1961). Indeed, even while expressing strong support for the Democratic party, about sixty percent of Portuguese-Americans now dismiss party affiliation as important to a candidate's ability to represent their interests.

This finding is particularly interesting since the Democratic party, nationally and statewide, is continuing its move toward a "neo-liberal" mix of fiscal conservatism and socio-cultural liberalism in response to national and state trends in voter behavior (Nie, Verba, Petrocik 1976; Ladd 1978; Pomper 2001). There have been two dominant trends in the American electorate over the last two decades with respect to party affiliation and ideological orientation. The number of persons who consider themselves Independents, rather than identifying with either major party, has increased consistently since the early 1970s, so that more persons now identify themselves as Independent than identify with either of the two major political parties.[16] The rising number of Independents has been accompanied by a shift in ideological orientation, where more and more voters, especially middle-class educated voters, have adopted an ideological orientation that is economically and fiscally conservative, but socially and culturally liberal. This perspective has certainly characterized electoral outcomes in Massachusetts during the last two decades, when socially liberal Republican governors and a fiscally conservative Democratic legislature have been elected.

The Portuguese-Americans responding to our surveys reveal an opposite mix of liberal and conservative views that stands in direct contrast to the nation's "changing American voter." Portuguese-Americans—at least those in southeastern Massachusetts—appear to be headed in the opposite direction. In general, Portuguese-Americans articulate a hybrid ideology that is best described as economically liberal, socially liberal (i.e., supportive of individual and group rights), but culturally conservative (i.e., traditional moral values). Indeed, such views are historically characteristic of the "lunch bucket Democrats" that were once the bulwark of the old New Deal coalition in the Northeast (i.e., blue-collar and Catholic).

As mentioned earlier, the Center's survey of economic opinions found that most Portuguese-Americans are optimistic about their economic situation, but are disturbed by the lack of progress on reducing poverty, and they strongly agree that inequalities of wealth and income are too wide in the United States. Moreover, Portuguese-Americans consider it government's responsibility to address issues of economic equity and economic opportunity. Portuguese-Americans in southeastern Massachusetts were also surprisingly liberal, given conventional wisdom, on a variety of social issues involving individual and group rights, such as support for bilingual education, the recognition of gender inequalities in employment, opposition to the death penalty, qualified support for abortion rights, and tolerance of same-sex civil unions. However, it is important to note that U.S.-born Portuguese were significantly more liberal on these social issues than foreign-born Portuguese.

At the same time, Portuguese-Americans express opinions on a variety of other issues that would ordinarily be described as culturally conservative, such as the belief that ethnic groups should assimilate into the mainstream of American society; support for prayer in public schools; support for public funding of parochial schools; a belief that becoming an "American" means becoming a U.S. citizen, speaking English, and living in the United States for most of one's life; support for the deportation of legal aliens convicted of felony crimes; and concern about exposing children to violence in movies and on television. Furthermore, most Portuguese-Americans in southeastern Massachusetts report that they do not feel discriminated against because of their ethnicity. Yet again, on many of these issues, it is the foreign-born Portuguese who anchor this conservative tendency, with many U.S.-born Portuguese adopting liberal views on most (but not all) cultural issues in the same proportions as Americans generally.

Depending on one's interpretation, this "Portuguese ideology" can be viewed as an anachronistic legacy of the New Deal—a cultural survival of the old politics determined by their disproportionate concentration in declining sectors of the regional economy—or as a reservoir of political support for a (economic) liberal renewal within the Democratic party. However, any potential impact on regional or statewide politics depends on the ability of Portuguese-Americans to enter the political system in greater numbers and to do so as a coherent political force with a unified voice. As noted earlier, Portuguese-Americans vote and register to vote in about the same proportions as other U.S. citizens, but of course, large numbers of Portuguese-Americans still cannot register to vote because they are not U.S. citizens. Thus, in addition to the problem of constructing a coherent political identity, targeting issues important to the Portuguese-American community, and mobilizing voters during elections, those interested in Portuguese-American political participation face the added burden of promoting citizenship among their cohorts. There are many ethnic legends about why so many Portuguese fail to become citizens, but our survey evidence does not support these claims in southeastern Massachusetts. Quite the contrary, a vast majority of the Portuguese interviewed for these studies express a desire to become U.S. citizens, but they simply do not know how to do so or even know how to initiate an application. The problem is not determined by "culture" or by a desire to return the old country, but it is a problem of immigrant assistance and government policy, as Bloemraad (2006) has demonstrated in her comparative analysis of immigrant political incorporation in Canada and the United States.

The survey findings also argue for the need to build (or rebuild) the social capital of the Portuguese community generally. While many of our survey findings replicate the expectations of the socioeconomic model of political behavior, the surveys also found that persons who belong to political organizations and civic associations, and who read newspapers are more likely to register to vote, more likely to vote, more likely to try to influence the voting of others, and likely to have a greater sense of political efficacy. Thus, while sports clubs, fraternal orders, and Portuguese language media outlets may all be non-partisan, or even non-political, on their surface, they provide cultural support mechanisms and institutional training grounds for political activity and political leadership. Significantly, a high percentage of Portuguese-Americans in our Taunton survey report that they still obtain political information from Portuguese-language media outlets, and our findings indicate that Portuguese-Americans have greater levels of trust and confidence in the mass media, as a result of this association, than other groups in the region.

From Immigrants to Ethnics

Rumbaut and Portes observe that a "color line" has historically "defined the boundary between two broad modes of ethnic incorporation into American social life" (2001, 4). One of these modes is epitomized by the traditional concept of assimilation, which purports to identify a single process that earlier "melted" tens of millions of European immigrants of heterogeneous national origins into a mainstream (largely Anglo-Saxon) American nation. In this view, ethnic identities in America are largely symbolic and, by the "third generation," survive only in the occasional homage to ethnic dress, dance, music, food, and holidays (Nahirny and Fishman 1996, 266).[17] The other mode of ethnic incorporation views certain groups as largely resistant to assimilation, whether by choice or exclusion, with a great deal of social distance and/or discrimination persisting in intergroup relations regardless of the groups level of acculturation or socioeconomic attainment (e.g., Hassidic Jews, African-Americans). However, as Rumbaut and Portes (2001, 5) observe, these conventional models of immigrant assimilation and ethnic self-identification are largely derived from processes that mirror the historical experience of Northern and Western European immigrants and their descendants, particularly those who arrived in the United States prior to World War II.

However, the Portuguese began arriving in the United States in large numbers during the 1920s as part of a larger wave of Southern and Eastern European immigration that consisted mostly of nationality groups—Italians, Poles, Greeks, and Russian Jews—who were often alleged to be unassimilable to American society. The establishment of national origin quota laws in the 1920s stemmed this flow, and the Portuguese did not immigrate to the United States again in large numbers until the 1960s and 1980s. In our own findings, we do find that assimilation is taking place among second-generation (i.e., U.S.-born) Portuguese-Americans, but extensive new comparative research on more recent immigrant groups in the United States finds that assimilation "is a process subject to too many contingencies and affected by too many variables to render the image of a relatively uniform and straightforward path convincing" (Rumbaut and Portes 2001, 5). Assimilation is no longer considered an either/or proposition as in previous models, but is now frequently viewed as a *segmented* process in which different immigrant groups and their children assimilate into different sectors of mainstream American society at different paces and by drawing on different levels of social capital and adaptive capacities in those sectors.

Assimilation to American society is certainly characteristic among the second-generation Portuguese, but the key question for all contemporary immigrant and ethnic groups is assimilation to *what sectors* of the society and under what conditions (Rumbaut and Portes 2001, 302). The theory of segmented assimilation views it as a complex process that hinges on at least four factors: 1) the history of the immigrant first generation, including the human capital brought to the United States by immigrants and the context of their reception; 2) the diffferential place of acculturation among parents and children; 3) the cultural and economic barriers confronted by second-generation youth in their quest for successful adaptation; and 4) the family and community resources available to the second generation for confronting these barriers (Rumbaut and Portes 2001, 5).

The comparative research published by Rumbaut and Portes (2001, 10) finds that some of the ethnic groups created by the new immigration "are in a clearly upward path, moving into society's mainstream in record time and enriching it in the process with their culture and energies. Others, on the contrary, seem poised for a path of blocked aspirations and downward mobility, reproducing the plight of today's impoverished domestic minorities." Indeed, the children of immigrants who live in poverty are regularly exposed to the lifestyle and outlook of the most downtrodden segments of the native population. Findings suggest that where there is not a well-structured ethnic community capable of reinforcing parental authority and "traditional values," the exposure of the second generation (most of our sample) to this lifestyle and outlook may well put them on a path of dissonant acculturation (i.e., non-assimilation) and downward mobility, particularly when these conditions are reinforced by external ethnic discrimination, the disappearance of industrial job ladders, and the increasing educational requirements of a technology-driven economy (Rumbaut and Portes 2001, 304-306).

While Portuguese-Americans face many of these barriers in southeastern Massachusetts, the continuing strength of Portuguese cultural identity and ethnic networks provides at least some insulation and counterforce to these barriers. Consequently, the Portuguese of southeastern Massachusetts seem to be pursuing the path that Rumbaut and Portes identify as selective acculturation. Selective acculturation steers a path between the traditional process of mainstream assimilation and the opposite process of exclusion, non-assimilation, and downward mobility into the underclass. Selective acculturation is defined by:

> a paced learning of the host culture along with retention of significant elements of the culture of origin. *Selective acculturation* is commonly associated with fluent bilingualism in the second generation.... [T]he key element in selective acculturation is the absorption by the second-generation youths of key values and normative expectations from their original culture and concomitant respect for them. (Rumbaut and Portes 2001, 308)

First-generation immigrants from Portugal continue to benefit from ethnic niches in the region's labor market, although their opportunities for social mobility are often blocked by poor mastery of the English language, the experience of ethnic discrimination, and exclusion from the formal political system by non-citizen status. Because of their ethnic niche in the region's labor market however, Portuguese-Americans in southeastern Massachusetts are still heavily slotted into declining (industrial) sectors of the region's economy, while they confront the challenge of moving into new sectors of the post-industrial economy with below average levels of educational attainment. However, these dissonant factors are partially offset, at least for now, by deep social capital; namely, ethnic networks that provide continuing access to jobs, social support, and political resources, as well as parental and family networks that echo the importance of a good education and a strong work ethic for future success.

The second generation (U.S.-born) has improved its level of educational attainment, even though it remains below that of other ethnic groups in the region. Furthemore, it is achieving a measurable level of representation in the political system, particularly at the local level, where Portuguese-Americans express their highest levels of political interest and knowledge. This progress is facilitated by strong ethnic networks and a persistent cultural identity rooted in family and religion. Selective acculturation is already taking place in the second generation (native-born), but not to the same extent in the first generation (foreign-born), which retains a stronger and more encompassing sense of ethnic identity that is based on exclusion from the opportunity to be completely "American." Thus, it is likely that the divergent views found among the foreign-born and U.S.-born Portuguese in our samples do not represent a long-term splintering of the community into divergent assimilation patterns, but these divisions may be as much "generational" (i.e., first and second or immigrant and ethnic), which allow us to observe the process of selective assimilation at "different times" simultaneously among these two groups of Portuguese-Americans. A lingering question is whether this pattern of selective acculturation can persist across another generation without further tangible economic and educational success in the next generation.

Future Research Directions

There are several important limitations to the empirical findings in our 1999-2000 surveys of Portuguese-Americans in southeastern Massachusetts. First, there is no inherent reason to assume that these findings can be generalized to other Portuguese-American communities, such as those in New Jersey, Rhode Island, Connecticut, California, and Hawaii. The cross-ethnic comparisons of Rumbaut and Portes find that "first-generation resettlement is decisively influenced by what immigrants bring with them in the way of skills, experiences, and resources and the environment that receives them." (2001, 207) These, in turn, create both barriers and opportunities for the second generation in their efforts to maintain an ethnic identity, while assimilating to mainstream culture. The combination of these factors allows for different modes of incorporation into the host society. While this concept (Rumbaut and Portes 1991, 83-93) has been used mainly to describe the different forms of acculturation and identity formation among different ethnic groups, it is certainly conceivable that state or regional sub-groups of the Portuguese-American community could develop distinct political cultures around the local politics, issues, and institutions of each location. It is equally conceivable that one might find an East Coast/West Coast divergence of political cultures. Given the explanatory power of the socioeconomic model in our surveys, it is also equally conceivable that class, or socioeconomic status, could be a common explanatory variable across these communities. Yet, until comparable behavioral and public opinion surveys are done in those communities, it is not possible to answer these questions.

Second, since a component of political culture is historical experience, it is potentially significant that most Portuguese-Americans in southeastern Massachusetts immigrated from the Azores. At a minimum, this fact warrants a comparison between "mainland" and "island" Portuguese, but given the small numbers of continental Portuguese among immigrants to southeastern Massachusetts, such a comparison was not possible in our surveys. Similarly, because Portuguese-Americans were surveyed as a single group for purposes of our analysis (i.e., to compare their views to non-Portuguese), neither the sample nor the survey was designed to fully capture and analyze differences within the region's Portuguese community. Nevertheless, such differences emerged in the data, but the sample sizes were often too small to draw anything but suggestive inferences. In particular, the distinction between native-born and foreign-born Portuguese was frequently the single most salient predictor of different opinions within the southeastern Massachusetts Portuguese community, and this topic warrants deeper analysis with appropriately designed surveys and samples. Indeed, on many items, the differences between foreign-born and U.S.-born Portuguese-Americans are larger than those between U.S.-born Portuguese-Americans and other ethnic groups. It also points to the need for additional analyses of how the assimilation process differentiates U.S.-born Portuguese from the foreign-born, as well as a comparison of those processes among the Portuguese and other ethnic groups.

Finally, it could prove interesting to probe the differences of attitude and background between those who view Portuguese ethnicity as "political" and those who view it as "cultural." In this respect, there is more work to be done in probing Portuguese-Americans' attitudes toward applying for official minority status and their attitudes toward affirmative action. It would be equally interesting to explore how other Americans perceive Portuguese ethnicity. However, these are questions that can only be posed by our research and addressed by further investigation.

Conclusion

Many of the oft-repeated assumptions about the Portuguese and politics are simply false, while the most salient characteristics about their political behavior and political beliefs are not explained by fixed historical or cultural characteristics of the group. Political behavior and ideological beliefs are significantly correlated with educational attainment, socioeconomic status, and generational status, and, as Bloemraad (2006) has effectively demonstrated, government policies to support immigrant groups can have a significant impact on whether these factors facilitate the political incorporation or socioeconomic exclusion of immigrant groups.

First, it should be emphasized that Portuguese-Americans are not less politically active than other ethnic groups, but rather Americans generally have low levels of political and civic participation. The same is true with respect to their levels of political knowledge, although Portuguese-Americans did reveal a higher level of interest in local politics, where Portuguese-American office holders are more numerous, than in state or national politics. They also did not show higher levels of distrust in government than other groups and, in fact, had greater trust in the mass media than other groups, based partly on their access to Portuguese-language newspapers, radio, and television programs. However, our findings did indicate that Portuguese-Americans generally do not define their ethnic identity in "political" terms in ways similar to that of other ethnic, racial, or nationality groups in the United States, although the Portuguese community is deeply divided on that question.

Thus, in reviewing these findings one is left wondering whether there is a distinct Portuguese-American interest in state and national politics. It is certain that our preliminary research cannot fully answer that question, but it does call for some rudimentary preliminary conclusions. The Portuguese-American interest in the U.S. political process derives from a combination of historical, cultural, and socio-economic factors. The historical and cultural factors largely define a "foreign policy" interest that includes immigration issues, deportation, cultural exchange, Portuguese language instruction, and greater engagement with other Lusophone nations. Any progress on these issues will require the combined foreign policy efforts of Lusophone governments and domestic lobbying from Portuguese-American political groups, because many of these issues do not command great support from most non-Portuguese voters. The Portuguese-Americans' socioeconomic status, in southeastern Massachusetts at least, largely defines a "domestic policy" interest that includes access to improved education and higher education, workforce development and worker displacement assistance, worker rights, a living wage, medical benefits, pension benefits, and a whole range of other issues that affect blue-collar workers in the new economy. It must also include immigration assistance and government facilitated access to citizenship. These two sets of issues merge for Portuguese-Americans in the process of economic globalization and trade liberalization, which is having a profound impact on the low-skilled manufacturing jobs in southeastern Massachusetts that have been the mainstay of Portuguese-American well-being for more than a century. Portuguese-Americans in southeastern Massachusetts, more than many other groups, are faced simultaneously with the problems of adjusting to economic globalization and deindustrialization, and the problems of identity and citizenship in a new country.

Consequently, it should be noted that there is a major structural impediment to the further advancement of Portuguese-American interests looming on the horizon. The Portuguese arrived in southeastern Massachusetts late in the industrialization process, and, in fact, they arrived just as the region's economic base was beginning to deindustrialize. The basic industries that sustained the economic, political, and cultural rise of previous immigrant groups—fishing, textiles, apparel, and automotive components—were relocating to other regions of the country or foreign locations, while later being replaced by firms in the new post-industrial economy (i.e., marine technology, medical devices, business and professional services, health care). It is possible that these economic disruptions could disrupt the "normal" dynamic of succession politics and social mobility.

This zero sum scenario means that one group—a new group—can only gain at the expense of older and more established groups, who are not likely to step aside quietly. A politics of economic decline, or economic stagnation, is one that inevitably breeds racial, ethnic, and class conflict as new groups demand equal access to the economic and political system. It is then no longer possible to distribute a share of economic resources and political opportunities to new groups, or incorporate them into the established power structure without de-distributing resources from established groups. Indeed, because the established groups control the major levers of power, they are in a position to protect their earlier gains even if it requires the exclusion of newer immigrant groups. Therefore, economic decline may effectively lock in the established power structure and lock new immigrant groups into their disadvantaged position in the economy and society even where they make political gains. Thus, the prospects for further advancement may not be promising without improvements to the Southeast region's overall economic outlook.

Notes

[1] For example, Gerstle (2001), Fuchs (1991), Bailey and Katz (1969), Litt (1970), Olzak and Nagel (1986), Walton, Jr. (1997), Pienkos (1978), Kantowicz (1975), Erie (1990), Bean (1994), González (2001), Suro (1998), Chapa, (1995), Cruz (1995), Zia (2000), San Juan (1994).

[2] The one notable exception is the important work by Bloemraad (2006).

[3] For the full results of these surveys, see Barrow (2002).

[4] Plymouth is technically a "town" as defined by the Massachusetts General Laws, but its population is larger than Taunton's and is therefore included as one of the region's major urban centers.

[5] The definition of the Portuguese Archipelago for this report is based on the Public Use Microdata Area (PUMA) definitions from the U.S. Census Bureau for 2000.

[6] For purposes of this study, Cape Verdeans were included as persons of Portuguese ancestry, but the survey does not include Brazilians as part of this ancestry group. In 2000, there were 11,057 Cape Verdeans and 1,233 Brazilians in the Portuguese Archipelago (U.S. Census 2000). Cape Verdeans were included as Portuguese because the island remained part of Portugal until 1975, and the timing of Cape Verdean immigration to southeastern Massachusetts coincides with immigration from the Azores and the mainland. In contrast, Brazil achieved national independence in 1822, and their arrival in southeastern Massachusetts began after the last major wave of Portuguese immigration in the 1980s.

[7] Ancestry refers to a person's ethnic origin or descent, cultural heritage, or the place of birth of the person or the person's parents or ancestors before arrival in the United States. In the U.S. Census, the term "primary ancestry" includes persons who report only Portuguese as their ethnic group or persons who report Portuguese first and then some other group. The term "secondary ancestry" includes persons who report Portuguese second and some other group first (U.S. Census 2000).

[8] The Genesys Sampling System was used to generate random telephone numbers for each of the three surveys. The Genesys Sampling System uses a list of all possible telephone numbers (listed and unlisted) in the United States and then randomly generates a telephone sample for a designated geographic area. The sample is generated using random digit dialing (RDD), which insures an equal and known probability of selection for every residential telephone number in the polling area. To facilitate efficiency in polling, the original list of possible numbers is "cleaned" so far as possible of disconnected numbers, cellular telephone numbers, facsimile machines, and business establishments. The telephone interviews were conducted between 9:00am and 9:00pm on weekdays and between 11:00am and 3:00pm on Saturdays. This range of hours provides interviewers with an opportunity to contact hard-to-reach respondents, and "no answer" telephone numbers were contacted at least seven times at varying times of the day, including weekends, before they were considered unreachable.

[9] As early as 1990, Portes and Rumbault noted that immigrants from Portugal "resemble those from Mexico in their low average educational attainment" (1990, 59).

[10] A Pearson Chi-square test of independence was conducted to determine if different variables, such as education, income, sex, native or foreign birth, and length of residence in the United States, had statistically correlated with respondents' answers to various questions. The Pearson Chi-square is the most common test for significance of the relationship between categorical variables. This statistic is used to test the measure of association between columns and rows in tabular data. It tests the hypothesis of no association of columns and rows in tabular data. The correlation between variables is considered statistically significant if the Pearson Chi-square and the Pearson Correlation coefficient is .05 and below. While the Pearson Chi-square value determines the correlation between two variables, correlation analysis alone does not allow the researcher to determine causality between variables. Furthermore, in some cases, two variables that move together may be driven simultaneously by a third variable. In cases such as these, partial correlations were run to control for, or partial out, the effects of a third factor thought to drive the relationship between the two variables of interest.

[11] See Barrow (2002) for the actual poll results that support these conclusions.

[12] The United States Department of Labor conducts a monthly survey to measure changes in the labor force and unemployment rates. To be counted as "unemployed," a person must not be employed, but must have also actively sought employment during the last four weeks. A person who is not actively seeking employment (e.g., discouraged workers) are not counted as part of the official labor force. This "disguised unemployment" simply does not register in the official unemployment statistics (Shim and Siegel 1995, 105-106).

[13] It was not possible to test this hypothesis directly, since the political efficacy, economic satisfaction, and political behavior surveys were conducted separately to prevent the surveys from becoming too long and losing respondents' interest.

[14] This finding could also explain why Portuguese-Americans simultaneously feel they need an intermediary or political connection to make direct contact with elected officials, particularly those who are not Portuguese-American.

[15] The terms liberal and neo-liberal are employed in their contemporary "American" usage, rather than in their classical "European" meanings (see Dolbeare and Medcalf 1993, 72-83). Liberalism, in its American usage, is an ideological orientation that seeks to promote social justice and equity through state action, while accepting the principle that such policies depend on the expansion and profitability of the private sector. This contrasts with American "conservatives," who advocate a laissez-faire economic policy or socialists who advocate public and social ownership of the means of production.

[16] There were 1,794,046 registered Democrats, 489,060 registered Republicans, and 1,909,491 registered as unenrolled voters in Massachusetts in 2000 (Massachusetts 2006). An unenrolled voter in Massachusetts is called an Independent voter in most other states.

[17] For example, as it is practiced in the United States today, Christmas is largely modeled on Dutch and German customs (e.g., St. Nickolaus and Christmas trees), but nearly everyone celebrates it in a similar manner. Likewise, most people celebrate St. Patrick's Day (Irish) and Columbus Day (Italian) so that ethnic symbolism is celebrated but also incorporated into the mainstream of the entire society.

CHAPTER 12

The Role of the School in the Maintenance and Change of Ethnic Group Affiliation[1]

ADELINE BECKER

Social scientists and educators have written extensively about the role of educational institutions in the creation of national identity. Seen as one of society's most important socializing agents, "elementary and secondary schools mold children into little Americans, little Germans, little Russians. They propagate the historical lore of the people, the myths, the beliefs and the faiths" (Key 1961, 315). This view does not take into account the realities of urban American school populations, which are comprised of children from diverse socioeconomic, racial, and ethnic backgrounds. While much attention has already been focused on the "hidden agenda," or informal ways in which the schools communicate a particular set of messages about gender, class, and race (see, e.g., Ogbu 1978; Tyack 1974; Rosenfeld 1971; Henry 1975), less is known about the ways in which schools mold, shape, and change the ethnic identity of recent immigrant children.

Mead (1973, 97) has asked, "What effects have the mingling of peoples—of different races, different religions and different levels of cultural complexity—had upon our concept of education?" With over five million foreign-born students in the public schools, one might also ask, "What effect has our educational system had upon these different peoples?" This study examines the effect of implicit educational policies on Portuguese immigrant students in an urban New England high school.

Structural and Cultural/Symbolic Ethnicity

My research has been formulated in relationship to both the literature on ethnicity and to educational analyses of the school as a socializing agent.

I have taken an approach which focuses on both the structural or group features of ethnicity and on the symbolic or identity-related features.

A view of ethnicity as a structural concept assumes a fixed set of attributes associated with the ethnic group. These attributes include reference to kinship, religion, language, and cultural tradition. Structural ethnicity encompasses group boundaries, conflict, and interaction, and is measurable through social network analysis, socioeconomic status, intermarriage, and participation in the political process. Implicit in this structural view is a shared pattern of normative behavior or uniformity that enables individuals to be identified and placed within boundaries that define group membership. When seen from this perspective, ethnicity

> subsumes a number of simultaneous characteristics which, no doubt, cluster statistically.... [this approach to anthropology] dichotomize[s] the ethnographic material in terms of ideal versus actual or conceptual versus empirical, and then concentrate[s] on the consistencies [the structure] of the ideal conceptual part of the data. (Barth 1969, 29)

By contrast, when ethnicity is seen as a cognitive or cultural/symbolic phenomenon, categories are determined by the people themselves. A combined approach is represented by Keefe, Reck and Reck (1983) who describe ethnicity in terms of structural, cultural and symbolic aspects in their research on ethnicity in Appalachian schools. They propose a set of definitions which I found particularly useful in guiding this research.

Cultural ethnicity is defined through behavior, values, styles of interaction, and material culture. The dimensions of symbolic ethnicity include ethnic identification, a sense of belonging to the group, a "recognition of and attachment to cultural symbols, linguistic markers" (Keefe, Reck and Reck 1983, 5) and feelings of either pride and positive affiliation or inferiority and discrimination. The system of classification that is significant to the members of the ethnic group becomes the one used for analysis. To discover this classification system, the people's own ethnic labels (or inferences of these labels derived from the data) are used. Boundaries, therefore, cannot be preconceived, but rather are drawn based on the rules established by the members of the group. These rules must be discovered in order to make sense of the established boundaries, and to distinguish between those who fall within them and those who fall outside.

It is possible to examine ethnicity from a variety of vantage points: as a reflection of self-identification (Barth 1969), as an external categorization by others (Braroe 1975), as a product of interaction with different groups (Geertz 1963; Cohen 1969), and from both macro and micro levels. I use a combination of objective (structural) and subjective (cultural/symbolic) methodologies in the following discussion.

My study of immigrant Portuguese populations also makes use of the literature on situational ethnic selection, which describes the individual's ability to assume more than one ethnic identity in order to optimize personal opportunity in varying social contexts. This literature includes, among others, Ogbu's (1983) discussion of research on the alternation behavior of Chinese, Cuban, Filipino, Japanese, and West Indian students attempting to cope through selective participation in two different cultures, as well as Gluckman's (1961) theoretical framework for studying migration through situational selection; Mitchell's (1956) discussion of stereotyping as part of the category reduction process; Mayer's (1962) characterization of alternation models or switching behavior; Hicks's (1977) description of role as a factor in ethnic identity; and Nagata's (1974) analysis of the complexity of individual oscillation in social interaction as illustrative of the situational ethnic selection process.

Much of this literature, however, concentrates on adults who are able to successfully employ alternating or switching behavior with no psychological damage. My research, on the other hand, is with high school students who are attempting to separate their home and school environments. As a result, I have had the opportunity to study both the process whereby situational ethnic strategies are developed and the effects that these strategies have on the students' ethnic identities.

My view of ethnicity incorporates ideas of ethnic survival as exemplified in the works of Glazer and Moynihan (1970), Yans-McLaughlin (1977), and Zinn (1979) with modified aspects of situational ethnic selection described by Gluckman (1961), Mitchell (1956), Mayer (1962), Nagata (1974), Hicks (1977), Keefe (l980a,b), and Ogbu (1978).

I see ethnicity as a set of resources and strategies which can be maneuvered or manipulated at will. These adaptive strategies develop as a response to urbanization and contribute to an ongoing process of ethnic transformation and renewal.

I also recognize the individual's ability to change identities to avoid cognitive dissonance or to move between different social fields and assume roles in each without producing stress or disorientation. This ability presupposes a repertoire of ethnic behavior used by people to manage seemingly conflicting demands. This flip-flop or context-dependent model underlies Adler's (1975) discussion of the five phases of adjustment in the immigrant transitional experience. The longer immigrants have been transplanted, the greater are their ethnic behavioral options.

In this paper, Portuguese ethnicity is characterized in structural and cultural/symbolic terms. These aspects of ethnicity are analyzed as part of a situational selection process whereby I focus attention on the behavior of recent and long-term Portuguese immigrant students in various social settings. By studying these two groups of students, I am able to record differential manifestations of alternating ethnic identification dependent on social context, i.e., the school, the home, or the community.

It is my contention that the Portuguese students use situational ethnicity more successfully in the cultural/symbolic realm than in the structural realm for achieving their goals. Many factors contribute to the maintenance of boundaries that constrain inter-group contacts. As Fernandes (1972) confirms, the establishment and maintenance of ethnic boundaries are consequences of a variety of historical and social situations, and not just products of individual choice. Through a combined focus on the features of structural and cultural/symbolic ethnicity and situational ethnic selection, it has been possible to assess the impact of implicit educational policies on Portuguese high-school students.

Research Design

The research described in this paper centers on eighteen Portuguese immigrant students enrolled in an urban New England high school. Comparisons are made between eight recent immigrants who were in the United States for less than two years, and ten early arrivals who were here from six to sixteen years at the time of the study. I observed these eighteen students in a variety of contexts over a period of one-and-a-half years. Using a combination of participant observation, personal interviews, and questionnaires, I was able to gather data from teachers, administrators, parents, siblings and other relatives, community members, friends, religious leaders, and of course, from the students themselves. Students were observed at different times of the day, on holidays, weekends as well as school days. Data were collected from social, athletic, religious, and academic settings. During school visits, documentation encompassed student participation in all of their subject classes, as well as from lunch, the library, physical education, and passing in the halls between classes. Observations were also made at athletic events, after-school detention, and homeroom.

Explicit vs. Implicit Policies Within the School

Like most urban high schools, East High School is a complex social institution with both implicit and explicit or formal policies vis-à-vis its Limited English Proficient (LEP) populations. Explicit or formal policies are designed to govern the decision-making process for both administrators and teachers by defining appropriate standards, procedures, and programs. They have the approval of the School Board.

Curriculum guides, subject area requirements, and policy manuals carry the official imprimatur of the school district, while implicit policies tend to develop in counterpoint to these formal ones. These implicit policies can be determined through an examination of teacher and administration attitudes and expectations as revealed through student placements, special program offerings, parent communications, and classroom practices. In order to understand the dynamic between East High School's explicit and implicit policies for LEP students, both the official doctrine and the actual practices were examined.

The official doctrine was revealed through the district's *Procedures Manual for Limited English Proficient Students* (Providence School Department 1984). This document represented the only policy approved by the School Board relative to the foreign-born student population. In part, the Manual stated that the School Department was "committed philosophically and financially":

1. to native language instruction;
2. to parental involvement in their children's educational program; and
3. to a "better understanding among ethnic groups" in the nation and the world (8).

The Manual further described the immediate objectives of the high-school bilingual program through "vernacular instruction in mathematics, social studies and science … . through retention of and respect for the mother culture, while becoming familiarized to and assimilating American culture" (24). The Manual also encouraged broadening the awareness of American students to other languages and cultures.

Investigation of the implementation of these written policies revealed that no math, science, or vocational training was offered in Portuguese. Only three hours per week of social studies were given in the vernacular. The Portuguese language-arts class was ironically scheduled in conflict with beginning English as a Second Language (ESL), so no recent arrivals could enroll. These students, in fact, received virtually no conceptual development in their native language.

In addition, while the Procedures Manual and other School Board documents referred to the availability of individual student counseling in all the city's high schools, only one of the guidance counselors was able to speak Portuguese, and he was only permitted to work with ninth graders. No other Portuguese students, therefore, received counseling services.

Even though the Procedures Manual discussed parental involvement, notices to parents were seldom sent home in Portuguese. Contact between the school and the home remained virtually non-existent.

While cross-cultural understanding was an explicit district-wide goal, no special in-service program was offered to either the staff or student body at the high school. Increased awareness of other languages and cultures was viewed as desirable by the School Board, but Portuguese was not offered as a foreign language in any of the high schools; neither was there a Portuguese cultural component to any other district-wide program or activity. When explicit policies were compared with actual program implementation, it became apparent that, despite claims to the contrary, no Portuguese bilingual program existed in the high school.

Teacher Expectations and Attitudes

Beyond these obvious discrepancies, teacher expectations and behaviors were the most serious contradictions to those written policies that proclaimed systemwide goals of cultural pluralism and "better understanding among ethnic groups."

Teacher attitudes and behavior reflected stereotypes of the Portuguese student as intellectually inferior, non-educationally oriented, socially backward, and marginal to American values of success, assimilation, and upward mobility. The teachers expressed feelings of alienation from these students, and frustration over their own inability to effect change. The teachers' desire that students be obedient and respectful promoted favoritism toward specific groups, e.g., Southeast Asians. They, like the Portuguese, represented no threat to the stability of the classroom but, unlike the Portuguese, expressed an interest in academic achievement.

The Portuguese, while frequently docile (particularly the girls), were not seen as intellectually motivated. Teachers' actions reflected their expectation that the Portuguese students would not do well academically and were therefore not worth spending too much time with. As one teacher stated, "The Portuguese kids will probably drop out of school, anyway." Little, if any, attempt was made to understand the cultural difference between the school and the home, or to reach parents, the majority of whom indeed held unsupportive attitudes about education.

When the teachers' feelings about the Portuguese were examined closely, many revealed patterns of racism, ethnocentrism, and cultural superiority. After mispronouncing one Portuguese student's name so badly that it was incomprehensible, a frustrated teacher commented, "This here Portagee doesn't even know his own name." Cynicism and helplessness in the face of overwhelming cultural difference pervaded the school. There was definite resistance to expressions of cultural diversity, an attitude which ran counter to explicit school department policies toward multicultural understanding and ethnic pluralism.

In another instance, an ESL teacher sitting in the Teachers' Room described the Azores Islands, a Portuguese archipelago 900 miles from Lisbon, as having "a weak incest taboo." He related a story in which an Azorean church had a north and south door. "The morons from the Azores come in from the north door, and everyone else comes in from the south." He concluded by saying that "the Azores are considered the armpit of Portugal." Ninety-eight percent of the Portuguese students at East High School are Azorean.

During a math lesson, the math teacher threw a basketball to the black boys in class. Occasionally an Anglo boy would catch the ball, but it was never thrown to a Portuguese student. The teacher said, "I like to horse around with the kids. The Portuguese kids don't know how to take it...you knock yourself out most of the year and they stop showing up."

The physical education teacher lamented the fact that the Portuguese boys don't ever try out for any sports, not even soccer. "They don't want to do anything."

A truant officer who described himself as "really overworked" commented that "When I drive around the city, I see these Portuguese boys hanging around outside. They're not really bothering anybody. Even if you bring them back to school one day, they'll be out again the next day. It's a losing battle."

A foreign language teacher called the Portuguese "low brow." He continued, saying, "The Portuguese fall short and always will. They are so well behaved that they get neglected.... They come to the United States with feelings of inferiority. Our society is a show-off system—a competition. They can't compete."

In many ways, the teachers' expectations echo American education policies circa 1920 regarding Anglo conformity and melting pot ideology (see Tyack 1974). Ironically, these attitudes survive at a time when the school system has publicly adopted cultural pluralism as an educational goal through its written statements promoting greater cross-cultural understanding and awareness. The implicit policies, as reflected in teacher attitudes, become implemented through preferential treatment to other groups, and self-fulfilling prophesies for poor Portuguese student performance.

In order to better understand the teachers' reactions to the Portuguese students, knowledge of both the teachers' ethnic background and that of the Portuguese immigrants is necessary. While the majority of East High School's students are members of either racial or linguistic minorities (sometimes both), the faculty is ninety-three percent Anglo. Most of the teachers at the high school are second- and third-generation Italian, Irish, and Jewish. The almost 1,000-member student body, however, is forty percent black, twenty-one percent Anglo, fifteen percent Portuguese, ten percent Hispanic, eight percent Southeast Asian, and six percent Cape Verdean and other groups.

Landes (1976, 401) has suggested that first- and second-generation American teachers, because of the insecurity of their newly converted status, "strive to invalidate a divergent one" by being highly judgmental, critical, and visibly disturbed by the presence of other minority groups in the school.

While highly judgmental and critical behavior characterized teacher interaction with Portuguese children, the teachers treated the black students as the most prestigious group in the school. As one of the Portuguese students in the study noted, "The teachers all like the black kids best." Teachers "rapped" with black students, teased them, and joined them in sports competitions. Association with the popular black students conferred status on the faculty, as well as non-black students.

By hanging around the black students, then, others established themselves as part of the school's most popular in-group. The guidance counselor confirmed this feeling by saying "[t]he blacks rule the school. There are more of them. They dance in the cafeteria and the hallways. They're more outgoing. They're performers. There's no question that they are the most popular kids. They also cause the most disturbances." The Portuguese, however, did not readily mix with blacks. As described by Almeida (1980), the Portuguese, Azoreans in particular, are deeply religious, submissive, pacific, orderly, and family-oriented. They transmit to their children a world view calling for adherence to a hard-work ethic.

The Portuguese come from a tradition of little formal education, of one of the highest illiteracy rates in Europe, of strong sexual role divisions, and of over fifty years of fascist dictatorships providing virtually no opportunity for political participation and very strong disincentives for defying authority. (Although a 1974 coup brought democracy to the country, its impact has not yet been clearly evidenced among the recent immigrants. It is expected that both education and political participation will be viewed as a greater priority among the newer immigrant populations.)

There are over half-a-million Portuguese in New England, the majority of whom are from the Azores. Like the blacks and Hispanics, the Portuguese occupy one of the lowest rungs in the socioeconomic ladder, competing for minimum wage jobs in the jewelry and textile industries. By encouraging an early entry into the labor market, the Portuguese family is ensuring its own economic survival, albeit at the expense of their children's education.

Despite the fact that most of the Portuguese immigrants have never seen blacks on the islands, many bring an anti-black prejudice with them. Fear of blacks is pre-adaptation, conditioned in large part by the subservient status of blacks in Africa under the Portuguese colonial empire. It also reflects a combination of anxiety toward the unknown, and reactions to tales told by returning Portuguese immigrants.

The expectations of both their American peers and their teachers contrasted sharply with those of the students' parents. Parents cautioned against association with blacks, but in the school, blacks were the most dominant and sought-after group. In the home, students, especially girls, were respectful, obedient and well-disciplined. These values, when transferred to the school, carried low esteem. In East High School, the defiant, raucous, academically indifferent student was admired. As Turner indicates in his 1983 study of the social world of the high school, getting into trouble signifies masculinity and confers prestige rather than shame. By openly defying a teacher, a student (usually male) obtained instant admiration and respect.

The Portuguese boys learned earlier than the girls to socialize outside the home. The skills acquired from meeting friends of their fathers or from relatively unrestricted forays into the community enabled them to adjust better than the girls to the diverse student body of the high school. It is not surprising, therefore, that in the school, the boys were more gregarious and had more Anglo friends than the girls. Neither the boys nor the girls, however, had any black friends.

Both teachers and peers conveyed to the students the idea that being Portuguese was not a mark of social esteem. The Portuguese language was not offered as an elective along with Spanish, French, and Italian. Recent Portuguese immigrants were segregated from mainstream classes. Portuguese parents were not involved in the school. The majority of guidance counselors not only could not speak Portuguese, but frequently mispronounced Portuguese names. Truant officers never followed up on Portuguese student latenesses or absences.

The faculty had reinterpreted Portuguese cultural concepts so that they now appeared undesirable. Values of hard work became viewed as anti-intellectual and non-educationally oriented. Close Portuguese family ties were seen as exclusionary and anti-assimilationist. Respect for authority was equated with docility and subservience. Protection of females was sexist and discriminatory. Fear of blacks was racist. Non-political involvement was un-American. In this way, teachers' attitudes and the resulting low expectations they had for Portuguese student achievement identified and separated the Portuguese as a distinct ethnic group within the high school.

Student Reactions

The recent Portuguese arrivals were not nearly as sensitive to this problem as the early arrivals. The early arrivals were keenly aware of the various forms of rejection of their ethnic heritage. One student said that she resented the fact that "Americans look down on the Portuguese." Another commented that "I get mad because I don't want people to make fun of me."

The early Portuguese arrivals observed the preferential treatment accorded other groups, and interpreted this behavior as rejection of them. Under these circumstances, there did not seem to be much point in remaining in school, a factor that accounted in large part for the Portuguese having the highest drop-out rate in the high school; more than half of them did not remain to graduate.

The early arrivals usually disassociated themselves from the recent immigrants. "We already paid our dues" was how one early arrival described this separation. "They'll learn how to get along on their own, just like we did" was another comment. In the hallways, the recent arrivals walked alone to their next classes. The early arrivals formed two groups, male and female, to walk to classes. On rare occasions one or two Anglo boys walked with the early Portuguese boys. The same pattern was evident in the cafeteria, where there were always separate tables for the early and recent arrivals. It was more common to see boys and girls mix if they were both recent or early arrivals than it was to see early boys or girls mix with recent ones.

Students in the recently-arrived group were socially stigmatized. Their inability to speak English, coupled with a respectful attitude toward their teachers, contributed to their general isolation from the mainstream and marked them as different. With black student behavior informally receiving the imprimatur of the school, the behavior of the recent Portuguese arrivals was farthest from the accepted norm. As one newly-arrived boy claimed, "I wish I wasn't Portuguese. Everybody likes the black kids. Nobody likes the Portuguese kids."

Without exception, the early student arrivals exhibited little sympathy for the recent immigrant, a feeling attributable, in large measure, to their own conflicting attitudes about their Portuguese heritage. These ethnic divisions were even further magnified by the fact that the Portuguese bilingual teacher was from continental Portugal and she, too, felt a linguistic and cultural superiority over the lower-status Azorean students.

Aspects of the early students' ethnic identity revealed an ambivalence stemming, in part, from ethnic pride nurtured in the home, and ethnic rejection as reflected in the implicit policies of the high school. Structural manifestations of ethnicity in the school were evidenced through intergroup relations. Even though the boys mingled with Anglos to a much greater extent than did the girls, especially in gym and in the halls, barriers were still evident between the Anglos and Portuguese. Students remained separate in their classes, in the cafeteria, walking to and from school, and generally between classes as well. These boundaries also existed between the recent and early arrivals.

A cultural/symbolic analysis of ethnicity revealed that the early arrivals had adopted English as the language of the school, and dressed, ate, and listened to music like their Anglo counterparts. At home, the early arrivals expressed strong feelings of pride and positive affiliation with the Portuguese, but in the school they exhibited negative feelings of inferiority and shame. It was, in fact, these negative feelings that prompted many of their other school-related behavior, e.g., speaking only English, avoiding the recent arrivals, using Anglicized versions of their names, and becoming bolder with their teachers. This last change in their relationship to authority figures was more evident among the boys than among the girls.

None of the recent arrivals had any Anglo friends, either in their neighborhood or in their classes. Group boundaries, as revealed through their intergroup relations, followed a pattern of almost total exclusivity. The greatest barrier for them was linguistic. The recent arrivals could not effectively communicate in English, and were therefore cut off from significant relationships with non-Portuguese speakers. This problem further accounted for the fact that the recent arrivals were conspicuously quiet in most of their classes. They remained well-behaved and obedient, rarely cutting classes and never answering their teachers disrespectfully.

More than the early arrivals, the recent immigrants sat together, walked to and from school together, ate together, and formed friendships. Boys and girls usually remained in separate groups and only occasionally interacted. There was, however, greater contact between the recent girls and boys in the school than between recent and early students of the same sex. In the home/community environment, however, there was greater recent and early student interaction, particularly at church and folk festivals, and for boys' street sports.

Unlike the early arrivals, all the recent arrivals expressed pride in their Portuguese heritage both at home and in school. They also expressed a mixture of fear and disdain for American permissiveness with regard to dating, interracial relationships, and lack of respect for teachers and parents. One recent arrival claimed that "In Portugal you have respect for teachers and teachers have respect for you. (Here) the kids are fresh and don't do work." She concluded that "I'll never be an American." The recent arrivals further pointed with dismay to the cavalier attitudes that Anglo students had about poor academic performance and personal behavior. Almost all the recent arrivals recounted stories of the shock they first experienced upon entering the high school. One boy commented that he "gets mad" when the kids make so much noise that he can't hear the teacher.

By contrast, one early arrival spoke about his "Portuguese blood" at home, but identified himself as an American in school. "I don't want people to make fun of me," he explained. Another early arrival told her father about colleagues who denied their Portuguese background; yet she refused to answer to her Portuguese name, Maria José, in the school, responding only to Mary Jo, the Anglicized version. At home, she is Maria José. One boy deliberately sought association with non-Portuguese in school. "I'm cool," he said. His Anglo companion added, "The Portuguese are uncool." In fact, all but one of the early arrivals identified themselves as Anglo in the school setting.

Because most of the early arrivals demonstrated feelings of inferiority about being Portuguese in the school setting, they often refused to acknowledge that they understood the Portuguese language. One boy went so far as to use only English even in his Portuguese social studies class. At home he spoke only Portuguese. Others admitted feeling shame when Anglos talked about Portuguese customs. One girl described the Anglos as being smarter than the Portuguese. The teachers, in fact, expressed surprise to learn that the early arrivals knew Portuguese because they never heard them use the language in school.

Despite student denials of their Portuguese background, most teachers were aware that the early arrivals were indeed Portuguese. While teachers mispronounced their names and underestimated their abilities, they were aware of their presence as a distinct sub-group of the school.

At home, by contrast, the early arrivals not only spoke Portuguese almost exclusively, but pointed with pride to their Portuguese heritage. They showed pictures of their homeland, told stories about their villages, and kept embroidery, special costumes for feast days, unique musical instruments, and even recipes on display. Although most of the early arrivals could speak English and Portuguese with equal ease, they used Portuguese with me at home and English in school, regardless of the language I used with them.

Total assimilation into the Anglo group was, however, prevented by the Anglo students' unwillingness to accept the Portuguese, and by the teachers' continued labeling of the early arrivals as Portuguese. A fairly common form of approbation used among Anglos and blacks alike in the school was the expression "quit acting like an immigrant" or its variant form "quit acting like a Portagee." The behavior in question could be anything from sloppy eating habits to an unattractive wardrobe. The expression was used as a general sign of disapproval and was not directed towards members of any ethnic group in particular.

One Anglo senior who tended to hang out with black students said that he does not even know any Portuguese kids. "They keep to themselves. They have all their classes together." His friend added that "Lots of cliques try to rule the school and be tough. That's not true of the Portuguese. They're close-knit, but they're not tough. They try to be as friendly as they can, but they feel more secure and comfortable together—it's like an extension of their family."

An Anglo girl commented that "Portuguese girls stick together and speak Portuguese, even though they know how to speak English. They don't participate in gym, or anything. They always seem embarrassed." Her girlfriend called them "meek, quiet nerds who dress in K-Mart polyester." A black girl noted, "it's hard to relate to Portuguese kids. Maybe it's the language barrier, although I don't have any trouble with Spanish kids." Her friend added, "they're always worried about their precious reputation." As Braroe (1975) has indicated, frequent contact between groups does not necessarily erase stereotypes or remove boundaries.

While other adult-focused research records the results of situational ethnic selection, this study observed the process. Through a series of trials and errors, students were testing the parameters of ethnic accommodation and change, but they had not yet resolved many of the conflicts inherent in the process. They were not always able to employ successful situational ethnic strategies to mediate between the disparities of their home and school cultures.

The Effects of Implicit Educational Policy on Ethnic Identity

The effects of implicit educational policies on the ethnic group became detrimental to the maintenance of ethnic identity in the school. While change in the cultural/symbolic aspects of ethnicity preceded the dissolution of structural barriers, assimilation of the ethnic group was simultaneously encouraged and thwarted by the educational hierarchy. Students continued to be regarded as Portuguese long after they'd chosen to identify themselves as Anglos. Because acceptance by Anglos was neither immediate nor total, group members still associated with each other, further increasing their identification with the ethnic group.

The eighteen students in this study lived in two cultures, both of which were important to their survival. The school was not assisting them in adapting to their bi-cultural reality. It was, instead, trying to negate one of these cultures, the Portuguese, while at the same time, discouraging acceptance into the other, broadly defined as "American." According to Fishman (1976) and others (e.g., Mehan 1981; Saville-Troike 1976) the bilingual program, if appropriately implemented, could have helped the students bridge this gap.

Rejection of the ethnic group by the school was neither blatant nor conspiratorial. It was, perhaps, all the more insidious because the teachers were acting out of the best of intentions—a desire to see the students become Americanized as quickly as possible. The result, however, was that students were renouncing their Portuguese ethnicity without being accepted as Americans. In a school strongly characterized by ethnic affiliations, the early Portuguese arrivals remained marginal.

The fact that the school's implicit policies served as the trigger for this behavior is significant. If the inferiority of the Portuguese was not implicitly sanctioned, then the early students would not be as eager to disassociate themselves from their heritage and more recently-arrived counterparts. Many of their home values, such as strong sex-role differentiation, an emphasis on economic advancement over educational achievement, unquestioned respect for authority, fear of blacks, and a lack of participation in schools and politics were unacceptable to the Anglo school majority. As a result, the early Portuguese students quickly lost their sense of ethnic pride. This loss also affected their school performance, as numerous studies on self-concept and academic achievement attest (see, e.g., Becker 1980; Cook 1972; Dimitroff 1972). Failing grades further encouraged early school dropout. Because ethnic identification was situationally selected, the early arrivals, most particularly the boys, opted for Anglo identification in the school.

Studies by Cortes (1986), Cazden (1985), and McDermott (1985), among others, document the social and academic consequences of low teacher expectations for specific ethnic minorities. In a similar vein, Walsh (1987, 204) notes that ethnicity was a major factor which contributed to the placement of "the Puerto Rican student in a position subordinate to the majority."

The Portuguese parents' own limited education and tradition of non-political involvement, coupled with a lack of contact with the high school, reinforced many of the attitudes held by the teachers. Convinced that the Portuguese did not care about their children's education, teachers perpetuated stereotypes of the Portuguese, which contributed to their continued position at the lower end of the education hierarchy. By showing favoritism to the more popular black students, or to the more studious Southeast Asians, the teachers confirmed these attitudes about the Portuguese.

To survive in East High School, the Portuguese students were forced to negate some of their home attachments and establish an identity apart from that deemed to be low-status Portuguese. To do so, they had to adopt different behavioral strategies in the home and the school so as to obtain acceptance in both.

But the early arrivals were not completely successful at making the transformation in the school. Strong Portuguese sex-role expectations persisted, as did other attitudes and behaviors inimical to acceptance by Anglo students and teachers. What emerged, instead, was a distinctly Portuguese-American identity, not totally acceptable to either group, yet not completely rejected by them either.

Portuguese students entered the public school with feelings of ethnic pride and left with notions of cultural inferiority and shame. They usually arrived both respectful and obedient but often left defiant and inattentive. Most Portuguese started their public-school careers with little faith in the power of education to redress social inequities. Unfortunately, they dropped out of school with the same conviction.

The school *was* socializing the Portuguese immigrants, but they were being socialized into an environment that was often hostile to their very existence as a group. This hostility may, however, eventually serve to create a new solidarity among the early arrivals, one which revives and transforms Portuguese ethnicity into what Bell (1975) calls a strategic choice.

If the school rejects Portuguese ethnicity while the home celebrates it, then the strategic choice made by the early arrivals is not an either/or choice (i.e., either identify as Portuguese or as Anglo). Rather, these ethnic choices become contingent on optimizing the advantages of being associated with one group in one context, and with another group in another context. It becomes just as important to minimize the disadvantages of identification with the less desirable group as it is to increase the advantages of association with the more desirable one. In this case, it was clearly more advantageous to be identified as Portuguese in the home and community and as Anglo in the school.

The early arrivals were in the process of transforming their Portuguese ethnicity in the high school through the incorporation of structural and cultural/symbolic features of Anglo ethnicity with aspects of Portuguese ethnicity. The result was a school-based ethnic identity that was neither Anglo nor Portuguese, but a combination of the two. The early arrivals in the high school interacted with Anglos, dressed and ate like Anglos, but did not socialize with them. They were more respectful than the Anglos. They called themselves Anglo but were classified by students and teachers alike as Portuguese. They had neither melted nor retained their cultural heritage. In the school setting, this ethnic limbo was seen by the early arrivals as preferable to being identified as Portuguese. Although they would rather be identified as Anglos, they were not able to do so.

Situational ethnic selection enabled the early arrivals to maintain the structural and cultural/symbolic aspects of Portuguese ethnicity in their home while adapting to aspects of Anglo ethnicity in the school. These attitudinal and behavioral changes in the school were a direct response to the school's implicit educational policies.

The school's role in shaping the ethnic identity of these immigrant students was both significant and invested with far-reaching social implications. The ambiguity of the public schools' response to the socialization of its LEP populations reflects a larger ideological tug-of-war being played out by the American people. While the numerous legislative initiatives that mandate bilingual education claim cultural pluralism as a goal of contemporary society, Anglo conformity and melting pot ideologies persist through implicit policies that undermine effective bilingual program implementation. Immigrant students are caught in the crossfire; they are subjected to programs designed to fail and teachers who anticipate the results.

Because this study dealt with a small number of students in only one school, future research is needed to determine whether there is wider applicability of these findings to other communities and other ethnic groups. If it is found to be systematically evident that explicit educational policies tout cultural pluralism while implicit practices do not, then school districts need to address questions regarding their own enforcement of written school board dictates. If cultural pluralism is, in fact, viewed as a goal of the district, then why are widespread counterproductive implicit practices allowed to flourish?

Note

[1] This article was originally published in *Human Organization* 49(1), 1990: 48-55.

WORK, GENDER AND FAMILY

CHAPTER 13

Portuguese Labor Activism in Southeastern Massachusetts[1]

PENN REEVE

The history of American immigration is also the history of the American labor movement. Immigrant men, women, and children, under economic and political pressure in their native lands, emigrated to the United States seeking work in the fields and factories. Finding less than ideal wages and working conditions, they began to struggle for greater power over their working lives by organizing and joining labor unions.

Southeastern Massachusetts was one of many centers of early industrialization on the Eastern Seaboard and therefore became a center for labor organizing. Fall River and New Bedford were leading textile mill towns during the late 19th and early 20th century. They experienced significant labor struggles that paralleled those occurring in other towns and cities throughout the nation. In southeastern Massachusetts, the largest group of immigrants during this period was the Portuguese. Their active participation in the labor struggles of the region is the subject of this paper.

In the first two decades of the 20th century, over 140,000 Portuguese immigrants arrived in the United States, settling mostly in California and southeastern Massachusetts (Williams 2005). They arrived from the mainland, the Azores, and Madeira. As part of the great influx of the so-called "new immigrants" to the U.S. from southern and eastern Europe, they were often disdained by the more established "old immigrants" from England, Scotland, Wales, and Ireland, who had become well-entrenched in the skilled factory jobs. The established immigrants also viewed "new immigrants" as culturally and even racially inferior and therefore unworthy of joining their established craft unions. Many chose to believe the Portuguese and other "new immigrants" were reluctant to engage in union activities and would work as "scabs" for low wages (Silvia 1976).

Some stereotypes of the Portuguese that became commonplace in the early 20th century have persisted until the present day. The prevailing view at the time was that the Portuguese were "hard working," but best suited for less skilled jobs requiring brute strength and little education (Silvia 1976, 228-230). Prejudices toward the newer immigrants from southern and eastern Europe were based on prevailing racist ideas that these were innately inferior immigrants compared with the more established northern and western European immigrants. The fear was that they would work at lower wages and that would depress all workers' wages. They were seen as culturally inferior because of their rural background and lack of formal education. The older immigrants preemptively excluded them from their craft unions.

One still hears some of these views expressed locally despite the current representation of Portuguese immigrants and their descendants at all levels of the region's economic and social life. The primary goal of this paper will be to demonstrate, contrary to past and present stereotypes, that Portuguese men and women have been actively involved in labor organizations, both as leaders and as rank-and-file participants. By examining secondary sources and the testimony of Portuguese workers and labor organizers at the time, this paper represents a preliminary attempt—as, to date, no other attempt has been made—to document their participation.

Women have always been recruited into factory work, often at less skilled jobs, with the owner's belief that they could be hired at lower wages and, because of family responsibilities, would be less apt to resist owner demands for long hours and low wages. Though women are sometimes stereotyped in the labor movement as more malleable and docile than males, women were active in the textile labor movement in southeastern Massachusetts as they have been elsewhere. This research indicates that women were represented in all labor organizing activities, and though men held most high-level positions in the labor organizations, some women assumed important leadership roles.

I have chosen to examine the issue of Portuguese labor participation between the 1920s and 1950s because it was during this period that the U.S. labor movement experienced a significant transformation. In the

1920s, the movement perpetuated an old struggle dating back to the 19th century between conservatives and radicals/leftists.[2] Workers in the 1920s continued to be subjected to repressive government and industry actions. Federal, state, and local laws and court actions limited workers' rights to organize unions and improve the harsh conditions of factory life. Factory owners demanded long hours of work for low pay in an extremely unhealthy working environment. During these difficult times, workers fought back in the only effective manner possible, by organizing themselves into unions—organizations that had the legal power to negotiate on their behalf. They demanded healthier working conditions, shorter workdays, and higher pay goals that are characterized here as part of a more conservative union agenda.

Some organizers incorporated these same goals but added more far-reaching ones, including workers gaining control over factories and using the unions as a political base for pushing society closer to socialism. For southeastern Massachusetts, the New Bedford Textile strike of 1928 was the clearest and most dramatic example of these massive organizing efforts that were also occurring throughout the U.S. Most workers and their leaders sought the right to be represented by a union and to gain higher pay and better working conditions. But the radical/leftist leaders of the strike and rank-and-file workers who followed them had the more radical goal of eventual worker control over the industry, a labor party and ultimately, a socialist economy. The radicals were most active during the 1920s and 1930s, although, as illustrated in this paper, their efforts were largely unsuccessful.

By the late 1940s and early 1950s, federal legislation, such as the Taft-Hartley Bill of 1947 and the McCarthyism of the early 1950s, as well as the conservative union leadership's own actions led to the elimination of radicals/leftists from the leadership of most unions. The year 1955 represents the conclusion of this process of "deradicalization" of the U.S. labor movement because in that year, the once more radical Congress of Industrial Organizations (CIO) joined with its long-time rival, the conservative American Federation of Labor (AFL) to form the largest labor federation in the U.S. From 1955 to the present day, the movement's conservative direction has been left virtually unchallenged. With unequivocal support of capitalism at home and abroad, and goals limited to improving wages and working conditions, the American labor movement continued on this more conservative path—one that came to set it apart from labor movements in all other advanced capitalist societies of the world (Stepan-Norris and Zeitlin 2002).

Elsewhere, labor organizations as well as distinct labor parties advocated a more left-leaning agenda, including more worker control in the factory and in society, socialized public services, including health care, and a labor party that would offer more power to workers. In the American two-party system, the Republican Party has been aggressively hostile to unions and the Democratic Party, where the movement placed all its hope, turned out to be a weak advocate for labor and strongly anti-socialist. All advanced capitalist countries, with the exception of the U.S., have a labor party and/or a socialist party that has a significant degree of political influence and has to led successful efforts to pass federal laws protecting workers' rights and health.[3]

To summarize, this paper will attempt to demonstrate 1) that despite stereotypes to the contrary, the Portuguese were active participants in the southeastern Massachusetts labor movement during this period and 2) that the particular character of their participation was shaped by the struggle between conservative and radical/left political forces within the unions and in the society at large.

Early Portuguese Migration and the Textile Industry

Prior to 1870, few Portuguese emigrated to southern New England. The official U.S. census of that year reported only 8,971 Portuguese-born individuals living in the U.S. (Williams 2005, 32). In the mid-1800s, the whaling industry attracted a few Portuguese to the East and West Coast, but it was not until the expansion of the textile industry that Portuguese immigration to southern New England accelerated. By 1900, 17,885 Portuguese were living in Massachusetts alone, and by 1920, the number increased to 50,294. A decade later, Massachusetts was home to more than 62,000 second-generation Portuguese (Williams 2005, 32).

In an effort to continue their traditional culture, some Portuguese who settled in Fall River and New Bedford opted for life on small farms, joined the New Bedford fishing fleets or engaged in traditional trades, such as carpentry or masonry. However, these opportunities were scarce in New England. The primary work was to be found in the textile mills, and that is where the overwhelming majority found jobs. In New Bedford, merchant families had transferred their investments from whaling to the production of fine cotton textiles. By the beginning of the First World War, thirty-two New Bedford cotton manufacturing companies employed 30,000 people. During the first thirty years of the 20th century, the cotton textile industry employed approximately ninety percent of New Bedford's manufacturing workers (Georgianna and Aaronson 1993). New Bedford mills were built along the railroad tracks and river in the north and south ends of the city. To this day, these areas are largely Portuguese-American communities.

Fall River, the "Spindle City," was a leading cotton textile manufacturing center in the 1800s, but very few Portuguese lived in the city during that time. Of the total Fall River population in 1870, only 132 individuals were from southern and eastern Europe, and only 104 were Portuguese immigrants. Over eighty percent of Portuguese mill workers in Fall River arrived after 1901. As late as 1880, all but forty of Fall River's textile employees were either native-born or born in northwestern Europe. The Portuguese and Polish immigrants generally entered mill jobs held by departing English and Irish who had advanced to higher paid, more skilled factory jobs. By 1900, 6,000 of Fall River's immigrants originated from Southern and eastern Europe, and that number exceeded 10,000 persons five years later. Azoreans comprised half this total. Almost the entire Portuguese and Polish population was working in the mills by 1910 (Silvia 1976, 224-226).

Transition to Factory Work

In the early years of the 20th century, most of the Portuguese who immigrated to southern New England were farmers from the Azores and Madeira, and had virtually no industrial work experience. The textile mills in the region could accommodate thousands of unskilled workers, placing them into the least skilled jobs that required only brief on-the-job training. Their typical tasks were tending machines as bobbin boys, doffers, carders, combers, sweepers, spoolers, and in many of the other less-skilled jobs (Silvia 1976, 224-226).

The transition from rural agriculture to urban industrial life was a shock for all of these immigrants. Textile work had always been difficult.

As Cumbler points out, "[n]ineteenth-century textile workers in Fall River rose daily in the early dawn to face exhausting, intensive labor, long hours, and low pay" (Cumbler 1979, 144-145). They endured ten-to-twelve hour shifts, six days a week at monotonous, tedious tasks, arriving home totally exhausted. Constant, close supervision, speed-ups, "stretch-outs"(adding more machines per worker) and dusty, poorly ventilated mills plagued the textile workers. In the early 20th century, conditions were only somewhat better, and periodic speed-ups and wage cuts led to great hardships for the workers (Cumbler 1979).

Many Portuguese-Americans have vivid memories of working in the mills. In 1931, at age fourteen, Manuel Medeiros left school to work in a Fall River textile plant. He recalls the hazardous health conditions in the plant: "It was rough in the mills where the cotton was processed through the machines. There was a heavy, musty odor. Miners work in the mines and they get all that coal dust. There's no ventilation of any kind. Today they call it black lung. Well, in those days we had the white cotton lung disease. I knew a man that worked in the picking room that died from that, just swallowed too much cotton" (Huse 1998, 38). In 1924, at age sixteen, Lydia Souza entered the mills to help support her family, which included nine siblings. She remembers when she was a little girl that her father missed lunch to tend machines twelve to fourteen hours a day. Visiting her father in the mills, Lydia was struck by the "deafening noise and the film of cotton in the room" (Huse 1998, 39). Joe Figueiredo's father was born in Lisbon and mother in São Miguel and both worked in the New Bedford mills. Joe was born in Boston in 1920 and started in the mills as a teenager. He later became very active in radical union politics including the 1928 New Bedford textile strike. He remembers visiting his mother who worked as a spool tender at City Mill in New Bedford: "In those days they did not permit the workers to use the freight elevators to go up to work in some cases four, five or six floors. There was no lunch room or chairs and tables to eat on, and most of the workers gathered around their machines sitting on boxes of bobbins, and even when the machines were shut down for lunch, there was still cotton dust in the air and cotton all over her eyebrows and around her ears and she would wipe it out and the sweat would still hold it."[4]

Like other "new immigrants," the Portuguese were subjected to the tyranny of skilled workers and hiring bosses. Skilled loom fixers and menders were often paid extra based on the output of the weavers in their sections. These were typically English, Welsh, Scottish, and, later, Irish and French-Canadian craft workers who often subcontracted piece work to the new Polish and Portuguese immigrants. Pushed to their limits, "Women fell ill and 'asked out,' that is asked to leave the machine because of illness or exhaustion although often the request was denied. This happened with such frequency that the companies in Fall River kept a crew of stand-by women" to immediately replace their colleagues (Montgomery 1977, 101-102).

Workers used many workplace strategies to alleviate their difficult conditions. Besides informal means of resistance, such as sabotage, sick-outs, slow-downs or quitting, many new immigrants joined labor organizations as a necessary means of improving their oppressive work situation. The 1928 New Bedford Textile Strike demonstrated the willingness of the Portuguese, regardless of their background and experience prior to arrival, to join organized labor actions.

The 1928 New Bedford Textile Strike

Though competition with southern textile companies intensified in the late 1920s, the fine cotton textile industry located in New Bedford was expanding and profitable. Yet, in 1928, the New Bedford textile manufacturers demanded a ten percent pay cut, a dramatic reduction in wages at the time. The mill owners were making a profit at the time but there was evidently a dip in demand and they decided to operate at the same rate of profit even though they were not operating at the same rate of production (Georgianna and Aaronson 1993, 50).

Wage cuts and speed-ups occurred throughout the textile industry's history. In 1898, New Bedford mill owner demands had been almost identical to those of 1928. In the earlier strike, owners demanded a ten percent wage cut, claiming competition from southern mills forced them to demand the cut. Many workers reacted to the wage cut immediately by walking off the job, and English-dominated craft union leaders, espousing a conservative political philosophy and strike goals, competed with leftist radicals advocating a more socialist ideology and militant actions for control of the strike (Georgianna and Aaronson 1993, 43-41).

In 1928, the Textile Committee (TC) representing craft unions did not represent the majority of mill workers, including the less-skilled, mostly Portuguese, Polish, and French-Canadian workers, who also walked off their jobs. As happened in 1898, a rival, more militant organization, the Textile Mill Committee (TMC), formed to represent them. The TMC was made up of local workers and outside organizers, including radicals with experience in other labor-organizing efforts, such as the 1912 Lawrence "Bread and Roses" Strike and the Passaic Strike in 1926.[5] The immediate goals of the TMC were to stop the wage cut and gain legal union representation for unrepresented workers. They did not declare their long-term future goals of having more workers in decision-making and management positions in the factory, except to more politically radicalized workers.[6]

A few Portuguese were already radicalized from prior political experience in the U.S. and in Portugal. Local members of the Industrial Workers of the World ("Wobblies"), a radical labor group formed in 1905, for example, advocated all workers be united in one single union and local anarcho-syndicalists, typically from central regions of mainland Portugal, advocated replacing capitalism, private ownership, wages and the federal government with a society managed by workers via their organizations.[7] Edward Mendes, for example, was blacklisted from millwork in Gouveia, Portugal for his radical politics, and in 1912, two years after Portugal's monarchy was overthrown, Mendes and many others fled Portugal. He obtained contract work in a cordage factory in Plymouth, Massachusetts, working alongside Bartolomeo Vanzetti, the martyred labor leader.[8] His daughter, Eula, remembers that, throughout her childhood, her father held political meetings in their house, and she became— in part, because of her father's influence—a union activist as well. The family was living in New Bedford at the time of the 1928 Textile Strike. Eula had been working in the City Mill since age thirteen and her father told her, "There is a strike. You must go on strike. You must be with the workers." She celebrated her eighteenth birthday walking a picket line.

Since most of the 20,000 unskilled and semi-skilled mill workers were Portuguese, and they were largely excluded from TC strike organizing activities, they found a home in the more militant TMC. Of the nine members of the TMC local leadership, six were of Portuguese extraction

(Georgianna and Aaronson 1993, 127). Some Portuguese played an active role in the daily strike activities of the TMC. They helped organize rallies, distribute food to striking workers, translate pamphlets, and attend rallies. Because of the large numbers of Portuguese participating in the strike, leaflets and pamphlets were translated into Portuguese. At the rallies, Joe Figueiredo, Eula Mendes and other Portuguese leaders gave speeches in Portuguese. Eula Mendes, for example, was a member of the strike committee, translating leaflets and speeches from Portuguese to English and vice versa. She became Secretary of the TMC and an active speaker, helping to organize Portuguese workers and maintain their morale.

While the Portuguese from the Azores were typically seen as more conservative and less willing to join the union than mainland Portuguese, the harsh conditions of mill work created an awareness of the need for protection and organization, and a readiness to join labor-organized activities. Regardless of whether they were from the islands or mainland, the Portuguese joined the TMC by the thousands. According to Eula Mendes:

> When the strike began, the Portuguese people got involved immediately.... They were the most active, not only Portuguese from Portugal, but from the islands, from the Azores, Madeira and from the Cape Verde Islands. The people from the islands were a little more conservative.... They had no background of working in factories when they came...but they became more active. The strike was pretty solid among the Portuguese people. (Interview by author and Jack Stauder, 1986)

Contrary to some claims as to the Portuguese reluctance to join the labor movement, the overwhelming majority participated in the strike.

The six-month strike ended when the TC and mill owners worked out an agreement for a five instead of ten percent per hour wage cut. The TMC was excluded from negotiations and the vote. During the strike and after the vote, the authorities attacked the TMC, arresting many leaders and members so they could not participate in the final settlement negotiations. The charges were dropped after the strike.

TMC organizers were accused of being dangerous outside agitators and un-American. The local media "red-baited" the TMC leadership and used the threat of deportation to intimidate radical leaders and discourage non-citizens from joining their cause.[9] Augusto Pinto, one of the strike picket captains, for example, was arrested many times during the strike and convicted twenty-two times. On appeal, Pinto's convictions, like those of most other defendants, were later dismissed. However, in his case—no doubt to make an example of him to the others—the U.S. Immigration Service forcibly placed Pinto on a ship bound for Salazar's Portugal, where labor militant's were treated harshly. He reportedly died under Portuguese military custody en route to prison in Cape Verde, "sending a shudder through New Bedford's Portuguese community" (Georgianna and Aaronson 1993, 142). One month after Pinto's deportation, William Murdoch, a key TMC labor leader, was deported to his native Scotland (Georgianna and Aaronson 1993, 142).

Though companies rehired many workers, they refused to rehire those who had been active in the TMC. Some left the area. Eula Mendes got a job for a while in the TMC, and in 1929, worked for the newly formed communist-led National Textile Workers Union. A few years later when the NTWU dissolved, she was hired as a part-time office worker and organizer by the local United Textile Workers (UTW) union office, but then was let go because of her membership in the Communist party. The union feared a "red-baiting" backlash if she remained.

By 1932, the southward movement of the textile industry and the depression had created mass unemployment in the New Bedford mills. Unemployment rose rapidly and wages fell. Radicals had been purged, blacklisted, and in a few cases, deported. Repression of radicals in the local labor movement left a vacuum of militant labor leaders. Portuguese workers were left in the hands of the conservative TC since the AFL craft unions largely excluded them.

The New Deal and the CIO

In response to declining wages during the depression and the hardships these economic and political shifts caused, there were continuous attempts to organize workers. The labor movement received a big boost from Franklin Delano Roosevelt's New Deal. Section 7(a) of the 1933 National Recovery Act permitted collective bargaining and ostensibly protected union organizing from retribution by employers. The

National Recovery Act also called for employers to set more reasonable limits on work hours and to set a minimum wage (Green et al. 1996, 140).

Adding to federal protections for workers, in the spring of 1935 Congress passed the Social Security Act and a sweeping new federal labor law, the National Labor Relations Act that created the National Labor Relations Board. For the first time, workers had the support of a federal board that protected their right to organize and be legally represented (Green 1996, 111). This was not a total victory for workers since the president appoints the Board, and few have strongly supported unions.

Though not taken seriously by industry, these federal protections of workers stimulated the largest union organizing drive in U.S. history. Hundreds of thousands of workers joined unions. The membership in the Textile Workers Union of America (TWUA) rose throughout this period and into the war years. By 1944, the TWUA could count 400,000 members, the largest CIO union in the country (Clete 2001, 138).

Competition for new members between the older, more conservative AFL and the new, more militant CIO generated great enthusiasm and a rise in the membership of both labor organizations. "The eruption of a socially conscious and broadly inclusive CIO movement attracted a whole new generation of union activists, including Poles, Russians, Lithuanians, Italians, Greeks, and Portuguese workers who had not found a home in the AFL craft unions. Despite the differences between the AFL and the CIO, the charges and the countercharges, a new spirit encompassed the labor movement" (Juravich et al., 118).

In 1936 and 1937, after breaking with the more conservative craft unions affiliated with AFL, the Congress of Industrial Organizations began to organize based on the principle of industry-wide unions, giving workers much more leverage in collective bargaining. The CIO targeted new immigrant workers in major industries—such as textiles, auto, steel and mining—who had not been welcomed in the AFL craft unions. In Massachusetts and throughout the country, the CIO often utilized militant tactics on the picket lines, though few entertained a radical labor agenda, such as giving workers more control in the factory or establishing a workers' party, as in most industrialized countries where the party serves as the base for gaining worker political power through the electoral process. The national TWUA, on the other hand, was the epitome of the "business union" model of unions, narrowly focused on the right to organize, wages, and working conditions.

From its inception, the TWUA was hierarchically arranged and not very democratic. Sidney Hillman and the CIO Textile Workers Organizing Committee intentionally created centralized and hierarchical unions without the possibilities of independent factions emerging within it. When unions merged or amalgamated, it was forced amalgamation from above (Stepan-Norris and Zeitlin 2002, 76). As Mariano Bishop told delegates to the 1939 UTWA convention, "We have heard a lot of talk about rank-and-file. There are some in the union who try to spread the impression that they are for the rank-and-file, while the rest of us are not [...] The finest thing that the union can do for the rank-and-file is to make the union administration stronger and [more] efficient" (Daniel 2001, 193).

Unlike some CIO unions, such as the United Packinghouse Workers Union, the United Auto Workers, and the United Electrical Workers, which had some socialists and communists in them, Hillman, as president of the Textile Workers Organizing Committee (TWOC-CIO) and future presidents of UTWA made no place for them (Stepan-Norris and Zeitlin 2002, 76). The UTWA, from which the TWOC-CIO emerged, had always been anti-communist in the 1930s. For instance, during the 1934 National Textile Strike, when the communists made overtures to join the strike effort, the head of the UTWA national strike committee, Francis J. Gorman warned, "Communist agitators are entering the conflict. [...] they would be fought to the limit. We will have to fight not only the employers and their hired thugs, but the Communists who are now trying to take advantage of the situation to promote their own philosophy."[10] Joseph A. Sylvia, regional strike director of New England, blamed communists for riots and deaths of workers in Rhode Island.[11]

During the mid-1930s, hundreds of Portuguese immigrants joined the Fall River and New Bedford labor unions, mostly those affiliated with the CIO. In Fall River, from the 1930s to the 1940s, Mariano Bishop, Manuel Melo, and Mike Botelho—all known labor activists of Portuguese descent—led organizing drives for the UTW locals to join the CIO and signed up many new members. New Bedford also became a stronghold of CIO organizing and successes, paralleling the successes in Fall River. Twenty-four shops made up the Joint Board of New Bedford and included over 15,000 union members (Interview, Manny Fernandes by author and Jack Stauder, 1986).

Mariano Bishop was typical of the more conservative UTWA union officials who became organizers for the UTWA-CIO in southeastern Massachusetts in the 1930s and 1940s. Bishop emigrated from the Azores and entered Fall River mills as a doffer at age ten. He lived in the Portuguese South End and socialized at the Liberal Athletic Club. In the 1920s, Mariano became president of the dyers unit of the UTWA. At the time of the 1934 strike, he was serving as organizer, business agent, and President of the New Bedford-Fall River Textile Council affiliated with the UTWA (Kelly 1956). He and his assistants closed down many plants throughout the region of Fall River and southern Rhode Island. They deployed pickets and stirred up lively protests. Once Bishop was arrested by state police, and then was pulled out of their hands by a group of angry women picketers.[12]

Although the 1934 strike failed to achieve its goals, Bishop continued to build the CIO's Textile Workers Union (TWUA-CIO) in the Fall River area. With Ed Doolan, he brought hundreds of workers into the CIO-UTWA. Eventually, he became Executive Vice President of the national union. He had long been the protégé of president Emil Rieve to succeed him as president of the national union. Tragically, in 1953, at the age of forty-six, just before this transfer happened, Bishop had suffered a massive heart attack and died (Daniel 2001, 237).

Despite union gains, the 1930s created many economic difficulties for most immigrants in southeastern Massachusetts. The Portuguese took a variety of jobs in the tight labor market. The garment shops hired only a fraction of the workforce that had been employed in the textile mills. Some individuals left for other parts of the country, such as California and New Jersey. Others took whatever jobs were available locally. These included working for clothing, synthetic fibers, rubber, or housewares manufacturers or taking jobs in the trades.

The Taft-Hartley Bill

Although the federal government made efforts to lift the country from its economic doldrums, it was not until World War II that the economy recovered and many people found work. Though unions expanded simply because of job growth and labor disputes occurred, unions and managers tempered their disputes and labor's militant voice was muted. Conservative labor leaders and management representatives on the National War Labor Board administered settlements.

After accepting frozen wages and long hours during World War II, in its aftermath increasing numbers of workers fought for improved wages and working conditions. Strikes were frequent. In retaliation, companies lobbied Congress for passage of Amendments to the Social Security Act of 1935. The amendments were written almost entirely by the National Association of Manufacturers, the most conservative business lobby in the nation. The amendments became known as the Taft Hartley Bill, or to many in the labor community, the "slave labor bill" and generally viewed by them as the most repressive federal labor laws of any advanced capitalist society. The bill was passed over Truman's veto with substantial support of the Democratic Party. Neither Truman nor leading democrats fought to defeat the bill (Green 1980, 198-199; Wagner 2002; Gordon 2006).

The 1947 Taft-Hartley Bill weakened labor's power on every front. The amendments allowed states to pass laws forbidding the "closed shop," which permitted workers to not join the union, thereby weakening its unity and power. The acts made unions and union leaders financially liable for losses incurred by businesses that were struck and made unions more vulnerable to court injunctions. Taft-Hartley outlawed secondary boycotts when workers in related plants strike in support of an existing strike. Wildcat strikes or spontaneous walkouts were declared illegal. Strikes had to be announced, voted on and not contradicted by contract. Strikes by federal workers, a growing part of the work force, were prohibited. The President was given the power to order workers back to work. Employers could sue workers for breach of contract (Zieger and Gall 2002; Green 1980, 189-190).

Most important for the radicals of the left and the conservatives on the right were the "loyalty oaths." All union officers had to sign an affidavit swearing they were not members of the Communist Party and that they did not advocate the overthrow of the government by force or by any unconstitutional means. The U.S. Supreme Court eventually declared the oaths themselves unconstitutional. The Cold War hysteria that was sweeping the nation precipitated the oaths, as well as the intention of business to kill the power of radicals and, thereby, weaken the labor movement.

The AFL and CIO purged unions with known communists in leadership or any union whose leadership refused to sign the loyalty oaths. The National Labor Relations Board would not certify any union election unless candidates had all signed. Communists and those leaders fearing that label withdrew from leadership or were forced out. Anyone who advocated ideas of worker power and equality was subject to the suspicion of being a communist and losing their standing. Fear spread through the union ranks squelching democratic debate (Stepan-Norris and Zeitlin, 271-277, 278-280; Gordon 2006).

The majority of locals in New Bedford and Fall River supported signing the loyalty oaths. The majority of Portuguese on the Board, including at least one communist member, were against signing. Manny Fernandes and others in leadership position led the effort to get the Board to accept signing the oaths. Cold War hysteria that was sweeping the nation established a likely context for business to build into the bill these repressive oaths.[13]

The conservative leadership of the national TWUA made the decision for Fernandes and other local leaders. They interpreted the amendments to mean that if a worker did not sign, he/she could not run for or remain in an official leadership position within the union. Knowing the communists on the board would be purged, they supported mandated signing of the oaths. If Fernandes and others wanted to stay in office or run for future office, they would have to sign. But Fernandes and the majority of the local leadership were not radicals, but patriotic Americans, and did not really object to signing the loyalty oaths. He made the motion to the Council in favor of signing the oaths. According to Fernandes, Portuguese labor leaders were actively involved in the "loyalty oath" debate and represented both sides of the issue. He noted that:

> [t]he so-called "active Portuguese" were against the signing of the affidavit. The more conservative ones would say well it's the law, I'm gonna sign it. The liberal ones said I don't care if it's the law, I don't have to sign it and I'm not a commie.... More Portuguese (members) than any other nationality were against signing the affidavit. We did have a

majority of Portuguese on the board but it was primarily (conservative) ones.[14]

The impact of the Taft-Hartley Bill, especially on the grievance procedure, was immediate. As Fernandes observed:

> From now on you just didn't take the so-called procedures of settling a grievance in the old way...because under the law if you...caused the company some hardship or loss of production...then there were damages...the union would be liable for damages. So, in my opinion, that made the union leadership cautious in how they settled a grievance.... In my opinion, it sort of weakened our grievance procedure.[15]

McCarthyism

Intensification of the Cold War mentality that led to McCarthyism and the political "witch hunts" of the early 1950s targeted many, including foreign-born union leaders who were socialists, anarchists, and communists. Many union members, like most Americans, embraced the anti-communist mood and the purges of radical union leaders that followed. But the repression had a general chilling effect on all union activism.

One tool the government used to sap union militancy was to deport or threaten to deport non-citizens who were active leftists in the labor movement, which caused anyone critical of the current economic and political situation to hesitate to voice their concerns. The tactic has a long history in the U.S., and we have already seen how it operated at the end of the 1928 strike to eliminate leftists from the scene.

The Smith Act of 1940 and The Subversive Control Act (McCarran-Walter Act) of 1950 became tools for removing militant labor leaders. Under the 1950 Act, at age forty-two, Eula Mendes was arrested at her home in New Bedford as a "subversive alien" due to her membership in the Communist Party. She was not a U.S. citizen, having been denied that opportunity because of her arrests during the 1928 strike. She had no family ties; her parents were dead, and her husband, also active in the 1928 strike, had recently divorced her. After losing appeals, Mendes was deported in May 1953. "I heard the iron [gate] clang behind me."[16] Portugal was a fascist state—the country Augusto Pinto had been deported to in 1929 and then allegedly killed by authorities. Mendes feared a similar fate. She thus sought and was granted asylum in Poland, where she lived until her death in 2003.

Mendes reflected on the chilling effect arrest and deportation threats had on the foreign-born workers in the unions at the time:

> The question of picking on foreign-born people was used during the McCarthy days as a pressure against people generally.... My arrest had an effect of creating a lot of fear amongst a lot of Portuguese people who were not citizens. And this question of arresting so many at that time all over the country also had an effect of trying to break the progress of the trade union movement.[17]

Despite repression of labor militancy throughout the 1950s, unions continued to organize and fight for wages and better working conditions. However, their militancy was muted by the purge of radical union members. With the merger of the conservative AFL and a "deradicalized" CIO in 1955, the union movement continued on its conservative path. In southeastern Massachusetts, the continued declining economy and dominance by the conservative CIO-affiliated UTWA, and its subsequent conservative incarnations (ACTWU, UNITE, and HERE-UNITE) that followed this period, have meant that a radical reemergence was unlikely to occur.

Conclusion

This purpose of this paper was to dispel certain stereotypes concerning Portuguese immigrants' historic involvement in the labor movement of southeastern Massachusetts. Arriving with the flood of "new immigrants" in the late 1800s and early 1900s, the Portuguese came primarily from a rural, uneducated, and politically conservative background. They entered the factories of New England. More established "old immigrants" from England, Scotland, Wales, and Ireland looked down on these new arrivals believing them culturally and racially inferior, lacking knowledge of factory regime, and too politically conservative to join unions.

Yet despite these imagined and real handicaps, the Portuguese, southeastern Massachusetts's largest immigrant group at the time, joined the labor movement by the thousands, and were quickly socialized into the hardships of industrial factory life. Often thought to shy away from the risks associated with labor activism, Portuguese women workers, too, joined the labor movement to improve their lives. Some, like Eula Mendes, rose to leadership positions. The active participation of Portuguese men and women was evident during the 1928 New Bedford Textile Strike and later in the CIO organizing of the 1930s and '40s.

This paper has focused on an important era in US labor history, a period of transformation. In the 1920s and 1930s the U.S. labor movement included both a conservative and significant radical/left radical strand. The 1940s and 1950s saw the rise of repressive labor legislation in the Taft-Hartley Bill and Cold War McCarthyism that led to the purging of radical/leftists from the labor movement. The merging of the once radical CIO with the always-conservative AFL in 1955 signified clear dominance by the conservatives that has continued to this day. David Caute reflects on the long-term impact of the events of this era on the U.S. labor movement: "So from the moment of its conception (1955), the AFL-CIO was—and would become during the second half of the century—the most conservative and ideologically acquiescent [central labor organization] among capitalist democracies" (Caute as quoted in Stepan-Norris and Zeitlin 2002, 274).

This is an initial attempt to document participation of Portuguese immigrants in the U.S. labor movement. Since their descendants continue to represent the largest ethnic group in the region, it would be useful to build on current research by documenting their participation in labor unions since the 1950s. Reflecting on the Portuguese-American contribution to the region's labor movement today, Peter Knowlton, United Electrical Workers Union organizer in New Bedford commented, "I can't think of a single union local in this area that doesn't have at least one person of Portuguese descent in its leadership" (Interview by author, April 14, 1996). Other leaders in the area I talked with confirmed this observation. In order to test this generalization and to analyze the current role of the rank-and-file Portuguese worker in the labor movement, it will be necessary to collect additional oral histories of contemporary Portuguese-American workers and labor leaders.[18]

Notes

[1] This essay is an adaptation of two earlier articles by the author, "The Portuguese Worker" and "Three Lives for Labor: Eula Mendes, Manny Fernandes and Tina Ponte," in *Portuguese Spinner: An American Story*, eds. Marsha McCabe and Joseph D. Thomas (New Bedford, MA, Spinner Publications, 1998), 230-245.

[2] The terms conservative and radical or leftist appear in labor studies literature and are not always clearly defined, nor is there full agreement on their meaning. Yet, they are useful terms because they differentiate two broad and divergent strands in the tactics and political agenda of the labor movement. The conservative labor leaders and organizations represented a greater level of worker accommodation to the demands of the owners and support for the capitalist system. In the period under consideration, the dominant representative of this strand is the American Federation of Labor and various unaffiliated skilled craft unions. They focused on obtaining legal recognition for unions and on improving working conditions, wages and benefits. The radicals, sometimes referred to as leftists, and here referred to as radicals/leftists were generally inspired by Marxist thought and practice. They also supported the legal right to organize unions and the improvement of working conditions, wages and benefits, but they had more far-reaching goals. They advocated increasing workers' control over running the factories and depending on which faction one considers, the reformation up to the total abolition of capitalism in favor of socialism, a shift in the structure of the U.S. economy from one based on the profit motive to one based on the needs of the workers and run by workers. These radical/leftist groups included the Industrial Workers of the World, the Socialist Party, the Communist Party, and others.

[3] Scholars have proposed various reasons for the conservative tradition of the U.S. labor movement in contrast to the more leftist character of those in other advanced capitalist countries. These include 1) the unique historical background of U.S. capitalism which militated against the formation of greater working-class solidarity ("American exceptionalism"); 2) greater opportunities for workers and/or their offspring to achieve upward social and economic mobility; 3) repression by the government and private industry policies and actions and finally; 4) divisive policies and strategies within the labor movement. Buhle (1999); Clawson and Clawson (1999); Goldfield, (2000).

[4] Joseph Figueiredo. Interview by Robert Shartery. Portuguese Oral History Project 1987-1992. The Ferreira-Mendes Portuguese American Archives. University of Massachusetts Dartmouth. March 14, 1983.

[5] "Bread and Roses" Textile Workers Strike in Lawrence, Massachusetts in 1912. Mostly women and new immigrants including Lithuanians, Armenians, Poles, Portuguese, and a dozen other nationalities came together for a nine-week strike. Strike meetings were held at ethnic clubs, such as the Portuguese center. The strike was organized by the radical Industrial Workers of the World (IWW, usually referred to as the "Wobblies"). It was one of the few successful strikes organized by the radical/left during the period. The strike demonstrated the potential for unity and unionizing among "new immigrant" workers. The 1926 Textile Strike in Passaic, New Jersey led by Communist Youth ended in failure. Some of the leaders of this twelve-month-long strike traveled to New Bedford, Massachusetts to help organize the New Bedford Textile Strike of 1928. See Juravich et al. (1996, 75-86); Georgianna and Aaronson (1993, 82-83).

[6] Eula Mendes interview by Penn Reeve and Jack Stauder. Portuguese Oral History Project 1987-1992. The Ferreira-Mendes Portuguese American Archives. University of Massachusetts Dartmouth. July 2-3, 1986.

[7] Ibid.

[8] Bartolomeo Vanzetti and Nicola Sacco were two Italian anarchists who were accused of robbery and murder in a 1920 Braintree, Massachusetts holdup. The case became one of the U.S.'s most well-known political trials because though the evidence was circumstantial, their political leanings and their militant anti-capitalist and pro-revolutionary views made them the target of attacks inside and outside of the court system. As the case gained notice around the world, many people from across the political spectrum saw it as the American justice system on trial. In 1927, they were put to death by electrocution.

[9] "Red-baiting" means accusing someone of being a communist or "red." It also can refer to accusing any leftist critic of the U.S. political or economic system. "Red-baiting" challenges leftists for their lack of patriotism to discredit their political ideas. The 1920s (First Red Scare) and the early-1950s McCarthy era (Second Red Scare) are the two primary historic examples of red-baiting

in American history.

[10] "Textile Strike is Extended to Silk and Rayon: Strike Leaders Fight Red Bid for Power" *Standard-Times,* September 1, 1934, 2.

[11] "U.T.W. Blames Reds for Riots: Union Strike Leaders Advises Workers Not to Tolerate Communists," *Standard-Times,* September 14, 1934, 1.

[12] "Strikers Fight Warren Police: Fall River Workers Picket Rhode Island Mill," *Standard-Times,* September 6, 1934, 3.

[13] Manny Fernandes. interview by Bela Feldman-Bianco and Penn Reeve, Portuguese Oral History Project 1987-1992. The Ferreira-Mendes Portuguese American Archives. University of Massachusetts Dartmouth. May 14, 1987.

[14] Ibid.

[15] Ibid.

[16] Eula Mendes. Interview by Penn Reeve and Jack Stauder, Portuguese Oral History Project 1987-1992. The Ferreira-Mendes Portuguese American Archives. University of Massachusetts Dartmouth, July 2-3, 1986.

[17] Ibid.

[18] The recently established Ferreira-Mendes Portuguese-American Archives at the University of Massachusetts Dartmouth, the repository containing many of the oral histories cited in this paper, is an excellent resource and location for future documentation of the Portuguese-American contributions to the labor movement.

CHAPTER 14

Kin Networks and Family Strategies: Working-Class Portuguese Families in New England[1]

LOUISE LAMPHERE, FILOMENA M. SILVA, JOHN P. SOUSA

Introduction

[...] We propose to examine the relationship among local economy, conjugal role, and kin network by focusing on the migration of Portuguese families to New England. Since special legislation encouraged the immigration of refugees from the 1957 volcanic eruption in Faial (one of the Azores Islands), and since the Immigration Act of 1965 lifted the restrictive quota system, large numbers of Portuguese, primarily from the Azores, have migrated to the United States, particularly California, southern Massachusetts, and Rhode Island. Many come from agricultural villages or working-class neighborhoods in the small towns of the islands. On arrival in New England, the Portuguese enter factory work. Both husbands and wives, as well as teenage children, are employed in labor-intensive low-wage industries. This constitutes a radical break with their past employment experience, since many husbands were previously employed in agriculture or in craft jobs (painters, stonemasons, carpenters). Most wives have had little work experience outside the home, garden, and fields, unless they have worked as maids or housekeepers. By examining the process of proletarianization (the transformation of rural agriculturalists and artisans to industrial wage workers), we can look closely at the impact of entering into a new economic position on family role relationships and kin networks.

Family Strategies

Throughout the chapter, we will argue that it is important to see couples as forging new strategies in the immigrant context, whether they are dealing with the daily tasks of living (housework, cooking, shopping, transportation, and financial management) or with more occasional, yet critical, activities (arranging for immigration, finding a job, renting a new apartment, or making new child-care arrangements). [...]

However, [...] strategies are not forged in a vacuum. We need to focus attention on the structural constraints that shape strategies and that may severely limit the options of actors within a system. Attention must be given to the political economy in which a few actors both control the means of production and dominate the social relations of production.

In the case of immigration, it is important to analyze factors that "push" migrants out of their original economic situation and those that "pull" them into particular places within a new local economy, shaping and limiting their access to economic resources and family strategies for coping with daily life. It is our contention that family migration and female labor-force participation are intelligible as family strategies. These strategies are a product of the Azorean economy that pushes families to migrate and the New England economy that, through the historical development of labor-intensive low-wage industries, has utilized female labor for 150 years, permitting as well as necessitating female employment. A wife's employment sets other forces in motion that begin to change the division of labor in the family, yet it is changed in a way congruent with other family values—male authority, family self-sufficiency, care of children by trusted persons. Some of these aspects are also beginning to change.

Entrance into an industrial economy sets up new tasks and problems that can be solved through the use of aid from members of a network of kin and eventually friends, neighbors, [...] or other ethnic group members. The process of immigration usually separates a nuclear family from its larger network of kin (i.e., from parents and siblings of the couple who migrate). However, in a situation where "chain migration" has been established and where there are substantial numbers of migrants from the same region, migrating couples often have access to some members of their respective kindreds, as well as contact with others from the same village or island. There is a dialectic here. On the one hand, kin are important in handling certain instrumental activities. On the other, given the low wages that Portuguese workers earn because they are recruited to jobs in the labor-intensive sector of the economy and given the instability of these jobs, there is incredible pressure put on these families to make sufficient income to meet expenses. Conflict may develop over issues of mutual aid in some families, while in others a rekindled unity grows through the sharing of goods and services in a new context. In addition, layoffs, new jobs in a distant town or city, and difficulties with housing often draw a family away from their closest kin, widening their social networks and encouraging the use of other ties and avenues of information, yet not shutting off the need for aid and contact with relatives altogether. Thus, the shape and interconnectedness of a social network is not just a function of the environment of the family and geographical mobility, as Bott suggests (1957, 1971), but also is related to the kind of local economy in which a couple finds themselves and their place within it, in terms of wages, job stability, and fringe benefits.

Research Setting

Data for this chapter come from a larger project, "Women, Work, and Ethnicity in an Urban Setting," which focused on women and their families in an industrial New England city of about 20,000 persons. The aim of the project was to provide a detailed understanding of the strategies used by working-class mothers to cope with their work and family roles. The study community is one in which the population mainly works in industry, a large proportion of married women are part of the paid labor force, and there are clearly defined ethnic populations. These features were present in the early decades of this century, when the town was dominated by cotton and silk textile mills. As the textile industry declined, first in the 1920s and 1930s, and later in the 1950s, jewelry, apparel, and other light industries have taken over the old mills, while some textile companies remain, mainly those in webbing and narrow fabrics. [...]

We completed fifteen Portuguese interviews, including eleven Azorean families and four continental families. The interviews, conducted separately with husbands and with wives included:

1. A description of the interviewee's current job and a complete work history;
2. A discussion of the structure of family life, including daily schedule, household division of labor, and finances;
3. A reconstruction of courtship, marriage, immigration, and residence patterns in the United States, as well as demographic material on parents, siblings, and in-laws;
4. A discussion of the role of relatives, neighbors, and friends in family life, including the exchange of goods and services, mutual aid, and visiting patterns.

360 [...] The Portuguese [...] have immigrated into an area where the Portuguese are already a well-established minority because of their immigration before 1924. In the area we studied, there are two Portuguese parishes, several Portuguese clubs, a Portuguese-language school, and a number of Portuguese small businesses. The older immigrants in this particular area tend to be from continental Portugal, whereas the new immigrants include some continentals but a large number from the Azores. [...]

The Push for Immigration

The work experience of the Azorean families we interviewed reflects the largely rural and underdeveloped nature of the islands' economy. An overview of the occupational structure makes clear that there are few opportunities for wage jobs outside of the rural sector. This sector, in turn, is dominated by large landowners, reducing most agriculturalists to the status of small holders, renters, or day laborers. One-half of the paid labor force is employed in agriculture and one-third in services, with an underdeveloped industrial sector (only seventeen percent of the labor force). Women work hard in their homes, caring for children, growing food in the family *quintal* (garden), washing clothes by hand, tending animals, or helping with the harvest and the processing of food. Only 10.6 percent of Azorean women are in the paid labor force, and of these 47.4 percent are in service jobs, including domestic service (twenty-nine percent) and other service work (nineteen percent). Of the female labor force only twenty-six percent are employed in the industrial sector, which means that women work in dressmaking or embroidery and knit shops or possibly in a brewery, a tobacco factory or a milk-processing plant.

A closer look at the rural sector reveals the very difficult situation that most Azorean families face. A 1965 agricultural census of the Azores shows that almost eighty percent of the land is held by individual families, but seventy-three percent of these holdings are considered insufficient to provide adequate incomes for the families that work them.[2] The proportion of insufficient holdings is higher for the island of São Miguel, which is also the most densely populated island with the highest birth rate. Here land is more heavily concentrated in the hands of a few large landowners, and there are more agricultural families who rent rather than own their own land. The Azorean rural economy is thus composed of small holders who have a difficult time supporting their families, a situation that is exacerbated on the largest island of São Miguel, where the domination of large landowners has reduced many rural families to the status of renters.

Thus, it is not surprising that 75,000 Azoreans immigrated between 1960 and 1970, about fifty-four percent to the United States and forty-three percent to Canada.[3] Also, it is not surprising that in any given year during this period, immigrants from São Miguel made up one-half to three-quarters of the total Azorean emigration.

Portuguese families come to the United States as part of family strategy to better their way of life (*melhorar a vida).* A woman from Terceira (Mrs. D.) stated the matter well:

> There we are raised as poor people. We immigrate for this reason: because we have the need to improve our standard of living. There the economy is very low right now. It's not that my land isn't beautiful, because it's absolutely marvelous. If we had the standard of living that we have in the U.S., no one would ever leave. I think most people feel the same way. We arrive here in order to improve our lives.

The Pull of the New England Economy and Female Labor Force Participation

Most Portuguese immigrant families entered the New England economy in the late 1960s at a time of economic expansion when unskilled and semi-skilled workers were badly needed. In the city that we studied, even the declining textile industry was in need of workers, since there were still a substantial number of small firms specializing in narrow fabrics, braiding, and synthetics or silk woven fabrics. The Colombian immigration, for example, was a direct result of recruitment by textile employers who needed skilled labor (loom fixers and weavers) during the expansion of the 1960s. These firms, as well as a number of jewelry, apparel, toy, wire, and cable plants, welcomed Portuguese migrants to their semiskilled and unskilled jobs. In the 1970s, the local economy saw a return to increased layoffs and unemployment, especially during the recession of 1974-1975; several textile firms, including two of the largest employers, closed their doors or moved to the South in 1975-1976.

Employers, especially in textiles and apparel, are faced with heavy competition from imports and realize that low wages are important to the survival of their businesses. They often complained about the difficulty of finding workers to fill their jobs, but several explicitly recognized the advantages of hiring Portuguese workers. The president of a small webbing company said that if there had not been an influx of Portuguese in 1970-1971, the company probably would have closed down and gone to the South. He said that nobody wants to do weaving except the Portuguese, and if he could get more weavers he would expand production and start a third shift. [...] [I]n the apparel company where I worked, the Portuguese women workers were described as "the backbone of the sewing operation." In other words, the Portuguese reputation for hard work fits well with the needs of industrialists in declining, low-wage industries.

Most of the families we interviewed immigrated when they were between thirty and fifty years of age, after having had several children or having completed a family of perhaps five to seven children. Two couples came to the United States as a young married pair and had all their children here. Most families had been in New England for five to ten years, although four families had been in the United States less than two years at the time of our study. Some came on work contracts, but most already had relatives living in New England and arranged their resident visas through them. The wives expected to take jobs to help their husbands meet the cost of the trip and to pay off the initial investment in a car and furniture. In some families, the oldest children had already completed school in Portugal (up through the fourth grade) and took jobs in the United States, whereas other children left school at sixteen to work and contribute to the family income.

In 1977, the Azorean and continental families interviewed were employed in a variety of textile, jewelry, wire and metal processing, and light manufacturing firms. [...] About forty percent work in small shops of 130 workers or less, all privately owned, often by several family members. The remainder work in shops of 150-500 workers, equally divided between privately owned local industries and subsidiaries of larger conglomerates. [...]

The husbands and wives we interviewed (both Azorean and Continental) are indeed making low wages.[4] Women in 1977 were making between $2.07 and $3.75 per hour, with an average of $2.70 an hour, only forty cents above the minimum wage of $2.35 per hour. The men were earning between $2.35 and $6.50 an hour, but only two of the eleven Azorean men were making $4.00 an hour or more. The average wage was $3.70 per hour. Some of the women and, particularly, the men worked substantial amounts of overtime. Some men worked eleven- and twelve-hour shifts, and one man, at the time of our interviews, was holding down two full-time jobs in order to make ends meet.

Almost all of the families have experienced repeated layoffs, industrial accidents, health problems, unforeseen major expenditures, and even the loss of their belongings in an apartment fire. Given the local wage structure, it is not only necessary that there be two wage earners in a family, but it is important that at least one if not both workers put in overtime hours in order to meet expenses. The stereotype of Portuguese immigrants as hard workers is a matter not only of cultural attitude but also of economic necessity.

This brief discussion of the economy of the Azores and New England helps us to see how families' strategies are shaped at both ends of the immigration process:

1. Immigration itself is part of a family strategy to better the family's way of life;
2. The entrance of the wife into a factory job is also "strategic" and follows from the family's economic situation on arrival and from the nature of the local economy; and
3. The low scale of male wages makes it almost certain that wives will

work. In addition, it is important for the husband who earns relatively higher wages to put in as much overtime as possible.

Conjugal Roles

The economic background of immigrant families and the niche they fill in the New England economy leads to a high probability that Portuguese married women will work even if they have young children. Once the wife is working, new considerations appear in terms of the daily management of the household, particularly in terms of how child care is handled and how household tasks are organized. In examining changes in conjugal role relationships, we see the complex interaction between traditional role relationships, the ideology of male-female roles within the family, and the new context of a dual-worker family.

Elizabeth Bott (1971) distinguished between complementary organization and joint organization of the activities in which husband and wife engage. In a complementary organization, activities of husband and wife are different and separate, but are fitted together to form a whole. Or, activities may be independent and carried out separately without reference to each other. In a joint organization of roles, activities are carried out by the husband and wife together, or the same activity is carried out by either partner at different times. In her research, Bott used the term "segregated conjugal role relationship" to indicate a relationship where complementary and independent organization predominated: "Husband and wife have a clear differentiation of tasks and a considerable number of separate interests and activities. They have a clearly defined division of labour into male tasks and female tasks. They expect to have different leisure pursuits, and the husband has his friends outside the home and the wife has hers" (Bott 1971, 54). In a joint conjugal role relationship, in contrast, joint organization is relatively predominant: "Husband and wife expect to carry out many activities together with a minimum of task differentiation and separation of interests. They not only plan the affairs of the family together, but also exchange many household tasks and spend much of their leisure time together" (Bott 1971, 54).

The traditional Azorean relationship between husband and wife is complementary for household division of labor, yet, because of the husband's role as head of the household and an ideology that women should be protected and within the shadow of the family, most leisure-time activities are done either as a family or in groups of same-sex individuals. In other words, families are male-oriented, and conjugal roles are segregated with regard to the division of labor but joint with regard to leisure activities. Under the impact of immigration and female labor-force participation, the segregated nature of role relationships has begun to change, but many aspects of traditional family ideology have remained, at least for the parents we interviewed.

Most of the Azorean couples we interviewed have gone through a traditional upbringing and courtship. As young women, girls are carefully watched and are not allowed to walk in public places unchaperoned. Mrs. N., age twenty-nine, recalled her upbringing, which she characterized as stricter than some other Azorean families:

> I remember...when I was there [in the islands] that I had a friend whom I liked very much and she sometimes would go to the park and she would say, 'are you coming with me?' And I would say, 'I will not go without asking my Father.' I would go home and I would say to my father, 'Ai, Father, may I go with that friend?' and he would say, 'No sir, you will go out when I go out.' See, the way I was brought up, I could not go out. I would not go out with anyone.... Now I go out more, but it would be very hard for me to be a popular girl, like the others for example, like my sister-in-law. My sister-in-law, I like her personality. She goes out, the husband goes out. She goes to a dance or to a feast. I like her temperament, but it would be very hard for me to adapt to this because I was not brought up this way.

Mrs. F., now forty-three and from a village on São Miguel, provides a good example of the way in which a traditional courtship progressed. She knew her husband since childhood. At fourteen she knew she liked her husband, who was then twenty-one years old. Once they began courting (became *namorados),* the relationship was closely supervised. They would talk formally to each other on Sunday afternoons. The duration of the encounter was supposed to be for an hour, but it usually lasted most of the afternoon. She would come to a window in the front part of the house, and he would speak to her from the sidewalk. Occasionally, they would be together in public, especially during feasts, but that was frowned upon by the parents. At no time were they allowed to be alone. In the Azores, the young man must have the father's permission to court "at the window," and, after he has approached the father a second time and has been granted permission for the couple to marry, the young man may enter the home.

Among younger couples, courting may be interrupted by immigration or a couple may begin to court by mail, first exchanging pictures and then, after receiving permission from the father, exchanging letters for an extensive period. As Mrs. E., age thirty-one, described her situation:

> He was courting a girl in my town and when he went there he saw me, and that was it. You know, he courted me for nine months there and then he came here to America. He was here for two years and a half. My father consented to the wedding and he returned there for the marriage. After we were married, I came back [to the United States] with him.... Before he came here, he talked to my father and everything was set so that I could receive his letters. But before he left he had set the time [for the wedding]—two or two and a half years.

In contrast, Mrs. N., another young wife, immigrated first with her parents and siblings. As Mr. N. described what happened:

> I had seen her but never spoke to her [in terms of courting] or anything. Later my sister's husband was friends with my wife's brother; they worked together. Her father came over with a work contract. Three years later, my brother-in-law [his sister's husband] used to get together with my father-in-law, and my sister sent a picture where my wife is together with the other family members. I recognized her and sent word asking if she had a boyfriend. That's how it started.

Mrs. N.'s interview took up the story from this point:

> Then I courted him for two months through letters, and after that I went there to marry. When I went it wasn't to get married; my sister was the one who was going to get married. I had the idea of going to get to know him and after, if I liked him, I would marry him; if not, I would stay single. My father said, "If you know the family...if the family is good, the guy is

> also good; but do what you want, I think you will get married. You will be married once and for all, instead of going back and forth!" So both of us got married. I got married on a Saturday and my sister on the Sunday.

In most of the Azorean families, the husband and father demands the respect of his wife and children, a respect that stems from their role as provider. Mr. M. commented on his role as head of the household:

> As long as they live under my wings I am the boss [i.e., the one who gives the orders is me]. No authority will boss my kids around because I am working. I am sacrificing my body to feed them, to clothe them, to get them shoes and to provide a bed for them to sleep in.... I'm not going to be sacrificing myself and watch them at the age of fifteen or sixteen going out for two or three days without coming home. If they ever did that, they would never step back into this house.

The ideal of family self-sufficiency is strong among Azorean families and is often verbalized by the men. Part of this is a commitment to hard work of any kind by the husbands, as indicated by Mr. F.: "I can do any kind of work here in America. Any kind of work that's doesn't matter ... nothing. No, the Portuguese, the Azorean, he is used to heavy work; he knows what work means [...]."

The older children usually follow Azorean custom and hand over their paychecks to their father. Often in the American context, the son or daughter may pay the bills because they have the English-language skills to do so, but the father often remains in charge of the allocation of funds. As Mr. F. described how financial arrangements work in his family with a working wife and a working sixteen-year-old son:

> No, I am the one who is in charge of the money. We all do it together. I come home, I tell them what's what, you see, but they do the same to me. For example, if my son goes shopping with his brothers he must tell me what is spent.

Mr. M.'s family works on a similar system:

> He [his seventeen-year-old son] comes home first, puts the check on the

> table or over there or here or there or any place. He puts it down first, then later he cashes it. Yes, he cashes it; I give him my check he cashes it. The bills—I give him the money then he leaves, pays everything, brings back the change, and there is never any problem. [...]

In some families decision-making is more jointly done. For example, Mr. D. handles the finances according to his wife, but they cash their checks together and then decide how to spend the money. In the N.'s case (a younger couple), the wife explained that Mr. N. took care of the money. Their paychecks are combined, and all the bills are paid; what, is left over is theirs. Mr. and Mrs. N. talked over the decision that Mrs. N. would work and that they would try to make important decisions together. Mr. N. says:

> Until this day, I never decided anything without talking it over with her together. And I enjoy it this way, because we can't blame the other. If it's good, it's for both of us, and if it's bad, the same.

The women in the household are responsible for cooking, cleaning, and child care. Usually the daughters in a family share some of these responsibilities. One father described his household routine, in which the sons as well as the daughters helped out:

> Well, we have seven people in the house but as we say, the parents are the ones in charge of all of this. But since I'm tired of working, and getting old, I'll tell Esmeralda [a twelve-year-old daughter] to clean the stove; I'll tell Mário [her twelve year-old twin] clean this or clean that. Or I'll tell Adriano [the ten-year-old son], "Come on guys, make our own beds. Mário will help," and so they do it.

The mother supervises bed-making and laundry and does the cooking, although the oldest daughter, age seventeen, cooks breakfast and dinner. In another household, the mother discouraged the adolescent girls from doing much of the housework, even though the father felt that they should help with these chores. Her point of view was: "No, inside the house I'm the boss," indicating her control over housework in the allocation of "female chores."

Most parents feel strongly that children should give respect to their parents. […] The G.'s had spent sixteen years in Brazil and felt that American culture supported entirely different relationships between children and parents in contrast to both Portugal and Brazil:

> There [in the Azores] we used to ask for our parents' blessing [kissing their hand] in the morning, very respectfully, everything…we used to talk in a lower voice than our parents. […] there [in Brazil] is much more respect for many things. That is, in Brazil, it is not already as respectful as in São Miguel, but in America it is much worse. […] Because in Brazil, my daughters at the age of my younger ones today, never spoke in a raised voice to me. […] My uncle told me, "You should have never come from Brazil. The person who comes to America to educate their kids only ends up with uneducated children."

Mrs. E., a young mother, felt, on the other hand, that she would be able to raise her children in the same way she would in the Azores. She said that the best she could teach her children is for them to be well-behaved, to be obedient to their parents, and not to misbehave. Mr. F. also emphasized the importance of respect in his philosophy of child-rearing: "We don't need to hit them; the child more or less follows the father's words, as long as they are polite words, words of obedience, words of respect, the child will follow also that road."

Some couples interviewed noted that they did things together, as a family. For example, Mr. N. said: "Americans have a different life from ours. We are more the type to stay home. For example, I go out, if I want to go out, I'll go with my wife. Americans, no. The wife goes one place and the husband goes someplace else. I don't buy that idea. Either we go out together or I stay home. […]"

Women's Paid Employment and Changing Roles

Given a strong ideology of family self-sufficiency, of male orientation, of control over children, and the importance of respect between parents and children, many of the rearrangements necessary because of the wife's paid employment have been handled within the nuclear family.

Rearrangement of husband-wife tasks has been possible because the local economy includes many firms that operate on two or three shifts. [...] Most couples have opted for handling child care by working on shifts, unless their children are all of school age. Since husbands and wives are often laid off, may leave a job because of childcare or health difficulties, or may seek a better job that is closer to home or on a better shift, there has been considerable adjustment of husband's and wife's jobs over an eight-to-ten-year period, with concurrent changes in child-care arrangements.

Family N., a young couple whose six-year-old child was born in this country, serves as an example. When the couple were first married, they lived with her parents in a city about fifty miles from the study area. They both worked first shift, he as a solderer and she in a knitting shop; her mother, who was not working, took care of the child. After a year they moved to the study town, and he worked for a brief three months at a second job; then he found a third job with better pay on first shift (7 a.m. until often 9 p.m.). He worked there until the workers went on strike and then found a fourth job through an advertisement in the paper. He worked first shift on this fourth job until he was laid off after three years. A fifth job was held for two years. This place closed and he found a sixth job. (All of these jobs were ten to fifteen miles commuting distance from his home). Finally, he was able to go back to his first job, a fifty-mile commute, but at high pay ($6.50 an hour).

Since coming to the study city, the wife has worked for five years at a textile company that makes elastic braid. She works on third shift, and since her job is close to home, she walks home in the morning, wakes her daughter and prepares her for school, walking her there as well. Her husband rises at 5:30 a.m. in order to get to his job fifty miles away by 7:30 a.m. This arrangement has worked well, except for a period when her husband was working from 5 a.m. to 3 p.m. He explains how they arranged babysitting with some Portuguese neighbors:

> One of these tenants had two young girls, the husband used to work second shift and the wife the first. So she used to leave at 3:00 p.m. [i.e., the wife would leave work at 3, and the husband would start at 2:00 p.m.]. So from 2 or maybe 1:30 until 3 they needed someone to stay with those two children, and since we lived in the same building my wife would stay with them. She used to pay me after. And often, since

> we did that for them, for example, when I worked in X for a short while, [about a month] for that time we had to start at 5 in the morning until 3, so I would take my girl the night before and I would take her there, she would sleep in my friend's house, instead of waking her up in the morning. So we helped each other.

[...] [M]ost couples work on different shifts unless there are already a number of older children to look after the youngest from the end of school until the parents arrive home. [...] Fathers who work third shift often get their children up and off to school after they arrive home. Some fathers will often look after a young child during the day, catching naps in between watching the child.

The household division of labor has changed in other ways in the United States. Few Azorean women drive, so the couple shops jointly for food and clothes. The husband often takes the washing to the laundromat. Some husbands make beds and participate in some of the housecleaning. There seems to be a wide range of variation here. For example, Mrs. N. reports that on Saturday mornings (after working all night) she may go to bed and sleep until 10 a.m. When she gets up, Mr. N. will have the house cleaned. Another husband who had been taking care of his children while the wife worked the second shift said he was *saturado* (he's had it) and encouraged his wife to change to the first shift, using a neighbor as a babysitter.

In most families, despite these changes, the wife takes the burden of a "second shift" and the responsibility for most of the work inside it in addition to her paid job. For example, Mr. M. said:

> The morning is the hardest part for Maria [his wife].... She has to prepare the children, their clothes and she has this thing about ironing. She had to iron their clothes before they go to school. She has to do it every day and it has to be well-ironed, for the girls as well as the boy. That's the only bad time for her. She always gets up around five o' clock in the morning to prepare everything.

Another husband said:

> Here in America a woman's life is more unpleasant than that of a man

> because I get home, even if I'm working only eight hours, on Sunday, I can't help anything at all around the house. I'm not one of those men who help their wives washing the clothes. Housework for me…maybe because I got married over there and you know that the customs there are different from those here…. I find it difficult to change.

In sum, the conditions immigrant families face in the New England economy make the wife's labor force participation an important family strategy for economic survival. This, in turn, sets off changes in the division of labor in the family, with increasing male aid in child care, shopping, laundry and even housecleaning. However, for these couples mainly in their thirties and forties, these changes are taking place in the context of maintaining a strong ideology of family self-sufficiency, as well as a commitment to respect for the father's authority, control over the children's behavior, and a proper upbringing for the children, especially the daughters, whose leisure-time activities are still carefully chaperoned.

The Reconstruction of Kin Networks

Migration into the New England economy, on the one hand, separates a couple from their kin, neighbors, and godparents, but, on the other hand, migration is made possible through kinship. One of the goals of the Immigration Act of 1965 was to reunite families, and preference is given to parents, children, and siblings of those who have already immigrated. This has set up a process of "chain migration" whereby some members of a family migrate and then are able to "call over" other family members, one at a time. […] Some families were able to immigrate in the late 1960s through a work contract, whereby an employer arranges immigration through guarantee of a job for a year or more.

Among the eleven Azorean families interviewed, most of the siblings and parents of one spouse are living in New England. Often members of the other spouse's kindred have immigrated to Canada or California or remain in the Azores. Some families are in the process of arranging the papers for a mother, sister, or married child. […] A number of parents are deceased, but there are some widowed mothers who have already immigrated and are living with a daughter or who plan to immigrate as soon as papers can be arranged.

In examining the role of close kin, that is, parents and siblings and spouse's parents and siblings, I have selected five instrumental tasks that are critical to setting up a life in the United States. These are 1) arranging for immigration (*carta da chamada*); 2) obtaining housing on arrival; 3) finding the husband a job; 4) finding the wife a job; and 5) arranging for childcare. This last item, as discussed earlier in the chapter, can be handled within the nuclear family, but for many of these families, at the point of immigration the youngest child was under school age, and some child-care arrangements had to be made if jobs on separate shifts were not obtained.

[...] In dealing with these five tasks, a variety of ties are sometimes used, for example, close kin in connection with contacts from the same village or town, *compadre* relationships, or more distant kin (i. e., cousins, aunts, and uncles). Thus, the A.'s found their first jobs because the foreman was from their town; their housing was arranged through a woman who knew the husband's mother. The house had very little heat and the baby was suffering during the cold winter months, so his sister found them jobs in the study town (thirty miles from where they originally located), and found an advertisement in the paper for the flat they eventually rented. The older daughter provided child care, at first, and after the family moved, the husband and wife worked on different shifts.

A family immigrates through relatives because of the way in which visas are obtained. However, a couple and children are often separated from their initial sponsors in the months and years following immigration. Much of this is due to the vagaries of finding and keeping jobs in the depressed New England economy. Most men and many of the women have experienced repeated layoffs, to say nothing of other job-related problems (sickness, difficulties with coworkers, conflict with a particular boss or supervisor). Siblings and their families tend to become scattered over several towns and cities in New England where there are substantial Portuguese populations. Thus, a couple may move to where another sibling is to get another job or better housing. Or they may simply strike off on their own because of an opportunity or a connection with a more distant relative (a cousin) or a coworker. As time goes on, both men and women begin to find jobs through other coworkers, through advertisements in the newspapers (often seen by relatives or coworkers), through unspecified word of mouth, and signs in shop windows. Sometimes husbands will encourage their wives to work in the same firm, especially in jewelry, where both men and women are employed in about equal numbers. Using more diverse sources for job information does not mean that for every family kin ties become irrelevant.

For example, Mrs. G. has held six jobs since the family has been in the United States. Her first job in 1968 was in a shop making billfolds: her brother's wife worked there and got her the job. She was laid off after one year and found a job at a shoestring factory through a newspaper advertisement. She worked second shift and was laid off after three months. Then in 1969, she went to work for a braiding company owned by a Portuguese man. She found this job through the mother-in-law of the man who had put up the money for their transportation to the United States. She worked first shift and left during the fourth month of her pregnancy. She stayed out of work for two years while her baby was small. She returned to work in 1972 at a jewelry company, where she packed jewelry on the first shift. Her sister saw the ad in the paper, and this woman's sister-in-law also worked there. She left this job after she had had a hysterectomy and the boss was unsympathetic to her absences due to visits to the doctor. In 1975, she went to work for another braid company, this time seeing a help-wanted sign on the door. She worked there for two years on first shift until an arm infection forced her to quit. Then in 1977, several months later, her husband found her a job at the jewelry shop where he worked. She left the job, which involved gluing jewelry-display casings, because the boss blamed her for work that had not been glued correctly. Throughout this work history, we see how Mrs. G. first relied on kin ties in finding a job, but subsequent jobs were found through a variety of means: advertisements, kin of friends, a sister, her husband, and even a help-wanted sign. Kin and other connections within the Portuguese community do not seem to drop out as potential sources of job information; rather, other more impersonal sources are added.

Portuguese families are under a fair amount of financial stress, especially during the first few years in the United States. Husbands and wives are earning low wages, and there are substantial expenses. These begin with paying off the debts incurred for plane fares and continue with furniture and car payments, as well as the weekly expenses of rent, food, and the ever-rising heating bills during the winter months. Portuguese families do not like to be in debt and prefer to pay cash for items. It takes a number of years for a family to be able to buy a house, even in working-class areas, where triple-decker frame housing is still relatively inexpensive.

Under these circumstances, considerable tension has developed in some families. Not only are families often physically separated by thirty to fifty miles but they also have experienced considerable conflict. For example, Mr. F. said of his family (most of whom are in New England):

> You know this was a poor family, and once this family came to America, money got to their heads.... There were several brothers and sisters and we never had any trouble...nothing. All married, on good terms with all. But ever since they came over to America, it's been hell.... Nowadays, I don't want to owe any favors to anyone, not because I am rich. It's because I already know what it is to live owing favors to others. I already lived here in America with my brothers as a favor; it was the worst time I ever lived.

Mrs. F. who remained in São Miguel for four years while her oldest son was serving in the armed forces, and who had just arrived in the United States a few months prior to our interviews, commented on her husband's difficulties during his first four years here: "My sister is the one that paid more attention to my husband when he was alone; the others—they are each in their own homes, and we also do the same... My husband was sick for three months and they never came to see if he needed a bit of tea."

The H.'s have had difficulties with the wife's relatives rather than with the husband's. Mr. H. commented:

> None of my brothers-in-law helped me, not even to look for work. I was the one who looked for a job...through a friend who had told me that his shop was looking for people. I went and asked; I didn't get it then, so about a week later I asked again, saying I had been without a job for six weeks and had five children, that I wanted to work, so they gave me a job the same week.

Mrs. H. described the way in which her large family of six siblings and her mother have grown apart since they have migrated to New England:

> In principle, we were very much together; one wouldn't go out without the other. The other wouldn't go to one side if the other wouldn't go. Now, it's not that way; things are all spoiled. Each one goes out when he wants and each one goes where he wants to go. Perhaps because there is jealousy among them.... [And friends? Are there differences between friends and family?] Well, I am going to speak frankly, I have at times more confidence in friends than in my own family. I do because in my life, I'm always trying to do the best for my family and my family now hasn't returned this kindness.

Other families seem to have had a different experience and have remained "united," visiting and exchanging goods and services often. For example, the E.'s, a young couple, visit her brother and family who live in Canada each summer. [...] Mr. E.'s parents and two brothers and a sister live about fifteen miles from the E.'s, and they visit regularly on weekends. [...] They also borrow a car occasionally from one of Mr. E.'s brothers, and another helps with auto repair work. [...]

In between these patterns are the I.'s. Mr. I's family (two married sisters and a married brother) live near the study town, but his wife's family has remained in São Jorge, one of the Azorean islands. When the I.'s first arrived, they stayed first with the brother and then one of the sisters. Mr. I. describes the changes that have taken place in visiting:

> We used to visit one another, but lately no, you know, they also have their lives taking care of things and we can't be always looking for them. Well, on special occasions, then we visit; we exchange gifts.... They used to come over to the house, and we used to go over there, but for quite some time they stopped doing it. They stopped looking for us and we have been doing the same. We don't know what is the reason. Sometimes it's outsiders, because of a word used in a conversation, they make a big thing out of it. People stop seeing each other and it's a shame seeing families not being as close as they should be.

Mr. I. expressed regret that his family is no longer united: "It's a very different life over there; we always used to visit, even dining during the week and on special days, and even on Sunday we used to all together." On the other hand, he felt that family members would turn to each other for assistance: "We, that is, we have sought each other; we always talk to each other and we keep in touch, but only a few times because we live far apart. […] When we have some special need, some great need of anything, they always help us."

In many cases distance and the pattern of family members working different shifts put restrictions on visiting. […] Many of the families are [also] at the stage in their developmental cycle where the parents are beginning to orient themselves to their teenage children, where five to seven children have become the relevant group for leisure-time interaction, and where visiting with other families takes more planning and preparation for an "occasion" than it would take for a young couple with only one or two children. Mrs. F. has five children and explains visiting her sisters who live thirty miles away:

> We visit my sisters in the morning [on Sunday]. We are seven people and they are seven people [the sister, her husband, and three children, as well as a second sister and her daughter]. We can't show up without them expecting us. Here in America we never run out of food, but when we go there or she comes, I take food and she brings food.

Although she is on good terms with these sisters, she expresses a philosophy of "everyone in their own home," a phrase used by many couples, which is indicative of both a strong ideology of family self-sufficiency in combination with the continuing separation and distance between families. This is ultimately traceable to the economy, which has scattered families over a fifty-mile range and has allowed family members to work different shifts and overtime hours on Saturday shifts, squeezing visits into a few hours on Sunday. As Mrs. F. said:

> Every one in his own home. The visits are when we can, and if we can't, we talk by phone and see if anyone needs anything; that is, here there is not time to visit a lot of people…sometimes around feasts…. You know

> I have only been here for a short while. They [the sisters] are also handy [*jeitosas*] meaning that they take care of their lives, and I also take care of mine.... Sunday is all too short; there isn't much time.... If we are going out, instead of going to someone's house, we go instead for a ride.

When asked about visiting other more distant relatives, she commented that it would be a miracle to make so many visits. That could only be done "when we get old and are out of work."

Conclusions

Among these Azorean immigrant families, as among many working-class families, primary relatives (i.e., parents, siblings, and their spouses) are important sources of aid and support, especially in the first phases of life in the United States. On the one hand, the history of Portuguese immigration to the United States and the requirements of the 1965 Immigration Act have made it possible for Portuguese families to reconstitute part of their kin networks through a process of chain migration.

On the other hand, the structure of the local economy encourages shift work for couples, and, because of layoffs and plant closings, pushes couples to relocate in nearby towns where jobs are available. These factors make it difficult to maintain a kin network of married siblings and parents. Distance and different schedules make visiting and exchange of goods and services more problematic and occasional. Their financial situation and their commitment to self-sufficiency (which includes owning a car, buying a house, and having all the bills paid) means that families are under pressure to maintain an orientation to their own nuclear families and remain "each in his own house." Among the eleven families we interviewed there is considerable variation in the amount of family unity that has been maintained, and it is important to recognize the variety of adaptations, rather than to try and find a generalization for "the Portuguese family" in general.

In conclusion, it seems more profitable to view conjugal role relationships and kin networks as directly impacted by economic variables rather than as primarily related to each other and only indirectly affected by an economic environment. In this chapter, I have shown how a wife's employment has changed the division of labor within the family, but many traditional Azorean patterns are being maintained or at least are not being altered dramatically in the first generation. Furthermore, kin networks are vital in helping couples solve instrumental problems in the process of immigration, but they too begin to change in the United States context. It is the basic structure of the declining industrial Northeast, rather than the immigrants' assimilation to "American values" or changes in their own attitudes and feelings, that pushes families apart. These findings support the general picture of working-class families that views their organization as a response to economic conditions and argues for a complex interrelationship between a local economy and strategic behavior in response to that economy. This clearer delineation of the relationship between family and economy should lead anthropologists away from focusing on how families adapt to an exploration of the kinds of public policies that might change the economic situation of families. Portuguese immigrant families deal daily with low-paying jobs, difficult work conditions, occupationally related health problems, and the pressures of the dual-worker situation. Their own lives might be easier and their goals more reachable if the nature of these industrial jobs were different (pay and conditions better) and if there were more support services available to them (better child care, transportation, and health care). Concrete research oriented to changing public policy around these issues seems to be the next area of fruitful investigation for anthropologists interested in family and kinship in its diverse forms in the United States.

Acknowledgments

Louise Lamphere would particularly like to thank Rebecca Matthews and Carlos Pato for their help in interviewing two of the Azorean families and four continental families. Their participation was particularly important in the initial stages of the project.

Notes

[1] This chapter is a shortened version of the original article which appeared in the collection, *The Versatility of Kinship*, Linda Cordell and Stephen Beckman (eds), Academic Press, 1980: 219-249. Brackets with ellipsis indicate cuts made by the volume editors.

[2] Figures from *Comissão de planeamento da região dos Açores, Relatório de Propostas Ponta Delgada*, São Miguel, Açores, March, 1972, vol. 2, 25-30

[3] *Comissão de planeanento da região dos Açores, Emigração. Subsídios para uma Monografia sobre os Açores* (n.d., 6-7). (Pamphlet available from the Commission of Regional Planning, Azores).

[4] Family incomes in 1977 ranged from $10,900 to $20,000 per year. It is important to note that those families with $18,000-$20,000 incomes are those with three or four full-time workers (either working children or a sister). In 1977, the medium income in the United States was $16,009. A number of these dual-worker families fell in the range of the lowest forty percent of family incomes (below $13,273).

CHAPTER 15

Unionization in an Electronics Factory: The Interplay of Gender, Ethnicity, and Class[1]

ANN BOOKMAN

This article is based on a two-year field study of union organizing at Digitex (a pseudonym), an electronics factory in the Boston, Massachusetts area. Of the four hundred union-eligible production workers, slightly over half were women and one-third were first-generation Portuguese immigrants. Thus, a majority of the work force was composed of groups that mainstream social scientists and some labor leaders have argued are resistant to unionization. However, the story of union organizing at Digitex reveals that a majority of women and immigrant workers did join the union, and that the factors that have been held responsible for the resistance of these groups to unionization—namely gender-related roles and strong ethnic identification—were the very factors that aided the unionization of Digitex.

This case poses many interesting questions about how women and immigrant workers become politically active in a workplace context. For example, what are the most important factors determining whether workers join a union? What is the interplay between such factors as gender, ethnicity, and class in shaping workers' response to unionization? This study allows a close examination of the changes that unionization produces in the social relationships and ideology found in an industrial workplace. It further shows how the process of social change that unionization sets in motion varies for different groups of workers.

There are several schools of thought, or bodies of literature, that address these questions. First of all, a number of studies conducted in the 1950s and early 1960s by mainstream social scientists are replete with the stereotypes of that era, and basically argue that women and immigrants are unorganizable. For example, Karsh *et al.* argue that "women are the group most resistant to labor organization." This is based on their view "that women are 'secondary wage earners' who enter the labor market for extra money and can leave it at any time, that they tend to be more dependent on and loyal to the company than men, and that internecine warfare constantly rages among them" (Karsch et al. 1959, 98). The essence of this and similar studies is that women do not take their jobs as seriously as they do their families and their interpersonal relationships, and therefore are unlikely to join unions. In a study of Italian immigrant workers and unions, Edwin Fenton states, "[t]hey were village-minded, fatalistic, and self-reliant, three qualities which made them poor union members" (1957, 30). Fenton concludes that as long as Italian immigrants maintained their ethnic identity, they would not choose to participate in or be effective members of trade unions. There appears to be a similar model underlying these studies of women workers' and immigrant workers' trade union activity. The family, in the case of women, and the community of origin, in the case of immigrants, are assumed to play a negative role vis-à-vis the receptivity of these groups to unionization.[2]

Second, studies influenced by classical Marxist tradition see all workers as organizable, with no distinctions among them in their responses to unionization, depending on their ability to develop class consciousness.[3] In this tradition, "class" is defined as a relationship embodied in groups of people and determined by their role in the production of goods or services. The development of "class consciousness," so the argument continues, occurs when people experience and articulate their relationship to production as something they hold in common with others like themselves, as distinct from or opposed to others with a different relationship to production.

Though the development of "class consciousness" is certainly a part of the process of social change that occurred at Digitex during the union drive, this study shows that there are other factors or central experiences that shape class consciousness beyond what happens at the point of production. In particular, I explore the intersection of gender and ethnicity as they affect the ability of women and immigrant workers to organize in their own class interests. Drawing on the work of historians like Alan Dawley, this study shows how "the labor movement in the city was a community affair" (Dawley 1976, 228). This was true both because jobs at Digitex were vital to the economic survival of the ethnic communities surrounding the factory and because family members of both sexes worked in the plant.

Third, there is a body of recent women's history and labor history that explores union organizing in a more complex and balanced manner than either of the aforementioned traditions. This scholarship, however, also has weaknesses. For example, some of the "new" labor history does not use gender as an important analytic category and has continued to obscure the multifaceted relationship of women to unionism. In the new women's history, some scholars have tended toward cataloguing and description, while others have painted a false and romanticized picture of women as supermilitants.[4] Ruth Milkman addresses these problems in her introduction to the anthology *Women, Work and Protest,* which makes a major break with both of these limiting tendencies:

> The old myths of women's lack of interest or involvement with labor struggle were effectively supplanted with new myths which were equally one-sided, and indeed the mirror-image of the old in the new feminist orthodoxy, each discovery of female militancy was taken as evidence of a virtually limitless potential lot for women's labor activism in the labor movement. (Milkman 1985, xii)

Milkman and a number of other feminist historians have called for an examination of the "conditions which have encouraged women's labor militancy, and those which have impeded it," as well as the need to analyze the "organizational forms and techniques ... rooted in women's own distinctive culture and life experience" (Milkman 1985, xiii). The study of union organizing at Digitex affords such an opportunity.

The macroeconomic and political conditions that contextualized the union drive were significant in both the inception and in the ultimate fate of unionism at Digitex. The dramatic growth of a largely nonunion electronics industry in and around the Boston area[5] provided a healthy economic climate and made wage and benefit improvements for Digitex workers seem possible. The upsurge of various progressive mass movements throughout the 1960s and early 1970s brought the United Electrical, Radio, and Machine Workers of America (UE) and a group of feminist trade unionists[6] together at the gates of Digitex in the fall of 1973. Their joint efforts began a process of unionization. However, it was the lives of Digitex women workers—inside and outside of the shop—that shaped the direction and outcome of the union organizing campaign. Women's roles in their families, their communities, and their workplace each had a particular and important bearing on their relationship to unionism. Women's ability to resist and change conditions they found undesirable and oppressive at work often involved transformations in their relationships to kith, kin, and community, as well as to their jobs.

Methodology

Before presenting the data from my fieldwork, I would like to make a few methodological points that differentiate this study from most studies of unionization. During the fieldwork period, I worked as a "light assembler" in the Coil Department of the Digitex Electronics Company and was a founding and active member of a union organizing committee affiliated with the UE. The standard method for conducting anthropological research is "participant observation," in which observation is the primary aspect and participation is secondary, being confined to those events and routines the anthropologist chooses to investigate. The method I utilized could better be termed "observation through participant activism," in which the primary aspect of my work was being an agent of social change within the factory as a union organizer, and the secondary aspect was being an anthropological observer with the same hours, pay, working conditions, and relationship to management as the other workers in the shop. For many people, the pursuits of social science and social reform are incompatible. Some social scientists argue that as a union activist one cannot possibly produce an objective or scientifically sound study of blue-collar women. Some union organizers argue similarly that social science research is simply a lot of complicated phrases and theories that have nothing to do with the day-to-day reality of workers' lives and problems, and serve only to obscure the need for action. My own view is that these pursuits are not only compatible but mutually necessary. I think that if social science is to have any social value, it must proceed from an engaged perspective on and position in social life. And if social reformers are to create real change, they must proceed on the basis of a systematic study of the social conditions they are seeking to transform.

My dual roles as activist and researcher are the basis for both the strengths and limitations of this study. The limitations stem from my assignment to a sex-segregated production area, which limited my access to male workers; my position as a worker, which limited my contact with management; and my role as a union organizer, which estranged me over time from some anti-union workers. However, for each door that was closed, a particular view of factory life was opened, vividly revealing the impact of unionization on the structure and content of social relationships at Digitex.

Industrial Ethnography: The Digitex Factory and the Work Force

The process of unionization, and the extent of social and political change that occurred during the union drive can best be understood with some background on the conditions that existed before the drive began. There are two sets of questions on which I would like to focus in this brief industrial ethnography. First, what were the sources of management's control before the union drive, and what, if any, were the sources of workers' control and potential resistance? Second, what were the sources of division and conflict among the workers, and what were the sources of cohesion?

The Digitex Electronics Company was originally a family-owned-and-controlled firm that manufactured products in the electronic components sector of the electrical industry (Digitex has since been taken over by a large multinational corporation). The company employed between 450 and 500 people of whom about 400 were union-eligible production workers. Of the production workers, about fifty-five percent were women and thirty-three percent were first-generation Portuguese immigrants. These two groups overlapped substantially; seventy-five percent of all Portuguese workers were women and forty percent of all women workers were Portuguese. The factory had a highly multinational character as there were also a fair number of African-American and Hispanic workers, Italian and Polish workers, and a small number of Greek, Haitian, and Asian workers.

The ethnic and national differences among workers were accentuated by the fact that many did not speak the same language. Degrading racial and ethnic stereotypes abounded in this atmosphere and centered on the Portuguese workers, most of whom had immigrated very recently and lived in two towns adjacent to the factory. They tended to be neighbors, to have friendship and kin ties which operated inside and outside of work, and to see each other in stores, social clubs, and churches on the weekends. For all their cohesiveness as a group, there were also divisions among Portuguese workers. Those from urban areas did not socialize with those from rural areas. The mainland Portuguese and the Azorean Portuguese were two distinct groups, and the Azoreans were further divided by their island of origin.

There were also divisions among women workers. Among non-Portuguese women, the divisions were generational, centering on dress and family values, and especially on family size and the appropriateness of divorce. Among the Portuguese women, there were tensions because some women were more traditional, wearing long hair, long skirts, and black clothes when in mourning, while the others were more "Americanized" in their dress, hair styles, and mourning customs.

The most obvious source of management's control came from the particular conditions of work and pay that were set up in the shop. The factory conformed in every respect to the commonly-held stereotype of a sweatshop. The production departments were housed in a long, one-story structure built during World War II when the company was founded. This building was dark, dirty, and very poorly ventilated; hot in summer and cold and drafty in winter. The majority of the workers were paid close to the minimum wage, which in 1973 meant a starting wage of $1.95 to $2.10 an hour. Management's control was also derived from the way in which production was organized. The most significant aspect of this organization was the social division of labor, as seen in the sexual and ethnic segregation of the work force. The workers in most production departments were either all men or all women, and the women's departments were predominantly Portuguese.

The women's departments were characterized by intricate assembly operations requiring "manual dexterity" and "good eyesight." Most women worked with fairly simple machinery or none at all, doing routinized tasks that repeated themselves tens or hundreds of times an hour. The women were paid for the most part on the piecework system. The company could easily enforce speed-up by raising the base rates, and the constant struggle to "make the rate" produced an atmosphere of competitiveness among the pieceworkers. The men, on the other hand, worked with more complex machinery, such as drill presses, punch presses, lathes, and screw machines, and were paid on an hourly basis at an average of two-and-a-half times what the women were making. These so-called skill and wage divisions were reinforced by the fact that the majority of supervisors in the women's production areas were non-Portuguese men.

Other aspects of production further extended management's control over the work force. The workers' degree of mobility during production hours varied tremendously. Male hourly workers often left their machines to get parts outside their department areas, whereas pieceworkers, who were mainly women, stood little chance of exceeding the base rate if they left their benches for even a few minutes. The extent of discipline and supervision in each production area also varied. The time-study man and the foreman of each piecework department were constantly watching and timing the pieceworkers, but the men in the machine shop and screw machine department worked on their own at their own pace. The degree of technical division of labor—that is, how isolated or interdependent workers were in the production of the electronics parts they made—also varied. In sum, the day-to-day life of male and female workers was strikingly different. Women were less mobile, more directly supervised, and more interdependent in the production process than their male counterparts.

The ideology of paternalism created further divisions among workers already divided by the structure and organization of production. The company insisted that Digitex was just like "one, big, happy family" in which every member was treated with care. But it was a classical patriarchal family in which the company owner "knew best" and treated all the workers like children who had no rights or bases on which to make decisions. Everything was done on a case-by-case basis, and there were no written policies that governed wage rates, benefits, hiring, or firing. This created a climate in which paternalism flourished, as each individual worker had to cultivate a good relationship with his or her supervisor to get a raise, a promotion, or even to keep the job.

While there were many aspects of factory life that created divisions among the workers and ensured management's control, there were other factors that created cohesion among workers, or at least, in the words of economist Richard Edwards, were "contested terrains," and therefore threatened management's control (Edwards 1979). One of the clearest examples of a contested terrain was non-production time during working hours. On the one hand, the sexual and ethnic segregation found in production areas was often reproduced in the composition of social groups during coffee breaks and lunch periods. The tables in the cafeteria, one of the few places where workers could intermingle, were more often than not composed of workers from the same production department. And ethnic divisions were fairly rigidly maintained in break groups within the production departments.

Yet the social life of the production departments also contained some examples of cross-cultural exchange and unity. For example, within the Coil Department there were "life crisis" parties held when someone was getting married or having a baby, complete with Portuguese sweet bread, Polish kielbasa, Italian meatballs, black-eyed peas, and other ethnic specialties. There were also "life crisis" collections taken up when someone was seriously ill or had died. Ethnic divisions were also bridged through the constant showing and sharing of photographs. Young Portuguese women showed pictures of their boyfriends fighting in Angola or of their grandparents and friends still living in Portugal. Non-Portuguese workers brought in wedding albums or pictures of family vacations. It was workers' relationships with their families, as well as with friends, church, and community organizations that provided the basis for contact and limited cohesion, especially among women of different ethnic and national backgrounds.

Another important contested terrain lay within the production process itself. In production areas where there was a high technical division of labor and workers were very interdependent in the production process, there was a strong feeling of solidarity amid cooperation among the workers involved. This was most evident on "the Belt," a primitive assembly-line in the largest women's production department, and could also be seen in the Coil Department, where women workers sat closely packed together at long benches doing the same routinized piece of the production process hour after hour, day after day. Laughing and pointing at the time-study man while he did his time-and-motion studies was often more powerful than the fact that the workers could not speak the same language. Furthermore, the ethnic and sexual segregation of the production areas had a dual effect, for though it kept men and women workers divided, it ultimately aided the organization of women workers as a group into the ranks of the union. The pattern of organization-building that emerged during the drive was one in which women often organized first as women within their departments and then joined the factory-wide cross-sex, multiethnic organizing committee. In a sense, each of the women's production departments had its own departmental organizing committee.

The Union Organizing Drive at Digitex

The unionization of Digitex may be viewed as a drama unfolding on three interrelated levels: the factory as a whole, the shop floor in particular production departments, and the experiences of individual workers. For the purposes of this article, I shall discuss all three levels simultaneously, focusing on the Coil Department and the experiences of women workers, both Portuguese and non-Portuguese.

The union drive that began at Digitex in 1973 was not the first unionization effort the shop had seen. There had been five other union drives that failed through the company's two-pronged strategy for dealing with pro-union workers—fire them or promote them to management. The company's success in containing and repressing unionization had resulted in a strong climate of fear and anti-unionism in the shop. As one woman worker put it:

> My first day at Digitex, I was told, 'Do not mention union. Never mention union. If you do, you'll be fired.' Matter of fact, I know of an instance—a girl came to get a job, she had union affiliations prior to coming to Digitex, and they wouldn't hire her.

It is also significant that trade unions were illegal in Portugal at the time that the union drive began, and many Portuguese workers and other immigrant workers in the shop were uninformed that their right to unionize was protected by American labor law.

The UE did not initiate this drive on its own. The union was approached by a woman who had taken a job in the shop with the specific intention of investigating whether or not it could be organized. Deciding it could be, she recruited a number of other people, including myself, to get jobs at Digitex. These "workers/organizers" were white, mostly middle-class, and all veterans of the anti-war, student, and women's movements of the late 1960s and early 1970s. On the part of the UE, the decision to organize Digitex was part of a comeback the union was experiencing locally and nationally as a result of the progressive mass movements of that period.

The union drive can be roughly divided into three periods, which correspond to important shifts in the balance of forces inside the shop, and the primary task of the organizers. Period One was in essence a period of "laying the foundation"; Period Two was a stage of "base building"; and Period Three was characterized by "consolidation and conflict."

During Period One both the union and the company operated in secret. The workers/organizers were responsible for identifying pro-union workers in the shop and then passing their names on to the union staff, who approached them individually outside of work by paying them "home visits."[7] For example, in the Coil Department, several women were identified as pro-union and visited at home. Three of these women were, in fact, very sympathetic. One of them was Maureen Agnati, an Italian-American pieceworker who had worked at Digitex on and off since dropping out of high school in her junior year. Although she admitted during her home visit that she hated the company and the piecework system, she was cautious about making a commitment to be active in the union. She was a mother with two small children and a difficult, and, at times, abusive husband. She said it was hard for her to get out of the house to see her girl friends, much less to attend a union meeting. Although neither Maureen nor the other women visited at home signed union cards, they did begin "talking union" in their respective sections of the Coil Department.

It was also during this period that Rose O'Brien, an Irish-American hourly worker in the "Special Coils" section of the department ("special" because all the workers were paid on an hourly, not piecework basis and performed a number of steps in the production process themselves), began talking against the union. She had worked at Digitex since 1959, was very friendly with many people in management, and was often the center of attention at the company Christmas party and in the company bowling league. She had no use for unions as a result of her negative experience in a union shop before coming to Digitex, and she used her influence to discredit the union among many long-service workers when the drive was just a rumor on the company grapevine. The views and activities of Maureen and Rose were consistent with those of short-service women pieceworkers and long-service women hourly workers throughout the plant. By the end of the first period, the majority of workers were still unaware of the drive, but there was a core of approximately twenty-five workers who had signed cards and begun to meet with the UE.

While the union drive was going on *sub rosa*, the company pretended to conduct "business as usual." However, they were busy trying to gather information on the union's activities. After the first open union meeting—at which the company must have had a spy—two young men who attended were fired. The union immediately filed charges against the company with the National Labor Relations Board (NLRB), knowing that it must be demonstrated that workers would have job protection if they joined the union.

The major turning point during the drive occurred in Period Two with a favorable NLRB ruling on the firings case. Both men were rehired and given back pay. The union took a picture of the two workers holding their back-pay checks. Union supporters posted copies of it all around the shop and took great pride in watching the faces of various supervisors as the photos turned up on every departmental bulletin board. Even anti-union workers were impressed that the company had had to back down on a firing. The union used the NLRB decision to stop the company's tactics of repression, and this, in turn, created the conditions for a change in the balance of forces inside the shop.

After the drive became public, the company was still on the offensive, sending workers a letter about the generosity of the "Digitex family" and the callousness of the UE, whose only interest was in collecting dues money. While the union staff prepared and distributed leaflets, making contact with workers at the plant gates, the workers/organizers began to do open union organizing inside the shop and make home visits. Most importantly, they began the production and distribution of a rank-and-file newsletter. The first appearance of *Union News,* passed out by Digitex workers during coffee and lunch breaks, was a very dramatic moment in the drive. There was great curiosity about who had written the newsletter and open enthusiasm about its contents.

The inception of *Union News* spurred a number of pro-union workers to attend organizing committee meetings outside work. Through these meetings they met with workers from other departments and began to learn what they had in common with workers who had different kinds of jobs or were of a different sex or ethnic group. Male workers began to see that their assumptions about "broads" and "Portagees" were not true, and that there were ways in which women pieceworkers from "the Belt" and men hourly workers from the stock room had more in common than either had with the company.

As women learned how male workers were paid and treated, they began to see two things: first, that their mistreatment was related to their gender; and, second, that they did have problems in common with men workers—particularly the company's paternalism, which deprived all workers of a plant-wide wage scale and seniority system and prohibited any formal procedure for dealing with grievances.

It was also during this time that there was a coup in Portugal. The repressive Caetano regime was toppled by the Armed Forces Movement, which named General António de Spínola as head of state and called for an end to Portuguese colonialism in Africa. The reaction of almost all the Portuguese workers in the shop was positive. Hatred of Caetano seemed universal, and events in Portugal had an observable and positive effect in countering the fears of Portuguese workers who wanted to support the union. The number of workers who became union members increased dramatically in this period. The union was able to sign up in a little over a month as many workers as had taken seven months to sign up previously.

Developments in the shop as a whole were again mirrored in the Coil Department, where twenty-four workers had signed cards by the end of Period Two (twenty of these were pieceworkers and half were Portuguese). These changes were evident in the composition of the break-time groups in the department as groups began to form on the basis of people's position on the union and not according to ethnic- or production-related divisions. It was also during this period that several women pieceworkers emerged as departmental union leaders and organizers. Maureen and a black pieceworker, named Belle Caldwell, were the first workers from coils to attend an organizing committee meeting. It was there that they met Lúcia Perreira, a Portuguese pieceworker from "the Belt." Lúcia was one of the first Portuguese people to have found employment at Digitex. As she was bilingual, she often translated for other Portuguese workers when they were called to the Personnel Office, and, in the Portuguese community, she often accompanied people to the Social Security office and various public agencies. When Lúcia spoke up at a union meeting about the situation in her own department, Maureen and Bella were moved by her indictment of the piecework system. They agreed with her about how unfair the rates were and were angered to learn that Lúcia had never received a promotion in her eight years of service with the company. They were also impressed with how rapidly she had been able to sign up women in her department and asked her for help in talking to workers in Coils. This was the beginning of the kind of cross-departmental, cross-ethnic cooperation that was crucial to building the union. These ties laid the basis for a form of social organization (the union) that was significantly different from the social organization that had characterized the factory before the drive.

There were several other factors that positively affected the participation of Portuguese women in the Coil Department. The first was a union meeting held at a social club in the Portuguese community, and the second was the coup in Portugal. Immediately after the coup, a young Portuguese woman, Isabel Sousa, became very active in the Coil Department. She confided that her uncle, with whose family she had just immigrated to the United States, had been exiled for illegal trade union activity. "Now that we have Spínola, I can tell you this," she said. "Now that we have Spínola, I can help you." She and Maureen both worked on *Union News*. Maureen, with help from the worker/organizers, wrote an article about the Coils Department that Lúcia translated. And Isabel and Maureen distributed each issue in the department. Other workers in Coils were impressed by the bilingual newsletter and commented on articles which showed the similarity between their own complaints about the company and those of workers in other departments whom they did not even know.

It was also during Period Two that Rose attended her first union meeting "out of curiosity," she said, never one to be far from the action. Immediately following the meeting she was given a promotion to the prestigious Inspection Department. This was not only a step up in the company but also removed her from the increasing flurry of pro-union activity in Coils. She was the first to say that the company was just trying to "buy her vote" and that she had deserved the promotion long before the UE had ever come along. By the end of Period Two she was truly "on the fence."

During the third and final period, the atmosphere inside the shop became highly politicized as all—be they production workers, office workers or managers—had to decide which side they were on. Was the company president "Boss Snidley" or "Mr. Snidley"? Were those who worked in the company "workers" or "employees"? These were not just questions of semantics but questions about the basic power relationships in the factory, and the terms you used told people which analysis you believed—the company's or the union's.

While the company had conducted its early antiunion campaign through selective repression, or polite letters from top levels of management, its tactics changed as the union gained in strength. First, company tacticians tried red-baiting after a particularly well-attended organizing committee meeting in April. When that did not work, they took their message to the shop floor. They enlisted technicians, office workers, foremen, and, most important, Digitex workers. They encouraged homemade anti-union leaflets, buttons, and signs, and condoned verbal intimidation of pro-union workers during production hours. They even hired a fancy downtown Boston firm that specialized in union-busting campaigns. The firm sent letters to workers' homes and set up display cases inside the shop with various goods, like canned food and children's clothes, worth $6.85—the amount of the union dues that would be taken out of workers' checks should the union win.

In the final weeks before the election, the UE staff concentrated on card-signing, while the workers/organizers focused on political education, trying to deepen workers' understanding of the meaning of unionism and the nature of class relations in the factory. They tried to prepare people for the fact that the election was just one step in a long process and that further struggle would be required to win a first contract. The final issue of "Union News," containing appeals to vote for the UE in seven different languages, impressively demonstrated that the union represented a broad cross section of workers who had resisted the company's efforts to divide them. As one article said in Italian, "Siamo venuti in America trovare una modo di migliore. Miglioramici la vita!" ("We came to America to make a better life for ourselves. Let's make a better life for ourselves!")

In the Coil Department, though only one more worker signed a union card during Period Three, many workers deepened their commitment to the union. This was demonstrated by a further realignment of the break groups reflecting workers' position on the union and by varying kinds of activism, especially inside the shop. For example, Isabel took on Beatrice Arruda, who was the lead woman in Coils and one of the most vocal anti-union Portuguese workers. Both Portuguese and non-Portuguese pieceworkers watched their verbal jousting matches with delight, especially when Beatrice threw up her hands and retreated to the foreman's desk. Maureen wrote more articles for "Union News," without any assistance, and her growing self-confidence was reflected in her announcement during one lunch break that she had enrolled in a General Education Diploma (GED) course and was preparing to take exams for her high-school equivalency diploma.

Both Maureen and Isabel faced tremendous odds against becoming and continuing as union activists. Isabel's boyfriend (who also worked at Digitex) refused to allow her to be seen without him in public, and would not accompany her to union meetings, despite the fact that he supported the union and had signed a card. Maureen's husband refused to take care of their children for even a few hours on the weekend so that she could attend organizing committee meetings. He was verbally abusive about her participation in the drive and often threatened her with physical abuse if she continued to be involved. But both women were able to define and develop a role inside the shop during working hours that more than compensated for the meetings they could not attend. Their commitment to the union was being constantly challenged, not only by their foreman and the time-study man, but by the men with whom they were personally involved. Their ability to remain involved went through constant ups and downs, but the value that their coworkers placed on their leadership served to build their self-esteem and renew their commitment to the union cause.

It was also during Period Three that Lúcia started actually coming into the Coil area during coffee and lunch breaks to talk to other pieceworkers. Such interdepartmental socializing was unheard of before the drive. Her purpose was not so much to sign up more workers as to allay the fears of those who had already signed cards and encourage their activism. Lúcia's efforts in her community reinforced her in-shop organizing. She obtained letters from two Portuguese community organizations and the priest of the largest Catholic Church in the Portuguese community in support of the union. This visibly bolstered the morale of Portuguese union supporters and infuriated Beatrice and other Portuguese anti-union workers.

The greatest change during Period Three occurred among long-service, non-Portuguese hourly workers like Rose. At this time she had a confrontation with the company vice-president, who had acted against her advice on some inspection-related matters. Rose had already been turned off by the company's packaged anti-union campaign, and this blatant disregard for her job-related experience and opinions crystallized her estrangement from management. She signed a union card about a month before the NLRB election and became a vocal and influential member of the organizing committee in its final days.

Though the core of workers who attended meetings remained small, many women fought against management's anti-union campaign on the shop floor. Whether it meant wearing a UE button on their blouse, taking ten minutes in the ladies' room (a *long* time for a pieceworker) to talk to someone who was frightened, or talking back to the foreman, all of the activities reflected a level of class-conscious behavior that would have seemed impossible in the shop only a year earlier.

When the ballots were counted on election day, the vote was 204 for the UE and 165 for the company. The majority of workers wanted union representation, and they had constructed a new type of social organization in the factory. Many factors that had formerly been the basis for division among the workers were now the basis for diversity in an all-worker organization. On the night of the election, I asked Isabel if she could come to the union victory party, a special one-time occasion. She answered, "My boyfriend is working second shift now. If you'll pick me up and bring me home by eleven, he will never know." When I arrived to pick her up, she led me into her room, and with a big grin, pointed above her bed to a large poster of General Spínola, on whom she'd pinned a UE button!

Findings and Analysis

By summarizing data collected after the union drive was over, the process of social change that occurred at Digitex can be further illuminated. Using both quantitative and qualitative data, two of the questions posed at the outset can be answered: 1) What were the significant factors determining whether or not workers became union members?; and 2) What was the process of social change that occurred during the course of unionization, and, particularly, what accounted for changes in the political activism and consciousness of women and immigrant workers?

In order to answer the first question, being a union member will be viewed as synonymous with signing a union card. Although signing a union card is an act associated with different levels of commitment to the union and different levels of participation in its activities, it does represent a conscious decision to join an organization of workers dedicated to confronting the company collectively on a range of job-related matters. Card signing is also an index for which there are data on all the workers in the factory.

It was found that women at Digitex, rather than resisting unionization, joined the union in equal proportion to men (65.00 percent of all women, 64.6 percent of all men). It was also found that first-generation Portuguese immigrants, rather than resisting unionization, joined the union in even greater proportions than indigenous workers (73.5 percent of Portuguese, 61.4 percent of non-Portuguese). Having established that these social characteristics of workers were not an impediment to unionization, it is possible to explore whether these factors or other job-related factors were more positively correlated with workers' union membership. Using data on the whole factory (N = 379), the factors that were most significant in determining union membership were related to workers' relationship to production. Union membership was correlated with data on method/amount of pay (piecework or hourly work/average rate of pay), and seniority, which determines the extent of benefits. Union membership was also correlated with data on the social relationships surrounding production (degree of technical division of labor, degree of mobility, degree of supervision). The data show in this case that workers with low pay and low seniority who were paid on a piecework basis were most likely to join the union, while workers with high pay and high seniority who were paid on an hourly basis were least likely to join the union. The data further show that workers whose jobs involved a high degree of technical division of labor (and were therefore highly interdependent on other workers in the actual manufacture of products) were more likely to join the union than workers who completed a number of phases of the production process by themselves, had high mobility during working hours, and experienced little supervision over their work.[8] The need for other studies to corroborate or further test these findings as a general proposition in a variety of industrial workplaces is suggested by the Digitex case.

Although the primacy of production-related factors was established in determining the receptivity to unionization of workers as an aggregate group, this was most true (that is, statistically significant) for non-Portuguese women, also true for non-Portuguese and Portuguese men, but not true for Portuguese women. In the case of Portuguese women, their ethnicity[9] was more important in determining whether or not they joined the union than their role in production. Although it has been established that a high proportion of Portuguese women were low-paid pieceworkers with low seniority, their social ties to people in their community seem to have been an even more positive force in creating the conditions for their joining the union than their role in production.

These findings raise serious questions about many of the mainstream social science studies summarized earlier. Much of that research assumed that women relate to work through the demands and pressures of their family roles. However, this study suggests that there is a greater disjunction, or at least a different relationship, between women's sexual/domestic roles and their experiences outside the home than has been supposed. The data suggest that for non-Portuguese women at Digitex, their job-related experiences were key in their deciding to join the union, whereas for Portuguese women at Digitex, their relationship to ethnically-defined groups and activities, both inside and outside the workplace, was key to their deciding to join the union.

Although this type of analysis may be useful for understanding which factors were most significant in determining whether women workers joined the union, it is much too simplistic and one-sided to explain the process of decision making and activity that preceded and followed card signing. In assessing the political experience of women workers during the organizing drive, many of the most important and interesting changes that occurred defy quantification. In fact, the only way to understand the process fully is to examine further quantitative data on the experiences of the four rank-and-file women—Lúcia, Isabel, Maureen, and Rose—described above.

In the cases of Lúcia, Isabel, and Maureen, their pro-unionism was immediate. There was little if any discrepancy between their view of worker-management relations and the view put forward by the union. But the reason for this was different in each case. Isabel came from a pro-union family in Portugal, so she had grown up with a heritage of involvement in trade union activity. Lúcia was indignant about the way the company treated Portuguese workers, taking advantage of their lack of familiarity with English and placing them in the lowest-paying, least-skilled jobs no matter what their level of education or previously acquired skills. Maureen's views stemmed mainly from her on-the-job experiences in the shop as a pieceworker who could never make much above minimum wage no matter how hard she worked.

The inclination of these three women to act on their views also differed. Lúcia was immediately ready to act and organize. She was used to fighting the company in the sense that she often complained to the general foreman or the Personnel Office on behalf of her Portuguese coworkers. Maureen, on the other hand, was held back from activity by a combination of factors including hostility, abuse, lack of help from her husband with child care, and very low self-esteem. Isabel, on the other hand, believed that what was illegal in Portugal was also illegal in the United States, and it was not until Spínola came to power that she felt free to organize inside the shop. But having surmounted that obstacle, she found that her domestic duties to her uncle's family, and her boyfriend's possessiveness and male chauvinism limited her pro-union activities to things she could do in the workplace. In Rose's case, the view of the company presented by the union was at odds with her own view. Her initial loyalty was to management, not to the workers. Despite some complaints, she had received certain privileges from and had social ties to management. It was management's refusal to continue to treat her as a "special" worker that changed her views.

The changes these workers experienced as they began to resist management's policies and control were also different and demonstrate that the process of becoming class-conscious is complex and variable even among women who belong to the same class. The major change in Lúcia's case was in her ability to work with others in fighting the company. She began to talk and strategize with workers in other departments and to fight for both Portuguese and non-Portuguese workers. Her role in her community was also transformed. Previously she had been a "go-between" facilitating communication. During the union drive she became an advocate, mobilizing important institutions in her own community against the company in support of the union.

In Rose's case, when she no longer identified with management she could relate to the grievances of unskilled, low-paid pieceworkers. She began to talk to workers with whom she had had no previous contact. Her social ties with management were replaced by social ties with an ethnically-diverse group of workers from a range of departments, including Portuguese workers. She was able to transcend her own negative experience with one union in one shop and see what the UE might accomplish for workers at Digitex.

With Maureen and Isabel, their ability to begin to question the confining, patriarchal relationship with husband or boyfriend was closely linked with their ability to develop a role in the union drive. For Maureen, support from other women in the department about her child-care problems was critical to her involvement, along with her growing sense of her own intelligence and ability through her success in organizing her coworkers and her writing efforts for *Union News*. For Isabel, the political activity of Portuguese people back in her homeland was pivotal, along with the support she received from her Portuguese coworkers when she took on anti-union harassment from the Portuguese lead woman in the Coil Department. Neither of these women could escape housework, child care, or other traditional female duties, but these traditional jobs did not prevent them from being activists during working hours or from beginning to define some limited autonomy outside the home.

There are two interesting points to be underscored here. First, without change and motion in the personal lives of rank-and-file women workers at Digitex, the union drive would not have succeeded or had the vitality it possessed. Second, the strength and contribution of many women union members lay in their in-shop organizing efforts, not in their participation in meeting's held after working hours outside the factory. Though this characteristic of women's political participation crossed ethnic lines, there were differences related to women's stage in the life cycle. This was more true for women like Maureen, with young children, and less true for women like Rose and Lúcia, who had grown children or no children.

One of the common threads in the lives of these four women and in the experience of other Digitex workers like them was the movement from an individual to a collective view of what it meant to be a worker at Digitex. In part, this was a view based on seeing that all workers, regardless of sex, ethnic group, or role in production shared a similar (if not the same) relationship to the company, which implied that their interests and those of management were in conflict. Equally important, it was a view based on seeing that particular subgroups of workers, such as women and Portuguese workers, had an additional set of problems with the company. Class consciousness therefore not only includes an ability to extend ideas about one's own job into an analysis of relations between the company and the workers, but also an ability to understand the relationship between the company and workers of different genders and different nationalities. When class consciousness is related to an appreciation of difference within the working class, it can transform both social relationships among workers and between workers and management. This transformation was apparent in the success of union organizing at Digitex.

To return to the work of those who insist that women in general and immigrant women in particular are resistant to unionization, their error lies in part, I think, in looking at the effects of patriarchy and sexual subordination only in the family context, where women are for the most part isolated from each other. In the workplace context, because of the sex-segregation of production departments, women work collectively with other women from diverse cultural backgrounds, and have opportunities for social contact with other women. Simply to assume that women's sexual subordination in the family will negatively determine their ideas and activity in every sphere is wrong on two accounts. First, this assumption adopts a narrow "gender model" for analyzing the totality of women's experience. Second, it fails to acknowledge that women can mount a successful campaign of resistance both in the family and in the workplace, and that their resistance in one area strengthens their ability to resist in another.

Having demonstrated that a woman's role in her family does not necessarily impede her becoming politically active in her workplace, how, in the case of the women at Digitex, did these two roles combine? The majority of non-Portuguese activists had no children or, had high-school-age or grown children. It is interesting that the two women at Digitex, Lúcia and Rose, who eventually assumed positions as shop-wide leaders, were both women without children who were close to the end of their childbearing years. One might assume this to be a particularity of this case, but a similar finding has been made by Carol Turbin in her study of women's industrial labor militancy in the late 19th century (Turbin 1984). Looking at the data more closely, we find that the age of their children did not seem to limit the activities of the majority of Portuguese women workers in quite the same way as it did the non-Portuguese women. The Portuguese workers with small children had a larger and more reliable network of female kin and friends on whom they could rely for help with their children. However, their husbands and boyfriends were often less willing to let them leave their homes and housework to attend union meetings or other union functions. The variability of child care and housework strategies among women of different ethnic groups, and their composite effect on women's political activism, certainly bear further investigation in our attempt to understand the relationship between work and family in women's lives.

Finally, how can a woman's ethnic group membership and her role in her community be integrated into a model that incorporates both family and workplace? In the case of women Portuguese workers at Digitex, their common language, kin ties, neighborhoods, and other bonds gave them a cohesiveness as a group that most workers lacked. Their common culture provided them with common standards by which to judge the changes they experienced upon becoming industrial workers in the United States. Many Portuguese workers, especially women, had not worked before, either in industry or in any other paid context. The unfavorable comparison between life at Digitex and their life in Portugal or the Azores proved an incentive for joining the union. Their common culture was both a source of resistance to the inhuman aspects of factory life and a source of continuity with more humane social forms. This was true for Lúcia, who was clearly a leader in both the community and the workplace before the union drive began, and also for women who were not leaders in either sphere.

For the majority of Portuguese women, their positive response to the union is clearly related to three community-related factors: some organizing committee meetings were held at clubs in the Portuguese community where these women felt comfortable and where their spouses felt comfortable; both the Catholic Church and Portuguese community organizations gave their sanction to the UE and encouraged voting for the union; and the Portuguese language was used and respected in union literature, including both UE leaflets and *Union News*, and at union meetings held outside the Portuguese community. It is hard to describe the impact that this had on the Portuguese work force. The fact that the company had never made any attempt to have its rules, regulations, benefit plans, or any kind of employee notices translated into Portuguese, and that the union had everything translated presented a dramatic contrast and favorably impressed even the "anti-union" Portuguese workers.

Thus, contrary to the, findings of Fenton and others, ethnicity was a positive and significant factor in determining the receptivity of Portuguese workers, and particularly Portuguese women workers, to unionization. Rather than acting to obscure class relations, the maintenance of strong ethnic groups became the social and cultural vehicle for interpreting common class experiences. This study also suggests that political movements linked to immigrant communities, such as the Armed Forces Movement in Portugal, can have a significant and positive impact on the receptivity of worker's to unionization and the extent and particular nature of their class consciousness.

Conclusion

A holistic approach to working women's empowerment and political activism is not just a question of remembering to look at two or three factors rather than one. It is fundamentally based in the way we conceptualize those factors and their interrelationships. To understand the impact of class, one must look beyond women's relationship to the production process as it occurs in the workplace. Class also affects the nature and scope of woman's subordination in the family and often the possibilities and limitations placed on her participation in her community. Gender likewise must not be narrowly viewed as restricted to woman's role in the family and how her domestic duties and obligations delimit her role outside the home. Sexual subordination in the workplace, including both the sexual segregation of production and the particular culture of production departments in which the work force is predominantly female, are important components for understanding gender oppression and gender identity. Similarly, ethnic and cultural differences must not be narrowly viewed as customs and traditions that comprise people's lives in their communities. National and cultural differences also affect the way people relate to their jobs and their ability to mobilize ethnically specific institutions to aid their activities in the workplace.

I want to conclude with two main points that are specific to the case of Digitex but that I believe have implications for a large number of industrial workplaces. First, unionization *is* a form of empowerment in which women and immigrant workers have and can play an important and leading role. In this study, women and immigrant workers not only joined the union but also built social groups in the workplace based on the sharing of important kin- and community-based experiences. Their ability to mobilize ethnically specific institutions in support of the union and to resist male chauvinism and anti-unionism in their families significantly aided the unionization of Digitex.

Second, there is great variability, in the pattern of empowerment for different groups of workers. For some women, their resistance began on the job; sharing their individual grievances against the company with female coworkers enabled them to participate in a collective fight against the company. This collective political experience, in turn, enabled them to transform their relationships with—and gain some autonomy from— men and their families. For other women, their resistance began in the community and in their identification with a resistance movement in their homeland. This, in turn, enabled them to become active in a workplace-based movement. There is, in sum, no single model that can explain the complex interplay of family, community, and workplace in shaping the political consciousness and activity of women workers. But we can make a commitment to a method of analysis that recognizes women's multiple roles and the importance of cultural and racial difference, as our methods will greatly affect what we learn from the struggle of Digitex workers and in other workplaces across the United States.

Acknowledgments

This study was funded in part by a National Institute of Mental Health Predoctoral Research Grant. I would like to thank my mentors and advisers, Beatrice and John Whiting, for their support of this project in the dissertation phase. I would also like to thank my colleagues in the Harvard Anthropology Department, Andrea Cousins, Sandy Davis, and Steve Fjellman, who listened and thoughtfully responded so many times during the conception and execution of my thesis.

The comments on and criticisms of my completed dissertation were very helpful in paving the way for this article, particularly those of Meredith Tak, Hal Benenson, and other members of the Sarah Eisenstein Series Editorial Board. I would also like to thank Paula Rayman and Roz Feldberg for their substantive comments on an early draft. Sandra Morgen, Martha A. Ackelsberg, and other contributors to this volume provided additional response and encouragement.

Notes

[1] This chapter appeared originally in 1988 in *Women and the Politics of Empowerment,* edited by Ann Bookman and Sandra Morgan, 1988, 159-179. Philadelphia: Temple University Press. Endnotes have been edited to conform to volume style.

[2] Although it is certainly true that working-class women have been socialized traditionally to view their family roles and duties as primary, it does not follow that their experience at work and their receptivity to unionization are completely and adversely determined by the sexual and domestic roles they play within their family units. It is interesting that in studies of working-class men, it is usually assumed and argued that work outside the home determines how they function in other spheres. The opposing assumptions underlying these studies of working-class men and women have led some critics of traditional social science, such as Feldberg and Glenn, to argue that sociology and other disciplines are "sex-segregated" and that there are two models of work and workplace behavior being used, one for men (a "job model") and one for women (a "gender model"). Feldberg and Glenn (1979).

[3] For a fuller discussion of such studies, see Banks (1970) especially chapters 4, 6, 7, 8.

[4] There are, of course, exceptions to this generalization, for example, the excellent book by Eisenstein (1983).

[5] For a fuller discussion of the history of the electrical industry and a history of electrical workers' trade unions, see Bookman (1977), chp. 3; and Schatz (1975, 4-5).

[6] There is a long, rich history of alliances and organizing between middle-class feminists and working-class women, and among the feminist, labor, and socialist movements. How this relationship functioned at Digitex, how it paralleled or diverged from its historical antecedents, is a fascinating topic beyond the scope of this article. For an excellent historical discussion of the issues involved, see Tax (1980).

[7] "Home visits" were a very important component of the methodology utilized in this study. It was the opportunity to make home visits to a broad spectrum of Digitex workers, male and female, that facilitated data collection on their domestic roles, responsibilities, and relationships.

[8] For a fuller explanation of the statistical methods and results, see Bookman (1977) especially chapters 8 and 9.

[9] "Ethnicity" was measured by a set of interrelated variables including location of residence, membership in particular social clubs, churches, neighborhood associations, and the like.

RACE, POST-COLONIALISM AND DIASPORIC CONTEXTS

CHAPTER 16

The Shadow Minority: An ethnohistory of Portuguese and Lusophone racial and ethnic identity in New England

MIGUEL MONIZ

In the late spring of 1973, during a peak period of popular political awareness of ethnic and racial identity in America, a group of Portuguese activists, community leaders, educators and business leaders convened the "Portuguese Congress in America" at Harvard University to take a wide-ranging look at the issues facing Portuguese immigrant communities. Participants discussed issues related to education, migration and citizenship, economic successes and struggles, and a prominent topic of the day: federal recognition of Portuguese minority status.[1]

The 1964 Civil Rights Act had initiated the creation of federal agencies such as the Equal Employment and Opportunity Commission (EEOC) to monitor compliance with anti-discrimination law. Essential, however, in policing discrimination against minority groups, was defining in law which groups were to be protected. Among federal-level deliberations defining protected minorities was the 1972 Ethnic Heritage Program which arrived at the classification of minority groups that exist in federal and state statute today—African-American, Hispanic, Native American, Native Hawaiian, Native Alaskan, Pacific Islander (Harney 1990, 117). There was another group, however, that was determined by the Ethnic Heritage Program to be a minority group and deserving of federal non-discrimination protection: the Portuguese.

How the Portuguese later came to be eliminated from the list of federally-defined minority groups, provides a little-known story in the ethnohistory of the Portuguese in America. The case also offers insight into the malleable nature of Portuguese ethnic and racial categorization, providing a departure point for a discussion of how social constructions of race and ethnicity intersect with the law.

New England's Portuguese communities were deeply involved in deliberations about the legal recognition of Portuguese minority status. The most public stance in the course of this debate was taken at the Harvard Portuguese Congress. Pointing to the difficulty of social integration, social marginalization, and discrimination against the group, participants at the concluding session of the Congress passed a key resolution by an overwhelming five hundred to three vote insisting that local, state, and federal authorities recognize the Portuguese as a legal minority. Another resolution passed at the Congress defined the Portuguese minority as a unitary group regardless of race. According to congress co-organizer, Ruben Cabral, all Portuguese "would be welcome—whether they are black or white."[2]

Not all of those present, however, were enamored with defining the Portuguese as a legal minority group. Leading the charge against minority status was Harvard University Professor and Dean of the Graduate School of Arts and Sciences, Francis M. Rogers. Of Portuguese/Azorean and Irish descent, Rogers was a broadly influential academic and one of the key figures in the founding of Portuguese Studies in America, writing various books, including some prominent English-language historiographies of Portugal, the Azores, and Madeira (Rogers 1979; 1992). Although his intellectual legacy may have been subsequently eclipsed, Rogers's effect on the emergence of Portuguese Studies within American academia cannot be discounted, and many of his former students—as well as adversaries—now lead the field.

Rogers was joined in his efforts by others, including the prominent Portuguese-American attorney, Joseph Freitas.[3] Using political connections with Congressional representatives, they worked to successfully derail Portuguese minority status. Part of the argument made to the local Congressional delegation was that the Portuguese should not be considered a minority group because the Portuguese were not Hispanics and, unlike other minority groups, they were "white."[4] Rogers's ability to shape the debate was certainly due to his political contacts, but, as influential as he may have been, his efforts were also facilitated by large numbers within the Portuguese-speaking communities who shared his opposition to Portuguese minority status.

Although the Portuguese were ultimately removed from the list of federally-recognized minority groups, the issue of Portuguese minority status has never been definitively settled in the law. The Portuguese are, in certain contexts, defined and treated as a minority by federal and state-level statues and programs, and in some cases explicitly enveloped into the definition of Hispanic, and protected by the anti-discrimination apparatus of the federal government.

The other fascinating aspect of the Portuguese case is that locally-grounded discourses about racial and ethnic identity have been, and continue to be, rife with ambiguities, disagreements, and contradictions. Even the seemingly simple questions of who—according to immigrants from Portugal and their descendants, as well as academics—is and is not "Portuguese" and who does and does not belong in which racial category yield murky answers. Assertions and arguments about identity are shaped by geographies of origin, individual biography and community dynamics, as well as historical shifts in the contours of the Portuguese state and American discourses about race and ethnicity.

The discussion traces the debates over Portuguese racial and ethnic identity in the U.S. and aims to make sense of the historical and contemporary contradictions in legal definitions and popular conceptualizations of Portuguese minority status. The intersection between self-definitions and definitions created by outsiders offers a unique opportunity for investigating the relation between codified state classification of identity—such as census categories, legal definitions in statutes protecting and offering entitlements to minority groups, and other forms of state-level codification through social policies, on the one hand, and on-the-ground ethnic and racial discourses on the other. The Portuguese example offers insight into the complex relationship between the law and social identity and moves us towards an understanding of how discourse and social practice are shaped by the law and vice versa. Understanding how migrants from Portugal and their descendants have forged and argued about group-specific social identities; how these groups have, or have not been codified by state-level laws and policies; as well as how these ethnic and racial categories have been debated and utilized over time reveals the instrumental nature of social identities,[5] the relevance of state policy for migrant social adaptation, and how collective social actors both work within and struggle against the confines of law and policy. The emergence of "the Portuguese" as a category in New England is, I will argue, a part of broader instrumental and socioeconomic processes that involve exclusion from social power and attempts to mitigate the consequences of that exclusion.

Relational Identities

Variability seems to be the only constant in how Portuguese ethnic and racial identity is perceived by non-Portuguese, how law and governmental policy codify this identity category, and how those who consider themselves Portuguese conceptualize their own categorization vis-à-vis other ethnic groups in the U.S. Immigrants from Portugal and their descendants have been treated in discourse, practice, and the law as both white and non-white, as something betwixt and between the binary categories characteristic of discourse and legal codification in the U.S. Since the first significant numbers of Portuguese national citizens began arriving in New England in the 1890s, and continuing over subsequent waves of migration to the present—with each historical period reflecting different political and social realities—the contradictory status of the Portuguese in U.S. legal statute has been informed by contradictory discourses playing out in the region's various ethnic communities. The perceptions by Portuguese immigrants and their descendants of their own racial and ethnic identity and how they have been identified by others have depended upon broader historical, political, and economic circumstances that have shifted over the past century, causing Portuguese racial and ethnic identity to shift as well.

The Portuguese in New England are comprised of individuals of different backgrounds, socioeconomic status, educational levels, geographic origins, and even preferred languages of expression. Most interesting for this treatment is that the population under discussion is also comprised of individuals of diverse phenotypes, situating them within different locally-defined and historically contingent racial categories.

Although definitions of the Portuguese are readily offered, there is no clear-cut consensus—among Portuguese themselves or among outsiders—on the group's racial identity and boundaries, especially in relationship to Cape Verdeans but also including the relationship to other Lusophone populations in the area, such as recent migrants from Brazil. This is reflected in the lack of agreement among ethno-historical treatments of the Portuguese in New England, in media accounts, and in popular discourse. These differences can depend upon the historical period under examination or the year of publication.[6]

A clear shift in the realities and discourses around identity occurred after the national independence of Cape Verde in 1975. Contemporary Cape Verdean racial identity (Halter 1993; Lobban 1995; Sánchez-Gibbau 2005a; 2005b) is situated both in contrast to African-American and Portuguese identities, where being Cape Verdean exists—using Halter's oft quoted descriptor—"between race and ethnicity." The Portuguese—a post-1975 gloss for non-Cape Verdeans usually from the Azores, but also from Madeira or continental Portugal—are generally treated as if their race—white—is an unquestioned given.

There has been little discussion of the complex and often contradictory construction of white identity among Lusophone migrants. Of particular interest is how Cape Verdean and Portuguese racial identities are historically and relationally dependent upon one other—how they have been defined in New England by reference and in contrast to each other, including state-level codification. The key dynamics in the communities in which migrants settled are predicated upon shifts in national identity and citizenship have intersected with articulations of racial difference. Settlement and work patterns of migrant groups from these various destinations also play into how racial and ethnic identities were forged in New England.

National Identity and Group Affiliation

The contours of Portuguese citizenship have evolved over the 20th century in complex ways and included, at various points in time, people living in continental Portugal, the Azores, Madeira, Cape Verde as well as the colonies in Africa and Asia. With the independence of Portugal's colonies after the colonial wars and the 1974 Revolution, those contours shifted dramatically. One of the challenges in defining the "Portuguese" in the diaspora is that people who were Portuguese nationals under colonialism were no longer considered Portuguese after the disintegration of the empire. Citizenship codes also created an inclusive category for geographically dispersed populations that included a wide range of phenotypes. The intersection of collective identities around race, ethnicity, and nationality within the American context was thus quite convoluted.

Only a relatively small percentage of the migrants come from continental Portugal: most originated from the Azores, with smaller numbers coming from Cape Verde and Madeira. Constructions of Portuguese identity in the archipelagoes have historically been shaped by economic and political disputes with continental Portugal, with discordant relations sometimes exhibited among islanders and those from the mainland, even in diaspora. The disputes culminated in the independence of Cape Verde and the emergence of the autonomous political status of the Azores and Madeira.[7] Despite political articulations of identity that favored regional identities over Portuguese, migrants arriving in the U.S. prior to 1974 from these places all held Portuguese passports. They were all thus officially Portuguese regardless of geographic location and divergent sentiments about their connection to Portuguese cultural or ethnic identity. Even though self-perception and perception by others are essential in social constructions of identity, national identity cannot be overlooked as a primary marker, especially in a migrant context where rights to entry and residence derive from official designations of citizenship.

The national citizenship of incoming migrants provided one basis on which others in the U.S. tended to perceive of the Portuguese as a collective, regardless of internal differences of geographies of origin and phenotype. That Portuguese migrants tended to settle in similar locales and work for the same companies or in the same professions also contributed to the salience of national identity in the migrant context.

Racial Identity of the Portuguese Migrants

Historical documents from the first half of the 20th century but ranging until the 1980s reveal that local populations classified Portuguese migrants as non-white in contrast to Anglophone populations and other European migrant groups. Leo Pap, the foremost mid-century scholar of the Portuguese in America writes, "the popular impression of many New Englanders earlier in this century was that the Portuguese ethnic group in general, including the Azorean majority, was more or less 'colored'" (Pap 1981, 114). Pap himself describes the "'racial' traits" of the Portuguese, writing of the "light skinned individuals along with the Negroid of Cabo Verde" and the "Negroid admixture [that] is present in the Azores" (Pap 1981, 113). Articles in various popular magazines in the U.S. during the early 20th century also described the Portuguese in California, New England, and Hawaii as all belonging in a "colored" category. Robert Harney (1990) compiled first-hand accounts from a range of sources, demonstrating that the Portuguese were considered to be a non-white racial group in the U.S. and Bermuda. Jack London, for example, referred to the Portuguese as "these small brown skinned immigrants" (1913, 10). An article in *Cape Cod Magazine*[8] stated, "Now the whole Cape Cod is dark with the dusty skins of the Portuguese 'White man'..." (note the author's inverted quotes around "White man"). Pap also cites newpaper reports of a 1920s soccer match in which a fracas erupted between the Lusitania club of Cambridge and an Irish team after a blond woman was quoted as shouting at the Portuguese, "You goddamn Negroes" (Pap 1981, 160). Harney (1990, 117), citing the *Harvard Encyclopedia of American Ethnic Groups*, calls attention to a 1976 classification in Barnstable, Cape Cod, that divided resident ethnic groups into white and non-white: the Portuguese were on the non-white side (see also Pap 1981). Other writing from the period treated the Portuguese as the exotic other: Mary Heaton Vorse, for example, referred to the "beautiful dark-eyed girls,"[9] whereas an official U.S. Government document entitled *Hawaii and its Race Problems* referred to the Portuguese as a "dark and handsome group."[10]

In other reaches of the Portuguese diaspora among Anglo populations, the Portuguese were also considered to be non-white. In Hawaii, for example, where some 30,000 Portuguese, mostly from Madeira, but also from the Azores, had migrated over the turn of the century, native Hawaiian islanders place the Portuguese in a separate category from Europeans and Americans. *Haole*, a term meaning any foreigner, but one that came to be used specifically to define whites, was not used in reference to Portuguese migrants. This Portuguese non-white status in Hawaii is clear from sources cited in both Pap and Harney, as well as elsewhere, noting that in the Hawaiian Census between 1910-1940, the Portuguese were not classified as "white" nor as "other caucasians," but rather had their own separate category. This status was mirrored in Bermuda, where the Portuguese were also not classified as white but again had their own category (Pap 1981, 114; Harney 1990, 114-115; Lamm 1933-1934; Felix and Senecal 1978; Rogers 1976,

54). Local perceptions of Azoreans and Madeirans as racially diverse (DuPuy 1932, 105), and patterns that found Portuguese marrying and working in plantations alongside native Hawaiians, Chinese, and East Indians placed the Lusophone migrants in a non-white category in local Hawaiian constructions of racial identity.[11]

One of the more authoritative academic voices defining racial perceptions of the Portuguese came from Donald Taft, whose 1923 Columbia University Ph.D. dissertation (*Two Portuguese Communities in New England*) examined, among other issues, the cause of high infant mortality rates among Portuguese populations living in New England. Although he collected a broad range of extraordinary demographic data, including rates of infant death, occupational distribution, arrest rates, literacy rates, level of education, etc., his problematic analysis hypothesizes that the negative trends characterizing a *Micaelense*-American community resulted from high levels of "black blood." Taft can be rightfully critiqued for positing that "Negroid blood" was the cause of a whole host of social problems, rather than the low-paying, long-hour, sweat-shop factory jobs and the unhealthy living conditions created by poverty. Shoddy analysis aside, the Portuguese phenotype described by Taft[12] (he devotes an entire chapter to the analysis of Portuguese racial composition) and others demonstrates the perception of Portuguese as non-white.

"Black" Portuguese, "White" Portuguese and Instrumental Adaptation

Mechanisms of state control over racial groups and national identity were codified in U.S. statute beginning with the Constitution. During the late 1800s and early 1900s, however, an unprecedented expansion of state codification of social identity emerged as the influx of migration to industrial centers caused nativist reactions against the new arrivals. This resulted in the enactment of a number of well-known statutes designed to bar migrants (i.e. the Chinese Exclusion Act of 1882) or to slow migration from particular locales, such as the Emergency Quota Act of 1921, followed by the even more restrictive Immigration Act of 1924, which limited southern European immigration while allowing for immigration from northern and central European countries such as England, Scotland, and Germany.

In both local popular discourse as well as academic analysis, Portuguese migration to America is seen as part of broader patterns of southern European migration. The case of the Portuguese is often lumped together with that of Italy or Greece without, however, much by way of critical analysis as to the comparability of these various migratory streams. It is important to note that this southern European gloss, along with supporting perceptions of the Portuguese as white, obscures several important distinctions. One key difference between these migrations from Southern Europe is the much later date of Portuguese arrival in North America. Portuguese migrated in repeated waves, the largest of which arrived during the 1960s and 1970s; whereas Italian migration, with the exception of 1921, began to abate after 1914. Secondly and significantly, Portuguese migration was European as a result of geopolitical considerations that enveloped the Atlantic islanders from Madeira, Cape Verde, and the Azores into the Portuguese nation, despite the fact that these island groups are geographically far-removed from continental Europe. Another important distinction is that Portugal, as was the case with Spain, yet unlike other European nations, stood as a geographic and cultural frontier between North Africa and Europe, having been part of the Moorish Empire for half a millennium. And only Portugal had extensive migratory, economic, and political contacts with South America, Asia, and Africa at the time of migration to the U.S. Another significant difference from other southern European migrant groups to which the Portuguese are often compared, was the racial diversity of the Portuguese migrants who self-identified as Portuguese and who settled within a tightly circumscribed geographic area in southeastern New England.[13]

The relationship between race and nationality current in discourse and codified in federal statute reinforced the notion that those from European nations were white (see for example, Haney-Lopez 1996). However, the Portuguese in New England, given the range of phenotype and diversity of geographic origin, presented perceptual conflicts for articulations of nationality writ as race. Migrants from the Atlantic archipelagoes of the Azores, Madeira and Cape Verde were, until 1975, treated as Portuguese for the purposes of migration quotas to the U.S. One effect this had on articulations of Portuguese migrant identity was that U.S. immigration law did not allow migrants from Africa to become

U.S. citizens until changes in the Immigration Act of 1952 abolished the prohibition. The bar on African migrants obtaining U.S. citizenship would of course not affect a Portuguese national citizen. This meant that immigrants from Cape Verde who might be considered African as a result of point of origin or phenotype would, in this case, have a prominent instrumental interest in asserting a Portuguese national identity.[14]

From the outset, local definitions of Portuguese racial and social identity were at odds with the law, given that a Portuguese passport meant that one was European and so was classified—at least under the polemic codified in law—as white in America. In local discourse, however, as pointed out in the examples above, the general perception of the Portuguese was as non-white. Discrepancies between Portuguese self-perceptions of racial identity and the perceptions of non-Portuguese led to interventions on the part of the state. One such issue arose in the early 1900s when census-takers, who were then responsible for filling out respondents' demographic information, including racial characteristics, were challenged by certain Portuguese who, upon their classification as both Portuguese and black, disagreed with the census-taker's ascription. Many disputes arose, given that Portuguese definitions of racial identity differed from that of the American census-takers (Halter 1993).

As various social theorists dealing with census categories and other forms of state-level identity codification point out, ethnic and racial categories on a census may reflect a particular social reality, but they may also contribute to the creation of that social reality.[15] Social identities are, of course, not reducible to state codification—and, of course, codification was not solely responsible for the racialization of the Portuguese category. Portuguese and non-Portuguese alike confronted definitions of racial identity that cast the Portuguese as both white and non-white, whether concomitant census categories existed, and whether the broader perception of the Portuguese as a group was consistent with more localized definitions. What the Portuguese treatment in the census provided, however, was a prominent means of codifying racial classification, adding one more source defining Portuguese racial identity that was confronted in practice.

In early-20th-century America, the implication of being classified as non-white, whether through legal codification or discourse, was not unimportant. Although overt apartheid existed to a lesser degree in the North than elsewhere, racial segregation and discrimination nonetheless existed, and classification as non-white carried with it serious ramifications. Certainly, there are prominent structural differences when examining the causes and function of discrimination levied against former black African slaves and their descendants when compared to voluntary migrant groups classified as non-white (see Fuchs 1990; Halter 1993). These differences notwithstanding, as the Portuguese migrants were treated as non-white in southeastern New England and suffered marginalization, they were subject to exclusion from factory jobs, from promotions, from housing, and confronted various apartheid policies such as segregated seating in movie theaters and the like.[16] Political rights were also at stake as those classified as non-white were denied "full social and political citizenship," barred from juries, participating in civic organizations, and holding public office, etc.[17]

Although contemporary discourses promote a collective "Cape Verdean" racial identity as distinct from that of all other Lusophone populations, racial distinctions were not always congruent with geographic origins. Depending on phenotype, many Cape Verdeans in the early 20th century were placed in the "white Portuguese" category, both in state discourse and social practice, even as migrants from the Azores and Madeira were considered non-white. Even individuals within the same family had, at times, different relations to phenotypically defined racial classifications. Those who were not able to be classified as white used their inclusion in the racially fluid Portuguese group to allow for the greatest malleability in their racial classification—individuals classified as black could mute stigmatization in law and social discourse by articulating a Portuguese, i.e. European, identity. Another fascinating example of the ambiguity of the Portuguese category is found in Southern segregation policy. The apartheid policy of the so-called separate but equal principle initiated by the Supreme Court's 1896 *Plessy vs. Ferguson* decision provided the legal standing for the creation of separate black and white schools. Prior to the Civil Rights Act of 1964, "Portuguese" were barred from attending white-only schools in North Carolina as they were considered to be non-white. Interestingly, however, the statute deemed that the Portuguese would also not be required to go to black schools.[18]

Assertions of Portuguese identity were often used by individuals of African and Native American descent in the South from the late nineteenth through the first half of the 20th century in court trials as a way to escape being classified as "Negro" and to "prove" their whiteness, necessary to secure citizenship and inheritance rights (Gross 2007). Considered Free Persons of Color in many southern states, Portuguese were nonetheless provided legal status as white, given Portugal's standing as a European nation. The nebulous nature of Portuguese racial identity—as non-white in discourse and white in the law—were essential aspects of this strategy. The transcript of a trial in Tennessee, for example, noted that "Samuel Bolton never claimed to be white, he claimed to be Portuguese…." (*Jack v. Foust.*, deposition of Rev. D. D. Scruggs, 315, 318. Quoted in Gross 2007). And by articulating his Portuguese identity, Bolton hoped to "prove" he was not black. Narratives of Portuguese identity were also essential to the efforts of certain groups of Native-American and African-American descent in the Carolinas and Tennessee, notably the Melungeons and the Croatans, to counter racial stigma.[19]

As other groups used Portuguese identity to escape classification as black, Portuguese migrants and their descendants went to great lengths to define themselves as white. Given local readings of phenotypes, Portuguese claims to "being white" were often tenuous. A strategy followed by some Portuguese to support the argument for inclusion in the white category was to distance themselves from Portuguese of other regions through racist discourses and to mobilize local readings of phenotypes. Gross (2007) describes this phenomenon among bi-racial descendants of Native-Americans and African-Americans where non-whites could "pass" through a performance of "whiteness," which in part depended upon the creation of distance from other lower status (read darker) groups. Conflicts arose, even within families, about segregation by phenotype and the discrimination from others to which most Portuguese had been subjected was wielded by some against compatriots. Continental Portuguese treated Azoreans as non-white; Azoreans treated Cape Verdeans as non-white; and even islanders from one island treated people from another island in the same archipelago as racially different and socially inferior (e.g. Faial and São Miguel). For example, the Portuguese Continental Union, the "largest Portuguese-American Fraternal organization in the East" excluded darker-skinned Azoreans from joining until 1931, and excluded Cape Verdeans from joining the club until 1959 (Pap 1981, 161).

The Civil Rights Act, Cape Verdean Independence and Changing Discourses of Identity

The 1964 Civil Rights Act provided many African-Americans who had suffered through both overt and covert apartheid practices with a positive sense of collective racial identity. The concomitant entitlement and affirmative action programs were put into place to break down the barriers to socioeconomic advancement and educational opportunities. These changes in U.S. law—in conjunction with the disintegration of the Portuguese colonial empire—created dramatic shifts in the dynamics of Portuguese ethnic and racial identity.

The cultural and political proto-nationalist movements begun earlier in the century in Cape Verde and Portuguese Africa culminated in national independence and political autonomy for Portuguese overseas territories, including the Azores and Madeira, after Portugal's 1974 revolution. Residents of the erstwhile colonies were given the choice of maintaining Portuguese citizenship or adopting the citizenship of the newly formed nations. Cape Verdean nationalist discourses de-emphasized Portuguese identity and focused on articulating the cultural and political connection between the independent Cape Verdean nation and Africa. These discourses found their way to New England by way of migrants' connections with relatives and friends in their homeland and through literature and reports on the war appearing in Portuguese-language newspapers in New England.

Positive expressions of black identity in America, together with Cape Verdeans' distancing themselves from Europe in favor of Africa, led to the fixing of discourses around a geographic basis for racial difference. Many Cape Verdeans, some of whose parents and grandparents had identified as white or as Portuguese, articulated black identities for themselves. Furthermore, embracing a black identity facilitated access to state entitlement programs designated for African-Americans.

It is in this context that participants in the Portuguese Congress in America, described at the beginning of this paper overwhelmingly argued for designating the Portuguese as a minority. Access to state-level protection and Congressional assistance by way of Civil Rights legislation and inclusion in the 1972 Ethnic Heritage Program were seen by many as effective ways to ameliorate Portuguese marginalization and social exclusion.

Some Portuguese however—especially those who were able to assert themselves as "white Portuguese" by distinguishing themselves from "black Portuguese"—were strongly opposed to minority classification of the Portuguese. As pointed out earlier, even though Professor Rogers spearheaded the move against minority status, other Portuguese supported his argument regarding the detrimental impact of such a designation. Escaping racial stigmatization by "being white" through asserting connections to other white ethnic groups such as the Italians or Greeks was, from this point of view, much preferred over being a "minority" and, through association with other minorities, being seen as "non-white."

As both Professor Rogers and Joseph Freitas have passed away, the published comments by Rogers's daughter, Sheila Ackerlind Rogers, a Professor of Spanish and Portuguese languages at West Point, help us better understand the debate about Portuguese minority status. In response to a piece summing up Rogers's role in the debate, Professor Ackerlind Rogers characterized her father's opposition in the following terms:[20]

> [W]hat prompted Prof. Rogers to speak out against minority status was...an abhorrence of any form of ethnic or racial classification. Such classification, in his opinion, only serves to divide what should be one American people and to fuel the fires of condescension and prejudice.... [M]y great-grandfather's name was..."Da Rosa," which an immigration official changed to Rogers when my great-grandfather immigrated to America in the 19th century.... [H]ow difficult it was, until the late 1940's for a person with an 'ethnic' surname to rise socio-economically. By giving my great-grandfather a WASP surname, the immigration official unwittingly did him the considerable favor of enabling him to enter and flourish in mainstream American society. Both my grandfather, Frank Rogers, and my father were convinced that Portuguese surnames would have hindered their pursuit of a quality education and of their respective professional careers. If their surname had been "Da

> Rosa," my grandfather would not have admitted [sic] to Georgetown college, and my father might not have been admitted to Harvard Graduate School of Arts and Sciences (of which he eventually became Dean). It might be incomprehensible to young students, raised in an environment of multiculturalism, that an "ethnic" surname could have been a factor in shaping one's destiny, but such was the sad reality of American society until after World War II. Although it can be argued that multiculturalism has tended to divide Americans rather than unite them, it has been instrumental in diminishing the social stigmas attached to "ethnic" names. (Rogers Ackerlind 2001)

Despite Rogers Ackerlind's claim, it seems it was not her father's "abhorrence of any form of ethnic or racial classification" that led him to argue against Portuguese minority status, but rather his opposition to what he considered to be the wrong kind of ethnic and racial classification. According to Rogers Ackerlind, if the Portuguese Da Rosas had not been given "the considerable favor" of deceiving influential individuals into thinking they were WASPS, they would have had a hard time making it.[21] Her comments underline Francis Rogers's belief that a perceptual inclusion in the dominant white group—and concomitantly downplaying one's Portugueseness and subsequent non-white status—was the most efficacious way of entering "mainstream American Society."[22] Many Portuguese, having witnessed the problems of social exclusion over the century and craving social and economic success in America, were reluctant to accept a legal status that they understood as non-white. For these Portuguese, to do so would invite discrimination, not redress it.

Continuing Ambiguities in Portuguese Racial and Ethnic Status

Current laws as well as popular discourse continue to perpetuate the ambiguous status of the Portuguese. They are, in some contexts, declared to be white and a non-minority group, in others as non-white and a legally-sanctioned minority group.

According to certain laws and programs in several states, the Portuguese are officially a minority. In Rhode Island and Massachusetts, for example, the Portuguese are included on a list of minorities eligible to participate in business development programs. A "minority" anti-smoking campaign organized by the Commonwealth of Massachusetts specifically targets the officially codified minority groups *and* the Portuguese. In the states of Indiana, Kentucky, Colorado, Florida, Washington, and Illinois, the Portuguese are included in certain definitions of "Hispanic" and eligible for minority business program preferences.

On the federal level, the Portuguese are also, at times, declared to be a minority in their own right or incorporated into the definition of other officially recognized minority groups. Data on "minority" groups in the Philadelphia metropolitan area presented at a 2002 U.S. Census Bureau conference, for example, included statistics on Portuguese and Brazilians in the Latino category. The American Red Cross programs to encourage minority bone marrow donations reaches out to all of the officially designated minority groups *and* the Portuguese. The Equal Employment Office also continues to address what the office holds as systematic discrimination against the Portuguese. For example, the affirmative action department of Rhode Island's largest non-government employer hired me to conduct research on reasons for the lack of advancement on the part of their Portuguese employees. They were mandated to address a federal report that found eighty percent of Portuguese male and ninety-nine percent of Portuguese female employees remained in the lowest level positions in the company without advancement for upwards of thirty years. Another example comes from the U.S. Congress's Republican Hispanic Conference, entitled "We the (Hispanic) people." It is penned by five "Hispanic" congressmen, one of whom is the Azorean-American California Representative, Devin Nunes. The goals of the caucus are to "promote policy outcomes that serve the best interests of Americans of Hispanic and Portuguese descent" and promote "principles that are of real importance to Hispanics and Portuguese in the U.S."[23]

Other forms of codifying the Portuguese as non-white are found in film and television. During the 2004 Presidential campaign, for example, the bi-racial actress Maya Rudolph played the role of Democratic nominee John Kerry's Portuguese wife (and 2005 Portuguese-American Women's Association "Woman of the Year"), Teresa Heinz Kerry,[24] on the comedy program *Saturday Night Live.* In the John Travolta film, *Phenomenon,* an Azorean agricultural laborer is thought to be Mexican until it becomes clear that he is speaking Portuguese. And one of the more frequent character actors in American film and television who has built a successful career out of playing Latin American villains with roles in *Miami Vice,* Robert Rodrigues's *Desperado*, along with numerous others, is the Portuguese actor Joaquim Almeida.

In both popular discourse and legal codification, the Portuguese are often incorporated into or placed side-by-side with the Hispanic category. For example, Luso-Canadian pop star, Nelly Furtado, who articulates a conscious Portuguese and Azorean identity,[25] was invited to perform at the Latin Grammy awards, an award show for Latino musicians. In the same show, Hispanic actor and host Jimmy Smits explained that Latinos include everyone from the Spanish-speaking countries, Portugal, and Brazil. (Incidentally, Smits' character on *NYPD Blue* is "half" Portuguese).[26] General opinion on the topic is given a rich airing on a fascinating website that poses the question "Hispanic or Portuguese?" (http://www.portuguesefoundation.org/hispanic.htm). The varied responses alternately articulate agreement and disagreement with the posed question, as others argue for a separate minority status for the Portuguese. Taken as a whole, the comments provide insight into the thinking reflecting the dichotomies around discourses that would characterize the Portuguese as both white and non-white.

Another example of how advantages offered by official group codification can shape social action is the process of university admissions. According to an article in *The Boston Globe*, Lusophone populations, including Portuguese and Brazilians, sought and were granted university admission and scholarships as "Hispanic" or "Black," even though they did not otherwise identify themselves with these categories (Rapoza 2001). Some universities, including for example, Brown University, explicitly include the Portuguese as a preferential group for the purposes of admissions. The practical ramifications of being classified as a minority is, for students, quite clear.

An odd Federal government document from the Attorney General acknowledges the disparities between participant-level discourses and state-level policy. The Justice Department noted in its official announcement of a recruiting drive for Hispanic applicants that, "Hispanic... does not include persons of Portuguese culture or origin."[27] The policy statement, used also for other governmental agencies, is clear enough; however, the Portuguese were the only group necessitating explicit exclusion from the definition of "Hispanic." There is no analogous statement that "Hispanics" do not include "White Anglo-Saxon Protestants" or "Italians" or "Greeks," as there are simply no discourses that treat WASPS or Italians or Greeks as Hispanics—whereas the classification of the Portuguese is ambiguous and inconsistent enough to warrant specific mention.

Whether Portuguese minority status or incorporation into the categories of Hispanic or Latino is accepted or rejected, the ambiguities and contradictions in both everyday discourse and action and state and non-governmental codified policy continue to shape contemporary Portuguese ethnic and racial status. Similar ambiguities and contradiction characterize the definitions and discourses around Cape Verdeans—who, in certain contexts are classified as neither black nor white nor Portuguese. They are recognized, at least in Massachusetts and Rhode Island, as a minority racial group, not as African-American, but specifically as Cape Verdean. Another complexity is introduced into contemporary definitions of Portugueseness by the recent influx of large numbers of Brazilian migrants into the region.[28] Shared points of reference include, of course, language, as well as work and residence patterns and socioeconomic networks. The interplay between the ethnic and racial identities of Brazilian and other Lusophone migrants and how on-the-ground identities are articulated and formed with state-codified categories remain key questions for future research.

Integrated and Relational Identities

Although prevailing wisdom suggests that state-level codification defining ethnic and racial groups merely recognizes a reality that already exists, in fact, the very act of codification works to create the social reality itself. State-defined social identities are not a natural given. The current definition of the Hispanic category, for example, came about through lobbying efforts on the part of activists and cultural elites who worked to expand earlier legal definitions that included only those born in Puerto Rico or Mexico (see Choldin 1986) to currently include anyone with a Spanish surname or with ancestry in a Spanish-speaking country. Hispanic identity, in contradistinction to the Portuguese case, has come to be categorized as a politically unified and undifferentiated group, even though both populations encompass a similarly wide range of phenotypes and geographic origins.

The process excluding the Portuguese from minority status was no less political, and the contours of ethnic or racial categories relevant to immigrants from Portugal and their descendants have come into being through a fluid process of social definition characterized by the interplay between state-created definitions and the strategies of social actors. The ethnohistory of Portuguese identity categories offers insight into how social actors strategically utilize and respond to these codified definitions of categorical identity. In various contexts, in various historical periods, individual actors have used the ambiguities in how their social identities have been construed to maximize their ability to respond to both state-level mandates and the challenges of their every-day lives.

If there has been little consensus over definitions of Portuguese social identity, given the differences in its participant-level construction and analytical treatment in different historical periods (with the perception that contemporary expressions of identity have always been so), this paper has argued that articulations of social identity among Lusophone migrants emerged through a relational and co-dependent social process that made the existence of a "white" Portuguese category dependent upon the existence of a "black" Portuguese category and vice versa. Contemporary racial and ethnic identities among Lusophone migrants and their descendants, both at the level of participant discourse and the law, have been shaped around this dichotomy.

A defining feature of Portuguese social identity is the ability to maintain multiple ethnic and racial identities that can be contextually articulated to either mark one as a member of the group, or conversely, to remove one from it. The relationship between Azorean islanders, Madeirans, continentals, and Cape Verdeans and the broader construction of a Portuguese category is neither inclusive nor is it binary. The same individuals who separate themselves from the Portuguese category by engaging in social networks and political and economic interest groups based on their belonging in one category also find themselves sharing political and social institutions within a broad Lusophone migrant group in other contexts.

The connections among Lusophone migrants also serve as counterpoints in the process of establishing distinct identities. Despite the post-independence rejection of Portuguese identity, it is, for example, the historical link to the "Portuguese" that allows Cape Verdeans in the present to maintain a separate non-African-American identity. The identities and networks of migrants from Brazil also are developed in relationship with, and in counterpoint to, the already well-established Lusophone population and pre-existing discourses around Portuguese racial identity. And being Azorean is what makes one Portuguese, but being Azorean is also used, in certain contexts, to define an identity in opposition to being Portuguese.

The law requires clear-cut definitions of social groups even though in discourse and practice the categories are not so clear-cut. Social actors are required to engage with state-level definitions of identity. One of the interesting features of the Portuguese case is the way the state itself helps create contradictions, providing in certain contexts codification that explicitly denies Portuguese minority status, while treating the Portuguese as a recognized minority in others.

Lusophone migrants and the social groups formed by their descendants today constitute a kind of "shadow minority."[29] That is, they have been subjected to the same kinds of social exclusion faced by legally codified minority groups (Barrow 2002), yet they lack the concomitant legal framework and political vocabulary that "minority" classification confers. This has been one result of Portuguese minority status undone. From a political standpoint, it is difficult to argue that the lack of minority status has been beneficial to the Portuguese efforts to address issues of economic, political, and educational marginalization. Rejecting minority status, however, maintained for those articulating belonging in the Portuguese category the legal status as white, which provided many with a means for avoiding a perceived subordinate status.

Notes

[1] Ethnographic data collected for the bulk of this paper was conducted through interviews and participant observation research among the Lusophone migrant communities in southeastern New England over 2001-2004, where I have also worked as an anthropologist on issues of Portuguese migration for several decades and where I have lived for much of my life.

[2] *The Boston Globe,* June 4, 1973.

[3] Freitas achieved notoriety in the trial of Dan White, who shot down San Francisco Assemblyman Harvey Milk and Mayor George Mascone. DA Freitas failed to convict White of murder in the first degree when his case was beaten by the infamous "Twinkie Defense."

[4] Onésimo Almeida, personal communication 2002.

[5] Instrumentalism here is situated in the anthropological tradition that views ethnic group

formation as situational, contextual, and ultimately adaptive. See Barth (1969); Cohen (1969); Colson (1967); Eller and Coughlin (1993); Gluckman (1958); Mitchell (1956); Moermon (1965). See Hicks (1977a), Eriksen (1993), and Banks (1996) for a summary of debates and approaches to contingent and instrumental social identities.

[6] The term "Portuguese" is not treated as a static category that always includes the same individuals, but is intended to refer to the group named in statutes regarding minority status and other forms of legal codification by the state, including those whose lives are affected by such classifications. As such, the "Portuguese" includes those individuals who self-identify as Portuguese, or who are classified as Portuguese by others. It is important to note that the composition of this group is malleable, depending upon historical period or instrumental context, including (or conversely excluding) those from diverse geographic points of origin (i.e. Cape Verde).

[7] Political autonomy in the Azores and Madeira provides the archipelagoes, respectively, with their own president and parliament, yet simultaneously envelops them through law and national identity within the Portuguese state.

[8] *Cape Cod Magazine,* Wareham, MA. no 16. (cited in Pap 1981).

[9] *Time and the Town: A Provincetown Chronicle.* New York, Dial Press 76, 1942.

[10] Dupuy, William Atherton. Washington DC. U.S. Department of the Interior, 1932.

[11] An example from Harney (1990, 115) makes this status clear. In impaneling the jury for a 1930s rape trial of Hawaiian and Chinese defendants, a dispute over fairness was settled by splitting the jury among "six white men" and six non-whites (two Japanese, two Chinese, one Hawaiian, and one Portuguese).

[12] First published in 1923 by Columbia University, the dissertation was reprinted in 1969 just prior to the legal debates around codified minority identity.

[13] Of course Portuguese pre-migration racial categories differed from the non-Portuguese in the post-migration period. Bastos's (2002) discussion of Goan medical doctors trained at the Medical School of Goa founded in the mid-1800s points out the disparity of identity narratives in which the Goans were seen as subaltern to medical doctors from the *Continente* but glorified for their work throughout the Portuguese African and Indian Empire.

[14] Haney-López (1996) demonstrates various instances in which migrants from certain nations attempted to "prove" that they were white in U.S. courts of law for the purposes of naturalization.

[15] Benedict Anderson (1993) broached the role of the Census in defining social identity in the reprint of his seminal work. However, the topic was treated in depth in a theoretically groundbreaking collection of essays, Kertzer and Arel (2001). Choldin (1986) examined the topic with the Hispanic category.

[16] See Halter (1993, 165-172) for a number of examples; for other patterns of discrimination and social exclusion, including against Azoreans factory workers, see Lauck (1912), Rodrigues (1990), and Silvia (1976).

[17] See Gross (2007). Skilled Anglophone mill workers, for example segregated themselves from the Portuguese, refusing to unionize with them (Lauck 1912).

[18] The policy was also mirrored in Bermuda, which also gave the Portuguese their own racial classification (Pap 1981).

[19] Two of anthropology's so-called "tri-racial isolates." Hicks (1977a) and Hicks and Kertzer (1972) offer a thorough discussion of the topic. See also Clifford (1988).

[20] The quotation is part of an exchange in *The Portuguese Times,* (a Portuguese-American weekly newspaper in New England) in response to a piece I wrote about the Harvard Conference and Rogers's subsequent role. Her full response and my rebuttal can be read in *The Portuguese Times* (May 23 and June 13, 2001).

[21] Rogers's desire to mute his association with Portuguese extended to other areas. Kenneth Maxwell, the eminent historian, political scientist, and frequent contributor to *The New York Review of Books,* recounted a story about Rogers from a professional meeting of Historians in America at which Rogers proposed banning all Portuguese (Kenneth Maxwell, personal communication, 2001).

[22] These attitudes were also reflected by Joseph Freitas who told a young scholar at another Ivy League university, "you aren't getting anywhere with a vowel at the end of your name" (Onésimo Almeida, Personal Communication, 2001).

[23] It is perhaps counter-intuitive that Republicans would form a caucus linking Hispanics and Portuguese, arguing for their interests as a unified group, while Democrats—who have been traditional advocates of Portuguese constituents and minorities—make statements on the topic as Massachusetts Representative Barney Frank did to me in an interview in his Fall River office saying,

"the Portuguese have never been discriminated against in systematic ways"; or as another Portuguese Democratic State representative told me, "the Portuguese are not a minority like the Spanish and the Blacks."

[24] An interesting example of the ambiguities of Portuguese racial identity in America in her own right, Heinz-Kerry, born in Mozambique, is the wealthy daughter of a Portuguese medical doctor and an Italian-French mother. Various news sources have referred to Heinz-Kerry as an "African-American" both in reference to her own self-identification or as a description (ie "Out of Africa," Maureen Dowd, *The New York Times,* July 18, 2004, 13; "A Whole Lot of Woman," Deborah Simmons, *The Washington Times,* March 5, 2004, A19; "Group Runs Anti-Kerry Ads on Black Radio Stations," Thomas B. Edsall, *Washington Post,* August 12, 2004, A01; "Not a Simple Matter of Black and White," Ruth Walker, *The Christian Science Monitor,* October 8, 2004, The Home Forum section, 18). According to a spokesman, Heinz-Kerry refers to herself as "African-American" as a geographic rather than a racial identity ("Pan Africa; an 'African" First Lady for the U.S.?" *Africa News,* March 16, 2004). This "African-American" identity raised some issues as the potential First Lady was introduced to America during the 2004 Presidential campaign. The campaign relied upon Heinz-Kerry's background in an appeal to black and Hispanic voters with various levels of success, prompting one nationally syndicated columnist to remark, "She may not be Black but she's a lot more African than most Americans are" (Clarence Page, "Blacks eye that John Kerry guy," *Chicago Tribune,* March 10, 2004, 21).

[25] As examples, the singer, called out to her father in Portuguese on the *Late Show with David Letterman* and plays an Azorean flag-painted guitar, surrounded by Hortensia flowers (a frequent Azores metonym) in a music video.

[26] The question of whether or not the Portuguese should or should not be incorporated into the Hispanic category was under debate at the Harvard Portuguese Congress in America.

[27] "Race and national origin identification." *Standard Form* 181 (Rev. 5-82) (EG), U.S. Office of Personnel Management, FPM Supplement 298-1; http://66.102.9.104/search?q=cache:bAYTg43fCOcJ:www.fsis.usda.gov/OM/HRD/pubform/SFForms/sf0181.pdf.

[28] 250,000 Brazilians reside in Massachusetts alone, often living in the same communities as earlier Portuguese-speaking migrants. In one study, Marrow (2003) examines racial and ethnic identity among the Brazilians in relation to other Portuguese-speaking migrants, as Brazilians fit and do not fit into participant and state-level definitions of Latino, Hispanic, and Portuguese identities.

[29] The use of "shadow" is intended to evoke the opposition "Shadow Cabinet" of a parliamentary system or the "Shadow Representative" used to refer (usually erroneously) to the non-voting Washington D.C. delegate in the House who participates in debate but has no legal standing to vote.

CHAPTER 17

Stereotypes of the Tropics in "Portuguese Newark": Brazilian Women, Urban Erotics, and the Phantom of Blackness

ANA Y. RAMOS-ZAYAS

> The Portuguese men think we're hot, that we can dance and move a certain way, that we are more expressive. The Portuguese women hate us for that, and think we're sluts. They criticize how we dress.... [They say] that we steal their husbands.... They live in fear of that. That's how it is here. That's how all Brazilian women are viewed in Newark. (Amélia Silva,[1] nineteen, from Belo Horizonte, Brazil)

A recent graduate of a public high school in Newark's Ironbound neighborhood, Amélia Silva's comment was in response to my request for a description of how Brazilians and Portuguese related to one another. In principle, the question was not posed in terms of gender relations and yet, whenever I asked either a Portuguese or a Brazilian in Newark to describe the relationship between the two groups, the first reaction was to talk about gendered tensions, romantic dramas, issues of infidelity, sexual repression, promiscuity, dress codes, and "the tropics."[2] This essay considers the everyday production of difference as these are transformed from rigid and inevitable categorizations to an ideological template. In particular, I examine how young Brazilian women living in "Portuguese Newark" articulated their relationship to a stigmatized urban space and racial landscape in their everyday interactions with Portuguese and Portuguese-American residents.

Examining the politics of "morality" and "respectability" that characterized Brazilian and Portuguese interactions in Newark provided a critical understanding of how the cultural representation of Brazilian (hyper)sexuality in the U.S. has in fact concealed a political economy that accommodated some Latin American migrant women in vulnerable occupational niches, including sex work. The employment niches available to Brazilian women contributed to and were viable because of everyday images of Brazilian women as "homewreckers," "loose," and morally corrupt, deployed in contradistinction to the more "traditional" and "respectable" Portuguese women in Newark's Ironbound, a neighborhood typically characterized as a quintessential "ethnic enclave" of good values, productive citizens, Old World traditions, and tightly-knit families.[3] While images of Brazilian hyper-sexuality date back to European constructions of "the tropics,"[4] the manifestations of stereotypes of the tropics in the context of Brazilian migration to Newark, New Jersey, offered an adequate analytical template through which to understand the everyday racialization of Brazilians as "closer to Hispanics" or even "closer to Blacks," especially in the intrinsically gendered readings that Portuguese and Brazilians had of one another.[5] Moreover, the fragility of working-class Portuguese whiteness further required that Portuguese women portray themselves as "decent" and "respectable," not only in traditional female roles as mothers and wives, but also in their capacity as owners of cleaning services that hired Brazilians as part of their staff of domestic workers. In this sense, Portuguese women's respectability in the productive realm was also evoked in contradistinction to the "indecent" jobs of barmaid, dancer, or sex worker more often associated with Brazilians in Newark.

A "majority minority" city etched in the U.S. national imagination as the site of the 1967 urban riots and epitome of urban decay, Newark is experienced by its residents in radically different ways from how it is nationally imagined.[6] Newark is, for the most part, lived at the scale of the neighborhoods or even certain streets or "mental territories" within them. While African-Americans constituted a majority of Newark's population in 2000 (53.5 percent), Latinos represent the fastest growing group (30.0 percent) during this time, with Puerto Ricans still constituting the largest nationality group in a state that also has the highest percentage of migrants from South America in the U.S.(Kaiser Foundation, March 2004).[7] Whites made up 26.5 percent of the city, concentrated mostly in two of the five main wards of the city—the North and East Wards. The neighborhood of the Ironbound, in the East Ward, has been historically considered a "Little Portugal" or a Portuguese "enclave" of Newark: a productive area that generated great revenue to the city because of its successful commodification of culture in the form of ethnic restaurants, specialty stores, and cafés.[8] In the late-1980s, the demographic dominance of the Portuguese in the Ironbound began to shift, as more Latin American migrants, especially from Brazil and other parts of South America, began to arrive in the area.[9] Despite claims of Newark as a "multicultural" city, it is critical to recognize that white and Latino residents alike develop "mental territories" (Morrisey 1997)—the social cartographies that individuals use to attach meaning to particular spaces—that are necessarily constituted against a centrality of a diverse blackness in which African-Americans represent both a powerful political elite and a highly stigmatized "underclass."

In this essay, I discuss the formation of "stereotypes of the tropics" in Newark's Ironbound by situating discussions of attractiveness, desirability, and emotionally-charged racial situations in a political economy of tenuous employment prospects, uneven urban development, inadequate housing conditions, and the racial tensions that needed to be negotiated at any given moment in the context of the extreme poverty that characterized New Jersey's most densely populated city.[10] This political economy also accounts for a fragile class and racial identity even among its Portuguese and other white European populations whose whiteness-in-the-making was unstable, compared to the less contested whiteness attributed to middle- and upper-class white suburbanites in other parts of New Jersey (see Barrett and Roediger 1997; Guglielmo 2003).

The Portuguese, whose whiteness is oftentimes challenged by Brazilians who did not see them as "real Americans" (a coveted term for whiteness and sometimes, in Newark, for blacks), were still viewed as "sort-of-white" by most U.S.-born Latinos around Newark. In the Ironbound, the Portuguese have engaged in a form of ethnic-based commercial development that depended on the deployment of "Portuguese"-ness as commercial strategy, thus increasing the residents' ambivalence toward terms suggesting any form of assimilation into whiteness. The normativity of whiteness and the equation of "Americanness" and whiteness, while perhaps not as taken-for-granted as in predominantly white settings, was still sustained in Newark precisely because of the limited contact that people of color have with whites in this city (see Delgado and Stefancic 1997). This fragile Portuguese whiteness oftentimes was viewed as being destabilized by the increase influx of Latin

American "immigrants" into what was otherwise considered a solid, working-class European "enclave" throughout the early-1900s.[11] Hence, whiteness in Newark was necessarily constituted against a "phantom of blackness," a blackness present even in the immediate absence of black bodies in an area like the Ironbound, where racial "minorities" were regarded with suspicion. Moreover, I want to challenge dominant views of the Ironbound as a "stable," organic, racially- neutral space by pointing to the increasing "Latinization" of the area and the complicated role that Brazilians, as "ambivalent Latinos," play in this process.[12] In this sense, and following Toni Morrison (1993), I want to highlight "invisibility" to denote ostensible absence but actual presence when analyzing "belongingness" in the Ironbound. Because while the Ironbound has traditionally been considered a Portuguese "ethnic enclave," it is necessarily constituted in light of "the rest of Newark" despite (or precisely because) of the railroad tracks that surround it.

Embodying the Tropics: Self-Presentations, Gendered Ideologies

When Myrian Caldeira and I arrived at the small boutique where Emília Ribeiro worked in the Ironbound, Emília had already done the daily accounting, folded the clothes that customers had tried on, and was in the process of ironing out the more delicate gowns with a hand vaporizer. It was almost the end of her workday and Emília, a tall, slim, and very stylish high school senior who had arrived from Recife as a young child, seemed happy with the commission she would be getting from selling a prom dress to a classmate that day. She explained:

> Let me tell you, a Hispanish girl came to buy a dress today. And this dress had a deep cleavage and no lining. So she buys this dress…but this girl is so fat! And wearing that skimpy dress! That's something I notice with Hispanish girls, they don't see that they wear those tight dresses and the fat is going to form like little rolls hanging. Now she's going to come to our prom wearing that dress.

Myrian, who was one of the Brazilian students most interested in exploring friendships with "Hispanics," would always intervene whenever something potentially insulting was said about a Latino. This time, she focused on the irony in Emília's description of the "Hispanish" customer in the skimpy dress, "Emília, what are you talking about? Our school's very dress code was instituted because of the skimpy clothes *you* wear!" Somewhat offended that Myrian and I could not help but chuckle at the idea that this was the very person who inspired the local high school's institutionalization of a dress code, Emília retaliated [to Myrian], "But you were the one who gave me the skimpy shirts when you got into the church!" And, in a no-nonsense fashion, she added, "Plus, I come from hot weather!"

The fact that Emília knew that Myrian and I were originally from Salvador da Bahia and Puerto Rico, respectively—and thus were both from "hot weather"—suggests how Emília's own explanation for wearing revealing clothes was less an effort to distinguish herself from us and more a rearticulation of a "moral-climatic idiom"(Livingstone 1993, 139) that characterized many everyday discussions in the Ironbound. By its naturalization of racial difference according to climatic classifications, this idiom placed those of "the dark races"—in the case of the Ironbound, the Brazilians and, to a lesser extent, the other Latin Americans and Latinos—at the bottom of geography's moral terrain (see Kobayashi and Peake 2000, 399). Nevertheless, this "moral-climatic idiom" operated in tandem with an alternative scale of desire that valued images of seduction in these complex "urban erotics," which was heavily accentuated in the relationship between Brazilian and Portuguese in the Ironbound (Ramos-Zayas 2007).

Although, as will be examined in this section, this relation was articulated around a discourse of morality, it is important to situate it within a broader context of feminized and racialized employment, particularly domestic work. Like the mothers and female relatives of several other Brazilian youth whom I met in Newark, Emília's mother worked for a cleaning service whose owner, a Portuguese woman, hired mostly undocumented Brazilian (and sometimes Ecuadorian) women, and assigned them to suburban houses that were on her "list."[13] This owner would drive the women in a van to different houses throughout suburban New Jersey, where they would clean from ten to fifteen houses on a given day. Multiple layers of subordination and misrecognition conditioned the exchanges between the domestic workers and the Portuguese owner, and further accentuated the very tenuous and highly controlled relationship with the "real American" suburban homeowners. Many of these Brazilian domestic workers, including Emília's mother, worked alongside "Hispanic" women, and even the Portuguese language was frequently not a significant marker of difference, particularly since the largely English-speaking suburban homeowners oftentimes did not recognize the language difference between Spanish and Portuguese. These very linguistic misrecognitions limited the possibility for many Brazilian domestic workers to distinguish themselves from the Spanish-speaking Latina co-workers, which sometimes raise concern about being stigmatized as "Hispanic." In such work contexts, the respectability of Portuguese women transcended traditional roles of mother and wife to include their position as supervisors or bosses in employment niches where Brazilians and other South Americans tended to predominate in the bottom ranks. What remained less visible in this labor cosmology was the ways in which the Portuguese female bosses and their Brazilian employees still worked for broader systems of dominance that also implicated class and racial subordination in relation to the wealthier suburban homeowners. These levels of inequality were oftentimes articulated in gendered and racialized discourses of "morality" or a politics of "respectability" in the Ironbound (see White 2001).[14]

Almost every single comment I heard during the five years of my fieldwork period, from Brazilians and Portuguese alike, as well as the mainstream media rendition of life in the Ironbound, ultimately reduced most conflicts between the two groups as having to do with presumed gendered differences in "dress codes," "temperament," and "the weather." The narrative by a Portuguese parent-volunteer at the Ironbound's high school is somewhat typical of this:

> The Brazilians are a whole different group, even different from the Hispanics, you know. They are South Americans, but they have their own… *joie de vivre.* It's just a whole other concept that they have. I think it definitely comes from the climate, because it is so hot, so humid there. They wear appropriate dress for that type of climate except that they want to bring it over here. We're more conservative, and they come from a warm climate…or from an island, in the case of the Hispanics. Showing belly and being dressed in a certain way comes natural to

them because of the climate. It's just natural to them. But [Portuguese] parents don't understand that.

In everyday conversations, Portuguese and Brazilians were viewed as discrete and somewhat homogenous groups that were distinct from one another. The shared Portuguese language, generally presumed to be a commonality between Lusophone populations, was deployed as yet another evidence of difference.[15] More significant here, an urban erotics operated to accentuate how Brazilians were "akin to Hispanics" ("from an island" here suggests the presence of significant numbers of Dominicans and Puerto Ricans), despite the initial comment on Brazilian exceptionalism (their *joie de vivre* articulated with certain sense of irony and disapproval).[16] By virtue of their increasing presence in the formerly "Portuguese" space of the Ironbound, Brazilians appeared threatening to the Portuguese at several levels, including a threat to their racial aspirations to white privilege. Brazilians introduced behaviors and attitudes associated with U.S. working-class and poor minorities—the "loudness," "revealing clothes," and racial markedness. They also introduced the possibility of increased state surveillance because of their more visible status as "illegal." Although undocumented Portuguese residents often lived with little harassment in the Ironbound,[17] the Brazilians had begun to gain visibility in U.S. nation-state discussions of "illegality" and "deportation." In fact, Brazilians in New Jersey have been central to incidents of local nativism, as evidenced in the massive deportation raids and hostility in the town of Riverside (Queiroz Galvão 2006). And yet, there is another element to be considered in the otherwise largely negative moral assessments of Brazilians by most Portuguese residents of the Ironbound: the valorization by most U.S.-born Latinos of images of the "seductress" they associated, somewhat enviously, with Brazilian women.[18]

A half-Dominican, half-Puerto Rican resident of North Newark who was a student in the Ironbound's public high school, Susana García was one of the many U.S.-born Latina women who definitively stated: "The most attractive people in this school are the Brazilians. All the guys agree that the Brazilian girls have great bodies, that they are hot. The Portuguese are very unattractive. Some Hispanic girls have J.Lo. bodies…but the Brazilians are the ones considered very, very pretty here." More significantly, Susana explained to her friend Vivian, a Puerto Rican resident of the Ironbound, and me that she had applied for the same coveted job at the boutique where Emília worked, but that "Emília has a better look to be clerk at that store." "That's a great job," Vivian acknowledged. To these two young women, who had extensive experience working in retail, it made "perfect sense" that Emília had been the chosen candidate not only because of her personal attractiveness, but also because she was from a nationality that was globally recognized for various gradations of "exotic beauty."[19] And from early on, U.S.-born Latinas recognized the professions, such as boutique work, in which "exotic" led to employment. I also heard comments by teachers at the Ironbound high school claiming that sometimes Portuguese girls tried to "pass" for Brazilians to get the attention of some of the guys, just like some Portuguese guys were hoping to become more "desirable" by pretending to be Puerto Rican. "They would pass for Black if they could, because being a Portuguese guy is not what most women here find attractive…unless these are Portuguese women," a young teacher mentioned. I examine these issues of who is considered "desirable" according to youth evaluations of "urban competency" elsewhere (Ramos-Zayas 2007). Nevertheless, what seemed quite clear among most of the U.S.-born Latino students with whom I spoke in Newark, and which appeared more ambiguous among some Portuguese adults in the Ironbound neighborhood, was that the image of Brazilian attractiveness appeared to be recurrent among high school youth and very well-protected by many Brazilians transnationally.[20]

Among U.S.-born Latino girls like Susana and Vivian, Brazilians' ability to be seductive was partly narrated and presented as evidence of Brazilian women's affective superiority in a context in which Portuguese women held a form of respectability inaccessible to other Latina and Latin American women; among U.S.-born Latinas, Brazilians were praised for having a valued form of "sexual capital" that Portuguese women presumably lacked.[21] A component of these "urban erotics" involved sustaining the impression that one could protect oneself against racism or even alter racial discrimination not necessarily by struggling for "rights," but by "behaving oneself."[22]

Despite the evaluation of these stereotypes of the tropics and "seductiveness" as alternative forms of cultural capital among U.S.-

born Latino youth, however, many Brazilian women actively aimed to disassociate themselves from an image of hypersexuality and, more generally, of leisure that other Central and South American migrants and Portuguese Ironbound residents attributed to them.[23] For many young Brazilian women, processes of secular and religious "conversions" constituted deliberate transformations and self-refashioning that were oftentimes in tacit dialogue with a broader image of Brazilian "cultural excess" (Ramos-Zayas 2005). For instance, the cases of Myrian Caldeira, Emília's friend and a devoted member of an evangelical youth group, and of Maura Montes, a "Goth" student who had just moved from the Portuguese bilingual program into the "mainstream" curriculum at the Ironbound public high school, illuminated these "conversions."

Myrian told me that she had begun attending a local Brazilian Evangelical church as a result of a brush with the police when, at fourteen, she had been caught "attending a club" a few weeks after arriving from Belo Horizonte. She had attended the club accompanied by some of her parents' friends in an effort to fight off the onset of a severe depression she had experienced upon migrating to the U.S. I was never fully clear about how to interpret Myrian's connection to this particular club, because in another instance she mentioned that she had worked as a barmaid, "getting involved with men," just a few months after arriving in Newark; but she never connected the two incidents and I always refrained from probing what I sensed was a very sensitive topic. Myrian made several comments about having "talked about the Lord" to a group of prostitutes that circulated near the area where she lived; she gave away all her "revealing" clothes and changed some of her friends, Emília being one of the few who remained from her original friendship group. While religious converts like Myrian were usually viewed as "judgmental" and even "ashamed of their own culture"—and associations with music, dancing, and even Catholicism[24]—secular converts presented themselves as more hyperindividualistic and "assimilated."

Maura Montes viewed the transformation to Goth in light of broader expectations that she had sensed from her parents growing up in Paraná and Newark, and which required that she transform herself to conform to more traditional gender roles whenever she would go to visit her family in Brazil. Maura explained:

> I never liked to wear what other girls were wearing or to be looking all pretty, you know. I started going to the vintage stores and seeing things that I liked, whatever clothes made me feel better.... In the beginning, my mom would tell me, "You'll never find a boyfriend dressing up like that." But now she leaves me alone, except when I go to Brazil to visit family. Then she tells me, "Tone it down." I don't like to be pigeon-holed, you know. I'm my own person. [AY: Do you feel...do you identify as Brazilian or do you...?] I don't care or not if they say I'm Brazilian. It's not something that I announce [by proclaiming] "I'm Brazilian, I'm Brazilian." If someone asks me, I'd say "Sure, I am." Sometimes people try taking guesses at what I am. [They guess] Italian, German.... Nobody guesses American. They also never guess Brazilian. Because a lot of people here have this misconception about Brazilian people. They think the girls are like, I don't know, they think they are really loud and they want attention, and they wear these skimpy clothes and, you know, that they just go out with lots of guys, stuff like that. I'm not like that. And even some of the Brazilian girls here are very smart, and they have been here for a while, so they are not as in touch with the whole Brazilian thing. I also think that I'm not like that because of where my family is from. Paraná is very different from the rest of Brazil. In Paraná we even have people that are German. They still speak German in their daily lives.

Maura identified always-already gendered stereotypes of Brazilians, but she adopted a somewhat "neutral" stance in relation to a presumed Brazilian identity (unless she's directly asked, she won't state that she's Brazilian or see this as a source of pride to be articulated openly). However, because Maura had developed a kind of sensitivity to overgeneralizations, given the marginality that she had occasionally experienced by "being Goth" in the Ironbound, she immediately emphasized that neither she nor many Brazilian women fit into the stereotype (using "very smart" in contraposition to "want[ing] attention" or wearing revealing clothes). She then proceeded to rearticulate the stereotype by explaining that the stereotype does not fit a particular sub-group of Brazilians (those who "have been here for a while" and, therefore, "are not in touch with the whole Brazilian thing"). Although Maura continued to sustain the Brazilian stereotype by explaining how some people did not fit into it (and thus presumed others did), she also challenged stereotypes of the tropics at an even more fundamental level, by removing Brazil (and some Brazilians like herself) from the tropics in the first place, by introducing a Europeanized "Paraná." Brazilians of German ancestry and Brazil's regional racial variation were viewed as a stance from which to launch a critique of the stereotype of the tropics which was presumably more in line with other areas of Brazil, particularly Rio de Janeiro and Salvador da Bahia, even when most of the Brazilians in Newark hailed from the interior state of Minas Gerais. It is also interesting to note the fact that nobody ever "guess[ed] American" in their description of Maura was viewed by her as positive; she had repeatedly commented, in relation to whites, that "Americans were too bland" (see Perry 2002).

The precarious line between "playfully seductive" and "inappropriate moral conduct" always seemed to permeate discussions of Brazilian exceptionalism and difference in Newark. Critical here is the idea that one could alter other people's racist attitudes by changing one's behavior; if one behaved "decently," changed one's clothes, adapted one's "temperament," then racism and social marginality would not exist and the American dream would be possible.

Dominant Narrative: Brazilians "Stealing Men" from Portuguese Women

Infidelity, amorality, and sensual prowess were the subject of many conversations in which the Portuguese and Brazilians attempted to define themselves in contradistinction to each other, and blamed local conflict on differences in "culture" or ideology that, at times, undermined a broader political economy of exploitative work (Rabinowitz 1997).[25] What may seem a benign stereotype of the tropics, particularly in relation to Brazilians, acquired a dangerous dimension in the context of a budding sex-work industry in Newark and surrounding New Jersey areas. Domestic minority and international women were actively recruited into this industry, oftentimes through deception or coercion, by falling prey to ambiguous job descriptions, seduced by the possibility of leaving poverty, and a general persistent sense that any job—as domestic workers, hairstylist, bartender, etc.—could, at the wrong turn or if things did not work out as expected, lead to a life in sex work. One's highly exoticized nationality always had the potential to be in itself a money-generating device in a context of capital accumulation that was highly sensitive to identity politics in the U.S. (Comissão Parlamentar Mista de Inquérito 2006). Likewise, these stereotypes, while exploitative to the most vulnerable women, were magnified in the context of the Ironbound, where "Brazilian"-ness was always-already a gendered referent to "temperamental" and "moral" distinctions from the more "traditional" Portuguese women.

Narratives of real-life dramas around Brazilian women "stealing men" from Portuguese women, for instance, appeared as a common theme among many of the adults and young adults in Newark, including Marcela de Souza, one of the few people whom I met in the Ironbound who was not connected to the Ironbound public high school in some way. I met Marcela somewhat unexpectedly, when I was having lunch and writing fieldnotes at a small Brazilian bakery on Ferry Street in May of 2003. Marcela struck up a conversation with me, by asking me, in Portuguese, if I was Brazilian. Also in Portuguese, I responded that I was Puerto Rican and, as if my response were inconsequential to her own trend of consciousness, Marcela almost broke down into tears, telling me how much she missed Brazil and how cruel every Brazilian and Portuguese person she had met in Newark had been to her since she first had set foot on the Ironbound nearly six months prior.[26] I asked her if she knew anyone in the area, and her despair, frustration, and sadness became even more evident as she explained that she had known some people at a Portuguese-owned bar where she used to work:

> The owner is Portuguese, a good Portuguese man, unlike all the others here, who are so rude to you when they know you're Brazilian.... I was friends with one girl who worked there, but she was fired. She was fired because a crazy Portuguese woman got in her head that my friend was trying to steal her husband. It wasn't true, but she thought it was. She got my friend confused with someone else.

"Why did she even think that?" I asked, trying to show support with a tone that pointed to the absurdity of the thought. And Marcela explained:

> They all think we want to take their husbands, all the Portuguese women think that! So that woman began calling the bar over and over again, threatening to call Immigration to have my friend deported. And the owner of the bar got tired. He said he didn't want any problems, that he didn't want his bar to get a bad reputation. Because the woman would follow her home, and then she even showed up at the bar and made a scene and accused my friend of being a slut. My friend got so tired that she is talking about going back to Brazil.

By the time that Marcela finished talking about her friend's experience, one of the Brazilian women working behind the counter of the tiny cafeteria had joined in the conversation to validate the fact that Portuguese women were rude to Brazilian women because they felt threatened. "It is not our fault if Portuguese men like Brazilian women, but they think it is. They are very prejudiced. The other day the manicurist from [one of the beauty salons in the area] told me that she had heard a Portuguese woman saying that Brazilians were sluts because we waxed the pubic area, the Brazilian bikini. But then, this same woman wanted to know how much it cost!" The women laughed and the conversation ended on a humorous note. While humor perhaps is itself an opportunity to express an alternative version of things or "tone down" the significance of any statements made,[27] Marcela's story was indeed very complex and situated in a political economy of gendered and racialized work.

As I later learned, Marcela's story was more "autobiographical" than she initially had admitted. Marcela had been the one "pursued" by the Portuguese woman's husband, though she always maintained that she never gave in to his advances.[28] Originally from the town of Governador Valadares in Minas Gerais, Marcela was quite frank about other aspects of her life, including a brief involvement in the "entertainment" industry as an exotic dancer and sometimes "girlfriend" of the owner of a bar in Portugal, where she had met the relative of the Portuguese owner of a bar in Newark who seemed to have been instrumental in her migration to the U.S.[29] There were several conversations that suggested Marcela's involvement in sex work without explicitly labeling it that, a tendency that seems in itself very reflective of the fluid boundaries of sex work, the slippage between certain kinds of employment niches and prostitution, and distinctions between sex work as employment or even occasional or supplemental employment versus as an assumed identity (Comissão Parlamentar Mista de Inquérito 2006).[30]

All these issues partly account for the limitations of employing "sex worker" as an analytical category. And yet, it was a category central to the gendered racialization of Brazilians in Newark, especially by the Portuguese. For instance, when I mentioned that I was researching Brazilian female employment in Newark, a young Portuguese woman at the Ironbound public library immediately commented that many Brazilian women ended up "in sex work" because they liked to make "fast money." She immediately qualified the statement by noting how these women were poor, and they wanted to go back to their families in Brazil. Nevertheless, following this relatively compassionate take on Brazilian women's economic predicament, she also added: "I would rather work twenty-hour days cleaning toilets than disrespecting myself like that."[31] I never heard other Latin American migrants or U.S-born Latinos characterizing Brazilian women in any way that suggested immorality or promiscuity, which only highlighted the particularity of these characterizations to the relationship with the Portuguese (and perhaps to other South American migrants) and, likewise, the very vulnerability that led Portuguese working-class women to use these characterizations to distance themselves from the precariousness associated with their own tenuous mobility prospects and ethnicized whiteness.

The sizeable sex industry in New Jersey is concentrated in big cities and suburbs, one of those high-density locations being Newark.[32] After New York created more stringent laws regulating sex work in the 1990s, more strip bars and their clients moved to New Jersey, particularly Newark, where the laws are less stringent (Meihy 2004, 184). "Some people claim that many of the women that used to dance in New York's bars now come to Newark because New York laws are getting tougher, but in New Jersey anything goes," João Soares, a Brazilian clergy working at an Evangelical church in the Ironbound, commented to the reporter of a *Star-Ledger* article (Patterson 2000). Many Brazilian and U.S. newspaper articles alike seemed to sustain the presumed "cultural predisposition" of Brazilian women toward various forms of entertainment industry work, including sex work, and oftentimes tended to draw these characterizations in contrast to Portuguese "traditionalism" in Newark (e.g., Dines 1989, 1991; Patterson 2000).

In her ethnography of Brazilians in New York, Maxine Margolis sees go-go dancing in New York and New Jersey as a primarily Brazilian employment niche for women (1994, 166), even when most Brazilian women tended to be more likely involved in domestic or restaurant work than in any other occupation. Margolis interviewed Brazilians who described continuous sexual harassment on the part of patrons and clients, and who acknowledged the complex connections between go-go dancing, violence against women, prostitution, and drugs (Margolis 1994, 165). According to Margolis, in 1990, Brazilians constituted eighty percent of the two or three thousand "exotic" dancers in the Greater New York Metropolitan area, including New Jersey (1994, 158). The connection between Brazilian "go-go dancers" in Newark and the town of Governador Valadares in Brazil was believed to have further sparked an export business of Brazilian-made string bikinis to dancers in New York, New Jersey, Connecticut, and Massachusetts in the 1990s (Dines 1989, 89).[33] Several agencies, including some owned by Brazilians, booked mostly Brazilian go-go dancers for bars and nightclubs, while other dancers operated independently and contracted with bars alone. Throughout the 1980s and 1990s, a majority of Brazilians, particularly recent-arrivals who did not speak English, worked as dancers in Newark, Elizabeth, and other towns in New Jersey that had Portuguese-speaking clientele (see Margolis 1994, 163); in fact, for Brazilian women in Newark, the only jobs available were as domestic servants, go-go dancers, and barmaids.[34]

Whether industries around sex work are more or less exploitative than any other employment niche available to Latin American migrants or U.S.-born minority women is a difficult question to answer, particularly given the precarious and exploitative work conditions to which most Latin American migrants are subjected in the U.S. At times, emotionally complex relationships ensconced sex work.[35] More significantly, sex work in the U.S. generally relies on racist and sexist representations that are deployed to market the women according to stereotypical behaviors and illusions of "exotic" difference. As Raymond, Hughes, and Gomez found:

> Men come to expect stereotypical behavior from the women they buy in prostitution. Also, buying women from different races and nationalities gives men the illusion of experiencing the 'different' or 'exotic.' Consequently, when men write [in internet sites dedicated to booking encounters] about buying women in prostitution, they frequently mention the race and nationality of the women.... Brazilian was among the most mentioned nationalities. (2001, 41-42)[36]

A 2001 report on the trafficking of women found that: "Even remotely located establishments [in New Jersey] were filled with Russian and Ukranian women...and a significant number of Brazilian women." (2001, 35).[37] In fact, the traffic of women was generally conveyed in the media as a quasi-competitive sport in which Brazilian and Russian women were vying for the prize of becoming the most sought-after sex worker in New Jersey. For instance, in the tourist guide *City Slicker*, author Daniel Jeffreys characterizes the Ironbound, not only as "the district immortalized in the Suzanne Vega song," but also as a "Portuguese and Brazilian district [where] descendants of pirates who live here have their own system of justice and do not tolerate gangs or street crime. But a turf war has begun between Russian and Brazilian call-girls. It seems many Brazilian men prefer the blond Russians" (1994, 2).[38] Likewise, the "insatiable appetite for Brazilian go-gos" (Dines 1989, 88) appeared to have accounted for the financial success of multiple booking agencies, including some Brazilian-owned ones, in New Jersey (Dines 1989, 88).

Rather than engaging in a more extensive description of Newark's sex industry, I want to focus on how the gendered tensions between Brazilian and Portuguese were framed around interpretations of the sexual desire of Portuguese men, like the one who pursued Marcela. These men's attraction to Brazilian women was read by the objects of desire as a sign of the men's liberal, even enlightened worldview and not as part of an economically and racially skewed system.[39] The belief that Portuguese men preferred Brazilian women—whether as girlfriends, lovers, or prostitutes—also was read as evidence of Brazilian's *innate* ability to seduce, in contradistinction to views of the Portuguese women as sexually "repressed" or as "traditional," depending on the interlocutor (see Goldstein 1999). The ambiguous and at times emotionally-loaded work relationships in which Brazilian women were implicated (and whatever fantasy may exist behind them) depended on the creation of a context in which Brazilian women, and some other U.S.-born Latina women, were asked to participate in their own sexual commodification partly for the purpose of sustaining an industry premised on their "exotic"-ness, and a widespread stereotype of the tropics. Many informants explained the existence of Brazilian sex workers in Newark and New York as a result of white and black American men favoring Brazilian "mixed-race" women, not only because of their "darkness" and "natural" sensuality, but also because they were not African-American. Hence, an examination of the exoticization of Brazilian women necessitates, by its very definition, an insertion into the labor market in which such images were possible as well as the migration context that sustained various forms of exploitative work conditions for these women. The work relations that developed in strip bars were complicated and very difficult to disentangle, because they were also entangled in complicated webs of love, affect, and desire that were oftentimes inseparable from financial need, illegal status, and limited employment options.[40]

These stereotypes of the tropics in fact belonged to a citywide gendered and racialized (and racializing) landscape in which the hypersexualized image of Brazilian women is deployed in connection to presumptions of "sexual work," existed alongside views of Puerto Rican women as "unwed mothers" and of African-American women as "violent" or "lesbians in gangs" (Ramos-Zayas, forthcoming). Traditional stereotypes of Brazilian-ness were sometimes contradicted by explicit everyday evidence of widespread participation of Brazilian women (including young women) in numerous Evangelical churches and youth groups. Nevertheless, this evidence did not impede new articulations of a U.S. "Brazilian"-ness in general, and an Ironbound-based "Brazilian"-ness in particular from surfacing in Newark, a city in which urban legends existed alongside people's recollections of particular incidents of "violence," "profanity," or real-life romantic drama. Intrigue over infidelity, attraction, and sexual expressions appeared in conversations that were really about social difference, downward mobility, and racial tensions. Teasing or friendly bantering about having the power to seduce any man, and multiple stories in which Latinas were presented as objects of desire of both Portuguese and African-American men, provided the context in which many of the Brazilian and Latin women whom I met racialized their own bodies, approximating an image of the "hot sexual mulata" that is part of traditional representations of "racial democracy" in Latin America, while also flirting with sexualized images of Black women in U.S. media and pop culture (Ramos-Zayas 2007).

An extension of discussions invoking conceptions of illegality—in terms of migrating without documents as well as becoming part of an "underground" industry—could be traced to the connection that the local media and some Portuguese businessmen and public officials drew between "violence" in the Ironbound and increased Brazilian migration and the presence of people of color in the area. Brazilians occupied a position of "constitutive outsiders" (Butler 1993) to Portuguese residents in the Ironbound, who alternatively racialized them in relation to other Latino groups and as "culturally" different from these other groups.[41] In this sense, Brazilians did belong to the Ironbound's cultural commodification and commercialization in a way that other Latinos perhaps did not. Even when Brazilian women were surveilled in light of their presumed promiscuity and ambiguous connection to an underground sex-work industry that posed emotional and familial threats to traditional Portuguese sensibilities, other U.S.-born Latinos and African Americans were monitored by law enforcement officers and their very presence was criminalized. For instance, in April of 2006, the Portuguese-led Ironbound Improvement District organization hired off-duty police officers to address "student rowdiness" on Ferry Street, the main commercial artery of the neighborhood. The organization was concerned about the "large numbers of students from [the Ironbound high school] harassing shoppers, littering, and damaging property on Ferry Street as they wait to catch buses on their way home after school *to other parts of the city*" (my emphasis, "IBID hires off-duty police officers"). The emphasis on how these students "did not belong" or "did not live" in the Ironbound appeared throughout the organization's communiqué; in the Ironbound, out-of-placeness almost invariably suggested "blackness," so that the bodies criminalized on the streets, those who interrupted commercial activity and social mobility aspirations and the well-being of "the shoppers," were those of young men of color.[42]

These images of difference sustained neo-liberal views of the city and of who fit and who did not into specific urban landscapes—about which bodies were productive, able to consume, valued, decent, and legal, and also white. Gendered stereotypes of the tropics were highly adaptable and malleable, and partly sustained by the fragility of the Portuguese's working-class whiteness. For many Portuguese whom I met, the prospect of being mistaken for Brazilians presented great anxiety because Brazilians, as a group, still possessed a very ambiguous standing in the U.S. racial system.

Conclusion: "Cultures of Poverty" and Stereotypes of Affect

The stereotype of the tropics and images of the "seductress" need to be read against a background of class and racial marginality, and the specific market niches that profited from the promotion of these images. These characterizations appeared to be outside the purview of the state and the local political economy because they were explained, in everyday interactions, as "cultural" and "innate" attributes. They were naturalized and manifested as moments that seemed instantaneous and unencumbered, and which appeared isolated from a before-or-after context. The seeming detachment of narratives of difference from political economy made such constitutive moments powerful. They safeguarded the "racial projects" of a state that supplied the conditions to naturalize constructions of Brazilian "promiscuity"—and of Puerto Rican welfare "dependency" and African-American "aggressiveness"—so that discussion of poverty, racism, and sexual exploitation remained concealed behind ideas of "culture" akin to the culture of poverty arguments of the 1960s (Lewis 1967).[43] A key tenet of this process is that working-class and poor Brazilian migrants, initially ambiguous enough to perhaps avoid being considered "Hispanic," were in fact becoming racialized as such when in relation to whiteness in the U.S.

Eugénia Segato, a Portuguese teacher and long-time resident of the Ironbound, insinuated the connection between Brazilian "promiscuity" and the "teenage pregnancy" attributed to U.S.-born Latinas, thus signaling how stereotypes of the tropics were never innocent but highly charged conceptions of difference and worthiness, and key elements of U.S. racial formation. When I asked her how she thought the Portuguese community viewed Brazilians, Eugénia explained:

> Their perspective on the Brazilians is that they are very loose, they are very fast, simply because they look a certain way, which may not always be true, but.... Here we have some second-generation Portuguese.... They still maintain those traditions and even their way of raising their children. They're still very Old World. But the Brazilian girls...you know...the tank tops, and uh...They're more...uh...*liberated.* We had, I think it was two years ago, we had this Brazilian girl. She was pregnant. We have pregnant girls here [at the high school in the Ironbound], not as much as they have at Barringer [high school in North Broadway, a predominantly Puerto Rican neighborhood]. I heard Barringer had a population explosion this year over there! But this girl, she was wearing a tank top and half of her belly was showing. So I said, "No, no, we can't have this." That was the end of that. So that happens here too.

The narrative proceeded in the following way: first, Eugénia acknowledged the stereotype and questioned it a bit by distancing herself from what most people thought ("simply because [Brazilians] look a certain way," they are judged with no other evidence other than their look and looks can be deceiving). Secondly, a presumably "positive" or at least nostalgic stereotype of the Portuguese was introduced without any questioning of it (they "still maintained [Old World] traditions" and child rearing practices). Then Eugénia moved on to provide concrete "evidence" that sustained the stereotype of Brazilian women, by introducing the comment on the Brazilian student who was attending the Ironbound's public high school while pregnant. Finally, Eugénia not only reinscribed a more concrete stereotype of Brazilian women in connection to "teenage pregnancy," but rearticulated the stereotype in reference to another population more frequently associated with being "unwed mothers" (an actual phrase she had used in many instances): the female student population at Barringer High School. Critical here is that Barringer was not simply a reference to a school building, but to a space invariably marked as "Puerto Rican," the Latino group that has come to denote "Hispanic" in Newark because of their higher numbers and longevity in the area, as well as emblematic of "danger," "proximity to black," and a cautionary tale to newer migrants of assimilation "gone wrong" (see Grosfoguel 2003; DeGenova and Ramos-Zayas 2003; Ramos-Zayas 2003, 2004).

Many Portuguese teachers and some parents alike commented that Brazilian migrant youth were going to "assimilate faster into American culture" (the "liberated" enunciated as a pejorative term) than even some of the U.S.-born, second-generation Portuguese youth. "The way Brazilians dress," a common detour in most conversations with the staff, teachers, and even students of the Ironbound high school, suggested that "dress code" and "getting pregnant" appeared as not-too-distant points in a continuum. Whenever conversations about "assimilation" as both desired and feared process emerged, the assimilation of Brazilian women was described in connection to a perceived hypersexuality akin to images of promiscuity and "unwed mothering" attributed to U.S.-born women of color, particularly Puerto Rican and African-American women, in the case of Newark. Brazilians in the U.S. have been invested in preserving their racial ambiguity and national uniqueness by avoiding a categorization as "Hispanic" or even "Latino," a term they have rightly understood as referent to foreign-ness, subordination, and marginality (see Beserra 2003; Marrow 2003). In Newark's Ironbound, however, Brazilians' desire to remain racially unmarked becomes complicated by a working-class Portuguese population that both reaped some socioeconomic benefits from their whiteness, but also often viewed un-hyphenated "Americans" as morally corrupt and a potentially bad influence on the Portuguese-American generation.[44]

Just like sex work happens not in isolated contexts but within the migration and job recruitment processes, the racialization of Brazilians in Newark unfolded through images of a Brazilian female worker who was the most undesirable product of a "traditional," "tight-knit," commercially viable white "ethnic enclave." Like many Puerto Ricans and Dominicans in the area, Brazilians were on occasion described in contradistinction to other South and Central American immigrants who were considered more "family-oriented" and "hardworking," and whose labor was exploited in more "family-friendly" employment venues.

Ironically, until recently, characterizations of Brazilians as ideal Latin American migrants had been oftentimes deployed, at least in the northeastern U.S., in contradistinction to the racialization of Puerto Ricans in general and Puerto Rican women, in particular, who were viewed as "lazy," "welfare-dependent," "parasites" of the system. In Framingham, for instance, Teresa Sales (1998) cites John Stefanini's claim that in addition to contributing to the "revitalization" of Framingham's downtown with their businesses, Brazilians possessed an "entrepreneurial spirit" that Puerto Ricans lacked:

> [A] sector of the Brazilian population that is coming here consists of people with high qualifications, that I would characterized as entrepreneurial. The Puerto Rican community lives here, for instance, for two or three generations and still has not set up businesses, whether these are family businesses or companies. Already the Brazilian population, that has been here for only ten years, they have opened companies, family businesses, they are doing things, not necessarily in the same fields in which they used to work in Brazil.... I'd say they are more educated and entrepreneurial people, opening businesses, take risks, work hard. (author's translation, Sales 1998, 67-68)

While in the case of Puerto Ricans, welfare "dependency" was predictably imagined in the form of unwed mothers who were liabilities to the state; in the case of Brazilians, the recurrent images of Brazilian culture and Brazilian women implicated sexual work and prostitutes, outside conservative "family values" discourse.[45] But these images were never entirely independent of each other; rather, they were points in a continuous gender logic that considered revealing dress style as just a few steps away from sexual work or from getting pregnant as a single woman, and which, in Newark, unfolded in connection to black majority and Portuguese influence. This continuum evoked enough stereotypes to leave a market-driven neo-liberal project unaffected and reinscribe the image of the U.S. as a Land of Opportunities and a meritocracy in which those who have not succeeded by being decent and productive workers were condemned for their "laziness," welfare "dependency" or "promiscuity."

Notes

[1] Following ethnographic protocol, all names of individuals in this essay are pseudonyms.

[2] This paper is part of a broader ethnographic project that I began in 2001 in Newark, New Jersey, and, to a lesser extent, Belo Horizonte (Minas Gerais, Brazil), and Santurce (San Juan, Puerto Rico). I conducted ethnographic research among Latino and Latin American youth, parents, teachers, and community activists in the neighborhoods of north Newark and the Ironbound; in particular, I focused on Puerto Rican and Brazilian youth and how discussions of "racial democracy" and

a politics of intimacy were shaped by urban development and "safety" projects in an aspiring neoliberal city. I considered the experience of Portuguese and Portuguese-Americans to the degree that these individuals were part of the everyday life of the Puerto Rican and Brazilian youth who are at the center of my project.

3 Relevant here is Cristoffanini's discussion of how "the other" gets to be represented as ideology, so that the behaviors and inclinations highlighted by the stereotype take away any historical referent and freeze the representation impeding alternative perspectives (2003, 12). These ideological forms generally prevented discussions of "race" in light of power inequalities (Ramos-Zayas, forthcoming). A subtext of such discussions is the privileging of "ethnicity" which is usually suggestive of "cultural distinctiveness" in ways that deny the continued significance of race and the special position of "blackness" in the U.S. As other scholars have eloquently argued, when applied to non-European immigrants, such conceptions of "culture" in fact repackage "culture of poverty" discourses that perpetuate stereotypes of U.S.-born Black experiences (Pierre 2004, 142-43; cf. Bashi and McDaniel 1997).

4 A major icon of "hot sexuality" in Brazil is the mixed-race woman. Brazilian understandings of race and color are intimately connected with Brazilian representation of their own sexual history in Freyrian terms; an unequal (and oftentimes not consensual) "love affair" of white men and dark women that does not take into account the context of violence and rape (cf. Goldstein 1999, 568). For a historically situated discussion of the figure of the mulatta ("mixed-blood" woman) or the "cult of the mulatta," particularly in Brazil, see Goldstein (1999); Sheriff (2001); and Skidmore (1993 [1974]). Beserra (2006) has also argued that the stereotypes of the tropics as applied to Brazilians in the U.S. dates back to Carmen Miranda, the "lady in the tutti-frutti hat" who also served as strategic link between Gertúlio Vargas's Estado Novo and Roosevelt's Good Neighbor Policy. Examinations of the processes of exoticization of "non-Western" women have also emphasized that these are directed to reconstituting feelings of dominance, wealth, power, and masculinity to Western men, whose traditional notions of masculinity have been diminished by modern cultural expectations.

5 I am following Omi and Winant's "racialization" framework, particularly its insistence that "race" or "racial difference" not be presumed as a "natural" characteristic of identifiable groups or the "biological" outcome of ancestry. Rather, "racial difference" is actively produced, reproduced, and transformed so that the key aspect of examining conceptions of "race" is the disentanglement of the social struggles—or "racial projects"—that constitute the foundation of how such racial distinctions between groups came to be naturalized and fixed

6 In "Roth, Race, and Newark," Larry Schwartz eloquently argues that the stereotype of post-1965 Newark as a crime-ridden, burnt-out city of blacks contributes to a liberal, racist mentality about Newark as an unlivable city especially when contrasted to the "good old days" of the 1940s and 1950s Newark "golden era." This "golden era," Schwartz rightly argues, is never examined as one built on long-term, cynical exploitation, racism, and deep, pervasive political corruption. Critical here, then, is Lefebvre's assertion, with specific regard to the city and the urban sphere, that space may be "the setting of struggle," but it is not only this; it is also "the stakes of that struggle" (Lefebvre 1991[1974]: 386).

7 The Henry Kaiser Family Foundation. Pew Hispanic Center. Survey Brief: Latinos in California, New York, Florida, and New Jersey. March 2004. According to the report, twenty-one percent of South American immigrants live in New Jersey, compared to thirteen percent, respectively, in New York and Florida, the second largest states with highest concentration of South Americans. Of people who reported to be Portuguese "foreign-born" in the 2000 Census, over 37,000 lived in New Jersey, the second state with the largest Portugal-born population after California. http://www.migrationinformation.org/USFocus/ whosresults.cfm

8 See Di Leonardo (1984) for an excellent critical discussion of the problematic concept of the "ethnic enclave," particularly its reliance on "women's work" and patriarchal ideologies to sustain notions of "culture" and authenticity.

9 A detailed discussion of the forces that contributed to Brazilian migration to the U.S., in general, and to Newark, in particular, deserves more attention than I can give here and are the subject of another project. Other works offer excellent discussions of Brazilian migration to various cities in the U.S., including Boston (Fleischer 2002; Martes 2000); Framingham (Sales 1998); San Francisco (Ribeiro 1997); Los Angeles (Beserra 2004); New York (Margolis 1994; Meihy 2004); South Florida (Souza Alves and Ribeiro 2002); and Washington, DC (Botelho 2004).

10 Statistics from Mara Sidney's "Urban Slums Report: The Case of Newark, USA": Newark's unemployment of 11.4% has been double the state average; "Poverty in Newark is widespread, with

high concentrations of poor people spreading throughout much of the city. Nearly thirty percent of Newark residents are poor, as are one in three children" (Sidney 2005, 7).

[11] When I use terms like "whiteness-in-the-making," I am not necessarily suggesting the Portuguese desire to "assimilate" into an unmarked "American"-ness at the expense of letting go of a "Portuguese" ethnic identity. Rather, I am highlighting the structural factors that shape how race in a white supremacy such as the U.S. has come to be historically extended to some groups and withheld from others. See, for instance, Bashi, Vilna, and Antonio McDaniel (1997); Pierre (2004); Barrett and Roediger (1997); cf. Ramos-Zayas (2001).

[12] According to Marrow (2003), successful Americanization for Brazilians means not becoming part of a stigmatized Hispanic/Latino group. The degree to which Brazilians control their own racialization, however, is not clear. Portuguese-language and heritage are the particularities most often cited by Brazilians to distinguish themselves from "Hispanics." It is important to recall that most of the populations that have been subsumed under the "Hispanic" or "Latino" categories initially attempted to reject it—for finding the label inadequate or outright offensive (Calderon 1992; Oboler 1995), and that many second- or third-generation Latinos do not see "Spanish" language as critical in being a Latino in the U.S (e.g. Flores and Yúdice 1993). Brazilians are not an exception to the general rejection of pan-Latino categories, though it may be critical to take into account variables in terms of class, race, and geographical location (in both "home" and "host" countries) to predict the "success" of Brazilians to avoid being racialized as Latinos in the U.S. In this work, as in others (De Genova and Ramos-Zayas 2003), I view "Latino" as a *racial* category that suggests power inequalities and subordinate status; to the degree that Brazilians in Newark experienced these inequalities, there will be, I believe, a possibility for them to be racialized as "Latino" or even "Hispanic." For a more extensive discussion of the relationships between Brazilians and "Hispanics," in the largely-Portuguese area of the Ironbound, see "Between Cultural Excess and Racial Invisibility" (Ramos-Zayas, Harvard Conference, 2005). For an interesting, informal discussion among Portuguese-Americans on their relation to the "Hispanic" label, see http://www.portuguesefoundation.org/hispanic.htm. Also, see reference to the 1970s decision to exclude the Portuguese from the U.S. Census "Hispanic" category.

[13] The relationships between domestic workers and employers are entangled in webs of affect that make identifying subordinate work conditions more difficult (cf. Fleischer 2002). Domestic work is sometimes ensconced in an emotive ambiguity, particularly in instances when the workers viewed their suburban patrons in positive terms. Many Brazilian (and other Latina) women described how unexpected it had been to encounter "nice" employers; ironically, because of this, the workers tended to be more reluctant to interpret an employer's behavior as "racist," even when they described instances of betrayal, threats or false accusations. Not only are these intimate contexts inherently saturated with emotional ambivalence; they are also situated in a political economy that allows and promotes certain interpretations—particularly nation-building mythologies of "meritocracy" and the "American dream"—over others. For an excellent study of Brazilian domestic workers in the U.S., see Fleischer, Soraya Resende (2002). See also Martes (2000, 77-112); Sales (1998, 115-128); Comissão Parlamentar Mista de Inquérito (2006).

[14] The eroticization of a Latinidad in Newark also shaped the experience of U.S.-born Latinas whose desirability and attractiveness were framed, not against that of the Portuguese women (as tended to be the case among Brazilians), but against that of African-American women. A *Star-Ledger* advertisement for Lancers, a club on Ferry Street, stated: "No matter how low the temperature drops, it's always halter top weather at Lancers, a sprawling restaurant and dance hall in Newark's Ironbound district....Even during deepest, darkest January, Lancers is awash in July fashions. As soon as women were buzzed in the front door, they peeled away their winter gear, revealing spaghetti-strap tops, leggy skirts and sheer things..." Lisa Rose; *Star-Ledger*, 31 January 2003.

[15] Language in the case of Brazilians and Portuguese adopted a similar politics to those examined by De Genova and myself in the case of Mexicans and Puerto Ricans in Chicago (see De Genova and Ramos-Zayas 2003). In that case, while both groups spoke Spanish, they used the particularities of idiomatic phrases, accents, and vocabulary to accentuate difference, rather than similarity. In such a case, the one leading factor presupposing a "Latinidad"—that is, the Spanish language—in fact served as a characteristic of difference.

[16] "Temperamental" distinctions were central even in public representations that aimed to also consider potential resolution to Portuguese-Brazilian conflict. For instance, a *Star-Ledger* article stated: "It's probably a one-generation-long conflict [between the Brazilians and the Portuguese]." And then the article proceeds to explain: "...friendships bloom between the [Brazilian and Portu-

guese] children, with some Portuguese teenage girls adopting Brazilian accents to better compete for boys in both groups...[T]heir [Brazilian Portuguese] language was familiar to the Portuguese, but [the Brazilian] temperament, body language, and looks were foreign...[F]or the old-time Portuguese in Newark, Brazilians represent a world full of light, laughter, and yes, bared flesh" (Patterson 2000). The sexualization of Brazilians, and very particularly of Brazilian women, interrupts the very speculations over future "harmony" between the two groups.

17 Some articles documenting Portuguese life in the Ironbound in the 1970s, emphasized that the community never really worried about deportation, despite occasional rumors of INS search for "illegals" in the neighborhood (REF.). This "invisibility" of the Ironbound as a site of "illegality" may have changed with the increase in the number of deportation cases involving Brazilians in Newark and the nearby New Jersey town of Riverside. See, for instance, Queiroz Galvão, Vinicius. "Ameaçados, brasileiros fogem nos EUA." *Folha de São Paulo*, August 21, 2006. Increased post-9/11 nativism, including anti-Mexican/Latin American sentiment, has also increased the visibility of Brazilians as "illegal" migrants. Brazilians entering the U.S. through the Mexico-U.S. border was a relatively new phenomenon in the 1990s. Before then, Brazilians were never really considered part of the "illegal" migrant stream. But by 2004, they constituted one of the largest "Other Than Mexican" or OTM, as the Department of Homeland Security now classifies them. The "illegal" migration of Brazilians across the Mexico-U.S. border decreased significantly in 2005 as a result of "immediate deportation" laws instituted and a visa requirement for Brazilians traveling into Mexico. Nevertheless, Brazilians acquired visibility in discussions of "illegality" when George W. Bush used them as example of the "effectiveness" of his immigration policy. See Comissão Parlamentar Mista de Inquérito (Brasilia, 2006) and Margolis (2006).

18 Brazilian gay men were also ubiquitous in Newark's "gay scene," as Emanuel Anzules noted in an undergraduate Senior monograph on homosexual life in Newark (2006, 8). In his monograph, Anzules interviewed the owner of Brasilia Grill, a family restaurant in the Ironbound during the day that becomes "B Lounge," a Latino gay club at night. Also in his interviews, Anzules found that Mexican and Central American day laborers in Newark were oftentimes propositioned for sex work. "Portuguese-speaking" gay men and gay men from outside the Ironbound participated in "Rainbow Night." Promotional advertisement cards were distributed throughout the neighborhood.

19 Although attractiveness hierarchies were generally contextual and somewhat fluid, specifically telling of this hierarchy was that white was not automatically equated with beauty or black with unattractiveness. Instead, a reconfiguration of an "erotic racial democracy" (cf. Goldstein), in which mixture was positively valued as long as the mixture was evident and identifiable in a way that dark-skinned Latinos could be separated from African-Americans (considered un-mixed) or light-skinned Latinos could be distinguished from American whites (considered bland) emerged. The African-Americans and the Portuguese, the two discrete "groups" viewed as standing at the margins of Latinidad in Newark, were oftentimes viewed as outside of this mixture because they were "pure" in what they were—black and white, respectively.

20 When *The New York Times* published a photograph of three "overweight" women on the beach in Ipanema to illustrate a report on the rise of obesity in Brazil, numerous postings appeared on an online Brazilian site in the U.S criticizing the article. The ultimate vindication happened when it was later discovered that the women in the photographs were not even Brazilian, but Czech tourists visiting Rio de Janeiro. When I mentioned the article to Paula, a Brazilian student at the Ironbound high school, she had heard about the incident through a TV Globo news magazine show. Paula's father, an outgoing and boisterous man, overheard us talking and said: "I have never seen as many fat people as in the U.S. Here everybody's so fat! E o *New York Times* para limpar a bunda!"

21 The view here is that Brazilian women who, in other contexts, were considered subordinate to Portuguese power, deployed an alternative, Lacanian form of (sexual) power that was defined not by domination but by the "manipulation of the dominant" (Lacan 1997; see Hartman 1999, 123). Lacanian perspectives make desire the central premise upon which understanding is based; it is what drives people's attempts to make meaning and is the essence of interpretation. In these instances, some individuals were turned into the object of desire, a strategy that somewhat compromised the possibility of experiencing the individual's subjectivity (cf. Murray 1999, 169). These instances are also a reminder of how narratives of desire are culturally constituted means through which the desire for a publically complete image of personhood may be achieved, but which also implies a sense of incompleteness or of something being lacking (see Fuery 1995, 8). Another key issue here is what Costa Vargas (2004, 443) has called the "hyper consciousness of race" and "racial negation," two concepts that operated in tandem. Race, in its negation, suggests that it lacks value as an analytically and

morally valid tool; it's presumed not to play a central role in determining or explaining subordinate status. Hence, a system seemingly devoid of racial awareness is in reality deeply immersed in racialized understandings of the social world.

[22] The racial composition of Newark neighborhoods influenced notions of attractiveness and desirability and produced "economies of desire" (Hennessy 2000) in ways that reproduced neoliberal versions of "racial democracy" among Latinos and Latin American migrant youth. A more thorough discussion is the subject of another project and beyond the scope of this essay (Ramos-Zayas, forthcoming).

[23] Pertinent here is Botelho's discussion of how Brazil and Brazilians have also been associated with images of "leisure," while Brazilian migrants in the U.S. aim to challenge these images by insisting on an identity as "hardworking" individuals (2006).

[24] For an interesting underside to youth religious conversions, see Armario's (2004) discussions of how young Latinas in Union City, NJ, explained a positive by-product of their conversions to Islam to be the respect they gained from men in the streets when they wore the veil. They avoided undesired whistling and felt less pressured to subscribe to fashion trends that favored revealing or provocative clothes (Armario 2004 in Christian Science Monitor). In the case of Brazilian women in Newark, I heard a few conversations in which "converts" judged "non-converts" for wearing revealing clothes and "non-converts" held on to the cultural "authenticity" of being Catholic (even in the case of non-practicing Catholics) over Evangelical. See also Beserra (2003, 79-116); Botelho (2004); and Martes (1999, 113-149).

[25] I do not want to overdetermine the tensions between Portuguese and Brazilians. Obviously, relationships were complicated and just as there were instances of great antagonism, there were also instances of cooperation. Many of the Brazilians with whom I spoke could cite having a Portuguese friend or were grateful to a Portuguese employer or landlord for helping them in a particular moment of vulnerability. Also, the fact that people use ideologies in surreptitious ways does not necessarily reveal how they really view them or to what extent they actually subscribed to them. Rather, my intention is to emphasize how the "ideologization of local conflict" (Rabinowitz 1997, 62) reflected a Portuguese knowledge about "Brazilian"-ness as a cultural form that developed ideologically, how new meanings and values were continually being created between historically dominant and subordinate groups, and how these values were always-already gendered (cf. Williams 1977).

[26] There was a sense that people "changed" with migration. I heard frequent comments on how Brazilians did not "get along" or help each other in the U.S. as much as other groups did, or as much as the Portuguese helped their own. To avoid glorified images of "community," it is important to recall Sarah Mahler's study of tensions within immigrant "communities" and her suggestion that we understand these communities not as folkloric entities of mutual assistance alone, but also as spaces oftentimes defined by competition, envy, debt, etc.

[27] Farr (1994) and Limón (1982), among others, have also examined "joking" as a verbal play capable of social inversion and anti-structural processes; this literature has emphasized the creative and performative power of such verbal play, while arguing for the transformative power of language. The jokes that Portuguese and Brazilians had of each other merit attention, but is beyond the scope of this essay.

[28] I want to emphasize the political economy of sexual work in this particular case not because I ever had concrete evidence that Marcela was involved in sex work in the most conventional sense of prostitution, though that may have been the case, but because she had arrived in the U.S. with the promise of work at a bar in which her gendered and sexualized Brazilian-ness was a prerequisite. These relationships (and whatever fantasy may exist behind them) provided a context in which Brazilian women, and many other U.S.-born Latina women, participated in their own sexual commodification (cf. Beserra 2006). Beserra (2006) found that some of the Brazilian women she interviewed in Los Angeles believed that the erotic stereotype they encountered in the U.S. "retain[ed] their movement, promotes the idea of prostitution, and have, consequently, a negative impact,..." while other interviewees argued that the image was "advantageously ambiguous" and allowed a space to distance themselves from groups that were even more stigmatized, especially Mexicans. This resonates with Foucault's claim that "we must not think that by saying yes to sex, one says no to power" (1990, 157).

[29] The increase in Brazilian sex workers in Portugal was reported in an article titled "When The Meninas Came to Town: Bragança was just an ancient, remote Portuguese outpost. Then the Brazilian prostitutes moved in—and the wives started fighting back" (October 12, 2003). In Bragança, a remote mountain town in northeast Portugal, some 300 *meninas brasileiras* began to arrive

in droves. Bragança's *meninas brasileiras*, or Brazilian girls, are part of the estimated $50 billion global sex trade that profits from the hundreds of thousands of women transported across national borders by human traffickers—often through coercion, sometimes willingly—to be sold or rented on the other side. To explain the hold these Brazilian women have over their husbands, the Portuguese wives tell themselves stories, accusing the prostitutes of using drugs and even witchcraft to seduce the men. In May, a group of Portuguese wives drew up a manifesto and brought their grievances to the mayor and the police chief, calling for a "war on prostitution." Some advocates argue that even when the women view sex work as an "option," this option more often than not is guided by economic desperation, thus making sex work jobs inherently coercive. The *meninas* made themselves more noticeable in Bragança by sticking together and wearing sexier clothing than the traditional Portuguese women. Forcing or tricking women into prostitution is illegal, as is "pimping," or facilitating prostitution. But these are hard crimes to prove. Any arrests that do get made usually stem from the women's immigration violations.

30 According to Kempadoo: "What the research shows is that coercion, extortion, physical violence, fraud, and detention take place within migratory processes or the employment recruitment process, and/or in places of employment in the receiving destination. Contemporary forms of forced work in the sex industry, that include aspects of consent and act in defense of the worker, are validated by research that document the active participation of the victims in migration across borders... What these women oftentimes do no know, or sometimes tacitly accept, are the dangers of the underground routes that they have to use to cross the border, the financial costs, the living conditions, etc." (in Comissão Parlamentar Mista de Inquérito da Emigração 2006, 329). Oliveira Silva (2005) also showed that there were as many sex workers involved in human trafficking as there were domestic workers in 2000. See also Leal (2002).

31 Several of the Portuguese women whom I met had worked as domestic employees, either individually or through cleaning agencies. This is an area of research that deserves great attention, as it could illuminate the economic vulnerability and social mobility prospects of working-class ethnic European women in the U.S.

32 East Brunswick, Red Bank, and Rockaway Township—towns that are close to Newark—were also reported to be high-density areas, but these were viewed as less appealing for non-English speaking women than Newark was. One police official reported that New Jersey has more go-go bars (strip clubs) than any other state in the country, as well as more "discrete" massage parlors or health clubs; and thousands of residences and other locations that house prostitution venues, including some hair and nail salons that were used as front businesses for brothels. Most sex establishments in New Jersey neither advertise nor display neon signs to draw attention to what they offer. See Raymond, Hughes, and Gomez (2001).

33 A 1991 article on go-go dancers in Newark noted a decline in earnings from tips which, in turn, urged former dancers to enter the bikini-import business while others sew go-go outfits to be sold for $100 a piece. "Lana, 'Go-go' em Newark, Queria Falar Inglês." *Folha de São Paulo,* June 10, p. D3.

34 Margolis dates the presence of Brazilian *dançarinas* in New York back to The Metropole, a go-go bar near Times Square that seemed to employ many Brazilian women from Minas Gerais in the mid-1970s. These women might have initially arrived in the U.S. to work as domestics but later learned through word of mouth that they could earn significantly more in the club business (1994, 158-59). See also Dines (1991).

35 In *Brasil Fora de Si: Experiências de brasileiros em Nova York* (2004), José Bom Meihy introduces the life history of a Brazilian woman from Belo Horizonte who falls in love with an American and moves with him to Elizabeth, NJ, a town adjacent to Newark. Once in the U.S., the American man kept her passport and induced her into prostitution by insisting that she sleep with his own friends. Eventually, the woman escaped the situation and decided to look for work at a bar in Queens (Meihy 2004, 202). The challenge here is to read such a situation in the context of structural exploitation while still recognizing subjectivity and agency. Meihy does not ask the woman more specifically about the decision to move to the U.S., and the degree to which other aspects may have informed the more immediate explanation of "falling in love" with an American man. Nevertheless, what is known is the widespread sexual trafficking in which Brazilians, along with other women from "Third World" countries, have been implicated. A 2006 report of the Parliamentary Commission on Emigration of the Brazilian National Congress, human trafficking generates close to $9 billion annually, with the most vulnerable groups being women who are "illegal" migrants, subjected to sexual exploitation and new forms of slavery (324). As Kamala Kempadoo argues, while one must consider

patriarchy in evaluations of the subordination of "Third World" women, this is not an absolute form of domination. Rather, this form of human trafficking is derived from capitalist, patriarchal, and racialized state relations, combined with the women's own desire to search for survival (Comissão Parlamentar Mista de Inquérito da Emigração 2006, 324).

[36] Many of the male customers' Internet writing examined by Raymond, Hughes, and Gomez (2001) mentioned the lack of English-language proficiency and recent-arrival status of the sex workers, and the most frequently mentioned racial identity in the New York and New Jersey area was "Hispanic/Latina" (32 percent). A greater number of South American women were noted in New York sex markets (2001, 42).

[37] According to law enforcement and social service providers, some venues were owned by prominent, local community members, while others are owned by Russian businessmen, including some who are considered member of organized crime networks (Raymond, Hughes, and Gomez, 2001, 35-36).

[38] Some of the popular and academic discussions about Brazilian sexual workers in Newark have focused on the competition between Brazilian and Russian strippers. An article titled "Brazilian Women Lose Their Place Among Strippers in the U.S.," which states that Brazilian dancers who had already made a name for themselves at night clubs were being "displaced by Eastern European blondes," appeared in the leading newspaper in São Paulo in 1999. Drawing from the research of José Carlos Meihy, an historian at the Universidade de São Paulo, the article examines how Brazilian female strippers and go-go dancers are being displaced by women from Eastern Europe, usually generically referred to as "Russians." The two main reasons given for this change in the world of sexual work were that "the average American" has come to devalue darker-skin strippers in favor of "Russians," and that the most successful strippers work under the auspices of an organization, not independently. In this sense, the women from Eastern Europe, who are blonde and who are supported by local organized crime have an advantage over Brazilian women: "The Brazilian women who would test their luck as independent strippers end up in serious situations with terrible consequences…Many of them end up in networks of prostitution, pornography, forced to take an uncontrollable path of drugs and alcohol, in an international crime circuit that uses dancing as the façade" (Meihy 2004, 176). See also Antunes de Oliveira (1999).

[39] The concept of "ethnosexual frontiers" is also pertinent here to describe how the race and ethnicity of sexual and romantic partners, though oftentimes quite actively inspected, are frequently transgressed and sometimes conspire with "heteronormative ethnosexual stereotypes" (Nagel 2000, 113). The transgressed "frontiers" of race and ethnicity in romantic partners also leads to a great deal of attention paid to the sexual demeanor of group members (by outsiders and insiders) in inspection and enforcement of both formal and informal rules of sexual conduct.

[40] Maxine Margolis noted that Brazilian *dançarinas* in New York were likely to tell relatives back in Brazil that they were employed as babysitters, housekeepers, barmaids, or waitresses (1994, 157), particularly if they were originally from the most "conservative" and "traditional" areas of Minas Gerais. Some of these *dançarinas* even lied to their Brazilian friends in New York about their profession, Margolis found, even though some of the Brazilians expressed suspicion about specific people working as "exotic dancers" (157-58).

[41] Butler used the idea of a "constitutive outside" in reference to the normative matrix that only functions in relation to abject others, those individuals who do not fit into the matrix. The "inside" is constituted only in relation to this outside, and the outsider can only be spoken about in terms of the process that led to their exclusion.

[42] Images of the Ironbound as a quaint ethnic enclave have been recently challenged by an increased incidence of crime in the area. However, the Portuguese residents still remain safeguarded from criminalization as local Portuguese authorities have generally attributed the increased crime rates to "people from the outside," particularly Black and Latino youth presumed to be "from other areas" of Newark or even to the increased migration of Brazilians. The housing projects at the outskirts of the Ironbound, where most African-Americans lived, were usually erased in narratives of commercial viability and "cultural richness" (cf. McCracken 1988). See "IBID Hires Off-Duty Police Officers to Address Student Rowdiness on Ferry Street" [April 6, 2006] In www.goironbound.com. See also Patterson (2000).

[43] I am using "culture of poverty" in reference to a set of sociopathological behaviors that have been historically attributed to racialized and colonial subjects to justify their subordination. In a variety of modalities, "culture of poverty" arguments have explained enduring poverty among some U.S. minority groups in terms of an inadequate "culture" while undermining structural and histori-

cal factors that contribute to creating "winners" and "losers" in societies organized around capital accumulation.

[44] I want to thank Kim Holton for urging me to problematize the concept of "Americanization" in relation to the Portuguese in Newark, and noting that Portuguese-American generations experienced great ambivalence toward considering themselves "American" (and, in fact, at times thought of themselves more akin to "Hispanics" or "Latinos").

[45] Teresa Sales (1998) notes that in Framingham, Massachusetts, Brazilians acknowledged that they preferred to remain distant from "os hispânicos," particularly Puerto Ricans, whom they stereotyped as individuals who did not work, lived off the U.S. welfare system, and were drug dealers (1998, 184-185). Like Brazilians in other Northeastern cities, including Danbury, CT and Boston, MA, Framingham Brazilians lived in neighborhoods of high Latino, particularly Puerto Rican, concentration (Sales 1998, 49-50, 61). In the case of Framingham, Brazilians are credited with having revitalized the commercial areas, and eliminated drug trafficking and prostitution from the deteriorated downtown (Sales 1998, 65). Images of Brazilians as "model migrants" prevailed around Brazilians well into the 1990s in Framingham (e.g. *The Boston Globe,* December 11, 1994). In October of 2005, Júlio César Gomes dos Santos, the Brazilian consul in New York, encouraged the Brazilian community in Danbury, CT, not to develop affiliations with the "Latinos," whom he called "cucarachos" (cockroaches) (Suwwan 2005).

CHAPTER 18

Contested Identities: Narratives of Race and Ethnicity in the Cape Verdean Diaspora[1]

GINA SÁNCHEZ GIBAU

Though the categories employed in the Census have changed intermittently throughout the years, the federal government is still motivated by economic and political factors to officially classify its citizens, legal residents, and undocumented occupants in racial and ethnic terms. In so doing, the Census homogenizes cultural groups into distinct racial and ethnic categories for statistical purposes. Whites, Blacks, Latinos, Asians, and Native Americans are counted, seemingly devoid of internal group diversity of culture, class, language, and national origin. Such categories are generally not perceived as the social constructs that they are; rather, as immutable indicators of human nature and behavior. This type of group essentializing is often met with resistance by people who relocate to the United States. Immigrants of African ancestry in particular are faced with the prospect of "racialization," defined by Michael Omi and Howard Winant as the process whereby racial meaning is imputed onto "a previously racially unclassified relationship, social practice or group" (Omi and Winant 1986, 64). For people migrating from countries as diverse as Nigeria, Barbados or Brazil, for example, racialization dictates their reassignment as "Black immigrants" and thus members of the larger African-American community in the United States.

This article focuses on Cape Verdean[2] immigrants living in the United States who represent one African diasporic population facing this dilemma of negotiating identity within a racialized society. With a small but significant historical role in the triangular slave trade, Cape Verde's legacy of colonization and slavery produced a population that today is approximately seventy-three percent "mixed" or mulatto. Since Cape Verdeans are primarily of mixed African and Portuguese ancestry,[3] they range in skin tone and phenotype—from light complexion with curly blond hair to dark complexion with straight black hair, and every variant in between. As a case study, this article explores the identity politics of Cape Verdeans living in Boston, Massachusetts, in particular, and the dialectical relationship between the processes of racial ascription and self-identification in the formation of individual and collective identities among this particular group.

The term "diaspora" is used throughout in my descriptions of the Boston Cape Verdean community. Diaspora studies have flourished into a burgeoning specialization within the social sciences. More recent studies have attempted to redefine the concept of diaspora as a "process" through which individuals and groups forge new, shifting identities out of multiple loyalties to various "home" and "host" locales. This trend in diaspora studies allows the inclusion of contemporary relocations of migrant workers, immigrants, refugees, and exiles as subjects of study. A major factor impacting this reconceptualization of diaspora, I argue, is the way in which diasporic populations are redefining themselves.

This article suggests that Cape Verdeans in Boston, both immigrant and United States-born, tend to negotiate their identities by situating themselves within both African and Cape Verdean diaspora communities (Sánchez 1998). This type of dual diasporic identity construction is observable in a range of experiences that embody the historical memory, cultural practice, politics, and everyday life lived by Cape Verdeans in the context of the United States. Cape Verdean diasporic identity formation incorporates the way Cape Verdeans are defined by state mechanisms (e.g., the Census), the way they are perceived by others, and the way they self-identify. This type of identity management entails the reconciliation of one's cultural identity with one's socially ascribed, racialized minority status. The conclusions that I draw concerning the Cape Verdean community of Boston, Massachusetts are not intended to be generalized to the entire Cape Verdean diaspora in the United States. Rather, my intent is to provide a window onto the lifeways of an internally diverse diasporic population.

From Whence They Came

July 5th, 2005 marked the thirtieth anniversary of independence from Portugal for the Republic of Cape Verde,[4] a ten-island nation approximately

350 miles west of Senegal. Cape Verdeans have been migrating from the Cape Verde Islands since the mid-18th century, first as crew members for the whaling industry and later as settlers and economic migrants escaping the ravages of poverty, drought, and famine. Despite this fact, many social scientists and the general public alike have never heard of nor have encountered Cape Verdeans. Since they are concentrated primarily within the southeastern New England area, Cape Verdeans have been rendered socially invisible (Arthur 2000; Bryce-Laporte 1972), relatively unknown to people living outside of this geographical area.

The Cape Verde Islands were discovered as uninhabited by the Portuguese during the mid-15th century and colonized soon afterward.[5] Extensive work conducted by Cape Verdean historian António Carreira (Carreira 1972; 1982) and most recently anthropologist Richard Lobban (Lobban 1995) reveals that Cape Verde, like other Portuguese colonies, endured an era of African enslavement, a legacy of "racial" and cultural miscegenation, an extended period of colonial neglect, and a struggle for independence. Out of this sociopolitical history came an island population that today is estimated at 450,000. The World Bank further estimates this number to reach 777,000 by the year 2030. Currently, there are more than 800,000 Cape Verdeans living abroad, with an emigration rate of approximately 2,000 per year.[6]

It would be easy to point to Portuguese colonization as the foundation of cultural differentiation in Cape Verde. After all, it produced a subsequent population that was ranked on a continuum of color and class. Yet, the effects of colonization were not widespread. The island of Santiago, in particular, witnessed the largest influx of enslaved Africans, some of whom were then transported to the New World while others remained, eventually escaping to inland areas. Contemporarily, this historical legacy is understood through popular discourse that constructs Santiago as the most "African" of all the islands. Conversely, Cape Verde's role in the whaling industry during the 18th and 19th centuries has led to the idea of Brava being the island that experienced the most European influence, with the ongoing contact of American seafarers.

The United States and Cape Verde have maintained strong historical ties from as early as the 19th century, when in 1816 an American consulate was established in Cape Verde (U.S. Department of State 2005). The Cape Verdean diaspora community of the United States first emerged as a byproduct of 19th- and 20th-century whaling expeditions. The so-called "Yankee whalers" of the East Coast acquired cheap labor from Cape Verde as well as from other Atlantic Islands, such as Madeira and the Azores. These crewmen would form the bases of settlement communities that emerged principally in the cities of New Bedford, Massachusetts, and East Providence, Rhode Island. Similar to other immigrant groups, Cape Verdean immigrants were first males, who—after years in the whaling industry and in other industries, such as fishing, textiles, and agriculture—eventually secured the economic means to transport their wives and other family members to the United States.

For those Cape Verdean migrants journeying to the United States, the promise of economic prosperity served as a stimulus for those seeking to escape the poverty and environmental severity of the islands. In addition to those entering into the United States, Cape Verdeans migrated to Portugal, Senegal, Brazil, Argentina, Holland, Sweden, and France. Others were forced to work on the coffee plantations of São Tomé and Príncipe, Angola, and Guinea-Bissau. These individuals were either kidnapped or tricked into what they thought were contractual labor agreements. Most left the islands never to see their families again (Foy 1988, 15; Silva 1993, 28).

In the United States, as they progressed "from immigrants to ethnics" (Portes and Rumbaut 1990) and became "Cape Verdean-Americans," early immigrants and the generations that followed faced the dilemma of maintaining their cultural practices within a society that advocated their abandonment in favor of assimilation. With succeeding generations came the opportunity for education and social mobility. The children and grandchildren of Cape Verdean immigrants attended public schools and acquired more education than their parents and grandparents who worked on cranberry bogs and in textile factories for less than minimum wage. These first- and second-generation Cape Verdean-Americans learned English and were encouraged to do so by their relatives. As a result, *Kriolu*[7] became transformed into a language of the elders, spoken only between parents and grandparents. Today, there exist multiple generations of Cape Verdean-Americans, particularly those born during the 1940s and afterward, who do not speak *Kriolu.* In addition, there are many more who do not know how to cook the traditional foods, nor do they listen to traditional Cape Verdean music.

Compounded by the ideology of assimilation during early settlement, early Cape Verdean immigrants also encountered an environment fraught with xenophobia and racial discrimination. Since the Cape Verde Islands were internationally recognized as part of the Portuguese colonial empire from the time of its settlement until its independence in 1975, Cape Verdean immigrants entering the United States and other countries during the 19th and 20th centuries did so with Portuguese passports or similar forms of documentation. Cape Verdeans in turn appropriated the label "Portuguese" to signify their status as Portuguese nationals under colonialism. Yet Cape Verdeans appropriated this label not only to indicate nationality, but also to distance themselves socially and culturally from the established African-American community of New England. This was done primarily to escape the stigmatization and racism waged against African-Americans, a group sharing with them similar skin tones and phenotypes. Cape Verdeans also enacted this distancing by establishing enclave communities and by publicly representing themselves as culturally distinct on the basis of language (*Kriolu*), religion (Catholicism), and other cultural practices (Halter 1993, 147). This early strategy of distancing has created deep-seated animosity between the two diasporic groups, with mutual misunderstanding continuing into the present.

Despite their efforts, Cape Verdean-Americans became aware of the "fact of blackness" (Fanon 1990), most acutely with the onset of Jim Crow legislation and during the World Wars as they ventured outside of their protective enclaves and into segregated realms of society, such as the military (Halter 1993, 163). Thereafter, during the sixties and seventies, Cape Verdean-Americans experienced the transformative effects of the Black Power and African Liberation movements. The evidence of politicized identities abounded as Cape Verdean-Americans began sporting Afros and participating in these movements. A new breed of Cape Verdean-American arose, one that identified as Cape Verdean and/or Black and not as Portuguese. For them and for other people of African descent living in the United States, these decades proved to be a watershed for the development of diasporic blackness.

With the establishment of the Republic of Cape Verde in 1975 came a new wave of immigration, one that has continued into the present. Whole communities emerged in the cities of Providence, Pawtucket, Brockton, New Bedford, and Boston that were qualitatively different from the earlier generations of Cape Verdeans living in these locales. The generations that followed were raised with the pride of having a distinct Cape Verdean heritage that took precedence over colonial schemes that had privileged Portuguese culture in the past. Previously suppressed cultural forms, such as music, dance, and language, were soon expressed for local and international consumption. This revitalized sense of Cape Verdean-ness was felt on both sides of the Atlantic and continues to feed the contemporary definitions of Cape Verdean diasporic identity.

The Cape Verdean diaspora of today is immensely complex in composition. It is marked by differences associated with generation, migration history, language, culture, and social-class status. Many Cape Verdeans coming to Boston acquire a job and spend their adult working years in the United States, with the intent of returning to the islands with their earnings upon retirement. Unlike the older Cape Verdean-American population, newer Cape Verdean communities, like the one in Boston, are characterized by residential and commercial enclaves and infrastructure that supports (albeit minimally) a bilingual clientele (Teixeira 1996, 21). Most importantly, they are very passionate in identifying themselves as Cape Verdean. "Cape Verdean" is understood as being based in language, cultural practice, and ties to the homeland. In fact, contemporary Cape Verdean immigrants often lay claim to cultural authenticity given their more recent and steady departure from the islands.

Boston Cape Verdeans

Most of the literature on the Cape Verdean diaspora in the United States has focused on the historic communities of southeastern New England, especially New Bedford, Massachusetts, and Providence, Rhode Island. I chose to focus my study in Boston because I felt it has received little attention despite its receipt of a significant number of Cape Verdean immigrants during the 1980s. Similar studies are warranted for Brockton, Massachusetts and Pawtucket, Rhode Island, two areas that have witnessed similar population increases in the last two decades.

I decided to conduct ethnographic research among Cape Verdeans living in the Roxbury and Dorchester neighborhoods of Boston specifically because these were the two areas which housed the greatest number of Cape Verdeans. Urban space is racialized in Boston, a historically and notoriously segregated city. Between 1940 and 1960, African-Americans from the South migrated north to Roxbury and Dorchester looking for work and to buy homes. By the mid-1960s, Roxbury and Dorchester were predominantly black neighborhoods, abandoned in the flurry of "white flight" by its previous Jewish and Irish residents who had moved into the suburbs of Randolph, Canton, and Newton. During the late 1960s into the 1970s, several banks in Boston established the Boston Bank Urban Renewal Group (BBURG) area in the wake of Martin Luther King, Jr.'s assassination, which served as a means to quell social unrest by helping African-Americans secure affordable housing. Cape Verdean immigrants to the area, at that time, were able to buy multi-family homes on the heels of the BBURG initiative.

Cape Verdeans in Boston are concentrated in predominantly black neighborhoods, which extend as a corridor from the South End, southward through Dorchester and Roxbury, and into Mattapan and Hyde Park. According to the Boston Redevelopment Authority (2002), Dorchester, a Boston neighborhood with about 92,000 residents (divided into North and South Dorchester), houses a racially, ethnically, and socially diverse population, with African-Americans representing the largest percentage (thirty-six percent) of the total population. Also noteworthy are Dorchester's "large pockets" of first-generation immigrants, including Cape Verdeans, Vietnamese, Haitians, and Dominicans. Dorchester and Roxbury are racialized as minority areas that enjoy a dubious reputation for crime and violence. Of course, as with all racialized spaces, however, there exist so-called "good" and "bad" parts, and residents comply with this discourse on an everyday basis in their circulation through and avoidance of such areas (De Genova and Ramos-Zayas 2003).

As Logan and Molotch note, "constraints on mobility contradict urban migration models that presume individuals can freely pick and choose the places [to live] that best serve their needs" (Logan and Molotch 1987, 41). The most critical of these constraints is the need to find a place to live where one can find work. Living near family and friends is also vital to sociocultural adjustment. The Boston Cape Verdean diaspora community is concentrated in a number of residential enclaves within Roxbury and Dorchester, each with its own distinct flavor. In the "Main

Street"[8] area of Dorchester, there are several Cape Verdean-owned businesses: a furniture store, hair salon, record store, and bakery. This same area is marked by the presence of a large health clinic whose clientele is largely Cape Verdean, as is evident in the number of *Kriolu*-speaking health practitioners on staff (at least one doctor, two nurses, one counselor, and numerous administrative staff). Main Street also has a regular flea market/yard sale that takes place in front of a local church and is frequented by Cape Verdeans and Latinos in the area.

Perpendicular to Main Street is Leland Avenue, which enters into Roxbury. This neighborhood, one of the poorest in Boston, houses a diverse population of approximately 24,000 including African-Americans (thirty-seven percent), Latinos (twenty-nine percent), Cape Verdeans (twenty-five percent), and Whites (seven percent) (Leonard 1999).This street is very popular and boasts the largest concentrated area of Cape Verdeans, with numerous residents living on side streets off the main thoroughfare. On this street there are Cape Verdean-owned grocery stores, sandwich shops, and a travel agency. Leland Avenue is also the street on which St. John's Church stands, a prominent marker in the community that beckons to hundreds of Cape Verdeans every Sunday for the Catholic mass that is performed in both Portuguese and *Kriolu*.[9] During the Boston school desegregation struggle (1974–1975), Cape Verdean and Haitian parents met at this church to organize ways of supporting their children (Almeida 1997).

Another well-known area is Haverly Road. This area also houses a local health clinic as well as various clothing shops, grocery stores, a Catholic church, insurance companies, hair salons, a travel agency, and now a popular Cape Verdean restaurant. On any given day on Haverly Road, one can see several Cape Verdeans speaking to each other on the corners, sitting outside doing their hair, crossing the streets with their children, riding by in cars blasting the latest contemporary *Kriolu* music, and shouting to each other in *Kriolu* from across the street. With the existence of ethnic businesses within the areas heavily populated by Cape Verdeans, it is possible that a person who has emigrated from Cape Verde in the last year could go an entire day without ever hearing English. This, of course, is not to say that they wouldn't encounter English, be it from their children and grandchildren, the local TV, or an occasional anthropologist. For the purposes of my research, I chose to live in an area on the south side of Haverly Road. This area was once predominantly a Jewish community, but is now home to African-Americans, Haitians, Jamaicans, Cape Verdeans, Puerto Ricans, and Southeast Asians. Many residents are those who bought the old Victorian homes and converted them into multi-family dwellings.

Michel Laguerre notes in his study of the Haitian diaspora of New York City that "diasporic culture has a material basis of support, and the business is one aspect of that infrastructure in the sustenance of the transnational identity of some immigrants" (Laguerre 1998, 112). Similarly, Cape Verdeans have made their presence felt through their entrepreneurial activity and, with the advent of ethnic entrepreneurs, "local business and social life become intertwined in a single support system" (Logan and Molotch 1987, 108). Yet, Cape Verdeans in Boston are situated at the margins of the state's economy. The businesses they own are located solely within a concentrated area of their neighborhoods. The community also suffers from a general lack of social services available to assist them in their everyday lives. There are few Cape Verdean doctors, lawyers, health practitioners, and other professionals providing social and emotional support to community members. Furthermore, the majority of Cape Verdeans in Boston are concentrated within labor, service, clerical, and lower-skilled occupations.

Logan and Molotch (1987, 107) contend that "a neighborhood provides its residents with an important source of identity, both for themselves and for others" (see also Williams 1988). Since Cape Verdeans reside primarily in the neighborhoods that are predominantly Black and Latino populated, they construct their identities in relation to how their neighbors perceive them as well as how they wish to be distinguishable from these neighbors. Whether born in the United States or in the islands, Cape Verdeans in Boston tend to formulate their identities in relationship to the people with whom they live in close proximity. The narrative examples to follow provide insight into the processes through which Cape Verdeans forge and negotiate diasporic identities in contradistinction to other racially defined groups that comprise their neighborhoods. In the midst of this identity management, the label "Cape Verdean" is appropriated, utilized, and disputed.

The construction and negotiation of identities is a process, subject to intensive legitimization and authentication. Some aspects of one's identity may prove more salient at times than others. Other aspects, which may be considered more obvious, may fail to form the basis of one's identity and of group solidarity (Appiah 1992; Gupta and Ferguson 1997, 14). Given these facts, the process of defining oneself within the sociocultural context of the United States is not an easy endeavor. I have been most interested in the self-identification practices of Cape Verdeans and how they "identify their identifications," what Eriksen (2001, 45) calls "reflexive identity politics." People of Cape Verdean descent have used various labels to identify themselves since their initial settlement in the United States. Cape Verdeans in Boston, as an African diasporic community, actively challenge the United States system of racial classification in their self-identification practices. The fact that this diaspora community is fractured in nature only adds to the complexity of this process.

Study of "My People"

Research conducted by scholars who have chosen to study a cultural group to which they belong or with whom they identify has been labeled "native" or "indigenous" anthropology (Abu-Lughod 1986; Altorki and El-Solh 1988; Golde 1996; Gwaltney 1980; Hurston 1970; Jones 1970). I chose to study Cape Verdeans because, like most other people of Cape Verdean descent, I am an enculturated community advocate. Given our obscure history, Cape Verdeans like myself who grew up in the southeastern New England area were almost charged from childhood to go forth and tell the world of our existence. Therefore, my decision was also both personal and political.

I wanted to study Cape Verdeans living in the Roxbury and Dorchester neighborhoods of Boston because I was interested in exploring the phenomenon of identity construction undertaken by people of African descent living in the United States. Cape Verdeans, I believed, would provide an interesting case study of African diasporic identity formation. This was not an easy decision, given my own Cape Verdean upbringing. My grandmother was the primary agent of my enculturation into Cape Verdean culture. She taught me to both love and hate my heritage. My grandmother taught me how to hold suspect darker-skinned Cape Verdeans (*badius*), to be cautious of African-Americans, and to absolutely despise our white Portuguese (*yambob*) neighbors. Obviously, my grandmother grew up in a society that privileged white over black, light over dark, which reinforced colonized racial understandings from "the old country" that filtered her own interpretations of her social position and that of her descendants. Yet, despite the weight of internalized oppression, I was also enriched by her love and knowledge of Cape Verdean culture through music, dance, food, and family communalization.

It was with that instilled passion that I pursued this project, though cognizant of the negative historical memory of my childhood looming in the background. Having to confront all that I embraced and rejected concerning Cape Verdean culture, I came to utilize my past experiences of growing up in a Cape Verdean-American community as a comparative lens through which to examine the contemporary Boston Cape Verdean community, comprised of both Cape Verdean-Americans and more recent Cape Verdean immigrants.

Before entering the field, I was advised to foreground my Cape Verdean ethnicity as a means of gaining entry into the community. However, given my resistance to monolithic categorizations, I could only do what I always do, which was to present myself as being of both Cape Verdean and Puerto Rican ancestry. Despite my self-representation, it ultimately was my partial identity as Cape Verdean that proved the most salient when establishing relationships with community members. This partiality was interpreted by my informants as being "good enough" to accept me into their homes and make me an honorary member of their families and social networks. My navigation of identities as researcher and native daughter subsequently rendered me a quasi-informant in my own study. De Andrade (2000) had a similar experience when she studied the Cape Verdean-American communities living in the Providence and New Bedford areas.

As I set out to delineate how Cape Verdeans deal with race in the United States context, I assumed that I would encounter Cape Verdeans like those with whom I had spoken at the Smithsonian's 1995 Festival of American Folklife, which featured Cape Verdean and Cape Verdean-American culture. There, I met young Cape Verdeans who talked of how they usually self-identified as both Cape Verdean and Black. They felt that privileging their "Cape Verdean-ness" was not a negation of their "blackness." I was not prepared for what I would discover, however. A Cape Verdean living in Roxbury warned me during an initial field site visit that no Cape Verdean person would talk to me if I did not speak

Kriolu. His warning became more significant to me once I learned that the majority of the 32,000 officially (under)counted Cape Verdeans living in the Boston area were island-born.

For the native anthropologist, examining one's position vis-à-vis the culture under study involves coming to terms with the fact that one is only a partial native. My experience involved the realization of my differentiation as a Cape Verdean-American, in contrast to those informants who are defined as Cape Verdean immigrants. From the moment I began the research, strangely enough, I felt as though I was in some exotic land, immersed in a foreign environment, surrounded by a people of a different culture who spoke a different language. I was a "familiar stranger" to this community.[10] I felt a distinct alienation from "my people." In short, most of the Cape Verdeans of Boston that I encountered were not the "Cape Verdean-Americans" with whom I most closely identified. "My people" were really those Cape Verdeans whose parents or grandparents were born in the United States. "My people" spoke English, not *Kriolu.*

Generational difference was a primary marker of my outsider status and became far more important to my study, allowing me to gain an understanding of the community as a fractured diaspora, composed of both island- and United States-born Cape Verdeans. As my presence within the community became more visible, so too did my ambiguity as a native researcher. Initially, I was perceived as an outsider, one with no (*Kriolu*) voice. In addition, as I occupied a subordinate position vis-à-vis my more authentic Cape Verdean immigrant informants, I was often introduced by my informants, who interpreted my presence as simply a person coming back to her roots, a person who was "*Kriolu e espanhol*" who wanted to learn more about Cape Verdean language and culture.

Another distinction made by the community was my status as a United States-born citizen. Despite my ancestry and my efforts at learning *Kriolu,* I was often referred to as "*merkanu*" or American. Others assumed I was either "Spanish" or Black (African-American) and not Cape Verdean at all. In the latter instances, people would subsequently warm up to me and even apologize once my Cape Verdean ancestry was discovered. I remember that at a birthday party, a gentleman barely acknowledged my presence as he was introduced to me. After walking away briskly, his niece followed him a few minutes later to explain to him that my mother's family was from Cape Verde. He just about fell over himself as he came back to me, embarrassed but warmly smiling as he shook my hand in recognition of his mistake. As an outsider gradually coming inside, and given my status as a researcher who is American by birth but *kriolu* by ancestry, I was often situated by members of the community between this cultural divide, between *kriolu* and *merkanu.*

I believe that I would not have had nearly as much access to the community as I was afforded had it not been for my Cape Verdean ancestry, partial as it may be. Yet, my status as an insider–outsider could never be taken for granted. Cape Verdean immigrants did not assume that I knew everything there was to know about the culture. This was mainly because my assertion that I was Cape Verdean was considered less authentic than that of a person born in the islands: a "fakeverdean," as I was once told. Therefore, my knowledge of Cape Verdean culture was considered lacking or even at times non-existent. The assumption was that Cape Verdean-Americans were lost souls, whose fundamental elements of Cape Verdean-ness (e.g., language) had been washed away by the waves of Americanization. A similar distinction is made among Latino subgroups; for example, United States-born Puerto Ricans are often seen as less authentic than island-born-and-raised Puerto Ricans. Language and cultural traditions are often used as indices of authentication (De Genova and Ramos-Zayas 2003, 20).

On the other hand, those representing the Cape Verdean-American population did take my cultural knowledge for granted. It was assumed that I had or knew of similar experiences given my ancestry and the fact that I am fourth generation. The history of Cape Verde, for example, was often not discussed in detail or at all because it was assumed that I already knew the script. This type of rapport forced me to interrogate that which I had taken for granted with respect to my own interpretations of Cape Verdean history and culture.

The native anthropologist has the unique opportunity to provide an in-depth ethnographic account of her community of identification while interrogating that which is often taken for granted. As a woman of Cape Verdean ancestry, I was afforded the opportunity to speak with people that may have been otherwise reserved were it not for the fact that my mother's family came from the islands of Fogo and Brava. My historical experience, generational difference, and regional nativity, in contrast to the Boston community, enabled me to engage the cultural meanings, values, and expressions of this Cape Verdean diasporic population from a place of knowing and unknowing.

Defining the Cape Verdean Diaspora

The Cape Verdean diasporic community of Boston can be described as a transnational community due to the constant influx of new migrants from the islands as well as increased communications via telephone and the Internet, improved airline transportation, and the ability of migrants to obtain dual citizenship, which has facilitated an ongoing dialogue between island and American cultural forms. Moreover, contemporary Cape Verdean "transmigrants" (Basch et al. 1994) maintain relationships that "cut across the configurations of cultural nationalism" (Hall 1997, 298). Thus, the Cape Verdean community of Boston, in particular, is considered part of a larger transnational "imagined" community (Anderson 1991), not only because of the constant flow of people, capital, technology, and commodities between diaspora and island-nation, but also because the government of Cape Verde recognizes the diaspora as such (Pires-Hester 1994).

I was made aware of this status of the diaspora as intricately connected to the transnational politics of Cape Verde in 1997 when I attended a gala dinner for the then Prime Minister of Cape Verde, Carlos Veiga. An estimated 700 people were expected to attend, most of whom were affiliated with the *Movimento para a Democracia* (Movement for Democracy) or MpD party. After Mr. Veiga arrived thirty minutes behind schedule, everyone stood and clapped, some even gave high-pitched shouts and hollers of recognition as the PM and his delegation (and secret servicemen) entered the hall. During his formal address, which lasted an hour and forty-five minutes (much to the dismay of the wait staff whose services were delayed), Veiga spoke of his gladness to be in Boston but spent the majority of his time speaking on the state of affairs in Cape Verde: the lack of rain, the economy, health conditions, transportation, public works fishery and other industries, and the plight of the poor. It was truly a political speech, one reminiscent of a person running for public office, and this was true to a large degree. In reality, he was campaigning for continued financial support from Cape Verdeans in the diaspora, offered through tourism and remittances. The Cape Verdean government facilitates this process of soliciting the economic power of immigrants (Cape Verdeans living abroad who return to Cape Verde frequently for visits or retirement) by offering them subsidies for purchasing property and building homes in the islands.

The Cape Verdean diaspora can also be described as multigenerational in composition, created out of an interruption in the flow of migration that occurred between the 1920s and 1950s, with the enactment of a series of restrictive immigration laws. Out of this interruption developed a cultural gap that has yet to be bridged between the Cape Verdean immigrants and the Cape Verdean-Americans, creating a social environment of cultural disaggregation. The Cape Verdean immigrant sector of the Boston community is comprised of people who immigrated to the United States directly or en route to other countries during the 1960s, 1970s, and 1980s. Another subgroup is the children of the immigrants, most who were born in the United States. Finally, there are the Cape Verdean-Americans whose ancestors migrated from the islands during the 19th and 20th centuries.

What has been compelling for me in my research, particularly as a person of Cape Verdean ancestry, are the ways in which the Cape Verdean diaspora of Boston, as fragmented into hyphenated American and immigrant segments, offer up competing definitions of "Capeverdeanness" through their social interaction with or avoidance of one another. For example, Cape Verdean immigrants identify the retention of the *Kriolu* language and the maintenance of familial connection to the islands as critical indicators of Cape Verdean identity. Conversely, the Cape Verdean-Americans contend that their historical presence in the United States and their ability to retain Cape Verdean cultural elements despite the pressure to become American render them just as Cape Verdean as the more recent immigrant. Interestingly, it is the adherence to the label "Cape Verdean" that both unites and divides this diversified community.

People of Cape Verdean descent in Boston are well aware of the cultural gap which has fostered animosity, resentment, and misunderstanding. Community leaders and state and local officials have initiated efforts to alleviate this situation by sponsoring events that encourage joint participation of United States- and island-born Cape Verdeans. One such event has been a community conference entitled "Common

Threads." Two years ago, I was asked to participate in this conference, on a panel that was charged to define the Cape Verdean nation. Toward the end of my presentation, I asked the Common Threads audience, "How can we ever come to one definition of a Cape Verdean nation—considering the ways in which we identify by island of origin? The ways in which we debate which island's *Kriolu* will be standardized? The ways in which we try to fix the criteria of who is and who is not *really* Cape Verdean? The ways in which we fight over *monchup* and *katxupa?"*

After the panel presentations, the audience members did not engage in a typical question-and-answer period, but rather offered their own personal stories of self-identification as a means of adding to the conversation. Ideally, this panel discussion was supposed to operate as a workshop in order to come up with this unified definition of Capeverdean-ness. In the end, the panel in practice illustrated how that goal is unattainable, given the processual nature of Cape Verdean identity formation. More importantly, it revealed for me how Cape Verdean identity is constructed not only on an individual basis, but also collectively, as illustrated by the panelists and audience participation. Historical legacy, language use, and cultural practice lie at the heart of the debate on Cape Verdean-ness that continues to be waged within the community.

Nos Povu Kriolu[11]

What has prompted Cape Verdeans to identify in particular ways has much to do with the social and political climate in which they find themselves as United States residents. Because of their "racially" and culturally mixed heritage, throughout the years, Cape Verdeans have been simultaneously embraced and ostracized by both dominant and minority groups in the United States. As a result, Cape Verdean attempts at self-identification have become, more and more, a matter of negotiation.

During my fieldwork, I spoke with Cape Verdean immigrants who argued that identity was a non-issue for them prior to coming to the United States. In the islands, they would say, there is no need to self-identify as Cape Verdean since everyone is Cape Verdean. However, upon further investigation, I discovered that most Cape Verdeans who have relocated to Boston also tend to refer to themselves and to each other in terms of their islands of origin and, most importantly, to their specific neighborhoods (e.g., "Fijon D'Agu" [Fajã D'Água]) or parishes (e.g., São Lourenço).[12] Overall, I found that Cape Verdean immigrants tend to adhere to a "Cape Verdean Only" identity. They invoke the Cape Verde Islands as their primary frame of reference and consistently conceptualize Cape Verde as home and the United States as their home-away-from-home.

Joãoana is a thirty-nine-year-old clerk employed by the City of Boston. She was born in Fogo and came to the United States with her younger brother in 1974. She had lived in Portugal briefly prior to her arrival in Boston. Once in Boston, she lived in Dorchester with family friends (a family of five) until she turned eighteen. Although Joãoana now lives outside of the Cape Verdean neighborhood of her youth, she is active in the community, especially through her participation in the local church. For Joãoana, racialized identities are not instrumental in forming and maintaining Cape Verdean group solidarity. Instead, she illustrates how Cape Verdean immigrants tend to negotiate their identities around ideas of nationality:

> I hear some people say "Oh, but there's white Cape Verdeans and there's black Cape Verdeans." I say, "No." Cape Verdeans to me they're Cape Verdean; they cannot be black or white. They can be lighter than the other one, but…like with my older sister, she's light-skinned, but she's not going to say she's white on her papers and I say I'm black…. [W]e just say we're Cape Verdeans.

As Cape Verdean immigrants attempt to assert their identities as "Cape Verdean, one hundred percent" in the United States context, they are faced with ambivalence and confusion. Despite the large and growing number of Cape Verdeans presently living in Boston and the surrounding areas, Cape Verdean immigrants who self-identify as Cape Verdean still face the challenge of having to answer the question, "What are you?" When further probed by questions of "What is that?" or "Where is it?" most Cape Verdeans are compelled to provide the inquirer with a brief history of the islands. In most cases, this explanation includes the mentioning of Portuguese colonization, the geographical location of Cape Verde, the importation of enslaved Africans, the development of the *Kriolu* language, and the year in which independence was achieved.

From this well-contained definition, the importance of history, nation, culture, and language figures prominently in the ways Cape Verdeans understand their identities and present them to others.

To define oneself as originating from Cape Verde or being Cape Verdean does not imply that this self-identification will be a sufficient explanation in the eyes of other social groups whom they encounter. Some Cape Verdean immigrants resort to identifying themselves as "mixed," emphasizing the historical influence of both Europeans and Africans in their genealogical makeup. Colleen, twenty-five years old, is a law school student born in São Vicente. She came to the United States when she was only seven months old. She offers an example of this mixed race discourse when answering the question, "What is a Cape Verdean?"

> For me...you know, a Cape Verdean is definitely...someone with...to some extent mixed lineage, like Portuguese and African, but although there were Jewish in the Cape Verde Islands and other groups as well, and so basically that is what a Cape Verdean, you know, is.

The practice of Cape Verdeans asserting an identity as mixed when faced with the popular discourse of a binary black/white classification is similar to the experience of people who define themselves as biracial in the United States. Psychologist, Beverly Daniel Tatum's explanation of the process of biracial identification in children is instructive:

> One such challenge [associated with biracial identity negotiation] is embodied in the frequently asked question, "What are you?" While the question may be prompted by the individual's sometimes racially ambiguous appearance, the insistence with which the question is often asked represents society's need to classify its members racially. The existence of the biracial person challenges the rigid boundaries between black and white, and the questioner may really be asking, "Which side are you on? Where do you stand?" (Tatum 1997, 175)

The act of self-identification, then, becomes an exercise of self-objectification for Cape Verdean immigrants, as they attempt to clarify their racial ambiguity and signify their social alliances. With respect to the latter, many of my Cape Verdean immigrant informants actually felt a greater affinity with the Latino population in particular because of the similarity of foreign status and linguistic issues experienced as residents of Boston.

Cape Verdean immigrants in Boston have maintained a strategic consumer relationship with their Spanish-speaking neighbors. Cape Verdeans rely heavily upon the Spanish-speaking community—for example, patronizing local markets for Goya products for cooking. Such ingredients as *Sazón* and *Adobo* are essential items for Cape Verdean cuisine. When I questioned Lola Pina as to this practice of buying Spanish spices, she revealed that Goya and other such brands were most similar to those found in the islands. Although many Cape Verdeans with whom I spoke admitted to having never received formal training in Spanish, they are nevertheless able to communicate with Puerto Ricans and Dominicans, and other Spanish-speakers. Cape Verdean immigrants are also fond of Spanish-language television. On several occasions in the Pina household, I have witnessed women seated in the foyer or in the kitchen, intently watching *telenovelas* or Spanish soap operas. These same persons may also watch the news or entertainment programs that are televised in Spanish.

The ongoing interactions between these two communities suggest a sense of affinity in life experience. Cape Verdean immigrants face similar challenges as do Latino immigrants in Boston. As foreign-language speakers, they are often concentrated alongside each other within lower economic niches, such as factories and domestic work. They experience socioeconomic discrimination on the basis of their foreign (and often illegal) status. Finally, because of their similar socioeconomic status, both groups are informally segregated into the poorest sections of Dorchester and Roxbury. As a result, the two communities often come in contact with each other when utilizing local service agencies as well, especially those targeting so-called "minorities."

This affinity with the Latino population is also related to the fact that many Cape Verdean immigrants experience the phenomenon of mistaken identity. For those Cape Verdeans who were born in the islands who have pronounced accents when speaking English, they are often marked automatically by those who presume their foreign nativity. Because of their unfamiliarity with the Cape Verde Islands, even in

Boston, many people believe Cape Verdeans to be Latinos or Spanish-speaking people. As Colleen explains:

> the first thing I'd say is that we don't speak Spanish in Cape Verde... because people...do assume that...all the time...they either...they see the color of your skin and you're not white, basically, [it] doesn't matter what hue of brown you are, and they just assume you're Spanish, and so I would make that distinction that we are, you know, *Kriolu* speakers, which is, you know, Portuguese and African languages mixed.

Because of their racially mixed phenotype and their acquisition of English as a second language, many Cape Verdean immigrants are specifically mistaken for Puerto Rican or Dominican given the large representation of these two communities in Boston.

In addition to racialization along linguistic lines, Joãoana provides the example of how her identity as Cape Verdean was misinterpreted as Puerto Rican given her presence within a particular social setting:

> People that probably never heard of Cape Verdean, or heard it but doesn't know... so they'll always say "Oh you're Puerto Rican" 'cause... where I worked [at a local health center], there was lot of Latinos and, or Black[s], but they say "Oh, you don't look black" like the native blacks or...mostly Latinos that goes there were Puerto Ricans so.... They talk to me in Spanish or Puerto Rican then...I'm like "speak it slow, I'm not Puerto Rican."

Apparently, this type of mistaken identity is not merely a contemporary phenomenon, as was confirmed to me more recently when I spoke to Ramiro Pereira, who related stories to me about his immigrant experiences in Boston during the early 1960s. He explained that since the Puerto Rican population outnumbered the Cape Verdean population at that time, much of the activities performed by Cape Verdeans were erroneously reported in the local newspapers as those of Puerto Ricans. He gave the example of several fights that broke out between Cape Verdeans that were reported as Puerto Rican rioting.

Yet, contemporary Cape Verdean immigrants are conscious of the fact that race matters in the United States. The ways in which Cape

Verdeans have had to negotiate their identities, as a result, has much to do with their close and historic associations with African-Americans in educational, occupational, and residential environments. For the younger generation of Cape Verdeans in Boston, this has facilitated the adoption of African-American styles of clothing, hairstyle, music (rap/hip hop), and speech patterns. For others, it has meant a general acceptance of one's racialized status as Black on the basis of skin color and common socioeconomic oppression.

Several informants conveyed their awareness of Cape Verdeans acquiring a racialized status of black in Boston. As "the only black kid" in her honors classes in middle school, and while living in subsidized housing, Colleen reveals that she became very aware of her blackness as she matured. Her interpretation of having a racial and an ethnic identity illustrates the manner by which she came to understand the process of racialization in the United States:

> When I was younger…if someone asked me you know "What are you?" that's a typical question, I guess I would just say Cape Verdean. But I think as you become more racial, like conscious of race, I understood, you know, who I am ethnically as a Cape Verdean but racially I'm black.… I think growing up here and also growing up in a like lower-income family or whatever, it's kinda like you are more influenced by popular culture, which is black culture, African-American culture, so I definitely identify more that way.… I'm proud of being black and at the same time it's something imposed on us as black people for other motives that I do see.… I don't agree with that part of it.… I mean like the whole…if you had this percentage of black blood in you, you're all black, and it was made to discriminate and all that other stuff.

Yet, such an acceptance is often followed by clarification; that is, calling oneself "Black" is understood as a racial identity, not to be confused with the term "Black American," which connotes a distinct, cultural group.

Indeed, recent Cape Verdean immigrants view themselves as culturally distinct from the larger African-American community in Boston, despite the fact that they can also be mistaken for African-American based on socially constructed ideas of physical appearance. Yet, it is not merely the act of disassociation with a socially oppressed group in the United States that prompts Cape Verdeans to identify in this manner, as was the case in the past. It is more importantly their reinterpretation of the label "Black." Cape Verdean immigrants refer to themselves as Black more as an indication of color and, at times, African ancestry. Although many of the Cape Verdean immigrants referred to themselves as Black, they did not want this disclosure to be misunderstood as an admission to being "Black American" or "African-American."

Lillian is a thirty-year-old nurse practitioner. She was born in Brava but left as an infant with her family to live in Portugal. She moved to Boston only five years ago. Many of her family members, including two sisters, remain in Portugal. To her, "Black" indicates a cultural group to which she does not belong:

> Lillian: I'm Black but at the same time I'm Cape Verdean.... I'm Cape Verdean, Black Cape Verdean.... Like here, they say "I'm Black American...."
> G: But... you don't identify as Black American though....
> L: No, I'm not Black American.... Definitely not.... I wouldn't get upset if someone identifies me as a black.... I am black.... but I would let them know that I'm Cape Verdean.

Similarly, Colleen clarifies her interpretation of "Black":

> When I'm saying "black" I mean race, but when I say "Black American" I mean an ethnic group. So, when I'm like "I don't identify as Black American" I don't mean I don't want to identify myself as black. To me, black means, encompassing of all groups that are of African descent basically, as opposed to Black American, which is yet another cultural group, it's not a race. And I think that people...some people that...like don't know you or don't know about your culture, they get automatically defensive about...if you say you're not Black American. But the fact of the matter is I am not Black American. If you speak of certain traditions that are carried on within the black, African-American community, I didn't grow up with that. I grew up listening to Bana, Cesária, eating *katxupa*, eating *kuskus*, I mean, it's very different. And so I think that a lot of times it's like saying Cape Verdean to some people con-

> notes or implies that your denying your blackness, but it doesn't. It just means I'm stating my cultural group, my ethnic background.

By incorporating "Black" into their self-presentations, both Colleen and Lillian illustrate their ability to identify *with* African-Americans but not *as* African-Americans. This diasporic reconfiguration of "Black" is nothing new, considering the strategies employed by post-1965 immigrants of African descent (Bryce-Laporte 1972; Butcher 1994; Foner 1988; Kasinitz 1992; Laguerre 1998; Margolis 1994; Ogbu 1991; Reid 1939; Waters 1999; Woldemikael 1989b).

Cape Verdean/Black Americans

The Cape Verdean-American population in Boston differs from their Cape Verde-born counterparts in their social interactions with African-Americans, their understanding of the racial classification system in place in the United States, and their awareness of racism and its effects on their lives as citizens of the United States. Indeed, many of the Cape Verdean-Americans I have encountered and interviewed have expressed to me the idea that as a person of Cape Verdean ancestry, one is both Black and Cape Verdean. Cape Verdean-Americans maintain a self-presentation that places them squarely within these two communities, and their everyday life activities reflect this dual membership. Such Cape Verdeans are and have been actively involved in African-American affairs, evident in their participation in African-American interest groups, churches, and social events, for example. Yet, they also feel legitimized in their assertion of their Cape Verdean identity and defend the implicit authenticity in this affirmation, much to the dismay of their Cape Verdean immigrant counterparts.

Many of my Cape Verdean-American informants grew up in the 1960s and spent their formative years (i.e., their early twenties) in Boston, relocating from the smaller communities of southern Massachusetts. Yet, as residents of Boston during the 1960s and 1970s, they experienced not only acute racism but also the transformative affects of the Black Power Movement. This made for a climate where racial ambiguity was not tolerated. Wanda, aged fifty, is a Cape Verdean-American professional in management. She is a divorced mother of one and identifies primarily as African-American. She was born and raised in Taunton, Massachusetts, and relocated to Boston in 1972 to attend college. Wanda was twenty-two years old when she discovered that her biological father was not her mother's light-skinned African-American husband, but was a Cape Verdean-American man. She traces her mother's ancestry to the island of Brava. She explains her early experiences in a racially divided Boston: "When I came to Boston, you couldn't say I'm something different. There are Black people and White people and you were trying to be Grey, somewhere in the middle, and there was no Grey. So, I identified with who, you know, I wanted to be like." As a result, many Cape Verdean-Americans integrated socially and culturally into the African-American community as a means of social survival in a racialized environment. For Wanda, survival meant downplaying her Cape Verdean heritage.

Other Cape Verdean-Americans offered stories of how racism had an impact on their identity development. Marlene, aged forty-three, was born and raised in Boston. Her father (deceased) was African-American and actively involved in the Black Power and Civil Rights movements. She currently lives with her mother, who is second-generation Cape Verdean from Hyannis, Massachusetts. Marlene identifies as Black and Cape Verdean. She recalls her earliest experiences of racial identity development:

> I felt very black in Catholic school 'cause I was the only Black person. But, my skin tone is so light that I never fit in the black community or the Cape Verdean community or the White community.... [M]y mother took me to school one day and she—I have a medical problem—so she had to tell the teachers about the medical problems, and at that time she worked in a hospital at night. And she worked in a mental institution, so she wore a white uniform. And the teacher asked if she was my nurse or my maid, because I was so white and she was so dark. And I looked [at her] and said, "That's my mother." And in that Catholic school, I faced so much racism that I was blown away. I was really, really shocked.

Margaret, aged forty-four, is a Cape Verdean-American middle school guidance counselor who has been working in the Boston Public

School system since 1988. She grew up in New Bedford, Massachusetts, and moved to Boston in 1976 to pursue a graduate degree. Margaret relates a similar story of racial differentiation experienced by her grandmother in the United States:

> My grandmother was extremely fair, and when she purchased her house she had problems with the English language so the family doctor helped and the area she lived in was predominantly Jewish. And so one day, this lady said to her, you know, "L... Who's this man that you have working for you? He's in and out of the house, he comes at all hours...What does he do? Does he take care of (you know), your garden? Is he cleaning? Is he repairing? Is he stoking the coal stove? What?" And she said, "There's no man in my house." And she was talking in broken English and she was like, "No man come my house, just my husband." And the woman was like, [gasps] because my grandfather was dark-skinned.

Tatum states that although "cultural identities are not solely determined in response to racial ideologies... racism increases the need for a positive self-defined identity in order to survive psychologically" (1997, 165). This may explain how experiences of racism have prompted many Cape Verdean-Americans like Marlene and Margaret to identify as African-Americans with a Cape Verdean background.

Lisa, a third-generation Cape Verdean-American, is a forty-five year-old local artist whose grandparents immigrated from Brava during the early 1920s. Recalling her experiences, she summarizes the process of identity formation and negotiation experienced by many Cape Verdean-Americans in Boston:

> With my experience in coming to age at adolescence, it was clear to me that I was a Black woman and I had been very proud of that and earlier on I was just a Cape Verdean and I went into the...got very, very Black in adolescence. I mean the Afro, the attitude, I joined the Black Panthers. On the other side of that, I started reaching back home to the Cape Verdean community, that's come within the last twenty years, where I started identifying how special a Black group this is... and that not only am I a Black woman, I can trace my roots back to a

> particular culture.... So clearly now it's sort of like clumped together, with the identity of being yes an African-American but also Cape Verdean-American.

Janice, aged forty-nine, is a housing inspector employed by the City of Boston. She is married to an African-American male and has two children. Janice identifies as Black yet acknowledges her Cape Verdean-American heritage simultaneously. Janice's grandmother (deceased) immigrated to the United States from Brava during the mid-1910s. Her father's family is of Portuguese and Cape Verdean descent. Like Wanda, her cousin, she was born and raised in Taunton, Massachusetts, and relocated to Boston during the late 1960s:

> I don't ever say I'm Cape Verdean; I say I'm Black. Unless you get in a conversation with somebody and...or they'll say, "you're not Black, you're Cape Verdean." I guess I don't deny it...you know what I mean? I mean, I wouldn't deny who I am or what I am...but I don't put a lot of emphasis on that I'm Cape Verdean. I guess when people ask me I say "I'm Black."...I wouldn't say, "Oh, I'm Cape Verdean." Probably, you know though, if I was sitting with somebody that I thought was a Cape Verdean, I would probably say "yeah, I'm one of you too or I'm a Cape Verdean also"...but I don't think I would ever say that at first. I don't even know if I act Cape Verdean.

The self-identification practice of withholding or concealing one's Cape Verdean identity is an indication of a degree of choice that influences Cape Verdean-American identity construction. Lisa explains this in terms of situationally-enacted identities:

> What tends to happen I think in the culture is that people, in order for us to really be successful in our field, we move, we have to move away from the culture somewhat, to go into mainstream. And when that happens, our people choose to identify in different ways. When I moved into the early parts of my career, I was an African-American woman. There was no reference or little references.... I know I was Cape Verdean but it wasn't...now I say I'm African-American–Cape Verdean. I mean clearly I link them together and that's it. And you want

> to know what that means, then I'll explain that. But, I think it's true that Cape Verdeans for a long time have mainstreamed without identifying themselves, and [they] let the world identify them. But every once in a while I'll stumble across someone who has been removed from the culture, who will admit to me that they're Cape Verdean but in the world not necessarily. It's not an emphasis and that's their choice.

Since many Cape Verdeans initially called themselves Portuguese and distanced themselves from the African-American community, African-Americans who perceive Cape Verdeans as Black people associate contemporary Cape Verdean cultural differentiation with wanting to be White or not wanting to acknowledge their African ancestry. For this reason, Cape Verdean-Americans have had to negotiate their diasporic blackness in light of this animosity. The persistence of Cape Verdean-Americans defining themselves as both Black and Cape Verdean highlights the ways in which the racial categories of "Black" and "African-American" are being actively reshaped in the post-Civil Rights era.

Diasporic Blackness

For Cape Verdeans, the struggle to be recognized as a distinct Black cultural group in the United States is waged on a daily basis. The distinction to be made between Cape Verdean immigrant and Cape Verdean-American assertions, however, lies in the conceptualization of the racial category "Black." For Cape Verdean-Americans, calling oneself Black implies an association with African-Americans based on acculturation and a shared experience with racism in Boston. Cape Verdean immigrants, on the other hand, refer to themselves as Black more as an indication of color and, at times, African ancestry. For Cape Verdeans living in the United States, then, diasporic blackness exemplifies the reformulation and redeployment of the racialized category "Black" in new, creative ways.

Included in this expression of what I am calling diasporic blackness is the reinvention of the islands as culturally, politically, and geographically tied to the African continent. Despite its close proximity to the mainland, the islands enjoyed a privileged position within the colonial schema that often placed them in an intermediate position of power, between Portugal and Africa. This position was complemented by the elevation of their phenotypically intermediate status within a racial hierarchy—that is, between White and Black. In other words, Cape Verdeans have historically benefited from disassociating themselves from other Africans in the past.

With the onset of independence, Amílcar Cabral's re-Africanization platform, and the globalizing effects of the United States Black Power and Civil Rights movements, more and more Cape Verdeans have abandoned this position of detachment from the mainland. Representing this generation, Colleen illustrates how some Cape Verdeans have come to self-identify in relation to their African heritage: "I see ourselves as Africans basically, I mean, our food, our music, our dance, physical features, all of that stuff, you see a lot of African attributes." Therefore, when contemporary Cape Verdean immigrants utilize the term "Black," they are also doing so as an affirmation of their African heritage and in recognition of the importance placed on skin color in the construction of racialized subjects in the United States context and in other global landscapes.

By defining Cape Verde as part of Africa, "African" becomes an acceptable identity used to broach the label of "Black" without taking it on completely and as a means of maintaining a Cape Verdean cultural identity. Yet, the ways in which Cape Verdean immigrants identify as Black or African can also be interpreted as a strategy of alignment with the diaspora communities of African descent. This alignment is fostered out of a common existence as Black people experiencing racial and economic discrimination on a daily basis in Boston.

The reinterpretation of *badiu* as a positive signifier of Cape Verdean culture, history, and identity can also be understood as an expression of diasporic blackness. The *Badius* are people who are believed to be the descendants of runaway slaves, primarily living in the island of Santiago. They are considered the "most African" in the Cape Verdean imagination. *Badius* also represent both the stigma of slavery and the power of resistance. During the colonial period, the Portuguese went so far as to ban African-influenced musical and cultural traditions of the *Badius*. Such politicized musical forms as *tabanka* and *batuku*,[13] for example, resurfaced from their underground manifestations only after independence in 1975. Prior to this reaffirmation of African heritage, the *Badius* were perceived negatively by the general Cape Verdean population. The pejorative connotation of *badiu* was reproduced in the diaspora, correlating with discourses of colorism that privilege light-skinned over dark-skinned representations.

Today, the term has been recuperated and is used by Santiago natives regardless of skin tone, as a means of expressing a political identity of authenticity nurtured in the wake of independence. I asked Mário, a "forty-something" musician originally from Praia, Santiago, who migrated from the islands during the late 1980s, why he called himself *Badiu* despite his light skin tone. He quickly stated that this was a stereotype, that he knew people fairer than himself, with blond hair, whose families had been in Santiago for generations. I found this apparent reinvention of *badiu* to be analogous to the way that the label "Black" was reborn here in the United States during the 1960s.

Diasporic blackness, as exhibited by the Cape Verdean diaspora in Boston, exemplifies how new politicized identities are being created and recreated in relation to processes of racialization. It is the way that Cape Verdeans reconfigure "Black" to mean "not African-American." It is the way Cape Verdeans self-identify as *badiu* to signify a deeper, more authentic connection to the islands. It is the adoption by Cape Verdean youth of African-American and Caribbean-stylized fashion and musical genres in the rearticulation of cultural identities in new social locales.

Music in particular is an instructive medium through which to examine diasporic blackness. Historically, Cape Verdean musical forms have been heavily influenced by genres from Africa, Europe, Latin America, and the Caribbean. Traditional Cape Verdean music that was previously deemed subversive and subsequently suppressed during the colonial period was revitalized during the 1970s and 1980s. Rural musical forms such as *funana* and *batuku* not only reemerged, but also underwent transformations in the form of electrical instrumentation. More recently, Cape Verdean popular music has borrowed heavily from a number of sources: Afro-pop, soukous, merengue, salsa, zouk, reggae, rhythm and blues, hip hop, and rap music.

The emergence of Creole (*Kriolu*) rap is a new, dynamic expression of Cape Verdean diasporic blackness. This budding musical genre is being produced on both sides of the Atlantic, though steadfastly on the East Coast and in Boston, specifically. Although Cape Verdean music has always functioned as an economic and cultural commodity in the European market, its marketability in the United States is contingent upon its demand within the Cape Verdean immigrant community.

Contemporary Cape Verdean music produced in Boston supplies the demand of the children of Cape Verdean immigrants, most who were born in the United States and are fluent in *Kriolu.* As Cape Verdeans continue to negotiate their cultural and racialized identities in the United States, the proliferation of Creole rap and other new forms of diasporic blackness will continue.

Politics of Resistance

The variety of ways in which the Cape Verdean diaspora community constructs itself racially and ethnically illustrates the internal diversity and complexity of this social group. Most importantly, the practice of Cape Verdean immigrants identifying as Cape Verdean only and Cape Verdean-Americans identifying as both Cape Verdean and Black signifies a distinct mode of resistance intrinsic to their self-identification practices. The politics of Cape Verdean identification, therefore, is one of resistance. Akhil Gupta and James Ferguson (1997, 19) define resistance as "an experience that constructs and reconstructs the identity of subjects." Although Cape Verdean self-identification practices may not necessarily dismantle the current racial hierarchy supported by the power of state mechanisms, it does challenge the process of racialized subject-making, if not on a "small or local" level (Abu-Lughod 1990).

For Cape Verdean immigrants in particular, daily interactions with non-Cape Verdean groups elicit a sense of self-preservation. When Cape Verdeans assert a "Cape Verdean Only" identity in response to external pressures to identify as Black, insist on speaking *Kriolu* instead of English, continue to refer to Cape Verde as home, and dress in ways typical of "the old country" (e.g., women wearing long skirts and *lenços* or kerchiefs), they do so as a means of resisting the ideology of racial hierarchy and racial hegemony that exists in the United States. They, likewise, self-identify as Cape Verdean in resistance to monolithic classification schemes that would otherwise situate them within homogeneous categories.

Similarly, the practice of Cape Verdean-Americans identifying as both Cape Verdean and African-American serves as an affront to the United

States system of racial classification. It works against the assumption that a person must identify themselves in "either/or" terms; that is, they must only check off one box. Although many Cape Verdean-Americans, when forced to do so, still check either "Black" or "Other," they assert a "both/and" identity in social situations. When Cape Verdeans do consistently check off "Other," they are participating in a political assault on the United States system of racial classification. The persistence of Cape Verdeans and other "Others" (e.g., multiracial individuals) engaging in this process has the potential to subvert current racial and ethnic categories and institute a change in the census classification schemes in the future.

Although racialization still occurs despite this affront, Cape Verdean self-identification practices illustrate how racial categories may eventually become more reflective of the cultural plurality characterizing the United States population. Specifically, Cape Verdean reinterpretation of the label "Black" as a marker of physical appearance and as an indicator of cultural distinction attests to this possibility.

Conclusion

The fact that the Cape Verde Islands are represented as mere dots on the world map does little to alter the general perception of Cape Verdeans as a relatively unknown United States cultural group. During my research, I was surprised to encounter people in Boston who were unfamiliar with Cape Verdeans. At one of the Cape Verdean Independence Day celebrations, held annually at City Hall Plaza, I participated as a vendor, selling photographs of Cape Verdeans taken by a Cape Verdean-American from California. I received at least two inquires from Euro-Americans who began with the intro, "I know this a stupid question but…" when admitting that they didn't know where Cape Verde was. I then went into the geographic description of the islands' location (at least one couple thought the "island" was located in the Caribbean, especially when observing the former green-red-and-black flag of independence I had displayed at my table). I also mentioned that the islands were colonized by Portugal, hence the "racial" composition of the people and the impetus of the *Kriolu* language, which I described as a Portuguese-based creole, in contrast to Haitian Kreyol as a French-based creole language. One man was not fazed by my efforts of explanation, resolved with the idea that Portuguese and Cape Verdean was "the same thing." When I asked another woman what was her impression of her co-worker before she found out her co-worker was a Cape Verdean, the woman replied, shrugging her shoulders, "you know, your generic, basic Black woman."

Cape Verdeans experience racialization not only casually but also through the United States Census and other institutionalized methods of documentation employed by federal, state, and local governments in the creation and definition of subject positionalities. These mechanisms of the nation-state are enacted in conjunction with social, economic, and political forces that determine the content and importance of racial categories in the United States (Omi and Winant 1986). In light of these facts, the politics of Cape Verdean diasporic identity formation involve a significant amount of contestation.

Cape Verdeans have much to offer us in terms of understanding the processes of social and cultural adjustment endured by immigrants in the United States. Cape Verdeans in Boston, like most other immigrant groups who have chosen the United States as a final destination, have had to manage their lives in the face of economic disparity, social exclusion, assimilative forces, and institutionalized discrimination. They have made strategic choices in order to enhance their lives in a new location: learning English as a means through which to secure employment; purchasing multi-family homes in order to reunify their families; and establishing residential enclaves in which to nurture cultural tradition.

Both Cape Verdean-Americans and immigrants identify themselves in various ways, in various social contexts, thus illustrating how diasporic Cape Verdeans enact situational identities on an everyday basis. For example, Cape Verdeans may enact one "racialized" identity in the workplace and another "cultural" identity in the home/enclave environment. Both Cape Verdean-Americans and Cape Verdean immigrants are thus cognizant of the impact that "racial" and "ethnic" classifications in the United States have on this process; they are conscious of the social forces that shape their lives and imbue their experiences with racial and ethnic meanings.

Given the persistence of racial categorization, Cape Verdeans have had to come to terms with the fact that they are often perceived as both foreign and Black in the United States context. Since Cape Verdeans are of African and Portuguese descent, their experiences have been one of constant negotiation of identity along racially ascribed and culturally defined lines. Other Black immigrants, from the Caribbean and Africa, have undergone similar experiences once confronted with the United States system of racial classification based on physical appearance and the demarcation of identity "boxes." However, Cape Verdeans who are comfortable with asserting multiple identities actively challenge ideas of racial categorization. The Cape Verdean diaspora community of Boston can be accurately described as being in a constant state of transformation, where identities are contingent upon the community's task of defining and redefining itself internally and to outgroup members. The individual and collective identities proffered by Cape Verdeans can be interpreted as identities of resistance in relation to the United States system of racial classification and its attendant ideology of racial hierarchy.

The present state of Cape Verdean diasporic identity formation raises the question of immigration patterns long relied upon to predict the lives of second and third generations. Contemporary Cape Verdean immigrants do not have the problem of disconnection from the islands or from their relatives, as did many 19th and 20th century immigrants. The Cape Verdean-Americans of my grandmother's and mother's generation, for example, may have had limited contact with the islands, in the form of providing goods through mutual aid projects, but they never made an actual visit to the islands. Ongoing contact with island culture through the steady stream of newcomers into the community has helped to maintain Cape Verdean culture, language, and identity thus far, albeit in dynamic forms. Moreover, because of the continual growth of the immigrant community, *Kriolu* may continue to be needed and thus utilized as a primary mode of communication among Cape Verdeans and implemented within bilingual education programs in the schools.

Due to the current persistence of *Kriolu* as a marker of Cape Verdean identity, the existence of Cape Verdean merchants and transnational entrepreneurs satisfying the hunger for the homeland, and the ongoing advances in the means with which to maintain contact with the homeland (e.g., phone cards, cell phones, internet, airline travel, ferries), the Cape Verdean diaspora remains a potential challenge to the ideas of cultural assimilation that structures American subjectivities. This challenge is also being posed by other immigrant, diasporic populations leading similar lives in the United States (Levitt 2001). In the near future, the Cape Verdean diaspora community of Boston may withstand the forces of Americanization that have irrevocably altered the culture and composition of immigrant groups in the past. Their historical memory of Cape Verdean cultural history, their persistence in asserting multiple identities, and their maintenance of *Kriolu* as a viable language may ensure this fate. To be sure, Cape Verdean diasporic identity formation, interpreted within its specific historical, cultural, and social contexts, provides a blueprint from which challenges to the static notions of race, ethnicity, and nationality can be waged.

Notes

[1] This article was previously published in *Identities* 12 (3), July 2005, 405-438.

[2] The term "Cape Verdeans" is used throughout as a general descriptor of a racial/ethnic community whose members identify themselves or are identified by others as such. Persons who self-identify as Cape Verdean trace their ancestry and/or that of their relatives to one of the nine inhabited islands comprising the Republic of CapeVerde. Although the term "Cape Verdean-American" has gained popularity as a way to define persons of Cape Verdean ancestry who were born in the United States, "Cape Verdean" is more often employed by the latter group as well as by the more recent migrants. For the purpose of this article, the term is therefore used to describe the diaspora community of Boston, Massachusetts, comprised of Cape Verdeans who are citizens (native and naturalized) and residents (legal and illegal) currently living (temporarily and permanently) in the United States.

[3] Along with the Portuguese, Cape Verde's European population also included settlers from France, Spain, and Italy during the colonial period. The islands underwent numerous raids by French and Spanish pirates as well. During the 16th and 17th centuries, Jews also sought refuge in the islands, their presence evident in the ruins of synagogues and in cemeteries, especially on the islands of Santo Antão and Boa Vista.

[4] The Sotavento (Windward) islands are comprised of Brava, Fogo, Santiago (São Tiago), and Maio. The Barlavento (Leeward) islands consist of Boa Vista, Sal, Santa Luzia (uninhabited), São Nicolau, São Vicente, and Santo Antão. There are also eight *ilhéus* or islets.

[5] For a discussion of the history of Cape Verde, see Carreira (1972), Davidson (1989), Foy (1988), Lobban (1995), and Meintel (1984). For the history of Cape Verdean immigration, see Halter (1993). See also Sánchez (1997).

[6] See *Economist Intelligence Unit* (1996, 95).

[7] *Kriolu* is the national yet unofficial language of Cape Verde. It is derived from 15th-century Portuguese and various West African languages. *Kriolu* is a distinct language that is often mistaken for a dialect of Portuguese. Efforts have been made in both the islands and in the United States to standardize the orthography of this orally transmitted language. As a result, in July 1998, the government of Cape Verde finally approved a five-year trial period for the use of *Alfabeto Unificado para a Escrita do Cabo-Verdiano* (ALUPEC) as the official alphabet to be used to standardize *Kriolu* in Cape Verde. Many community members, both island- and United States-born, refer to the language as "Capeverdean" (e.g., "I speak Capeverdean").

[8] The names of all interviewees, streets, and local landmarks have been changed throughout to protect the privacy of the informants. Names of major cities, however, remain identifiable.

[9] Although a large portion of the Cape Verdean global community is Catholic, there is an increasing influence of Protestantism, both in the United States and in the islands. Many Cape Verdeans in Boston have also joined the *Igreja Universal* (Universal Church), a fundamentalist church formed and promoted by the Brazilian immigrant population.

[10] I use this term similar to how Karen Blu (1980, xi) used it when discussing native anthropology: "an anthropologist studying his own society is more aware of his possible cultural blinders and is likely to take for granted much less about his own society than those without that training. At the same time, the anthropologist studying his own culture is a 'familiar stranger,' one somewhat apart,

yet at least partially versed in the sensibilities and outlook of those he desires to understand and potentially able to delve deeply into their nuances because he is so versed."

[11] "We, Cape Verdean people."

[12] See also Machado (1981).

[13] *Tabanka* is a tradition usually celebrated in conjunction with religious festivities commemorating particular Catholic saints. The tradition includes Cape Verdeans dressing in costumes that mock colonial society and men playing drums and conch shells. *Batuku* is a tradition composed of a lone singer/dancer surrounded by a call-and-response choir of women. The dance performed consists of the intense swinging of the hips in rhythm to the beat kept by the other women, who pound out the beat on a strip of *pano* (traditional woven cloth) that is wrapped and placed between their thighs. The rhythmic pounding on the pano is referred to as *txabeta*. See Rodrigues (1995).

CHAPTER 19

Angola Dreaming: Memories of Africa Among Portuguese Retornados in Newark, NJ[1]

KIMBERLY DACOSTA HOLTON

Introduction: Decolonization and Taboo

The decolonization movements that swept across Africa during the mid-20th century sparked the widespread return of five to seven million European colonials to their native continent. Characterized by Andrea Smith (2003) as "invisible migrants," this large group of repatriates has received surprisingly little scholarly attention. It is only in the last five to ten years that scholars of migration are turning their attention to the transcontinental movements of European repatriates following decolonization and the circumstances that have conditioned their arrival and reception in native contexts.

The Portuguese who left Africa following the independence of Angola, Mozambique, and Guinea Bissau in the mid-1970s numbered over half-a-million people, and their return to Europe produced a five percent increase in Portugal's total population. These repatriates, termed *retornados* (returnees), comprised mostly of white settlers, some Portuguese-born, others African-born, as well as smaller numbers of mixed race and indigenous black Africans, all of whom fled rising violence and political instability in 1975-1976. Given the size of this migratory stream—indeed the "largest populational movement in the history of 20th-century Portugal" (Pires 2003, 1)—and the momentous historical period in which this repatriation occurred, a period marking the end of forty-eight years of authoritarianism and four centuries of Portuguese colonialism, it is, again, surprising that *retornados* have been the object of so few studies. To date, there are only a handful of full-length published works, unpublished theses, and academic articles dedicated to the topic.[2]

What explains the dearth of research on *retornados* and the "invisibility" of this population today? Andrea Smith (2003) argues that scholarly inattention can be attributed in part to biases within the fields of history and anthropology toward the study of migratory trajectories of formerly colonized people following independence. Rui Pena Pires argues that it took merely a decade (1975-85) for *retornados* to become "invisible as a collective" within Portugal (Pires 2003, 1). He attributes this to *retornados's* successful socioeconomic reintegration into Portuguese society, government policies which discouraged group identification and mobilization, and the support of family in native towns who provided financial and emotional assistance while *retornados* started new lives on Portuguese soil. Other scholars have pointed to the racial and ideological stigmatization of the term "*retornado*" (Lubkemann 2002; 2003; 2005; Ovalle-Bahamon 2003) and the selective disavowal of this label among newly-arrived repatriates. This, at the level of discourse and language, could explain the quick disappearance of the term and subsequent "invisibility" of the term's referent. In addition, cost-saving strategies prompted the Portuguese government to take measures limiting those who might officially be deemed *retornados*, declaring in 1977 that Portugal's responsibility to help resettle ex-colonists from Lusophone Africa was officially over, and from that point forward those repatriates needing state assistance would be termed "homeless" rather than "*retornado*" (Pires 2003, 232). Lastly, and perhaps most importantly, there is the shame of the colonial project, and the pervasive silence among scholars, politicians and the general public surrounding the colonial wars and African decolonization which make *retornados*—sometimes referred to as convenient "colonial scapegoats"—a taboo topic of discussion and research.

In his book *Silêncios do Regime*, António Barreto states:

> The uncomfortable silence about the Portuguese colonial war, on the part of almost everyone, is a flagrant example of complicity. Studies, books, memories, films or debates about the war, its antecedents and its end, are extremely rare. Rare are the people who dare express themselves totally and freely on the topic. The two powerful orthodoxies, the colonial and the independent, remain, more or less unchecked. Above all else, they are protected by the founders of the new regime: the military leaders and civilians who, having made a war in the name of State

> legality and historical legitimacy, rose up against both. Portugal did a good job of carrying out a bad war and a bad job of carrying out a good decolonization. No one was left without guilt or contradiction. This is the silence which will slowly be broken. (1992, 10)[3]

Although the dynamics Barreto describes in 1992 still exist today and the silence regarding the colonial project is far from broken, there are now fledgling civic movements, documentaries, and TV programs sprouting up in Portugal agitating for public discussion of 20th-century Portuguese colonialism, the colonial wars, and the Estado Novo dictatorship which provided the ideological foundation for forty-eight years of colonial policy.[4] A group calling themselves "Don't Erase the Memory," led by an eighty-seven-year-old activist who spent sixteen years in jail as a political prisoner during the Estado Novo dictatorship, plans to build monuments commemorating those who fought against the repressive policies of António Salazar. An AP article documenting the activities of this group explains that "vestiges of the regime were expunged by those who had suffered under it, fought it and hated it.... Portugal hastily pushed its dictatorship out of its collective memory and still has not exorcised its ghosts" (Hatton 2006). It is in the spirit of silence-breaking that this essay unfolds, exposing uncomfortable memories of Portugal's colonial past in the words of white settlers who lived in Angola until independence, then moved to Portugal as *retornados*, and then moved again to the United States.

In keeping with the dynamics described above, New Jersey's population of *retornados* entered my research quietly. In 2000, I founded The Ironbound Oral History Project, whose objectives were to teach undergraduates ethnographic methodologies in order to document the immigrant experiences of the large Portuguese-speaking population of New Jersey. Over the last seven years my students and I have conducted and transcribed over 250 interviews with Portuguese and Brazilian immigrants. Several years ago, as I sifted through the rich testimonies, trying to gain a broad understanding of the material, I noticed a surprising trend. In answer to the question, "have you ever lived anywhere else other than New Jersey and Portugal," a large proportion of the Portuguese interviewed for the project described living in Africa. At first, I dismissed this Africa link as one that was tied solely to military service.

But upon further investigation, I realized that many who had lived in Africa had either settled there after leaving the military or had moved there independent of military obligations. Even though this Africa link is rarely mentioned in Newark's Portuguese-language newspapers or in the cafés and social clubs of Newark's "Little Portugal," a surprising number of New Jersey's Portuguese immigrants have had intense personal contact with Angola, Mozambique, and Guinea Bissau, either as native-born Luso-Africans, ex-soldiers in the colonial wars, escapees from military service or as *retornados.* This experience has gone virtually undocumented and unexamined.

Retornados who left Africa for Portugal in 1975 to 1976 were initially the victims of an inhospitable reception from their fellow countrymen (Lubkemann 2002; 2003; 2005; Ovalle-Behamon 2003). However, now, thirty years later, scholars have lauded their reintegration into Portuguese society as an economic success story—one with a rocky start but a resoundingly positive ending (Pires et al 1987; Pires 2003). Given the twists and turns of this historical narrative, I set out to research why and when the *retornado* population of New Jersey arrived in the U.S. After having fled Africa in the midst of anti-colonial violence, and reentered Portugal during a time of political instability, what would motivate these families to pack up yet again and move to a third continent? What did America promise them? What kind of feelings did *retornados* have toward Portugal? Toward Lusophone Africa? Where did their national affections and cultural affinities lie? What was their experience of colonialism and how has this experience conditioned views on race and ethnicity in a diverse Northeastern state like New Jersey? Following an experience of serial migration, how permanent do they view their lives on American soil?

In order to begin answering these questions, my students and I conducted lengthy life-history interviews with six people—three men and three women—who had lived in Angola and returned to Portugal during the mid-seventies. Several sat for three and four different interview sessions, so as to better express the richness of their experience and the complexity of their stories. I have also conducted fieldwork with several of these interviewees, accompanying them to family gatherings and other social events where the topic of Africa continually emerged. My paper will examine the testimony of these six New Jersey residents against recent theories that *retornados* from Africa reassimilated successfully into native Portuguese towns following the 1974 revolution.

All six of my interviewees identify as white, bearing a phenotypical resemblance to other continental Portuguese immigrants who populate northern New Jersey. However, despite racial and ethnic similarities to this community, not one of the interviewees identifies as simply "Portuguese." Four interviewees were born in Angola and call themselves "Angolans" or "Africans," while the other two were born in Portugal and refer to themselves as "Portuguese who lived in Angola" or sometimes just "refugees." All report socializing more frequently with Luso-Africans in New Jersey than with Portuguese immigrants who have no connection to Africa. Two of the six have actively rejected the companionship of non-African Portuguese, and have instead sought out friendships among other ethnic and racial groups that populate northern New Jersey such as Brazilians, African-Americans and Latinos. One interviewee even embraced a new religion in order to frequent a Brazilian Evangelical parish where she had friends. Four of the interviewees report having joined official associations, online communities, and/or social clubs of Luso-Africans, and report celebrating Angola Independence Day each year.

The life history narratives of these six *retornados* living in New Jersey—narratives dominated by an unwavering identification with Angola—complicate the portrayal of seamless cultural adaptation and marked economic success among white Angolan settlers who remained in Portugal following 1974. These six New Jersey interviewees report a vastly different experience, one of social rejection in Portugal, intense emotional ties to Angola, and an embrace of serial migration in search of a surrogate Africa. This essay examines the sociopolitical dynamics, affective ties, and personal decision-making processes that catalyzed a triangular migrational trajectory from between Portugal, Angola, and the United States.

Inhospitable Reception and Emotional Ruin

During the final phase of Portuguese colonialism, dictator António Salazar and his Estado Novo government (1926-1974) dealt with increasing international criticism of its prolonged colonial rule in Africa by encouraging Portuguese settlement, passing legislation which abolished previous racial categories, and promoting the colonies as egalitarian multiracial societies which, as "overseas provinces," were merely an extension of the Portuguese nation. The majority of Portuguese colonial emigration occurred from 1950-1970, the precise period when other European nations were concentrating their efforts on decolonization. Portugal's "archaic settler colonialism was an artifact of the Salazarian regime's attempt to counter mounting international pressure" to decolonize (Lubkemann 2002, 192).

Following the Portuguese revolution of 1974 and the handing over of power to African anticolonial groups, the vast majority of white Portuguese settlers and a portion of the mixed race and indigenous black population, escaped rising violence and the nationalization of private property by either fleeing to neighboring countries, or, in the case of over 505,000 people, moving to Portugal. Sixty-one percent of the returnees arrived from Angola, and thirty-three percent from Mozambique (Pires et al. 1987).

As might be expected, the mass return of colonial settlers at a time of dramatic political change—Portugal went from entrenched authoritarian rule to a fledgling communist government in just a few days—added another layer of instability and flux. In addition to the sweeping political changes, rampant unemployment and poor economic conditions plagued the country in the early seventies. The arrival of a half-million people, many of whom had lost all of their savings and possessions in Africa and needed assistance finding housing, work, and medical care, strained an already taxed national operation.

The handful of scholars who have studied *retornados* can be divided up according to two somewhat conflicting research foci. On the one hand, Lubkemann (2002; 2003; 2005) and Ovalle-Bahamón (2003) concentrate on the difficulties *retornados* encountered upon reentry into Portugal, and Droux (1986) concentrates on the psychological trauma resulting from repatriation. On the other hand, Rui Pena Pires (2003), taking a more longitudinal approach, focuses on the way in which *retornados* were able to overcome initial obstacles and ultimately succeed economically in Portugal, due to higher rates of formal education and professional experience gained in Africa. Pena Pires (2003) attributes some of this success to state policies designed to short-circuit the mobilization of a group identity, by encouraging *retornados* to disperse themselves back into the wider population with the help of family, and facilitate rapid reentry into the larger Portuguese workforce through special credit and job placement programs. Pena Pires argues that, generally, these *retornado* policies accomplished their goals of a swift and positive reentry into Portuguese society and the Portuguese economy.

My research with *retornados* living in New Jersey affirms some of Pena Pires's findings, but the global view of their experiences deviates dramatically from the overarching narrative laid out in Pena Pires's work. Generally, these New Jersey *retornados* were unable or unwilling to adjust to life in Portugal. Presently, they are all living in working-class neighborhoods throughout northern New Jersey and, in all but one case, working blue-collar jobs and living very frugal lives. Their present circumstances would not constitute an economic success story. They have never "gotten over" Angola, and contrary to commonly held perceptions, this longing for past lives has little to do with material wealth. Some came to the United States in search of a surrogate Africa. Others came to escape what they characterized as the social toxicity of Portugal manifested in family feuds, soured business relationships, and a general environment of narrow-mindedness and critique. All still dream of returning to Angola, either permanently or for a visit. Many New Jersey *retornados* socialize together, have sought out spouses and roommates of varying races from Angola, Mozambique or Brazil, and attend official and unofficial gatherings of Luso-Angolans in the U.S. Unlike the findings in Pena Pires's study, the New Jersey *retornados* have indeed formed a group identity, albeit a somewhat subdued one, laden with painful collective memories.

So, where and when did the New Jersey *retornados'* alternate path begin? All report difficult times in Portugal, along the lines of Lubkemann and Ovalle-Bahamón's studies which argue that *retornados* were generally greeted by the Portuguese public—strangers, neighbors, friends, and family alike—with suspicion and hostility. In addition to the economic burden caused by the reintegration of colonial settlers, the political climate of revolutionary Portugal made for the swift and energized disavowal of all symbols associated with the old fascist colonial regime, and the *retornados* were roasted in the press as just such a symbol. Ovalle-Bahamón analyzes this dynamic as part and parcel of a post-revolutionary impulse to reimagine colonialism as:

> the sum total of individual actions in the colonies, distanced from continental Portugal: a discursive strategy of temporal and spatial containment.... If blame for colonialism was to fall on anyone, it would be the *retornados.* Even though debate and politics continued to show signs of confusion regarding colonialism..., at the level of lived experience *retornados* tended to shoulder the burden of colonialism. (2003, 166)

In addition to serving as a symbolic scapegoat for the colonial project, *retornados* were also faulted for not having kept in close enough contact with Portuguese family members and friends once they had settled in Africa. Steve Lubkemann (2002) analyses this dynamic as a rupture in the "moral script"—norms which dictate that emigrants maintain strong emotional ties to those left behind in Portugal through visits, letter-writing, gifts, remittances, and investment in Portuguese retirement homes. Colonial settlers in Africa failed to retain roots in native towns and were thus seen as having shirked important social, economic, and moral commitments to home communities. Failure to meet these expectations contributed to the difficult reentry of *retornados* in Portugal during the revolutionary period.

Ana Maria[5], a secondary school teacher who currently resides in Elizabeth, New Jersey and was born in Nova Lisboa, Angola in 1955, recalls her family's clean break from Portuguese friends and family and a complete reconstitution of social ties in Angola. Even though her parents moved to Angola in the early fifties knowing no one, they quickly found friends and neighbors that Ana Maria later came to call "cousins and aunts and uncles." She says:

> You see in Angola we didn't even talk a lot about family [in Portugal]. Because you have to understand that all the people that were with us [in Angola], my parents' best friends, they became our aunts. And like my godmother's mom became my Vovó.... So our real family in Portugal they were strangers to us, we had no connection with these people in another country. So, yes, I remember getting pictures once in a while but we didn't pay attention to them.... [M]y cousins were my friends in Luanda.

The lack of contact between Portuguese relatives and settlers in Angola makes Rui Pena Pires's findings that sixty percent of *retornados* moved back to native towns in 1975 surprising (Pires et al. 1987; 2003). Pires explains that the Portuguese government encouraged *retornados* to move in with family members in native towns, as a cost-saving measure and as a way to short-circuit the mobilization of group solidarity and identity (Pires 2003). How did this policy succeed in the face of the family estrangement Lubkemann posits and my interviewees confirm? Pena Pires's statistical portrait of familial benevolence does not specify the quality of and conditions under which family assistance occurred. In the case of Joana, who was born in Catumbela, Angola in 1950, and returned with her family to the town of Mangualde, Portugal in 1975, their welcome was anything but hospitable:

> My father had an aunt and uncle in Portugal that had a good situation.... They had a house, that was really more of a silo where they kept corn and bags of seeds...and in that space they made a house to shelter my father and my mother, and later I came and stayed there too. But it was more of a storage building that she then made into a house, but it was in no shape [to live in]. The water ran down the walls, the floor was always full of water and you could barely live there. So the moment came when they had given us things and it was time for us to pay them back.... Not in money. But I made a lot of crochet and sold it out of the home to survive, because we didn't have any financial help from anyone. And my aunt made me work for her for free, making crochet, and my mom—the same thing—a free seamstress for her. Working. And so we reached a point we couldn't take it anymore, and my parents went to Lisbon.

Despite being well off, Joana's paternal relatives housed her family in a silo and put them to work without paying them. This type of arrangement, bearing more than a passing resemblance to indentured servitude, lasted for four years. Joana's experience, surprisingly similar to other interviewees' tales of moving first to native towns, and then later to other cities in Portugal and elsewhere in order to sever hometown ties, would not have shown up in the census data used to narrate a generally successful reentry into Portuguese society with the help of hometown friends and family.

Carlos, born in Angola in 1968, returned with his parents to Portugal in 1975 as a seven year old. From 1975 to 1985, Carlos attended secondary school in northern Portugal in the hometown of paternal relatives. Carlos says that his father was so offended by the way Portuguese relatives treated him that he left in 1975 to find work outside the country, first in Spain, then in France, then finally in the U.S. In 1985, Carlos and his mother moved to New Jersey to join his father who had found steady work in construction. Carlos had not seen his father in ten years. Although he spent more of his youth in Portugal than in Angola, Carlos does not consider himself Portuguese. He reports that the ten years spent in northern Portugal were extremely lonely and painful. Despite being a talkative, charismatic child, Carlos says he only had one or two friends there, neither of whom he has kept in touch with as an adult. He details what it was like in Portuguese secondary school as a white Angolan:

> When I left Angola, and I was seven years old, I didn't want to go to Portugal. I wanted—a lot of our friends [from Angola], they went to Brazil. If you don't want to change [your life], go to Brazil. They speak Portuguese too. So you going to another tropical country. I was never welcomed in Portugal because I was an outsider. Although I was born under the Portuguese flag, but I was an outsider. And I got pretty sick of the Portuguese people, not the country or the culture, but the attitude of those people. I remember I was in school, and people used to beat the crap out of me because I was from Angola. And there were three kids from Angola, me and two other kids. And those parents, those Portuguese parents, would tell their kids to do that to us. [The parents] would say, "Don't come home from school until you do it." So when we left school—because we had to walk home—there was no buses to pick us up or drop us off. I had to walk an hour to go home through the woods. So when I got my feet in the woods, you know, someone would come down on me with a stick to the head. Everyday for me,... it was like an adventure just to get from point A through the woods to point B. But me and those two kids, we used to get beat up. I mean once you get beat up everyday, you lose your mind and you go crazy.... I used to come home all beat up and my mother won't even recognize me, that's all, I had to go straight to the hospital. My face looked like the elephant

> man. I mean we're talking fifteen to twenty kids between kicking you and doing you with the sticks.

Carlos's experience of childhood abuse in Portugal clearly marks him as an adult. He says that despite the difficulty of packing up at seventeen years old to move to yet another country, and despite his regret at never having finished high school, he is glad he's not living in Portugal. He finds the linguistic and ethnic diversity of the U.S. comforting after his experience of hostile intolerance to difference in Portugal. The lasting impact of school-age trauma has caused Carlos to view himself as a self-professed "black sheep" for eschewing typical Portuguese-American traditions like going to Mass, drinking wine at lunch, going to immigrant social clubs, and getting together with Portuguese family and friends on Christmas. He lives his life in opposition to these practices and says that if he ever has kids, he's not sure if he will teach them his mother tongue.

Steve Lubkemann (2003), following Werbner (1989), suggests that *retornados* were treated as "internal strangers" upon arriving in Portugal due in part to racialized Portuguese ideologies of nationhood. Lubkemann (2002) also argues persuasively for the way in which white *retornados* fought to differentiate themselves from black or mixed-race *retornados* in order to mitigate the stigma of "ethnic otherness" associated with the term. What is different in Carlos's experience as narrated above is that as a white Angolan whose parents still had active ties to their native towns, his internal strangerhood did not involve overt racial prejudice nor prior estrangement from Portuguese family and friends. And as an adult, he has rejected a white Portuguese identity, preferring instead to affiliate with and reside near immigrants of color, mostly post-1964 immigrants from Latin America and the Caribbean. His experience of childhood rejection in Portugal caused him to look for affiliation and friendship across racial lines as an adult in New Jersey and to embrace a certain social marginality as the family "black sheep." This move is significantly different from the white repatriates who stayed in Portugal and attempted to reappropriate a white-washed version of the term *retornado* "as a claim to prestige and centrality" (Lubkemann 2002, 208).

José, a man born in Nova Lisboa in the 1950s whose mother died when he was six, had almost no contact with extended family in Portugal.

So when he left Angola in 1975, he relied on government welfare distributed by IARN (*Instituto de Apoio ao Retorno de Nacionais*—Institute for the Support of Returning Nationals) to settle temporarily in Lisbon. His experience in Lisbon, living off government hand-outs was so difficult that he immediately set his sights on leaving the country. Now a construction worker and musician resident of Elizabeth, New Jersey, José continues to write about his experience leaving Africa for Portugal, thirty years after the fact, in poems he sets to music.

In these poems, Africa is represented as a maternal force enveloping newcomers in the startling beauty of her natural landscape, an embrace that begins to enter the body, overtaking one's inner cells. In contrast, José describes post-revolutionary Lisbon as an inhuman, mechanized wasteland that vomits outsiders. Even though, logistically, it was Angola he was expelled from in 1975, José's more memorable experience of rejection and repulsion takes place on Portuguese soil, according to the following poem:

Angolano
Still in the early dawn
With the subway vomiting out all that human meat
Rolling rolling

If you feel hate, you do
I'm also
like you
I come from somewhere else

Get in line, my brother,
On the *Junqueira* of disgrace
In the incandescent cold
The Angolan has no race

If you feel hate, you do
I'm also
like you
I come from somewhere else

Go Angolan without bread
Go Angolan without work
Keep walking along the streets
Keep walking without pardon

José documents the hostile, "hateful" reception he confronted upon entering a country he considered foreign. By bringing in the phrase "the Angolan has no race," he refers to the public assistance lines both white and black Angolans waited in together along Lisbon's "Junqueira Avenue (of disgrace)"—IARN headquarters. José also projects the desire for a raceless Angola, a wishful vision which would facilitate his return there. In other poems, he continues the personification of Africa as mother wondering, "Isn't there somewhere you could fit me in on your face, Mother Africa, a small piece of your white smile?" His poetic bloodlines clearly do not include Portugal, which is always portrayed as a hostile foil to his broken but loving Angolan family.

José came as quickly as possible to the U.S. from Lisbon, using his government assistance not for food or housing in Portugal, but to buy a plane ticket to a new world. When he arrived in the U.S., he sought out other *retornados* from Lusophone Africa, and ended up marrying a white Angolan woman who was also born in Nova Lisboa.

Ana Maria views her move to America as therapeutic for processing emotional pain and as a corrective to politically enforced ignorance: "Our family was separated. My parents and sister and I left Africa not knowing if we would see my brother again, and knowing we would never see neighbors and friends again. My brother survived, but is still a broken person." Ana Maria's brother, who had been drafted into the Portuguese army and sent to war in the early seventies, was not able to leave Angola for Portugal with the rest of his family. He survived the war, though when he arrived in Portugal with a pregnant white Angolan wife, things started to fall apart. He was employed as a manager in his father-in-law's new manufacturing plant in northern Portugal. Although he had steady and lucrative employment, a new wife and baby, Ana Maria's brother could not adjust to living in Portugal. Missing his parents and sisters who were already in the U.S., and perhaps also suffering from undiagnosed post-traumatic stress disorder, her brother began acting erratically—crashing cars, drinking, cheating on his wife, gambling money away. Eventually, he moved to the U.S. without his wife and baby and has lived the last several decades in New Jersey fighting substance abuse, sometimes unemployed and occasionally homeless.

Ana Maria talks about coming to America as a therapeutic fresh start for her sister and parents, though the move did not help her brother. "It allowed us to heal," she said. When she used the term "fresh start," Ana Maria wanted to make clear she was not talking about money. Her father went from a white-collar job at the Bank of Angola to a janitor cleaning New York City public schools, and this did not seem to bother him. She says, "After you lose everything, possessions and money don't matter anymore." Ana Maria and her parents invested everything they had in education. Ana Maria wanted to learn about Portuguese colonialism in Angola because during her youth, under the Estado Novo and its censors, she says she never knew what was really happening. She and her husband have decided not to have children. Instead, her substantial store of physical energy, intellectual drive, and compassion has been directed toward researching and teaching others about Lusophone Africa. "To me," she says, "the only way to heal the wounds of the past is through learning." By reading uncensored accounts of the war, Estado Novo policy, and post-independence literature, Ana Maria also tries to come to terms with what happened to her brother. Moving to the United States, throwing herself into the public education system, and earning a doctorate in Lusophone-African Literature has allowed Ana Maria to connect with Angola from afar as well as work through painful family experiences.

Financial Crises

In addition to stories of inhospitable receptions and emotional trauma, four out of six interviewees also experienced financial crises following relocation to Portugal. All of the interviewees except for one arrived in Portugal with little or no money and possessions. In Angola in 1975, Ana Maria and José were high school students from upper middle-class families; Carlos was a third grade student from a middle-class family; Joana was working as an office assistant from a lower middle-class family; Judite was working as a retail clerk in a clothing store and Nuno was working as a welder. Regardless of their varied economic circumstances in Angola, all six interviewees and their nuclear families arrived in Portugal having abandoned bank accounts, household goods, personal effects, and, in some cases, properties in Angola. Joana, Judite and Nuno, and Ana Maria's brother took advantage of Cifre[6] and other programs either to start new businesses or resuscitate failing businesses in Portugal. In the end, all of these ventures faltered or failed.

In the case of Nuno and Judite, a married couple who had moved to Angola as young adults, political allegiances caused them to have a rocky economic reentrance into Portugal. Nuno left Angola six months before his wife because she harbored hopes that Angola would find stable political leadership and would ultimately accept the presence of whites in a post-independence society. Nuno, who had witnessed the murder of a white colleague and his pregnant wife at the hands of MPLA guerillas, held out no such hope, and reluctantly left his wife behind in Luanda.[7] In the ensuing six months, Judite became increasingly disillusioned with both the communist-led government in Portugal and Angola's communist-backed MPLA party that continued to solidify its power. After heeding warnings from black friends and co-workers who felt Judite's life was in danger in Luanda, she packed up and returned to Portugal, blaming the communist party on both continents for Angola's rising violence and botched decolonization.[8] In Portugal, Judite and her husband's anti-communist convictions cost Nuno his job as a welder when he was "blacklisted" and denied work. Judite describes this period of unemployment:

> My husband was an excellent welder, and he was a good professional. Now those people on the left wanted to organize strikes. But as we in Angola are used to working, we didn't even know what a strike was, my husband didn't want a strike. So they put him on the black list so that he would be defeated and unemployable when we arrived in Portugal. So after six months, I went to get…I asked my father for a gun, because I said, "I'll kill you, because not even in Angola and certainly not here will you bring me down," and I never accepted those politics.

As the above statement demonstrates, Judite's anger at the communist party which, from her perspective, destroyed her life in Africa, was also preventing her husband from starting over financially in Portugal.

Her anger was so intense that she went so far as to obtain a gun and contemplate what she termed a blend of vigilante justice and political revenge.

Ultimately, in 1976 and 1977 as rumors of other communist initiatives and rebellions spread throughout Portugal, Judite prepared her passport and those of her two infant sons and husband to apply for political asylum in the United States. While awaiting their paperwork, they also applied for Cifre funds to resuscitate Nuno's father's trucking business near Lisbon. Over time, Nuno and his father grew the business. The family stayed in Portugal until 1985 when the business started to falter, and Nuno discovered that a close childhood friend had been stealing money from him for years, jeopardizing his company.

Just as he had done in Africa, Nuno moved to the U.S. without knowing anyone and started a new life with Judite and their two young sons. He reports having found Portugal small, corrupt, and dominated by ideologues who were ruining the country. Details about souring business ventures in native towns parallel testimony from other interviewees about returning to Portuguese communities of petty, narrow-minded people who had never experienced other ways of life, did not know how to conduct business, and did not know how to sustain an authentic friendship. In the stories surrounding Nuno's business problems, he described an environment of suspicion, jealousy, and greed, perhaps brought on by the fact that *retornados* had access to government loans while others did not. While in some instances government subsidies and credit programs eased the economic burden of having lost everything in Angola, they did not, in the case of Nuno and other interviewees, ease social reintegration into native towns and villages. To the contrary, *retornado* benefits created antagonistic relationships between those who had lived in Africa and those who had stayed in Portugal. While the targeted objectives of government interventions like Cifre were, according to Pena Pires's research, to short-circuit *retornado* group identity, prevent collective reparation demands, thwart "disidentification" with Portuguese society, and encourage rapid reintegration, many New Jersey interviewees outline the way in which these programs created hostility, mistrust, transience, and marginalization, and ultimately sped their emigration out of the country—dynamics in complete conflict with what was initially intended.

Nuno's discovery that he had been cheated by a friend was the straw that broke the camel's back, a culminating moment in his unhappiness with Portuguese society, business, and politics. For Nuno, the Northeastern U.S. promised anonymity, social diversity, and expanded horizons of the same kind he remembered from Africa. By moving to the U.S., Nuno hoped to escape the small-minded, petty ways of the Portugal he had returned to, and hoped to recreate the more expansive dynamics he had so appreciated in Angola.

Race and Affective Ties to Angola

In his book, *Angola Under the Portuguese: The Myth and the Reality,* Gerald Bender (2004 [1978]) dismantles the myth of lusotropicalism, a conceptual paradigm spawned by Brazilian sociologist Gilberto Freyre in the 1940s, first used to describe Brazil and later applied to Lusophone Africa. Lusotropicalism frames the lusophone colonial world as exceptional in its incidence of interracial mixing and relative absence of racist attitudes. Bender's pioneering study employs demographic evidence to show that Angola's rate of miscegenation was no higher than that of other African colonies. Bender engages other sets of historical data such as Estado Novo laws which facilitated forced labor of rural black Africans—a system described by one mid-century observer as "worse than slavery"—(Galvão cited in Birmingham 2006, 84) to demonstrate that lusotropical claims of interracial harmony bore little resemblence to colonial reality in Angola. Bender's systematic dismantling of a powerful and enduring set of ideas is clearly a seminal contribution, and his general argument is one I agree with. However, the *retornado* testimony gathered for this paper conflicts with his assertion that white colonists were generally not exposed to and did not identify with native Angolan culture.

Bender states, "[w]ith the exception of occasional *sertanejos* [frontiersmen] and bush traders, the Portuguese in Angola have been largely impervious to African influences, even in such aspects as music, food, and language ..." (2004 [1978], 28). The overwhelming throughline of all six interviews conducted for this paper, however, deals with the acute longing for life on African soil. Contrary to what Bender's study might have predicted, memories of this life include the smells of African cuisine, the sounds of African music, the distinctive Angolan accent in Portuguese, and in the case of one interviewee, the Kimbundu language which her white Portuguese father spoke fluently and which, to this day, peppers her memories and dreams.

Among the handful of scholarly studies of late colonial Angolan society, analyses of the complexities of race and class differ somewhat as to the role of white civilian settlers.[9] Patrick Chabal notes that except for the elite coffee plantation owners, "the Portuguese settlers were poor, unskilled, uneducated and on the whole … failed to succeed as agriculturalists" (2002, 109). He states that most of these settlers, unable to compete with Africans and without resources, moved to cities to labor alongside other races in blue-collar jobs. Chabal describes the presence of this underclass of white settlers as a "bar to the progression of Africans into the kind of jobs which they might have expected to have in other, non-Portuguese colonies"—a dynamic which led to an environment of "petty discrimination and racism which affected the ordinary Africans and Creoles of the cities" (2002, 109). While Chabal underscores the conflict and competition caused by the presence of uneducated whites in Angolan cities, Bender describes a dynamic of limited contact. The societal portrait of Angola in the 1960s and 1970s painted in Bender's study consists of three primary populational swathes: a small but relatively wealthy class of white colonists who settled along Angola's littoral strip of cities and towns; a large black African majority who maintained residence in the rural interior; and a third group of mixed race and "assimilated" blacks who served the colonists in the cities having generally abandoned ties to native communities and families in the interior. Though he does acknowledge the presence of a small proportion of white Portuguese living among black Angolans in the urban *musseques* (ghettoes), Bender's argument focuses on a distinct lack of interracial contact.[10] It is precisely this contact which conditions many of my interviewees' memories of and longing for Africa.

Joana, a domestic worker who currently resides in Newark, New Jersey was born in Catumbela, Angola in the province of Benguela in 1950. Her father had been born in Angola in 1924, whereas her mother was born in Portugal and came to Angola as a young girl. Joana comes from a lower middle-class family; both parents possessed only four years of formal education and Joana left school after the sixth grade to seek employment. Joana grew up in Catumbela and Lobito and, at age twenty-five, moved to Portugal just before Angolan independence in 1975. After ten years of what Joana characterizes as hostility and maltreatment by Portuguese family and friends, she and her husband—a white army official who grew up in São Tomé and Angola—left Portugal and moved back to Angola where they lived from 1986 to 1993 in relatively impoverished and violent circumstances. After Joana's husband died suddenly in 1993, following complications from a routine surgical procedure, she again moved from Angola to Portugal for one year and then decided to relocate to the U.S. in 1995, where she has been ever since. She describes her experience of Angolan return as the result of an ever-present and urgent desire to live in Angola under any economic and political conditions. She reports that she kept trying to go back, not to recapture her youth, nor for financial gain, but for the simple pleasure of living among a familiarly diverse array of people and against the unique topographical landscape that Angola offers. She says she has just wanted to "go home."

Joana's small, tidy apartment in a working-class neighborhood of Newark is overflowing with objects from Angola. On her coffee table and bookshelves she shows me her Angolan library—books of poetry by family friends like the popular writer Goia and Agostinho Neto, the first president of independent Angola. She has large books of photographs of Angolan landscapes, scholarly books by a cousin about the proliferation of political parties in post-independence Angola, and diaries and essays about the colonial wars. The books on permanent display throughout Joana's apartment, arranged in almost altar-like fashion, do not contain romanticized images of colonial Angola and white privilege, but rather a multifaceted portrayal of Angola's last fifty years, rife with war, destruction, hunger, and poverty—interspersed with photographic representations of monumental beauty and literary portrayals of hope for a brighter future.

As I sit on her sofa and leaf through the closest book, she points out the fact that Bonga is playing on her CD player. Bringing forty to fifty cassettes and CDs of Angolan music to the coffee table, she confesses that Bonga is her favorite. She shows me letters from friends who are still in Angola, careful to set aside all of the letters from one close friend who works in a post office in Luanda. She wants me to read years' worth of correspondence from this friend—a black Angolan with a wife and children who sends many updated family photographs and asks when she might return to Angola. She told me later that she has periodically helped this friend in hard financial times, sending him money or goods that he can sell such as cameras and calculators. She also says that he and his wife have, in turn, helped her by sending souvenirs and handicrafts from Angola and offering to help her find a job, should she decide to return. Joana's apartment and the life experience it reflects hardly represent Bender's claim that white settlers had limited contact with other races and remained untouched by or indifferent to native Angolan culture.

As Joana's story unfolds over many meals and afternoons of dialogue and interviews, it is clear that the sights, sounds, and smells of Angola—an Angola of diverse races—haunt her to the point where she seems somewhat disinterested in her American present. She defines herself solely as "an African from Angola," and dreams of returning there before she dies. When asked what it is about Angola that so captivates her, she, finding it hard to settle on one element, decides it is mostly the sociability and camaraderie that existed among people she knew. Most of these narratives describing Angolan sociability are placed against the backdrop of her negative experience in Portugal where she felt "people were cold, conservative, paranoically closed, and would do their best to see you fail or even to cause your demise." In contrast, Joana's community in Benguela featured intense interchange among people, extensive periods of time socializing outside in the street, yards or patios and tight-knit communities where neighbors banded together in hard times:

> We Angolans have a saying: "Whoever drinks from the Catumbela River, will never abandon Angola." Because that there is a land, the climate is perfect. You work, you live, you play, well, there is everything. Even in times of shortages and lack, there are always friends that have a little to help others. I mean, within that circle of friendship there aren't difficulties, because if one has something s/he gives it to the other, if the other has it, he gives it, and there are no problems.

Asked how race figures into these memories, she neither whitewashes the situation nor ignores her own personal attachments to black and mixed-race Angolans. She talks of her experience in an integrated secondary school, a *mestiço* uncle who inherited half of her grandfather's business, of friends and neighbors of different races, and of *bailes* (dances) and other festivities where revelers of all colors danced together. The way she describes the scene makes it clear, however, that certain criteria conditioned the acceptance of non-whites in the 1950s and 1960s, when she was growing up:

> When I went to school, we had all kinds—every race that there was in Angola, blacks, mulattos, *cabritos*.... We had parties and dances [where] the musicians were black, and the parties were full of white, blacks, and mulattos, dancing together. As long as they were people of a certain level, there was no problem at all. [If they were] well-dressed and educated, there was no difference based on color. But, well, a guy with no shoes, who was drunk, would not be let in.

According to Joana, she often experienced interracial conviviality and white tolerance toward blacks and mulattos, so long as certain class markers were in place. According to her testimony above, well-dressed well-brought-up people of color would be accepted, though folks bearing a lower-class status—marked by a shabby appearance or public drunkenness—would not.

Between the lines of Joana's explanation of race/class dynamics in late colonial Angola lies the Estado Novo policy, implemented in 1954, of forcing non-whites to prove they had become "assimilated" in order to be issued a Portuguese Identity Card and consequent access to Portuguese citizenship. In order to be deemed "assimilated," black and mixed-race Angolans had to be fluent in Portuguese, had to have reached a designated level of formal Portuguese schooling, had to produce documents attesting to a positive moral and civic comportment, and pass muster during home inspections where Portuguese officials verified whether or not African residents used European-style furniture and ate Portuguese food. In the words of Angolan writer, Raul David, assimilation was tantamount to the "complete humiliation of the black man" where "Portuguese colonization disqualified all African behavior in order to solely valorize what could be identified as European, and more particularly Portuguese" (cited in Laban 1991). Following David,

Alfredo Margarido states, "[w]hat is at work here is the frank rejection of any form of reciprocity, where [indigenous African traditions constitute] a simple manifestation of savagery to the point where they are clearly prohibited by Portuguese legislation" (Margarido 2000, 43).

When asked about the effects of such legislation, Joana admitted she was not familiar with the particulars of the assimilation process but clearly witnessed the societal rewards for looking and behaving like an idealized version of a middle-class Portuguese. Clearly "assimilated" Angolans populated the interracial *bailes* Joana remembers from her youth.[11] However, when asked about the legislated erasure of African tradition, Joana said that this had not been her experience. In fact, she said, as an adult she and her husband, who had been born in São Tomé, listened almost exclusively to lusophone African music and ate primarily African dishes. Following their move to Beira Alta, Portugal in 1975, their Portuguese neighbors complained about the smells of their "African barbecues" and critiqued their habits of cultural consumption, saying "with so much Portuguese music, all these *retornados* play is music from Angola."

Joana and almost of all of the others interviewed contrasted Angola's conditional white acceptance of assimilated blacks with the dynamics of Mozambique, whose practices and attitudes they felt were influenced by South African apartheid. Joana states:

> In Mozambique, I don't know [if they were so tolerant] because…they had apartheid close by. Once my parents went from Angola to Mozambique to see a soccer game between Benfica and Porto and they stayed in a hotel there. Traveling with them was a woman of color, who was a friend with a degree in languages, and she did not have access to the hotel where my parents and aunt and uncle stayed. She had to go to another hotel because she was of color.

Unlike what Robin Sheriff (2000) documents in Brazil, however, Joana does not mute or "silence" stories of white racism and violence in order to paint a lusotropicalist portrait of interracial harmony in colonial Angola. In addition to contextualizing white acceptance of black and *mestiço* Angolans along class lines, Joana also described the abuses of what she characterized as a "minority of white exploiters." She talked at length of her boss who was said to have murdered black Angolans in order to take over their lands:

> I will tell you about a case of this boss of mine. This guy, in order to have the plantations he had, he stole from the blacks. Sometimes he even had them killed, there are people that say he did this. I never saw it, but there are people that say that he can't sleep with the light off anymore. Because they say that his guilt and remorse are so great that he can't sleep with the light off, thinking of all the evil he'd done to the blacks. There were half-a-dozen more like him [that I knew]. We can't say that every Portuguese that went to Angola did bad things, but there were cases, yes sir, of people that exploited, killed, in order to have the possessions that belonged to them.

As demonstrated by this testimony, Joana's memories of Angola include recalling nightmarish rumors of elite white brutality toward black Africans and practices of land seizure motivated by greed and enabled by unchecked colonial power. In the world that Joana remembers, this violent exploitative white faction was also accompanied by people like herself who were tolerant of racial difference and wanted to better their lives through hard work and sacrifice, often alongside people of color. When probed further on these memories, Joana invokes her more recent history to try to elaborate. She described returning to war-torn Angola in 1986 to 1993 and living in an enormous apartment building in Lobito where "there were only three white couples, the rest were all black. And we never had problems. I always acted as if nothing had ever happened—it was my hometown and no one ever did anything bad to me." She recounts handing out many of the medical supplies that she had brought from Portugal to homeless Angolans who needed them. She also describes the way in which currency had no value during this period of civil war and neighbors of all races had to barter with each other in order to put food on the table. She often traded flour and handmade crochet linens for other neighbors' produce.

Joana's affective ties to Angola are dominated by stories of intense sociability and interchange in a society where during peaceful periods, people spent their leisure time outdoors in public spaces. In her testimony, there existed a dynamic of intersection and interchange among lower middle-class white, black, and mixed-race Angolans in several cities and towns of her native Benguela province. Such memories are tempered by recognition of the European class markers which conditioned multiracial coexistence and which must be viewed in tandem with Portuguese colonial policies of forced African assimilation. However, despite the brutal requirements of assimilation which forced Africans to abandon indigenous languages, culinary habits, traditions of dress, and ways of furnishing a home, Joana came into contact with and internalized fragments of the Kimbundo lexicon, and left Angola with a passion for African food and music. She considered these indigenous traditions to be part of her upbringing, an irreplaceable part of her own Angolan culture. At one point she tells me, "You know the expression—'I'm *dying* to go back there.' Well, my husband literally died as a consequence of having returned to Angola. And I could have died too. Angola and the people of Angola were worth that kind of risk."

Conclusion

What explains the gap between the scholarly record and the experience of the *retornados* living in New Jersey? Are we to mistrust their testimony as overly romanticized when dealing with memories of Africa and overly harsh when dealing with memories of Portugal? Should we be skeptical of these testimonies because they have been influenced by contemporary norms of political correctness and multicultural ideologies of racial tolerance, therefore skewing and manipulating memories of the past? Has the shame of the colonial project and the scapegoating of *retornados* caused white colonists, consciously or not, to recast their experiences according to more acceptable norms of comportment and conceptualization? Or, is this gap the result of a disciplinary vacuum where post-*25 de Abril* scholarship on Angola has been dominated by monographs out of history, quantitative sociology, political science, and literary studies, with, as Miguel Vale de Almeida (2004) points out, surprisingly few from anthropology? In other words, has qualitative research focused on in-depth testimony and participant observation come into conflict with studies based on different forms of "evidence" by teasing out the slippage between top-down intent and bottom-up practice? Or, finally, does this swathe of the *retornado* population living in New Jersey represent a distinct group of individuals whose experience differs from those who adapted successfully to life in Portugal after 1975? Were they unable and unwilling to adapt to Portuguese society due to a different kind of—and perhaps more enduring attachment to—Angola?

While all these explanations are worth considering and probably all contribute in varying degrees toward an understanding of *retornado* experience in New Jersey, I believe the individuals I have worked with in New Jersey have had, in fact, experiences that differ substantively from accounts of the *retornados* who reassimilated to Portuguese society. The testimonies of these six individuals indeed complicate and often contradict recent studies showing the seamless integration of *retornados* into post-revolutionary Portuguese society following a temporary phase of difficult adjustment. Generally, the New Jersey *retornados* have rejected a Portuguese identity in favor of an Angolan one. Many associate their Angolan identity with indigenous musical, culinary, and linguistic traditions they try to recreate in an American context. These practices are incongruent with the scholarly record which argues that the majority of white Portuguese had little or no contact with black African traditions. Unlike the white *retornados* who stayed in Portugal, most of the New Jersey *retornados*—particularly the four born in Angola—did not attempt to distinguish and separate themselves from a black African identity, but instead sought out a multiracial, multiethnic environment in which to reside, forging friendships and affiliations among the diverse immigrant groups that populate northern New Jersey. They have embraced the financial and social uncertainty that comes with immigrating to an entirely new country in order to escape Portuguese society which they felt was petty, small-minded, hostile, and intolerant of difference—racial and otherwise. And, finally, in opposition to the Portuguese post-colonial legislation which was meant to prevent *retornados* from identifying as a collective, New Jersey *retornados* have organized themselves into associations and clubs and have joined online listserves and websites dedicated to reconnecting with Angola and old Angolan friends and contacts.

Those *retornados* who decided to leave Portugal following decolonization do not appear in *retornado* scholarship, save for a few paragraphs in Pena Pires's work.[12] The U.S. *retornado* community has not appeared in any of the literature on Portuguese immigration to the U.S. or, more specifically, to New Jersey.[13] *Retornados* who left Portugal in the late seventies and eighties constitute an important and virtually unexplored area for future research, implying the need for a more internally differentiated understanding of the category of "*retornados*" beyond Lubkemann's work analyzing experiential divisions along racial lines. The New Jersey *retornados* suggest a significant demographic release of those unwilling to accept the social, political, and economic conditions of post-colonial Portugal, and seem to comprise a distinct category of white colonists whose intense affective ties to Angola hampered an easy integration into Portuguese society.

The New Jersey *retornados's* collective notion of America as a surrogate for Africa facilitates a sense of continuity—a social throughline which mitigates the disruptive, fragmenting effects of *retornado* migration. For José, Carlos, and Ana Maria, a move to America allowed healing. For Ana Maria, a move to the U.S. also facilitated the pursuit of an "unbiased" education into Lusophone-African literature and culture—a way to reconnect to her roots and understand Portuguese colonialism without the obfuscating propagandistic filters of the Estado Novo. For Joana Nuno and Judite, a move to the U.S., and more specifically, to the largely African-American city of Newark, allowed for the re-creation of a diverse community where heterogeneity was the norm. For all of the interviewees, both Angola and America were described in tropes relating to twin landscapes—social and natural—offering broad sight lines and possibility. In the words of Judite, "We wanted a big sky kind of life."

Notes

[1] Portions of this research were supported by Rutgers University, Newark's Diversity in Undergraduate Education Grant, for which I am very grateful. I would like to thank my undergraduate research assistants, Tatiana Nogueira and Diana Escudeiro, for their careful transcription work and Janki Patel for her cross-cultural interviewing skills. I would also like to thank the six people whose life histories provide the foundation for this article for their openness and generosity.

[2] Portuguese sociologist, Rui Pena Pires, has been the primary contributor to *retornado* scholarship. He wrote his doctoral dissertation on the topic, portions of which appeared in *Os Retornados: Um Estudo Sociográfico* (Pires et al. 1987). He has since published a new book, *Migrações e Integração* (2003) which includes a case study chapter on *retornado* integration. Rocha-Trindade (1995); Lubkemann (2002; 2003; 2005);and Ovalle-Behamon (2003) have all published articles on aspects of *retornado* migration, integration, and stigma. Arnaldo Droux (1986) wrote an unpublished masters thesis on the psychological costs of *retornado* reintegration.

[3] Unless otherwise noted, all translations are my own.

[4] For the very latest example of a silence-breaking television series, aired in December 2007 on RTP and viewed regularly by more than one million people, see Barry Hatton's (2007) AP article, "Ordinary Portuguese Confront a Colonial Past," which details the response to journalist Joaquim

Furtado's controversial programs.

[5] Names of interviewees have been changed in order to protect anonymity.

[6] In July 1976, the Portuguese government created the Commisão Interministerial de Financiamento a Retornados—Cifre [Interminesterial Commission for *Retornardo* Financing] in order to make credit available to *retornados* and administer loan programs. The Cifre programs were designed to make up for *retorandos's* loss of capital through the availability of loans to finance "new economic projects, giving preference to homeless *retornados* in order to build wealth and create new jobs" (Pires 2003, 235). Pena Pires argues that the Cifre program must be analyzed as one of a handful of government initiatives and interventions designed to mobilize and redistribute collective resources and thereby minimize the disidentification with Portuguese society (2003). For more on Cifre and other programs, see Moniz and Pisco (1987).

[7] According to Judite, Nuno had been traumatized not only by the barbaric murder of his longtime colleague and the colleague's wife, whose womb had been sliced open and fetus butchered, but he had also been disillusioned by the Portuguese troops who had set fire to hundreds of warehouses of food, provided by humanitarian relief agencies for the Angolan poor, before returning to Portugal. She said, "[h]e became so traumatized by this, because here it is, they went and destroyed the very thing that the people were lacking, that the city was lacking. Because it was the fear, it was the massacres, it was the attacks, it was the horrible things that happened in the city. He became so traumatized, so changed, that he went everywhere trying through any means possible to arrange a way to leave."

[8] In Pena Pires's research on *retornados* in Portugal, he finds that many share negative views of the political left due to the way in which these parties handled decolonization (2003, 197-99). As a result, *retornados* tend to support Portugal center-right party PSD. Although this is certainly the case for Nuno and Judite, it does not hold true for all of the other New Jersey interviewees. Ana Maria and Joana, for example, support the Democratic Party in the U.S. and are critical of rightest ideologies and policies in the U.S. and Portugal.

[9] David Birmingham offers a statistical portrait of Angola's demographics. "In 1960, ninety percent of Angola's sparse population lived in rural areas, on plantations, around scattered farmsteads, and in small villages. Only the other ten percent lived in sixteen officially designated colonial towns. Of these townspeople, a quarter-million lived in provincial cities such as Nova Lisboa and Benguela or in remote administrative posts.... The other quarter-of-a-million urban Angolans lived in the city of Luanda. The late colonial population of Angola consisted of two million black adults, two million children, and a rising tide of white immigrants from unlettered peasant communities in northern Portugal and Madeira.... Total immigration rose to around 200,000 people" (2006, 83-84). For more on the demographics of white settlement, see Castelo (2007), and more on the complexities and diversity of Angolan social identities, see Messiant (2006).

[10] Comparing interracial contact in Brazil and Angola, Bender states, for example, "throughout their history in Brazil, blacks have been in close contact with the white population. Precisely the opposite is true in Angola, where the overwhelming majority of Africans have always lived on their own or communally-held lands in the rural areas. In 1970, only ten percent of Africans lived in urban centers—a little more than half of them in Angola's capital, Luanda—whereas over fifty percent of whites lived in Angola's major cities. Until recent decades, then, most Africans have had little or no association with whites" (2004, 27).

[11] The official categories of colonial Angola that Joana mentioned more frequently were the designations of "first-class and second-class whites." Joana's mother, having been born in Portugal, was a "first-class white," while her father, a native Angolan, was a "second-class white." These differences manifested themselves, according to Joana, for example, when packing up to leave in 1975. Her mother was entitled to take her belongings with her to Portugal, while her "second-class" father had no such rights.

[12] Citing a dearth of reliable data for quantifying the number of Portuguese colonists who opted not to return to Portugal following 1975, Pena Pires estimates that approximately 60,000 people left Lusophone Africa for other countries (2003, 198). Another smaller swathe of people, estimated at approximately 12,000, was shown to have left Portugal sometime between 1975 and the early eighties, perhaps indicating "a refusal to accept the repatriation solution, following a negative experience of temporary integration into Portuguese society" (2003, 1999). I would include the New Jersey *retornados* in this second group, although their emigration timelines differ somewhat in that three of them came to the U.S. in 1985, and one reemigrated several times between the U.S., Portugal and Angola throughout the 1980s and 1990s. Obviously, further research needs to be done to identify whether or not the *retornados* who moved to the U.S. have other unifying features and to try to get

some sense of the numbers, though U.S. Census categories make this difficult.

[13] For more on Portuguese immigrants in New Jersey, see Holton (2005a; 2005b).

CHAPTER 20

Diasporic Generations: Distinctions of Race, Nationality and Identity in the Cape Verdean Community, Past and Present

MARILYN HALTER

Beginning in the 19th century, when the initial wave of newcomers from the Cape Verde Islands, located off the coast of Senegal and long-colonized by Portugal, began arriving to southeastern New England, they held a unique place in the nation's immigrant mosaic, representing the first voluntary mass migration from Africa to the United States in American history. More than a century later, Cape Verdeans are still making the transatlantic journey to the region, establishing permanent settlements while maintaining strong transnational ties, but today the contemporary flow is joined by migrants from several other African nations and by a variegated Caribbean and Latino diaspora that includes a large and ever-growing Brazilian population. Drawing on my earlier work on the classical period of Cape Verdean migration, as well as new empirical research on the post-independence influx, this chapter compares the two eras of settlement especially with regard to issues of race, ethnicity and cultural identity formation, as well as the generational dynamics of intergroup relations.

The Cape Verdean settlers of the first wave brought with them a distinctive cultural identity, migrating freely to New England as Portuguese colonials, thereby initially perceiving themselves in terms of ethnicity: they were Portuguese. However, when they migrated to the United States at the turn of the last century, they arrived in a society entrenched in fixed notions of black and white, and because of their mixed African and European ancestry, they were looked upon as an inferior racial group. Throughout this phase of adaptation, the strategy of being recognized as a distinctive cultural group—as Cape Verdean-Americans—was met with stiff resistance as it coincided with a period in

American history when racial segregation was at its height and notions of racial identity were rigidly cast in black and white. Contemporary migrants, however, are settling into a society where the social climate has become more accepting of cultural hybridity. Furthermore, during the last two decades, the demography of southern New England, still the overwhelming destination of recent Cape Verdean arrivals, has been dramatically transformed from communities comprised primarily of people of European descent, to a much more diverse and multiracial social landscape. A century before the notion of "the browning of America" gained popularity as a way of describing the increasingly *mestizo* complexion of the United States, the Cape Verdean diaspora was testing the waters of American pluralism. Issues of identity have continued to figure prominently in the Cape Verdean-American experience, but today the range of affiliations has broadened, making the permutations of multiple identifications more multifaceted and complex.

Then and Now

For well over a century, the United States has hosted the largest proportion of the worldwide Cape Verdean diaspora residing in any one nation, a population that includes immigrants and their descendants, and it continues to do so today (Halter 1993; Carling 2002). The first mass migration occurred in the late 19th and early 20th centuries when approximately 40,000 newcomers arrived by packet boat on the shores of New England. The islands of Brava and Fogo comprised over sixty percent of the influx and, at 83.4 percent, the overwhelming majority of the migrants were male (Halter 1993, 40-47). During the half-century between passage of the restrictive Immigration Control Act of 1924 in the United States and the attainment of independence in 1975 of Cape Verde, migration went into steep decline. Even after 1965, when new U.S. legislation opened the doors up again to large-scale immigration, Cape Verdeans were not able to take advantage of the liberalized policy because it was so difficult to navigate the crumbling Portuguese colonial bureaucracy or even get to a diplomatic post to make an application. All that changed considerably when Cape Verde became independent and established a U. S. Embassy in the capital city of Praia, greatly facilitating the process of obtaining a visa. In the thirty-three years since the islands became an independent nation, approximately 65,000 Cape Verdeans have arrived. The estimated number of Cape Verdeans and their descendants living in the United States today stands at several hundred thousand, more than the total population of the home country itself.[1]

One demographic difference between past and present flows is that contemporary migrants have more diverse island origins. While the influx from the last century came almost entirely from the islands of Brava, Fogo, and São Nicolau, today there are newcomers from all the islands with increasing numbers especially coming from Santiago and São Vicente, now that it is no longer necessary to apply under Portuguese immigration policy. Still, the largest population of Cape Verdeans hails from Fogo. These arrivals represent both those who are starting new chains of migration and those who relocate under family reunification allotments. Another significant demographic shift concerns the gender composition of the diaspora. Whereas men overwhelmingly predominated in the first wave, today the gender ratio is much more balanced.

Cape Verdeans in the U.S. are still heavily concentrated in the New England region, especially the states of Massachusetts and Rhode Island with smaller communities in Connecticut. The city of New Bedford, Massachusetts remains the historic hub of the Cape Verdean-American community, while areas of the smaller towns of upper Cape Cod are populated by residents of Cape Verdean descent. However, the post-1975 newcomers began to stream into the city of Boston, Massachusetts, especially the Dorchester and Roxbury neighborhoods, metropolitan areas where low-income and minority populations are concentrated. They also began settling in large numbers in the city of Brockton, about thirty miles southeast of Boston as well as in Pawtucket, Rhode Island. One of the biggest draws of both Brockton and Pawtucket has been the affordable housing that these cities offer, primarily in two- and three-family homes that can accommodate extended families. By the post-Independence era, employment in maritime-related work, the cranberry industry, and textiles—the jobs that had pulled the earlier influx to southeastern New England—had all but disappeared so that the post-1975 wave gravitated to the larger urban centers hoping to find work in manufacturing and other industries. Immigration really picked up in the 1980s when the Massachusetts economy was flush but has continued strong right through the 1990s until today. Furthermore, transportation between Boston and the Cape Verde Islands has improved greatly since independence, easing the process of migration. As of the 2000 Census tabulations, eighty-seven percent of Cape Verdean-Americans were residing in New England. Outside the region, the state of California is home to clusters of Cape Verdeans in the Sacramento, San Francisco, and Los Angeles metropolitan areas while Cape Verdeans from New England have been relocating in recent years to central Florida, especially the cities of Orlando and Kissimmee. Though highly assimilated into local culture, a Cape Verdean presence also exists in Hawaii. In fact, when trying to capture the multiplicity of nationalities and the model of pluralism that characterize the archipelago today, one interviewee cleverly remarked, "Cape Verde is the Hawaii of Africa."[2]

Cape Verdeans, past and present, have been pushed and pulled by similar factors. Economic necessity at home and economic opportunity abroad, as well as family reunification, drive the dynamics of diaspora. However, the desire to seek a better education plays a more significant role today in motivating migration than it did a century ago. Moreover, recent Cape Verdean arrivals are already much more widely educated—most adults enter having completed a high school education in Cape Verde—than those who came in the first wave. At that time there were only two high schools on the entire archipelago, one in Mindelo, São Vicente and one in Praia, São Tiago. Neither island was home to the great majority of Cape Verdeans who actually immigrated to the United States in those days. Thus, only the children of the wealthiest would have had the opportunity to be sent to another island or abroad for a high-school education. As a result, on average most of the immigrants in the past arrived with minimal schooling, usually only a fifth-grade education. Women were even less likely to be educated; whereas since independence in Cape Verde, girls are going to school right alongside the boys. With secondary schools in place on all of the islands today, unprecedented numbers of young people of both sexes complete high school. In addition, current newcomers are much more likely to be able to speak English since English language classes are a required part of the curriculum in Cape Verdean schools beginning in ninth grade. Once in the United States, like their Cape Verdean-American counterparts, many more are going on to college. Consequently, for the first time in the history of Cape Verdean settlement in the United States, a significant proportion of young adults is receiving higher education. The wide network of Cape Verdean student organizations on New England college campuses testifies to this trend. Despite these gains, however, according to 2000 Census findings, Cape Verdeans in the eighteen to twenty-four age cohort were still the least likely of the minority groups in the city of Boston to be enrolled in college or graduate school (Leith 2007).

One constant of the Cape Verdean experience has been the predominance of Catholicism as the primary religious affiliation. However, recent immigrants are more likely than in the past to become followers of evangelical Christianity, which has experienced an ongoing and unprecedented surge in Africa and in other parts of the developing world, and has been transplanted to the United States. Thus, the longstanding Cape Verdean Protestant minority is being joined today by newcomers who experience religious conversion and become active members of Pentecostal storefront congregations.

Employment patterns between the old and new immigrants have shifted largely because of changes in the socioeconomic structure of American society. Cape Verdeans of the first influx filled the need for low-wage labor working the cranberry bogs and the docks, sometimes procuring manufacturing jobs in the textile mills of industrial America. Today, new immigrants are still finding employment in factories housed in old mill buildings, but the nation's increasingly post-industrial, service-oriented economy often requires other kinds of technical and occupational skills. Since the 1970s, increasing numbers of Cape Verdean-Americans have attained success as professionals in management positions or in civil service jobs.

Although Cape Verdeans have not established an ethnic employment niche such as the West Indian immigrant population has done in the healthcare industry, one aspect of their occupational structure that has changed significantly in the current period has been the development of a robust Cape Verdean business sector. The first wave of Cape Verdeans was rarely self-employed, and when they did operate small businesses they were in the traditional category of personal services to the co-ethnic community, such as barbershops and funeral parlors. These were enterprises that white proprietors shunned because the level of intimate contact with minority customers that they required was too great. Contemporary migrants are much more entrepreneurial, in some cases arriving with enough resources and a systematic business plan that enables them to open up shop without much difficulty. A high percentage of the entrepreneurs come from the island of Fogo. Particularly in the Dorchester neighborhood of Boston and in Brockton and Pawtucket, Cape Verdean shopkeepers have developed viable commercial sectors offering a wide range of goods and services, including restaurants, grocery stores, clothing boutiques, gift shops, insurance agencies, real estate businesses, hair and skin care salons, record stores, auto-body shops, and computer repair services. Indeed, enough enterprises have opened in the Greater Boston area for the Cape Verdean Community Task Force to publish an annual business directory.

These are typically small-scale establishments, often family-owned and catering to the immigrant community. Nonetheless, their proliferation is noteworthy in the changes they have brought to the urban landscape. For the first time, Cape Verdeans are establishing bona fide ethnic enclaves where residential concentration in combination with the existence of a versatile business district enable the immigrants to work and live in close proximity. This is especially true in the city of Brockton. Indeed, the number of immigrant vendors as well as in-language health and social service agencies and media outlets, including television and radio stations, enables newcomers to go about their daily lives without having to immediately master English. The Cape Verdean Association of Brockton is now the largest service organization in Massachusetts for this ethnic group, offering counseling, referrals, ESL and citizenship classes, assistance with immigration problems, computer training, home-buying seminars, and youth recreation activities. In fact, approximately a third of the students at Brockton High School, the largest high school in New England, is Cape Verdean.

Identity Matters

In the first decades of the 20th century, although Cape Verdean settlers sought recognition as Portuguese-Americans, white society, including the other Portuguese immigrants in the region, excluded them from their social and religious associations. At the same time, the Cape Verdeans chose not to identify with the native-born black population. Cape Verdean-American Joaquim A. "Jack" Custodio, born in New Bedford, Massachusetts in 1914, put it bluntly:

> The white Portuguese never, never accepted us in any way, shape or form.... We had our own separate little areas. Cape Verdean Band Club, St. Vincent's Sporting Club.... And God forbid, if you married *American d'cor* [pejorative term for African-American]. If my mother were alive right now knowing that both of my surviving daughters have married Afro-Americans, my mother would turn over in her grave.[3]

As another child of Cape Verdean immigrants, the late Lucille Ramos, a life-long resident of New Bedford who was born in 1935, explained the identification of her parents' generation: "The older people may still say 'We're Portuguese.' That is how they were raised. But I think the New Bedford Portuguese always objected to us saying we were Portuguese, because they felt we really weren't" (Ramos 1981, 34). Jack Custodio echoes this interpretation:

> There is a distinction. I have to bring in the white Portuguese here. The white Portuguese have been labeled *nhambobs* by Cape Verdeans. In the context of the *nhambobs*, though, we never referred to ourselves as Portuguese.... [I]t was a concession. I can see that so clearly now, to the fact that we, as Cape Verdeans were not white like *nhambobs* were. Now that I look back on it, we professed to be white. If you asked me my race, I would tell you white, if you pin me down, I would tell you Cape Verdean or Portuguese.[4]

By the mid-20th century, and especially for the generation of Cape Verdean-American men of the age to enlist in the armed forces during World War II, a new set of identity issues emerged. Joining the military meant a first step out of the protective shelter of their local communities in southern New England and brought them face to face with the existence of segregated troops and a wider society that did not know or care about the ethnic identity of a Cape Verdean. Most were sent to black regiments where they were forced to deal directly with racism. As one Cape Verdean veteran remembered:

> I grew up thinking of myself as a brown-skinned Portuguese, not black at all. I remember telling this sergeant, a black guy, that I was Cape Verdean. He said, "You ain't Portuguese nothing. You're a nigger." It sounds incredibly naïve, but I'd never thought of myself as black or white. I was both, and neither. I was Cape Verdean. America wants you to choose sides.[5]

Some were assigned to white units where they were not accepted either. For those stationed with white troops in the southern states, it was especially painful to try to come to terms with the ambiguity of their own ethnic background and the rigid racial barriers of their surroundings. The immigrants and their children had largely been raised to think of themselves as Portuguese, thus white, but once outside the ethnic community, they faced an indifferent, often hostile world that labeled them black.

The social and political events of the postwar era also penetrated the cocoon of the Cape Verdean enclave. Beginning with the Civil Rights movement, the 1960s were watershed years for Cape Verdean-Americans as the rise of Black Nationalism, and its attendant emphasis on pride in one's African heritage had a transformative effect on many. Thus, the struggles for liberation from Portuguese colonialism on the continent of Africa coincided with turbulent social change on the domestic front. The process of rethinking racial identifications touched most Cape Verdean-American families in this period, often creating intergenerational rifts between the parents and grandparents, who were staunchly Portuguese, and their children, who were beginning to ally themselves with the African-American struggle not only in political thought but also in cultural expression. Some, who could, would let their hair grow out into Afros; others dressed in colorful dashikis, much to the dismay of their Portuguese-identified parents. In her memoir, Cape Verdean-American Belmira Nunes Lopes, who grew up in Wareham, Massachusetts in the early years of the 20th century, considers the changes that came about in the 1960s:

> At that time, our idea of Portuguese culture was Cape Verdean culture, and that was the thing that we really wanted to stress. To us, to be Portuguese was synonymous with being Cape Verdean.... The Cape Verdeans have been saying they were Portuguese all along. I was brought up to believe that I was Portuguese. My parents said they were Portuguese. Whenever anybody asked us what we were because we spoke a foreign language or because we looked different from any other group, we always said that we were Portuguese. All of a sudden to be told that you are an African, I think, is a shock to most people, certainly to my generation and to many of those of this generation also, the children of Cape Verdean parents who have made their children feel that they had some reason to be proud of the Cape Verdean heritage. (Nunes 1982, 144, 201)

Similarly, in the early 1980s, reflecting back on the generational shifts over the years, Lucille Ramos asserted:

> When I was younger our country was still ruled by the Portuguese government.... When we were young we were Portuguese because that was our mother country, and then we went through the Black part of our lives in the sixties. And now I think we finally know who and what we are, which is Cape Verdean, and it is something special. And we are different, we're different from the American Blacks and we're different from the Whites. We've taken from both cultures, and that makes us unique.
>
> In the sixties, we had lots of problems here locally with the labels "Black" and "White." You see, up until then the kids identified themselves as Cape Verdean. But at that point they had to take a stand, especially in high school. You were either Black or you were White, there was no in-between...and nobody wanted to hear whether you were Cape Verdean or not. It was just Black or White. The kids had a difficult time then because they had to make that decision. (Ramos 1981, 34-35)

Her assessment of the post-1960s cohort underlines the shift to a more black-identified stance and calls attention to the intergenerational tensions that such reformulations prompted:

> I think the majority of the kids now are coming around to saying they are Cape Verdean. But if it is a choice of identifying White or Black, I think they would choose Black. I think it was more difficult for the older ones, the parents and grandparents, to accept that their children identified as Black. Some of the kids were even dropping the Cape Verdean altogether and it was just Black. There was lots of peer pressure and they felt you couldn't be in-between, you had to be one or the other, and if the color of your skin wasn't pure white, that didn't give you much choice to begin with anyway.
>
> But it was very difficult for the parents and grandparents to accept this. Take my father-in-law for instance. He is an extremely dark man, and looking at him there would be no doubt in your mind that this is a Black man. But he does not consider himself a Black man. He was born on the Cape Verdean islands. He is now in his eighties, and he considers himself Portuguese—he does not identify as Cape Verdean. He is Portuguese and Portuguese is White. Do you know the ridicule that a Black man faces when he says, "I'm White, I'm Portuguese"?
>
> But you see the kids were not going to be ridiculed that way. They knew what they were, and the thing is, they have been able to accept the pride in it, which is the important thing. Whereas for the older people being White meant being...special. They didn't want to be in the minority. But our kids don't feel that way, they're Black and they're proud. That came about in the sixties. (Ramos 1981, 36-37)

Whether migrants from the earlier period or contemporary arrivals, identity concerns have been paramount in the life stories of members of the Cape Verdean diaspora. The legacy of both colonialism and creolization has continued to divide the population over conceptions of race, color, and ethnicity. As was the case a century ago, many Cape Verdeans today still wrestle with these fundamental questions of identity. What is most apparent about the contemporary Cape Verdean diaspora in the United States is that it is no longer possible to speak of a monolithic Cape Verdean community. Apart from the continuity of regional geographic concentration in southern New England, from the newly arrived to fourth-generation Cape Verdean-Americans, this population represents a multiplicity of educational backgrounds, socioeconomic positions, ethnoracial affiliations, religious beliefs, political perspectives, and island and national origins. Individual biographies typically reflect these complex diasporic histories. As one immigrant, who had been born on the Cape Verdean island of Brava, migrated to Dakar, Senegal, when she was two years old, and then moved to the United States at age five and who is trilingual in Cape Verdean Creole, English, and French put it, "I'm a well-seasoned salad."[6]

Among the long-standing American-born segment, there are those, especially of lighter skin color, who continue to refer to themselves as ethnically Portuguese while others, particularly those who live in predominantly black communities who themselves identify as black. The position of being "in-between peoples" continues to manifest itself among the current wave (Barrett and Roediger 1991). As one immigrant, now in his early thirties but who had arrived as a teenager in the 1990s, succinctly phrased the dilemma:

> We aren't accepted being Black because I am Cape Verdean and my culture is different and I am lighter. We know we are from Africa, but we are from Cape Verde. We are not accepted in the white culture because we are dark and speak Portuguese. We are caught in the middle of Blacks and Whites.[7]

And despite over thirty years as an independent nation of Africa, the great majority of both Cape Verdean immigrants and the American-born still resist the label of African. There are some exceptions, however, especially among those families who were active in the revolutionary struggle or who have lived in continental Africa en route to migrating to the United States. One such individual who was eight years old when he arrived in this country explains:

> The difference for us, we were more conscious of our Cape Verdeanness, number one, and secondly, I remember when coming here [to the U. S.] being really proud of my Africanness. Cape Verdeanness in my household was not even an issue. We knew who we were because our parents lived through that. They lived in a predominantly African community in Guinea-Bissau...especially coming here when the

> image of Africans as a whole from the continent is already Tarzan and jungle and those types of things. And the other kids would ask, "How can you be proud of being African?" Because we heard those stories at home in terms of the revolution, in terms of Amílcar Cabral, so our roots were already there.[8]
>
> What was most difficult for me was sifting through the racism coming from outside.... There was that disconnect when I was young, but we got over it...identifying more as we grew up with the African-American culture and tradition but never really losing sight because we spoke Cape Verdean at home, we had a chance to go back [to Cape Verde] and we were really immersed in our community.... At no point did I ever negate any part of my Cape Verdeanness.[9]

For his younger brother, hip-hop culture was the vehicle through which his multiple black, African, and Cape Verdean identities could be expressed:

> For me Cape Verdean and black were synonymous...never that difference of Cape Verde and black being something else.... I think it was being young and wanting to just fit in as being a young kid.... The hip-hop culture had a lot to do with that, and hip-hop at that time was about being black and proud and being African and all of that so it was a way for me to say, well I know I'm African, I know I'm proud of my Africanness, and now there's this here that's emerging that everyone wants to be down with, showing that they're black and proud, too, so cool, I'm going with this.[10]

Faced with the complexities of ethnoracial social dynamics, in a variation of the notion of situational ethnicity, individuals sometimes have used several different identity strategies at once in the course of negotiating daily life (Gans 1979; Okamura 1981; Waters 1990). An American-born daughter of Cape Verdean and West Indian parents who grew up in a sheltered Cape Verdean neighborhood in the Cape Cod community of Onset, but who, beginning in the fourth grade, attended an all white parochial school in nearby Fairhaven, Massachusetts, described it this way:

> I was very outgoing in Onset. I knew everyone and everyone knew me. It was very comfortable but…at St. Joseph's not only was I the new kid but I was the only student of color and, right away, from the first day of school, it was a horrible experience. No one would let me sit down next to them, no one would play with me at recess or sit with me at lunch.… [P]eople turned their back on me and would point and whisper and snicker. I started to put two and two together and decided that the reason they were doing this was because I was different and there were only one or two things that were different about me—the color of my skin… and my hair. I got into a lot of fights. That was the first time I was called "nigger." That was the first time that I started to have to deal with race, and I was only eight years old, and I remember becoming really withdrawn and depressed because I went from being a social butterfly who was very well-liked and respected to being a social outcast.
>
> My parents—their philosophy was—you are a beautiful, black child, and we aren't going to let you run away. We want you to stay there and do your best. You're there to get the best education so just persevere. I remember talking to my grandmother about it…and her rationale was, "I don't know why they're calling you nigger because we're different from African-Americans. We're black but we're *Kriolu*, so don't let it bother you, because they don't know. Just go to school and study hard and you'll be OK." But it never really got better, and then I went to Bishop Stang [high school] and the racism just started all over again. I had many confrontations with teachers as well as students.
>
> [Thanks to my upbringing] I never really felt that I had to choose. At school, I saw myself clearly as black and African-American because that was what was impressed on me. That's how people saw me. That's how they dealt with me. But at home it was clear that our culture was both West Indian and Cape Verdean.[11]

The approach of socializing children to think of themselves as different from African-Americans exemplified in the response above of the young woman's grandmother was a common pattern for the pre-1975 generation. Another American-born Cape Verdean woman who was a teenager in the late 1950s reiterated this strategy:

> A seed that was planted in all of us, especially the American-born, growing up in the South End [of New Bedford], the one thing that they always said to us is, "you are different, not like the negroes, not like the colored folks." And we all felt different until we learned better, but that got us through.... [I]t gave us an out, so that we wouldn't have to deal with it...even though it was putting blinders on, it helped to get through.[12]

At the intragroup level, contested identities reflect shifts in meaning based on changing historical circumstances and the contrast between pre- and post-independence generations of the Cape Verdean diaspora. For example, in recent years a complete reversal has taken place in the how the label of *badiu* has been employed. The term refers to those who are believed to be descendants of runaway slaves from the southern *sotavento* island of Santiago who escaped their masters to settle in the interior region. Historically it was typically utilized by Cape Verdeans from the more Portuguese-identified northern *barlavento* islands as well as the island of Brava as a slur against the population of the archipelago that has been most closely associated with Africa and whose inhabitants were perceived by them as more backward. However, in contemporary Cape Verde and reproduced in the diaspora, a turnaround has occurred, where especially the young people employ *badiu* as a label of pride and as a symbol of toughness and resistance to authority. These teenagers contrast the authenticity of their *badiu* identity with what they view as the diluted Cape Verdeanness of those who hail from the islands in the north. They have turned the hierarchy of intraethnic, intraisland name-calling on its head, making the expression *sampadjudu*, which refers to the migrants from the northern *barlavento* islands, the new derogatory term. Young people in Cape Verde today, raised on revolutionary pride, are much more likely to be African-identified than were the earlier generations who came of age under Portuguese rule. This transformation has seeped into the diaspora populations with the result that many more adolescents abroad have slowly come to own their Africanness and, with larger numbers from the *sotavento* islands, such as Santiago and Fogo, they use it to intimidate the smaller group (Gibau 2005; Laporte 2007; Leith 2007, 23).

Such levels of internal diversity can result in intragroup segmentation that challenges the creation of a cohesive community. The deepest divisions are generational. Given that there was a fifty-year hiatus in migration flows, differences related to education, culture, and social levels separate those families who have been in New England for generations and those who immigrated after Independence. The results of ethnographic research conducted several years ago on identity structures among the Cape Verdean diaspora in Boston also underscore the division between immigrants and the American-born (Sánchez 1999). For starters, the immigrant community tends to continue to converse in Cape Verdean Creole, while the American-born residents speak English. But the splintering is much more complex than that.

Cape Verdeans of the first settlement tended to identify with their particular island of origin, forming social organizations such as the Brava club and the São Vicente Sporting Club. An additional source of tension in the years of the protracted armed conflict to procure independence from Portugal was the position the immigrant community took on the revolutionary movement. The revolutionaries did find some support for their cause among Cape Verdean-Americans, but there was also much resistance to the idea of Cape Verde breaking its long-standing ties with Portugal and switching to an African-identified political and cultural ideology. While island rivalries still exists today, they are far less pronounced among recent immigrants, largely because of the greater numbers among this population who have attained higher levels of education. Especially among college students, such cliquishness is minimal. Differences based on the politics of Cape Verde remain persistent, however. Loyalty to the Party for African Independence-Cape Verde (PAICV) versus the Party of the Democratic Movement (MPD) can shape the shared vision of the diaspora population and influence how alliances are built on this side of the Atlantic. Typically there is a direct correlation with PAICV partisanship and a more African orientation, while those who are followers of MPD identify most strongly with their European Portuguese roots.

Cultural fragmentation stemming from the long-standing issue of the extent to which diaspora Cape Verdeans identify as Portuguese versus as African-Americans does persist, but more recently the intergenerational struggles have centered, instead, on what is viewed as an erosion of traditional family control. The past decade has witnessed a significant upsurge in drug- and gang-related violence among Cape Verdean youth, especially in the cities of Boston and Brockton, Massachusetts, which has often been attributed to this generation's lack of respect for its elders and the community itself. Such concerns speak directly to the fear that the immigrant children will fall into the oppositional culture that has developed among some disaffected American-born adolescents, especially among the black and Latino populations, whose attempts to attain upward mobility through educational pursuits have been so thwarted by the dire socioeconomic circumstances that they find themselves in that it has led them to reject academic aspirations and to scorn scholastic achievement among their peers.[13] By contrast, a recent hip-hop initiative among a group of young Cape Verdean musicians, known as The Movement, seeks to address the troubles vexing their communities with a positive message. Their promotional literature describes them as:

> Inspired by Cape Verde's own revolution and born out of a spirit of collaboration among Cape Verdean artists who are exploring new directions in the *Kriolu* sound. Through music, the artists tackle issues that face the Cape Verdean community and the African diaspora at large with a positive approach and a conscious mentality.[14]

The phenomenon of cross-generational discord is not new or unique to Cape Verdean immigrants, however. Similar dynamics among other populations of African descent have been identified and examined by scholars such as Mary Waters in her study of West Indians in New York, *Black Identities.* Waters discusses the parents' hopes and convictions for continuity and their fierce cultural pride while the realities of their children's lives, especially peer influences, often lead the young ones to assimilate, instead, into a broader ghetto-youth subculture. Sociologist, Milton Vickerman, looking mostly at the first generation, in his work, *Crosscurrents: West Indian Immigrants and Race,* analyzes some of these same dynamics (Waters 1999; Vickerman1999). Thus, initial trends suggest that the adaptation patterns of contemporary Cape Verdean youth resemble those of other foreign-born people of color such as West Indians, whereby the immigrant generation attempts to emphasize distinctive cultural traditions and defies being grouped with African-Americans while the second generation, is much more likely than their parents to associate and identify with native-born minorities. Alternatively, research on Dominican youth in Providence, Rhode

Island, has led one scholar to argue that post-1965 immigrants and especially the second generation are transforming entrenched notions of black/white racial categorization altogether. The young people in the study privileged their ethno-linguistic and cultural background as their racial designation whether as Dominican, Spanish or Hispanic rather than identifying in terms of black or white (Baily 2001). Related to intergenerational strife is an increasingly pronounced conflict between the American-born diaspora and the newest immigrants. Barriers between newcomers and those born in the United States are especially high among the adolescent population. Clearly the complexities of Cape Verdean identity formation, as is the case with other non-white immigrants, are forged not only by the debates and changing circumstances within their own cultural group, but also by the discourses of black and mainstream America.

The Ethnic Revival

Certainly American society has changed in many ways in the decades between the two waves of Cape Verdean immigration. One of the most striking contrasts concerns attitudes toward ethnic differences and the vision of what it means to be an American. The Cape Verdean newcomers at the turn of the last century arrived at a time when the foreign-born were expected to suppress their cultural distinctiveness and shed their Old World customs either through conformity to the Anglo-Saxon way of life or by fusing and melding such differences into a unified American character. Both such approaches, Anglo-Conformity and the Melting Pot ideal, called for the renunciation of the newcomers' native languages and cultures in exchange for full integration into American society. Yet, these were models of assimilation that, if they worked at all, were based on a prototypically white immigrant of European heritage. Nonetheless, these earlier generations of arrivals typically wanted to become part of the mainstream as rapidly as possible.

By the mid-1970s, after decades in which assimilation was the leading model for the incorporation of diverse populations, cultural pluralism emerged to take its place as the reigning paradigm. Unlike Anglo-Conformity or the Melting Pot, which assumed the disappearance of the immigrants' original culture and communal life, the ideology of cultural pluralism advocated the preservation of the immigrants' heritage, including language, religious beliefs, foods, customs, history and so forth. During the same period, initially driven by a backlash against minority group movements for racial power, white descendants of immigrants who had arrived primarily from southern and eastern Europe, at the same time as the first influx of Cape Verdeans in the late 19th and early 20th centuries and who had also faced discrimination from the native population at the time, began to assert their own brand of ethnic pride. At first construed largely as a defense against the perceived threats of black power and the encroachment of African-Americans into white ethnic neighborhoods, the ethnic resurgence ultimately went beyond such narrow aims to encompass a cultural alternative to assimilation and a political alternative to individualism for both black and white ethnics.

Thus, these early, often reactive impulses to reclaim roots had evolved by the century's end into a full-blown and multifaceted ethnic revival across a broad spectrum of the population that carries a much more benign rhetoric of rainbows and salad bowls to explain these dynamics. When Congress passed the Ethnic Heritage Act in 1974 to support the funding of initiatives that promote the distinctive cultures and histories of the nation's ethnic populations, it was clear that this philosophy had taken hold at even the highest levels of government, while the enthusiastic reception to the publication of Alex Haley's *Roots* in 1976 demonstrated the extent to which the ethnic revival had permeated popular culture. The so-called roots phenomenon accounts for such developments as the growth of ethnic celebrations, a zeal for genealogy, increased travel to ancestral homelands, and greater interest in ethnic artifacts, cuisine, music, literature, and, of course, language (Halter 2000).

The ethnic revival and the emphasis on cultural pluralism were just taking hold when Cape Verdeans began to arrive again in larger numbers in the wake of independence at home and a more liberal immigration policy in the United States. Thus, post-1975 newcomers have been migrating in an age of multiculturalism where claiming a hyphenated identity has become normative, even fashionable. Furthermore, the influx of large numbers of non-white immigrants from many parts of the globe in the last three decades combined with the increase in rates of mixed–race marriages and reproduction have transformed the United

States from a largely black and white world to a kaleidoscopic ethnoracial landscape where the boundaries between groups are becoming less and less sharp. Some call it the browning of America—a palette on which Cape Verdean brush strokes much more readily blend in. As Belmira Nunes Lopes elucidates in the closing chapter of her autobiography:

> It is more a question of having my culture recognized as opposed to the whole blanket viewing of all non-white people as black. I belong to a black sorority, and I like the Afro-Americans immensely, but I just don't happen to be an Afro-American, and I want people to recognize me for what I am.... If when people ask me if I am black, the answer is, "yes, I'm black." If anybody who has African blood is black, I am black because there is no question about the fact that I have African blood in me.... Nevertheless, I want to be recognized as a person with a distinct culture. In keeping with the tendency in American society nowadays for ethnic groups to reclaim their roots, this is precisely what I feel Cape Verdeans are doing. It is the basis from which Cape Verdeans are going forward and asking to be recognized as a minority group. (Nunes 1982, 202-3)

In this current environment of ethnic pride and reclamation of roots as well as greater acceptance of multiracial identities, Cape Verdeans have had less difficulty asserting their cultural distinctiveness than those who settled in the early 1900s when notions of racial identity were rigidly cast in black and white and the anti-immigrant movement for one-hundred percent Americanism carried much political clout. Perhaps nothing illustrates this sea change better than the Smithsonian-sponsored Festival of American Folklife held on the National Mall in Washington D.C., a multicultural extravaganza that, in 1995, featured the culture of the Cape Verdean diaspora as a centerpiece of their program.

At the local, regional, and national level, Cape Verdean-Americans are proudly calling attention to their cultural heritage. Like many other third- and fourth-generation ethnics who have lost native language skills, American-born Cape Verdeans are eagerly signing up for *Kriolu* language classes. For those students who are matriculating at area colleges, the well-organized Cape Verdean student networks provide both an academic support system and opportunities to celebrate their members' ancestry and promote greater awareness of Cape Verdean history though a full schedule of conferences, fundraisers, social events, and lecture series. Usually at least one program on the school calendar pays tribute to the legacy of Amílcar Cabral, as young Cape Verdeans today, whether new immigrants or American-born, are likely to be familiar with the monumental role that Cabral played in the history of Cape Verdean Independence.

Indeed, the most public displays of the political culture of recent African immigrant groups are Independence Day festivities marking the overthrow of colonialism in their respective home countries. Thus, the most widely celebrated holiday among Cape Verdeans in the United States occurs on July 5th, Cape Verdean Independence Day, commemorating the successful ousting of Portuguese colonial rule in 1975. Parades, picnics, pageants, and cultural performances are held in Cape Verdean-American communities throughout the country. The occasion provides an opportunity to acknowledge the historic significance of the event but, increasingly, also to highlight and legitimize Cape Verdean culture to the broader community. For Cape Verdeans in New Bedford, Massachusetts, that wider recognition has already been accomplished. Since the holiday falls on the day after the 4th of July, American Independence Day, the cultural merger has been so complete that the city's annual parade is designed to simultaneously commemorate the back-to-back Independence Day celebrations. Cape Verdean community leaders, youth groups and entertainers wave from floats or march alongside city officials, high-school bands, and representatives of other civic associations while the parade route is mapped to culminate in the South End neighborhood that is the heart of the Cape Verdean enclave. Ironically, in Providence, Rhode Island, the annual Cape Verdean Independence Day festival is held in Fox Point: an area of the city that once was the vibrant center of this ethnic community but because of the decimation that resulted from 1970s urban renewal, Cape Verdeans were pushed out and no longer live there. Rather, this neighborhood has become merely a symbolic site of Cape Verdean-American settlement.

The vast improvements in transportation and global telecommunications technology of the last two decades have facilitated the transnational quality of day-to-day lives in the Cape Verdean diaspora, dynamics that also help to sustain strong cultural identifications. Indeed, one sociologist studying these patterns characterized the primary sites of Cape Verdean transnationalism—Boston, Providence, Lisbon, and Rotterdam—as "islands in a migratory archipelago" (Góis 2005, 270). Maintaining a strong dual identity has become much more feasible for members of the Cape Verdean diaspora in recent years. The government of Cape Verde now defines a Cape Verdean as someone born in the islands or having a parent or grandparent born there, while members of the diaspora community can vote in Cape Verdean national elections and have had representation in the National Assembly. In fact, Cape Verdean presidential candidates routinely include southern New England on their campaign trails. Moreover, virtual communities online promote the Cape Verdean connection worldwide. For example, the editor of the online journal *Crème Magazine*, the daughter of a mixed marriage, recently wrote on her website:

> I was born of two cultures and identify myself as a Cape Verdean and Black Woman. My father is Black and my mother is Cape Verdean. Long ago I stopped checking boxes about my nationality because Cape Verdean was never there, yet our country is definitely on the map!
>
> It was not until recently, that I've connected with my Cape Verdean roots, and in the oddest place—Myspace! While on Myspace, a young artist reached out to us to review his music. Suddenly, I started meeting Cape Verdeans everywhere including another journalist here in New York. I can't tell you how great it was to connect with people that defined who I was and what was missing.[15]

Intergroup Relations

Although not as rigidly stratified as was the case at the turn of the last century, today the relationship between Cape Verdean-Americans and those from the Azores and mainland Portugal still remains uneasy. Interactions occur primarily at the commercial level, such as Cape Verdean restaurant owners purchasing Portuguese food and wine to stock their kitchens, thereby limiting their associations to the realm of business transactions. Furthermore, despite some mutual residential aggregation, Cape Verdeans still resist identification with African-Americans as well as foreign-born populations of African descent, such as those in the Haitian or Dominican communities, whose cultural backgrounds and native languages differ from the Cape Verdean heritage; such circumstances have not been conducive to building alliances. And while increasing numbers of immigrants from West Africa, especially Liberians, are settling in New England, Cape Verdeans do not associate with these groups either. Not surprisingly, given their mutual histories of Portuguese colonialism, the only other African newcomers with whom Cape Verdeans interact are arrivals to the region from Angola. As for other groups within the Lusophone diaspora in New England, Cape Verdeans are beginning to form connections with the burgeoning Brazilian immigrant community as well. Such intergroup exchanges, particularly with Angolans and Brazilians, are most pronounced in the cultural arenas of religious participation, music, and soccer.

A striking example of transnationalism within the Lusophone world involves the migratory patterns of Cape Verdeans and Angolans. As former Portuguese colonies, the shared language and cultural elements of the two nations triggered a large-scale migration of Cape Verdeans to Angola in the 1950s. There, the two populations intermingled, marriages occurred, and new multinational families were formed. Many were working for the Portuguese colonial government, so that after Angola won its independence in 1975, they were propelled to leave the country, relocating back to the Cape Verde Islands. Later they became migrants once again as they sought visas to the United States. By the late 1990s, pushed by the ravages of political unrest at home, many more Angolans began to flee their war-torn country seeking refuge through migration. Some Cape Verdeans, who were either born in Angola or came there at a young age, migrated to Portugal and some among this population have also become twice migrants and made the transatlantic journey to New England. Finally, a sprinkling of Cape Verdean-Angolans as well as non-Cape Verdean-Angolans have been able to come directly to the United States through political asylum, holding refugee status. Because of their long-standing ties, these diverse Angolan settlers to the region have moved into the same neighborhoods and communities where Cape Verdeans were already residing, a pattern that is especially evident in Brockton, Massachusetts. There they have been able to take advantage of a Portuguese language infrastructure, social services, medical professionals and co-ethnic employment and housing networks originally set up for the Cape Verdean newcomers.

While the relationship of Cape Verdeans and Angolans in Portugal itself is often antagonistic due to intensive competition for jobs, especially in construction work, and the scarcity of resources available to these two recent populations that constitute significant numbers, in Brockton the Angolans are a small minority, compared to the Cape Verdean settlement, and are much newer to the Lusophone community. Thus, in order to benefit from the resources available through the already well-established Cape Verdean enclave, they readily recognize that they need to get along and adapt to local norms. As one Cape Verdean teacher at Brockton High School declared:

> So here they are, you find them, a lot of them, and sometimes you can't even tell that they come from Angola because they are very integrated into the community—a lot of them never spoke *Kriolu* when they were in Angola but now that they are here, because Cape Verdeans are the majority in this community, they are learning *Kriolu*, because everywhere you go, you find Cape Verdeans, they are socializing with Cape Verdeans and they end up eventually speaking the language. It's a good relationship—a very good relationship. Not much tension at all.[16]

Indeed, an Angolan, DJ Adilson, is the top Cape Verdean deejay in the community. Such adaptations are not unprecedented in the history of migration and settlement in this country. For example, the governments of Japan and Korea have been in conflict for hundreds of years, and hostility toward the Korean-Japanese population living in Japan is still manifested today, yet once these groups migrated to the United States, their relationship shifted. Now Korean-Japanese restaurants are proliferating and have become familiar metropolitan landmarks. Typically it is Korean ownership offering the more familiar and popular Japanese fare as a way of bringing customers in; nonetheless, it shows a level of cross-cultural collaboration that would not be easily replicated in the respective home countries of these two historical enemies.

Although not a case of full-blown integration, of the array of other ethnic groups in New England, Cape Verdeans are beginning to form connections with the burgeoning Brazilian population, particularly in the area of cultural exchange. One basis of affinity grows out of the shared legacy of Portuguese colonial rule and a common resentment of the power and control that the Portuguese government had wielded over them in the past. Another commonality is in religious participation, not only because of the overarching influence of the Catholic Church, but also because many Brazilians are worshipping at the same new Evangelical congregations to which the Cape Verdeans belong and where Portuguese-speaking pastors conduct services. These dynamics may actually, in part, be the result of transplanted religious practices rather than wholly new associations being made in the United States. Evangelical and Pentecostal groups originating in Brazil have become very active in establishing new congregations in Cape Verde in recent years, thus, Brazilians are heavily involved in the current religious life of the archipelago. Contemporary immigrants to the United States, thus bring their newfound faiths with them, seeking to join such churches as they settle into their new surroundings. Whereas within the history of Catholicism, followers have been well served by either Cape Verdean or Portuguese priests, and among the long-standing Protestant Nazarene denomination, Cape Verdeans have had their own clergy, in the case of the new Evangelical churches, Cape Verdean congregants have relied upon the leadership of the Brazilian ministry both in the United States and the Cape Verde islands. Transnationally, Brazilian religious leaders are exhibiting a fervent missionary zeal, energetically starting up storefront churches, raising significant sums of money—enough to buy considerable radio and television time to get their message out—and bringing in sizeable numbers of new converts.

However, the strengthening of the link between the Republic of Cape Verde and the nation of Brazil in recent years has not only occurred in the arena of religion. In both government and the private sector, Cape Verde has been partnering with Brazil to cultivate closer ties in trade and foreign investments—in some cases, eclipsing historical levels of economic cooperation with Portugal. How much of this trend of solidifying mutual relations with Brazil is influencing intergroup dynamics in the diaspora remains to be seen. One factor working against the development of a strong Brazilian-Cape Verdean connection in the United States is that Brazilians have typically considered their migration to this country as temporary, while Cape Verdeans (and Angolans) are much more likely to put down permanent roots. Thus, the Brazilians are simply less invested in establishing long-standing communities, whether multiethnic or not. In fact, in recent months a noteworthy pattern of return migration among Brazilians has been occurring, a response to the weakening value of the dollar, while the economy in Brazil has been on the upswing. Furthermore, a significant proportion of Brazilians are undocumented, and the recent nationwide crackdown on illegal immigrants is another worrisome factor in explaining the Brazilian exodus. Estimates suggest that last year between 5,000 and 7,000 Brazilians left Massachusetts to return to Brazil, which is about twice the total of those who had gone back in 2006.[17]

In the arena of musical performance, the contemporary cachet of Cape Verdean and Afro-Portuguese rhythms and sounds as well as the intersecting cultural forms represented by both the world music and hip-hop genres have triggered a sense of camaraderie between Brazilians and Cape Verdeans and attracted mixed Portuguese-speaking audiences. For example, a recent event sponsored by the Massachusetts Alliance of Portuguese Speakers (MAPS) featured entertainment by the Dorchester Cape Verdean group, *Txuba di Kultura,* as well as *Capoeira* and other Brazilian dances performed by the Somerville Youth Program. Music has also been the catalyst for the unlikely opening up of a cultural space where Cape Verdeans are even collaborating with Haitians, two groups with significant histories and sizeable communities in the Greater Boston area, but whose members have rarely intersected. Last year, an enterprising Brockton resident, Djovany Pierre, started a new radio station, Brockton Heat, dedicated to conjoining Cape Verdean and Haitian music. The connection can especially be heard in the similarities between the genres of Haitian *compas* and Cape Verdean *zouk* music. Pierre explained that, "he saw the need for a community radio station for both his people and Cape Verdeans. They share the same issues of immigration, deportation, jobs, and health issues … .This is why, through music, we understand each other."[18] The local station has become extremely popular; while the music is the primary draw, as outreach to both populations, community announcements as well as programming on health issues and youth violence are interspersed with the rhythms of *zouk* and *compas*. Yet while the cultural hybridity represented by Brockton Heat is a relatively new feature of the urban landscape, Brockton-based and Cape Verdean-born musicians, the Mendes Brothers, have been melding the sounds of Cape Verde, Angola, and Haiti for over twenty-five years. Hailing from the island of Fogo, João and Ramiro Mendes immigrated to the United States in 1978 and soon after formed a band, inviting Haitian keyboardist Nono to serve as their musical director. Their debut album was an amalgamation of Cape Verdean *bandera* (festival music) with Angolan *semba* and a sprinkling of Haitian *konpa*. Working out of a Brockton basement studio for many years, they established the MB record label with the goal of producing a broad cross-section of the music of Lusophone Africa. The success of the Mendes Brothers' uniquely globalized and multilayered sound was recognized in 2006 by the Prime Minister of Cape Verde when he presented them with a Medal of Merit for their outstanding contributions to Cape Verdean culture.[19]

Finally, participation in sports, especially soccer, has facilitated closer intergroup relations. The Luso-American Soccer Association which later became the New England Luso-American Soccer Association had always been run by the Portuguese with teams comprised almost totally of Portuguese players. However, over the years, more and more Cape Verdeans began to join these clubs. With fewer immigrants arriving from the Azores and the continent, while many more young Cape Verdean athletes were making New England their home, the Cape Verdean players became too dominant and the older Portuguese team members could not compete. As a result, the Portuguese clubs began leaving the league and established their own association. In fact, Cape Verdean leagues are a relatively recent phenomenon, starting up only in the last five years.[20] Currently, for example, Brockton alone supports several soccer teams made up primarily of Cape Verdean players but also including Angolans, while interleague play among Cape Verdean and Brazilian clubs naturally attracts fans from each group. Since Cape Verdeans and Angolans are almost evenly divided in their representation on the three main soccer clubs in Portugal—Porto, Benfica, and Sporting—their mutual participation on New England diaspora teams is nothing out of the ordinary. When, in 2002, friends and family of the late Jorge Fidalgo, a much admired Cape Verdean community leader and avid soccer player who had been murdered in Dorchester the previous year, initiated the first soccer challenge to honor his legacy, it was sponsored by the Boston area Cape Verdean Community Task Force (now CVC UNIDO). For the first two years of this now annual event, only Cape Verdean teams participated. In 2005, however, the organizers featured a match between the Cape Verdean All Stars and the Caribbean All Stars. In the last two years CVC UNIDO has partnered with the Massachusetts Alliance of Portuguese Speakers and invited the Brazilian All Star Team to face the Cape Verdean All Stars. This kind of globalizing trajectory may well portend broader trends within the Cape Verdean community.

For the most part, however, residential patterns keep the Cape Verdeans and Brazilians apart. In the Greater Boston area, Brazilians are living in the communities of Allston-Brighton, Cambridge, Somerville, Framingham, and Maynard, not in the Dorchester and Roxbury neighborhoods where Cape Verdeans reside, which prohibits daily interaction and the opportunity for the immigrant children to attend the same schools. There are exceptions, however. Although the number of Brazilians residing within the Brockton school district is small, not surprisingly those young people who attend Brockton High School are eager to fit into the dominant Cape Verdean social group. In the case of one Brazilian family, the mother of a student in the school's bilingual program removed her son on the grounds that he was socializing too much with the Cape Verdean kids and was learning *Kriolu* faster that he was learning English. Apparently her strategy failed as the young man went on to try to record a *Kriolu* rap album and still keeps up close ties with his Cape Verdean friends.[21] Another exception to residential disaggregation can be found in the North End district of New Bedford, an area that is beginning to be populated by both Brazilians and Cape Verdeans, where for generations only immigrants from the Azores and Madeira lived. It is in this North End neighborhood that signs of a broader Lusophone enclave are emerging. Not only do the classic triple-decker structures now house those from Brazil and Cape Verde in addition to the long-standing Azorean population, but the many shops and restaurants that line the area's main avenue have diversified in recent years. Across the street from Café Europa, a gathering spot for those of various Lusophone backgrounds who usually can be found speaking

Portuguese together rather than English, a new store has opened, Africa Unite, owned by Cape Verdeans, while around the corner is a Brazilian restaurant, Café Rio. Nightlife in North End neighborhood clubs is now as likely to feature Cape Verdean or Brazilian music as Portuguese groups. And the New Bedford celebration of the annual Day of Portugal festival routinely includes Cape Verdean and Brazilian performers along with musicians from Portugal and the Azores on center stage.

In Brockton, the case of one of the leading Cape Verdean dining spots is perhaps indicative of this changing Lusophone landscape. Restaurante Luanda, just as their name signals, is run by an Angolan-Cape Verdean family. The global Lusophone network represented by this local community site of Cape Verdean proprietorship becomes even more intricately connected when the large sign in the parking lot is taken into account. Underneath the name of the restaurant, in big yellow letters, the owners advertise that Saturdays are Brazilian night. Always in flux, as this example illustrates, the Cape Verdean diaspora community, past and present, has continued to defy strict cultural classifications, challenging notions of race, ethnicity, color, and identity. Historically, the primary interconnections that Cape Verdean immigrants struggled to negotiate within the Lusophone world were with the Azorean and continental communities, an already complicated set of sociocultural circumstances. Yet with the more recent influx of Angolan and Brazilian newcomers to the region, intergroup relations within the broader Portuguese diaspora have become even more intricate and complex. How the dynamics of these various constituencies play out in a post-colonial era are still unfolding, offering rich contexts for future study and in-depth research.

Notes

[1] For example, official figures from the capital city of Praia, Cape Verde show that 1,225 Cape Verdeans emigrated to the US in 2005, while another 2,000 traveled to the U.S. for business or tourism.

[2] Interview with Maria Fernandes Andrade by Marilyn Halter, June 25, 2004, Fairhaven, Massachusetts.

[3] Interview with Joaquim A. Custodio by Marilyn Halter, July 28, 1988, Fairhaven, Massachusetts.

[4] Interview with Joaquim A. Custodio.

[5] Charles Andrade, Jr. quoted in Colin Nickerson, "Black, White or Cape Verdean?" *The Boston Globe*, 29 Sept. 1983: 16.

[6] Interview with Maria Andrade Fernandes.

[7] Paul De Barros quoted in Johnny Diaz and Scott Greenberger, "Not White, Not Black, Not

Hispanic—Boston's Cape Verdeans Have Long Been Misunderstood," *The Boston Globe*, 15 February 2004: B1

[8] Amílcar Cabral was the leader of the Cape Verdean independence movement.

[9] Interview with Adonis Ferreira by Marilyn Halter, May 18, 2004, Fairhaven, Massachusetts.

[10] Interview with Temistocles Ferreira by Marilyn Halter, November 19, 2004, Fairhaven, Massachusetts.

[11] *Kriolu* is the term used to name the Cape Verdean language and culture.

[12] Interview with Jeanne M. Costa by Marilyn Halter, June 25, 2004, Fairhaven, Massachusetts.

[13] See Carter (2005); Rong and Brown (2001); Suárez-Orozco (1991); Ogbu (1991).

[14] http://www.myspace.com/themovementcaboverde

[15] Dominga Martin, http://www.creme-magazine.com/Issue16/editorialletter/

[16] Interview with Herminio Furtado by Marilyn Halter, February 26, 2008, Brockton, Massachusetts.

[17] Brian Ballou, "Hardships in Mass. Spur Brazilian Exodus," *The Boston Globe,* 6 January 2008.

[18] Milton J. Valencia, "One Radio Station, Two Communities," *The Boston Globe*, 8 January, 2008.

[19] "The Mendes Brothers, PRI's The World, Global Hit," February 26, 2007: http://www.theworld.org/?q=node/8338; Mendes Brothers Profile, MySpace: http://profile.myspace.com/index.cfm?fuseaction=user.viewprofile&friendid=74299065

[20] Interview with Herminio Furtado. Interestingly, however, Portuguese managers have still maintained their organizational control over the Cape Verdean league until only this year when, for the first time, Cape Verdeans are running the league.

[21] Interview with Herminio Furtado.

REFLECTIONS

Current Trends and Future Directions in Portuguese-American Studies

CAROLINE B. BRETTELL

Few Americans outside the Eastern seaboard were aware of immigrants of Portuguese origins in the United States or of the sizeable growth of this population after the United States reopened its doors to immigration in 1965. Indeed, the Portuguese were the only southern Europeans who migrated to the United States in large numbers in the latter 20th century. As the essays in this volume suggest, they have settled in and sometimes remade communities from New Jersey to Boston. Yet, despite the so-called "Portuguese Archipelago" of southeastern Massachusetts, an ethnic enclave in the full sense of the word, the Portuguese have been and, as several authors in this volume suggest, remain an "invisible minority."

Portugal is a small country located on the westernmost edge of Europe and yet its global impact is large. At one time, the Portuguese and Lusophone world extended from Macau in China, to Goa in India, to the African countries of Mozambique, Angola, and Guinea-Bissau, to the islands of São Tomé, Cape Verde, and the Azores, and to Brazil. In the 19th century, Portuguese immigrants arrived in New England as well as in northern California. And in the 20th century, the Portuguese emigrated to France, Germany, Switzerland, and England, drawn by the employment opportunities of a post-war northern Europe that was rebuilding itself. They also settled in Canada, particularly in the cities of Toronto and Montreal, and Australia. Clearly this global diaspora calls for systematic scholarly attention, just as the omission of the Portuguese from discussions of both the third wave of immigration to the United States that occurred between 1880 and 1924 and the fourth wave that began in 1965 needs to be rectified.

This volume and other work (Brettell 2003a) that has recently appeared begin the process of rectification by making the case for what the Portuguese emigration/immigration experience can add to our understanding of broad themes and trends in immigration history and in the settlement of immigrants in various receiving societies, including the United States. I address here some of these broader themes and how they emerge in this collection of essays. I do so, however, with one cautionary note. Although it is important to understand the Portuguese case, it is also important not to treat it as unique. Admittedly, some aspects of the Portuguese migratory experience are distinctive, but there is also much that the Portuguese have in common with other immigrant populations of the 19th, 20th, and 21st centuries.

The Importance of Context and Cross-National Comparison

The fact that the Portuguese are dispersed across the globe makes it possible to compare processes of incorporation in different contexts of reception, something that has become increasingly important to scholars of migration in the early 21st century (Reitz 2003; Foner 2005; Tsuda 2006). Early in my own work on Portuguese immigration, I engaged in such a comparison, delineating differences between Portuguese immigrants who settled in Toronto, Canada and those who settled in Paris, France at roughly the same period of time in the 1960s (Brettell 2003b). In their essays in this volume, Bloemraad and Klimt engage in similar cross-national comparisons. Bloemraad begins with this question: Why do Portuguese immigrants in the city of Toronto become citizens at a higher rate than Portuguese immigrants in Boston, Massachusetts, and why are they more politically visible? She suggests that government support of community organizations, including ethnic media, as well as a stronger and more competitive party system and more localized nomination procedures are among the factors that lead to greater political mobilization of the Portuguese in Toronto by contrast with their counterparts in Boston. Further, the discourse of race and ethnicity in the United States and Canada differs, and this too has an impact. Canadian multiculturalism puts the Portuguese on an equal footing with other ethnic groups, each with its own voice; in the United States, by contrast, the Portuguese are grouped with other white ethnics and in some contexts they, like Brazilian immigrants, might even be grouped with Latinos. They have no distinct voice. Clearly the context of settlement matters to processes of incorporation for any national-origin immigrant population, but we only understand this if we pursue the kind of controlled comparison that Bloemraad undertakes.

Klimt's comparative question is somewhat different. She asks why the Portuguese in Hamburg, Germany have organized their lives and feelings of belonging in different ways from those in the northeastern United States. Until recently, German citizenship was based on *jus sanguinis,* or ancestry, rather than *jus solis* or residence. The children of immigrants born in the country did not automatically acquire citizenship and hence were denied the right to belong. Portuguese immigrants in Germany, like those in France (Brettell 2003c), have maintained a desire to return home over decades. However, as Klimt points out, this has changed in relation to the emergence of a European identity. "As it is becoming increasingly commonplace for 'Europeans' to live in one national space while 'belonging' to another, the Portuguese could remain in Germany without calling their commitment to being Portuguese into question" (Klimt, this volume, 103). By contrast, the orientation to the home country is much weaker among the Portuguese in southeastern New England who are residentially concentrated and have constructed their own institutions of incorporation and a place that even the second generation can call home.

Context is also central to de Sá and Borges's analysis of the absence of upward social mobility among the Portuguese who arrived during the third wave of immigration. While the children and grandchildren of Italian immigrants moved into the middle class, this has not been the case for the offspring of Portuguese immigrants. Fewer than ten percent of the Portuguese had a Bachelor's degree or higher in 2000, compared with twenty-four percent of non-Portuguese in southeastern Massachusetts. These authors are critical of classic explanations that have emphasized a culture that did not value education and instead focus on the fact that the Portuguese arrived largely at the tail end of the industrial expansion when traditional ladders to social mobility were becoming more limited. A further constraint to upward mobility derives from the residential concentration of the Portuguese in a local region where opportunities for employment are limited. This has particularly impacted the post-1965 wave because they entered a region where unemployment rates rose sharply after 1985. As de Sá and Borges put it, the Portuguese archipelago is both a gateway and a trap. What is most intriguing about this point is that it has been made elsewhere in the migration literature in association with other national-origin immigrant groups. Ethnic enclaves can have negative as well as positive effects (Portes and Manning 1986; Zhou 1992; Logan, Alba, and McNulty 1994; Kwong 1997; Fong and Ooka 2002; Valdez 2007; Chiswick and Miller 2008). Yet no one has thought to include the Portuguese case as part of this debate, a case that is particularly illustrative when one realizes that in other regions of the United States (for example, California), the Portuguese do better and have higher rates of college graduates and higher income that those who reside in the "archipelago." Intra-U.S. comparisons are as important as cross-national comparisons in our research on the immigrant experience.[1]

Political and Social Incorporation

In recent years, increasing numbers of scholars have become interested in the social and political incorporation of fourth-wave immigrants. Theoretical conceptualizations have moved away from the straight-line assimilation model (Gans 1992) to models of segmented assimilation (Rumbaut 1996; Portes and Zhou 1993: Heisler 2007) and hybridity (Kasinitz, Mollenkopf, and Waters 2002; Werbner and Moodod 1997; Werbner 2004). There are those who still argue that the assimilation model (whether straight-line or segmented) is important (Glazer 1993; Morawska 1994; Alba and Nee 1997), while others are focused on transnational and multicultural lives as the dominant form of incorporation in a global and flat world (Levitt, DeWind, and Vertovec 2003; Dhingra 2007).

Studies of social incorporation are often organized around analyses of social networks and social capital (Massey, Alarcon, Durand, and Gonzalez 1987; Zhou and Bankston 1994; Pessar 1999; Aguilera and Massey 2003; Brettell 2005). Tamar Wilson (1994) uses the phrase "network-mediated migration" to describe the role of kinship and friendship ties in the process of migration. But family, friendship, and other co-ethnic networks are also used by newcomers to find jobs and housing, as well as information about how to adapt to a new society.

In 1965, the United States introduced an immigration policy based on family reunification. As Feldman-Bianco in this volume observes, webs of kinship made way for the continuous arrival of new Portuguese contingents to the United States. Kinship played itself out not only in transnational marriages that involved finding spouses in the homeland, but also in paternalistic labor strategies that facilitated employment in factories where kin were already employed. Louise Lamphere and her colleagues examine the impact of the local economy on family and social networks among working-class Portuguese families in New England. More specifically, they explore how individuals draw on kinship networks to help them solve problems, including finding child care and arranging immigration visas.

More recently, social scientists and historians of immigration have been looking at the process of political incorporation (Gerstle and Mollenkopf 2001). As Plotke (1999, 299) has argued, research on political incorporation opens up thorny questions about citizenship: What should citizenship mean? What kinds of citizens should newcomers become, and how might that happen? Do newcomers threaten democratic politics? Bloemraad, in her essay, in this volume and elsewhere (Bloemraad 2006) has explored these questions for the Portuguese by investigating how different receiving societies such as Canada and the United States "make" citizens. As she suggests, the political incorporation of immigrants "carries significant repercussions for states that derive their legitimacy from notions of equality and democratic involvement" (2006, 11). Political incorporation is also addressed by Barrow in this volume. He opens his discussion of the political culture of Portuguese-Americans in southeastern Massachusetts by emphasizing that most of the Portuguese who entered the United States after 1965 had grown up under an authoritarian dictatorship and hence came with very little experience with politics. Although he appears to suggest that the Portuguese of Fall River and New Bedford have a higher level of political participation than those described by Bloemraad who live in Boston, it is participation in local politics, within the Portuguese enclave and in relation to co-ethnics. For the most part, the Portuguese are less politically active than other groups, particularly those who are foreign-born and not citizens. And yet, Correia's essay in this volume,

"Salazar in New Bedford," suggests that during the 1930s there was a highly-politically engaged Portuguese-American community in southeastern Massachusetts that was wrestling with homeland politics much as other immigrant populations are wrestling today with the politics of their sending societies.

Local activism is also the subject of the chapter by Reeve. He describes Portuguese men and women who joined the labor movement by the thousands in order to fight for decent conditions in the mill context. Similarly, Bookman writes about unionization in an electronics factory in the Boston area, where over half of the workers were women and one-third first-generation Portuguese immigrants. These essays are particularly interesting and important for their emphasis on the role of immigrant women in political activities in the workplace—a very significant form of political incorporation. In the last twenty to thirty years, a good deal of emphasis has been placed on the role of women in the migration process (Hondagneu-Sotelo 2003; Brettell 2003d; Gabaccia, Donato, Holdaway, Manalansan, and Pessar 2006) and on gender as an important analytical category (Mahler and Pessar 2001; Pessar 2003). Although not as well developed as analyses of the labor force participation of immigrant women or the impact of work on domestic life (Lamphere et al. in this volume but also, for example, Kibria 1993; Foner 1997; Parreñas 2001), there are some studies of the collective political empowerment of women (for example, Groves and Chang 1999; Goldring 2003). The Reeve and Bookman essays in this volume offer valuable insights about important forms of female empowerment and political incorporation—that which occurs in the workplace in relation to the assertion of rights to decent wages and working conditions. Coalition-building can occur on the shop floor more easily than it can among women who spend their days in the domestic spaces of their own homes.

Cultural Versus Political Identity

In his essay in this volume, Barrow draws a distinction between cultural and political identity and calls for more research on the differences of attitude and background between those who view Portuguese ethnicity in political terms and those who view it in cultural terms. Another way to look at this is to draw a distinction between forms of political belonging and forms of cultural belonging (Brettell 2006). Recently, theorists such as Renato Rosaldo and William Flores have coined the term cultural citizenship to refer to "the right to be different in terms of race, ethnicity, or native language with respect to the norms of the dominant national community, without compromising one's right to belong, in the sense of participating in the nation-state's democratic processes" (1997, 57). Processes of cultural citizenship include the claiming of public spaces and the construction of sacred places. Immigrant communities often claim space through street festivals and cultural performances.

Several essays in this volume focus our attention on the role of such performances among Portuguese immigrants. Holton's argument that dance troupes (*ranchos*) and revivalist folklore are forms of civic participation in the U.S. context certainly underscores the necessity to evaluate closely the relationship between cultural and political belonging. Her point is made even stronger when we understand the role of the Portuguese State in sustaining such activities among their citizens abroad. Klimt describes Azorean politicians who participate in community parades and celebrations in New England in order to sustain the ties with the homeland. Halter describes public displays of political culture among Cape Verdeans who celebrate their Independence Day.

One of the most prominent celebrations among the Portuguese in America is the feast of the Holy Ghost. As Leal writes, around such festivals an Azorean-American identity is constructed, and through such festivals ties to the homeland are sustained. These festivals are the fulcrum for both the continuity of traditions as well as creative changes that mark the development of an immigrant community as it emerges in the host country. Leal picks up on the bifocal outlook that Vertovec (2004) has described in association with transnationalism. He writes: "migrants are involved with the host country as they are with their country of origin; [they] maintain multiple relations and identities that cross national borders, and construct their identities in a context of structural ambiguity (this volume, 134). Leal captures the essence of an immigrant America that has been, as he puts it, in dialogue with its immigrants for several centuries, appropriating or absorbing aspects of other peoples' cultures into its own culture. If we understand this deeply-rooted process of absorption, we are better armed to address the anti-immigrant backlash of the latter half of the first decade of the 21st century. People seem to be afraid that American culture is being lost, yet what is American culture but the sum of the contributions of all the populations who have come to these shores since 1776?

Portuguese and other immigrants also claim space by taking over and rejuvenating neighborhoods in major cities. Across the United States, Asian and Latino immigrants are reenergizing old strip shopping malls along major thoroughfares and making them centers of ethnic community life (Wood 1997; Brettell 2008). The Ironbound area of Newark described by Baptista in this volume is such a neighborhood, a "site of memory" akin to the Lower East Side of Manhattan (Diner 2000). The exhibition of images of the Virgin Mary mounted in Newark helped the Portuguese to overcome their insularity and connect with the broader community. Encoded in this event, according to Barcliff Baptista, were all the tensions of becoming an American and remaining Portuguese—of both cultural and political identities.

The cultural performances of Portuguese-Americans in communities along the Eastern and Western United States are echoed by those that they bring to or reinvigorate in their sending communities, whether on the mainland (Brettell 2003f) or in the islands. Certainly, these activities are equally characteristic of other immigrant populations in the United States and elsewhere (Orsi 1985; Kasinitz and Freidenberg-Herbstein 1987; Schneider 1990; Cruces and Diaz De Roda 1992; Cohen 1993; Werbner 1996; Levitt 1998). Brucher develops this cultural link to the homeland further in her essay about the Portuguese-American Bands that return to Portugal to perform in local village communities. Here too, the tension between Portuguese and American identities played out as authenticity is both negotiated and challenged.

Race, Ethnicity, and Identity

Scholars of late 20th-century U.S. immigration have begun to document how first-generation immigrants and their children are reworking racial and ethnic categories (Stafford 1987; Bailey 2001; Vickerman 2001; Hackshaw 2007). The literature is particularly rich in studies of the Haitian immigrant experience (Stafford 1987; Stepick 1998). Waters (1994), in her research on Haitian and other West Indians in New York City, delineates three types of identities among the second generation—a black American identity, an ethnic or hyphenated national origin identity, and an immigrant identity. These identities, she suggests, are influenced by the way that adolescents perceive and understand race relations in the United States.

Historians have contributed to this discussion of the mutability of racial and ethnic categories and identities through their analysis of "whiteness" (Roediger 1991; Frankenberg 1993). The Irish who came to America were first defined as racially other, but were eventually absorbed into the white category when other newcomers—Southern and Eastern Europeans—began to arrive on America's shores (Allen 1994; Ignatiev 1995). But eventually the Italians (Guglielmo 2003) and the Jews (Brodkin 1998) also became white as their economic and political position improved (Smith et al. 2001, 6).[2]

Like the Italians, the Portuguese who emigrated to the United States in the late 19th and early 20th centuries were also treated as colored. Those from the Azores and the mainland who came after 1965 were not confronted by this category, but immigrants from the Cape Verde Islands had to wrestle with their blackness as well as with their Portugueseness. Indeed, the whiteness of Azorean Portuguese in the archipelago could be reinforced by contrast with the blackness of Cape Verdeans.

The complexity and diversity of the Portuguese immigrant population offers rich insight on the fluidity of racial and ethnic categories, as well as on what Isajiw has called the double boundaries of identities: "those from within and those from without, self-identifying and being identified by others" (1997, 90).

In this volume, Moniz discusses the malleability of Portuguese ethnic and racial categories in the U.S., beginning with a fascinating description of a debate over recognizing the Portuguese as a legal minority that occurred at the 1973 Portuguese Congress in America. Some participants were for it; some were against it. In the early 1980s, a similar debate took place among Asian Indians in the United States (Bhalla 2006), with a similar degree of dissension between those who saw it as an advantage—for access to resources—and those who were steadfast in not wanting to be perceived in this way by Americans. Some Portuguese, Moniz observes, rejected the minority status category because to accept it was to embrace a Portuguese and non-white status just when they wanted to become Americans and be included in mainstream society.

Two essays in this volume deal with the racialized identities of Cape Verdean Portuguese, who have to choose, as Gibau puts it, between associating with their ethnic/cultural group (the broader Portuguese community) or with the larger racialized groups (i.e. African-Americans). Yet, there is also a third alternative: constructing a new space for themselves which is neither Portuguese or African-American and that recognizes the special characteristics of their own culture which is Cape Verdean and African rather than African-American. Gibau, like other immigration scholars, suggests that these tensions of identity are particularly strong among the second generation.

In her very rich essay for this volume, Halter analyzes changes between the society into which Cape Verdeans entered in the 19th and early 20th centuries, and that they have entered today. Among other differences, the more recent Cape Verdean immigrants are more entrepreneurial than those of previous generations of immigrants, and they have entered an America that has created space for ethnic pride, cultural pluralism, and multiracial identities. And yet, she describes Cape Verdeans who still struggle with their Portuguese, African, and African-American identities in a manner similar to that which has been described for West Indian immigrant populations (Foner 2001).

The diversity and complex identities of the Portuguese immigrant population is further enhanced when consideration of the *retornados* who have settled in New Jersey, as described by Holton in her essay, is brought into play. There are interesting comparisons to be drawn between this population and that of the Indians born and raised in Uganda and Zambia who have also ended up settling in cities around the United States—another population that is understudied by comparison with the wealth of new monographic studies that now exist that deal with Asian Indians in America. For the *retornado* population, like the Cape Verdean population, the connection to Africa needs to be further explored; but in this latter case, race may be of less importance than the *saudade* that these immigrants have for what they consider to be their real homeland. The narratives that Holton has collected clearly suggest that, beyond a shared language, these people do not feel they have much in common with the Portuguese either on the continent or in New Jersey.

Where We Go From Here?

How unique is the Portuguese immigration experience? While I have attempted here to tease out characteristics of this experience that are shared with those of other immigrant populations, it is still worth asking whether there is another country of Europe that makes as much effort as Portugal does to remain in touch with its overseas populations and to encode this relationship in various ways. Is there another country with something equivalent to the *saudade* described in this volume by Feldman-Bianco, or with a national identity so deeply rooted in its past as a seafaring nation and its present as a deterritorialized nation? The answers to these questions require further and rigorous comparative work. Scholars of the Lusophone world must heed the warning of "methodological nationalism" outlined by Wimmer and Glick Schiller and move beyond the study of a single group as it is defined by the "geographic and political boundaries of a particular nation-state" (2003, 578). But in doing so, they will be better able to understand the unique characteristics of the Portuguese immigrant experience. Certainly one question worth pursuing is what the diversity of places of origin of Portuguese migrants means for processes of incorporation and community-building. In this volume, Portuguese from the mainland, from the Azores, from Cape Verde, as well as the *retornados* from Africa are included. Clearly they do not necessarily form one unified Portuguese community, and yet there is evidence of bridges being built—bridges that extend to the Brazilian immigrant community on the basis of language and, as Halter suggests, also on the basis of race. By contrast, however, Ramos-Zayas's chapter in this volume explicitly explores how young Brazilian women living among the Portuguese in Newark negotiate their relationships with the Portuguese and Portuguese-Americans, many of whom see them (applying a "stereotype of the tropics") as hypersexual and less respectable. The hierarchies within the Portuguese-speaking immigrant populations, by comparison with other immigrant populations, as these are based on class, race, and/or gender, are certainly worth further investigation. Furthermore, the Portuguese case should be better integrated with broader debates on whiteness—several essays in this volume suggest how important this question is within this particular community. Finally, more work needs to be done on how Lusophone populations situate themselves in relation to the large Hispanic immigrant populations in this country. As I suggested a few years ago (Brettell 2003a, 199), Salvadorans, Guatemalans, Nicaraguans, and other immigrants from Spanish-speaking countries who are in the United States do make efforts to differentiate themselves from the massive Mexican immigrant group and consider the Hispanic or Latino label one that is imposed from the outside. How do the Portuguese in the United States confront these issues, particularly in comparison with those in Germany, Canada, France or Australia where the Latino presence is less?

Other topics are also well-suited to a broader comparative approach that includes the Portuguese case. For example, several authors in this volume (Barrow, Becker, Feldman-Bianco, and Klimt) touch on the second generation, if not the third generation. Outcomes for the second generation have captured the attention of a number of social scientists working on the current fourth wave of immigration to the United States (Portes and Zhou 1993; Portes and Rumbaut 2001; Rumbaut and Portes 2001). Lusophone scholars need to bring their knowledge of Portuguese and Brazilian immigrants into this debate and particularly to take advantage of the global Portuguese diaspora to explore how outcomes might differ in different host societies. Does the bifocality of outlooks mentioned above manifest itself differently depending on where immigrants settle? And, does the possibility of a European identity shape the outcomes for Portuguese in France and Germany in a different fashion than for those in the U.S. or Canada?

Notes

[1] The "city as context" model (Brettell 2003e) emphasizes this intranational comparative approach.

[2] The literature on the construction of "whiteness" is quite extensive and extends well beyond the immigration literature. See, for example Twine (1996); Jackson (1998); Perry (2001); Kolchin (2002).

BOOKS AND PERIODICALS

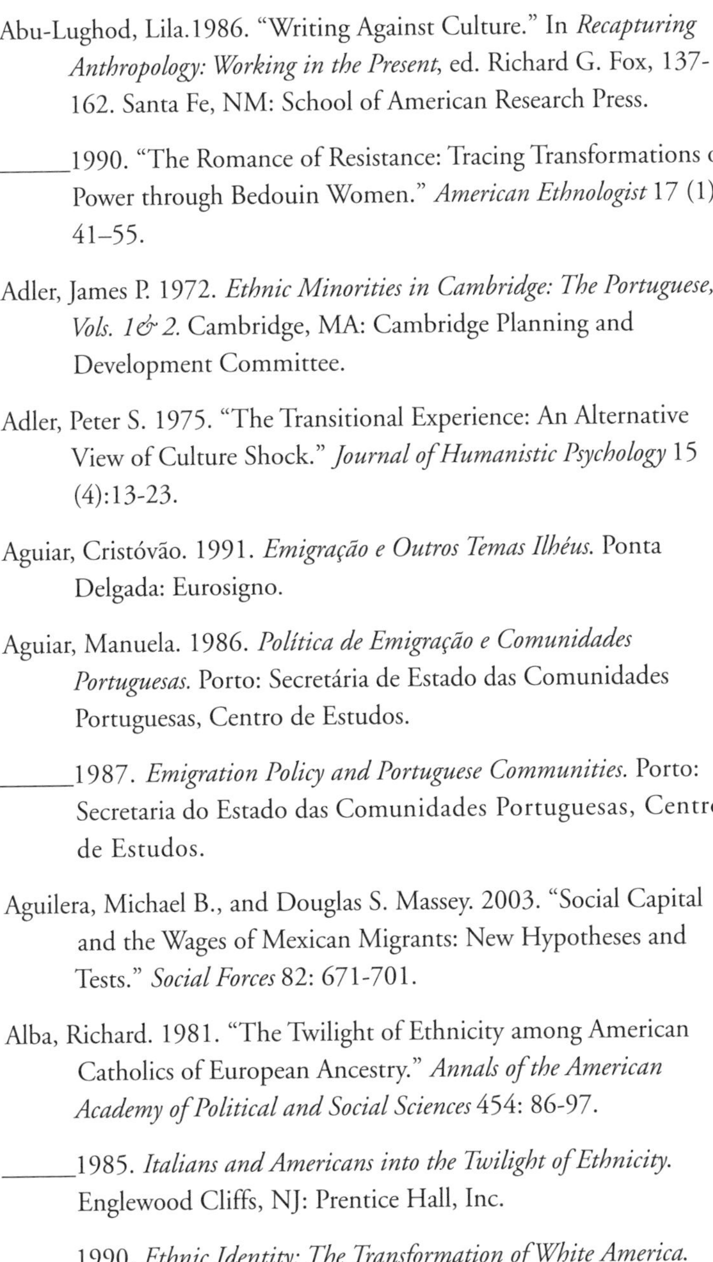

Abu-Lughod, Lila.1986. "Writing Against Culture." In *Recapturing Anthropology: Working in the Present,* ed. Richard G. Fox, 137-162. Santa Fe, NM: School of American Research Press.

______1990. "The Romance of Resistance: Tracing Transformations of Power through Bedouin Women." *American Ethnologist* 17 (1): 41–55.

Adler, James P. 1972. *Ethnic Minorities in Cambridge: The Portuguese, Vols. 1& 2.* Cambridge, MA: Cambridge Planning and Development Committee.

Adler, Peter S. 1975. "The Transitional Experience: An Alternative View of Culture Shock." *Journal of Humanistic Psychology* 15 (4):13-23.

Aguiar, Cristóvão. 1991. *Emigração e Outros Temas Ilhéus.* Ponta Delgada: Eurosigno.

Aguiar, Manuela. 1986. *Política de Emigração e Comunidades Portuguesas.* Porto: Secretária de Estado das Comunidades Portuguesas, Centro de Estudos.

______1987. *Emigration Policy and Portuguese Communities.* Porto: Secretaria do Estado das Comunidades Portuguesas, Centro de Estudos.

Aguilera, Michael B., and Douglas S. Massey. 2003. "Social Capital and the Wages of Mexican Migrants: New Hypotheses and Tests." *Social Forces* 82: 671-701.

Alba, Richard. 1981. "The Twilight of Ethnicity among American Catholics of European Ancestry." *Annals of the American Academy of Political and Social Sciences* 454: 86-97.

______1985. *Italians and Americans into the Twilight of Ethnicity.* Englewood Cliffs, NJ: Prentice Hall, Inc.

______1990. *Ethnic Identity: The Transformation of White America.* New Haven: Yale University Press.

______, and Victor Nee. 1997. "Rethinking Assimilation Theory for a New Era of Immigration." *International Migration Review* 31: 826-74.

______1999. "Rethinking Assimilation Theory for a New Era of Immigration." In *The Handbook of International Migration: The American Experience*, ed. Charles Hirschman, Philip Kasnitz, and Josh DeWind, 137-160. New York: Russell Sage Foundation.

Allen, James Paul, and Eugene James Turner. 1988. *We the People: An Atlas of America's Diversity.* New York: Macmillan.

Allen, Theodore W. 1994. *The Invention of the White Race.* London: Verso.

Almeida, Miguel Vale de. 2004. *An Earth-Colored Sea: 'Race,' Culture and the Politics of Identity in the Post-Colonial Portuguese-Speaking World.* New York: Berghahn Books.

Almeida, Onésimo T. 1980. "A Profile of the Azorean." In *Issues in Portuguese Bilingual Education*, ed. Donald Macedo, 113-164. Cambridge: NADC.

______1983. *(Sapa)teia Americana.* Angra do Heroísmo: Direcção de Serviços de Emigração.

______1987. *L(U.S.A.)lândia: A Décima Ilha.* Angra do Heroísmo: Direcção de Serviços de Emigração.

______1999. "The Portuguese-American Communities and Politics: A Look at the Cultural Roots of a Distant Relationship." *Gavea-Brown: A Bilingual Journal of Portuguese-American Letters and Studies* 19-20: 229-43.

______2000. "Value Conflicts and Cultural Adjustments in North America." In *The Portuguese in Canada: From the Sea to the City*, ed. Carlos Teixeira, and Víctor M.P. da Rosa, 112-124. Toronto: University of Toronto Press.

Almond, Gabriel A., and Sidney Verba. 1963. *The Civic Culture: Political Attitudes and Democracy in Five Nations; An Analytic Study*. Princeton: Princeton University Press.

______. 1980. *The Civic Culture Revisited: An Analytic Study*. Boston: Little, Brown, and Co.

______, and G. Bingham Powell, Jr. 1978. *Comparative Politics: System, Process, and Policy*, 2nd edition. Boston: Little, Brown, and Co.

Alpalhão, J.A., and Víctor M.P. da Rosa. 1980. *A Minority in a Changing Society: The Portuguese Communities of Québec*. Ottawa: University of Ottawa Press.

Altorki, Soraya, and Camillia F. El-Solh, eds. 1989. *Arab Women in the Field: Studying Your Own Society*. Syracuse, NY: Syracuse University Press.

Alvarez, Robert R. 1987. "A Profile of the Citizenship Process Among Hispanics in the United States." *International Migration Review* 21 (2): 327-51.

Anderson, Benedict. 1991 [1983]. *Imagined Communities: Reflections on the Origin and Spread of Nationalism*. New York: Verso.

Anderson, Grace M., and David Higgs. 1976. *A Future to Inherit: The Portuguese Communities of Canada*. Toronto: McCelland and Stewart.

______1983. "Azoreans in Anglophone Canada." *Canadian Ethnic Studies* 15 (1): 73-82.

Andrade, Laurinda C. 1968. *The Open Door*. New Bedford, MA: Reynolds-DeWalt.

Appadurai, Arjun. 1990. "Topographies of the Self: Praise and Emotion in Hindu India." In *Language and Politics of Emotion*, ed. Catherine A Lutz and Lila Abu-Lughod. Cambridge: Cambridge University Press.

______1996. *Modernity at Large: Cultural Dimensions of Globalization*. Minneapolis: University of Minnesota Press.

Appiah, Kwame Anthony. 1992. *In My Father's House.* Oxford, U.K.: Oxford University Press.

Arenas, Fernando. 2003. *Utopias of Otherness: Nationhood and Subjectivity in Portugal and Brazil.* Minneapolis: University of Minnesota Press.

Arendt, Hanna. 1978. *O Sistema Totalitário.* Lisboa: Publicações Dom Quixote.

Arroteia, Jorge. 1983. *Emigração Portuguesa: Suas Origens e Distribuição.* Lisboa: Instituto de Cultura e Língua Portuguesa.

______1985. *Atlas da Emigração Portuguesa.* Porto: Secretaria de Estado da Emigração, Centro de Estudos.

Arthur, John A. 2000. *Invisible Sojourners: African Immigrant Diaspora in the United States.* Westport, CT: Praeger.

Asad, Talal. 1972. "Market Model, Class Structure and Consent: A Reconsideration of Swat Political Organization." *Man* 7: 74-94.

Athayde, Roberto. 1996. *Brasileiros em Manhattan.* Rio de Janeiro: Topbooks.

Baganha, Maria Ioannis Benis. 1991. "The Social Mobility of Portuguese Immigrants in the United States at the Turn of the Nineteenth Century." *International Migration Review* 25 (2): 277-302.

______ 1998. "Portuguese Emigration After World War II." In *Modern Portugal*, ed. António Costa Pinto, 189-205. Palo Alto, CA: Society for the Promotion of Science and Scholarship.

______, and Pedro Góis. 1998. "Migrações Internacionais de e para Portugal: O Que Sabemos e Para Onde Vamos?" *Revista Crítica de Ciências Sociais* 52: 229-80.

Bailey, Benjamin. 2001. "Dominican-American Ethnic/Racial Identities and United States Categories." *International Migration Review* 35 (3): 677-708.

Bailey, Harry A., and Ellis Katz. 1969. *Ethnic Group Politics.* Columbus, Ohio: Merrill and Co.

Balakrishnan T.R., and John Kralt. 1987. "Segregation of Visible Minorities in Montréal, Toronto and Vancouver" in *Ethnic Canada: Identities and Inequalities*, ed. Leo Driedger, 138-157. Toronto: Copp Clark Pitman.

Bannick, Christian. 1971. *Portuguese Immigration to the United States: Its Distribution and Status.* San Francisco: R&E Research Associates.

Banks, J.A. 1970. *Marxist Sociology in Action: A Sociological Critique of the Marxist Approach to Industrial Relations.* Harrisburg, PA: Stackpole.

Banks, Marcus. 1996. *Ethnicity: Anthropological Constructions.* New York: Routledge.

Barreto, António. 1992. *Os Silêncios do Regime: Ensaios.* Lisboa: Imprensa Universitária, Editorial Estampa.

Barrett, James, and David Roediger. 1991. "In Between Peoples: Race, Nationality and the 'New Immigrant' Working Class." *Journal of American Ethnic History* 16 (3): 3-44.

Barrow, Clyde. 2005. "Portuguese-Americans in the Massachusetts Power Structure: A Positional Analysis." North Dartmouth, MA: University of Massachusetts Dartmouth, Center for Policy Analysis.

______, and Nina Galipeau. 2005. *Portuguese-Americans in the Power Structure: A Positional Analysis.* North Dartmouth, MA: University of Massachusetts Dartmouth, Center for Policy Analysis.

______ ed. 2002. *Portuguese-Americans and Contemporary Civic Culture in Massachusetts.* North Dartmouth, MA: University of Massachusetts Dartmouth, Center for Portuguese Studies and Culture and the Center for Policy Analysis.

______, and Borges, David R. 2001. "Greater New Bedford Economic Base Analysis: Critical and Emerging Industries and Work Force Development Target." *Economic Research Series* 29. University of Massachusetts Dartmouth, Center for Policy Analysis.

Barth, Frederick, ed. 1969. "Introduction." In *Ethnic Groups and Boundaries: The Social Organization of Culture Difference*, 9-38. Boston: Little, Brown and Co.

Basch, Linda, Nina Glick Schiller, and Cristina Blanc-Szanton, eds. 1994. *Nations Unbound: Transnational Projects, Postcolonial Predicaments, and Deterritorialized Nation-States.* Amsterdam: Gordon and Breach.

Bashi, Vilna, and Antonio McDaniel. 1997. "A Theory of Immigration and Racial Classification." *Journal of Black Studies* 27 (5): 668-82.

Bastos, Cristiana. 2002. "The Inverted Mirror: Dreams of Imperial Glory and Tales of Subalternity from the Medical School of Goa." In *Mirrors of Empire*, ed. Rosa Maria Perez and Clara Carvalho. *Etnográfica* IV (1): 59-76.

Bastos, Cristina, Miguel Vale de Almeida, and Bela Feldman-Bianco. 2002. *Trânsitos Coloniais: Diálogos Críticos Luso-Brasileiros.* Lisboa: Imprensa de Ciências Sociais. Campinas: Editora da Unicamp.

Bean, Philip A. 1994. "The Irish, the Italians, and Machine Politics, A Case Study: Utica, New York (1870-1960)." *Journal of Urban History* 20: 205-39.

Becker, Howard. 1993. *Human Capital: A Theoretical and Empirical Analysis, with Special Reference to Education.* Chicago: University of Chicago Press.

Bedford, Henry F. 1966. *Socialism and the Workers in Massachusetts, 1886-1912.* Amherst: University of Massachusetts Press.

———, ed. 1995. *Their Lives and Numbers: The Condition of Working People in Massachusetts, 1870-1900.* Ithaca, N.Y.: Cornell University Press.

Bender, Gerald. J. 2004 [1978]. *Angola Under the Portuguese: The Myth and the Reality.* Trenton, NJ: Africa World Press.

Benedict, Helen. 1992. *Virgin or Vamp*. Oxford: Oxford University Press.

Bernard, Miguel A. 1991. "Five Great Missionary Experiments and Cultural Issues in Asia." *Cardinal Bea Studies* 11: 88.

Beserra, Bernadette. 2003. *Brazilian Immigrants in the United States: Cultural Imperialism and Social Class*. New York: LFB Scholarly Publishing LLC.

Bessa, A. Marques et al. 1988. *Identidade Portuguesa: Cumprir Portugal*. Lisboa: Instituto Dom João de Castro.

Bhalla, Vibha. 2006. "The New Indians: Reconstructing Indian Identity in the United States." *American Behavioral Scientist* 50 (1): 118-36.

Birmingham, David. 1993. *A Concise History of Portugal*. Cambridge: Cambridge University Press.

______2006. *Empire in Africa: Angola and Its Neighbors*. Athens, OH: Ohio University Press.

Blau, Peter, and Otis Duncan. 1967. *The American Occupational Structure*. New York: John Wiley & Sons, Inc.

Bledsoe, Caroline. 1980. *Women and Marriage in Kpelle Society*. Stanford, CA: Stanford University Press.

Bloemraad, Irene. 2002. "The North American Naturalization Gap: An Institutional Approach to Citizenship Acquisition in the United States and Canada." *International Migration Review* 36 (1): 193-228.

______2005. "The Limits of Tocqueville: How Government Facilitates Organizational Capacity in Newcomer Communities." *Journal of Ethnic and Migration Studies* 31 (5): 865-87.

______2006. *Becoming a Citizen: Incorporating Immigrants and Refugees in the United States and Canada*. Berkeley, CA: University of California Press.

______Forthcoming. "Of Puzzles and Serendipity: Doing Research with Cross-National Comparisons and Mixed Methods." In *Research Methods Choices in Interdisciplinary Contexts: War Stories of New Scholars*, ed. Louis DeSipio, Manuel Garcia y Griego, and Sherrie Kossoudji. New York: Social Science Research Council.

Blu, Karen. 1980. *The Lumbee Problem.* New York: Cambridge University Press.

Borges, Aluísio Medeiros da Rosa. 1990. *The Portuguese Working Class in the Durfee Mills of Fall River, Massachusetts:* A *Study of the Division of Labor, Ethnicity, and Labor Union Participation, 1895-1925.* New York: Binghamton.

Borges, David R., and Clyde W. Barrow. 2000. *Fall River Community Report Card 2000.* North Dartmouth, MA: University of Massachusetts Dartmouth, Center for Policy Analysis.

Borjas, George J. 1985. "Assimilation, Changes in Cohort Quality, and the Earnings of Immigrants." *Journal of Labor Economics* 3: 463-89.

______1994. "Long-run Convergence of Ethnic Skill Differentials: The Children and Grandchildren of the Great Migration." *Industrial and Labor Relations Review* 47 (4): 553-73.

Botelho, Paula. 2004. "In the Service of the Community: The Roles of the Brazilian American Church in Reconstructing Identity." *National Association of African-American Studies and Affiliates* (NAAAS) *Monograph Series*, Vol. II.

Bott, Elizabeth. 1957. *Family and Social Network.* London: Tavistock Publications.

______1971. *Family and Social Network*, 2nd. ed. London: Tavistock Publications.

Bourdieu, Pierre. 1977. *Outline of a Theory of Practice.* Cambridge: Cambridge University Press.

Boxer, Charles. 1969. *Four Centuries of Portuguese Expansion 1415-1825: A Succinct Survey.* Berkeley: University of California Press.

Boym, Svetlana. 2001. *The Future of Nostalgia.* New York: Basic Books.

Braroe, Niels W. 1975. *Indians and Whites: Self-Image and Interaction in a Canadian Plains Community.* Stanford, CA: Stanford University Press.

Breton, Raymond, and Maurice Pinard. 1960. "Group Formation among Immigrants: Criteria and Processes." *Canadian Journal of Economics and Political Science* 25: 465-77.

______,Wsevolod W. Isajiw, Warren E. Kalbach, and Jeffrey G. Reitz. 1990. *Ethnic Identity and Equality: Varieties of Experience in a Canadian City.* Toronto: University of Toronto Press.

Brettell, Caroline B. 1982a. *We Have Already Cried Many Tears.* Cambridge, MA: Schenkman Publishing Company.

______1982b. "Is Ethnic Community Inevitable: A Comparison of Settlement Patterns of Portuguese Immigrants in Toronto and Paris." *Journal of Ethnic Studies* 93: 1-17.

______1986. *Men Who Migrate, Women Who Wait: Portuguese Immigration and History in a Portuguese Village.* Princeton, NJ: Princeton University Press.

______2003a. *Anthropology and Migration: Essays on Transnationalism, Ethnicity, and Identity.* Walnut Creek, CA: AltaMira Press.

______2003b. "Is the Ethnic Community Inevitable? A Comparison of the Settlement Patterns of Portuguese Immigrants in Toronto and Paris." In *Anthropology and Migration: Essays on Transnationalism, Ethnicity, and Identity,* 109-126. Walnut Creek, CA: AltaMira Press.

______2003c. "Emigrar para Voltar: A Portuguese Ideology of Return Migration." In *Anthropology and Migration: Essays on Transnationalism, Ethnicity, and Identity,* 57-74. Walnut Creek, CA: AltaMira Press.

______2003d. "Gender and Migration." In *Anthropology and Migration: Essays on Transnationalism, Ethnicity, and Identity,* 139-151. Walnut Creek, CA: AltaMira Press.

______2003e. "Bringing the City Back In: Cities as Contexts for Immigrant Incorporation." In *American Arrivals: Anthropology Engages the New Immigration,* ed. Nancy Foner, 163-196. Santa Fe: School of American Research Press.

______2003f. "Emigration, the Church, and the Religious Festival in Northern Portugal." In *Anthropology and Migration: Essays on Transnationalism, Ethnicity, and Identity.* 75-100. Walnut Creek, CA: AltaMira Press.

______2003g. "Ethnicity and Entrepreneurs: Portuguese Immigrants in a Canadian City." In *Anthropology and Migration: Essays on Transnationalism, Ethnicity, and Identity,* 127-138. Walnut Creek, CA: AltaMira Press.

______(1993) 2003h. "The Emigrant, the Nation, and the State in Nineteenth- and Twentieth-Century Portugal: An Anthropological Approach." In *Anthropology and Migration: Essays on Transnationalism, Ethnicity, and Identity,* 9-22. Walnut Creek, CA: AltaMira Press.

______2005. "Voluntary Organizations, Social Capital and the Social Incorporation of Asian Indian Immigrants in the Dallas-Fort Worth Metroplex." *Anthropological Quarterly* 78: 853-83.

______2006. "Political Belonging and Cultural Belonging: Immigration Status, Citizenship, and Identity Among Four Immigrant Populations in a Southwestern City." *American Behavioral Scientist* 50 (1): 70-99.

______2008. "Meet Me at the Chat Corner': The Cultural Embeddedness of Immigrant Entrepreneurs." In *From Arrival to Incorporation: Migrants to the U.S. in a Global Era,* ed. Elliott R. Barkan, Hasia Diner, and Alan M. Kraut, 121-142. New York: New York University Press.

Brodkin, Karen. 1998. *How Jews Became White Folks and What that Says about Race in America.* New Brunswick, NJ: Rutgers University Press.

Brubaker, Rogers. 1992. *Citizenship and Nationhood in France and Germany.* Cambridge: Harvard University Press.

Bruneau, Thomas C., et al. 1984. *Portugal in Development: Emigration, Industrialization, the European Community.* Ottawa: University of Ottawa Press.

Bryce-Laporte, Roy Simon. 1972. "Black Immigrants: The Experience of Invisibility and Inequality." *Journal of Black Studies* 3 (1): 29–56.

Buhle, Paul. 1999. *Taking Care of Business: Samuel Gompers, George Meany, Lane Kirkland and the Tragedy of American Labor.* New York: Monthly Review Press.

Butcher, Kristin F. 1994. "Black Immigrants in the United States: A Comparison With Native Blacks and Other Immigrants." *Industrial and Labor Relations Review* 47 (2): 265–84.

Butler, Kim. 2001. "Defining Diaspora, Refining a Discourse." *Diaspora* 10 (2): 189-219.

Butler, Judith. 1993. *Bodies that Matter: On the Discursive Limits of "Sex."* New York: Routledge.

Cabral, Stephen L. 1989. *Tradition and Transformation: Portuguese Feasting in New Bedford.* New York: AMS Press.

Calderón, José. 1992. "'Hispanic' and 'Latino': The Viability of Categories for Panethnic Unity." *Latin American Perspectives* 75 (4): 137-144.

Cardozo, Manuel da Silveira. 1976. *The Portuguese in America, 590 B.C.-1974: A Chronology and Fact Book.* Dobbs Ferry, NY: Oceana Publications.

Carling, Jorgen. 2002. "Migration in the Age of Involuntary Immobility: Theoretical Reflections and Cape Verdean Experiences." *Journal of Ethnic and Migration Studies* 28 (1): 5-21.

Carreira, António. 1972. *Cabo Verde: Formação de Uma Sociedade Escravocrata, 1460–1878.* Porto, Portugal: Impresa Portuguesa.

______1982. *The People of the Cape Verde Islands: Exploitation and Emigration.* C. Fyfe, trans. Hamden, CT: Archon.

Carter, Prudence. 2005. *Keepin' It Real: School Success beyond Black and White.* New York: Oxford University Press.

Carty, Maria da Ascensão. 2002. "Festa Queens." In *Holy Ghost Festas: A Historic Perspective of the Portuguese in California*, ed. Tony Goulart, 451-462. San Jose CA: Portuguese Chamber of Commerce.

Carvalho, Eduardo de. 1931. *Os Portugueses da Nova Inglaterra.* Rio de Janeiro: A Leitura Colonial.

Cassola Ribeiro, F. G. 1986a. *Emigração Portuguesa: Algumas Características Dominantes dos Movimentos no Período de 1950 a 1984.* Porto: Secretaria do Estado das Comunidades Portuguesas, Série Migrações, Sociologia. Centro de Estudos.

______1986b. *Emigração Portuguesa: Aspectos Relativos às Políticas Adoptadas no Domínio da Emigração Portuguesa, desde a Última Guerra Mundial.* Porto: Secretaria de Estado das Comunidades Portuguesas. Instituto de Apoio à Emigração e às Comunidades Portuguesas, Série Migrações, Política. Relações Internacionais, Porto.

Castelo, Cláudia. 2007. *Passagens para África: O Povoamento de Angola e Moçambique com Naturais da Metrópole, 1920-1974.* Porto: Edições Afrontamento.

Castelo-Branco, Salwa, and Jorge Freitas Branco, eds. 2003. *Vozes do Povo.* Oeiras, Portugal: Celta Editora.

Castro, Augusto de. s/d. *Subsídios para a História da Política Externa Portuguesa durante a Guerra.* Lisboa: Livraria Bertrand.

Caute, David. 1979. *The Great Fear: The Anti-Communist Purge Under Truman and Eisenhower.* New York: Simon and Schuster.

Cazden, Courtney B. 1985. "Social Context of Learning to Read." In *Theoretical Models and Processes of Reading,* ed. H. Singer, and R. Ruddell, 595-610. Newark, DE: International Reading Association.

Center for Policy Analysis. 2001. "Greater New Bedford Economic Base Analysis: Critical and Emerging Industries and Workforce Development Targets." Dartmouth, MA: University of Massachusetts.

Chabal, Patrick. 2002. "Lusophone Africa in Historical and Comparative Perspective: The Limits of Nationhood." In *History of Postcolonial Lusophone Africa,* 88-134. Bloomington, IN: Indiana University Press.

______ et al. 2002. *A History of Postcolonial Lusophone Africa.* Bloomington, IN: Indiana University Press.

Chapa, Jorge. 1995. "Mexican-American Class Structure and Political Participation." *New England Journal of Public Policy* 11 (1): 183-98. Spring/ Summer.

Chapin, Wesley. 1996. "The Turkish Diaspora in Germany." *Diaspora* 5: 275-301.

Chiswick, Barry R. 1979. "The Economic Progress of Immigrants: Some Apparently Universal Patterns." In *Contemporary Economic Problems,* ed. William Fellner, 357-399. Washington: American Enterprise Institute.

______and Paul W. Miller. 2008. "Immigrant Enclaves, Ethnic Goods, and the Adjustment Process." In *From Arrival to Incorporation: Migrants to the U.S. in a Global Era,* ed. Elliott R. Barkan, Hasia Diner, and Alan M. Kraut, 80-93. New York: New York University Press.

Cho, Wendy K. Tam. 1999. "Naturalization, Socialization, Participation: Immigrants and Non-Voting." *Journal of Politics* 61 (4): 1140-55.

Choldin Havey M. 1986. "Statistics and Politics: The 'Hispanic Issue' in the 1980 Census." *Demography* 23 (3): 403-418.

Clawson, Dan, and Mary Ann Clawson. 1999. "What Has Happened to the US Labor Movement?" *Annual Review of Sociology* 25: 95-119.

Clifford, James. 1988. "Identity in Mashpee." In *The Predicament of Culture: Twentieth-Century Ethnography, Literature and Art*, 277-334. Cambridge, MA: Harvard University Press.

Cohen, Abner. 1969. *Custom and Politics in Urban Africa: A Study of Hausa Migrants in Yoruba Towns*. Berkeley: University of California Press.

______1993. *Masquerade Politics: Explorations in the Structure of Urban Cultural Movements*. Berkeley, CA: University of California Press.

Cole, Sally. 1991. *Women of the Praia: Work and Lives in a Portuguese Coastal Community*. Princeton: Princeton University Press.

Coles, Tim, and Dallen J. Timothy, eds. 2004. *Tourism, Diasporas, and Space*. New York: Routledge.

Collier, Jane. 1974. "Women in Politics." In *Women, Culture and Society*, ed. Michele Rosaldo and Louise Lamphere, 89-96. Palo Alto, CA: Stanford University Press.

Colson, Elizabeth. 1967. "Contemporary Tribes and the Development of Nationalism." In *Essays on the Problem of Tribe: Proceedings of the 1967 Annual Spring Meeting*, ed. June Helm, 201-206. Seattle: University of Washington Press.

Cook, Cleo O. Hearnton. 1972. "Self Concept and the Culturally Different Learner." In *Culture and School*, ed. Ronald Shinn, 121-126. Scranton, PA: The Haddon Craftsmen, Inc.

Cortés, Carlos. E. 1980. *Portuguese Americans and Spanish Americans*. New York: Arno Press.

______1986. "The Education of Language Minority Students. A Contextual Interaction Model." In *Beyond Language: Social and Cultural Factors in Schooling Language Minority Students*, ed. Evaluation Dissemination and Assessment Center, 3-34. Los Angeles: California State University.

Costa-Pinto, António. 1998. "Twentieth-Century Portugal: An Introduction." In *Modern Portugal*, ed. António Costa-Pinto, 1-40. Palo Alto, CA: Society for the Promotion of Science and Scholarship.

Costa Vargas, João. 2004. "Hyperconsciousness of Race and Its Negation: The Dialectic of White Supremacy in Brazil." *Identities* 11: 443-470.

Cristoffanini, J. 2003. "The Representation of 'the Others' as Strategies of Symbolic Construction." In *Intercultural Alternatives: Critical Perspectives on Intercultural Encounters in Theory and Practice*, ed. Maribel Blasco, and Jan Gustafsson, 79-102. Copenhagen: Copenhagen Business School Press.

Cruces, Francisco, and Angel Diaz de Roda. 1992. "Public Celebrations in a Spanish Valley." In *Revitalizing European Rituals.* ed. Jeremy Boissevain, 62-79. London: Routledge.

Cruz, Jose. 1995. "Puerto Rican Politics in the United States: A Preliminary Assessment." *New England Journal of Public Policy* 11 (1): 199-219.

Cumbler, John T. 1979. *Working-Class Community in Industrial America.* Westport, CT: Greenwood Press.

Cunningham, John T. 2002. *Newark.* Newark: New Jersey Historical Society.

Dahl, Robert A. 1961. *Who Governs?* New Haven: Yale University Press.

Daniel, Clete. 2001. *Culture of Misfortune: An Interpretive History of Textile Unionism in the United States.* Ithaca: Cornell University Press.

daRosa, Victor, and Carlos Teixeira. 2000. "The Portuguese Community in Québec." In *The Portuguese in Canada*, ed. Carlos Teixeira, and Victor DaRosa, 191-206. Toronto: University of Toronto Press.

Davidson, Basil. 1989. *The Fortunate Isles: A Study in African Transformation.* Trenton, NJ: African World Press.

Dawley, Alan. 1976. *Class and Community: The Industrial Revolution in Lynn.* Cambridge: Harvard University Press.

De Andrade, Lelia Lomba. 2000. "Negotiating from the Inside: Constructing Racial and Ethnic Identity in Qualitative Research." *Journal of Contemporary Ethnography* 29 (3): 268–290.

De Genova, Nicholas, and Ana Y Ramos-Zayas. 2003. *Latino Crossings: Mexicans, Puerto Ricans, and the Politics of Race and Citizenship.* New York: Routledge.

Delgado, Richard, and Jean Stefancic. 1997. *Critical White Studies: Looking Behind the Mirror.* Philadelphia, PA: Temple University Press.

De Montfort, St. Louis, and Mary Barbour. 1954. *The Secret of the Rosary.* Rockford, Illinois: Tan Books and Publishers.

Derrick, Michael. 1939. *The Portugal of Salazar.* New York: Campion Books.

de Sá, Maria da Glória. 1985. *A Posição Socioeconómica dos Imigrantes Portugueses e seus Descendentes nos Estados de Massachusetts e Rhode Island (U.S.A.).* Porto: Secretaria de Estado da Emigração -Centro de Estudos.

______2008. "The Azorean Community on the East Coast." In *Capelinhos: A Volcano of Synergies-Azorean—Emigration to America,* ed. Tony Goulart, coord., Marilyn Harper, 159-170. San Jose: Portuguese Heritage Publications of California, Inc.

Dhingra, Pawan. 2007. *Managing Multicultural Lives: Asian-American Professionals and the Challenge of Multiple Identities.* Stanford, CA: Stanford University Press.

Dias, Eduardo Mayone. 1983a. *Coisas da LUSAlândia.* Lisboa: Instituto Português de Ensino à Distância.

______1983b. "A Literatura Emigrante Portuguesa na Califórnia." *Arquipélago: Revista da Universidade dos Açores.* Separata.

______ ed. 1988. *Portugueses na América do Norte.* Rumford, RI: Peregrinação Publications.

______1989. *Falares Emigreses: Uma Abordagem ao Seu Estudo.* Lisboa: Ministério da Educação. Instituto de Cultura e Língua Portuguesa.

______1992. *Crónicas da Diáspora.* Lisboa: Salamandra.

______1993. *Escritas de Além-Atlântico.* Lisboa: Salamandra.

Dimitroff, Lillian. 1972. "Concept of Self and Teaching Culturally Different People." In *Culture and School,* ed. Ronald Shinn, 209-227. Scranton, PA: The Haddon Craftsmen, Inc.

Diner, Hasia. 2000. *Lower East Side Memories: A Jewish Place in America.* Princeton: Princeton University Press.

Dines, Deborah. 1989. "Go-Gos: Os (As) Brasileiros (as) Entram na Dança do Dolor." *Ele Ela* 21: 88-92.

Dodds, Jerrilynn D., and Sullivan, Edward J., eds. 1997. *Crowning Glory: Images of the Virgin in the Arts of Portugal.* Maria de Lourdes Simões de Carvalho and Julia Robinson, coords. Newark: The Newark Museum.

Dolbeare, Kenneth M., and Linda J. Medcalf. 1993. *American Ideologies: Shaping the New Politics of the 1990s,* 2nd edition. New York: McGraw-Hill.

Drewal, Margaret Thompson. 1992. *Yoruba Ritual: Performers, Play, Agency.* Bloomington, IN: Indiana University Press.

DuPuy, W.A. 1932. *Hawaii and Its Race Problem.* Washington.

Duval, David Timothy. 2002. "The Return Visit-Return Migration Connection." In *Tourism and Migration,* ed. C. Michael Hall and Allan M. Williams, 257-276. Boston: Kluwer Academic Publishers.

Economist Intelligence Unit (EIU). 1996. *Country Profile: Congo, São Tomé and Príncipe, Guinea-Bissau, Cape Verde, 1995–96.* London: EIU Limited.

Edwards, Richard. 1979. *Contested Terrain: The Transformation of the Workplace in the Twentieth Century.* New York: Basic Books.

Eisenstein, Sarah. 1983. *Give Us Bread but Give Us Roses: Working Women's Consciousness in the United States, 1890 to the First World War.* London: Routledge & Kegan Paul.

Eller, Jack, and Reed Coughlin. 1993. "The Poverty of Primodialism." *Ethnic and Racial Studies* 16: 183-202.

Emery, Edwin. 1972. *The Press and America.* New Jersey: Prentice-Hall.

Enes, Carlos. 1994. *A Economia Açoriana entre as Duas Guerras Mundiais.* Lisboa: Edições Salamandra.

Erie, Steven. 1990. *Rainbow's End: Irish Americans and the Dilemmas of Urban Machine Politics.* Berkeley: University of California Press.

Eriksen, Thomas Hylland. 1993. *Ethnicity and Nationalism: Anthropological Perspectives.* London: Pluto Press.

______ 2001. "Ethnic Identity, National Identity, and Intergroup Conflict: The Significance of Personal Experiences." In *Social Identity, Intergroup Race and Ethnicity in the Cape Verdean Diaspora Conflict, and Conflict Reduction,* ed. Richard D. Ashmore, Lee Jussim, and David Wilder, 42-70. New York: Oxford University Press.

"Estudos sobre a Emigração Portuguesa, Cadernos." 1981. *Revista de História Económica e Social.*

Evangelista, J. 1971. *Um Século de Emigração Portuguesa (1864-1960).* Lisboa: CED-INE.

Faist, Thomas. 1999. "Developing Transnational Social Spaces: The Turkish German Example." In *Migration and Transnational Social Space,* ed. Ludger Pries, 36-72. Aldershot: Ashgate.

Fanon, Frantz. 1990. "The Fact of Blackness." In *Anatomy of Racism,* ed. David Theo Goldberg, 108-126. Minneapolis: University of Minnesota Press.

Faragher, John Mack, et al. 1994. *Out of Man: A History of the American People, Vol II.* New Jersey: Simon & Schuster.

Farr, Marcia. 1994. "Echando Relajo: Verbal Art and Gender among *Mexicanas* in Chicago." In *Cultural Performances: Proceedings of The Third Berkeley Women and Language Conference,* 168-186. Berkeley: University of California.

Feldberg, Roslyn, and Evelyn Glenn. 1979. "Male and Female: Job versus Gender Models in the Sociology of Work." *Social Problems* 26 (5): 524-38.

Feldman-Bianco, Bela. 1992. "Multiple Layers of Time and Space: The Construction of Class, Race, and Ethnicity, and Nationalism among Portuguese Immigrants." In *Towards a Transnational Perspective on Migration: Race, Class, Ethnicity, and Nationalism Reconsidered,* ed. Nina Glick-Schiller, Linda Basch, and Cristina Szanton-Blanc, 145-75. New York: New York Academy of Sciences.

______1994. *Saudade, Immigration and the Politics of Reterritorialization and Deterritorialization.* Coimbra: Centro de Estudos Sociais, University of Coimbra.

______2001. "Brazilians in Portugal, Portuguese in Brazil: Constructions of Sameness and Difference." *Identities: Global Studies in Politics and Culture* 8(4): 607-650.

______2004. "Globalización: Antiguos Imaginários y Reconfiguraciones de Identidad." In *La Antropologia Brasileña Contemporânea,* ed. Alexandre Grimson, Gustavo Lins Ribeiro, and Pablo Séman, 71-94. Buenos Aires: Prometeo Libros.

______2007. "Empire, Postcoloniality and Diasporas (Feature)." *Hispanic Research Journal* 8 (3): 267-278.

______, and D. Huse. 1996. "The Construction of the Immigrant Identity: The Case of the Portuguese of Southeastern Massachusetts." In *Spinner: People and Culture in Southeastern Massachusetts,* Vol. 5, ed. Joseph D. Thomas and Marsha McCabe, 60-73. New Bedford, MA: Spinner Publications, Inc.

Felix, John Henry, and Peter F. Senecal, eds. 1978. *The Portuguese in Hawaii.* Honolulu, Hawaii: Sturgis Printing Co.

Félix, Pedro. 2003. "O Concurso 'A Aldeia Mais Portuguesa de Portugal' (1938)." In *Vozes do Povo: A Folclorização em Portugal.* ed. Salwa Castelo-Branco and Jorge Freitas Branco, 207-231. Oeiras, Portugal: Celta Editora.

Ferreira de Castro, José Maria. 1978 [1928]. *Emigrantes.* Lisbon: Guimarães.

______1930. *A Selva.* Lisbon: Guimarães.

Fijalkowski, Jürgen. 1998. "Incorporating Immigrants and Expanding Citizenship." In *Immigration, Citizenship, and the Welfare State in Germany and the United States: Welfare Policies and Immigrants' Citizenship,* ed. Herman Kurtner, Jürgen Fijalkowski, and Gert Wagner. Stamford, CT: Jai P.

Fishman, Joshua A. 1976. *Bilingual Education: An International Sociological Perspective.* Rowley, MA: Newbury House Publishers, Inc.

Fleischer, Soraya Resende. 2002. *Passando a América a Limpo: O Trabalho de* Housecleaners *Brasileiras em Boston, Massachussets.* São Paulo, Brasil: Annablume Editora.

Flores, Juan, and George Yúdice. 1993. "Living Borders/ Buscando América: Languages of Latino Self-Formation." In *Divided Borders,* ed. Juan Flores, 199-224. Houston: Arté Publico Press.

Foner, Nancy. 1988. *New Immigrants in New York.* New York: Columbia University Press.

______1997. "The Immigrant Family: Cultural Legacies and Cultural Changes." *International Migration Review* 31: 961-974.

______ ed. 2000. *Islands in the City: West Indian Migration to New York.* Berkeley, CA: University of California Press.

______2005. *In a New Land: A Comparative View of Immigration.* New York: New York University Press.

Fong, Eric, and Emi Ooka. 2002. "The Social Consequences of Participating in the Ethnic Economy." *International Migration Review* 36: 125-146.

Foucault, Michel. 1977. *Discipline and Punish: The Birth of the Prison.* trans. Allan Sheridan. New York: Vintage.

Foy, Colm. 1988. *Cape Verde: Politics, Economics, and Society.* London: Pinter.

Frankenberg, Ruth. 1993. *White Women, Race Matters: The Social Construction of Whiteness.* Minneapolis: University of Minnesota Press.

Freitas, Pedro de. 1946. *História da Música Popular em Portugal.* Lisbon: Custódio Cardoso Pereira & Ca.

______1965. *O I Concurso Nacional de Bandas Civis.* Lisboa: L. C. G. G.

Freitas, Vamberto. 2001. *Jornalismo e Cidadania: Dos Açores à Califórnia.* Lisboa: Edições Salamandra.

Fuchs, Lawrence. 1991. *The American Kaleidoscope: Ethnicity and the Civic Culture.* Hanover, NH: University Press of New England.

Fuery, Patrick. 1995. *Theories of Desire.* Carlton, Australia: Melbourne University Press.

Gabaccia, Donna, Katharine M. Donato, Jennifer Holdaway, Martin Manalansan IV, and Patricia R. Pessar, eds. 2006. "Gender and Migration Revisited." *International Migration Review* 40. Special Issue.

Gans, Herbert. 1962. *The Urban Villagers.* New York: The Free Press.

______1979. "Symbolic Ethnicity: The Future of Ethnic Groups and Cultures in America." *Ethnic and Racial Studies* 2: 1-20.

______1992. "The Second-Generation Decline: Scenarios for the Economic and Ethnic Futures of Post-1965 American Immigrants." *Ethnic and Racial Studies* 15: 173-192.

Geertz, Clifford. 1963. "The Integrative Revolution: Primordial Sentiments and Civil Politics in the New States." In *Old Societies and New States: The Quest for Modernity in Asia and Africa,* 105-157. New York: Free Press.

Gemzoe, Lena. 2000. *Feminine Matters: Women's Religious Practices in a Portuguese Town.* Stockholm, Sweden: Stockholm University Publications.

Georgeanna, Daniel, and Roberta Hazen Aaranson. 1993. *The Strike of '28.* New Bedford, MA: Spinner Publications.

Georgianna, Daniel, and Debra Shrader. 2008. "The Effects of Days on Sea on Employment, Income and Hours of Work: Some Preliminary Evidence." *Human Ecology Review* 15(2): 185-193.

Gerstle, Gary. 2001. *The American Crucible: Race and Nation in the Twentieth Century.* Princeton: Princeton University Press.

______ and John Mollenkopf , eds. 2001. *Et Pluribus Unum? Contemporary and Historical Perspectives on Immigrant Political Incorporation.* New York: Russell Sage Foundation.

Geschwender, James A., Rita Carroll-Seguin, and Howard Brill. 1988. "The Portuguese and Haoles of Hawaii: Implications for the Origin of Ethnicity." *American Sociological Review* 53 (4): 515-27.

Gilbert, Dennis L. 2003. *The American Class Structure in an Age of Growing Inequality,* 6th Edition. Belmont, CA: Wadsworth Publishing.

______, and Joseph A. Kahl. 1998. *The American Class Structure: A New Synthesis,* 4th Edition. Belmont, CA: Wadsworth Publishing.

Gilbert, Dorothy A. 1989. *Recent Portuguese Immigrants to Fall River, Massachusetts: An Analysis of Relative Economic Success.* New York: AMS Press, Inc.

Giles, Wenona. 2002. *Portuguese Women in Toronto: Gender, Immigration, and Nationalism.* Toronto: University of Toronto Press.

Gilroy, Paul. 1993. *The Black Atlantic: Modernity and Double Consciousness.* London: Verso.

Glade, Mary Elizabeth. 1989. *Immigration: Pluralism and National Identity.* Boulder, CO: Social Science Education Consortium Publications.

Glazer, Nathan, and Daniel Moynihan. 1970. *Beyond the Melting Pot,* 2nd edition Cambridge, MA: Massachusetts Institute of Technology Press.

Glazer, Nathan. 1993. "Is Assimilation Dead?" *Annals of the American Academy of Political and Social Sciences* 530: 122-136.

Glick-Schiller, Nina. 1999. "Transmigrants and Nation-States; Something Old and Something New in the U.S. Experience." In *Handbook of International Migration: The American Experience,* ed. Charles Hirschman, Philip Kasinitz, and Josh DeWind,
94-119. New York: Russell Sage.

Glick-Schiller, Nina, Linda Basch, and Cristina Szanton-Blanc. 1992. "Transnationalism: A New Analytic Framework for Understanding Migration; Towards a Definition of Transnationalism, Introductory Remarks and Research Questions." In *Towards a Transnational Perspective on Migration: Race, Class, Ethnicity, and Nationalism Reconsidered,* ed. Nina Glick Schiller, Linda Basch, and Cristina Szanton-Blanc, 1-24. New York: Annals of the New York Academy of Sciences, Vol. 645.

______1999. "From Immigrant to Transmigrant: Theorizing Transnational Migration." In *Migration and Transnational Social Spaces*, ed. Ludger Pries, 74-105. Aldershot, UK: Ashgate.

Gluckman, Max. 1958. *Analysis of a Social Situation Modern Zululand.* Manchester: Manchester University Press for the Rhodes-Livingstone Institute.

______1961. "Anthropological Problems Arising From the African Industrial Revolution." In *Social Change in Modern Africa*, ed. A. Southall, 67-82. London: Oxford University Press.

Goethe Society of New England. 1981. *Germans in Boston.* Boston, Massachusetts.

Góis, Pedro. 2005. "Low Intensity Transnationalism: The Cape Verdean Case." *Vienna Journal of African Studies* 8: 255-76.

Golde, Peggy, ed. 1986. *Women in the Field: Anthropological Experiences.* 2nd edition. Berkeley: University of California Press.

Goldfield, Michael. 2000. "Union Democracy and the U.S. Labor Bureaucracy." *New Politics* 7 (4): 87.

Goldring, Luin. 2003. "Gender, Status, and the State in Transnational Spaces: The Gendering of Political Participation and Mexican Hometown Associations." In *Gender and U.S. Immigration: Contemporary Trends*, ed. Pierrette Hondagneu-Sotelo, 341-358. Berkeley, CA: University of California Press.

Goldstein, Donna. 1999. "'Interracial' Sex and Racial Democracy in Brazil: Twin Concepts?" *American Anthropologist* 101 (3): 563-578.

Gomes, Francisco António N. P. 1991. *O Canal da América.* Lages das Flores: Câmara Municipal.

Gonzalez, Juan. 2001. *Harvest of Empire: A History of Latinos in America.* New York: Penguin.

Goulart, Tony, ed. 2002. *Holy Ghost Festas. A Historic Perspective of the Portuguese in California.* San Jose, CA: Portuguese Chamber of Commerce.

Green, James. 1980. *The World of the Worker: Labor in Twentieth-Century America.* New York: Hill and Wang.

Greenblatt, Stephen. 1991. "Resonance and Wonder." In *Exhibiting Cultures: The Poetics and Politics of Museum Display*, ed. Ivan Karp and Steven D. Lavine, 42-56. Washington: Smithsonian Institution Press.

Greer, Collins. 1972. *The Great School Legend.* New York: Viking Press.

Grogan, Paul S. and Tony Proscio. 2001. *Comeback Cities: A Blueprint for Urban Neighborhood Revival.* Boulder, CO: Westview Press.

Grosfoguel, Ramón. 2003. *Colonial Subjects: Puerto Ricans in a Global Perspective.* Berkeley: University of California Press.

Gross, Ariel. 2007. "'Of Portuguese Origin': Litigating Identity and Citizenship Among the 'Little Races in 19th Century America.'" *Law and History Review* 25: 3.

Groves, Julian McAllister, and Kimberly A. Chang. 1999. "Romancing Resistance and Resisting Romance: Ethnography and the Construction of Power in the Filipina Domestic Worker Community in Hong Kong." *Journal of Contemporary Ethnography* 28: 235-265.

Guglielmo. Thomas A. 2003. *White on Arrival: Italians, Race, Color, and Power in Chicago, 1890-1945.* Oxford: Oxford University Press.

Guimarães, Norma. 1993. *Febre Brasil em Nova Iorque.* Belo Horizonte: Record.

Gupta, Akhil, and James Ferguson. 1997. "Culture, Power, Place: Ethnography at the End of an Era." In *Culture, Power, Place: Explorations in Critical Anthropology*, ed. Akhil Gupta and James Fergusen, 6-23. Durham, NC: Duke University Press.

Gwaltney, John L. 1980. "The Propriety of Fieldwork: A Native Assessment." *The Black Scholar: Journal of Black Studies and Research* 11 (7): 32–39.

Hackshaw, Alana C. 2007. "Black Ethnicity and Racial Community: African-Americans and West Indian Immigrants in the United States." In *Constructing Borders/Crossing Boundaries: Race, Ethnicity, and Immigration*, ed. Caroline B. Brettell, 149-184. Lanham, MD: Lexington Books.

Hall, Elkton W. 1982. *Sperm Whaling from New Bedford.* New Bedford, MA: Old Dartmouth Historical Society & The Whaling Museum.

Hall, Stuart. 1992. "The Question of Cultural Identity." In *Modernity and Its Futures*, ed. Stuart Hall, David Held and Tony McGrew, 273-316. Cambridge: Polity Press-Open University.

______1997. "Subjects in History: Making Diasporic Identities." In *The House That Race Built: Black Americans, U.S. Terrain*, ed. Wahneema Lubiano. New York: Pantheon.

Halter, Marilyn. 1993. *Between Race and Ethnicity: Cape Verdean-American Immigrants, 1865-1960.* Urbana: University of Illinois Press.

______2000. *Shopping for Identity: The Marketing of Ethnicity.* New York: Schocken Books.

Handlin, Oscar. 1977. *Boston's Immigrants: A Study in Acculturation*, New York: Atheneum.

Haney-Lopez, Ian F. 1996. *White by Law: The Legal Construction of Race.* New York: New York University Press.

Hansen, Marcus L. 1996 [1938]. "The Problem of the Third Generation Immigrant." In *Theories of Ethnicity: A Classical Reader*, ed. Werner Sollors, 202-215. London: MacMillan Press.

Hardy-Fanta, Carol. 1993. *Latina Politics, Latino Politics.* Philadelphia: Temple University Press.

Harney, Robert P. 1990. "'Portygees and Other Caucasians': Portuguese Migrants and the Racialism of the English-speaking World." In *Portuguese Migration in Global Perspective*, ed. David Higgs, 113-135. Toronto: The Multicultural History Society of Ontario.

Harnish, David. D. 2005. *Bridges to the Ancestors: Music, Myth, and Cultural Politics at an Indonesian Festival.* Hawaii: University of Hawaii Press.

Harris, M. 1969. *Patterns of Race in the Americas.* New York: Columbia University Press.

Hartman, Saidiya. 1999. *Scenes of Subjection: Terror, Slavery, and Self-Making in Nineteenth-Century America.* New York: Oxford University Press.

Heisler, Barbara Schmitter. 2008. "The Sociology of Immigration: From Assimilation to Segmented Assimilation, from the American Experience to the Global Arena." In *Migration Theory: Talking Across Disciplines,* ed. Caroline B. Brettell and James F. Hollifield, 83-111. New York: Routledge.

Hennessy, Rosemary. 2000. *Profit and Pleasure: Sexual Identities in Late Capitalism.* New York and London: Routledge.

Henry, Jules. 1975. "Golden Rule Days: American Schoolrooms." In *The Nacirema: Readings on American Culture,* ed. James P. Spradley, 30-42. Boston: Little, Brown, and Co.

Henry Kaiser Family Foundation. 2004. Pew Hispanic Center. *Survey Brief: Latinos in California, New York, Florida and New Jersey,* March.

Hicks, George L. 1977a. "Introduction: Problems in the Study of Ethnicity." In *Ethnic Encounters: Identities and Contexts,* ed. George Hicks and Philip Leis, 1-20. North Scituate, MA: Duxbury Press.

______1977b. "Separate but Similar: Adaptation in Two American Indian groups." In *Ethnic Encounters: Identities and Contexts,* ed. George L. Hicks, and Philip E. Leis, 63-83. North Scituate, MA: Duxbury Press.

______, and David I. Kertzer, 1972. "Making a Middle Way: Problems of Mohegan Identity." *Southwestern Journal of* Anthropology 1 (28): 1-24.

Hobsbawm, Eric, and Terence Ranger, eds. 1983. *The Invention of Tradition.* Cambridge: Cambridge University Press.

Holton, Kimberley DaCosta. 2003. "Fazer Das Tripas Coração: O Parentesco Cultural nos Ranchos Folcóricos." In *Vozes do Povo: A Folclorização em Portugal*, ed. Salwa El-Shawan Castelo Branco and Jorge Freitas Branco, 143-52. Oeiras: Celta Editora.

______2004. "Dancing Along the In-Between: Folklore Performance and Transmigration in Portuguese Newark." *Portuguese Studies Review* 11 (2): 153-82.

______2005a. *Performing Folklore: Ranchos Folclóricos from Lisbon to Newark.* Bloomington, IN: Indiana University Press.

______2005b. "Pride, Predjudice and Politics: Performing Portuguese Folklore amid Newark's Urban Renaissance." *Etnográfica* 9 (1): 181-101.

Hondagneu-Sotelo, Pierrette. 2003. *Gender and U.S. Immigration: Contemporary Trends.* Berkeley, CA: University of California Press.

Huff, Toby E. 1989. "Education and Ethnicity in Southeastern Massachusetts." In *New England Board of Higher Education: Issues in Planning and Policymaking*, 1-8. Boston: New England Board of Higher Education.

Hurston, Zora Neal. 1970. *Mules and Men.* New York: Harper and Row.

Huse, Donna. 1998. "Growing up in the Mills." In *Spinner.* Vol. II 38-39. New Bedford, MA: Spinner Publications.

Ingraham, Chyrs. 1996. "The Heterosexual Imaginary: Feminist Sociology and Theories of Gender." In *Queer Theory/Sociology*, ed. Steven Seidman, 168-93. New York: Blackwell.

Isajiw, Wsevolod W. 1997. "On the Concept and Theory of Social Incorporation." In *Multiculturalism in North America and Europe*, ed. Wselvolod W. Isajiw, 79-102. Toronto: Canadian Scholars Press.

Ito-Alder, James P. 1980 [1972, 1978]. *The Portuguese in Cambridge and Somerville (Combined Edition).* Cambridge, MA: Cambridge Department of Community Development.

Jackson, Peeter. 1998. "Constructions of 'Whiteness' in the Geographical Imagination." *Area* 30 (2): 99-106.

Jennings, James, and Mel King, eds. 1986. *From Access to Power: Black Politics in Boston.* Cambridge, MA: Schenkman Books, Inc.

João, Maria Isabel. 2002. "Public Memory and Power in Portugal (1880-1960): Reflections on Centenary Commemorations." *Portuguese Studies* 18: 96-121.

Jones, Delmos. 1970. "Towards a Native Anthropology." *Human Organization* 29 (4): 251–59.

Jones-Correa, Michael. 2001. "Institutional and Contextual Factors in Immigrant Naturalization and Voting." *Citizenship Studies* 5 (1): 41-56.

Juravich, Tom, William F. Hartford, and James R. Green. 1996. *Commonwealth of Toil: Chapters in the History of Massachusetts Workers and Their Unions.* Amherst, MA: University of Massachusetts.

Kantowicz, Edward R. 1975. *Polish-American Politics in Chicago, 1888-1940.* Chicago: University of Chicago Press.

Karp, Ivan. 1991. "Festivals." In *Exhibiting Cultures: The Poetics and Politics of Museum Display,* ed. Ivan Karp and Steven Lavine. 279-287. Washington: Smithsonian Institution Press.

Karsh, Bernard, Joel Seidman, and Daisy Lilienthal. 1959. "The Union Organizer and His Tactics." In *Unions and Union Leadership: Their Human Meaning.* ed. Jack Barbash, 98. New York: Harper & Brothers.

Kasinitz, Philip, and J. Freidenberg-Hjerbstein. 1987. "The Puerto Rican Parade and West Indian Carnival: Public Celebrations in New York City." In *Caribbean Life in New York City: Sociocultural Dimensions*, ed. Constance Sutton and Elsa Chaney, 327-349. New York: Center for Migration Studies.

Kasinitz, Philip. 1992. *Caribbean New York: Black Immigrants and the Politics of Race.* Ithaca, NY: Cornell University Press.

______, John Mollenkopf, and Mary C. Waters. 2002. "Becoming American/Becoming New Yorkers: Immigrant Incorporation in a Majority Minority City." *International Migration Review* 36: 1020-36.

Kay, Hugh. 1970. *Salazar and Modern Portugal.* New York: Hawthorn Books.

Kearney, Michael. 1991. "Borders and Boundaries of the State and Self at the End of Empire." *Journal of Historical Sociology* 4 (1): 52-74.

Keefe, Susan E. 1980a. "Acculturation of the Extended Family among Urban Mexican Americans." In *Acculturation Theory, Models, and Some New Findings*, ed. Amado M. Padilla, 85-110. Boulder, CO: Westview Press.

______1980b. "Personal Communities in the City: Support Networks among Mexican-Americans and Anglo-Americans." *Urban Anthropology* 9 (1): 51-76.

Kelly, Richard. 1956. *Nine Lives for Labor.* New York: Praeger.

Key, V. O. 1961. *Public Opinion and American Democracy.* New York: Alfred A. Knopf.

Kibria, Nazli. 1993. *Family Tightrope: The Changing Lives of Vietnamese Americans.* Princeton: Princeton University Press.

Kirschenblatt-Gimblett, Barbara. 1991. "Objects of Ethnography." In *Exhibiting Cultures: The Poetics and Politics of Museum Display*, ed. Ivan Karp and Steven D. Lavine, 386-443. Washington DC: Smithsonian Institute Press.

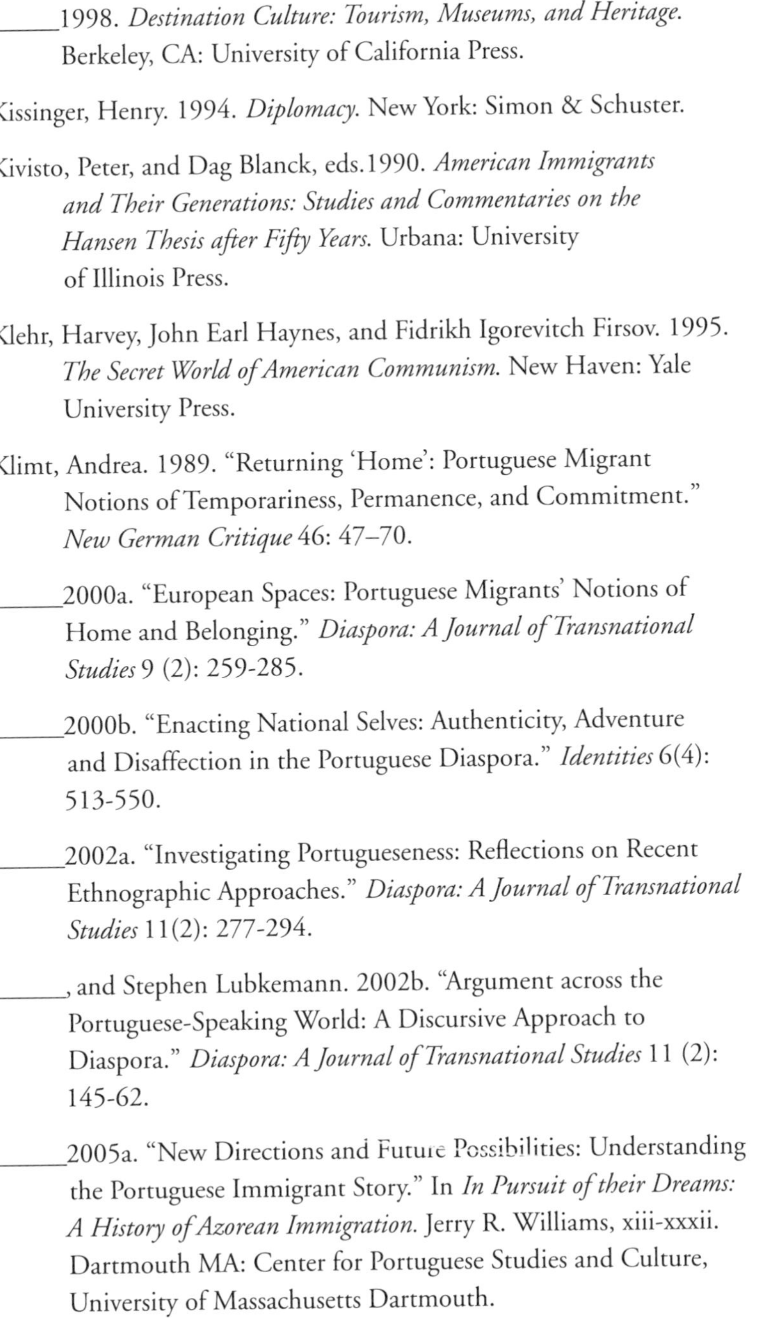

______1998. *Destination Culture: Tourism, Museums, and Heritage.* Berkeley, CA: University of California Press.

Kissinger, Henry. 1994. *Diplomacy.* New York: Simon & Schuster.

Kivisto, Peter, and Dag Blanck, eds.1990. *American Immigrants and Their Generations: Studies and Commentaries on the Hansen Thesis after Fifty Years.* Urbana: University of Illinois Press.

Klehr, Harvey, John Earl Haynes, and Fidrikh Igorevitch Firsov. 1995. *The Secret World of American Communism.* New Haven: Yale University Press.

Klimt, Andrea. 1989. "Returning 'Home': Portuguese Migrant Notions of Temporariness, Permanence, and Commitment." *New German Critique* 46: 47–70.

______2000a. "European Spaces: Portuguese Migrants' Notions of Home and Belonging." *Diaspora: A Journal of Transnational Studies* 9 (2): 259-285.

______2000b. "Enacting National Selves: Authenticity, Adventure and Disaffection in the Portuguese Diaspora." *Identities* 6(4): 513-550.

______2002a. "Investigating Portugueseness: Reflections on Recent Ethnographic Approaches." *Diaspora: A Journal of Transnational Studies* 11(2): 277-294.

______, and Stephen Lubkemann. 2002b. "Argument across the Portuguese-Speaking World: A Discursive Approach to Diaspora." *Diaspora: A Journal of Transnational Studies* 11 (2): 145-62.

______2005a. "New Directions and Future Possibilities: Understanding the Portuguese Immigrant Story." In *In Pursuit of their Dreams: A History of Azorean Immigration.* Jerry R. Williams, xiii-xxxii. Dartmouth MA: Center for Portuguese Studies and Culture, University of Massachusetts Dartmouth.

______2005b. "Performing Portugueseness in Germany." *Etnográfica* IX (1): 103-122.

Kobayashi, Audrey, and Linda Peake. 2000. "Racism out of Place: Thoughts on Whiteness and an Antiracist Geography in the New Millennium." *Annals of the Association of American Geographers* 90 (2): 392-403.

Kolchin, Peter. 2002. "Whiteness Studies: A New History of Race in America." *Journal of American History* 87: 154-173.

Kostecki, Anita. 1987. "Pointing the Finger: Portuguese Identity and the Big Dan's Rape Case." *Cleavage: The Brown Undergraduate Journal of Women's Studies* 1: Spring.

Kurtz, Howard. c1995. "The Vigilant Press: A Love-Hate Relationship." In *America's Media: Are They Out of Control?/ Providence Journal/Brown University Public Affairs Conference, February 27-March 9, 1995, Salomon Center for Teaching, Brown University.* Providence, RI: Office of University Relations, Brown University.

Kvistad, Gregg.1998. "Membership without Politics? The Social and Political Rights of Foreigners in Germany." In *Immigration, Citizenship, and the Welfare State in Germany and the United States: Welfare Policies and Immigrants' Citizenship.* ed. Jürgen Fijalkowski, 141-157. Stamford, CT: Jai Press.

Kwong, Peter. 1997. "Manufacturing Ethnicity." *Critique of Anthropology* 17: 365-387.

Laban, Michel, ed. 1991. "Interview with Raul David." In *Angola: Encontro com Escritores,* vol. 1, 45-76. Porto: Fundação Eng. António de Almeida.

Lacan, Jacques. 1997. *The Language of Self: The Function of Language in Psychoanalysis.* Baltimore, MD: Johns Hopkins University Press.

Ladd, Everett Carl. 1978. *Where Have All the Voters Gone?: The Fracturing of America's Political Parties.* New York: W.W. Norton and Co., Inc.

Laguerre, Michel S. 1998. *Diasporic Citizenship: Haitian Americans in Transnational America.* New York: St. Martin's.

Lameiro, Paulo. 1997. "Práticas Musicais nas Festas Religiosas do Concelho de Leiria." In *Actas dos 3ºs Cursos Internacionais de Verão de Cascais (8 a 13 de Julho 1996)*, 213-254. Cascais, Portugal: Câmara Municipal de Cascais.

______1999. "'*Coretos Sagrados' Algum Repertório Litúrgico das Filarmónicas do Concelho de Leiria.* Lisboa: Universidade Nova de Lisboa.

Lamm, M. 1933-1934. "Baseball and Racial Harmony in Hawaii." *Sociology and Social Research* 18: 58-66.

Lamphere, Louise. 1987. *From Working Daughters to Working Mothers: Immigrant Women in a New England Industrial Community.* Ithaca: Cornell University Press.

Landes, Ruth. 1976. "Teachers and Their Family Cultures." In *Schooling in the Cultural Context*, ed. Joan I. Roberts and Sherrie K. Akinsanya, 401-417. New York: David McKay Company.

Lang, Henry Roseman. 1989. *O Elemento Português na Nova Inglaterra.* Horta, Açores: Câmara Municipal da Horta.

Lauck, W. Jett. 1912. "The Cotton Mill Operatives of New England." *Atlantic Monthly*, 109, May.

Laumann, Edward, et al. 2004. *The Sexual Organization of the City.* Chicago: University of Chicago Press.

Lavigne, Gilles, and Carlos Teixeira. 2000. "Building a Neighborhood in Montréal." In *The Portuguese in Canada*, ed. Carlos Teixeira and Victor da Rosa, 175-190. Toronto: University of Toronto Press.

Leal, João. 1984. *Etnografia dos Impérios de Santa Bárbara: Santa Maria, Açores.* Lisboa: Instituto Português do Património Cultural - Departamento de Etnologia.

______1994. *As Festas do Espírito Santo nos Açores: Um Estudo de Antropologia Social.* Lisboa: Publicações Dom Quixote.

______1996. "Festa e Emigração numa Freguesia Açoriana." In *O Voo do Arado,* ed. Fernando Oliveira Baptista, Joaquim Pais de Brito, and Benjamin Pereira, 582-589. Lisboa: Museu Nacional de Etnologia.

______2000a. "The Making of *Saudade*" in *Roots and Rituals: The Construction of Ethnic Identities,* ed. Ton Dekker, John Helsloot, and Carla Wijers, 267-287. Amsterdam: Het Spinhuis.

______2000b. "Traditions Locales et Émigration: les Fêtes du Saint-Esprit aux Açores." *Ethnologie Française* XXX (1) : 51-60.

______2002. "Identities and Imagined Homelands: Reinventing the Azores in Southern Brazil." *Diaspora: A Journal of Transnational Studies* 11 (2): 233-254.

______2005. "We Are Azorean: Discourses and Practices of Folk Culture in Santa Catarina (Southern Brazil)." *Etnográfica* IX (1): 171-194.

Leal, Maria Lúcia, org. 2002. "Pesquisa sobre Tráfico de Mulheres, Crianças e Adolescentes para Fins de Exploração Sexual Comercial no Brasil." In *PESTRAF: Relatório Final—Brasil.* Brasília: CECRIA.

Lee, Alfred McClung. 1973. *The Daily Newspaper in America.* New York: Octagon Books.

Lefèbvre, Henri. 1991 [1974]. *The Production of Space.* Oxford: Basil Blackwell.

Leonardo, Micaela di. 1984. *The Varieties of Ethnic Experience: Kinship, Class and Gender among California Italian-Americans.* Ithaca: Cornell University Press.

______1998. *Exotics at Home: Anthropologists, Others, American Modernity.* Chicago: University of Chicago Press.

Levitt, Peggy. 1998. "Social Remittances: Migration Driven Local-Level Forms of Cultural Diffusion." *International Migration Review* 32: 926-948.

______2001. *The Transnational Villagers.* Berkeley: University of California Press.

______Josh DeWind, and Steven Vertovec, eds. 2003. "Transnational Migration: International Perspectives." *International Migration Review* 37. Special Issue.

Lewis, Oscar. 1966. *The Culture of Poverty.* New York: Scientific American.

Lieberson, Stanley. 1980. *A Piece of the Pie: Blacks and White Immigrants Since 1880.* Berkeley: University of California Press.

Lieberson, Stanley, and Mary C. Waters. 1988. *From Many Strands: Ethnic and Racial Groups in Contemporary America.* New York: Russell Sage Foundation.

Lien, Pei-te. 2002. "Ethnicity and Political Adaptation: Comparing Filipinos, Koreans, and the Vietnamese in Southern California." In *Asian Pacific American Politics Reader*, ed. Don Nakanishi and James Lai, 193-210. Lanham, MD: Rowman and Littlefield Publishers.

Limón, José. 1982. "History, Chicano Joking, and the Varieties of Higher Education: Tradition and Performances as Critical Symbolic Action." *Journal of the Folklore Institute* 19: 141-66.

Lionnet, Françoise. 2004. "The Mirror and the Tomb: Africa, Museums and Memory." In *Museum Studies: An Anthology of Contexts*, ed. Bettina Messias Carbonell, 92-103. Malden, MA: Blackwell Publishers.

Litt, Edgar. 1970. *Ethnic Politics in America: Beyond Pluralism.* Glenview, Illinois: Scott Foresman.

Livingstone, David. 1993. *The Geographical Tradition: Episodes in the History of a Contested Enterprise.* Malden, MA: Blackwell.

Lobban, Richard. 1995. *Cape Verde: Crioulo Colony to Independent Nation.* Boulder, CO: Westview.

Logan, John R., and Harvey L. Molotch. 1987. *Urban Fortunes: The Political Economy of Place.* Berkeley: University of California Press.

______, Richard Alba, and T.L. McNulty. 1994. "Ethnic Economies in Metropolitan Regions: Miami and Beyond." *Social Forces* 72: 691-724.

London, Jack. 1913. *Valley of the Moon.* New York: Macmillan.

Lourenço, Eduardo. 1978. *O Labirinto da Saudade.* Lisboa: Publicações Dom Quixote.

Lubkemann, Stephen C. 2002. "The Moral Economy of Portuguese Postcolonial Return." *Diaspora: A Journal of Transnational Studies* 11 (2): 189-213.

______2003. "Race, Class and Kin in the Negotiation of 'Internal Strangerhood' among Portuguese Retornados 1975-2000." In *Europe's Invisible Migrants.* ed. Andrea Smith, 75-93. Amsterdam: Amsterdam University Press.

______2005. "Unsettling the Metropole: Race and Settler Reincorporation in Postcolonial Portugal." In *Settler Colonialism in the Twentieth Century: Projects, Practices and Legacies,* ed. Caroline Elkins and Susan Pedersen, 257-270. New York: Taylor and Francis.

MacCannell, Dean. 1999. *The Tourist.* Berkeley, CA: University of California Press.

Machado, Deirdre Meintel. 1981. "Cape Verdean-Americans." In *Hidden Minorities: The Persistence of Ethnicity in American Life,* ed. Joan H. Rollins, 233-256. Washington, DC: University Press of America.

Mahler, Sarah J., and Patricia R. Pessar. 2001. "Gendered Geographies of Power: Analyzing Gender across Transnational Spaces." *Identities: Global Studies in Culture and Power* 7: 441-459.

Margarido, Alfredo. 2000. *A Lusofonia e os Lusófonos: Novos Mitos Portugueses.* Lisboa: Edições Universitárias Lusófonas.

Margolis, Maxine. 1994. *Little Brazil: An Ethnography of Brazilian Immigrants in New York City*. Princeton: Princeton University Press.

Marinho, Rita. 2002. "Portuguese-Americans in the Political Process: A Quarter-Century Retrospect." In *Portuguese-Americans and Contemporary Civic Culture in Massachusetts,* ed. Clyde Barrow, 159-170. North Dartmouth, MA: Center for Portuguese Studies and Culture, University of Massachusetts Dartmouth.

______1992. *Os Luso-Americanos No Processo Político Americano: Estudo duma Situação Concreta.* Angra do Heroísmo: Gabinete de Emigração e Apoio às Comunidades Açorianas.

Marques, A. H. Oliveira. 1982. *Correspondência Política de Afonso Costa, 1896-1910.* Lisboa: Editorial Estampa.

______ coord., Paulo Guinote, Pedro Teixeira Mesquita, and João José Alves. 2000. *Parlamentares e Ministros da 1ª República, 1910-1926.* Lisboa: Edições Afrontamento.

Marques, Domingos, and Manuela Marujo. 1993. *With Hardened Hands: A Pictorial History of Portuguese Immigrants to Canada in the 1950s.* Etobicoke, ON: New Leaf.

Marrow, Helen. 2003. "To Be or Not to Be (Hispanic or Latino): Brazilian Racial and Ethnic Identity in the United States." *Ethnicity* 3 (4): 427-464.

Martes, Ana Cristina Braga. 2000. *Brasileiros nos Estados Unidos: Um Estudo Sobre Imigrantes em Massachusetts.* São Paulo: Paz e Terra.

Martin, Philip L. 1994. "Germany: Reluctant Land of Immigration." In *Controlling Immigration: A Global Perspective*, ed. Wayne Cornelius, Philip Martin, and James Hollifield, 189-225. Palo Alto, CA: Stanford Univeristy Press.

Marwell, Nicole P. 2004. "Privatizing the Welfare State: Nonprofit Community Organizations." *American Sociological Journal* 69 (2): 265-291.

Massey, Douglas S., Rafael Alarcón, Jorge Durand, and Humberto González. 1987. *Return to Aztlan: The Social Process of International Migration from Western Mexico.* Berkeley: University of California Press.

Mayer, Adrian C. 1966. "The Significance of Quasi-Groups in the Study of Complex Societies." In *The Social Anthropology of Complex Societies,* ed. Michael Banton, 97-122. London: Tavistock Publications.

Mayer, Philip. 1962. "Migrancy and the Study of Africans in Towns." *American Anthropologist* 64: 576-592.

McCarthy Brown, Karen. 1998. "Mimesis in the Face of Fear: Femme Queens, Butch Queens, and Gender Play in the Houses of Greater Newark." In *Passing: Identity and Interpretation of Sexuality, Race, and Religion*, ed. Maria Carla Sanchez, and Linda Schlossberg, 208-227. New York: New York University Press.

McCracken, Grant. 1988. *Culture and Consumption: New Approaches to the Symbolic Character of Cultural Goods.* Bloomington, IN: University of Indiana Press.

McDermott, R. P. 1985. "Achieving School Failure: An Anthropological Approach to Illiteracy and Social Stratification." In *Theoretical Models and Processes of Reading,* ed. Harry Singer and Robert Ruddell and Martha Rapp Ruddell, 558-594. Newark, DE: International Reading Association.

Mead, Margaret. 1973. "Our Educational Emphases in Primitive Perspective." In *The Myth of Cultural Deprivation,* ed. Nell Keddie, 95-101. Middlesex, UK: Penguin Edition.

Medeiros, António. 1995. "Minho: Retrato Oitocentista de uma Paisagem de Eleição." *Revista Lusitânia* (Nova Série) 13-14: 97-123.

Mehan, Hugh. 1981. "Ethnography and Bilingual Education." In *Culture and the Bilingual Classroom,* ed. Enrique Trueba, Grace Guthrie, and Kathryn Au, 36-55. Rowley, MA: Newbury House Publishers.

Meihy, José Carlos Sebe Bom. 2004. *Brasil Fora de Si: Experências de Brasileiros em Nova York.* São Paulo: Parábola.

Meintel, Deirdre. 1984. *Race, Culture, and Portuguese Colonialism in Cabo Verde.* New York: Maxwell School of Citizenship and Public Affairs, Syracuse University.

Mendonça, Luís, and José Ávila. 2002. *Emigração Açoriana, sécs. XVIII a XX.* Lisboa: Edições Autores.

Messiant, Christine. 2006. *L'Angola Colonial, Histoire et Société: Les Premisses do Mouvement Nationaliste.* Bâle: Schlettwein Publishing.

Milkman, Ruth, ed. 1985. *Women, Work and Protest: A Century of U.S. Women's Labor History.* Boston and London: Routledge & Kegan Paul.

Miller, Warren E., and J. Merrill Shanks. 1996. *The New American Voter.* Cambridge, MA: Harvard University Press.

Mitchell, J. Clyde, ed. 1959. *The Kalela Dance. Aspects of Social Relationships Among Urban Africans in Northern Rhodesia.* Manchester, UK: Humanities Press.

______1969. *Social Networks in Urban Situations.* Manchester: Manchester University Press.

Moermon, Michael. 1965. "Who are the Lue? Ethnic Identifiacation in a Complex Civilization." *American Anthropologist* 67: 1215-30.

Mohanram, Radhika. 1991. "Woman-body-nation-space." In *Black Body: Women, Colonialism and Space.* 56-86. Minneapolis: University of Minnesota Press.

Moniz, Fernando, and Manuel Pisco. "Avaliação dos Programas de Apoio Financeiro à População Retornada." In *Os Retornados: Um Estudo Sociográfico.* Lisboa: Instituto de Estudos para o Desenvolvimento.

Montepio Luso-Americano (organization). 1932. *Os Portugueses de New Bedford.* New Bedford, MA.

Montgomery, David. 1977. "Immigrant Workers and Managerial Reform." In *Immigrants in Industrial America*, ed. Richard L. Ehrlich, 101-102. Charlottesville: University of Virginia Press.

Morwaska, Ewa. 1994. "In Defense of the Assimilation Model." *Journal of American Ethnic History* 13: 76-87.

______1996. *Insecure Prosperity: Small Town Jews in Industrial America, 1890-1940.* Princeton: Princeton University Press.

Morrison, Toni. 1992. *Playing in the Dark.* New York: Vintage Books.

Morrissey, Katherine. 1997. *Mental Territories: Mapping the Inland Empire.* Ithaca, NY: Cornel University Press.

Murray, David. 1999. "Laws of Desire? Race, Sexuality, and Power in Male Martinican Sexual Narratives." *American Ethnologist* 26 (1): 160-172.

Nagata, Judith A. 1974. "What is a Malay? Situational Selection of Ethnic Identity in a Plural Society." *American Ethnologist* 1:331-350.

Nagel, Joane. 2000. "Ethnicity and Sexuality." *Annual Review of Sociology* 26:107-133.

Nahirny, Vladimir C., and Joshua A. Fishman. 1996. "American Immigrant Groups: Ethnic Identification and the Problem of Generations." In *Theories of Ethnicity: A Classical Reader*, ed. Werner Sollors, 266-281. New York: New York University Press.

Neto, Félix. 1986. *A Migração Portuguesa Vivida e Representada: Contribuição para o Estudo dos Projectos Migratórios.* Porto: Secretaria do Estado das Comunidades Portuguesas.

Nie, Norman H., Sidney Verba, and John Petrocik. 1976. *The Changing American Voter.* Cambridge, MA: Harvard University Press.

Noivo, Edite. 1993. "Ethnic Families and the Social Injuries of Class, Migration, Gender, Generation and Minority." *Canadian Ethnic Studies* 25(3):166-176.

______1997. *Inside Ethnic Families: Three Generations of Portuguese–Canadians.* Montréal: McGill-Queen's University Press.

______2000. "Diasporic Identities at Century's End" in *The Portuguese in Canada*, ed. Carlos Teixeira and Victor da Rosa, 158-174. Toronto: University of Toronto Press.

______2002. "Towards a Cartography of Portugueseness: Challenging the Hegemonic Center." *Diaspora: A Journal of Transnational Studies* 11 (2): 158-174.

Nunes, Fernando. 2004. "Portuguese-Canadian Youth and their Academic Underachievement: A Literature Review." *Portuguese Studies Review* 11 (2): 41-88.

Nunes, Maria Luísa. 1982. *A Portuguese Colonial in America: Belmira Nunes Lopes, The Autobiography of a Cape Verdean-American.* Pittsburgh: Latin American Literary Review Press.

Oboler, Suzanne. 1995. *Ethnic Labels, Latino Lives: Identity and the Politics of (Re)Presentation in the United States.* Minneapolis: University of Minnesota Press.

O'Connor, Thomas H. 1995. *The Boston Irish: A Political History.* Boston: Northeastern University Press.

Ogbu, John U. 1978. "Minority Status and Schooling in Plural Societies." *Comparative Education Review* 27 (2):168-190.

______1983. *Minority Education and Caste.* New York: Academic Press.

______1991a. "Immigrant and Minorities in Comparative Perspective." In *Minority Status and Schooling: A Comparative Study of Immigrant and Involuntary Minorities*, ed. Margaret Gibson and John U. Ogbu. New York: Garland.

______1991b. "Low School Performance as an Adaptation: the Case of Blacks in Stockton, California." In *Minority Status and Schooling: A Comparative Study of Immigrant and Involuntary Minorities*, ed. Margaret Gibson and John Ogbu, 249-286. New York: Garland.

Okamura, Jonathan. 1981. "Situational Ethnicity." *Ethnic and Racial Studies* 4: 452-465.

Oliveira, César. 1989. "Oliveira Salazar e a Política Externa Portuguesa: 1932-1968." In *Salazar e o Salazarismo*. Lisboa: Publicações Dom Quixote.

Oliveira, Manuel Armando, and Carlos Teixeira. 2004. "Second Generation, Cultural Retention and Ethnic Identity: Young Portuguese and Portuguese-descendants in Canada." *Portuguese Studies Review* 11 (2): 1-23.

Olzak, Susan, and Joane Nagel, eds. 1986. *Competitive Ethnic Relations.* Orlando: Academic Press.

Omi, Michael, and Howard Winant. 1986. *Racial Formation in the United States: From the 1960s to the 1980s.* New York: Routledge.

O'Neill, Brian Juan. 2003. "Folclorização e Identitdade Crioula no Bairro Português." In *Vozes do Povo*, ed. Salwa Castelo-Branco, and Jorge Freitas Branco, 587-598. Oeiras, Portugal: Celta Editora.

O'Rourke, Kevin H., and Jeffrey G. Williamson. 1999. *Globalization and History: The Evolution of a Nineteenth-Century Atlantic Economy.* Boston: Massachusetts Institute of Technology.

Orsi, Robert Anthony. 1985. *The Madonna of 115th Street: Faith and Community in Italian Harlem, 1880-1950.* New Haven: Yale University Press.

Ovalle-Bahamón, Ricardo E. 2003. "The Wrinkles of Decolonization and Nationness: White Angolans as Retornados in Portugal." In *Europe's Invisible Migrants,* ed. Andrea Smith, 147-168. Amsterdam: Amsterdam University Press.

Pap, Leo. 1976. *The Portuguese in the United States: A Bibliography.* New York: Center for Migration Studies.

______1981. *The Portuguese-Americans.* Boston: Twayne Publishers.

Parenti, Michael. 1967. "Ethnic Politics and the Persistence of Ethnic Identification." *American Political Science Review* 61 (3): 717-726.

Parreñas, Rachel S. 2001. *Servants of Globalization: Women, Migration, and Domestic Work.* Palo Alto, CA: Stanford University Press.

Paulo, Heloísa. 2000. *Aqui Também é Portugal: A Colónia Portuguesa do Brasil e o Salazarismo.* Coimbra: Quarteto.

Pelletier, Alain. 1991. "Politics and Ethnicity: Representation of Ethnic and Visible-Minority Groups in the House of Commons." In *Ethno-Cultural Groups and Visible Minorities in Canadian Politics: The Question of Access,* Vol. 7, ed. Kathy Megyery, 101-59. Research Studies, Royal Commission on Electoral Reform and Party Financing. Toronto: Dundurn Press.

Peniston, William A., ed. 1999. *The New Museum: Selected Writings by John Cotton Dana.* Washington D.C.: American Association of Museums.

Pereira, Maria do Carmo. 1996. "Segundo Caderno: Um Século de Actividade Comercial Portuguesa em Newark, New Jersey." *Luso-Americano,* June 7: 25-63.

Pereira, Miriam Halpern. 1981. *A Política Portuguesa de Emigração, 1850-1930.* Lisboa: A Regra do Jogo.

Pereira da Costa, Dalila, and Josué Pinharanda Gomes. 1976. *Introdução à Saudade.* Porto: Lello & Irmão.

Perlmann, Joel, and Roger Waldinger. 1997. "Second Generation Decline? Immigrant Children Past and Present—A Reconsideration." *International Migration Review* 31 (4): 893-922.

Perry, Pamela. 2001. "White Means Never Having to Say You're Ethnic." *Journal of Contemporary Ethnography* 30 (1): 56-91.

______2002. *Shades of White: White Kids and Racial Identities in High School.* Durham: Duke University Press.

Pessar, Patricia. 1999. "The Role of Gender, Households, and Social Networks in the Migration Process: A Review and Appraisal." In *The Handbook of International Migration*, ed. Charles Hirschman, Philip Kasinitz, and Josh De Wind, 53-70. New York: Russell Sage Foundation.

______2003. "Anthropology and the Engendering of Migration Studies." In *American Arrivals: Anthropology Engages the New Immigration*, ed. Nancy Foner, 75-98. Santa Fe: School of American Research Press.

Pienkos, Angela T., ed. 1978. *Ethnic Politics in Urban America: The Polish Experience in Four Cities.* Chicago: Polish American Historical Association.

Pierre, Jemima. 2004. "Black Immigrants in the United States and the 'Cultural Narratives' of Ethnicity." *Identities* 11:141-70.

Pires, Rui Pena. 2003. *Migrações e Integração: Teoria e Aplicações à Sociedade Portuguesa.* Oeiras, Portugal: Celta Editora.

______ et al. 1987. *Os Retorndos: Um Estudo Sociográfico.* Lisboa: Instituto de Estudos para o Desenvolvimento.

Plotke, David. 1999. "Immigration and Political Incorporation in the Contemporary United States." In *The Handbook of International Migration*, ed. Charles Hirschman, Philip Kasinitz, and Josh De Wind, 294-318. New York: Russell Sage Foundation.

Pomper, Gerald M. 2001. *The Election of 2000: Reports and Interpretations.* New York: Chatham House Publishers.

Portes, Alejandro, and Robert Manning. 1986. "The Immigrant Enclave: Theory and Empirical Examples." In *Competitive Ethnic Relations*, ed. Joane Nagel and Susan Olzak, 47-68. Orlando, FL: Academic Press.

______1992. "Gaining the Upper Hand: Economic Mobility Among Immigrant and Domestic Minorities." *Ethnic and Racial Studies* 15: 491-522.

______1999. "O Enclave Emigrante." In *Migrações Internacionais: Origens, Tipos e Modos de Incorporação*, ed. Alejandro Portes, 41-63. Oeiras, Portugal: Editora Celta.

______, and Rubén G. Rumbaut. 1990. *Immigrant America: A Portrait.* Berkeley: University of California Press.

______, and Min Zhou. 1993. "The New Second Generation: Segmented Assimilation and its Variants among Post-1965 Immigrant Youth." *Annals of the American Academy of Political and Social Sciences* 535: 74-96.

______, and Rubén G. Rumbaut, eds. 2001. *Legacies: The Story of the Immigrant Second Generation.* Berkeley: University of California Press.

Price, Mary Sue Sweeney. 2004. "Embracing the Spiritual at the Newark Museum." In *Stewards of the Sacred,* 71-80. Washington, D.C.: American Association of Museums in cooperation with the Center for the Study of World Religions, Harvard University.

Pye, Lucian W., and Sidney Verba. 1965. *Political Culture and Political Development.* Princeton: Princeton University Press.

Rabinowitz, Dan. 1997. *Overlooking Nazareth: The Ethnography of Exclusion in Galilee.* Cambridge: Cambridge University Press.

Rae-Turner, Jean and Richard T. Koles. 2001. *Newark New Jersey.* Charleston, SC: Arcadia.

Ramakrishnan, S. Karthick, and Thomas J. Espenshade. 2001. "Immigrant Incorporation and Political Participation in the United States." *International Migration Review* 35 (3): 870-907.

Ramos, Lucille. 1981. "Black, White or Portuguese? A Cape Verdean Dilemma." In *Spinner: People and Culture in Southeastern Massachusetts,* Vol. 1 34-37. New Bedford, MA: Spinner Publications.

Ramos-Zayas, Ana. 2001. "Racializing the 'Invisible' Race: Latino Constructions of 'White Culture' and Whiteness in Chicago." *Urban Anthropology* 30 (4): 341-380.

______2003. *National Performances: The Politics of Class, Race, and Space in Puerto Rican Chicago*. Chicago: The University of Chicago Press.

______2004. "Delinquent Citizenship, National Performance: Racialization, Surveillance, and the Politics of 'Worthiness' in Puerto Rican Chicago." *Journal of Latino Studies* 2: 26-44.

______2007. "Becoming American, Performing Blackness?: Cultural Competency, Racialized Spaces, and the Politics of Citizenship among Brazilian and Puerto Rican Youth in Newark." *Identities* 14 (1): 85-110.

______Forthcoming. "Urban Erotics and Racial Affect in a Neoliberal 'Racial Democracy': Brazilian and Puerto Rican Youth in Newark, New Jersey." *Identities*, ed. Maria Elena Cepeda and Carlos Alamo.

Rapp, Rayna. 1978. "Family and Class in Contemporary America: Notes Toward an Understanding of Ideology." *Science and Society* 42: 278-300.

Reeve, Penn. 1998. "The Portuguese Worker," In *Portuguese Spinner: An American Story*, ed. Marsha McCabe, and Joseph D. Thomas, 230-235. New Bedford, MA: Spinner Publications.

______1998. "Three Lives for Labor: Eula Mendes, Manny Fernandes and Tina Ponte." In *Portuguese Spinner: An American Story*, ed. Marsha McCabe, and Joseph D. Thomas, 236-245. New Bedford, MA: Spinner Publications.

Reid, Ira De. A. 1939. *The Negro Immigrant: His Background, Characteristics and Social Adjustment, 1899–1937*. New York: Columbia University Press.

Reitz, Jeffrey G. 1998. *Warmth of the Welcome: The Social Causes of Economic Success for Immigrants in Different Nations and Cities*. Boulder, CO: Westview Press.

______, ed. 2003. *Host Societies and the Reception of Immigrants.* La Jolla, CA: Center for Comparative Immigration Studies, University of California, San Diego.

Ribeiro, José Luís. 1982. *Portuguese Immigrants and Education.* Bristol, RI: Portuguese-American Federation.

Roach, Joseph. 1996. *Cities of the Dead: Circum-Atlantic Performance.* New York: Columbia University Press.

______2003. "Culture and Performance in the Circum-Atlantic World." In *Readers in Cultural Criticism: Performance Studies,* ed. Erin Striff, 124-136. New York: Palgrave Macmillan.

Rocha-Trindade, Maria Beatriz. 1973. *Immigrés Portugais.* Lisboa: Instituto de Ciências Sociais e Política Ultramarina.

______, ed. 1981. *Estudos sobre a Emigração Portuguesa.* Lisboa: Sá da Costa.

______1995. "The Repatriation of Portuguese from Africa." In *The Cambridge Survey of World Migration,* ed. Robin Cohen, 337-341. Cambridge: Cambridge University Press.

______2000. "The Portuguese Diaspora." In *The Portuguese in Canada,* ed. Carlos Teixeira and Victor da Rosa, 15-36. Toronto: University of Toronto Press.

Rodrigues, Gabriel Moacyr. 1995. "Traditional Festivities in Cape Verde." In *Smithsonian Institution 1995 Festival of American Folk Life Program,* 29-32. Washington, DC: Smithsonian Institution.

Roediger, David R. 1991. *The Wages of Whiteness: Race and the Making of the American Working Class.* London: Verso.

Rogers, Francis M. 1974. *Americans of Portuguese Descent: A Lesson in Differentiation.* Beverly Hills: Sage Publications.

Rogers, Sheila Ackerlind, ed. 1979. *Atlantic Islanders of the Azores and Madeira.* North Quincy, MA: Christopher Publishing House.

_____ed. 1992. *Internationalism and the Three Portugals.* New York: Peter Lang.

Rong, Xue Lan, and Frank Brown. 2001. "The Effects of Immigrant Generation and Ethnicity on Educational Attainment among Young African and Caribbean Blacks in the United States." *Harvard Educational Review* 71 (3): 536-565.

Rosaldo, Renato and William V. Flores. 1997. "Identity, Conflict, and Evolving Latino Communities: Cultural Citizenship in San Jose, California." In *Latino Cultural Citizenship: Claiming Identity, Space, and Rights,* ed. William V. Flores, and Rina Benmayor, 57-96. Boston: Beacon Press.

Rosas, Fernando, and J. M. Brandão de Brito, eds. 1996. *Dicionário de História do Estado Novo,* 2 Vols. Lisboa: Círculo de Leitores.

Rosen, Ellen Israel. 1987. *Bitter choices.* Chicago: University of Chicago Press.

Rosenfeld, Gerald. 1971. *Shut Those Thick Lips: A Study of Slum School Failure.* New York: Holt, Rinehart and Winston.

Rosenstone, Steven J., and John Mark Hansen. 1993. *Mobilization, Participation, and Democracy in America.* New York: Macmillian.

Rouse, Roger. 2002 [1991]. "Mexican Migration and the Social Space of Postmodernism." In *The Anthropology of Globalization: A Reader,* ed. Jonathan Inda and Renato Rosaldo, 155-171. Malden, MA: Blackwell.

Ruggles, Steven, et al. 2004. *Integrated Public Use Microdata Series: Version 3.0.* Minneapolis, MN: Minnesota Population Center.

Rumbaut, Rubén G. 1996. "The Crucible Within: Ethnic Identity, Self-esteem, and Segmented Assimilation among Children of Immigrants." In *The New Second Generation,* ed. Alejandro Portes, 119-170. New York: Russell Sage Foundation.

______1999. "Assimilation and Its Discontents: Ironies and Paradoxes." In *The Handbook of International Migration: The American Experience*, ed. Charles Hirschman, Josh DeWind, and Philip Kasnitz, 173-195. New York: Russell Sage Foundation.

______, and Alejandro Portes. 2001a. "Introduction—Ethnogenesis: Coming of Age in Immigrant America." In *Ethnicities: Children of Immigrants in America,* 1-19. Berkeley: University of California Press.

______2001b. "Conclusion: The Forging of a New America: Lessons for Theory and Policy." In *Ethnicities: Children of Immigrants in America,* 301-317. Berkeley: University of California Press.

______, eds. 2001c. *Ethnicities: Children of Immigrants in America.* New York: Russell Sage Foundation.

Ryan, Mary. 1989. "The American Parade: Representations of the Nineteenth-Century Social Order." In *The New Cultural History*, ed. Aletta Biersack and Lynn Hunt, 131-153. Berkeley: University of California Press.

Sales, Teresa. 1998. *Brasileiros Longe de Casa.* São Paulo: Cortez Editora.

Sánchez, Gina E. 1997. "The Politics of Cape Verdean-American Identity." *Transforming Anthropology* 6 (1/2): 54–71.

______1998. "Between Kriolu and Merkanu: Cape Verdean Diaspora Identities." *Cimboa: Revista Caboverdiana de Letras, Artes e Estudos* 5: 22–25. Spring.

Sánchez Gibau, Gina. 2005a. "Contested Identities: Narratives of Race and Ethnicity in the Cape Verdean Diaspora." *Identities: Global Studies in Culture and Power* 12 (3): 405-438.

______2005b. "Diasporic Identity Formation Among Cape Verdeans in Boston." *The Western Journal of Black Studies* 29 (2): 532-539.

San Juan, Karin Aguilar, ed. 1994. *The State of Asian America: Activism and Resistance in the 1990s.* Boston: South End Press.

Santos, Isaías Gomes dos. 1999. *Os Portugueses na América do Norte.* Lisboa: Sociedade de Geografia.

Saraiva, António José, and Óscar Lopes. 1985. *Para a História da Cultura em Portugal.* Lisboa: Publicações Europa-América.

Sardo, Susana. 2003. "Cantar em Português: o Papel da Música na Reconstrução da Identidade Goesa." In *Vozes do Povo,* ed. Salwa Castelo-Branco and Jorge Freitas Branco, 579-586. Oeiras, Portugal: Celta Editora.

Sarkissian, Margaret. 2000. *D'Albuquerque's Children: Performing Tradition in Malaysia's Portuguese Settlement.* Chicago: University of Chicago Press.

______2002. "Playing Portuguese: Constructing Identity in Malaysia's Portuguese Community." *Diaspora: A Journal of Transnational Studies* 11 (2): 215-232.

Saville-Troike, Muriel. 1976. *A Guide to Cultures in the Classroom.* Washington, DC: National Clearinghouse for Bilingual Education.

Schatz, Ron. 1975. "The End of Corporate Liberalism: Class Struggle in the Electrical Manufacturing Industry, 1933-1950." *Radical America* 9: 4-5.

Schneider, Jo-Anne. 1990. "Defining Boundaries, Creating Contacts: Puerto Rican and Polish Presentation of Group Identity Through Ethnic Parades." *Journal of Ethnic Studies* 18: 33-57.

Schudsen, David. 2002. "How Culture Works: Perspectives from Media Studies on the Efficacy of Symbols." In *Cultural Sociology,* ed. Lyn Spilman, 141-148. Malden, MA: Wiley-Blackwell.

Scott, James C. 1985. *Weapons of the Weak: Everyday Forms of Peasant Resistance.* New Haven: Yale University Press.

Sennet, Richard. 1999. *The Corrosion of Character: The Personal Consequences of Work in the New Capitalism.* New York: Norton.

Serrão, Joel. 1982. *A Emigração Portuguesa: Sondagem Histórica.* 4th edition. Lisboa: Livros Horizonte.

Sewell, William, and Robert Hauser. 1975. *Education, Occupation and Earnings: Achievement in Early Career.* New York: Academic Press.

Sheriff, Robin E. 2000. "Exposing Silence as Cultural Censorship: A Brazilian Case." *American Anthropologist* 102 (1): 114-132.

______2001. *Dreaming Equality: Color, Race, and Racism in Urban Brazil.* New Brunswick, NJ: Rutgers University Press.

Shim, Jae K., and Joel G. Siegel. 1995. *Dictionary of Economics.* New York: John Wiley and Sons, Inc.

Sieber, Timothy. 2005. "Popular Music and Cultural Identity in the Cape Verdean Post-Colonial Diaspora." *Etnográfica* IX (1): 123-148.

Siemiatycki, Meyer, and Engin Isin. 1997. "Immigration, Diversity and Urban Citizenship in Toronto." *Canadian Journal of Regional Sciences* 20 (1/2): 73-102.

Silvia, Philip T., Jr. 1973. *The Spindle City: Labor, Politics, and Religion in Fall River, 1870 - 1905*, 2 vols. New York: P.T. Silvia.

______1976. "The Position of 'New' Immigrants in the Fall River Textile Industry." *International Migration Review* 10 (2): 2221-32.

Skidmore, Thomas. 1993a[1974]. *Black into White: Race and Nationality in Brazilian Thought.* Durham: Duke University Press.

______1993b. "Bi-racial USA vs. Multi-racial Brazil: Is the Contrast Still Valid?" *Journal of Latin American Studies* 25: 373-86.

Slobin, Mark. 1993. *Subcultural Sounds: Micromusics of the West.* Middletown, CT: Wesleyan University Press.

Smith, Andrea, ed. 2003. *Europe's Invisible Migrants.* Amsterdam: Amsterdam University Press.

Smith, Estellie M. 1974. "Portuguese Enclaves: The Invisible Minority." In *Social and Cultural Identity: Problems of Persistence and Change*, ed. Thomas K. Fitzgerald, 81-91. University of Georgia: Southern Anthropological Society Proceedings.

Smith, Robert C., Hector R. Cordero-Guzman, and Ramon Grosfoguel. 2001. "Introduction: Migration, Transnationalization, and Ethnic and Racial Dynamics in a Changing New York." In *Migration, Transnationalization and Race in a Changing New York*, ed. Hector R. Cordero-Guzman, Robert C. Smith, and Ramon Grosfoguel, 1-32. Philadelphia: Temple University Press.

Souza Alves, José Cláudio, and Lúcia Ribeiro. 2002. "Migração, Religião e Transnacionalismo: O Caso dos Brasileiros no Sul da Flórida. *Religião e Sociedade* 22 (2): 65-90.

Stafford, Susan Buchanan. 1987. "The Haitians: The Cultural Meaning of Race and Ethnicity." In *New Immigrants in New York*, ed. Nancy Foner, 104-107. New York: Columbia University Press.

Stansfield, Jr., Charles A. 1998. *A Geography of New Jersey: The City in the Garden.* New Brunswick, NJ: Rutgers University Press.

Stepan-Norris, Judith, and Maurice Zeitlin. 2002. *Left Out: Reds and America's Industrial Unions.* Cambridge: Cambridge University Press.

Stepick, Alex. 1988. *Pride against Prejudice: Haitians in the United States.* Boston: Allyn & Bacon.

Stokes, Martin. 1994. "Place, Exchange and Meaning: Black Sea Musicians in the West of Ireland." In *Ethnicity, Identity, and Music: The Musical Construction of Place,* ed. Martin Stokes, 97-115. Providence, RI: Berg.

Strom, Elizabeth. 2002. "Converting Pork into Porcelain: Cultural Institutions and Downtown Development." *Urban Affairs Review* 38 (1): 3-28.

______2003. "Cultural Policy as Development Policy: Evidence from the United States." *International Journal of Cultural Policy* 9(3).

Suárez-Orozco, Marcelo. 1991. "Immigrant Adaptation to Schooling: A Hispanic Case." In *Minority Status and Schooling: A Comparative Study of Immigrant and Involuntary Minorities*, ed. M. Gibson, and J. Ogbu, 37-61. New York: Garland.

Suro, Roberto. 1998. *Strangers Among Us: How Latino Immigration Is Transforming America.* New York: Alfred A. Knopf.

Taft, Donald R. 1923. *Two Portuguese Communities in New England, 1910-1920.* New York: Columbia University.

Tatum, Beverly Daniel. 1997. *Why Are All the Black Kids Sitting Together in the Cafeteria? And Other Conversations about Race.* New York: Basic Books.

Tax, Meredith. 1980. *The Rising of the Women: Feminist Solidarity and Class Conflict, 1880-1917.* New York: Monthly Review Press.

Teixeira, Carlos, and Gilles Lavigne. 1992. *The Portuguese in Canada: A Bibliography.* Toronto: Institute for Social Research, York University.

Teixeira, Carlos. 1999. *Portugueses em Toronto: Uma Comunidade em Mudança.* Açores: Direcção Regional das Comunidades, Governo Regional dos Açores.

______2000. "On the Move: Portuguese in Toronto." In *The Portuguese in Canada,* ed. Carlos Teixeira, and Victor Da Rosa, 207-222. Toronto: University of Toronto Press.

______, and Victor M. P. Da Rosa, eds. 2000. *The Portuguese in Canada: From the Sea to the City.* Toronto: University of Toronto Press.

Thomas, Joseph D., and Marsha L. McCabe, eds. 1998. *Portuguese Spinner: An American Story.* New Bedford, MA: Spinner Publications, Inc.

Thompson, E. P. 1967. "Time, Work-discipline and Industrial Capitalism." *Past & Present* 38: 56-97. December.

Tolman, Deborah. 1994. "Doing Desire: Adolescent Girls' Struggles for/with Sexuality." *Gender & Society* 8 (3): 324-342.

Tosta, António Luciano de Andrade. 2004. "Latino, Eu? The Paradoxical Interplay of Identity in Brazuca Literature." *Hispania* 87 (3): 576-585.

Tsuda, Takeyuki. 2006. *Local Citizenship in Recent Countries of Immigration: Japan in Comparative Perspective.* Lanham, MD: Lexington Books.

Twine, France Winddance. 1996. "Brown-Skinned White Girls: Class, Culture and the Construction of White Identity in Suburban Communities." *Gender, Place & Culture* 3 (2): 205-224.

Tyack, David E. 1974. *The One Best System: A History of American Urban Education.* Cambridge: Harvard University Press.

Urry, John. 2002. *The Tourist Gaze.* 2nd ed. London: Sage Publications.

Valdez, Zulema. 2007. "Beyond the Ethnic Enclave: The Effect of Ethnic Solidarity and Market Opportunity on White, Korean, Mexican, and Black Enterprise." In *Constructing Borders/ Crossing Boundaries: Race, Ethnicity, and Immigration*, ed. Caroline B. Brettell, 243-272. Lanham, MD: Lexington Books.

Vasconcelos, Carolina Michaëlis de. 1922. *A Saudade Portuguesa,* 2nd edition. Porto: Livraria Guimarães Editores.

Verba, Sidney, and Norman H. Nie. 1972. *Participation in America: Political Democracy and Social Equality.* New York: Harper and Row, Inc.

Vertovec, Steven. 2004. "Migrant Transnationalism and Modes of Transformation." *International Migration Review* 38: 970-1001.

______, Kay Lehman Schlozman, and Henry E. Brady. 1995. *Voice and Equality: Civic Voluntarism in American Politics.* Cambridge: Harvard University Press.

Vicente, António Luís. 1999. *Os Portugueses nos Estados Unidos: Política de Comunidades e Comunidade Política.* Lisbon: Fundação LusoAmericana Para o Desenvolvimento.

Vickerman, Milton. 1999. *Crosscurrents: West Indian Immigrants and Race.* New York: Oxford University Press.

______2001. "Jamaicans: Balancing Race and Ethnicity." In *New Immigrants in New York*, ed. Nancy Foner, 201-228. New York: Columbia University Press.

Viers, David J. 1989. *The Portuguese in the United States.* Durham: International Conference Group on Portugal.

Waldinger, Roger. 1996. *Still the Promised City? African-Americans and New Immigrants in Post-Industrial New York.* Cambridge: Harvard University Press.

Wallerstein, Emmanuel. 1974. *The Modern World-System: Capitalist Agriculture and the Origins of the European World-Economy in the Sixteenth Century.* New York: Academic Press.

Walsh, Catherine.1987. "Language, Meaning and Voice: Puerto Rican Students' Struggle for a Speaking Consciousness." *Language Arts* 64 (2): 196-206.

Walton, Hanes, Jr. 1997. *African American Power and Politics: The Political Context Variable.* New York: Columbia University Press.

Warrin, Donald, and Geoffrey L. Gomes. 2001. *Land as Far as the Eye Can See: Portuguese in the Old West.* Spokane, WA: The Arthur H. Clark Company.

Waters, Mary. 1990. *Ethnic Options: Choosing Identities in America.* Berkeley: University of California Press.

______1994. "Ethnic and Racial Identities of Second-Generation Black Immigrants in New York City." *International Migration Review* 28: 795-820.

______1999. *Black Identities: West Indian Immigrant Dreams and American Realities.* New York: Russell Sage Foundation.

Werbner, Pnina. 1996. "Stamping the Earth with the Name of Allah: Zikr and the Sacralizing of Space among British Muslims." In *Making Muslim Space in North America and Europe*, ed. Barbara Daly Metcalf, 167-185. Berkeley: University of California Press.

______, and Tariq Modood. 1997. *Debating Cultural Hybridity: Multi-cultural Identities and the Politics of Anti-Racism.* London: Zed Books.

______2004. "Theorizing Complex Diasporas: Purity and Hybridity in the South Asian Public Sphere in Britain." *Journal of Ethnic and Migration Studies* 30 (5): 895-911.

Werbner, Richard.1989. *Ritual Passage: Sacred Journey.* Washington DC: Smithsonian Institution.

Werneck, José Inácio. 2004. *Com Esperança no Coração: Os Imigrantes Brasileiros nos Estados Unidos.* São Paulo, Brasil: Augurium Editora.

Weston, Kath. 1995. "Do Clothes Make the Woman? Gender, Performance Theory, and Lesbian Eroticism." *Genders* 17: 1-21.

Wheeler, William Bruce. 1994. *Discovering the American Past,* Vol. 2. Boston: Houghton Mifflin Company.

White, E. Frances. 2001.*Dark Continent of Our Bodies: Black Feminism and the Politics of Respectability.* Philadelphia: Temple University Press.

White, Jenny. 1997. "Turks in the New Germany." *American Anthropologist* 99: 754-69.

Williams, Brett. 1988. *Up Scaling Downtown: Stalled Gentrification in Washington, D.C.* Ithaca, NY: Cornell University Press.

Williams, Jerry R. 1982. *And Yet They Came: Portuguese Immigration from the Azores to the United States.* New York: Center for Migration Studies.

______2005. *In Pursuit of Their Dreams: A History of Azorean Immigration to the United States.* Dartmouth, Massachusetts: Center for Portuguese Studies and Culture, University of Massachusetts Dartmouth.

Williams, Raymond. 1973. *The Country and the City.* Oxford: Oxford University Press.

Wimmer, Andreas, and Nina Glick Schiller. 2003. "Methodological Nationalism, the Social Sciences, and the Study of Migration: An Essay in Historical Epistemology." *International Migration Review* 37 (3): 576-610.

Woldemikael, Tekle Mariam. 1989a. *Becoming Black American: Haitians and American Institutions in Evanston, Illinois.* New York: AMS Press.

______1989b. "A Case Study of Race Consciousness among Haitian Immigrants." *Journal of Black Studies* 20 (2): 224–239.

Wolfinger, Raymond E., and Steven J. Rosenstone. 1980. *Who Votes?* New Haven: Yale University Press.

Wolforth, Sandra. 1978. *The Portuguese in America.* San Francisco: R. & E. Research Associates.

Wood, Joseph. 1997. "Vietnamese American Place Making in Northern Virginia." *Geographical Review* 87: 158-172.

Yans-McLaughlin, Virginia. 1977. *Family and Community: Italian Immigrants in Buffalo 1880-1930.* Ithaca, NY: Cornell University Press.

Young, Michael, and Peter Willmott. 1957. *Family and Kinship in East London.* London: Penguin Books.

Zia, Helen. 2000. *Asian-American Dreams: The Emergence of an American People.* New York: Farrar, Straus, and Giroux.

Zieger, Robert H., and Gilbert J. Gall. 2002. *American Workers, American Unions: The Twentieth Century*, 3rd edition. Baltimore: The Johns Hopkins University Press.

Zinn, Maxine Baca. 1979. "Chicano Family Research: Conceptual Distortions and Alternative Directions." *Journal of Ethnic Studies* 7 (3): 59-72.

Zhou, Min. 1992. *Chinatown: The Socioeconomic Potential of an Urban Enclave.* Philadelphia: Temple University Press.

______, and Carl L. Bankston III. 1994. "Social Capital and the Adaptation of the Second Generation: The Case of Vietnamese Youth in New Orleans." *International Migration Review* 23 (4): 821-845.

GOVERNMENT PUBLICATIONS

A Comparative View of Housing and Household Characteristics in Boston and its Neighborhoods, 1990–2000, Publication 555. 2002. Boston Redevelopment Authority.

Background Note: Cape Verde, 2005. U. S. Department of State. Bureau of African Affairs. http://www.state.gov/r/pa/ei/bgn/2835.htm.

Brownfields Show Case Community Fact Sheet. http://www.epa.gov/brownfields/slocat.htm#new.

Comissão Parlamentar Mista de Inquérito. 2006. *Brasil, 'celeiro de vítimas': O Tráfico Internacional de Pessoas para Fins de Prostituição: Relatório Final da Comissão Parlamentar Mista de Inquérito.* República Federativa do Brasil, Congresso Nacional, Comissão Parlamentar Mista de Inquérito da Emigração. Brasília.

Comissão de Planeamento da Região dos Açores. 1972. *Relatório de Propostas.* Ponta Delgada, São Miguel, Açores.

Comissão de Planeamento da Região dos Açores. n.d. *Emigração: Subsídios para uma Monografia sobre os Açores.* S. Miguel, Açores.

Emigração Portuguesa: Aspectos Relevantes Relativos às Políticas Adoptadas no Domínio da Emigração Portuguesa desde a Última Guerra Mundial: Contribuição para o Seu Estudo. 1986a. Secretaria de Estado das Comunidades Portuguesas, Centro de Estudos, Instituto de Apoio à Emigração e às Comunidades Portuguesas, Série Migrações, Política. Relações Internacionais. Porto, Portugal.

Emigração Portuguesa: Algumas Características Dominantes dos Movimentos no Período de 1950 a 1984. 1986b. Secretaria de Estado das Comunidades Portuguesas, Centro de Estudos, Instituto de Apoio à Emigração e às Comunidades Portuguesas, Série Migrações, Sociologia. Porto, Portugal. Porto, Portugal.

Emigração Portuguesa: Regulamentação Emigratória do Liberalismo ao Fim da Segunda Guerra Mundial. 1987. Secretaria de Estado das Comunidades Portuguesas. Instituto de Apoio à Emigração e às Comunidades Portuguesas, Série Migrações, Política. Relações Internacionais. Porto, Portugal.

Massachusetts Secretary of the Commonwealth. 2006. "Massachusetts Registered Voter Enrollment: 1948-2004." http://www.sec.state.ma.us/ele/eleenr/enridx.htm

Ornstein, Michael. 2000. *Ethno-Racial Inequality in the City of Toronto: An Analysis of the 1996 Census.* Report Prepared for the Access and Equity Unit, City of Toronto. Toronto: City of Toronto.

Portugal: Grandes Opções dos Planos 2005–2009. 2005. Conselho de Ministros, June 14. Lisboa, Portugal.

Providence School Department. 1984. *Procedures Manual for Limited English Proficient Students.* Providence, RI: Providence School Department.

Raymond, Janice, Donna Hughes, and Carol Gomez. 2001. "Sex Trafficking of Women in the United States: International and Domestic Trends." Coalition Against Trafficking in Women. Jersey City, East Brunswick, Red Bank and Rockaway Township, March.

Salazar Perante o Mundo. 1944. Editora Portugal Ultramar. Lisboa.

Settlement and Integration: A Sense of Belonging, "Feeling at Home," Report of the Standing Committee on Citizenship and Immigration Communication. 2003. House of Commons. Canada.

World Festival I: Portuguese Words and Ways/Rumos e Sons Portugueses. 1997. New Jersey Performing Arts Center/ Portuguese Ministry of Culture.

U.S. Census, 2000. Census of Population and Housing. 2000. www.census.gov

U.S. Census Bureau. http://factfinder.census.gov

UNPUBLISHED MATERIAL

Almeida, Onésimo T. 1984. "On the Ethics of Media-made Events." Letter to the Editor of *The New York Times* on March 1984.

Almeida, Ray. "The Church and the People of Cape Verde." http://www.umassd.edu/specialprograms/caboverde/cvchurch.html.

Anzules, Emanuel. 2006. "Latino Homosexuality in the 'Brick City'." Undergraduate Monograph for *Seminar in Latino and Hispanic Caribbean Studies: Latino Newark.* Department of Latino and Hispanic Caribbean Studies, Rutgers University.

Baganha, Maria Ioannis B. 2001. "Keynote Address," given at the "Race, Culture, Nation: Arguments Across the Portuguese Speaking World," conference at Brown University and University of Massachusetts—Dartmouth, March.

Baptista, Lori Barcliff. 2001-2007. Unpublished field notes and video recordings documenting ethnographic fieldwork on Portuguese culture, Newark and Portugal.

Basch, Linda, Nina Glick Schiller, and Cristina Szanton-Blanc. 1991. "Transnationalism and the construction of the Deterritorialized nation: An Outline for a Theory of Post-National Practices." Paper presented at the Meeting of the American Anthropological Association, Chicago, November.

Bates, Aryana. 2001."Religious Despite Religion: Lesbian Agency, Identity, and Spirituality in Truth Union Fellowship Churches in Newark. Ph.D dissertation, Drew University.

Becker, Adeline. 1980. "Family and School Interactive Processes as Success Determinants Among Portuguese First Grades: A Study in the Anthropology of Education." M.A. thesis, Brown University, Providence, RI.

Beserra, Bernardette. 2006. "In the Shadow of Carmen Miranda and the Carnival: Brazilian Immigrant Women in Los Angeles." Latin American Studies Associaiton XXVI International Congress. San Juan, Puerto Rico, March 15-18.

Bookman, Ann. 1977. "The Process of Political Socialization among Women and Immigrant Workers: A Case Study of Unionization in the Electronics Industry." Ph.D. dissertation, Harvard University.

Borges, David. 2005. "Ethnicity and Education in Southeastern Massachusetts: 1980-2000, A Continuing Challenge." Paper presented at "Portuguese-Americans and the 2000 U.S. Census," University of Massachusetts, Dartmouth, MA, September 2005.

Botelho, Paula. 2006. "The Construction of Brazilian and American Identities by American Art Reviewers and Newspapers." Latin American Studies Association Presentation. San Juan, Puerto Rico, March.

Braga, Manuel S. 2006. *Holy Ghost Brotherhood Mariense*, manuscript. "Breves Apontamentos Biográficos da Banda do Clube Juventude Lusitana, Cumberland, Rhode Island." 2006. Cumberland, Rhode Island.

Brucher, Katherine. 2005. "*A Banda da Terra: Bandas Filarmónicas* and the Performance of Place in Portugal." Ph.D. dissertation, University of Michigan, Ann Arbor.

Carvalho, João Soeiro de. 1990. "*Ranchos Folclóricos:* A Strategy for Identification Among Portuguese Migrants in New Jersey." M.A. thesis, Columbia University.

Dimas, Ana-Maria. 2005. *Higher Education in Portugal—Country Report.* University of Twente, the Netherlands. Center for Higher Education Policy Studies. (http://www.utwente.nl/cheps/documenten/portugal.pdf)

Dodds, Jerrilynn D. 2005-2007. Correspondence.

Droux, Arnaldo. 1986. "Os Repatriados da Descolonização Portuguesa: Alguns Aspectos Psicossociais da Sua Reintegração." M.A. thesis, Faculdade de Medicina da Universidade do Porto.

Feldman-Bianco, Bela. 1991. "A Reinvenção da Memória em Festas Migrantes." Paper presented at the International Seminar "Festas: Tradição e Inovação" Universidade Aberta, Lisboa, on Nov. 11-13.

______1994. "Immigration, Saudade, and the Dialectics of Deterritorialization and Reterritorialization." Wenner Gren Foundation for Anthropological Research, *Symposium #117: Transnationalism, Nation-State Building, and Culture*, Mijas, Spain, on June 14.

______1996. "The Politics of Dual Citizenship." Paper presented at the panel *Transmigrants, Transnational Processes and the Refurbishing of Nation-States* (org. Nina Glick Schiller), Annual Meetings of the American Ethnological Society, San Juan, Puerto Rico, April 18-21.

Fenton, Edwin. 1957. "Immigrants and Unions, A Case Study: Italians and American Labor, 1870-1920." Ph.D. dissertation, Harvard University.

Fernandes, Ronald Louis. 1972. "Ethnicity as a Symbol System: A Theoretical Discussion Exemplified by Case Studies of Spaniards in Montreal." M.A. thesis, McGill University, Montreal, Canada.

Gordon, Jerry. 2006. "The Taft-Hartley Act: Why the American Labor Movement Called it a 'Slave Labor Bill.'" Open World Conference of Workers In Defense of Trade Union Independence and Democratic Rights, January 11. <http://www.owcinfo.org/campaign/ILWU/Slave%20Labor%20Act.htm>.

Harder, Ronald J. 1989. "Between Two Worlds: A Case Study of Capitalism and Migration in the Central Azores." Ph.D. dissertation, University of Florida.

Heuer, Madalena Costa Leal. 1995. "Saudades Am Tor zur Welt: Lebessituation und Zukunftsperspektiven Junger Portugiesen in Hamburg." M.A. thesis, University of Hamburg, Germany.

Holton, Kimberly DaCosta. 1999. "Performing Social and Political Change: Revivalist Folklore Troupes in Twentieth-Century Portugal." Ph.D. dissertation, Northwestern University.

______2003. "Post-Colonial Conflict and Community in a US Urban Enclave: Brazilian and Portuguese Immigrants in Newark, NJ." Paper Presented at the Oral History Association Annual Meeting. Bethesda: Maryland, October 9.

"IBID Hires Off-Duty Police Officers to Address Student Rowdiness on Ferry Street." www.goironbound.com.

Keefe, Susan E., U. M. L. Reek, and G. G. Reek. 1983. "Ethnicity and Education in Southern Appalachia." Addendum to a proposal funded by National Science Foundation, January.

Klimt, Andrea. 1992. "Temporary and Permanent Lives: The Construction of Identity Among Portuguese Migrants in Germany." Ph.D. dissertation, Stanford University.

Lang, Scott W. 2007. "State of the City Address," City of New Bedford on March 1.

Laporte, Laurie. 2007. "The Continuities of Modernity: Cape Verdean Identity and Emigration." Ph.D. dissertation, Boston University.

Leith, Chad. 2007. "First-Generation Immigrant Adolescents from Cape Verde: Ethnic Identities, Socioeconomic Backgrounds, and Educational Outcomes." Unpublished paper.

Leonard, Margaret A. 1999. "We Need to Stand Together, the Impact of Welfare Reform on the Dudley Neighborhood and the Community's Response to Challenge." Dudley Street Neighborhood Initiative, Roxbury.

Margolis, Maxine. 2006. "Brazilian Immigration to the U.S. after 9/11." Unpublished Conference Paper. Second Conference on Brazilian Immigration to the West Coast of the U.S., Brazilian Consulate in San Francisco. City College of San Francisco, Nov 4-5.

Matos, Maria Cristina de Abreu da Costa. 1979. "Whom We Shall Welcome? *As Políticas de Imigração Americana.*" Unpublished Manuscript, Universidade Aberta.

McGowan, Owen T. P. 1976. "Factors Contributing to School Leaving among Immigrant Children: The Case of the Portuguese in Fall River, Massachusetts." Ph.D. dissertation, Catholic University of America.

Meireles, Maria de Fátima de Sacadura Calado. 1994. "Entre dois Universos Culturais: O Conceito de Identidade no Discurso Autobiografado de Laurinda de Andrade." Unpublished Manuscript, Universidade Nova de Lisboa.

Moniz, Miguel. 2004. "Exiled Home: Criminal Deportee Forced Return Migrants and Transnational Identity: The Azorean Example." Ph.D. dissertation, Brown University, Providence.

Moniz, Rita. 1979. "The Portuguese of New Bedford, Massachusetts and Providence, Rhode Island: A Comparative Micro-Analysis of Political Attitudes and Behavior." Ph.D. dissertation, Brown University.

Mulcahy, Maria. 2001. "The Portuguese in the US: An Overview." Invited Paper given at the "Race, Culture, Nation: Arguments Across the Portuguese Speaking World," Conference at Brown University and University of Massachusetts Dartmouth, March.

______2003. "The Portuguese of the U.S. From 1880 to 1990: Distinctiveness in Work Patterns Across Gender, Nativity and Place." Ph.D. dissertation, Brown University.

Oliveira Silva, Jacqueline, ed. 2005. Pesquisa "Tráfico de Seres Humanos para Fins de Exploração Sexual no Rio Grande do Sul." Porto Alegre, June. Coordenação. In Comissão Parlamentar Mista de Inquérito. Brasil, celeiro de vítimas: O tráfico internacional de pessoas para fins de prostituição. República Federativa do Brasil. Congreso Nacional. Comisso Parlamentar Mista de Inquérito da Emigração. Relatório Final da Comisso Parlamentar Mista de Inquérito. Brasília 2006: 339.

Pereira, Maria G. 1985. "The Socioeconomic Achievement of Portuguese Males in Massachusetts and Rhode Island." M.A. thesis, Brown University.

Pires-Hester, Laura J. 1994. "A Study of Cape Verdean-American Ethnic Development: The Emergence of Bilateral Diaspora Ethnicity and its Impact in a Southeastern New England Locality." Ph.D. dissertation, Columbia University.

Ramos-Zayas, Ana. 2005. "Between Cultural Excess and Racial Invisibility: Brazilian and Latino Youth in Newark's Ironbound." Harvard Conference on Brazilian Immigration to the United States, March 8-10.

Ribeiro, Gustavo L. 1997. "Street Samba: Carnaval and Transnational Identities in San Francisco." Paper presented at the Brazilian Studies Association IV Congress, Washington, DC, November 12-15.

______n.d. "Vulnerabilidade e Ambiguidade. Cidadania na Situação de Emigrante em São Francisco, Califórnia." Institute for Global Studies in Culture, Power and History, The Johns Hopkins University.

Rodrigues, Linda M.A. 2005-2007. Correspondence.

Rodrigues, Rose Pearl. 1990. "Occupational Mobility of Portuguese Males in New Bedford, Massachusetts: 1870-1900." Ph.D. dissertation, New School for Social Research.

Sánchez, Gina. 1999. "Contested Identities: Negotiating Race and Culture in a Cape Verdean Diaspora Community." Ph.D. dissertation, University of Texas, Austin.

Schwartz, Larry. 2005. "Roth, Race, and Newark." *Cultural Logic* 8. <http://clogic.eserver.org/2005/schwartz.html>. Accessed on 12 April 2008.

Sharkansky, Ira. 1960. "The Portuguese of Fall River: A Study of Ethnic Acculturation." Honors Thesis, Wesleyan University.

Sharp, James. 2002. Keynote Address. "Os Lusíadas" Portuguese American Student Group of Rutgers University Newark Annual Awards Dinner. Newark, NJ, March 2002.

______2004. Welcome Statement. The Official Website of the City of Newark, NJ (www.ci.newark.nj.us).

Silverman, Sydel. 1976. "Comments on Symposium on Social Structure, Ideology and Women's Choices." Paper presented at the annual meeting of the American Anthropological Association, Washington, D.C.

Sidney, Mara. 2005. "Urban Slums Report: The Case of Newark, USA." Department of Political Science, Rutgers University.

Sullivan, Edward J. 2005-2006. Correspondence.

Teixeira, Aldaberto J. 1996. "Cape Verdeans in Boston: An Urgent Call for Unity and Civic Participation." The McCormack Institute of Public Affairs, University of Massachusetts at Boston.

The Newark Museum. 1998. Report to the Geraldine R. Dodge Foundation, Feb. 27. Photocopies.

______1998. Education Department Highlights. An Internal Report, January. Photocopies.

Turbin, Carol. 1984. "Women's Life Cycles and Nineteenth-Century Labor Militancy." Paper presented at the Sixth Berkshire Conference on the History of Women, Smith College.

Wagner, Steven. 2002. "How Did the Taft-Hartley Act Come About?" *History News Network*, 14 Oct.

FILMS

Crowning Glory: Images of the Virgin Mary in the Arts of Portugal. 1999. Hispanic Telecommunications Network, Inc. Boston: Distributed by Pauline Video, Videocassette.

Ironbound Ties to Portugal. 1999. New Jersey Network television video documentary.

O Caso do Big Dan's. 1994. Directed by Diana Andringa, RTP, Lisbon, Portugal.

The Accused. 1988. Directed by Jonathan Kaplan. Written by Tom Torpor. Produced by Stanley R. Jaffe and Sherry Lansing. Paramount Pictures.

NEWSPAPERS AND POPULAR MAGAZINES

Almeida, Onésimo. 1983a. "Contra Argumentos Não Haja Factos." *O Jornal*, Nov. 5.

______1983b. "Letter to the Editor." *Boston Magazine*, Vol. 75, no. 11.

______1984. "Ainda o Caso do Big Dan's e as Sucessivas Confusões." *O Jornal*, March 29.

______1995a. "A Violação de Uma Comunidade." *Açoriano Oriental*, July 1.

______1995b. "Carta ao Açoriano Oriental." *Açoriano Oriental*, July 5.

Antunen de Oliveira, Renan.1999. "Brasileiras Perdem Espaço entre Strippers nos EUA : Dançarinas que já Fizeram a Fama nos Clubes Noturnos Estão Sendo Substituídas por Loiras do Leste Europeu." *O Estado de São Paulo*, June14.

Antunes, Conceição. 2000. "Emigrantes & Turistas." *Expresso*. Dec. 12. http://www.portugalnews.pt/icep/artigo.asp?cod_artigo=52485.

"A Performing Arts Center Takes A Bow: In Newark, a Strong First Season Raises Hope," *The New York Times Special*. Jul. 6 1998. Supplement.

Armario, Christine. 2004. "Latinas and Islam in Union City." *Christian Science Monitor*. Dec. 27, Features Living.

Buros, Marian. 1987. "Little Portugal: Page of History in Newark." *The New York Times*, Oct. 7.

Cotter, Holland. 1997. "ARTVIEW: A Gently Captivating Superstar Who Helped Rule an Empire," *The New York Times*, Dec. 21.

"Com Onze Tarefas para Cumprir: Conselho das Comunidades Portuguesas Reune em Lisboa de 8 a 13 de Setembro." 1997. *Luso-Americano*. June 25: 3.

"Conselho das Comunidades Portuguesas: Reunião Amanhã e Sexta-Feira em Mass. Prepara Plenário de 26 a 28 de Junho." *Luso-Americano*. June 4: 4.

Diana, Victor. 2001. "The Brazilians Among U.S." *O Jornal.*

Diaz, Johnny, and Scott Greenberger. 2004. "Not White, Not Black, Not Hispanic—Boston's Cape Verdeans Have Long Been Misunderstood." *The Boston Globe,* Feb. 15, B1.

Dines, Deborah. 1991. "Mineiros e Portugueses Disputam a 'Baixada Fluminense' dos EUA." *Folha de São Paulo,* June 10, D1.

______1991. "Lana, 'Go-go' em Newark, Queria Falar Inglês." *Folha de São Paulo,* June 10, D3.

DuLong, Jessica. 2003. "Young and in Danger in New Jersey: Incident of Black Lesbian from Newark Beating a Guy who Made an Offensive Comment to Her in the West Village." *The Advocate Report,* June 24.

El-Ghobashy, Tamer. 2003. "Jersey Teen Killed in Gay Bias Attack." *New York Daily News,* May 13. http://www.nydailynews.com/front/v-pfriendly/story/83225p-76120c.html.

Feng, Clifford. 1974. "Portuguese Overthrow is Felt in Newark," *The Star-Ledger,* May 19.

Friendly, Jonathan. 1984. "New Bedford Rape Case: Confusion Over Accounts of Cheering at Bar," *The New York Times,* April 11.

Godinho, Joana. 1984. "O Direito de Dizer Não," *O Jornal,* April 19.

Hatton, Barry. 2002. "Portuguese Fear Irrelevancy in Europe," *Associated Press,* Dec. 24.

"IBID Hires Off-duty Police Officers to Address Student Rowdiness on Ferry Street." April 5, 2006. http://www.goironbound.com/html/press/04-05-06.htm.

Jefferys, Daniel. 1994. "City Slicker: Newark." *The Independent,* Dec.

Kong, Deborah. 2002. "30 States Have Multilingual Ballots," *The Washington Post* (A) 25, Sept. 1.

Mano, Henrique. 2003. "Martins da Cruz Defende Consulados Itinerantes." *Luso-Americano.* September 24: 8.

"Martins da Cruz Quer Luso-Descendentes Mais Envolvidas na Vida Cívica e Política." 2003. *Luso-Americano.* April 30: 9.

Medeiros, João Luís. 1995. "O Tristemente Famoso Caso 'Big Dan's': Uma Disputa em Família," *Açoriano Oriental,* July 1.

Moniz, Rita, 1981. "Azoreans in America: Political Assimilation." *Atlântida* 26 (3). Julho–Setembro.

Nickerson, Colin. 1983. "Black, White or Cape Verdean?" *The Boston Globe,* Sept. 29: 16.

Rapoza, Kenneth. 2001. "College-bound Know What's in a Name." *The Boston Globe,* March 18, 3rd edition, Learning Section. L1.

Ripley, Amanda. 2003. "When the *Meninas* Came To Town: Bragança Was Just an Ancient, Remote Portuguese Outpost. Then the Brazilian Prostitutes Moved in—and the Wives Started Fighting Back." *Bragança.* Oct. 12.

Rose, Lisa. 2003. "Latin Dance Scene Turns up the Heat." *Star Ledger,* Newark, NJ, Jan. 31. 21.

Santos, Fernando. 2002a. "A Prática do Conselho das Comunidades Passará Sempre Pela Capacidade de Afirmação dos Seus Membros." *Luso-Americano.* Sept. 25: 2-3.

______2002b. "Censo 2000 Dá Mais 9 Mil Pessoas às Comunidades Portuguesa de NJ." *Luso-Americano.* May 29: 4.

______1997. "Abre Hoje ao Meio Dia, No Museu de Newark, A Exposição Sobre a Virgem na Arte Portuguesa." *Luso-Americano.* Nov. 26.

Silva, Luiz. 1993. "Gold of Atlantis." *Revue Noire* 10: Sept – Nov.

Smothers, Ronald. 1997. "In Newark's Museum, an Exhibit Honors the City's Portuguese." *The New York Times.* Dec. 4: 15. Late edition East Coast.

______1998. "A Performing Arts Center Takes A Bow: In Newark, a Strong First Season Raises Hope," *The New York Times Special.* July 6. Supplement.

The Newark Museum. 1997. "Newark Museum Exhibitions and Events." Newsletter of the Newark Museum. November/ December.

The Newark Public Library. 1999. "Trustee President: A Community Leader." Official Newsletter of the Newark Public Library. *The Second Century* 10: 1.

O'Brien, Greg. 1983. "Rape in New Bedford." *Boston Magazine*, Vol. 75, no. 8.

Patterson, Mary Jo. 2000. "Cultures Collide in Ironbound—City's Portuguese and Brazilians Find Life is a Lesson in Tolerance." *Star-Ledger*, May 14.

Queiroz Galvão, Vinicius. 2006. "Ameaçados, Brasileiros Fogem nos EUA." *Folha de São Paulo*, August 21.

Suwwan, Leila. 2005. "Para Cônsul, Hispânicos são 'Cucarachos'." *Folha de São Paulo*. Oct. 20.

Tierney, John. 1990. "Urban Epidemic: Addicts and AIDS—A Special Report; In Newark, A spiral of Drugs and AIDS." *The New York Times*, Dec.16.

Valdés, Alisa. 1995. "Proclaiming Their Presence: In Mass. Potential Clout." *The Boston Globe*, Thursday, Apr. 20, 61, 64-65.

Onésimo Teotónio Almeida is Professor of Portuguese and Brazilian Studies at Brown University. He doubles as a scholar and author, having written short stories, plays, and *crónicas* along with numerous scholarly books, articles, and essays. His most recent publications are: *Livro-me do Desassossego* (2006); *Onze Prosemas* (2004); and *Viagens na Minha Era, dia-crónicas* (2001). His well-known book of Portuguese-American short stories, *(Sapa)teia Americana,* was first published in 1983. He has also written hundreds of articles for newspapers and other periodicals, and for many years was a regular columnist for the literary journal LER. He continues to write frequently for the *Jornal de Letras*, and is a frequent contributor to the Portuguese press in the US and Canada. He is currently finishing a book on national identity, *A Obsessão da Portugalidade.*

Lori Barcliff Baptista is a Ph.D. Candidate in the Department of Performance Studies at Northwestern University. She specializes in food studies, the adaptation of literature, and a broad range of performance practices. Her most recent publication, "Peixe, Patria e Possibilidades Portuguesas/Fish, Homeland and Portuguese Possibilities," is forthcoming in a special issue of *Text and Performance Quarterly.* Her dissertation project: *Stirring the Melting Pot: Food and the Performance of Inclusion of Newark's Ironbound Community* considers how Portuguese and Brazilian immigrants in New Jersey's largest city use food to negotiate issues of civic engagement, entrepreneurship, and cultural continuity and change.

Clyde W. Barrow is Chancellor Professor of Policy Studies and Director of the Center for Policy Analysis at the University of Massachusetts Dartmouth where he specializes in public policy and political economy. His most recent book (co-edited) is *Class, Power and the State in Capitalist Society: Essays on Ralph Miliband* (2008). His other books include *Critical Theories of the State* (1993) and *Universities and the Capitalist State* (1990). Dr. Barrow has also authored numerous policy reports for federal, state, and local governments, trade associations, labor unions, and non-profit organizations.

Adeline Becker is Executive Director of The Education Alliance for Equity and Excellence in the Nation's Schools and Adjunct Associate Professor in the Department of Portuguese & Brazilian Studies at Brown University. She works in the areas of urban school reform, second-language acquisition, bilingual education, first- and second-language literacy, and cross-cultural studies of language acquisition.

Irene Bloemraad is Assistant Professor of Sociology at the University of California, Berkeley. She studies the intersection of immigration and politics, with particular emphasis on citizenship, immigrants' political and civic participation, and the impact of migrants on state ideologies. She is the author of *Becoming a Citizen: Incorporating Immigrants and Refugees in the United States and Canada* (2006), a study of Portuguese and Vietnamese migrant communities in the Boston and Toronto areas. She has published numerous articles, a number focused on Portuguese migrants. Her current research, funded in part by the Russell Sage Foundation, examines intergenerational political socialization in immigrant families and the visibility and influence of immigrant community organizations in local decision-making.

Ann Bookman is Executive Director of the MIT Workplace Center. She is a social anthropologist who has authored a number of publications in the areas of women's work, work and family issues, unionization, and child and family policy. Her new book, *Starting in Our Own Backyards: How Working Families Can Build Community and Survive the New Economy* (2004), extends the discourse on work-family integration to include issues of community involvement and civil society.

David Borges is Assistant Director and Senior Research Associate at the University of Massachusetts Dartmouth Center for Policy Analysis. His research focus is on applied policy research in the areas of program evaluation, survey research, economic impact analysis, and public management.

Caroline Brettell holds the title of Dedman Family Distinguished Professor in the Department of Anthropology at Southern Methodist University and is an internationally-known specialist on immigration.

She is the author of numerous books including: *Men Who Migrate, Women Who Wait: Population and History in a Portuguese Parish* (1986); *We Have Already Cried Many Tears: The Stories of Three Portuguese Migrant Women* (1982, 1995); and *Anthropology and Migration: Essays on Transnationalism, Ethnicity and Identity* (2003); and *Crossing Borders/ Constructing Boundaries: Race, Ethnicity and Immigration* (2006); co-editor of *International Migration: The Female Experience* (1986); *Migration Theory: Talking Across Disciplines* (2000 and 2008); *Citizenship, Immigration and Belonging: Immigrants in Europe and the United States* (2008); and *Twenty-First Century Gateways: Immigrant Incorporation in Suburban America* (2008). She was co-principal investigator on the project (2001-2005) "Immigrants, Rights and Incorporation in a Suburban Metropolis" and the project "Practicing Citizenship in a New City of Immigration: An Ethnographic Comparison of Asian Indians and Vietnamese" (2005-2008).

Katherine Brucher is Assistant Professor of Music at DePaul University. She received her Ph.D. in ethnomusicology from the University of Michigan. She is interested in music and migration and has conducted fieldwork on Portuguese music traditions in both Portugal and New England. Her current research projects include an ethnographic study of *filarmónicas* in Portugal and the United States.

Rui Antunes Correia is a historian and teaches high school. The focal point of his research is community-level political and social dynamics from the 18th to the 20th century. He has been director of a teachers' national magazine, author of several history school books, editor of a national award-winning school newspaper, and an ITC/didactics teacher trainer since 1992. He currently works as an independent assessment expert for the Education, Audiovisual, and Culture Executive Agency in Brussels.

M. Glória de Sá is Assistant Professor of Sociology and Faculty Director of the Ferreira-Mendes Portuguese-American Archives at the University of Massachusetts Dartmouth. Her research interests intersect the fields of immigration, race, and ethnicity as they relate to Portuguese-speaking groups in the U.S. Her recent work includes "The Azorean

Community on the East Coast" (forthcoming), "The Portuguese in the United States Census of 2000" (forthcoming), and "Mobility Ladder or Economic Lifeboat? Self-Employment among Portuguese Immigrant Women in the U.S." (forthcoming). She is currently working on an ethnography of the Portuguese in Westport, Massachusetts.

Bela Feldman-Bianco teaches Social Anthropology at UNICAMP (The State University of Campinas), Brazil, where she also directs The Center for the Study of International Migration (CEMI). Her research projects have focused on issues related to culture and power, with emphasis on identities, transnational migration, colonialism, and post-colonialism in comparative perspective (Portugal, Brazil, and the U.S.). In addition to the internationally acclaimed ethnographic video, *Saudade* (1991), she has edited, among others, *Colonialism as a Continuing Project: The Portuguese Experience* of *Identities: Studies in Culture and Power* and co-editor of *Trânsitos Coloniais: Diálogos Críticos Luso-Brasileiros* (2002).

Gina Sánchez Gibau is Associate Professor of Anthropology at Indiana University Purdue University Indianapolis. Her research interests include race and ethnicity, identity, migration, gender studies, and the African diaspora. She has published articles in *Transforming Anthropology, Identities,* and *The Western Journal of Black Studies.*

Marilyn Halter is Professor of History and Research Associate at the Institute on Culture, Religion, and World Affairs at Boston University. An interdisciplinary scholar, she specializes in the history and sociology of American immigration, race, ethnicity, entrepreneurship, and consumer society. Her books include *Between Race and Ethnicity: Cape Verdean-American Immigrants, 1860-1965* (1993) and with Richard Lobban, *The Historical Dictionary of the Republic of Cape Verde* (1988) as well as *Shopping for Identity: The Marketing of Ethnicity* (2000) and her edited collection, *New Migrants in the Marketplace: Boston's Ethnic Entrepreneurs* (1995). Her current research project focuses on recent West African immigrants and refugees to the United States.

Kimberly DaCosta Holton is Associate Professor and Director of the Portuguese and Lusophone World Studies Program at Rutgers University Newark. She is author of *Performing Folklore: Ranchos Folclóricos from Lisbon to Newark* (Indiana 2005), as well as articles in scholarly journals and edited volumes. As an interdisciplinary scholar with a Ph.D. in Performance Studies from Northwestern University, Holton's research interests focus on the intersection between performance, politics, and immigration. Holton is the founder of the Ironbound Oral History Project, a store of over 250 oral history transcripts and other primary documents collected from within the Portuguese-speaking communities of New Jersey.

Andrea Klimt is Associate Professor in the Department of Sociology, Anthropology, and Crime and Justice Studies at the University of Massachusetts Dartmouth. She is the author of numerous articles on identity and community in the Portuguese diaspora and focuses on comparisons between the Portuguese in Germany and the U.S. She has also guest edited special journal volumes for *Diaspora* and *Etnográfica* that bring together analyses of culture, politics, and identity formation in various corners of the Portuguese diaspora. She is the social science editor for the Portuguese in the Americas Series published at the University of Massachusetts Dartmouth.

Louise Lamphere is Distinguished Professor of Anthropology at the University of New Mexico and past president of the American Anthropological Association. Among her numerous publications on gender and work in the U.S. is her book exploring the experiences of Portuguese immigrant women, *From Working Daughters to Working Mothers: Immigrant Women in a New England Industrial Community* (1987).

João Leal is Associate Professor of Anthropology at Universidade Nova de Lisboa. He is the author of several ethnographies on Portugal and the Portuguese diaspora, including *As Festas do Espírito nos Açores. Um Estudo de Antropologia Social* (1994), and *Açores, EUA, Brasil. Imigração e Etnicidade* (2007). He is currently involved in a research project on the Holy Ghost Festivals in North America.

Miguel Moniz is a Senior Associate Investigator at the Centro de Estudos de Antropologia Social (CEAS) at ISCTE and the Centro em Rede de Investigação em Antropologia (CRIA) as a Post-Doctoral Fellow of the Fundação para a Ciência e a Tecnologia (FCT). His areas of research are race, ethnicity, and the nation, and he is focusing on the effect of state policy and the law on the formation of social identity with particular focus on Portuguese and Lusophone migration to North America. His current project examines similar processes treating Portugal as a destination for international migration.

Ana Y. Ramos-Zayas is Associate Professor of Anthropology and Latino & Hispanic Caribbean Studies at Rutgers University in New Brunswick. She is the author of *National Performances: Class, Race, and Space in Puerto Rican Chicago* (2003) and co-author of *Latino Crossings: Mexicans, Puerto Ricans and the Politics of Race and Citizenship* (2003). Ramos-Zayas has written articles on alternative education, citizenship, race, urban ethnography, and youth culture in the U.S., Puerto Rico, and Brazil. She is currently writing an ethnography on U.S.-based "racial democracy," the anthropology of emotion, and urban neo-liberalism among Brazilians and Puerto Ricans in Newark, NJ.

Penn Reeve is Professor of Sociology and Anthropology at the University of Massachusetts Dartmouth. He specializes in social inequality, ethnicity, and labor issues, and has conducted research in Brazil, the Azores, and the Alentejo, Portugal, and among Portuguese-Americans in southeastern Massachusetts.